TOOLS FOR AGRICULTURE

TOOLS FOR AGRICULTURE

*A guide to appropriate equipment
for smallholder farmers*

Introduction by Ian Carruthers and Marc Rodriguez

Fourth edition

Intermediate Technology Publications *in association with* CTA and GRET • 1992

Intermediate Technology Publications Ltd,
103-105 Southampton Row, London, WC1B 4HH,
UK

© Intermediate Technology Publications 1992

Tools for Progress first published 1967
Tools for Agriculture first published 1973
Second edition 1976
Third edition 1985
Fourth edition 1992

Cover photograph by Jeremy Hartley

A CIP catalogue record for this book is available from the British Library

ISBN 1 85339 100 X

Printed by Russell Press, Nottingham, UK

CONTENTS

How to use this guide   vi

Preface   vii

Smallholder farming: strengths and constraints by Ian Carruthers   1

Agricultural equipment: the maintenance myth by Marc Rodriguez   5

1. **Field power**
   Introduction by Frank Inns   9

2. **Soil preparation**
   Introduction by Andy Metianu   23

3. **Sowing, planting and fertilizer distribution**
   Introduction by Peter Munzinger   49

4. **Pest control and operator safety**
   Introduction by Bill Radley   65

5. **Harvesting and threshing**
   Introduction by Ian Johnson   91

6. **Crop processing and storage**
   Introduction by Brian Clarke   115

7. **Water lifting**
   Introduction by Bernard Gay   141

8. **Transport and materials handling**
   Introduction by IT Transport   165

9. **Livestock husbandry and health**
   Introduction by Alastair Mews   181

10. **Beekeeping**
    Introduction by Nicola Bradbear   199

Sources of further information   213

Manufacturers' index   223

Equipment index   237

User questionnaire   239

HOW TO USE THIS GUIDE

This Guide will be of particular use to:
- farmers' representatives who purchase equipment for smallholder farmers;
- advisers who seek to assist farmers and farmers' organizations with the purchase of equipment;
- development agency personnel who need to purchase equipment for farmers, farmers' organizations or development projects;
- prospective manufacturers or manufacturers' agents who wish to have information about the range of equipment currently available;
- development workers, students and others who wish to learn about the types of equipment available;
- equipment information services who wish to provide advice to enquirers about specific equipment or the range of equipment available.

The Guide can be used in a number of different ways:
- to find the name and address of the manufacturer of a specific piece of equipment whose generic name is known, e.g. triangular harrow or rice transplanter;
- to find the name and address of the manufacturer of a piece of equipment whose general purpose is known, e.g. a machine for cleaning grain or a machine for weeding crops;
- to find out about specific types of equipment or equipment for specific purposes;
- to find out about the range of equipment available from specific manufacturers or manufacturers in a particular country;
- to learn more about equipment used for crop and livestock production and processing;
- to find the addresses of further information resources which can be contacted.

The information has been clearly labelled and indexed, and laid out as follows:
- the *Contents page* guides the reader to one of ten chapters;
- the *Manufacturers' index* gives the page numbers of equipment supplied by a particular manufacturer. This index is organized in alphabetical order by country, e.g.:

CAMEROON

CENEEMA, *123, 133*
B.P. 1040 Nkolbisson
Yaounde
CAMEROON
Tel: 23 32 50

TROPIC, *29, 30, 75, 98, 135, 171, 175, 195*
BP 706
Douala
CAMEROON

- the *Equipment index* gives the page numbers of specific types of equipment listed under their generic and functional names, e.g.:

hoes 25, 28, 30, 78, 79
    chopping 67
    digging 67
    motorized 81
    pushing and pulling 67
    rotary 14-15, 67, 79
    tined 25
    wheeled 79

- the *chapter headings* and accompanying photograph give the title and contents of each chapter;
- the *page headings* indicate the contents of each page, or at least some of the major items on each page;
- the *Sources of further information* pages give the names and addresses of organizations active in the fields of agricultural engineering, crop protection and beekeeping. These are organized by country.

Within each chapter the information is presented in three ways:
- *Introduction.* This details the most important points to consider when purchasing a particular type of equipment (the emphasis varies from chapter to chapter — showing the difficulty of decision-making when selecting equipment for smallholder farmers).
- *Tables.* Clear, easy-to-read tables list the ranges of certain types of equipment produced by different manufacturers. The addresses of the manufacturers are not included in the tables; these can be looked up in the Manufacturers' index.
- *Equipment pages.* The equipment is presented in the order that operations are carried out and, within each type of operation, a progression from hand-powered through animal-powered to engine-powered. Each type of equipment is illustrated and there is a brief description followed by the name and address of the manufacturer of the machine. Where several manufacturers make very similar machines, these addresses are grouped together.

When you have identified the equipment that you are interested in, it is advisable to contact the manufacturer directly for further details such as current models, model performance, current prices, and delivery times.

Please also mention that you found the address in *Tools for Agriculture*, as this may encourage the manufacturer to supply more information to us for the next edition.

This guide is compiled entirely from information supplied by manufacturers. Inclusion in the guide does NOT imply any recommendation by ITDG of the equipment illustrated or guarantee that the equipment performs to the standard claimed. The publishers and compilers cannot accept responsibility for any errors which may have occurred. In this connection it should be noted that specifications are subject to change without notice and should be confirmed when making enquiries and placing orders with suppliers. If you do find any errors in this book, please inform ITDG's Agricultural Equipment Programme Manager so that they can be corrected in future.

PREFACE

Since 1965 ITDG has been producing buyers' guides to appropriate equipment for smallholder farmers. The first included only manufacturers of UK origin, whereas later editions have broadened their scope to include other countries. The most recent edition, produced in 1985, particularly emphasized developing country manufacturers, with the majority of entries in the book coming from such companies. All these books were produced on a one-off basis and have provided the most comprehensive store of such information available in the world at that time. However, no facility existed for the continual updating and expansion of the information resource which quickly became out of date, necessitating large searches for information for each new edition — a time-consuming and expensive exercise.

Accordingly, in 1989 a decision was made to set up an agricultural tools computer database which would form the basis of an active and continually updated resource to supply information about manufacturers of appropriate equipment. A database like this makes possible the systematic and continuous updating of information, and allows new information to be stored and made available immediately without having to wait for the production of a new book. In collaboration with GRET, we have collected information from more than 1200 manufacturers from over 90 countries to be stored on the computer database. This information will in due course be made available electronically, a form of particular use to information services. Any organization interested in this database should write to ITDG for further information.

Electronic databases are not accessible to many of the users of *Tools for Agriculture*, however, and so the need to produce updated versions of the book is paramount. This is the first edition to be produced from the new database. Great care has been taken to ensure the accuracy of the information in the book and through the use of the database many of the errors of the last edition have been avoided. Parallel with this book GRET are producing their own French language edition using the same database as a source.

Many useful comments and suggestions have been made as to how the last edition could be improved. Where appropriate these have been acted on. A new chapter on power sources has been added. This primarily deals with how to make choices of field power sources (human, animal and engine, including tractors), and provides advice about the appropriateness of those sources. Since most of the information in the book is hand- or animal-powered, the equipment section of this chapter has been kept short. The increasing use of lower powered tractors (up to 60kW) in developing countries has led us to discuss tractors in the introduction, but tractors from major manufacturers are not included in the equipment section.

Other changes from the last edition include the incorporation of the Intercultivation and Crop protection chapters into the new *Pest Control and operator safety*, which now includes much more information on non- or reduced-chemical control techniques. Multi-purpose toolbars and Seedbed preparation have been combined to form a new chapter on *Soil preparation* and the wool harvesting chapter has been amalgamated into the chapter on *Livestock husbandry and health*. All the chapter introductions have been updated or totally rewritten.

This Guide is by no means exhaustive. We have tried to include all relevant equipment and manufacturers from the database, the emphasis being on the range of equipment described and the accuracy of the information included. However, the content is limited to those companies who provided us with information. While every attempt has been made to include all suitable manufacturers, it should be understood that we have not necessarily included all the products available from all the listed manufacturers.

There is an expanded and amended section on Sources of further information. Names and addresses of institutions have been included for as many countries as possible. These institutions should be able to provide further information, particularly on aspects of equipment use and choice. If not able to help with a particular enquiry themselves, they may well be able to direct you to a more appropriate source of information. Please help us to make future lists as useful as possible by telling us of omissions of institutions which should be included, and also where we have inappropriate inclusions.

With each new edition we are attempting to improve on the previous one. For this we rely on advice and suggestions from you, the user, and in this edition you will find a short questionnaire. Please take the time to fill it in and send it to us.

A new companion guide, *Small-scale Food Processing*, is also available, providing extensive information about the tools, techniques and procedures for numerous different types of food products. For details please contact IT Publications.

Tim Ogborn
Programme Manager, Agricultural Engineering
ITDG

Improvements to this Guide

Tools for Agriculture is only as good as the information provided by manufacturers. You can help us to improve the quality of this Guide by doing any or all of the following.

❍ Please fill in the short questionnaire at the back of this book and send it to us. This is most important as it will tell us what you want from this Guide.

❍ If you use the book to contact a manufacturer, please tell them that you found the address in *Tools for Agriculture*. They will then be more than likely to supply us with more information next time round.

❍ Please send us details of any manufacturers of appropriate equipment which do not appear in this edition (name, address and, if possible, equipment brochures).

❍ Please write and tell us any suggestions, criticisms or comments you have on the book

❍ Please tell us of any errors you find in this edition.

❍ Please tell us of any sources of information that we should be using to increase our coverage of manufacturers.

It is only through **your** help that this unique information resource can be improved to provide you and other users with what you require.

Acknowledgements

Producing a book like this requires the help of an enormous number of people. It is impossible to list all who have contributed their time and effort and we apologize to those who have been omitted. First, we have to correct an omission from the last edition by thanking Ian Goldman who designed the basic structure of that edition, a structure which still forms the basis for this edition.

We wish to thank the hundreds of companies around the world who took the time and effort to reply to our letters and send information about their products. Without their efforts there would have been no information to include in this Guide. In addition we would like to thank all the companies who sent in information, but whose products are beyond the scope of the book, and the numerous people in organizations, embassies, consulates, research and educational institutions, and business organizations who took time to send information about companies.

It is not possible to mention everyone who has helped in the production of this edition, but in particular we wish to thank the following: the authors of the ten chapters; Jeremy Herklots and Christophe Beau for the mammoth job of data collection and Richard Holloway for the equally enormous task of organizing and writing the equipment pages; Patrick Mulvany for his guidance and experience from the last edition, Marc Rodriguez for masterminding the French end of the work; Ranatunge Bandara (Sri Lanka), Fowzal Kamal (Bangladesh), Pawlo Florés and Luis Vargas Soto (Peru), Nowkezi Moyo (Zimbabwe) and Songsak Wong Bhumiwat (Thailand) for the collection and provision of information in the named countries; Ruth Fairman and Ann Hampton for shared information, advice and support; Siân Jones for translations from French; Vince Driver, Matthew Whitton and Geoff Brownlow for their illustrations; and also all the following for their time, effort and assistance: Kim Daniel, Rosy Herklots, Sue Holloway, Anthony Holloway, James Ogborn, Amanda Ogden, Charles Pegge, Rachael Ratcliffe, Maureen Sewell, and Chris Wylem.

Our particular thanks also go to CTA and ODA for their financial support during the preparation and publication of this book. Without their assistance none of this could have been a achieved.

SMALLHOLDER FARMING: STRENGTHS AND CONSTRAINTS

Simple innovation using a log to add weight to an inverted harrow for seedbed levelling

Paul Starkey/ITDG

The survival of smallholder farmers in developing countries is dependent on them making rational and intelligent decisions in the difficult circumstances that they face. Their capacity to do this is evident from the continued existence of smallholder farmers in many of the most marginal situations. When circumstances have dictated the need, technology change and improvements in farming systems have taken place. These changes have only been able to take place at the speed dictated by the farmer's risk-minimizing strategies, which usually depend on the spreading of risk rather than increasing production. However, when outside forces on the farming systems change rapidly and beyond the control of the farmer (as in the present day with vastly growing demand from increasing numbers of non-food producers), it may seem that the farmer's response is slow, that technological change stagnates and that the farmer is not maximizing production.

This can be explained by understanding several unusual characteristics of smallholder agriculture. First and foremost, agriculture is a biological process, subject to various risks of weather, pests and disease which can affect the supply of the product in an unpredictable fashion. In order to meet their reasonable goals of maintaining or even increasing their existing low levels of income, farmers are being forced to adapt their farming systems at ever increasing rates: they must increase yields, which in turn requires the use of purchased inputs such as extra labour or fertilizers. These inputs can only be obtained with cash, which means that farmers rely increasingly on cash sales of the crop in order to survive.

Agricultural products have consumer demand patterns which can turn even good production years — when biological constraints are conquered — into financial disasters because of the resulting glut. The biological nature of production also results in a large time-gap, often months or even years, between the expenditure of effort or cash and the returns. Once cash inputs are used, an unusually high proportion of working capital is required, compared with industry. These constraints are all further complicated by the marked seasonality of agricultural production. The peaks of labour input create management problems, and perishable commodities are produced intermittently; both create additional financial and technical storage problems.

A second characteristic of smallholder agriculture is the scale of production. The small scale of most farming operations, often coupled with a lack of access to educational resources, gives farmers little economic power as individuals and little opportunity to seek such remedial measures as do exist.

A third characteristic of smallholder agriculture which constrains production is the political dimension. It is in some ways ironic that in countries with very large numbers of smallholder farmers, producers tend to command little political power despite their combined voting strength. Indeed they are often seen as the group to be directly and indirectly taxed to support other, generally urban-based, state activities. As a contrast, in rich countries, we generally see minorities of farmers with little voting power receiving massive state subsidies, part of which is provided to support technological advancement. The lack of political power of the smaller-scale farmers in developing countries results in the exploited smallholder farmers having to compete with rich, large-scale farmers producing food excesses that can only be sold at further subsidized prices, often depressing the prices obtainable by the smallholder farmer.

The various food crises of the last two decades, the recent failure of agriculture to match rising food demands in many countries, particularly in sub-Saharan Africa, and the failure of industry to fulfil its promise of creating employment and wealth have turned the attention of policy-makers back to the long-neglected and often despised small-scale agriculture sector. Smallholder farmers will need to have access to the wider technological options that exist if they are to respond to the new opportunities and challenges presented.

TECHNOLOGY CHANGE AND OPTIONS

The economics of smallholder farming are undergoing a process of more and more rapid change: farm size is halving every twenty years or so in some regions (as a result of population growth, land appropriation and so on) and there is an increasing demand for cash from farming activities for production and consumption items. This results in new challenges to the traditional rationale and the old system optima. Traditional systems have always had to adapt to change in order to survive; now these changes are having to be made at an increasingly rapid pace and, in the main, in response to factors outside the farm. This requires the adjustment of existing resources to find new optima; however, in order to make substantial gains, the input of new technologies may be required, which in turn may alter — even radically — current methods and systems. A change in the resource base or the introduction of a new piece of technology into an inter-dependent agricultural system may alter various other constraints and opportunities within the farm system. In this way, innovation and technology change continue to be the driving force behind agricultural development.

Reference books like this publication can act as an encyclopedia, illustrating alternative ways of coping with these challenges. Readers do not have to reinvent the wheel each time a new transport problem arises. Farmers need the opportunity to choose and adapt technology for themselves.

This new edition of *Tools for Agriculture* displays a very wide range of agricultural equipment and describes what the technology can achieve as well as how and where more information can be discovered. It shows that there is already a mass of equipment for small-scale farmers. The farm technology itself provides numerous opportunities for sustaining the returns to land, water, labour and other crucial resources.

THE ROLE OF INFORMATION

In the theory of classical economics, information on the contents of the technology itself is assumed to be readily available to all. This is clearly absurd in any industry, but particularly so in agriculture. Smallholder farmers' capacity for research and experimentation is constrained by the limited scale of their activity and their need to minimize risk. Therefore, one of the main justifications for public support of agricultural research and extension, in developed and developing countries alike, is to push research beyond the point which the farmer can risk.

However, knowledge alone of the existence of appropriate technology will not be sufficient to ensure adoption. Attitudes towards it may need to change; the hardware has to be physically available; and those convinced of its value need financial resources to acquire it. Local testing of the appropriateness of equipment is essential and should be done by smallholder farmers. This, in turn, will require more agricultural researchers and toolmakers to accept responsibility for forging closer links with farmers so that adaptive research and technology testing can truly be of benefit to farmers.

THE IMPACT OF TECHNOLOGY

Selection of equipment for inclusion in this book does not imply endorsement of a particular product. Indeed, supporters of the appropriate technology concept often have an ambivalent attitude towards any modern systems and in particular those which are likely to change the beneficiaries. Appropriate Technology advocates believe on the whole that cheap, simple, small-scale, locally produced, reliable or at least mendable technology will generate income and improve — or at least avoid worsening — income distribution. This is possible, but it remains difficult to prove that any technology can be considered 'appropriate' outside of the economic, social and physical context in which it will be used. No technology has the ideal intrinsic qualities that will somehow create wealth and at the same time favour the poorest groups in society. On the contrary, experience shows that the income-distribution consequences of change are generally unpredictable. New technology normally requires access to resources and it therefore generally favours the better off, particularly when the objective of an intervention has been the introduction of that technology, rather than the strengthening of farmers' ability to choose.

If societies wish to accept the benefits of new technology, they must devise means for its introduction that reduce the social costs associated with any worsening of income distribution. An understanding of the context of technology use and its possible consequences is all the more important given that the direct users of the book will seldom be the smallholder farmer whom the contributors and compilers generally have in mind when selecting equipment.

HOW TO CHOOSE

Numerous criteria can be devised to aid judgement in selecting new applied technology, either for testing or promotion. These will include the degree of technical effectiveness, financial profitability, the economic and social returns, health and safety factors, and the administrative and legal compatibility with existing conditions. The criteria will not necessarily be independent or even compatible. A piece of equipment which is financially profitable for the farmer may depend upon underpriced foreign exchange or tax allowances and may be economically unattractive for the country as a whole. It may also substitute capital expenditure on machinery for unskilled or low-income labour and be socially unattractive.

A particular criterion such as technical efficiency may have several elements to aid judgement — such as the technology's simplicity and labour-intensity, its environmental appropriateness, its scale and flexibility, its complementarity with existing equipment and so forth. These elements are not inherently equal and in some circumstances one of them will be regarded as carrying most weight, in other circumstances another. Choice of technology is a matter of judgement and understanding of the context in which it will be used; all the modern aids for technology assessment, for cost-benefit analysis and the like cannot hide this fact. Such analyses can only be used as a guide to possible options. The actual choice must remain with the farmer who, as the one who must live with the consequences of the decision, is the best judge.

The equipment presented in this book reflects the belief that while all technology has the potential to alter the economic status of large numbers of people (sometimes in the direction of greater inequality of income, greater commercialization, more wage labour and increasing landlessness) some types of equipment are more likely to do so than others, and the overall impact of any change will vary from time to time and from place to place. Consequently, you will find few tractors or combine harvesters in this book, but great emphasis on, for example, animal-drawn ploughs and small threshers.

Low-income farming groups are a key component of the rural economy. There may perhaps be a cost of lost output through using less 'efficient' or labour-saving equipment — handpumps rather than tubewells, hand-tools rather than tractors, small livestock rather than cattle and buffaloes — but this is likely to be very small. Furthermore, new technology does not actually guarantee increased farm production. The productivity of labour-intensive gardening and allotments can often exceed that of modern capital-intensive farming systems, as was shown in Britain during and after the Second World War. Research in many countries has shown that modernized peasant-based systems are generally equally or even more efficient and to most views more equitable. It is, therefore, the smallholder farmers who are seen as the main beneficiaries of *Tools for Agriculture* — even if they are unlikely themselves to be the main readers of this book.

Patrick Mulvany/ITDG

Investment in machinery may have socially unattractive consequences such as reduced employment

FEEDBACK

While there are people who know and understand the type of hardware described in this book, there is less understanding of the ways in which smallholder farmers can increase their technological options and have the opportunity to gain benefits from such hardware. We need much better appreciation and knowledge of the management of technology and its maintenance and modification by farmers. ITDG is therefore always pleased to have critical and appreciative feedback — from the aid agencies, extension workers, credit agencies, schoolteachers, businessmen and women, politicians, farmers themselves and others who use this text — on the content and format, equipment that is missing, new problems, the effectiveness of the equipment, the context of its use, the service of the manufacturers, and new ideas. The hardware available grows rapidly in diversity and power but, just like computers, it will be useless without the software support. In the case of agriculture, this software stems from the efforts of smallholder farmers and artisans and from the interested individuals and groups who work closely with and for such farmers.

In order to improve the quality of this book with each edition, we need to know your thoughts about the publication — how you use it, for what purpose, which sections are most useful, etc. At the end of the book there is a short questionnaire which will help us to begin to answer some of these questions: please take a minute to fill it in and send it to us.

Ian Carruthers
Professor of Agrarian Development
Wye College

AGRICULTURAL EQUIPMENT: THE MAINTENANCE MYTH

The failure of mechanization in developing countries has been explained by many as a result of shortcomings in maintenance. It has been claimed that the difficulties in finding spare parts and competent technicians to repair machines, and the shortage, or complete lack, of minimum maintenance (oil, grease, changing worn parts) have reduced the service life of the equipment and its economic profitability.

This has been an excellent excuse for those responsible for agricultural mechanization development policies, an excuse often tinged with an air of disdain. The diagnosis has led to minimalist philosophies of agricultural mechanization, possibly including the 'do it at home' concept in Appropriate Technology. It is comforting to conclude that your maintenance problems will be reduced if farmers are not so dependent on supplies from outside.

There are more fundamental reasons for the failure of mechanization strategies which are often adopted by governments and international agencies who do not pay sufficient attention to the interests of the farmer and to the processes of technical change. Such failures and strategic errors are found both in heavy mechanization approaches (tractorization) and in those recommended by the proponents of light equipment (animal-drawn multi-purpose toolbars).

Why should farmers maintain a piece of equipment at a cost which can never be recovered from increased production? Have they been consulted about the changes which the machine will cause in the production system? Why buy this equipment in the first place? Often the only answer is that subsidies have been used for persuasion. This results in adoption which is ill thought out and, in the long term, will undermine all the costly efforts made by projects and governments to train users and install maintenance systems.

Seen from this viewpoint the maintenance problem is a result of inappropriate choice of equipment. Once the farmer decides that new equipment has potential benefits, the maintenance problem is on its way to being solved.

Lack of maintenance is therefore an effect, not a cause, of the failure of mechanization strategies. When a piece of equipment meets the needs of users they will find a way to deal with its maintenance and servicing requirements. Numerous examples could be cited to illustrate this thesis at all levels of mechanization.

Tractors

Tractor graveyards, a symptom of so many failed development projects, often exist alongside thriving fleets of operational lorries and transport vehicles of all kinds. If people know how to maintain and repair road vehicles, why not tractors too? It is indeed possible to maintain a healthy tractor population, even a long way from the capital city; for example, in Zimbabwe, India and some West African countries.

Increased use of tractors is potentially a viable component in the development of production systems and technical programmes. In many places the technical skills already exist to enable such changes to proceed. Complete tractorization is not necessarily appropriate. Analysis of individual cases should indicate suitable target levels.

Irrigation pumping sets

In Africa the number of skilled workers involved with motorization has shown the greatest increase in connection with irrigation services. A gradual improvement in the service life of machinery can be observed, but maintenance problems are complicated by the structure of user organizations. Wherever individual responsibility is clearly established the actual service life will usually equal, or exceed, the manufacturer's estimates.

Often, however, users choose to buy the cheapest machine even though they know it will bring greater maintenance problems in the long run. Where engine-driven pumps are concerned, the maintenance problem has been completely turned around in the past ten years by the introduction of small motorized pumpsets designed in Asia. They cost very little and are reasonably effective technically so that the average market gardener can recover their cost in three months. At this level it may be more attractive to replace the equipment when it breaks down, rather that repair it. However, many local mechanics manage to make necessary repairs to small petrol engines, though not so often to diesel engines.

Animal draught equipment

The supply and maintenance of animal draught equipment is completely self-sustaining in many countries. In Pakistan, where there is a long tradition of animal cultivation, implements are manufactured and maintained by local artisans working in close relationship with the users and responsive to their special requirements.

In Guinea Conakry, where the introduction of animal draught systems is more recent, the government has lost interest in any support for the development of animal traction. Artisans have been left to fabricate ploughs themselves. They have succeeded in producing them and the hundreds of parts needed to maintain them in use.

Milling equipment

Grain mills are the most popular items of small-scale processing equipment currently in use in Africa. There has been an extraordinary growth in their local manufacture. In Senegal many dozens of artisans are manufacturing Engleberg-type mills at various places throughout the country.

In these cases, successful maintenance systems have been built up as the result of interaction directly between the manufacturer and the user. On the other hand, systems set up by governments have rarely achieved such success.

THE FAILURE OF CENTRALIZED SYSTEMS

At independence the governments of many developing countries inherited centralized government-run maintenance systems. Everything — supply of spare parts, repair services, user training — was the responsibility of the administration and its technical services. After independence, international aid 'projects' often attempted to provide technical support to continue these centralized services.

In theory, centralized maintenance should have certain advantages through savings in initial investment and training. In practice such systems quickly collapsed as soon as international aid stopped financing them, leading to poor stock levels, small numbers of qualified repairers and poor overall profitability. The economic viability of the system proved to be a fiction.

It is now realized in most countries that the supply of spare parts and distribution of manufactured goods is really a job for a free-market trader. This discovery has been made only recently in some countries which have continued to live with centralized supply systems. Now these monopolies are being broken down. However, many governments impose high customs duties on imported parts. Dealers use this argument to sell equipment and parts at astronomical prices. Although untaxed supplies are very common in some countries they usually suffer from a lack of reliability.

Motorization has increased the need for sound, practical technical training. Governments have progressively failed to fulfil this need, perhaps because of low priority or difficulty in providing adequate staff and facilities. It is quite exceptional for technical colleges to provide the practical further training which is needed. It is no exaggeration to say that most mechanics are trained on the job. In addition mechanics have virtually no access to credit facilities for the purchase of tools and equipment, whether from government or private bank loans.

Thus in nearly all areas of agricultural production and rural development the hope of long-term agricultural equipment maintenance by government services was effectively abandoned long ago. In the current context of structural

Jeremy Hartley/Panos

Rice threshers can be manufactured and repaired locally

adjustment it is no longer even considered, except in certain international projects which are able to reproduce the same errors *ad infinitum*.

While these centralized systems were foundering, or their costs remained at a high level which the state could not maintain, the farmers, users, artisans and traders were finding their own *ad hoc* solutions. The private sector is the only certain by which technical change can be maintained in the countryside.

MAINTENANCE STRATEGIES

Public sector involvement in the manufacture, maintenance and repair of hand-tools, machinery, engines and tractors has declined rapidly in recent years. Most state-run facilities have become financially unsupportable and have been dramatically scaled down.

The size of the private sector, in many countries, was limited at first because of competition from state-owned companies and technical services which were highly subsidized and protected. More recently, with the decline of these facilities, the private sector has expanded rapidly to fill the gap.

This expansion extends both to the local manufacture of equipment and spare parts, and to the importation of equipment.

Locally manufactured equipment

The local manufacture of agricultural equipment is encouraged by most governments, although with varying degrees of enthusiasm. In some countries, such as India, the importation of manufactured goods is virtually prohibited, encouraging the development of a protected local agricultural engineering industry.

Local manufacturing ideally results in a very close and responsive relationship between local, usually small, artisanal workshops and the user. This is combined with intensive competition between workshops. The user usually benefits through low prices and good quality of service. The good reputation of the manufacturer depends upon the quality of the product and the after-sales service provided. In Pakistan, for instance, the manufacturer may provide free after-sales maintenance for a year.

Changes in the production and supply system must be made when manufacturing capacity is expanded to satisfy provincial or national markets rather than the purely local one. Customer loyalty depends on the ability to supply a reliable piece of equipment supported by good after-sales service. Two possible solutions to this problem are evolving.

Firstly, the main agricultural equipment manufacturers may appoint dealers to stock, sell and service their equipment. Initially the dealers may be confined to the larger towns, but in time they will also set up stockists in the user areas. Dealers must take the training of their local stockists seriously so that they can provide an effective maintenance and repair service. Governments should accept and encourage this trend.

Secondly, specialist trader/repairers may set up in businesses dealing in particular types of equipment. This arrangement is well advanced in the field of village water supplies. Projects should encourage the emergence of such enterprises and work with them to extend equipment use, treating them as artisan-run businesses. Services provided should be calculated and paid for on the basis of economic costs, with provision for phasing out of any residual subsidies. A permanent service can only be guaranteed by paying attention to the true costs.

Imported equipment

Usually it is the more complex equipment which must be imported. This may include tractors, harvesting and processing machinery.

Often such equipment has been supplied without a realistic assessment of user need (technical and economic benefits and burdens) and without setting up an effective organization for training in its use and maintenance, or for supply of spare parts. Shortsighted 'aid' projects and opportunist manufacturers have both contributed to the resulting graveyards of equipment.

One response to this situation has been to emphasize the supply of spare parts, with each workshop aiming at self-sufficiency in the availability of every individual machine component. Alternatively, manufacturers have been asked to supply a selection of 'recommended spares' when equipment is first purchased. Because the demand for the majority of spare parts is erratic and quite unpredictable the result in most cases has been large quantities of unused spare parts gathering dust in project stores.

A more rational solution is to categorize spare parts as:
○ consumables: items specified as necessary for routine servicing at specified intervals — e.g. filters, spark plugs — and items which will wear in operation such as tyres and soil-engaging parts of cultivation implements;
○ predictables: items most subject to wear which will need replacement at some time during the life of the equipment — e.g. drive belts, steering joints, light bulbs;
○ erratics: items for which the demand is unpredictable — parts which should last the life of the equipment, but may fail in a random manner (e.g. gears and bearings) or be broken in unforeseeable accidents. Replacement assemblies (e.g. gearboxes, engines) would generally be included in this category.

Workshops should concentrate on maintaining good stocks of consumable and predictable items while the importers must, in addition, be set up to meet the demand for erratic items, mostly by immediate delivery from their own stocks or otherwise very quickly indeed by urgent order and express delivery from the manufacturer.

In these circumstances the duties of the machinery importer are clear:
○ to introduce equipment for which there is a specific demand or for which there is judged to be a technically and economically viable future, sustainable by user demand;
○ to provide training in equipment use as and when required.
○ to provide appropriate training in equipment maintenance to the user and to mechanics employed by dealer workshops;
○ to operate efficient repair and maintenance services centrally and through a dispersed dealer network;
○ to maintain a highly responsive spare parts supply service.

The responsibilities outlined above are well known to most manufacturers of tractors and other agricultural machinery, who realize that an export market cannot be sustained in the longer term if these duties are neglected. They take care to appoint agents who will maintain a high level of service. In the past their efforts have often been made difficult by the actions of governments which have been biased against private enterprise businesses.

Customer-orientated private enterprises are already operating successfully in a number of countries, and many governments now accept that these arrangements provide the best prospect for the solution of current and future maintenance problems. Government action may be necessary to ensure that these enterprises are not encountering unfair competition from organizations receiving direct or indirect subsidies from government or international funds.

ADVICE TO USERS AND PURCHASERS

Action needed to keep equipment going

○ Regular maintenance is essential and must comply exactly with the manufacturer's recommendations, especially with regard to routine checks, adjustments and replacements (filters etc.), the frequency of lubrication and the quality of

Notice the tools ready for users to make repairs to the pump

oils and greases used. Manual equipment also requires maintenance if it is to last for its normal service life.
○ Replace worn parts in good time. Excessive wear results in lost performance and can also cause damage to neighbouring components leading to unnecessary extra costs.
○ Employ competent craftsmen. Unskilled repairs or incorrect spare parts only lead to additional trouble and expense. Do not expect repairers to do the impossible.
○ Think ahead. Plan for maintenance to be done in good time — not in the middle of a busy season. Buy consumable parts and replacements for wearing parts in advance so that they are ready as soon as needed.

Buying equipment

If the use of a machine is fundamentally unprofitable, no amount of good maintenance can keep it going.
○ Examine the farming system to identify potentially profitable improvements which machinery could help to bring about.
○ Find out what equipment is available: this catalogue will help to initiate ideas.
○ Check the financial viability of possible machines: this must be done using realistic estimates of work output, costs and extra income generated.

Having chosen a viable machine, draw up a guideline specification for the machine:
○ functional requirements according to the job it is intended to do;
○ quality requirements to ensure reliability and minimize maintenance costs: good design and high quality materials for strength and to resist wear;
○ maximum purchase price which will allow a good financial return to be made.

Evaluate service back-up for available machines which come nearest to meeting the specification.
○ Find out which local dealers have a good reputation for after-sales service and availability of spare parts at reasonable prices.
○ For what period will the supplier carry out repairs and maintenance free of charge under guarantee?
○ Local artisans will be better able to repair machines which are already available on the local market.

Locally manufactured machines or imported ones?

Don't overlook the potential of existing local machines.

❍ Existing traditional designs have already proven that they fulfil a need and that they are sustainable in use.

❍ Adaptation and change is a continuing dynamic process. This catalogue may provide some new ideas on improvements to existing machines or on new machines which could be made locally.

❍ Improvements to technical performance, construction and materials, supply of spare parts and training should all be thoroughly investigated.

Dialogue between users, manufacturers and would-be innovators is essential. Full weight must be given to the opinions of all participants in change. The enthusiastic backing of all parties, freely given, is the best recipe for progress.

Check that importers have a strong commitment to service at point-of-sale and afterwards. They should:

❍ provide instruction, given by competent demonstrators, in use and maintenance of equipment, preferably on-farm;

❍ maintain a network of local dealers to provide a prompt and efficient service for repair, maintenance and supply of spare parts, all at reasonable prices;

❍ provide a comprehensive spare parts service:

— all consumable and predictable wearing parts should be immediately available locally;

— 'erratic' spare parts which may be needed from time to time may be stocked centrally, but should be available without delay through a local dealer.

Some additional points

Choose the right size of equipment. Obtaining equipment of the right size at purchase may prevent a lot of problems. Equipment that is too small is likely to break down quickly; if it is too large, apart from the pointless extra cost, it will be under-used to the detriment of performance and with faster wear and extra maintenance problems.

Compare 'total life' costs. When comparing tenders from suppliers for different pieces of equipment it is advisable to take account not just of the purchase price, but also of the costs of servicing, the life and costs of wearing parts and the cost of other basic spare parts. Some manufacturers exploit users by selling their spare parts at very high prices when the initial prices for their machines and equipment are average.

Marc Rodriguez
Agricultural Co-ordinator
GRET

Rob Nichols/Oxfam

1. FIELD POWER

This chapter looks at the need for power in farming operations and the sources available for the provision of that power for smallholdings. Most of the equipment in this book is powered by humans or by animals; however, with the increasing use of tractors in some countries, these are briefly discussed too.

The equipment section has been kept small since most equipment for harnessing animals is and should be made by local artisans and much of the engined equipment in this book is sold with an integral power source. No attempt has been made to list the numerous smaller tractors made by major tractor manufacturers since they are best sourced through agencies in country.

POWER FOR PRODUCTION

A mechanized farming operation is one which is carried out with the help of a machine. The machine may be a hand-tool such as a hoe, an implement such as an animal-drawn plough, or a complex machine such as a combine harvester.

The machine, of whatever type, requires a *power input* to make it produce a specified *output effect* such as cultivation, seed planting, or weeding. The power input defines the rate at which energy is supplied and so controls the rate at which the output effect is achieved.

Most agricultural operations are time-sensitive and crop yields suffer if they are not completed with due *timeliness*. Timeliness depends upon good management backed up by suitable equipment and adequate levels of power.

These relationships are illustrated in Figure 1.

A timely and effective mechanized operation depends upon:
○ a clearly specified output, i.e. the desired effect;
○ an adequate, available and sustainable input of mechanical power;
○ a machine, matched to the available power source, which can produce the desired output effect.

What type of power?

For a machine to function, it must be provided with an input of mechanical work; i.e. a pushing, pulling or turning force must be supplied to it. The mechanical work input is supplied by a source of mechanical power.

For field operations such as cultivation, planting and harvesting, the power source must be mobile. The need for in-field mobility limits the choice to:
○ humans;
○ animals;
○ engines — usually a diesel or petrol engine installed in a tractor with its own self-contained fuel supply.

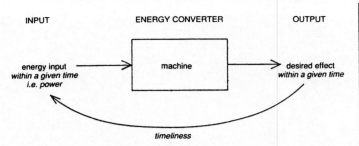

Figure 1 Timeliness and the need for power in an agricultural operation

Essentially all of these power sources are heat engines which convert chemical energy (food or fuel) to mechanical energy by oxidation processes.

HUMAN LABOUR

Human labour is characterized by limited power output compensated by versatility, dexterity and judgement. Thus human labour has superior capability for operations requiring these skills, such as transplanting seedlings, weeding and selective harvesting of fruit, vegetables and some fibre crops. It is less competitive for operations demanding brute power rather than skill, such as water lifting and heavy soil cultivation.

Limitations on human power production

Consumption of energy

From the point of view of power production, the human being is in essence a heat engine with built-in regulators against overload. An input of chemical energy in the form of food is converted into energy outputs in useful forms, including work, together with by-products and waste products such as excess heat and food waste with reduced energy content.

The sustainable rate at which the body can use up energy in this way is about 300W for a reasonably fit person in temperate conditions. In hotter climates heat stress may reduce this value, perhaps to about 250W.

Many agricultural activities demand higher rates of energy consumption (Table 1). Rest periods are then necessary.

Table 1   Human power consumption for various farming activities

Activity	Gross power consumed (Watts)
Clearing bush and scrub	400 - 600
Felling trees	600
Hoeing	300 - 500
Ridging, deep digging	400 - 1000
Planting	200 - 300
Ploughing with animal draught	350 - 550
Driving tractor:	
single axle tractor	350 - 650
conventional four-wheel tractor	150 - 300
Driving car on-farm	150

Source: mainly from Durnin and Passmore, 1967, *Energy, work and leisure* Heinemann

The energy consumption for various field tasks may be estimated by measuring heart rate. Energy consumption is correlated with the rise of heart rate above the 'at rest' level, which varies from person to person. A rise of about 30 beats per minute corresponds approximately to the maximum sustainable rate of energy consumption of 300W.

Rest periods

A rate of energy consumption exceeding 250-300W cannot be sustained for very long. A rest period will be necessary to allow the body to recover. If the rate of energy consumption is known, then the required rest period can be estimated from the equation

$$t_R = 60 (1 - 250/P) \text{ minutes per hour's work}$$

where t_R is the required resting time and P is the actual rate of energy consumption in watts.

As an example, suppose that a person is engaged in hoeing which calls for a power consumption of 300-500W (Table 1). The formula indicates that rest periods of

$$t_R = 60 (1 - 250/300) = 10 \text{ minutes per hour}$$

to

$$t_R = 60 (1 - 250/500) = 30 \text{ minutes per hour}$$

will be needed, depending on whether light or heavy hoeing is being undertaken.

Usually the worker will adopt a working mode which incorporates rest periods. It is important to understand that appropriate rest periods are physiologically necessary and it should not be assumed that the worker is slacking.

Efficiency of energy conversion

The efficiency with which consumed energy is turned into a physical work output is about 25 per cent in free-flowing activities such as walking, pedalling, pushing and pulling. The efficiency may be much lower (5 per cent or less) when the action is intermittent and/or the working posture is strained.

Physical work output

At the maximum continuous rate of energy consumption of 300W and conversion ratio of 25 per cent, the physical power output (force × distance/time) will be approximately 75W sustainable throughout a working day of eight to ten hours. Higher rates can be maintained only for shorter periods, as shown in Figure 2.

Ergonomics

Working methods can usually be improved, e.g. by reducing fatigue and improving control through a better interaction between human and machine. Ergonomics is the study of work design, based on the sciences of anatomy, physiology and psychology. It is closely associated with optimizing human performance as a power source (Grandjean, 1988).

General characteristics of human labour

The maximum sustainable power output which a person can produce is approximately 75W. Limitations have already been discussed. The input to any human-powered machine should not exceed this potential supply. Preferred methods for applying the power are by pedalling at about 30 to 40 revolutions per minute or by simulated walking as in treadle-operated pumps.

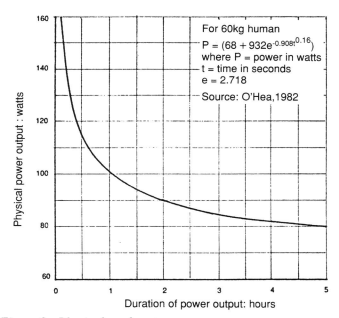

For 60kg human

$$P = (68 + 932e^{-0.908t^{0.16}})$$

where P = power in watts
t = time in seconds
e = 2.718

Source: O'Hea, 1982

Figure 2 Physical work output

Other relevant human characteristics which can compensate in very considerable measure for a rather low physical power output are that s/he:
○ can think and make decisions;
○ can control hand-tools with precision and judgement;
○ can control additional sources of power;
○ is versatile in his/her actions.

Work which requires much physical effort but not much thought is in general better undertaken by alternative sources of mechanical power, if the farmer has access to them and their use is economically sustainable.

ANIMAL POWER

Animal power is of enormous importance throughout Asia and in South America. Its use in Africa, particularly south of the Sahara, is limited but the potential is correspondingly greater. The main limitation in this region is that many farmers have restricted access to animal power. Restrictions arise because:
○ farmers may not own cattle because mixed farming is not traditional in many areas;
○ trypanosomiasis is endemic in many regions;
○ government agencies often lack interest in, and commitment to, encouraging the use of animal power.

Power potential of draught animals

Optimum pull

The power which a draught animal can provide is dependent upon the pull developed and speed of movement:

Power = Pull × Speed.

If the pull is measured in newtons (1 kilogram force = 10N) and the speed in metres per second (1m/s = 3.6km/h) the power will be given in watts.

The pull depends mainly on species and body weight but is also influenced by condition, temperament and training. In general the optimum pull for bovines (ox, cow, buffalo) is about 10-12 per cent of body weight. For equines (horse, donkey, mule) and camels the optimum pull is about 12-15 per cent of body weight.

The working speed for most draught animals when working at optimum pull is about 1m/s: rather lower for oxen and buffalo. A large increase above the optimum pull (say 50 per cent) will lead to a significant reduction in working speed. Table 2 shows guideline figures for typical animals.

Energy consumption and work output

The consumption of energy by draught animals may be assessed using the same basic methods as for human energy consumption. The Centre for Tropical Veterinary Medicine (CTVM) at Edinburgh has monitored the oxygen consumption of animals working on a treadmill to gain much useful data. Shetto (1983) pioneered the use of an earlobe transducer to monitor the heart rate of work oxen in the field. The Overseas Division of Silsoe Research Institute has developed a comprehensive data-logging system for field studies on the energy consumption of draught animals.

The following information arising from these studies is of value in assessing animal power.
○ A draught ox (Brahman) consumes about 3.3J for every newton of pull applied through a distance of one metre (i.e. 1J of mechanical work output). The corresponding energy consumed by a buffalo is about 2.6 J.
○ A draught ox consumes about 2 J of energy per metre travelled for each kilogram of its live weight. An additional 3J is consumed for each kilogram carried on the shoulders or 5J if the weight is carried in the middle of the back.
○ The rise in heart rate above its 'at rest' level corresponds approximately to increased power output. For oxen the mechanical power output (W) is given approximately by the rise in heart rate (beats per minute) multiplied by 50/3.

Table 2   Sustainable power of individual animals in good condition

Animal	Typical weight kN (kgf)	Pull-weight ratio	Typical pull N (kgf)	Typical working speed m/s	Power output W	Working hours per day	Energy output per day MJ
Ox	4.5 (450)	0.11	500 (50)	0.9	450	6	10
Buffalo	5.5 (50)	0.12	650 (65)	0.8	520	5	9.5
Horse	4.0 (400)	0.13	500 (50)	1.0	500	10	18
Donkey	1.5 (150)	0.13	200 (20)	1.0	200	4	3
Mule	3.0 (300)	0.13	400 (40)	1.0	400	6	8.5
Camel	5.0 (500)	0.13	650 (65)	1.0	650	6	14

Note: For animals of different weight the power output and energy output per day may be adjusted proportionately

Table 3 Feed requirements for work oxen

Weight of ox kN (kgf)	Maintenance ration	Light work		Medium work		Heavy work	
		Work ration	Total ration	Work ration	Total ration	Work ration	Total ration
2.5 (250)	2.3	1.2	3.5	2.3	4.6	3.5	5.8
3.0 (300)	2.6	1.3	3.9	2.6	5.2	3.9	6.5
3.5 (350)	2.9	1.5	4.4	2.9	5.8	4.4	7.3
4.0 (400)	3.2	1.6	4.8	3.2	6.4	4.8	8.0
4.5 (450)	3.5	1.8	5.3	3.5	7.0	5.3	8.8
5.0 (500)	3.8	1.9	5.7	3.8	7.6	5.7	9.5

Source: FAO, 1972, *The employment of draught animals in agriculture*, FAO, Rome.

Note: Feed requirements are given in terms of feed units (FU), based on a typical high quality carbohydrate foodstuff, e.g. 1 FU = 1kg of maize of other cereal grain and is equivalent to about 13 MJ ME (metabolizable energy)

Feed requirements

Feed requirements may be considered in two parts. The maintenance ration, which depends upon body mass, is used to sustain basal metabolism and normal activity of the animal. An additional 'work ration' is needed depending upon the energy consumed by the animal in walking, pulling and carrying a load.

Table 3 shows how the feed requirement for draught oxen varies with the intensity of their work output. The feed requirement is shown in FU (fodder units, equivalent to 1 kilogram of good quality grain). Available grazing must usually be supplemented by high grade foodstuffs (grain, oilseed cake etc.) FAO (1972) gives further details, including FU equivalent of various foodstuffs.

Limitations on the performance of draught animals

Major factors which influence the performance of draught animals include:
○ weight and condition, which depend upon breed, age, nutritional status and health of the animal;
○ conformation, which is mainly a function of the animal's genetic make-up;
○ temperament, which is influenced by a range of genetic and environmental factors: an alert, positive and cooperative temperament is desirable;
○ husbandry and training.

It is important to maintain the weight and condition of animals which have been selected and trained for draught work. Their most demanding workload often occurs when the rains break at the end of a dry season, when grazing and other feedstuffs are in short supply. Their condition will deteriorate rapidly if high workloads are demanded without an adequate supply of good quality feedstuffs.

Animal-powered implements

Types of operation

Work animals are used in a number of roles:
○ transport by pulling carts or sledges, as pack animals or for riding;
○ field work, pulling agricultural implements;
○ water lifting and processing operations such as sugar cane crushing, usually by moving in a circular path to drive the device through animal-powered gears.

The following discussion concentrates on the use of draught animals for field work.

Types of implement

Animal draught implements for field work may be classified in three broad categories:
○ beam-pulled or 'pole-pulled' implements;
○ chain-pulled implements;
○ wheeled tool carriers with a range of attachments.

The most widely used implements are grouped in the first two categories. In each category a range of implements is available to deal with basic cultivation operations (soil breaking, ploughing, ridging etc.), weeding, planting and harvesting for particular crops. The characteristics of specific implements are discussed in later chapters.

Beam-pulled implements have been in use for 4000-5000 years. During this time empirical development has resulted in many extremely sophisticated implements, locally manufactured from readily available materials, which are relatively cheap to buy and maintain. They should certainly not be rejected as 'old-fashioned'.

Beam implements are normally pulled by a pair of animals (oxen or buffalo) harnessed by a shoulder yoke (see below). The yoke supports the implement's beam at the front, making it easy to control and lift. Thus beam-pulled implements are particularly well suited to use in small and/or irrigated fields where frequent lifting is necessary for turning or jumping over partition bunds.

Beam-pulled implements must be light to lift (about 12kgf to 15kgf at the handle) if they are to be acceptable to the farmer. Their light weight also ensures that they have a relatively low draught so that a pair of oxen in good condition can normally work for a full day without becoming too tired.

Chain-pulled implements originated in Europe, and they have been introduced into much of sub-Saharan Africa.

In general, chain-pulled implements are heavier than traditional beam-pulled implements, with a tendency to higher draught and a deeper working depth in consequence. This can be an advantage if relatively deep working is required, particularly on heavier soils.

The potentially high draught of chain-pulled implements may make it necessary to use a team consisting of several pairs of animals to pull them. Suitable harnessing arrangements can be made but manoeuverability will suffer.

Chain-pulled implements are well suited to heavier soil conditions and longer working runs, but are not as well adapted as beam implements to working in confined and/or irrigated areas.

Wheeled tool carriers have been the subject of much research and development effort over the past forty years or so. Two major features are that they can be fitted with alternative attachments for a range of field operations (including cultivation, ridging, weeding, seeding, and transport) and that in most cases the machines are intended for 'ride-on' operation. In these respects they might be considered as a desirable half-way stage between conventional animal draught power and tractorization, providing an improved technical performance and an enhanced status for the owner/operator.

Although wheeled tool carriers have been used to good effect on research and demonstration farms in many countries, their adoption and use by farmers have been limited, even when supplied at subsidized prices. The 'improved' technology has not proved to be effective or acceptable at farm level (Starkey 1988). A cautious approach to its promotion is advisable.

Harnessing

Types of harness

The main types of harness may be classified as:
- ○ yoke: head yoke (sometimes called neck yoke); shoulder yoke (sometimes called neck yoke or withers yoke);
- ○ collar: full collar; split collar;
- ○ breastband.

These harnesses are illustrated in Figure 3.

The head yoke is traditional in some areas but is not a favoured type. It is only of use with non-humped cattle (*bos taurus*) and buffalo. Humped cattle (*bos indicus*), equines (horse, donkey, mule) and camels have weaker necks which make the head yoke quite unsuitable.

The double shoulder yoke has been used to harness oxen and buffalo for thousands of years. It is not suitable for equines. It is easy and cheap to make using local timber, but it has been criticized as inefficient and for causing sores and injury. These problems can be largely overcome by shaping the yoke beam to the animal's neck, padding it if necessary, and by ensuring that implement draught does not exceed the levels recommended in Table 2.

Collar harnesses may be classified as either full-collar or split-collar. The full-collar harness has been widely used with horses but tends to be expensive. The split-collar harness, with two vertical hames joined at the top and bottom, is versatile and has been used for oxen, buffalo and donkeys.

The breastband harness can be adapted to suit most animals' various work functions such as pulling a cart or a cultivation implement. It is relatively cheap and easy to make but care is needed to ensure that it is a good fit on the animal and does not cause sores or discomfort.

Selection of harness

In areas where draught animal power is traditionally practised, a particular type of harness will already be in use. The type of harness is usually a rational response to a complex set of local circumstances, and in such cases it will be advisable to investigate possible improvements to the existing harnesses rather than attempt to introduce radically different types, at least in the initial stages.

Where draught animal power is being introduced for the first time, the choice of harness will depend upon the draught animals and types of implement to be used and the skills, materials and money which are available.

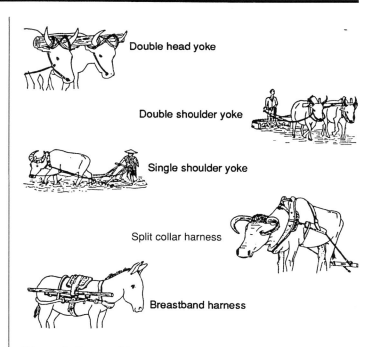

Figure 3 Types of harness

Beam-pulled implements are normally used in conjunction with a pair of oxen or buffalo harnessed with a shoulder yoke.

Chain-pulled implements can be used with other animals and other types of harness. Alternatives which can be considered are the breastband and the split-collar harness. A well made and fitted split-collar or full-collar harness is probably the most efficient for any animal. It is also the most expensive and requires more training and higher levels of skill in its construction and use.

Operation of cultivation implements

Fundamental forces and their relationships

Most cultivation operations are aimed at changing the soil condition in a way which will enhance crop production and bring financial benefits to the farmer, in the short and long term, without detriment to the environment. The implement, the draught animals and the operator all have important roles to play. For optimum results the inter-relationships between these three components must be carefully considered.

The harness forms the link between the animals and the implement. Figure 4 shows the relationship between the force systems acting on the implement and on the animals. Forces P_1 and P_2 are equal in magnitude, being the tension force in the pull chain or beam attachment ropes. The draught force on the implement, H_1, is matched exactly by the horizontal pull from the animals, H_2, while the effective vertical force, V_1, acting on the implement is transferred and carried, depending on the harness design, on the animal's shoulders, back or haunches (force V_2).

Adjusting the implement in work

The implement draught force depends on:
- ○ the weight of the implement;
- ○ the angle of pull from the chain;
- ○ the extent to which the effect of implement weight is counteracted by support forces, mainly from the soil, acting in an opposing (upward) direction.

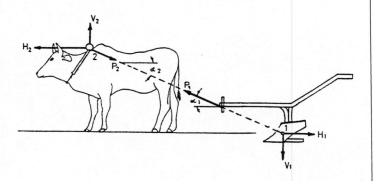

P₁ = P₂ = pull force on chain
H₁ = H₂ = draught force/pull force
V₁ = V₂ = effective vertical force on implement
       = vertical force at yoke beam
∝₁ = ∝₂ = angle of pull

Figure 4 Fundamentals of harnessing showing relationship between force systems acting on the implement and the animals

The implement will move deeper into work until the draught force builds up to an equilibrium value in accordance with these draught-controlling factors. How deep this will be depends upon the specific soil resistance (Inns 1990).

It may be necessary to adjust the implement draught in order to:

○ reduce the pull to a level which the draught animal(s) can comfortably exert: this is particularly critical when working with a single animal;
○ reduce or increase the depth of work.

To *reduce* implement draught and depth of work:

1. use the lightest implement consistent with required strength and function;
2. adjust the harness or implement attachment to give a steep angle of pull;
3. counteract a greater proportion of the implement's weight by increasing the support forces acting on it.

To *increase* implement draught and depth of work:

1. reduce support forces so that implement weight has its maximum effect in causing penetration;
2. adjust the harness or implement attachment to give a shallow angle of pull;
3. add weight to the implement at a point near its centre of gravity.

It may also be necessary to adjust the point of attachment of the pull chain to the implement, in order to ensure that the implement is in good balance under the forces acting on it.

Support forces may be increased by adjusting any components provided for this purpose, possibly including a heel, sole or slade on a plough or ridging body, or by lowering depth wheels or skids (if fitted) to make earlier contact with the ground. They may be reduced by reversing any such adjustments, but it is necessary also to ensure that there are no undesirable support forces resulting from worn shares or badly set or shaped mouldboards.

A moderate draught force is particularly necessary for single animal working. A system developed for this purpose in the Sudan combines a lightweight plough and steep angle of pull to achieve the desired effect.

TRACTOR POWER

Tractors with a power rating of 25kW or less are variously described as 'low-power', 'compact' or 'small' tractors. To identify possible uses for small tractors on small farms in developing countries it is necessary to examine their technical and economic characteristics and management requirements.

Four-wheel tractors

Drawbar pull

Tractors are primarily intended for pulling. Most tractors are also designed with a rotating 'power take-off' drive shaft to provide power to a variety of machines such as rotary hoes, pumps, and threshing machines (see below).

The term 'drawbar pull' refers to the pull which the tractor applies to an implement, either through a three-link attachment system or by a drawbar. The drawbar pull produced by a tractor depends upon the interaction between its driving wheels and the soil at their area of contact.

The main factors which influence drawbar pull are the vertical load carried on this contact area, the strength and deformability of the soil when subjected to a shearing action, and the size and shape of the contact area.

These factors impose a severe limitation on the ability of small tractors to provide adequate pull for many field operations. Primary cultivation in particular is a high-draught operation for which a sustainable pull of at least 5kN (500 kgf, 1100 lbf) is desirable.

To develop a reliable pull of 5kN (500 kgf) in the range of soil and field conditions to be expected in rainfed agriculture, a 'heavy duty' small tractor will generally be needed. It is necessary to look for the following features:

○ minimum bare weight 1200 kgf;
○ minimum rear (driven) axle load 800 kgf;
○ provision for adding rear wheel ballast;
○ minimum drive wheel size 11.2/10-24 (traction type tyres);
○ minimum engine power 20kW (25hp);
○ at least four well-spaced gear ratios;

Harness for working with a single donkey. The lightweight plough and steep angle of pull help to keep draught to an acceptable level

○ sound design and construction;
○ accessible and reliable service back-up: maintenance, repair, replacement parts.

Engine power on its own is not a satisfactory guide to drawbar performance. The ability of the tractor to transform power into drawbar pull depends upon the ground drive characteristics.

Power from the power take-off

Power can be delivered to an implement much more efficiently through the power take-off (pto) than through the drawbar. Consequently many small tractors use a pto-driven rotary hoe as the main primary cultivation implement.

The rotary hoe is undoubtedly efficient mechanically but has a number of practical and agronomic limitations which must be taken into account:
○ it is not suitable for use in dry soil conditions;
○ the depth of work is limited;
○ continued use often leads to formation of a compacted layer ('hard-pan') at working depth;
○ the soil is left in a loose and fluffy condition which is vulnerable to capping and erosion;
○ the cost of replacement hoes and maintenance may be high.

The tractor power take-off is useful for driving other machines such as sprayers, fertilizer distributors (spinning-disc type) and stationary machines such as pumps and threshers. Costs may be high if it is used exclusively for these operations.

Single axle (two-wheel) tractors and rotary cultivators

The use of single axle tractors and rotary cultivators is associated mainly with the production of irrigated rice in Asian countries and of horticultural crops in temperate and tropical countries. These are relatively high-value crops and it may be difficult to justify the use of single axle tractors for general agricultural production.

Traction is very limited because of the tractors' low weight and small wheels. Consequently, the potential of these machines for primary cultivation is limited mainly to rotary hoeing, which does not depend on high tractive forces from the wheels.

The ability of single axle tractors to work in ridged fields is limited. In general their ground clearance is too low to straddle a ridge, and they are too wide to work between ridges unless these are widely spaced.

The single axle tractor is often used with a trailer attachment for transport (mainly on-road) or for spraying in conjunction with a tanker-trailer. It may also be used as a power source for stationary machines such as threshers, using a power take-off shaft or belt drive.

'Small and simple' tractors

It has long been argued that tractors manufactured for use in the more industrialized countries are too sophisticated, too expensive, too powerful and not robust enough for viable use in smallholder production systems in less developed areas of the tropics and sub-tropics. As a result, many attempts have been made to design tractors specifically for manufacture and use in less developed countries. These attempts have originated and been pushed along by various organizations and individuals from and within both industrialized and developing countries (Holtkamp 1990).

The aim of indigenous design and manufacture is still pursued in many developing countries. Some progress has been made with a number of pioneering designs. Local

Single axle tractors can be used for seedbed preparation in level fields for higher value crops

Jeremy Hartley/Panos

production under licence of adapted models from major manufacturers has, in general, proved more successful to date.

SELECTION OF POWER SOURCE AND MACHINERY

Operations to be mechanized

More power becomes available as the progression is made from human labour to animal power and then to engine power. The fundamental question arises of how to use the extra power to best advantage.

Power cannot substitute fully for the skill, judgement and experience which people can bring to delicate operations such as transplanting seedlings. Relatively sophisticated machines are needed to undertake such operations, but not much power. On the other hand, routine operations such as water lifting consume much power but little intelligence once the system has been installed.

Binswanger (1984, 1988) calls operations of the former type 'control-intensive' and of the latter type 'power-intensive'. In between these extremes are many operations requiring various mixes of control and power. Binswanger observed that, historically, when new sources of power are introduced (first animal power, then engine power) they are used initially for power-intensive operations such as transport, water lifting and primary cultivation.

When the owners of new sources of power have satisfied their own needs in basic power-intensive operations, they have usually found it advantageous to sell surplus capacity to non-owners, often neighbours or tenants, and buy in the skills needed for their more control-intensive work. Thus new power sources tend to be used for operations in which they have the greatest comparative advantage (Binswanger).

Based on these observations, some guidelines may be suggested concerning the potential viability of particular mechanized operations, as shown on Table 4.

Selection of power sources for field operations

Selection of a suitable source of mechanical power for a particular operation is specific to local circumstances. Major factors, which can be used as a check-list in selection, are that the power source should be:

○ accessible to the farmer;
○ available when needed;
○ user-friendly;
○ sufficiently powerful;
○ sustainable in use;
○ economically viable;
○ socially acceptable.

These factors must be evaluated from the farmers' point of view, according to their own position in a social and economic hierarchy.

Accessibility

Ownership of a power source by its user is obviously desirable. Most farmers have some family labour available. If they do not own draught animals or a tractor, farmers must rely upon services which may possibly be available from the landlord, a neighbour, a local contractor, or a hire service.

Availability

It is important to the farmer that the power source should be available to start work as soon as it is needed. Delays may give rise to costly timeliness penalties. If the farmer has to buy in power (labour, draught animals or tractor), its availability at the appointed time is likely to be less reliable with increasing remoteness of the supplier and with any associated bureaucracy.

User-friendliness

The power source and equipment should be compatible with the knowledge, skill and experience of the user. These may be supplemented by additional training if necessary, but the training must be sound and readily available.

Power sufficiency

Timeliness in completing an operation depends upon having sufficient power available. The sources selected must be powerful enough to undertake the required tasks with due timeliness. The overall farming and social system should be examined to identify additional work which the new power source might undertake on a commercially viable basis, so helping to minimize unit power costs.

Table 4   Relative power intensity and control intensity of various operations

Power intensive: viable mechanization at an early stage

Transport
Water lifting/pumping
Land forming
Primary culitivation
Seedbed preparation
Weed control
Harvesting grain
Seeding
Harvesting rootcrops
Planting tubers, sets, etc.
Transplanting seedlings
Harvesting fruit and vegetable crops

Control intensive: viable for mechanization at a later stage

Sustainability

There are three major aspects to sustainability:
○ physical;
○ operational;
○ financial.

Physical sustainability It must be possible to keep all equipment in efficient working condition. This applies equally to human, animal or tractor power sources and all associated tools and implements. Human and animal power sources require food and a healthy environment, with medical and veterinary services when needed. Engine use must be supported by readily available consumables (fuel, oil, filters etc.) together with replacement parts, maintenance and repair services as required.

Operational sustainability This depends upon using equipment to its best advantage, which requires well-trained and skilled operators together with managers who are aware of the technical capabilities of the power sources and machines under their control, and who have the expertise to ensure that these capabilities are used to the full.

Financial sustainability The power and machinery should be used within a system which is profitable to the farmer as judged by its actual performance. Projected performances commonly have a tendency to over-optimism.

Social acceptability

The equipment and working methods should be socially and culturally acceptable, enhancing the dignity and status of the user. A primary social duty of the farmer is to ensure that the family is fed. The farmers' assessment of the reliability with which any new equipment and practices can help them to achieve this target must be respected — they have more to lose than their advisers.

Subsidies

Subsidies are payments made as a matter of policy to influence or assist the actions of a target group of people. Many governments use subsidies in an attempt to increase food production.

Farming subsidies are of two main kinds. Input subsidies encourage the farmer to use particular inputs such as fertilizer, improved seed, or tractor services by providing them at an artificially low price. Output subsidies are usually paid to the farmer in the form of guaranteed high purchase prices as an incentive to produce particular crops.

Subsidies distort the market with the intention of producing a desirable outcome but their overall effects are not always fully considered. Input subsidies influence the farmers' freedom of choice. For instance, if subsidized fertilizer is available cheaply to farmers they will be influenced to use it although in a free market other inputs might be more cost-effective and desirable on a sustainable basis.

Mechanization inputs are often subsidized by low prices for tractors and machinery or by providing tractor hire services at less than their true cost. In many countries animal power and equipment are not given similar support and encouragement. The smallholder farmer, and the national economy, may be disadvantaged in consequence.

Output subsidies, on the other hand, encourage farmers to produce more of a particular crop without biasing choice o inputs. They can make their own 'grass roots' judgements about whether and how to grow the crop according to specific circumstances. Their judgements are likely to be more rational, perceptive and sustainable then those brought about by the effects of input subsidies decided off-farm.

Costs

It is difficult to assess the costs of power in near-subsistence farming where human labour and, in some areas, draught animal power are likely to be the dominating power sources. Consequently it is not possible to make a convincing exact comparison of costs for alternative farming systems under varying degrees of mechanization and with a variety of power sources.

Smallholder farmers react mainly to costs paid in cash and cash-equivalent costs involving payments in kind. Government and its various agencies will probably be more interested in economic costs, often involving subtle variations in definition.

The availability of cash, and cash flow, are major problems which limit the farmers' ability to use more power to expand or intensify their production system.

Selection of power source from the farmers' viewpoint

Factors influencing the selection of human labour

For most smallholder farmers, personal and family labour is the most readily available, reliable and cheap source of power. The cost of such labour is not readily identifiable unless there is alternative employment which would bring in a cash income. It will usually be regarded as free. Direct cost is limited to the extra food which may be needed to replace energy used while working.

The cost of basic hand-tools is relatively low, although the purchase and maintenance costs of more sophisticated human-powered equipment (seeders, sprayers) may well be prohibitive.

Factors influencing the selection of animal power

A distinction must be made between areas where mixed farming is customary and areas where livestock raising is a specialist activity limited mainly to a particular, often nomadic, group of people.

Where mixed farming is customary it is likely that at least some farmers will already use their animals on draught work, possibly for transport or irrigation water lifting. Others will have experience of livestock husbandry and will generally accept draught animal power as a user-friendly technology. The cost of using these already-owned power sources will be that of extra feed, additional health care and the purchase of harnesses and implements.

There is an increasing awareness of the potential for using single animals for draught work on smaller farms. The introduction and feasibility of single-animal working depends upon careful selection of suitable harnesses and implements, together with effective training. Weeding and primary cultivation are the main operations targeted for single-animal working.

Owners of draught animals enjoy considerable benefits arising from self-sufficiency and operational control over their power inputs. Compared with tractor owners, their power source depreciates very little with use and is less demanding of bought-in inputs such as fuel and replacement parts.

The introduction of draught animal power into areas where arable farming and livestock ownership are separate ways of life presents many problems, however; arable farmers will lack

Single animal working: note simple adaptation of wooden framed ard, and very simple breastband harness

experience of good animal husbandry and may find it difficult to work with and exercise sympathetic control over draught animals. An alternative line of development exists when livestock-owning groups become aware of benefits which might arise from mixed farming and the potential for using their animals in draught work. In some areas there is already a tendency for nomadic livestock owners to adopt a more settled way of life.

Factors influencing the selection of tractor power

Individual ownership of a tractor is not a viable option for most smallholder farmers. The total cost of tractorized operations (capital plus running costs) is such that, even with good yields and selling prices, a power intensity of 0.5kW/ha is the maximum which is likely to be economically viable.

On this basis about 40ha of well-cropped arable land will be needed to support the costs of a 20kW tractor — the minimum power at which a tractor is considered technically feasible. It will be necessary for a number of smallholder farmers to participate in the use of such a tractor, a concept usually referred to as 'multi-farm use of agricultural machinery' (FAO 1985).

An individual smallholder farmer may have access to tractor power through a variety of 'multi-farm use' arrangements:
○ individual ownership and supply of contract services to neighbouring farmers: the owner becomes a farmer-contractor;
○ buying in services from a neighbouring farmer-contractor;
○ buying in services from the landlord;
○ group ownership of a tractor through a cooperative or syndicate;
○ buying in services from a commercial contractor;
○ making use of a government-sponsored tractor-hire service.

The farmer will judge the effectiveness of contract services by criteria such as those already discussed. Experience has shown that in general the most satisfactory service is provided by a neighbouring farmer-contractor. Government-sponsored contracting services are cheaper than those provided by private contractors, but their record for reliability and responsiveness is generally poor in comparison.

It is essential whenever it has been decided to use tractor power that full back-up services are available. These include efficient maintenance and repair facilities and the prompt and reliable supply of replacement parts. Without such facilities it is only too likely that any tractors purchased, or supplied under 'aid' schemes, will quickly join the graveyards of derelict equipment which are an unwelcome feature of attempted tractorization in many countries.

The best guide to good back-up services is the reputation of the local agents for particular manufacturers. The best safeguard of continuing support is to purchase only from agents who show commitment and organization in providing an efficient service to the customer.

SELECTIVE MECHANIZATION

The introduction of a new and more powerful power source should lead naturally to a process of selective mechanization, starting with power-intensive operations. Its economic use for less power-intensive operations will depend upon the rate at which the agricultural system evolves within the framework of national development, and should not be unduly forced.

Selective mechanization is not a second-rate alternative to complete mechanization. It is a realistic process which, when properly applied, allows mechanization to evolve in response to economic realities with a high degree of flexibility and precision.

PURCHASING EQUIPMENT

The following pages provide information on the sources of mechanical power for tools and equipment mentioned in the later chapters. The equipment is laid out in this order: animal harnessing, walking tractors, four-wheel tractors, stationary engines.

Animal harnessing

This section contains the little information on animal harnessing equipment that has been sent to us. However, most harnessing is made by local artisans who are not represented in this guide. Accordingly, before approaching the manufacturers mentioned here, it is important to look at what is being produced and used locally and try to source your requirements there.

Single axle (two-wheel) tractors

The list of walking tractors here should be read in conjunction with the powered cultivators in Chapter 2. Most of the powered cultivators can also be used as general walking tractors.

Four-wheel tractors

This introduction has described some of the main points to consider when purchasing a tractor. It is not in the scope of this book to go into greater detail and so no information is included on four-wheel tractors made by the large number of international manufacturers. The existence of a good local agency is the most important factor to be considered when purchasing a tractor, and information on the range of tractors produced by such manufacturers will be available from their agencies. However, some information is included about tractors made by manufacturers from developing countries.

Information is not given on the large number of mini, compact or 'garden' tractors available. These do not provide a viable option for smallholder farmers in developing countries. The only exception to this are mini tractors with rotovators used for paddy cultivation in Asia, and accordingly they have been included.

Stationary power sources

Most powered equipment is sold with a power unit already installed. Mentioned in this chapter are the manufacturers of engines that informed us that they sell power units separately. Again, as for tractors, the existence of a local agency is a major factor in the choice of power unit.

Frank Inns
Consultant

REFERENCES

Hamzar Elharith Battran (1990). Unpublished MSc thesis, Silsoe College, MK45 4DT, UK.

Binswanger, H.P. (1984) *Agricultural Mechanization: a comparative historical perspective*, World Bank working paper No. 673, The World Bank, Washington DC, USA.

Binswanger, H.P. et al (1988) *Agricultural Mechanization: issues and options*, The World Bank, Washington DC, USA.

Durnin, J.V.G.A., and Passmore, R. (1967) *Energy, work and leisure*. Heinemann, London.

(FAO) (1972) *The employment of draught animals in agriculture*, FAO, Rome.

(FAO) (1985) *Multifarm use of agricultural machinery*, FAO agriculture series No 17.

Grandjean, E. (1988) *Fitting the task to the man — a textbook of occupational ergonomics*, 4th edition, Taylor and Francis, London.

Holtkamp, R. (1990) *Small four-wheel tractors for the tropics and sub-tropics: their role in agricultural and industrial development*, GTZ, Eschborn, Germany.

Inns, F.M. (1990) 'The mechanics of animal draught cultivation implements, part 1, chain-pulled implements', *The Agricultural Engineer*, 45 (1) 13-17.

Inns, F.M. (1990) 'The mechanics of animal draught cultivation implements, part 2, beam-pulled implements', *The Agricultural Engineer*, 46 (1) 18-21.

O'Hea, A. (1982) 'Performance index for man-powered pumps', *Appropriate Technology*, 9 (4), 10-11.

Shetto, R.M. (1983) 'Work assessment of draught animals', unpublished MSc thesis, Silsoe College, MK45 4DT, UK.

Starkey, P. (1988) *Animal-drawn wheeled toolcarriers: perfected yet rejected*, GTZ/GATE, Eschborn, Germany.

DONKEY HARNESS

This harness is based on a collar with specially shaped hames and canvas pads filled with animal hair. It is used with implements such as the Rumptstad plough or with carts.

The cart harness has a saddle to support part of the load and a breeching strap which connects to the cart shafts for 'braking'. The harness was designed by the Department of Agricultural Engineering, University of Nairobi.

MUTOMO TECHNICAL CENTRE
P.O. Box 147
Mutomo
Kitui
KENYA

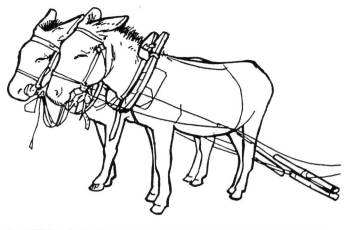

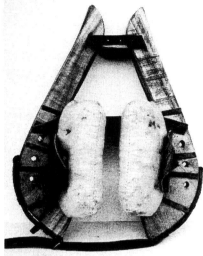

OX COLLAR AND TREK CHAINS

This ox collar is of similar design to the donkey collar described above. Specially shaped hames, fitted with canvas pads filled with animal hair, make this harness more efficient than a neck yoke. Designed by the Department of Agricultural Engineering, University of Nairobi.

MUTOMO TECHNICAL CENTRE
P.O. Box 147
Mutomo
Kitui
KENYA

TREK CHAINS
A variety of chains are available from:

ZIMPLOW LTD
P.O. Box 1059
Bulawayo
ZIMBABWE

HITCH EVENER

The normal arrangement for hitching two animals to implements is by means of a hitch evener comprising a curved brace to which two swingle trees are linked. The position of this link can be adjusted to compensate when one animal is more powerful than another. Traces from the swingle trees attach to the animal's harness.

ZIMPLOW LTD
P.O. Box 1059
Bulawayo
ZIMBABWE

ANIMAL-DRAUGHT POWER UNIT

This is a capstan type power unit, to which one or two large animals can be harnessed. It can be used as a power source for crop processing and water pumping. One animal revolution provides 18.5 revolutions of the drive shaft. Gearing is provided by sprocket and chain.
Weight 400kg.

ALVAN BLANCH DEV. CO. LTD
Chelworth
Malmesbury
Wilts SN16 9SG
UK

HORSE AND PONY HARNESSES

Regular and Welsh type pony harness and horse buggy harness.

C.H. DANA COMPANY INC.
Hyde Park
Vermont
05655
USA

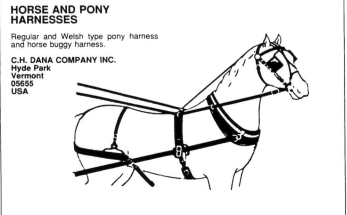

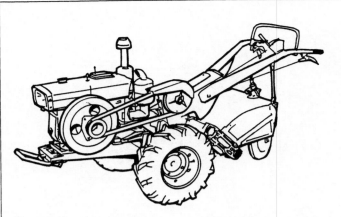

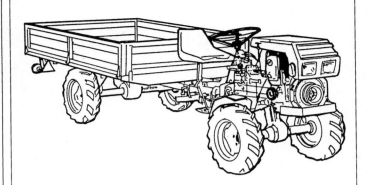

DONGFENG-12 WALKING TRACTORS

Several versions of Dongfeng walking tractors are made at Jiangxi. The basic DF-12 model is supplied with a rotary tiller which incorporates a single rear wheel. As the DF-12C it is produced as a transportation tractor and is fitted with a steering wheel and permanently attached to a small open-top truck body. This can achieve a maximum speed of 29.2 km/hour. The same body is available in trailer form which can be hitched to the DF-12A model, similar to the DF-12 but without the tiller.

Power take-off for use with free-standing implements is by belt drive from the same flywheel-mounted pulley used to drive the tractor.

Attachments are :

- Rotary tiller incorporating rear wheel and driver's seat;
- Single share plough;
- Paddy harrow;
- Rolling harrow.

Rubber road wheels are standard as is a single headlight, mounted on top of the fuel tank. The 9kW diesel engine is water cooled.

RED STAR MACHINE WORKS OF JIANGXI
Bong Xiang Si
Jiangxi
CHINA

WALKING TRACTOR
This walking tractor is fitted with a horizontal single cylinder four-stroke diesel engine rated at 8.82kW. It is suitable for a range of uses, including rotary tillage, ploughing, paddy field operations, seeding, harvesting and transport when coupled to a trailer. The tractor can be used as a power source for electricity generating, water pumping, threshing and fodder processing. Weight 470kg (with tiller).

BEIJING TRACTOR COMPANY
1 Xinfeng Street
Beijing
100088
CHINA

WALKING TRACTORS

This tractor is powered by a 9kW diesel engine driving the wheels via a three-speed gearbox. A single reverse gear is also provided. The power take-off can be synchronized with the forward gear selected, left in neutral or run independently of the gears at 750 rev/min. The handlebars are adjustable laterally and vertically with a quick locking device and a 'deadman's handle' provides safety by stopping the engine if it is released by the operator.

In addition to the standard soil-engaging implements available with the machine, the company supplies a trailer with a steering wheel, operator's seat and a two-wheel axle driven from the tractor's power take-off. This provides optional two- or four-wheel drive and has a rear-facing power take-off point to drive extra equipment such as a pump or generator.

S.E.P. FABBRICA MACCHINE AGRICOLE S.R.L.
42018 S. Martino in Rio (R.E.)
ITALY

Similar tractors are made by:

AYUTTHAYA TRACTOR FACTORY
63/4 Moo 1, Rojana Road
T.Pai-Ling, A.Muang
Ayutthaya 13000
THAILAND

GEBR HOLDER GmbH & CO.
Stuttgarter Strasse 42-46
Postfach 1555
D-7430 Metzingen
GERMANY

CENTRE FOR DEVELOPMENT OF APPROPRIATE AGRICULTURAL ENGINEERING TECHNOLOGY
Situgadung, Legok
Tromol Pos 2,Serpong
15310
INDONESIA

C.V. KARYA HIDUP SENTOSA
Jl. Magelang 144
Yogyakarta
55241
INDONESIA

NEW RUHAAK INDUSTRIES
Jl. Pintu Besar Utara 11
Jakarta
INDONESIA

P.T. RUTAN MACHINERY TRADING CO.
P.O. Box 319
Surabaya
INDONESIA

V.S.T. TILLERS TRACTORS LTD
P.O. Box 4801
Mahadevapura Post Office
Bangalore
560 048
INDIA

AGRIA-WERKE GmbH
Postfach 1147
D-7108 Moeckmuehl
GERMANY

AYUTTHAYA NANAPHAN
68/3 Moo 1, T.Pai-Ling
A.Muang
Ayutthaya
THAILAND

CHOR CHAROENCHAI FACTORY
59/7 Rojana Road
T.Pai-Ling, A.Muang
Ayutthaya
THAILAND

JAKPETCH TRACTOR CO. LTD
14 Moo 3, Soi Orn-Nuch,
Ladkrabang
Bangkok
10520
THAILAND

DM INVESTMENTS GROUP CT+U (T) LTD
P.O. Box 820
Mwanza
TANZANIA

IMT BEOGRAD
Fabrika Opreme I Pribora
Industrijska zona bb.
23272 Novi Becej
YUGOSLAVIA

AGROTECHNICA
Karlova
4300
BULGARIA

TINKABI TRACTOR

This unit was specially developed for licensed manufacture overseas, to give power to the subsistence farmer. It is a four-wheeled tractor with a 34kW, water-cooled diesel engine and hydrostatic transmission. Speed, direction of travel and braking are controlled by a single hand lever, no foot controls being fitted. The tractor has a maximum speed of 15 km/hour and has a maximum drawbar pull of 818kg. It is 2.5m in length, with a fabricated chassis and an integral oil reservoir and fuel tank. The engine and driver are to the rear, and in front of the driver is a load platform with a 1000kg carrying capacity. Implements include: drawbar, plough, hammer mill, planter, spring-tine cultivator and ridger, harrow, circular saw bench, generator, pump and irrigation set, crop sprayer, and transport trailer.

VICTORWARD LTD
Bury Farm
Sandridgebury Lane
Sandridge
St. Albans AL3 6JB
UK

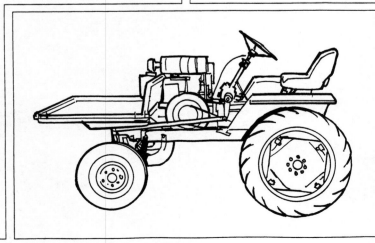

'TE' TWO-WHEEL DRIVE TRACTOR

This tractor was developed in France, primarily for use on cotton farms in West African countries. It is powered by an 18 or 22kW air-cooled four-stroke diesel engine which drives the rear wheels. The tractor has a hydraulically operated three-point linkage, two-speed power take-off (540 and 1000 rev/min) and a gearbox with six forward speeds in two ranges and three reverse speeds. A front load deck is one metre square and has a capacity of 500kg. The tractor has a high ground clearance, 580mm, and a wide track which enables it to straddle two rows of cotton.

C.F.D.T.
13 rue de Monceau
Paris
75008
FRANCE

FRONT-WHEEL-DRIVE FOUR-WHEEL TRACTOR

This is a small, front-wheel-drive tractor with rear-wheel steering. Power is provided by a 7kW single cylinder diesel engine with a belt and pulley drive to the gearbox. The tractor is fitted with a toolbar but has no hydraulic system or power take-off.
Weight 1100kg

AYUTTHAYA NANAPHAN
68/3 Moo 1
T.Pai-Ling, A.Muang
Ayutthaya
THAILAND

A similar tractor is available from:

AYUTTHAYA TRACTOR FACTORY
63/4 Moo 1, Rojana Road
T.Pai-Ling, A.Muang
Ayutthaya
13000
THAILAND

SMALL FOUR-WHEEL-DRIVE TRACTORS

The following companies offer small, sophisticated four-wheel-drive tractors that can be used in wet- and dry-land farming. The model illustrated is supplied with a rotary tiller.

VST TILLERS TRACTORS LTD
P.O. Box 4801
Bangalore 560 048
INDIA

KUBOTA LTD
2-47 Shikitsuhigashi 1-chome
Naniwa-Ku, Osaka 556-91
JAPAN

REAR-WHEEL-DRIVE FOUR-WHEEL TRACTOR

This is a small, rear-wheel-drive tractor with conventional front-wheel steering. Power is provided by a 7kW single cylinder diesel engine with a belt and pulley drive to the gearbox. The tractor is 2.9m long, has a track of 1330mm and a ground clearance of 330mm.
The tractor is fitted with a toolbar but has no hydraulic lift system or conventional power take-off.
Weight 1100kg.

AYUTTHAYA TRACTOR FACTORY
63/4 Moo 1, Rojana Road
T.Pai-Ling, A.Muang
Ayutthaya 13000
THAILAND

A similar tractor is available from:

AYUTTHAYA NANAPHAN
68/3 Moo 1
T.Pai-Ling, A.Muang
Ayutthaya
THAILAND

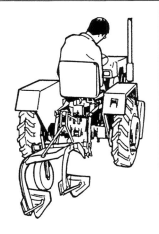

SWARAJ 724 TRACTOR

The 18.5kW tractor illustrated is one of a range produced by this company. This model is fitted with a twin cylinder four-stroke water-cooled diesel engine. It has a 1⅜" 1000 rev/min power take-off and a Category I three-point hitch. The hydraulic system provides position, draught and mix control and has a lifting capacity of 800kg. The transmission has six forward and two reverse gears. A 12V electrical system is fitted, providing lights and engine starting.
Weight 1800kg.

Other tractors in the range have power outputs of 15kW, 29kW and 40kW.

PUNJAB TRACTORS LTD
P.O. Box 6, Phase IV
SAS Nagar
Near Chandigarh
160 055
INDIA

GOLDEN LION TRACTOR

This company produces two models of a small, four-wheel tractor fitted with one of two single cylinder diesel engines. The engines are water-cooled four-strokes rated at 8.8 or 11kW (2000 rev/min) and drive the tractor via a gearbox with six forward speeds and one reverse. Specific fuel consumption is 251g/kW/hr.
Both models are provided with hydraulic systems to raise and lower implements mounted on the three-point hitch. The tractors are not provided with roll-over protection for the operator.
Weight 785kg.

BEIJING TRACTOR COMPANY
1 Xinfeng Street
Beijing
100088
CHINA

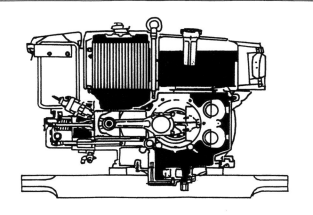

SELF-CONTAINED DIESEL POWER UNITS

The following companies all produce self-contained four-stroke diesel engine units which can be used to provide power for many agricultural implements. The units have integral fuel tanks, water cooling systems and headlights. Typical power outputs are in the range 6 to 12kW.

YANMAR AGRICULTURAL EQUIPMENT CO. LTD
1-32, Chayamachi
Kita-ku, Osaka 530
JAPAN

MITSUBISHI CORPORATION
Central P.O. Box 22
Tokyo 100-91
JAPAN

KUBOTA LTD
2-47 Shikitsuhigashi 1-chome
Naniwa-Ku
Osaka 556-91
JAPAN

AIR-COOLED DIESEL ENGINES

These are cold-starting, vertical, air-cooled four-stroke engines, with totally enclosed overhead valves and direct injection. They can be started by hand with a detachable handle.

RAJAN UNIVERSAL EXPORTS (MFRS) LTD
P.O. Box 250
Madras
600 001
INDIA

LISTER PETTER LTD
Long Street
Dursley
Glos GL11 4HS
UK

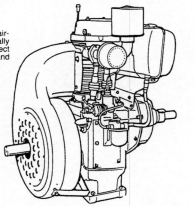

TWIN CYLINDER WATER-COOLED DIESEL ENGINES

This company produces a range of twin cylinder vertical four-stroke diesel engines fitted with two cast iron flywheels, spring-loaded governor and Bosch-type fuel pumps.

RAJAN UNIVERSAL EXPORTS (MFRS) LTD
P.O. Box 250
Madras
600 001
INDIA

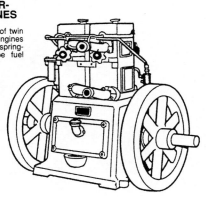

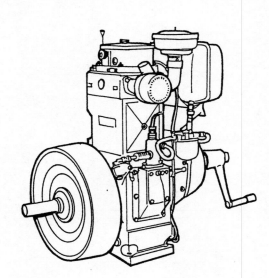

SINGLE CYLINDER WATER-COOLED DIESEL ENGINES

This is a range of single cylinder, vertical, four-stroke water-cooled diesel engines fitted with large flywheels. They have both splash lubrication and pumps to provide oil to the main bearings. These engines are cold starting, controlled by a spring-loaded governor and fitted with Bosch-type fuel injection.

RAJAN UNIVERSAL EXPORTS (MFRS) LTD
P.O. Box 250
Madras
600 001
INDIA

DIESEL ENGINES
A range of single cylinder water cooled four-stroke engines, with the following maximum outputs:

Power kW	Revs/min.
4.5	2400
6.3	2200
8.2	2200
9.7	2400
10.5	2200

Weights from 78 to 156kg.

KOREA FARM MACHINERY & TOOL IND. CO-OP
11-11 Dongja-Dong
Youngsan-Gu
Seoul
KOREA

AGRICO DIESEL ENGINES
This company produces a range of vertical, totally enclosed, cold starting, four-stroke, water-cooled diesel engines.

Model code	Power kW
VW	3.75
MW	5
SW	6

AGRICULTURAL ENGINEERS LTD
Ring Road Industrial Area
P.O. Box 12127
Accra North
GHANA

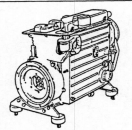

MULTI-CYLINDER AIR-COOLED DIESEL ENGINES

This company produces a range of two, three and four cylinder diesel engines with power outputs from 5kW to 57kW.

MOTORENFABRIK HATZ GmbH
D-8399 Rhustorf a.d. Rott
GERMANY

HIGH-SPEED FOUR-STROKE PETROL ENGINE

This is a portable 3.75kW engine, suitable as a prime mover for grinding mills, maize shellers and rice hullers or for pumping purposes. It has a close-grained cast iron cylinder block with deep cooling fins and an aluminium alloy cylinder head. The crankshaft is one piece, heat-treated high grade forged steel alloy with an induction hardened crank pin, supported on ball bearings at both ends. There is an enclosed fully lubricated and adjustable governor. Splash lubrication from 1.12 litre capacity sump. The unit is air-cooled by fan in the flywheel magneto.

RAJAN UNIVERSAL EXPORTS (MFRS) LTD
P.O. Box 250
Madras
600 001
INDIA

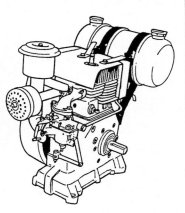

ENFIELD MK25 ENGINE

This is a high-speed four-stroke petrol or petrol-kerosene engine which develops 2.5kW at 3000 revs/min. It has pulley start and can be used to run compressors, pumps, alternators, power dusters and power sprayers. Optional extras available are choice of crankshaft ends, crankcase modified for close coupling, variable speed control. The engine is air-cooled. Weight 26.8kg.

ENFIELD INDIA LTD
Thoraipakkam Division (Engines)
Post Bag 892
Madras 600 096
INDIA

Similar engines are manufactured by:

KOREA FARM MACH. & TOOL IND. CO-OP
11-11 Dongja-Dong
Youngsan-Gu, Seoul
KOREA

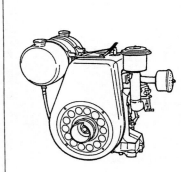

ENFIELD MK12 ENGINE

High-speed four-stroke petrol and petrol/kerosene engine. Pulley start. It can be used for powering compressors, pumps, alternators, grass cutters and concrete vibrators.
Weight 17kg.

ENFIELD INDIA LTD
Thoraipakkam Division (Engines)
Post Bag 892
Madras
600 096
INDIA

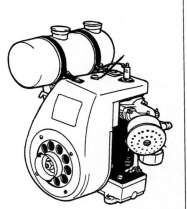

Oxfam

2. SOIL PREPARATION

The first operation the farmer has to undertake in growing a crop is to use a soil-engaging implement to prepare the soil. The term 'soil-engaging implement' covers all implements whose primary function it is to work soil, either in routine cultivation or in the process of developing and laying out land for agriculture.

Details of a range of animal- and simple tractor-drawn implements are given in this chapter. When selecting equipment it is important to consider the details of the farming system, the cropping cycles, and for what purpose the implements will be used, in order to get the right equipment of the appropriate size. This introduction discusses some of the objectives of cultivation, and the functions of the implements available.

OBJECTIVES

It is important to consider what the farmer is trying to achieve by soil preparation before considering the tools available. The objectives are usually numerous and inter-related, and vary according to the climate, soil, and crop. Some basic objectives are listed below:
○ preparation of a seedbed into which seed may be sown or plants transplanted;
○ control of weeds;
○ incorporation of surface trash (and manures);

○ reduction of compaction, especially associated with trafficked areas;
○ control of drainage;
○ increasing the infiltration rate of rainwater;
○ control of the adverse effects of erosion on cultivated soils;
○ to achieve the above using the power sources available on the farm.

The cultivation requirements for flooded rice are somewhat different from those for dryland crops and are discussed separately.

Seedbed preparation

The preparation of a seedbed is a major objective of most cultivation. The purpose is to provide enough loose soil, of appropriate clod size, to sow seeds or plant crops. The type of seedbed required is directly related to the type of crop and its method of establishment. A crop with small seeds, such as carrots, needs a very fine seedbed, while larger seeded crops such as cereals or pulses can be sown into a cloddier tilth. Crops that are established by vegetative propagation, such as sweet potato or sugar cane, can be planted in a rougher seedbed, containing considerable amounts of trash and clods, so long as there is enough tilth in which to plant. Producing over-fine seedbeds is not only expensive in terms of unnecessary operations, but can lead to soil capping and increased soil erosion.

Weed control

Weed control is usually the other major objective of cultivation. If weeds are not controlled they will compete with the crops for scarce resources — water, nutrients and light — resulting in reduced crop yields or even complete crop failure. Primary cultivation is an appropriate point in the crop cycle to start on the process of weed control. If weed control is effective at this stage it will reduce the requirement for subsequent weed control measures.

During soil preparation weed control can take several forms, depending principally on the weed types and the climate. In European farming systems, weeds have traditionally been controlled in primary cultivation by burying them through inversion of the furrow slice with a mouldboard plough. Although this may be effective in the soft moist soils of Europe, it is not necessarily the best choice for the range of conditions encountered in the tropics and may even have adverse effects. In hot, dry conditions weeds can be controlled by cutting the roots below the soil surface in a range of operations from hoeing to discing. When stoloniferous weeds are a problem these can be controlled by raking and burning. If annual weeds are a major problem some control can be achieved by preparing a seedbed early, allowing first rains to fall and weed seeds to germinate, then killing them by a final light cultivation. However, when growing seasons are short this technique may not be possible.

Weeding and weed control are discussed in greater detail in Chapter 4.

Trash incorporation

Before cultivation starts, the surface of the soil will frequently be covered with trash, probably the residue of the previous crop. For many crops it will be necessary to deal with this in some way, in order to be able to prepare a seedbed. Here implements such as rotary cultivators or discs which chop and mix the trash with the soil, or ploughs which bury the trash are useful. An alternative approach is to plant the new crop through the covering of 'trash', but this is only applicable to certain types of farming operations.

Compaction reduction and drainage control

Soil compaction occurs for a variety of reasons. Some structureless soils compact naturally, while better structured soils are frequently compacted by trafficking. This trafficking may be by tractor, implement wheels, or by the repeated passage of animal and even human feet, and will have the greatest effect when the soil is moist. Localized compaction may occur at different depths in the soil profile, for example just below the depth of ploughing, caused by the smearing effect and pressure from the 'heel' of the plough when used repeatedly.

The effects of compacted soil can be seen in impeded drainage, reduced water-holding capacity of the soil, and in poor root development of the crop, restricting its search for water and nutrients. Tined implements are normally used for combating compaction, but the draught requirements go up exponentially as working depth increases.

Where possible compaction should be avoided by limiting trafficking, especially when the soil is damp. An alternative approach where trafficking is an essential part of the farming system is to limit it to well defined areas, forming semi-permanent wheel- or walkways as used in some bed systems or in 'tramlining'.

Seedbed preparation using a camel

Jeremy Hartley/Panos

Increased infiltration rate and erosion control

In dryland farming systems, where catchment of seasonal rains is important, 'opening up' the soil prior to the rains is sometimes done with the objective of increasing the infiltration rate. This can be done in the dry conditions before the rain, or possibly at the end of the growing season when, if there is any moisture left in the soil, the operation will be easier and require less power.

In the process of cultivation, soil is exposed to the effects of rain and wind, with the risk of erosion. This risk will vary with a number of factors, including the severity of the climate, the soil type, and the slope of the land. In order to combat erosion the farmer can adopt a number of cultural practices which include maintaining a cloddy, trashy seedbed, cultivating along the contour, and contour bunding in order to reduce rainwater runoff and subsequent erosion of the soil. As pressure on land increases and farmers move into marginal and hilly areas, the need to conserve soil and combat the effects of erosion increases in importance, to a point where it becomes the major objective in hillside 'hedgerow' farming systems.

Land forming

A certain amount of land forming is typically associated with cultivation, as the land-forming operation is done in between or in association with cultivation operations. Operations such as ridging, bed making, and maintenance levelling fall into this category. The objective of this type of operation is usually quite specific in terms of preparing the field for irrigation, or for a particular system of row crop farming.

Flooded rice cultivation

Unlike other crops, irrigated rice requires a hard pan or bottom to the field in order to impede drainage, maintain the water level in the field, and provide a hard base for subsequent cultural operations. This pan is built up by the smearing together of soil particles caused by implements, and slipping wheels operating repeatedly at the same depth.

Many of the other objectives of cultivation, such as the preparation of a seedbed, weed control and incorporation of trash, are the same for irrigated rice as for other dryland crops. However, because the soil conditions are so different the techniques used to achieve these objectives are also different.

POWER SOURCES FOR CULTIVATION

There are currently three basic choices of farm power that may be available to the farmer for operating soil-engaging implements. These comprise: human power; animal power; and power from the internal combustion engine (tractor power).

These are discussed in detail in Chapter 1. The reality of most situations is such that the farmer has very little choice, at least in the short term, with regard to the form of power available. However, where some choice is possible the requirements of soil preparation, as probably the most energy intensive of all farm operations, are an important consideration.

Cultivation by hand is essentially hard physical work, and slow, and will severely limit the area of land brought under cultivation by individual farmers. It is suitable for limited areas, perhaps in gardens, or for high-value crops. Hand-cultivation of a growing crop, in the form of hoeing or weeding operations, is however frequently used in conjunction with animal-, or even tractor-cultivation, as the 'power' input is very low, but more control over the operation is possible.

With the use of draught animal power the area a farmer can cultivate is increased considerably. Draught animals that are owned and under the control of the farmer will provide a reliable and sustainable form of farm power, and with appropriate equipment will be able to complete all the necessary cultivation requirements.

It is clear that with the use of the internal combustion engine as a power source for a range of tractors the process of cultivation can be completed rapidly over large areas. Two-wheel, pedestrian-controlled tractors have been most successful in wetland farming, for flooded rice production, where used with rotary implements their small size and low weight make them suitable for use on small fields in soft ground conditions. However even here the 'ride-on' four-wheel tractor is gaining ground.

Four-wheel tractors, from around 20kW upwards, are suitable for cultivation of dry ground, with larger units in particular being well suited to heavy cultivation work. However, if the infrastructure of the country is not adequate to support tractor mechanization fully, it is likely to become unreliable and its use, particulary for timely, or routine operations, suspect. Even if tractors can be operated successfully the cost of ownership of such equipment may be beyond the means of the small or medium-sized farmer.

TECHNIQUES AND EQUIPMENT

Having given some thought as to what is to be achieved by soil preparation it is appropriate to consider the range of equipment available and select suitable items.

Cultivation equipment is frequently grouped into primary, secondary and inter-row equipment. Primary cultivation comprises the first step in the soil preparation process, which is typically breaking up a hard surface with a plough of some type, while secondary cultivation is typically breaking down the ploughed surface using a cultivator or harrow. Inter-row cultivation is the cultivation of the soil between rows of growing crops, usually with the objective of weed control. Although this classification is useful it is by no means universal, as in many farming systems a single implement such as a hoe or tined cultivator is often used for primary, secondary and inter-row operations.

Hoes

Hoes are widely used by small farmers in most developing countries as a tool for both primary and secondary cultivation, and for other operations such as ridging, bunding, planting and weeding. Many designs of hoes have developed to suit local farming conditions and manufacturing facilities. Broad-bladed digging hoes are widely used for primary cultivation and a range of subsequent operations. Where conditions are particularly hard, narrower blades like the mattock are favoured for primary cultivation. In stony conditions tined hoes are sometimes used.

Primary cultivation

The plough is the main implement used for primary cultivation. The term 'plough' covers several types of implement, which can be grouped into traditional, mouldboard, disc and chisel ploughs.

Traditional ploughs

Traditional animal-drawn ploughs are typically made in the village, principally of wood, but usually with a metal point. Although the designs vary considerably, they are usually of the 'pole' type, where a long pole is used both to attach to the hitch at the front and to carry the soil-engaging parts and handle at the rear. These ploughs open up the soil, but do not invert it. 'Improved' versions of the traditional design use steel soil engaging parts, but retain the wooden pole.

Mouldboard ploughs

The distinguishing feature of the mouldboard plough is its ability to invert or turn over the soil, thus burying surface weeds and trash. The action of the plough is dependent upon the shape of the mouldboard, which can be designed for complete or partial inversion, to give different degrees of break-up of the furrow slice and to work at different depths. The basic mouldboard is designed to turn the furrow to the right, which necessitates ploughing in 'lands'. As this is not always convenient in small areas, or where a level surface is important, reversible ploughs have been developed with either right- and left-hand mouldboards or a reversible mouldboard.

The simplest type of animal-drawn mouldboard plough is the pole plough, with a share and mouldboard fitted in place of the traditional plough point. However, the usual type is descended from the European ox-drawn plough. It is pulled by a chain attached to the yoke of the draught animal(s) and comprises a beam carrying a wheel or skid at the front, and share, mouldboard and handles at the rear. In order to resist the side thrust developed by the mouldboard, such ploughs have

Tim Ogborn/ITDG

Traditional plough

A Metianu

Clod breaking using a plank

a long landside. A knife or disc cutter, to make the vertical cut in forming the furrow slice, is usually available. Whereas animal-drawn ploughs are usually single furrow — occasionally two-furrow — tractor ploughs are usually multi-furrow, with wider furrows, and have the ability to work at greater depth because of the additional power available.

Disc ploughs

Disc ploughs are usually tractor-drawn and multi-disc. Their action is similar to the mouldboard, but inversion is less complete. They are able to work in conditions with considerable surface trash, so long as under-beam and inter-disc clearance is large. They are able to penetrate hard ground, so long as they have sufficient weight (or weight can be added) and they must roll over stones, stumps etc. For these reasons they are a suitable choice for the small to medium tractor in tropical conditions. Because of the weight required to make these implements penetrate the ground, and because of the cost associated with the disc bearing, this type of plough has not been developed for animal use.

Chisel ploughs

The chisel plough is again usually tractor-drawn, although animal-drawn models are available. The typical implement comprises a number of ridged tines, raked forward, with chisel-type points. The action of the implement is to break up the surface, to a depth of around 200mm, with little if any inversion of the soil. The action is more akin to the traditional plough than the mouldboard or disc plough. On some designs alternative tines are available to fit the same frame. These may include sub-soil tines, or heavy spring tines.

Secondary cultivation

Most of the implements used for secondary cultivation are described as cultivators or harrows. These two terms are similar, but a cultivator is usually a heavier implement. When considering disc implements the term harrow is used irrespective of weight. The main types of soil-engaging components used for secondary cultivation can be broken down into tines, discs, rotary cultivators, rolls and levellers.

Tined cultivators and harrows

Tined cultivators and harrows are the major secondary cultivation tools. The simplest tined harrows consist of a framework, carrying numerous vertical steel spikes or tines,

which when pulled through the soil break down clods, or uproot small weeds. Many types are available for animal or tractor use, some with flexible frames, others with ridged frames, sometimes incorporating soil-levelling bars. This type of equipment is simple, and lends itself to local manufacture.

Cultivators use a number of types of tine, and tine point or share. Tines can be rigid, spring-loaded, or made in a range of shapes from spring steel. Some manufacturers offer a range of tines on a standard frame. The spring and spring-loaded tines are used in stony conditions while, for higher speeds associated with tractors, the vibration caused by the spring tine increases the shattering of clods and the formation of the seedbed.

Alternative points can be fitted for cultivation, mixing of trash, or weeding operations. Many cultivator frames allow the positioning of tines for inter-row work.

Disc harrows

Disc harrows differ from disc ploughs in that a number of discs are arranged on one axle. The action of the disc is to chop and mix, which is useful for breaking down clods and mixing in surface trash. Although usually considered as a secondary cultivation implement, large tractor-pulled discs — often termed 'ploughing harrows — are used for primary cultivation in sugar cane and similar industries. These are however beyond the scope of this guide. The type of work done by the disc is dependent on the disc diameter, the disc spacing along the axle, disc angle and the weight per disc. For animal or small tractor draught, discs of 400-500mm diameter, spaced at 200mm apart, with 15-30kg weight per disc would be used for secondary cultivation purposes. As the disc harrow is more expensive than the tined implement it is usually cheaper to use tined implements if they will do the job.

Rotary cultivators

A selection of rotary cultivation equipment is available. This includes ground-driven rotary cultivators of patent design through to power-driven rotary cultivators. All such implements will generally do more work in preparing the seedbed in a single pass than a tined implement and the power-driven rotary cultivators are very useful at incorporating trash. However, this is at the expense of increased cost and complexity and consequently increased maintenance requirements in comparison with simple tined implements.

Other equipment

In addition to the above, mechanisms such as rolls, levelling bars, or heavy wooden planks are frequently used in the preparation of a seedbed, with the objective of breaking down clods and producing a smooth and level surface for sowing seed or planting a crop. An item such as a levelling plank, because of its simplicity, is likely to be made in the local village, rather than be sold by a manufacturer, and so would not appear in a catalogue of this sort.

Ridgers and bed makers

Simple equipment is available for a range of landforming operations. For field operations like ridging or bed making mouldboard ridgers and bed makers are used. Single row double mouldboard ridgers are suitable for animal use, while multi-row ridgers are used with small and medium tractors. Discs can be used as an alternative to mouldboards for ridge formation, and will give better service in stony ground or soil containing a large number of roots. The single furrow mouldboard ridger actually cuts a furrow, although by repeated passes the overall effect is to form ridges. Where a single ridge is required, perhaps to retain water on irrigated land or for erosion control, a bund former can be used. These can be mouldboard or disc types, and essentially move soil to the centre thus forming a ridge or bund.

Land development

Where land development is taking place, and perhaps more soil has to be moved, simple scrapes and levelling blades are available for animal or small tractor draught. A blade, as used in a grader or leveller, is useful for reducing high spots and filling adjacent low areas, but is not satisfactory for transporting soils over any distance. A scraper or scoop has the ability to collect, transport, and deposit soil and so is more useful for intermediate transport distances, such as when building an earth dam, or excavating a fish pond.

Multi-purpose toolbars

Most simple implements are single purpose, i.e. as a traditional plough. An alternative is the multi-purpose frame which can carry a number of different attachments so that different farm operations can be undertaken. Such an implement is usually referred to as a multi-purpose toolbar. The range of animal-drawn toolbars varies from simple frames which will take cultivation tools — including ploughing bodies, ridging bodies and a selection of tines that can be spaced to suit the crop conditions — through to wheeled toolbars, with a range of attachments for almost all farm operations.

The uptake of animal-drawn toolbars has not been as great as was initially expected when this type of equipment was under development. The cost of the wheeled tool carriers tends to be high in comparison with traditional single purpose implements, and the benefits from the wide selection of tools available are frequently not realized as farmers tend not to change the tooling. The toolbar can end up as a very costly plough or cart if this happens. The pros and cons of such equipment in comparison with single purpose implements need to be considered carefully in relation to the specific needs of the farming system and individual farmers involved before equipment in purchased.

Cultivation of irrigated rice

The main operations that will need to be carried out are the incorporation of the residue from the previous crop, puddling to produce a surface for transplanting, and levelling while reinforcing rather than disturbing the soil pan. Incorporation can be done by a number of means, from traditional ploughs and tines, to rotary cultivators, depending on the power source available and the soil conditions. Rotary cultivation is very important in rice growing, especially in south-east Asia, where a range of light two- and four-wheel tractors are used to prepare the field for planting. The simplest single axle tractor can be fitted with cage wheels and usually pulls a simple plough or tined implement. The cage wheels are themselves effective at puddling the soil. On larger two-wheel tractors a second axle carries a rotary cultivator, which increases the machine's effectiveness.

MAINTENANCE REQUIREMENTS

Soil-engaging parts wear as a result of abrasion from the soil. The most important aspect of maintenance is replacing these wearing parts before they are completely finished, when the implement could be damaged or cease to be effective. Most cultivation implements are designed in such a way that the point where wear occurs can be easily changed, e.g. the plough

share or the cultivator point. Cultivation points, for example, are often reversible, and if changed in good time can give double life. If they are not changed the result can be damage to the end of the tine, which would require an expensive replacement.

On more complex cultivation implements, such as discs or rotary cultivators, there will be bearings, and with power-driven machines a power transmission. The maintenance requirements here are basically greasing/oiling as advised by the manufacturers, and ensuring that dirt is kept out of bearings, chain cases etc. by checking regularly the condition of seals and for accidental damage.

The use of more complex implements will necessitate the demand for inputs such as parts, and lubricants. The availability and cost of such inputs should be considered before purchase of a new machine. A 'one-off' machine perhaps for trial purposes can be supported in the short term by a package of spare parts supplied by the manufacturer with the machine. However if the implement is to be viable in the long term, then parts need to be stocked locally and, in the case of fast-moving items like cultivator points, manufactured locally.

ALTERNATIVES

Although this section is concerned with tillage equipment, mention should be made of zero or minimum tillage techniques, since these offer the most rapid method of crop establishment. Weeds, controlled by herbicides or shallow cultivation, then form a mulch with crop residues from the previous season, through which seeds are planted. The mulch eventually breaks down and helps to maintain the soil's organic matter, so that the productive life of land can be extended without the need of a fallow period. Mulch on the surface of uncultivated soil also reduces the incidence of soil erosion.

COSTS AND BENEFITS

The costs and benefits of particular items of equipment need careful consideration in relation to the needs of the particular farmers who will use this equipment.

The first thing to consider is the capital cost. Simple hand-tools, such as a hoe, will be low cost, low output, and will not require additional expenditure on a mechanical power source. This makes them well suited to ownership by small-scale farmers. The capital cost of animal-drawn equipment is higher than that of hand equipment, typically by

Rice cultivation using a single axle tractor

Jeremy Hartley/Panos

a factor of 5-10, but in addition the capital cost of purchasing draught animals has to be added. However, as a pair of draught animals can cultivate 5-10 times the area of a man with a hoe, fewer individual units of equipment will be required. A similar relationship arises with the next technological step into tractor power, where again both the capital cost per unit and the output per unit go up.

It is therefore clear that the capital cost must be seen in relation to the amount of work to be undertaken and specifically to the area to be cultivated.

In addition to the capital cost the operating cost must be considered. This will comprise the labour of the operator (wages if employed labour is used), plus the running costs of animal or mechanical power if used. For animals this would comprise food, housing, vet bills; for tractors fuel, oil, parts, maintenance and repairs. Clearly the labour productivity for cultivation is low in hand systems, increasing through animal draught systems to tractor-powered cultivation. Therefore as labour rates increase animal- and tractor-powered systems become increasingly financially attractive to farmers.

IMPACT

The adoption of different systems of cultivation based on different power sources, i.e. manual, animal or tractor, and to a lesser extent the selection of tools within the system, will affect not only the individual farmers but also the farming community.   If more efficient cultivation tools are used they should improve both the quality of work and the amount of work possible. In conditions where land is not a limiting factor,

additional land may be cultivated with the same labour resource, resulting in increased output and labour requirement for subsequent weeding and harvesting operations. Where additional land is not available, benefits may be possible from increasing cropping intensity, i.e. growing a second or third crop in a year. However, other inputs such as irrigation may be necessary to do this.

There may well be a conflict of interest in developing countries between farmers and labourers over mechanization. As an economy develops labour rates are likely to rise, and labour becomes less willing to undertake some of the physically more demanding tasks such as soil preparation. As such conditions develop it becomes increasingly attractive financially for farmers to increase their level of mechanization, with subsequent loss of labouring jobs. In addition, richer farmers may well be able to purchase or take over the land farmed by poorer farmers unable to invest in the new technology. Once a new form of farm power has been introduced for cultivation purposes it will probably be financially attractive to farmers to extend its use to other farm operations, such as transport, weeding, and threshing. The result is increased levels of mechanization, increased labour efficiency on the farm, but labour displacement from agriculture. This may be satisfactory where the economy is growing quickly and re-employment is possible, but where it is not unemployment and landlessness can increase.

Andy Metianu
Overseas Division
Silsoe Research Institute

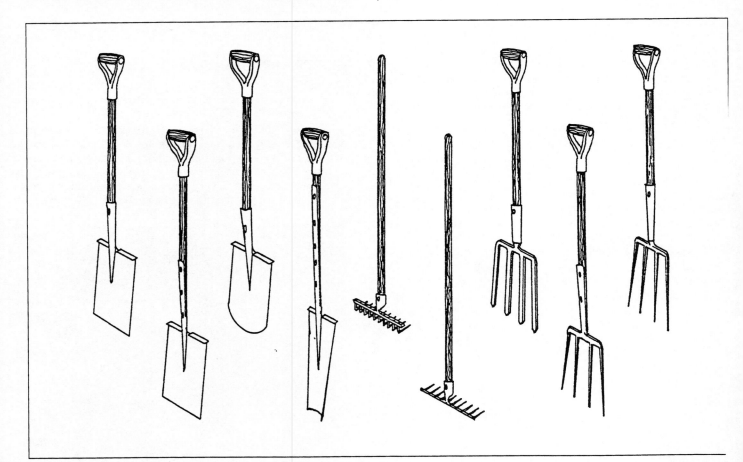

From left: solid socket treaded spade; strapped treaded spade; open socket treaded round-nose spade; strapped treaded drainage spade; shaped-tine rake; garden rake; tang and ferrule broad-tine digging fork; strapped fork; solid socket digging fork

Spades, forks, and rakes

Country	Manufacturer	Implements		
		Spades	Forks	Rakes
Belgium	Ateliers Jules Marcelle S.A.	●		
	Madear B.V.B.A. Gereedschappen Outi	●		●
	S.A. Chanic	●		
Brazil	Acotupy Industrias Metalurgicas Ltd	●		
Cameroon	Tropic		●	●
Chile	Famae	●		
Finland	Gripit Oy Ab	●	●	
Germany	Schwabische Huttenwerke GmbH	●	●	
India	Kumaon Nursery		●	
	Kumar Industries	●	●	
	Yantra Vidyalaya	●		●
Italy	Eurozappa S.P.A.	●		
	Falci S.P.A.		●	
Kenya	Datini Mercantile Ltd		●	
Nepal	Agricultural Tools Factory Ltd			●
Peru	Fahena S.A.	●	●	●
	Herramientas S.A.	●	●	●
	Herrandina			●
Portugal	Verdugo Ernesto L. Matias	●	●	●
Spain	Patricio Echeverria S.A.	●		●
Sri Lanka	Kanthi Industries		●	
Tanzania	Ubungo Farm Implements Manuf. Co. Ltd			●
UK	Bulldog Tools Ltd	●	●	●
	Fiskars Ltd	●	●	●
	Samuel Parkes & Co. Ltd	●	●	●
	Spear & Jackson Garden Products	●	●	
	The Stockton Heath Forge Ltd	●	●	
	Wolf Tools Ltd	●		●
Yugoslavia	Gorenje Muta		●	●
Zimbabwe	Temper Tools (Pvt) Ltd		●	●

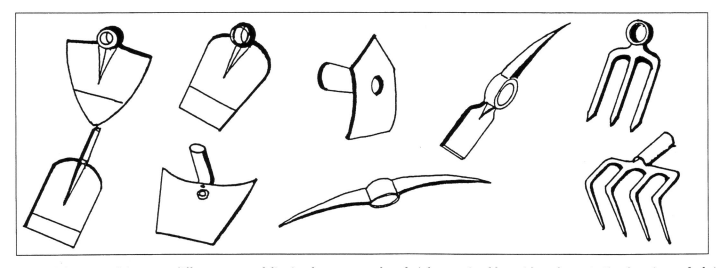

From left: some of the many different types of digging hoes; mattock and pickaxes; tined hoes (these have similar function to forks)

Hoes, picks, and mattocks

| Country | Manufacturer | Implements | | |
		Hoes	Picks	Mattocks
Austria	Sensenwerke Krenhof A.G.	●		
Bangladesh	Zahed Metal Industries	●		
Belgium	Madear B.V.B.A. Gereedschappen Outi	●		
	S.A. Chanic	●		
Brazil	Acotupy Industrias Metalurgicas Ltd	●	●	●
Cameroon	Tropic	●	●	
Chile	Famae	●	●	
China	China Nat. Imp. & Exp. Corporation	●		
Finland	Gripit Oy Ab	●		
Germany	Schwabische Huttenwerke GmbH	●		
India	Bharat Industrial Corporation	●		
	Cossul & Co. Pvt Ltd	●		
	Kumar Industries			●
	Yantra Vidyalaya	●		
Kenya	Oyani Christian Rural Serv. Centre	●		
Malawi	Chillington-Agrimal (Malawi) Ltd	●		
Nepal	Agricultural Tools Factory Ltd	●		●
Peru	Herramientas S.A.	●	●	●
	Herrandina	●		
Philippines	Agricultural Mechanization Dev. Prog	●		
Portugal	Verdugo — Ernesto L. Matias	●	●	
Rwanda	Rwandex-Chillington Sarl	●		
Spain	Patricio Echeverria S.A.	●	●	
Sri Lanka	Agricultural Implements Factory	●		
	Sarvodaya Kandy	●		
Tanzania	Ubungo Farm Implements Manuf. Co. Ltd	●		
	Zana Za Kilimo Ltd	●		●
Thailand	Chillington Tool (Thailand) Co. Ltd	●		
Uganda	The Chillington Tool Co. (Uganda) Ltd	●		
UK	Alfa-Laval Agri Ltd			●
	Bulldog Tools Ltd	●		●
	Burgon & Ball Ltd	●		
	Fiskars Ltd	●		
	Samuel Parkes & Co. Ltd	●		
	Spear & Jackson Garden Products	●		●
	The Stockton Heath Forge Ltd	●	●	●
	Wolf Tools Ltd	●		
USA	Lehman Hardware & Appliances Inc.	●		
	Seymour Manufacturing Co. Inc.	●		
Yugoslavia	Gorenje Muta	●		
Zimbabwe	Bulawayo Steel Products			●
	Garba Industries (Pvt) Ltd	●		
	Zimplow Ltd	●		

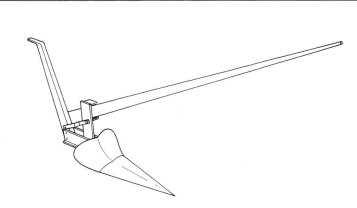

TRADITIONAL PLOUGHS

Animal-drawn traditional ploughs are usually designed and produced at village level from locally available materials. When cutting a furrow they break the surface rather than invert the soil.

The following examples are based on such designs but are available commercially.

MACO SOIL-STIRRING PLOUGH
Pulled by a pair of animals, this plough opens the soil to aid aeration.
Width of work 175mm.
Depth of cut 110mm.
Weight 14kg.

MOHINDER & CO. ALLIED INDUSTRIES
Kurali district
Rupnagar dist. (Ropar)
Punjab
INDIA

ANIMAL-DRAWN PLOUGH
This is a standard design of single share steel plough. Interchangeable plough bodies allow greater flexibility of use.

FAMAE
Casilla 4100
Santiago
CHILE

SUDAN TYPE PLOUGH
This plough is made from high-grade steel. The handle and beam are adjustable and the landside is fitted with a heel for better control.
Weight 25kg.

COSSUL & CO. PVT LTD
123/367 Industrial area
Fazalgunj
Kanpur
U.P.
INDIA

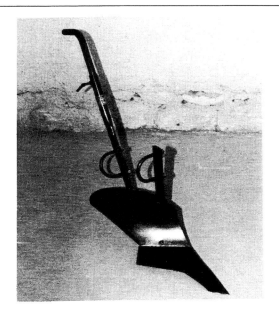

SIMPLE MOULDBOARD PLOUGHS

These ploughs are of simple design: the body is mounted below a straight beam and controlled with a single handle. The mouldboard is intended to invert the soil, thus burying weeds and trash.

ANIMAL-DRAWN MOULDBOARD PLOUGHS
Standard designs of single share steel plough with wooden beams.

FAMAE
Casilla 4100
Santiago
CHILE

SOIL-INVERTING PLOUGH
This bullock-driven plough inverts the soil burying surface trash and weeds. The plough also pulverizes the soil.
Working width 150mm.
Depth of cut 100-125mm.
Weight 15kg.

MOHINDER & CO. ALLIED INDUSTRIES
Kurali district
Rupnagar dist. (Ropar)
Punjab
INDIA

RAJA CAST IRON PLOUGH SET
Cast iron and steel construction with detachable share and mouldboard.

RAJAN UNIVERSAL EXPORTS (MFRS) LTD
P.O. Box 250
Madras
600 001
INDIA

ANIMAL-DRAWN MOULDBOARD PLOUGHS
There are models both for mountain farming and for the tropics (illustrated). They are of metal construction with wooden drawbar. Weights 9.5kg, 11kg.

CENTRO DE INVESTIGACIÓN, FORMACIÓN Y EXTENSIÓN EN MECANIZACIÓN AGRÍCOLA
Casilla 831
Cochabamba
BOLIVIA

EC1 LIGHT PLOUGH
This plough is for use with one or two draught animals. It is made from steel tube and can be fitted with either a skid or wheel for depth control. Wearing parts are made from heat treated boron steel.
Working width 152mm.
Weight 18kg.

Note: As with all Project Equipment products, workshops can be set up to manfacture this implement locally.

PROJECT EQUIPMENT LTD
Industrial Estate
Oswestry
Shropshire SY10 8HA
UK

CARE PLOUGH
The body of this plough is made of cast iron and the U-clamp, standard and share are all steel. Two sizes are available weighing 14.5kg and 10.5kg.

COSSUL & CO. PVT LTD
123/367 Industrial area
Fazalgunj
Kanpur, U.P.
INDIA

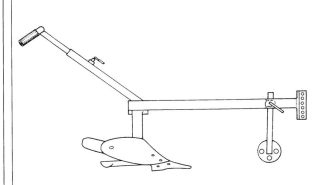

THE PECOPLOUGH

This is a strong, lightweight plough built of modern materials. The main beam is of rectangular, hollow-section steel tube and the all-welded construction minimizes maintenance tasks. There is a choice of four plough body sizes: 112, 152, 190 and 230mm, and two sizes of depth-control wheel: 175 and 240mm.
Weight is 24kg for the smallest combination and 36kg for the largest.

PROJECT EQUIPMENT LTD
Industrial Estate
Oswestry
Shropshire SY10 8HA
UK

Similar implements are manufactured by:

COBEMAG
B.P. 161
Route de Djougou
Parakou
REPUBLIC OF BENIN

MEKINS AGRO PRODUCTS (PVT) LTD
6-3-866/A Begumpet
Greenlands
Hyderabad
500 016
INDIA

UPROMA
B.P. 1086
Lomé
TOGO

RUMPTSTAD BV
Postbus 1
Stad Aan't-Haringvliet
3243 ZG
NETHERLANDS

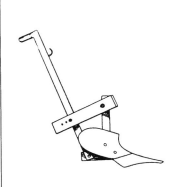

SUBHASH PLOUGH

This general purpose 150mm mouldboard plough is made of steel. Its working depth can be adjusted and the big throat clearance provided makes it useful for ploughing weed-infested fields. Available in right- and left-hand mouldboard types. A workrate of 0.25ha/day can be achieved.
Weight 11kg.

COSSUL & CO. PVT LTD
123/367 Industrial area
Fazalgunj
Kanpur
U.P.
INDIA

GENERAL PURPOSE MOULDBOARD PLOUGHS

These ploughs are manufactured and used in many parts of the world. The important feature of this type of plough is that a slice of soil is cut from the ground and inverted, so that weeds and surface trash are buried and the soil is exposed to weathering agents and further cultivation.

The soil-working parts of the ploughs are in the main fabricated from steel and worn parts can be replaced when required. The ploughs are usually supplied with an adjustable depth wheel and may also be fitted with knife or disc coulters to aid penetration in difficult or trashy conditions. The hitch points supplied with these ploughs are often adjustable both vertically and laterally to accommodate different sizes of draught animal.

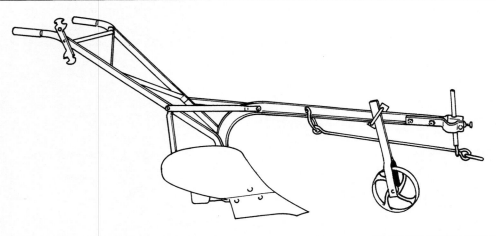

VIJAYA PLOUGH
Best suited to breaking virgin soil. Comes with headwheel to adjust depth. Cuts furrows of about 225mm wide and 100mm to 150mm deep.
Weight 38kg.

COSSUL & CO. PVT LTD
123/367 Industrial area
Fazalgunj
Kanpur
U.P.
INDIA

ANIMAL-DRAWN PLOUGHS
All-steel construction, complete with drawbar hitch. Available in three sizes, 200, 250 and 300mm.
Weights 37kg, 38kg and 43kg.

ISICO
P.O. Box 417
Mbabane
SWAZILAND

OX PLOUGHS
Standard and heavy duty models.

DATINI MERCANTILE LTD
Enterprise Road
Box 45483
Nairobi
KENYA

PLOUGH
Forged main frame with fabricated handle guide bars. Hitching shackle point and guide wheel depth are both adjustable. Various optional shares are available.

UBUNGO FARM IMPLEMENTS MANUFACTURING CO. LTD
P.O. Box 20126
Dar es Salaam
TANZANIA

SINGLE FURROW PLOUGH
This plough can be pulled by horse, ox or donkey. It has a frame made of mild steel and a share of carbon steel. This is a traditional model, suitable for general use in all types of soil.

ZIMPLOW
P.O. BOX 1059
Bulawayo
ZIMBABWE

SINGLE FURROW MOULDBOARD PLOUGH
This plough has a forged main frame with fabricated handle guide bars. Hitching shackle point and guide wheel depth are both adjustable. It can be fitted with either 200 or 250mm flat shares.
Weight 38kg.

AGRIMAL (MALAWI) LTD
Makata Road
P.O. Box 143
Blantyre
MALAWI

SINGLE FURROW PLOUGH
Simple design with guide wheel and harness hitch.

ALVAN BLANCH DEVELOPMENT CO. LTD
Chelworth
Malmesbury
Wilts SN16 9SG
UK

OX-DRAWN PLOUGH
Drawn by two oxen. This plough is available with a heavy and light mouldboard for heavy or light soil.
Working width 220mm.
Working depth 50-150mm.
Weight 32kg.

RUMPTSTAD BV
Postbus 1
Stad Aan't-Haringvliet
3243 ZG
NETHERLANDS

ANIMAL-DRAWN SINGLE FURROW PLOUGH
All-steel plough complete with 200mm sweep, flat or upset share.

BHARAT INDUSTRIAL CORPORATION
Petit Compound
Nana Chowk, Grant Road
Bombay
400 007
INDIA

Similar ploughs are manufactured by:

DANDEKAR BROTHERS & CO.
Shivajinagar
Sangli
Maharashtra
416 416
INDIA

AGRICULTURAL TOOLS FACTORY LTD
P.O. Box No.2
Birganj
NEPAL

SISMAR
20 rue Dr. Thèze
B.P. 3214
Dakar
SENEGAL

S.M.E.C.M.A.
Zone Industrielle
Route de Sotuba
B.P. 1707
Bamako
MALI

HERCULANO ALFAIAS AGRICOLAS
Loureiro
Oliveira de Azemeis
3720
PORTUGAL

PILTER FRANCE
12 rue Gouverneur
B.P. 3
Dreux
28100
FRANCE

BALDAN-IMPLEMENTOS AGRICOLAS S.A.
Avenida Baldan, 1500
CP 11
Matão S.P.
15990
BRAZIL

BKF TECH TERRE
3814
Ouagadougou
BURKINA FASO

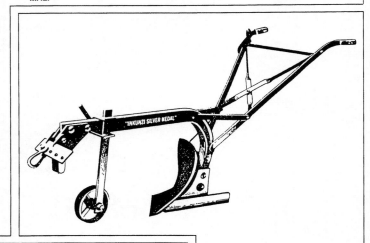

SILVER MEDAL SINGLE FURROW PLOUGH

This single furrow plough has three bolt-on attachments to provide greater versatility. These are:

- ridger;
- groundnut (peanut) lifter;
- ripper tine.

BULAWAYO STEEL PRODUCTS
P.O. Box 1603
Donnington
Bulawayo
ZIMBABWE

WALKING PLOUGH

Available in either left- or right-hand models in three widths, this plough has a hitch which can be adjusted vertically for any size horse, and horizontally for two- or three-horse teams. Features include a fully adjustable depth gauge wheel.
Working widths 300mm, 350mm or 400mm.
Weight 114kg.

PIONEER EQUIPMENT INC.
16392 Western Road
Dalton
OHIO 44618
USA

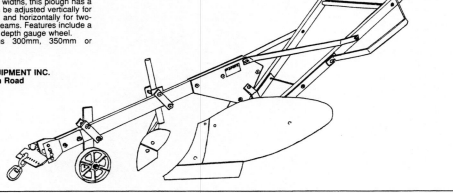

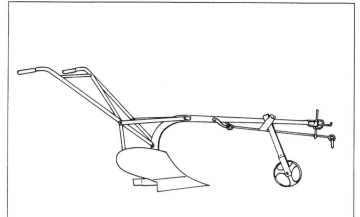

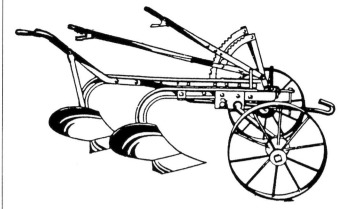

MARCHESAN AT10 PLOUGH

This single-bodied mouldboard plough can cut a furrow to a depth of 150mm. A depth wheel is supplied as standard equipment and the plough has two control handles. The hitching point is adjustable both vertically and laterally to allow fine tuning between the draught animal team and the plough.
Working width 300mm.
Weight 34kg.

MARCHESAN
IMPLEMENTOS E MAQUINAS
AGRICOLAS 'TATU' S.A.
Av. Marchesan 1,979
Matão SP
BRAZIL

REVERSIBLE PLOUGH

Nardi of Italy produce a range of heavy duty reversible ploughs with working widths of up to 550mm. Depth of work is controlled by a lever acting on the axle which supports the wheels.

NARDI FRANCESCO & FIGLI
06017 Selci Lama
Perugia
ITALY

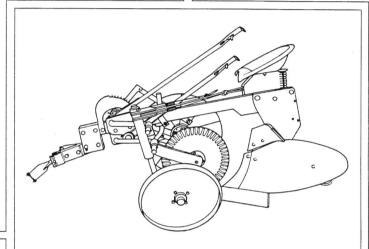

SULKY PLOUGHS

HORSE-DRAWN SULKY PLOUGH
This is a steel plough with landwheel and large, spring-loaded driver's seat, designed for teams of two, three or four horses. The hitch has a wide range of vertical and lateral adjustment and the ploughing width can be adjusted from 350mm to 500mm. All wheels have tapered roller bearings and a cover board is standard equipment. Options include 430mm rolling coulter, right- or left-hand jointers, and spring hitches.

D.A. HOCHSTETLER & SONS
R.R.2 Box 162
Topeka
IL 46571
USA

SULKY PLOUGH
Horizontal adjustment for two, three or four horse teams. All levers and controls are easily reached from the driver's seat. Features include a safety bolt which breaks if the plough hits a solid object in the ground, and fully adjustable foot-operated lever to assist in lifting of the plough out of work.
Weight 200kg.

PIONEER EQUIPMENT INC.
16392 Western Road
Dalton
OH 44618
USA

DOUBLE FURROW PLOUGHS

DOUBLE FURROW PLOUGH
This is a light, double furrow plough weighing 135kg. It has widely spaced wheels to prevent overturning, and is fitted with a hand lever for landwheel control and with a furrow lever for control of furrow depth. Each share cuts a furrow 250mm wide. The plough requires the draught power of eight oxen.

ZIMPLOW LTD
P.O. Box 1059
Bulawayo
ZIMBABWE

ANIMAL-DRAWN PLOUGH SETS: TWIN FURROW
Fabricated from angle iron and designed to be used with either the Raja ordinary type, deluxe type or master type plough shares, these are available from Baby to Giant size. These ploughs are of very simple construction.

RAJAN UNIVERSAL EXPORTS
(MFRS) LTD
P.O. Box 250
Madras
600 001
INDIA

A similar plough is available from:

G. NORTH (PVT) LTD
P.O. Box 111
Southerton
Harare
ZIMBABWE

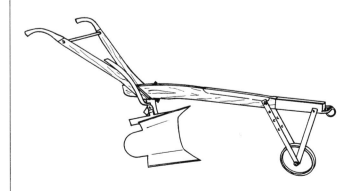

REVERSIBLE MOULDBOARD PLOUGHS

The ability to turn the furrow slice either to the left or to the right adds greatly to the efficiency of the ploughing operation in areas where ploughing in lands is not practical, such as on narrow terraces in hilly areas. The ploughs described vary in complexity from the most simple design in which a symmetrical plough body can be rotated about its horizontal axis to those ploughs fitted with both left- and right-hand bodies in which the whole frame is rotated.

ARN4 REVERSIBLE PLOUGH
This wooden-beamed plough has a simple lever release mechanism to reverse the pivoted body, and an adjustable depth wheel.

Working width 300mm.
Working depth to 150mm.
Weight 36kg.

MARCHESAN IMPLEMENTOS E
MAQUINAS AGRICOLAS 'TATU' S.A.
Av. Marchesan 1,979
Matão S.P.
BRAZIL

REVERSIBLE SINGLE FURROW PLOUGH
Weight 54kg.

ZIMPLOW LTD
P.O. Box 1059
Bulawayo
ZIMBABWE

REVERSIBLE MOULDBOARD PLOUGHS

The Alghesa plough is suitable for mountainous conditions where its reversing capability will significantly improve productivity. The plough is reversed by turning the mouldboard on its horizontal axis and securing it with a lever. The frame is fabricated from tubular steel. A harness is available.
Working depth to 180mm.
Working width 230mm.
Weight 16kg.

ALGHESA
Monte Umbroso 140
Santiago de Surco
Lima 33
PERU

REVERSIBLE ANIMAL PLOUGH
Adjustable hitching point.
Ploughing depth 200mm.
Weight 40kg.

I.C.A. PROG. DE MAQUINARIA AGRICOLA
Instituto Colombiano Agropec.
Apartado Aéreo 151123
Bogotá
COLOMBIA

THE PECOPLOUGH REVERSIBLE
This plough is simply constructed from heavy gauge steel tube. The reversing mechanism has a spring-loaded locking pin. A choice of plough body sizes and depth wheels are available.
Working width 152 or 226mm.
Weight 40 or 52kg (depending on size).

PROJECT EQUIPMENT LTD
Industrial Estate
Oswestry
Shropshire SY10 8HA
UK

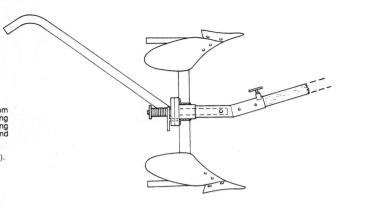

DISC PLOUGHS

Disc ploughs differ considerably from mouldboard ploughs in that the coulter, share and mouldboard are replaced by a large concave disc fabricated of steel which is free to rotate. Owing to the form of construction, the implement's weight can be substantial, and so all the ploughs described are of the tractor-mounted type. The disc is set at an angle to the direction of travel and turns a slice of soil to one side. The lateral force generated by the plough is counteracted by both the wheels of the tractor and a furrow wheel attached to the frame. Disc ploughs are well suited to working in hard soils and can operate in trashy conditions where a mouldboard plough could not.

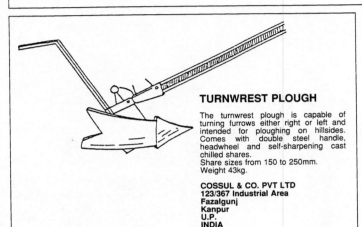

TURNWREST PLOUGH

The turnwrest plough is capable of turning furrows either right or left and intended for ploughing on hillsides. Comes with double steel handle, headwheel and self-sharpening cast chilled shares.
Share sizes from 150 to 250mm.
Weight 43kg.

COSSUL & CO. PVT LTD
123/367 Industrial Area
Fazalgunj
Kanpur
U.P.
INDIA

DISC PLOUGH
There are three models with one, two and three discs respectively. They are tractor mounted and require Category I or II three-point hitch. The furrow wheel is spring-loaded and the heat-treated steel discs are mounted on double, heavy duty precision taper roller bearings. A choice of three working angles for the disc and lateral shift on the cross-shaft enable the optimum setting to be achieved. Individual disc scrapers are adjustable. There is a kit for converting the two-disc model to three-disc.

PUNJAB TRACTORS LTD
P.O. Box 6, Phase IV
SAS Nagar
Chandigarh
160 055
INDIA

CHISEL PLOUGHS

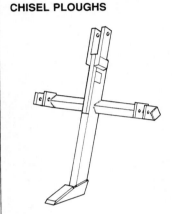

RIPPER
A single tined implement for breaking compacted ground, it is designed to be mounted on a standard three-point hitch and requires a tractor with at least 15kW. 225mm reversible point, rips to a depth of 350mm.

KANGA FARM EQUIPMENT
P.O. Box 1177
Dandenong
Victoria 3175
AUSTRALIA

The Steel Structures chisel plough has a mild steel frame with a straight centre beam, alloy steel chisel/blade and a cast iron guide wheel.
Weight 42kg.

STEEL STRUCTURES LTD
Dandora Road
Box 49862
Nairobi
KENYA

REVERSIBLE DISC PLOUGH
This has a Category I three-point hitch attachment to a tractor and is mechanically reversed by hydraulic cylinder.
Working depth 300mm max.
Disc diameter 660mm.
Weight 260kg.

FIANSA
Apartado Postal 5017 Lima 100
Avenida Industrial 675
Lima
PERU

REVERSIBLE DISC PLOUGH
This two-disc plough with Category I three-point hitch is manufactured by:

JARC DEL PERU S.A.
Santa Natalia 119
Urb. Villa Marina-Chorrillos
Lima 9
PERU

DISC PLOUGH
Twin disc assembly for use with hand tractor.

AYUTTHAYA NANAPHAN
68/3 Moo 1, T.Pai-Ling
A.Muang
Ayutthaya
THAILAND

DISC PLOUGHS
Two-disc and three-disc adjustable disc ploughs for use with the TKS series of walking tractors.

JAKPETCH TRACTOR CO. LTD
14 Moo 3, Soi Orn-Nuch
Ladkrabang
Bangkok 10520
THAILAND

AGRICULTURAL ENGINEERS LTD
Ring Road Industrial Area
P.O. Box 12127
Accra North
GHANA

SPARE PARTS FOR PLOUGHS

ATTACHMENTS FOR AGRICULTURAL MACHINERY
Various parts are made of steel for agricultural machinery, including springs, tines and plough parts.

CARS LTDA
Casilla 2279
Correo Central Santiago
San Bernado
CHILE

Metalurgica Sudamericana produce a range of metal discs and attachments for agricultural machinery, in particular ploughs and harrows, including 'Horseman' discs which are produced under the technical and quality control of W.A. Tyzack and Co. Ltd of Sheffield.

METALURGICA SUDAMERICANA S.A.
Las Violetas 5926
Santiago
CHILE

CHISEL PLOUGH SHARES
Three shapes of steel plough shares.

CENTRO DE INVESTIGACIÓN, FORMACIÓN Y EXTENSIÓN EN MEC. AGRICOLA
Casilla 831
Cochabamba
BOLIVIA

Plough spare parts also available from:

ZIMPLOW LTD
P.O. Box 1059
Bulawayo
ZIMBABWE

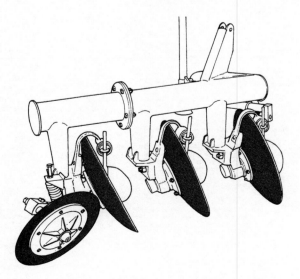

SQUARE HARROW

The harrow is constructed in three sections and each section has eight hardened steel tines. A levelling strip is attached to the front to help smooth the surface of the seedbed. The harrow can be drawn by two oxen and has a working width of 1300mm.

RUMPTSTAD BV
Postbus 1
Stad Aan't Haringvliet
3243 ZG
NETHERLANDS

WINGED RAKE

Two rows of blades are set vertically one behind the other on a simple frame. The blades in each row are set at a slight and opposite angle to the direction of travel to impose a soil mixing action and the frame can be loaded with ballast to increase penetration.

The implement is principally used for breaking up the soil after ploughing or for covering the seeds of wheat, oats or barley.

The rake requires the draught power of one or two oxen.

**CENTRO DE INVESTIGACIÓN,
FORMACIÓN Y EXTENSIÓN
EN MEC. AGRICOLA**
Casilla 831
Cochabamba
BOLIVIA

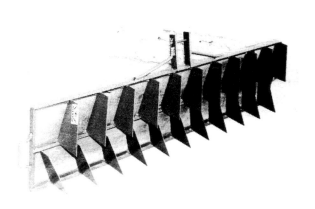

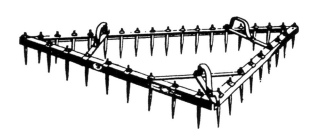

TRIANGULAR HARROWS

This is a lightweight harrow, with a mild steel frame and replaceable carbon steel teeth 16mm square in section and 150mm long. It can be pulled by two donkeys and is fitted with side handles to aid handling.

BULAWAYO STEEL PRODUCTS
P.O. Box 1603
Donnington
Bulawayo
ZIMBABWE

This all-steel triangular harrow has thirty-five tines made from 16mm square section steel and held in place with nuts. Weight 34kg.

COSSUL & CO. PVT LTD
123/367 Industrial Area
Fazalgunj
Kanpur
U.P.
INDIA

TRIANGULAR TINE HARROW
This harrow consists of a triangular fabricated frame from which seven 200mm tines protrude on each side. Width 1500mm.

HERRANDINA
Marte 581
Brena
Lima 5
PERU

Similar implements are manufactured by:

**MARCHESAN
IMPLEMENTOS E MAQUINAS
AGRICOLAS 'TATU' S.A.**
Av. Marchesan 1,979
Matão SP
BRAZIL

AGRIMAL (MALAWI) LTD
Makata Road
P.O. Box 143
Blantyre
MALAWI

SISMAR
20 rue Dr. Thèze
3214
Dakar
SENEGAL

DANDEKAR BROTHERS & CO.
Shivajinagar
Sangli
Maharashtra
416 416
INDIA

HARROW FRAME

This harrow is mounted on a folding frame which allows the two outer sections to be lifted out of work for ease of transport. The working width is 3100mm when all the sections are folded down. The central frame has a Category I three-point hitch for mounting on a conventional tractor.
Weight 135kg including harrows.

**ZALAGEP BAGODI
MEZŐGAZDASÁGI
GÉPGYÁRTÓ VÁLLALAT**
8992 Bagod
Gépállomás út 9
HUNGARY

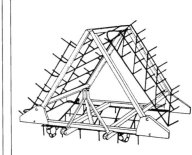

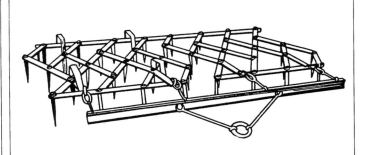

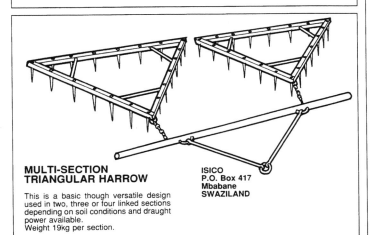

MULTI-SECTION TRIANGULAR HARROW

This is a basic though versatile design used in two, three or four linked sections depending on soil conditions and draught power available.
Weight 19kg per section.

ISICO
P.O. Box 417
Mbabane
SWAZILAND

DIAMOND HARROWS

DIAMOND HARROW
With a diamond pattern frame of twenty tines, this harrow can be used for pulling out weeds and grass from light or ploughed land, available in light, medium and heavy section.
Weights 26kg, 28kg, 31kg.

COSSUL & CO. PVT LTD
123/367 Industrial Area
Fazalgunj
Kanpur
U.P.
INDIA

DIAMOND HARROW
Designed for use in two, three or four sections, depending on the soil type and number of draught cattle. Teeth size 16mm square.
Each section has twenty tines.

BULAWAYO STEEL PRODUCTS
P.O. Box 1603
Donnington
Bulawayo
ZIMBABWE

OX-DRAWN DIAMOND HARROW
Can be adapted to take two, three or four sections with a drawbar, each section is fitted with twenty 16mm carbon steel forged teeth, 150mm long.
Weight 23kg per section.

ZIMPLOW LTD
P.O. Box 1059
Bulawayo
ZIMBABWE

Similar harrows are availble from:

AGRIMAL (MALAWI) LTD
Makata Road
P.O. Box 143
Blantyre
MALAWI

SISMAR
20 rue Dr. Thèze
3214
Dakar
SENEGAL

COBEMAG
B.P. 161
Route de Djougou
Parakou
REPUBLIC OF BENIN

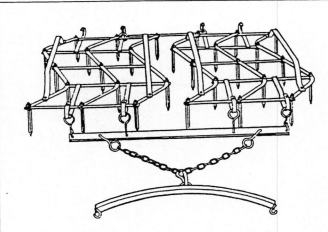

ZIG-ZAG HARROWS

ANIMAL-DRAWN HARROW

This is a simple three-section zig-zag harrow on a single crossbar. Each section has fifteen tines and is linked to the crossbar with short chains.

FAMAE
Casilla 4100
Santiago
CHILE

ZIG-ZAG HARROWS

Diamond and zig-zag section harrows with two-, three- and four-section drawbars available. All-steel construction with heat-treated teeth.

ISICO
P.O. Box 417
Mbabane
SWAZILAND

ZIG-ZAG HARROW

The zig-zag pattern of tines allows each tine to cut a separate track. There are twenty tines in total. The harrow is available in light, medium or heavy sections. Weights vary from 20kg to 32kg.

COSSUL & CO. PVT LTD
123/367 Industrial Area
Fazalgunj
Kanpur
U.P.
INDIA

OX-DRAWN ZIG-ZAG HARROW

Made in two sections, coupled side by side for free movement, this harrow has a mild steel frame with forty hardened steel tines and comes complete with a drawbar.

GARBA INDUSTRIES (PVT) LTD
P.O. Box 90
Norton
ZIMBABWE

OX-DRAWN HARROWS

This is a lightweight zig-zag harrow of all-steel construction.

G. NORTH (PVT) LTD
P.O. Box 111
Southerton
Harare
ZIMBABWE

OX-DRAWN HARROW

This is a lightweight ox-drawn harrow, suitable for the preparation of seedbeds. It is fitted with 150mm-long carbon steel teeth. Weights can be added on top of frame for deeper penetration, and sledge attachments are available to aid transport.

ZIMPLOW LTD
P.O. Box 1059
Bulawayo
ZIMBABWE

HEAVY DUTY ANIMAL-DRAWN ZIG-ZAG HARROW

The basic unit is fitted with 20mm square section carbon steel teeth 200mm long. Two-, three- or four-sections can be coupled together and used with a drawbar.
Weight 40kg.

COBEMAG
B.P. 161
Route de Djougou
Parakou
REPUBLIC OF BENIN

ZIG-ZAG HARROW

Heavy duty, for use with light tractors or a team of oxen, this harrows working width can be adjusted from 1m to 2m. Two, three or four sections can be joined together as required. Teeth size 30 x 12mm.
Weight 97.9kg per section.

BULAWAYO STEEL PRODUCTS
P.O. Box 1603
Donnington
Bulawayo
ZIMBABWE

Similar harrows are available from:

SISMAR
20 rue Dr. Thèze
3214
Dakar
SENEGAL

S.M.E.C.M.A.
Zone Industrielle
Bamako
MALI

CEMAG
Rua João Batista de Oliviera 233
06750 Taboao de Serra
São Paulo
BRAZIL

UPROMA
B.P. 1086
Lomé
TOGO

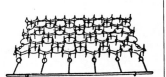

CHAIN HARROW

The chain harrow comprises up to five rows of interlinking 'tridents' (three spiked teeth mounted on a ring). Two working widths of 1.5 and 1.75m are available with weights ranging from 32 to 77kg.

NARDI FRANCESCO & FIGLI
06017 Selci Lama
Perugia
ITALY

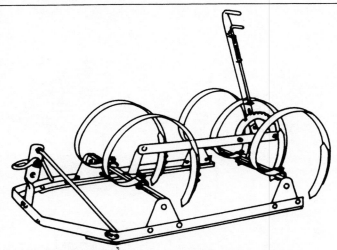

SPRING-TINE HARROW

Spring-tine harrows are a versatile cultivation tool. By adjusting the depth of work (usually with a simple lever mechanism) the curved spring tines present a different angle of attack to the soil. Thus at shallow settings the tines are almost vertical while at full depth the tips are nearly horizontal.

SPRING-TOOTH HARROW

The spring-tooth harrow is an implement for deep tillage. It will work to a depth of 150mm. It is suitable for work in ground filled with stones and roots. The frame is made of angle steel and turns up in front enough for clearance. A hand lever adjusts the depth of the harrow.
Weight: five-tine 35kg, seven-tine 57kg.

COSSUL & CO. PVT LTD
123/367 Industrial Area
Fazalgunj
Kanpur
U.P.
INDIA

RAKER-TYPE SPRING-TOOTH HARROW

Each section is an individual unit available in 900mm and 1200mm sections up to 4.8m: eight teeth per 900mm section; eleven teeth per 1200mm section. Heat-treated and tempered spring teeth, drilled in order to fit reversible tips after original tips wear down. Weights are 76kg and 89kg respectively.

PIONEER EQUIPMENT INC.
16392 Western Road
Dalton
OH 44618
USA

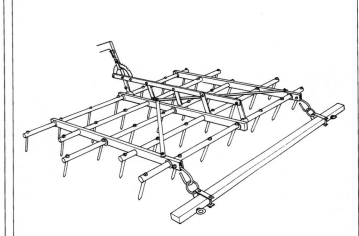

ADJUSTABLE TOOTH HARROWS

SPIKE-TOOTH HARROW

The spike-tooth harrow is available in any combination of 1520mm and 1830mm sections up to 5.5m wide. The rake angle of the tines is adjustable by means of a lever on each section and the tines are arranged in a diamond formation. Thirty-five tines per 1520mm section, Forty tines per 1830mm section.
Weights are 50kg and 54kg respectively.

PIONEER EQUIPMENT INC.
16392 Western Road
Dalton
OH 44618
USA

PEG-TOOTH LEVER HARROW

All-steel construction for cultivation. The rake angle of the tines is adjustable (by means of a lever) in order to vary the amount of penetration. There are thirty tines on each section of harrow.
The harrow can be pulled by a pair of bullocks.
Working width 1200mm.
Weight 50kg.

COSSUL & CO. PVT LTD
123/367 Industrial Area
Fazalgunj
Kanpur
U.P.
INDIA

SINGLE ROW DISC HARROWS

Disc harrows consist of a number of dish-shaped discs mounted on two axles or gangs. The angle between the line of draught and the gangs is adjustable over a small range, and each gang's angle is set opposite and equal to eliminate side forces. The action of the harrow on the soil is dependent both on the set angle and also upon the weight of the implement as this directly affects the amount of penetration. Gangs of discs can be mounted side by side or in tandem.

DISC HARROW
This harrow is fitted with six discs (made in India), and a seat is provided for the driver. Two small road wheels are fitted above the frame and the whole harrow is inverted for road transport.

AGRICULTURAL TOOLS FACTORY LTD
P.O. Box No. 2
Birganj
NEPAL

RIGID FRAME DISC HARROW
This harrow has two gangs of four discs mounted on a heavy steel frame. The angle between the frames can be adjusted to a maximum of 22 degrees. Weight 160kg.

I.C.A. PROGRAMA DE MAQUINARIA AGRICOLA
Instituto Colombiano Agropec.
Apartado Aéreo 151123
Bogotá
COLOMBIA

A similar implement is manufactured by:

AGRO MACHINERY LTD
P.O. Box 3281
Bush Rod Island
Monrovia
LIBERIA

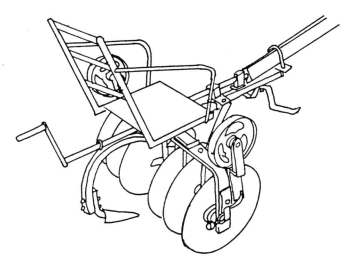

BULLOCK-DRIVEN DISC HARROW
This harrow is drawn by two bullocks or oxen and is usually used after ploughing to chop weeds and pulverize the soil. It can be used in both dry and wet conditions.
Working width 760mm.
Working depth 25mm to 90mm.
Approximate weight 85kg.

MOHINDER & CO. ALLIED INDUSTRIES
Kurali District
Rupnagar Dist. (Ropar)
Punjab
INDIA

DISC HARROW
Used for preparing seed beds and puddling rice fields, this harrow comes with disc scrapers and driver's seat.
Weight: six-disc version 38kg, eight-disc version 92kg.

COSSUL & CO. PVT LTD
123/367 Industrial Area
Fazalgunj
Kanpur
U.P.
INDIA

BULLOCK-DRIVEN DISC HARROW
Six 406mm discs. Single action with depth control lever, seat for operator while ploughing and cast iron road wheels when inverted. Suitable for light and medium soils and for puddling paddy fields.
Weight 100kg.

STANDARD AGRICULTURAL ENG. CO.
824/5 Industrial Area B
Ludhiana
Punjab
141 003
INDIA

THREE-DISC HARROW
Each disc is 609mm in diameter and 3mm thick. The maximum working depth is 228mm. The distance between discs is 762mm.
Weight: 160kg.

HAMDARD AGRO ENGINEERS
Circular Road
Daska
Dist. Sialkot
PAKISTAN

DISC HARROW
Eight discs on simple frame for attaching to a walking tractor.

JIANGMEN DITY FARM MACH'Y FACTORY
25 Gangkou Rd
Jiangmen
Guangdong
CHINA

DISC HARROWS
For use with small tractors.

SO'MTOSS'
55 Hristo Botev bul.
Sofia
BULGARIA

TANDEM DISC HARROWS

TANDEM DISC HARROW
This harrow has two gangs of six discs in tandem with maximum coupling angle of 38 degrees.
Total weight without ballast 200kg.

I.C.A. PROGRAMA DE MAQUINARIA AGRICOLA
Instituto Colombiano Agropcuario
Apartado Aéreo 151123
Bogotá
COLOMBIA

TRACTOR-DRIVEN DISC HARROW (TRAILING TYPE)
The front gang of discs are notched enabling the implement to dig better. This implement can often replace the ploughing operation in soft irrigated soil. Range of disc harrow sizes with gangs of five, six, seven and nine discs. Disc diameter 610mm.

MOHINDER & CO. ALLIED INDUSTRIES
Kurali District
Rupnagar Dist. (Ropar)
Punjab
INDIA

DISC HARROW
Flexible, four-gang, mounted type. Twenty discs, diameter 460mm, at 165mm spacing. Working width 1.85m. Maximum working depth 120-150mm. The front and rear gangs can be inclined to five basic positions by levers which are within reach of the driver.
Weight 300kg.

OLT - PROMET
54000 Osijek (P.O.B. 222)
P. Svacica 4
YUGOSLAVIA

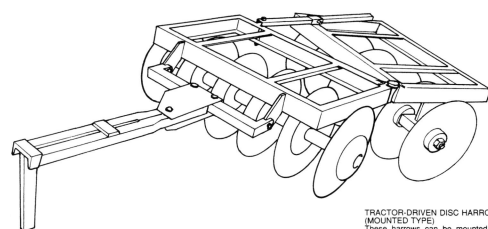

OFFSET DISC HARROW
Three models with ten, twelve and fourteen discs respectively, fitted with self-lubricating, sealed, deep-groove ball bearings. The harrows are tractor mounted requiring a Category I or Category II hitch.
Cutting width 900, 1120 and 1340mm.
Weight 280, 300, 340kg.

PUNJAB TRACTORS LTD
P.O. Box 6, Phase IV
SAS Nagar
Chandigarh
160 055
INDIA

DISC HARROW
This Category I three-point hitch-mounted implement has sixteen 400mm discs in two gangs of eight; the front gang has serrated discs to aid penetration. The discs are made from high carbon steel. Minimum power required is 22.5kW.
Weight 330kg.

JARC DEL PERU S.A.
Santa Natalia 119
Urb. Villa Marina - Chorrillos
Lima 9
PERU

AGRICULTURAL TOOLS FACTORY LTD.
P.O. Box No. 2
Birganj
NEPAL

TRACTOR-DRIVEN DISC HARROWS (MOUNTED TYPE)
These harrows can be mounted offset from the centre line of the tractor to enable cultivation to take place beneath the overhanging branches in an orchard. In order to counteract the side thrust caused by such a set-up, the second gang of discs can be set at a greater angle to the line of draught than the first. A range of disc sizes is available:
Two gangs of four 560mm diameter.
Two gangs of five 560mm diameter.
Two gangs of five 610mm diameter.
Two gangs of six 610mm diameter.

MOHINDER & CO. ALLIED INDUSTRIES
Kurali District
Rupnagar Dist. (Ropar)
Punjab
INDIA

ROTARY HARROWS

Similar in principle to the disc harrow, the rotary harrow comprises a frame into which one or more rows of either spiked (starred) teeth or chopping blades are mounted. The movement of the harrow over the ground causes the teeth or blades to rotate and break up the soil.

SISMAR
20 rue Dr. Thèze
3214
Dakar
SENEGAL

COSSUL THREE-TINE CULTIVATORS

R.N. CULTIVATOR
This three-tine cultivator has reversible carbon steel tines and the width can be adjusted across the beam. The depth of work can also be altered by changing the angle of the drawbar. Various attachments can be supplied as extras. Weight 16kg.

VIKAS JR. CULTIVATOR
Three-tine all-steel cultivator similar in appearance to the R.N. cultivator; its working width is adjustable. A mould-board plough, seeding attachment and sweeps of different sizes can be used with the cultivator and are supplied as extra attachments.
Weight 16kg.

COSSUL & CO. PVT LTD
123/367 Industrial Area
Fazalgunj
Kanpur
U.P.
INDIA

RIGID-TINE CULTIVATORS

The fixed tine cultivators described are similar in function to harrows but have fewer tines. These can be set to work at greater depths than those of harrows. These cultivators can be used for several tasks, including the preparation of seedbeds as a secondary operation to ploughing, inter-row cultivation and weed control.

MACO ADJUSTABLE TRIPHALI (BULLOCK-DRIVEN)
The Adjustable Triphali has three tines and is pulled by two animals.
Working width 450-600mm.
Depth of cut 50-100mm.
Approximate weight 18kg.

MOHINDER & CO. ALLIED INDUSTRIES
Kurali District
Rupnagar Dist. (Ropar)
Punjab
INDIA

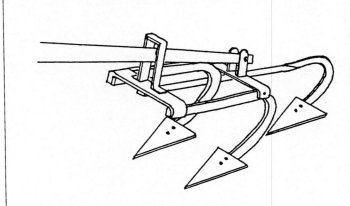

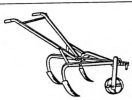

MASTER FARMER LIGHT CULTIVATORS

The BS2 is a very lightweight cultivator for sandy soils which one animal can pull. The BS3 is a three-tine lightweight cultivator for lighter soils, using two smaller draught cattle or donkeys.

BULAWAYO STEEL PRODUCTS
P.O. Box 1603
Donnington
Bulawayo
ZIMBABWE

SIMPLE THREE-TINE CULTIVATORS

ROW CROP HOE
This is a simple design of three-tined light cultivator, with adjustable working width.

ALVAN BLANCH DEV. CO. LTD
Chelworth
Malmesbury
Wilts SN16 9SG
UK

Similar implements are manufactured by:

AGRICULTURAL TOOLS FACTORY LTD
P.O. Box No. 2
Birganj
NEPAL

CECOCO
P.O. Box 8
Ibaraki City
Osaka 567
JAPAN

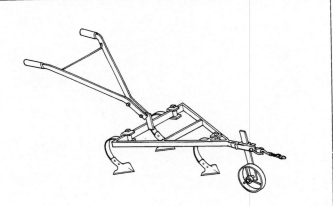

TRIANGULAR THREE-TINE CULTIVATORS

This ox-drawn cultivator is one of a range produced by C.N.E.A. and Uproma. The basic frame can be fitted with either three- or five-spring or rigid tines, and the distance between the tines can be adjusted by sliding them along the frame to the required position. A wheel is provided to control the depth of the implement in work.

CENTRE NATIONAL D'EQUIPEMENT AGRICO
B.P. 7240
Ouagadougou 03
BURKINA FASO

UPROMA
B.P. 1086
Lomé
TOGO

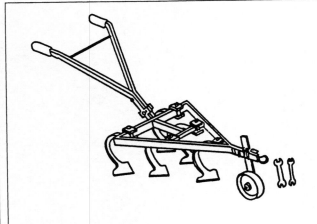

FIVE-TINE CULTIVATORS

The 'HOUE SICAMIA' (illustrated) has a square frame fabricated from rectangular section steel bar. Various implements can be attached to this frame using the simple clamps provided. The attachments available include spring tines, rigid tines, groundnut lifter and ridging plough. Weight 50-100kg.

MARPEX
1 rue Thurot
44000 Nantes
FRANCE

NUBA GRECO HOE
This is a cultivator with five spring-tines. The working width and depth are both adjustable.

E.B.R.A.
28 rue de Maine
B.P. 915
49009 Angers Cedex
FRANCE

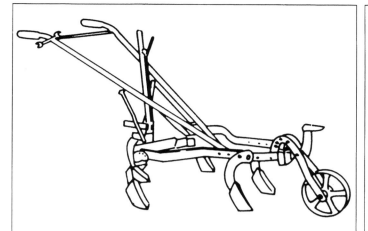

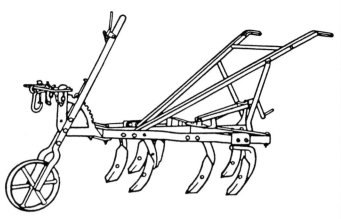

FIVE-TINE LEVER ADJUSTABLE CULTIVATORS

ANIMAL-DRAWN CULTIVATORS
Two all-steel models in which the operating width can be adjusted by means of a lever. Model S51 has two tines, two hillers and one duck foot sweep. The 'Light' has four tines and one duck foot sweep. Both have a 150mm diameter cast iron depth wheel. The S51 is a heavy model suitable for row crops between 610 and 1070mm. The light cultivator is suited to narrow row cultivation and is adjustable between 475 and 750mm.

ZIMPLOW LTD
P.O. Box 1059
Bulawayo
ZIMBABWE

ANIMAL-DRAWN CULTIVATOR
An all-steel construction with five tines and an adjusting lever to change the operating width. It can be used for working already ploughed land, as well as cultivating between row-crops such as sugar cane, cotton and maize. A full range of spares is available.

FAMAE
Casilla 4100
Santiago
CHILE

This all-steel cultivator has five tines and can be adjusted for width from 300 to 625mm by means of a lever. Mouldboard shares are available for earthing up ridges and making irrigation channels.

RAJAN UNIVERSAL EXPORTS
(MFRS) LTD
P.O. Box 250
Madras
600 001
INDIA

SCREW-ADJUSTABLE SEVEN-TINE CULTIVATOR

This implement is designed for preparing seed beds or inter-row cultivation of crops such as sugar cane, cotton, maize, tobacco and potato. The seven points made in steel are reversible. Right/left mouldboards are available as extras. Working width 300 to 625mm. Weight 35kg.

AGRIMAL (MALAWI) LTD
Makata Road
P.O. Box 143
Blantyre
MALAWI

Similar implements are manufactured by:

G. NORTH (PVT) LTD
P.O. Box 111
Southerton
Harare
ZIMBABWE

BHARAT INDUSTRIAL
CORPORATION
Petit Compound
Nana Chowk, Grant Road
Bombay
400 007
INDIA

ISICO
P.O. Box 417
Mbabane
SWAZILAND

MARCHESAN
IMPLEMENTOS E MAQUINAS
AGRICOLAS 'TATU' S.A.
Av. Marchesan 1,979
Matão SP
BRAZIL

COSSUL & CO. PVT LTD
123/367 Industrial Area
Fazalgunj
Kanpur
U.P.
INDIA

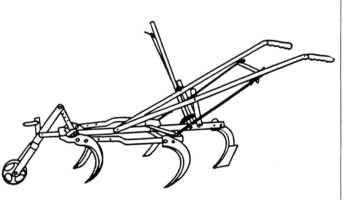

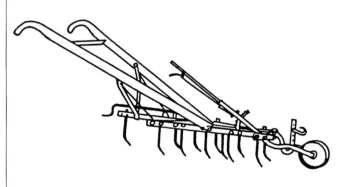

MASTER FARMER CULTIVATORS

The BS221 cultivator is for use in heavy soils and row crops, and has a mild steel frame with carbon steel teeth. It has side hillers which deposits soil on both rows to support plants. Width is adjustable. Spare parts are interchangeable with the BS41 described below.
Weight 36kg.

The BS41 cultivator is similar to the BS221 but has tines between the frames to loosen soil between plant rows and is for general use on medium to light soils.
Weight 36kg.

BULAWAYO STEEL PRODUCTS
P.O. Box 1603
Donnington
Bulawayo
ZIMBABWE

HORSE-DRAWN CULTIVATORS

These steel cultivators can be used for soil tilling or inter-row cultivation. They have stepless adjustment of working width between 250 and 800mm. Penetration depth is also adjustable.

FORTSCHRITT LANDMASCHINEN
Berghausstraße 1
Neustadt
DDR-8355
GERMANY

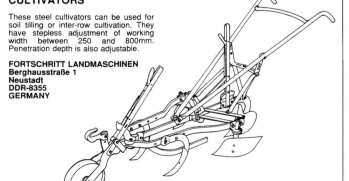

14-TOOTH CULTIVATORS

The Orchard Harrow is made of steel and may be furnished with wooden handles. Designed principally for destroying weed seedlings, it has a lever for adjusting width and an adjustable wheel to regulate depth. The harrow weighs 31kg, with a working width of 800mm and a working depth of 50mm.
It can be drawn by one animal.

BALDAN IMPLEMENTOS
AGRICOLAS S.A.
Av. Baldan 1500
C.P.11 15990 Matão SP
BRAZIL

MARCHESAN
IMPLEMENTOS E MAQUINAS
AGRICOLAS 'TATU' S.A.
Av. Marchesan 1,979
Matão SP
BRAZIL

TRACTOR-MOUNTED CULTIVATORS

FIVE-TINE CULTIVATOR
Five-tine cultivator with replaceable shares and adjustable depth wheels is tractor mounted using a standard Category I three-point hitch.
Working width 1400mm.
Weight 120kg.

V.S.T. TILLERS TRACTORS LTD
P.O. Box 4801
Mahadevapura Post Office
Bangalore
560 048
INDIA

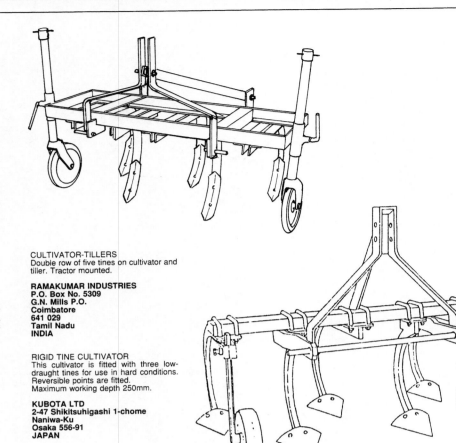

TINED-CULTIVATOR/RIDGER
This is a series of rigid tine toolbars (with three, five, seven or nine tines) from which the tines can be removed in order to attach a ridging tool. For use with a tractor with a Category I three-point hitch.
Toolbar length 1800mm.
Weight 230kg.

AGROMONFER S.A.
El Santuario 1035
Zarate
Lima 36
PERU

CULTIVATOR
This is a rigid-tine cultivator designed for use in breaking compacted ground. A tractor power of between 15 and 22kW is required for operation.
Width of work 1000 to 1600mm.

HELWAAN MACHINE TOOLS FACTORY
Ein Helwaan
Cairo
EGYPT

CULTIVATOR-TILLERS
Double row of five tines on cultivator and tiller. Tractor mounted.

RAMAKUMAR INDUSTRIES
P.O. Box No. 5309
G.N. Mills P.O.
Coimbatore
641 029
Tamil Nadu
INDIA

RIGID TINE CULTIVATOR
This cultivator is fitted with three low-draught tines for use in hard conditions. Reversible points are fitted.
Maximum working depth 250mm.

KUBOTA LTD
2-47 Shikitsuhigashi 1-chome
Naniwa-Ku
Osaka 556-91
JAPAN

FIXED-SHARE CULTIVATOR
This cultivator has eight fixed shares with two adjustable wheels for depth control. Mounts on the hitch of the MT8-050 tractor.
Working depth 80mm.
Working width 1260mm.

AGROZET PROSTEJOV K.P.
MOTOKOV FOREIGN TRADE CORPORATION
Na strži 63
140 62 Praha 4
CZECHOSLOVAKIA

RIGID TINE CULTIVATORS
A range of cultivators with from five to fifteen tines.

JECO (PRIVATE) LTD
P.O. Box 46
G.T. Road
Gujranwala
PAKISTAN

A similar implement is manufactured by:

S.C.A.D. BOURGUIGNON
B.P 37 Les Tordières
26301 Bourg-De-Peage Cedex
FRANCE

SIX-TINE CULTIVATOR
This implement has six tines, individually clamped on a single toolbar. Tine spacing can be readily changed by loosening the clamps and sliding the tines along the bar. Depth control wheels are also provided at each end of the bar.
Working width 1000mm.
Weight 40kg.

ALDO BIAGIOLI & FIGLI
52037 Sansepolcro (Arezzo)
ITALY

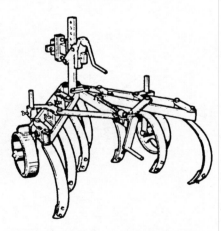

SEVEN-TINE ADJUSTABLE CULTIVATOR

This cultivator has been designed for use with a walking tractor. The seven spring tines are mounted on a pantograph frame which keeps them parallel to the direction of travel at any width setting. Two depth control wheels are provided and the tractor coupling is also adjustable vertically.
Working width 750mm (maximum).
Weight 42kg.

S.C.A.D. BOURGUIGNON
B.P. 37 Les Tourdièr
26301 Bourg-De-Peage Cedex
FRANCE

CULTIVATOR FOR USE WITH MAESTRAL WALKING TRACTOR
Five-tine cultivator adjustable for depth and width.
Working width 300-600mm.
Working depth 100mm.

GORENJE MUTA
62366 Muta
YUGOSLAVIA

ADJUSTABLE FIVE-TINE CULTIVATOR
This cultivator has been designed for use with a walking tractor; it has reversible tips and a depth control wheel.
Working width 300 to 600mm.
Weight 28kg.

ALDO BIAGIOLI & FIGLI
52037 Sansepolcro (Arezzo)
ITALY

INTER-ROW CULTIVATOR

This inter-row cultivator is tractor-mounted on a Category I three-point hitch. A separate cultivator unit for either side of the crop row is attached to a frame on a spring suspension mechanism, and each rotary cultivator is driven by chain from a cross-shaft which is itself driven from the tractor power take-off.
Depth of cultivation 120mm.
Weight 146kg.

ZALAGÉP BAGODI
MEZŐGAZDASÁGI
GÉPGYÁRTÓ VÁLLALAT
8992 Bagod
Gépállomás út 9
HUNGARY

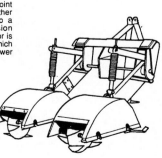

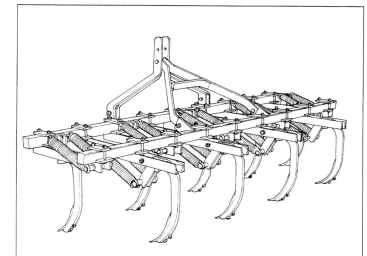

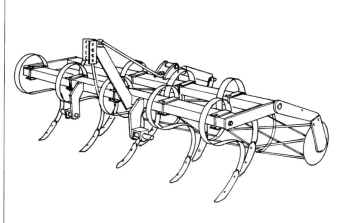

SPRING-LOADED TINE CULTIVATORS

CULTIVATOR
Tractor mounted using Category I or II three-point hitch, three models with seven, nine or eleven 920mm tines respectively. The tine spacing is adjustable for inter-row cultivation and the high carbon steel tips are reversible.
Width 1650, 2160 and 2670mm.
Weight 180, 220 and 260kg.

PUNJAB TRACTORS LTD
P.O. Box 6, Phase IV
SAS Nagar
Near Chandigarh
160 055
INDIA

MACO CULTIVATOR (TILLER), SPRING-LOADED
A spring-loaded, tractor-mounted cultivator, this can carry up to nine tines with an approximate draught of 320kg.

MOHINDER & CO. ALLIED INDUSTRIES
Kurali District
Rupnagar Dist. (Ropar)
Punjab
INDIA

CULTIVATOR
Five-tine spring-loaded type with replaceable shares, adjustable tine angle and wheel depth.
Width 720mm.
Weight 130kg.

V.S.T. TILLERS TRACTORS LTD
P.O. Box 4801
Mahadevapura Post Office
Bangalore
560 048
INDIA

Similar implements are manufactured by:

AGRICULTURAL TOOLS FACTORY LTD
P.O. Box No. 2
Birganj
NEPAL

IMT BEOGRAD
Fabrika Opreme I Pribora
Industrijska zona bb.
23272 Novi Bečej
YUGOSLAVIA

ALDO BIAGIOLI & FIGLI
52037 Sansepolcro (Arezzo)
ITALY

S.C.A.D. BOURGUIGNON
B.P. 37 Les Tourdièr
26301 Bourg-De-Peage Cedex
FRANCE

SPRING-TINE CULTIVATORS

These implements are similar in operation to spring-loaded tine cultivators but each tine is itself manufactured from spring steel and therefore requires no separate spring or pivot.

SPRING-TINE CULTIVATOR
Nine spring tines mounted on a frame and pulled by an 11kW tractor, used for loosening soils and small farms. Width of cultivation 1500mm.
Weight 80kg.

ZALAGEP BAGODI
MEZÖGAZDASÁGI
GÉPGYÁRTÓ VÁLLALAT
8992 Bagod
Gépállomás út 9
HUNGARY

SEEDBED CULTIVATOR
Tractor-mounted, this cultivator has fifteen or twenty-one replaceable tines.
Working width 2100mm.
Working depth to 150mm.
Weight 330kg.

IMT BEOGRAD
Fabrika Opreme I Pribora
Industrijska zona bb.
23272 Novi Bečej
YUGOSLAVIA

Similar implements are manufactured by:

ALDO BIAGIOLI & FIGLI
52037 Sansepolcro (Arezzo)
ITALY

S.C.A.D. BOURGUIGNON
B.P. 37 Les Tourdièr
26301 Bourg-De-Peage Cedex
FRANCE

RIDGERS

THE OD2 RIDGER
This ridger has a frame of square section bars and steel tubing, and the ridging body is adjustable for use in crop lifting.
Working width 970mm.
Weight 42kg.

PROJECT EQUIPMENT LTD
Industrial Estate
Oswestry
Shropshire SY10 8HA
UK

ANIMAL-DRAWN RIDGER
This ridger is made from steel and the soil-engaging parts are all replaceable.
Working width 300mm.
Working depth 200mm.
Weight 38kg.

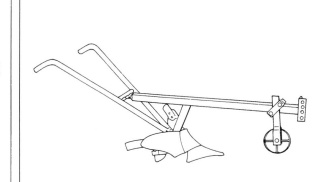

I.C.A. PROGRAMA DE MAQUINARIA AGRICOLA
Instituto Colombiano Agropec.
Apartado Aéreo 151123
Bogotá
COLOMBIA

ADJUSTABLE LIGHTWEIGHT RIDGER
This ridger is constructed of steel with adjustable handles and adjustable ridger bodies.
Working width 300 to 650mm.
Working depth 120 to 200mm.

ALVAN BLANCH DEVELOPMENT CO. LTD
Chelworth
Malmesbury
Wilts SN16 9SG
UK

Similar implements are produced by the following companies:

ZIMPLOW LTD
P.O. Box 1059
Bulawayo
ZIMBABWE

MEKINS AGRO PRODUCTS (PVT) LTD
6-3-866/A Begumpet
Greenlands
Hyderabad
500 016
INDIA

FAMAE
Casilla 4100
Santiago
CHILE

RAJAN UNIVERSAL EXPORTS (MFRS) LTD
P.O. Box 250
Madras
600 001
INDIA

AGRO MACHINERY LTD
P.O. Box 3281
Bush Rod Island
Monrovia
LIBERIA

AGRICULTURAL ENGINEERS LTD
Ring Road Industrial Area
P.O. Box 12127
Accra North
GHANA

AGRICULTURAL TOOLS FACTORY LTD
P.O. Box No. 2
Birganj
NEPAL

UBUNGO FARM IMPLEMENTS MANUFACTURING CO. LTD
P.O. Box 20126
Dar es Salaam
TANZANIA

OYANI CHRISTIAN RURAL SERV. CENTRE
Box 771
Suna
KENYA

COBEMAG
B.P. 161
Route de Djougou
Parakou
REPUBLIC OF BENIN

BHARAT INDUSTRIAL CORPORATION
Petit Compound
Nana Chowk, Grant Road
Bombay
400 007
INDIA

SUPER TATU RIDGER PLOUGH

This animal-drawn ridger is of steel construction with a wooden beam and handles. The adjustable wings enable the implement to produce ridges of different widths.
Working width 400 to 750mm.
Weight 31kg.

**MARCHESAN
IMPLEMENTOS E MAQUINAS
AGRICOLAS 'TATU' S.A.
Av. Marchesan 1,979
Matão S.P.
BRAZIL**

Similar ridgers are available from:

**NARDI FRANCESCO & FIGLI
06017 Selci Lama
Perugia
ITALY**

**HERCULANO ALFAIAS AGRICOLAS
Loureiro 3720
Oliveira de Azemeis
PORTUGAL**

**DEL MORINO S.P.A.
52033 Caprese Michelangelo
ITALY**

**BALDAN IMPLEMENTOS
AGRÍCOLAS S.A.
Av. Baldan 1500
C.P.11 15990 Matão SP
BRAZIL**

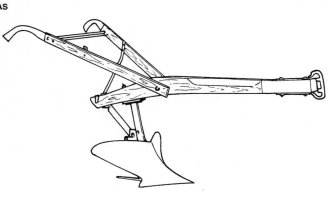

KAPAS (EMCOT) RIDGER

This ridger is supplied with depth control wheel, mouldboard and handles all made of steel. Breasts with tailpieces can be fitted to the mouldboards to extend the furrow width.
Weight 44kg.

**COSSUL & CO. PVT LTD
123/367 Industrial Area
Fazalgunj
Kanpur
U.P.
INDIA**

**BULAWAYO STEEL PRODUCTS
P.O. Box 1603
Donnington
Bulawayo
ZIMBABWE**

Similar implements are manufactured by:

**G. NORTH (PVT) LTD
P.O. Box 111
Southerton
Harare
ZIMBABWE**

**AGRIMAL (MALAWI) LTD
Makata Road
P.O. Box 143
Blantyre
MALAWI**

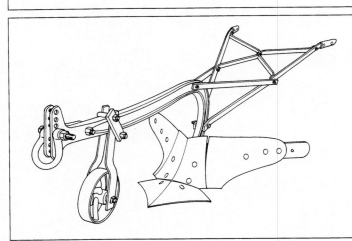

TRACTOR-DRAWN RIDGERS

This implement comprises a row of three ridger bodies mounted on a toolbar coupled to a tractor using a Category I three-point hitch. This is capable of producing three parallel ridges in one pass.

**RAMAKUMAR INDUSTRIES
P.O. Box No 5309
G.N. Mills P.O.
Coimbatore 641 029
Tamil Nadu
INDIA**

RIDGING PLOUGH
This steel mouldboard plough has an adjustable working width from 260 to 440mm.

**GORENJE MUTA
62366 Muta
YUGOSLAVIA**

RIDGER FOR POWER TILLER
This implement can form 900mm wide furrows.

**V.S.T. TILLERS TRACTORS LTD
P.O. Box 4801
Mahadevapura Post Office
Bangalore
560 048
INDIA**

Similar implements are manufactured by:

**ALDO BIAGIOLI & FIGLI
52037 Sansepolcro (Arezzo)
ITALY**

**S.C.A.D. BOURGUIGNON
B.P. 37 Les Tourdièr
26301 Bourg-De-Peage Cedex
FRANCE**

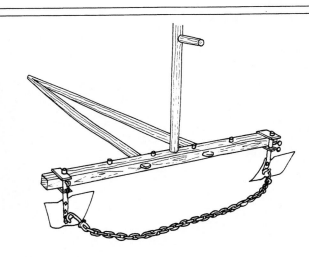

BROAD BED FORMERS

There are various types of bed former based on iron or wooden T-bars, to which standard ridger bodies are attached at either end, the distance between them determining the bed width. A drag chain is sometimes hitched between the bodies to smooth the surface of the bed and help to retain moisture.
These implements have been developed by:

**THE INTERNATIONAL CROPS
RESEARCH INSTITUTE FOR THE
SEMI-ARID TROPICS
Patancheru P.O.
Andra Pradesh
502 324
INDIA**

These implements are available commercially from the following manufacturers.

**KALE KRISHI UDYOG
S31/2/2, Hinge Khurd
Vithalwadi, Sinnagad Road
Pune
411 051
INDIA**

**MEKINS AGRO PRODUCTS (PVT)
LTD
6-3-866/A Begumpet
Greenlands
Hyderabad
500 016
INDIA**

**BALAJI INDUSTRIAL &
AGRICULTURAL CASTINGS
4-3-140 Hill Street
P.O. Box 1634
Secunderabad
500 003
INDIA**

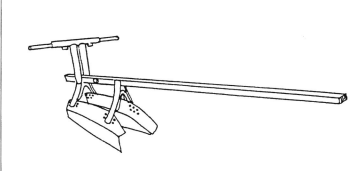

BUND FORMERS

A simple labour-saving implement for forming bunds (ridges) helps in the preparation of fields for irrigation and can be used in dry farming areas to preserve moisture. On steep slopes bunds are made along the contour to prevent soil erosion during heavy rains.

COSSUL BUND FORMER
The main parts are a pair of collecting mouldboards made of steel. They are fitted so as to collect soil and throw it on the centre to make a bund. Size of bund and soil-collecting capacity can be increased or decreased by adjusting the mouldboards.
Weight 16.5kg.

COSSUL & CO. PVT LTD
123/367 Industrial Area
Fazalgunj
Kanpur
U.P.
INDIA

BUND FORMER
This implement can be pulled by a pair of animals.

MOHINDER & CO. ALLIED
INDUSTRIES
Kurali District
Rupnagar Dist. (Ropar)
Punjab
INDIA

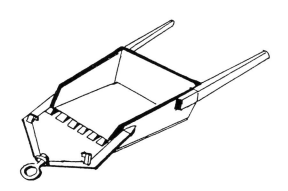

ANIMAL-DRAWN SCRAPERS AND LEVELLERS

ANIMAL-DRAWN SCRAPER
This scraper is suitable for use in tropical conditions and can be pulled by two draught animals. The capacity is between 0.1 and 0.15 cubic metres.
Weight 53kg.

RUMPTSTAD BV
Postbus 1
Stad Aan't-Haringvliet
3243 ZG
NETHERLANDS

Similar implements are made by:

DANDEKAR BROTHERS & CO.
Shivajinagar
Sangli
Maharashtra
416 416
INDIA

COSSUL & CO. PVT LTD
123/367 Industrial Area
Fazalgunj, Kanpur
U.P.
INDIA

ZFE COMPANY (PVT) LTD
P.O. Box 1180
Harare
ZIMBABWE

ANIMAL-DRAWN LAND SCRAPER
This leveller comprises a hopper cut from an ordinary 200-litre oil drum to which a steel blade is attached. A U-shaped steel rod and wooden beam is used for hitching the implement to animals. The blade position is controlled by a hand lever.
Working width 850mm.

INSTITUTE FOR AGRICULTURAL
RESEARCH
Samaru
P.O. Box 1044
Zaria
NIGERIA

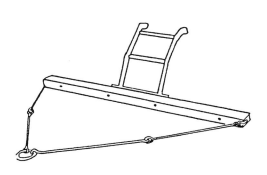

SOIL LEVELLERS

This is a basic design consisting of a long beam with a pair of handles and solid-link hitching arrangement.

ALVAN BLANCH DEVELOPMENT CO.
LTD
Chelworth
Malmesbury
Wilts SN16 9SG
UK

ANIMAL-DRAWN LAND LEVELLING BOARD
Designed at the Department of Agricultural Engineering, University of Nairobi, who are willing to put enquirers in touch with small local manufacturers. This wooden construction is strongly reinforced, with metal levelling blade, edge vane and fabricated guide bar, complete with chains to attach to animal harness.

ANIMAL POWER DEVELOPMENT
PROJECT
Department of Agricultural
Engineering
University of Nairobi
Box 30197
Kabete Campus
Nairobi
KENYA

WOODEN LEVELLER
The leveller consists of two wooden planks hinged together. A steel handle is provided to control scraping and dumping.
Working width 1225mm.
Weight 57kg.

COSSUL & CO. PVT LTD
123/367 Industrial Area
Fazalgunj
Kanpur
U.P.
INDIA

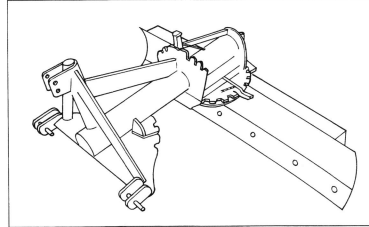

TRACTOR-MOUNTED LEVELLERS

HEAVY-DUTY GRADER BLADE
For back blading, vee draining, and so on, it can be offset left or right. Angle and tilt adjustment is provided as is a reversible cutting edge.

KANGA FARM EQUIPMENT
P.O. Box 1177
Dandenong
Victoria 3175
AUSTRALIA

REAR BLADE LEVELLER
Multi-position for grading and levelling.

JECO (PRIVATE) LTD
P.O. Box 46
G.T. Road
Gujranwala
PAKISTAN

LEVELLER FOR POWER TILLER
For dry land levelling.

V.S.T. TILLERS TRACTORS LTD
P.O. Box 4801
Mahadevapura Post Office
Bangalore
560 048
INDIA

RAKING BLADE
Intended for raking materials in areas with compacted surface. Steel blades are for raking bulk materials like soil or sand. Coupled on to a tractor using a three-point quick-release hitch.
Working width 1650mm.
Weight 106kg.

AGROZET PROSTEJOV K.P.
Motokov Foreign Trade Corporation
PSC 792 21
CZECHOSLOVAKIA

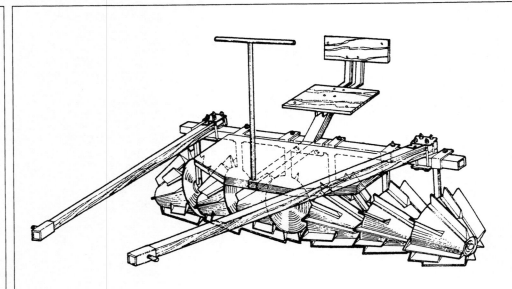

PUDDLERS

COSSUL PUDDLER
The Cossul puddler has three axle-mounted cast iron hubs each with four blades which act on the soil to break up clods and stir the surface layer. The draught power of one animal is required to pull the implement.
Weight 39kg.
Workrate 1-1.5 ha/day (8hrs).

COSSUL & CO. PVT LTD
123/367 Industrial Area
Fazalgunj
Kanpur
U.P.
INDIA

A combined puddler and harrow requiring the draught of two oxen is manufactured by:

DARMO METAL INDUSTRIES
Tepaurel Compound
Barrio Putatan
Mantinlupa
Metro Manila
PHILIPPINES

CONO-PUDDLERS

ANIMAL-DRAWN CONO-PUDDLER
The design uses the concept of conical-shaped rotors for wetland preparation. The blades on the rotors puddle the top 100mm by a differential soil displacing motion which also buries weeds and trash with a rolling action. There are six rotors individually clamped to a toolbar for easy removal and spacing adjustment. Two wooden beams are rigidly fixed to the toolbar for hitching to the yoke. A removable seat is provided for the driver, whose additional weight will assist with penetration on harder soils.
Draught required 30-80kg.
Working width 1.6m.
Workrate 0.8ha/day (8hrs).
Weight 40kg.

POWER-TILLER-MOUNTED CONO-PUDDLER
Similar in design and use to the animal-drawn unit previously described, the toolbar of this implement can be fitted to a walking tractor by means of a special hitch adaptor. The mounting has a free side-swinging arrangement to aid turning.
Working width 1.6m.
Workrate 1.5ha/day (8hrs).
Weight 38kg.

INTERNATIONAL RICE RESEARCH INSTITUTE
Agricultural Engineering Department
P.O. Box 933
Manila
PHILIPPINES

IRRI WETLAND CULTIVATION EQUIPMENT

Equipment designed by the International Rice Research Institute (IRRI) is produced by a number of manufacturers in India and South-east Asia. Particularly appropriate for wetland cultivation, the IRRI-designed implements are of a simple construction which enables them to be fabricated in machine shops using widely available materials.

There are three IRRI-designed wetland cultivators currently available. The Rotary Tiller is a medium-powered walking tractor which may be used for both primary and secondary tillage. The Power Tiller has a slightly lower power output, but is equipped with a wider range of attachments which, in addition to the standard tillage equipment, include a one-metre wide reaper. The Power Tiller may also be adapted for use as transport and as a power source for a water pump. The IRRI Hydro Tiller has been designed to overcome the problems of excess water or mud in wetland farming systems, which can cause delays in planting because traditional tillage equipment cannot cope with the conditions.

In addition to these powered implements, other wetland equipment which has been designed by IRRI is also included both here and in later chapters.

POWER TILLER
Powered by 3.5kW petrol or diesel engine via V-belt to roller chain and sprockets. The transmission runs in an oil bath to reduce wear and therefore maintenance. Manual steering.
Width with puddling wheels 1290mm.
Speed 2.5-4.5km/hr
Fuel consumption 1.1l/hr (petrol).
Workrate 0.6ha/day ploughing.
Weight 88kg (petrol).

ROTARY TILLER
This IRRI design has 3-4.5kW diesel or 4-6kW petrol engine. Transmission is by V-belt from the engine to chain and sprockets drive to the cage wheel axles. There are two forward gears giving a maximum field speed of 3km/hr and road speed of 12km/hr. Individual side clutch mechanisms provide the means of steering by cutting the drive to an individual wheel.
Fuel consumption 0.6l/hr diesel or 0.86l/hr petrol.
Workrate 1-1.5ha/day.
Weight 178kg (petrol) 200kg (diesel).

INTERNATIONAL RICE RESEARCH INSTITUTE
Agricultural Engineering Department
P.O. Box 933
Manila
PHILIPPINES

JCCE INDUSTRIES
242 Mayondon
Los Baños
Laguna
PHILIPPINES

SV AGRO INDUSTRIES ENTERPRISES INC.
65 Commission Civil Street
Jaro
Iloilo City
PHILIPPINES

POYING'S WELDING SHOP
262 National Highway
Brgy, Anos, los Baños
Laguna
PHILIPPINES

C.V. KARYA HIDUP SENTOSA
Jl. Magelang 144
Yogyakarta
55241
INDONESIA

P.I. FARM PRODUCTS INC.
Km.16 Malanday
Valenzuela
Metro Manila
PHILIPPINES

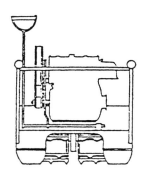

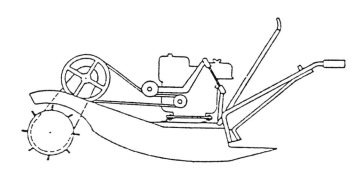

HYDRO TILLER

This tiller has twin pontoon and tunnel construction designed to cope with extreme field conditions of deep mud and/or water. The pontoons aid operation and handling and are intended to reduce the formation of unwanted furrows. The rotor both acts as the means of propulsion and has a rotovating and puddling action.

The power requirement is for a 7kW petrol or 5-6.5kW diesel engine with a maximum weight of 50kg. Power is delivered by V-belts from the engine to the roller chain and sprocket transmission to the rotor. Pneumatic tyred wheels can be fitted to the ends of the rotor for road transportation.

Fuel consumption is approximately 1.5l/hr petrol or 1.0l/hr diesel.
Workrate 1.8-2.0ha/day (8 hrs).
Weight without engine 105kg.

INTERNATIONAL RICE RESEARCH INSTITUTE
Agricultural Engineering Department
P.O. Box 933
Manila
PHILIPPINES

JCCE INDUSTRIES
242 Mayondon
Los Baños
Laguna
PHILIPPINES

SV AGRO INDUSTRIES
ENTERPRISES INC.
65 Commission Civil Street
Jaro
Iloilo City
PHILIPPINES

C.V. KARYA HIDUP SENTOSA
Jl. Magelang 144
Yogyakarta
55241
INDONESIA

P.I. FARM PRODUCTS INC.
Km.16 Malanday
Valenzuela
Metro Manila
PHILIPPINES

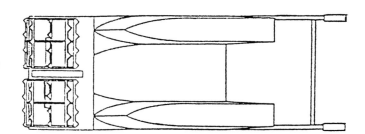

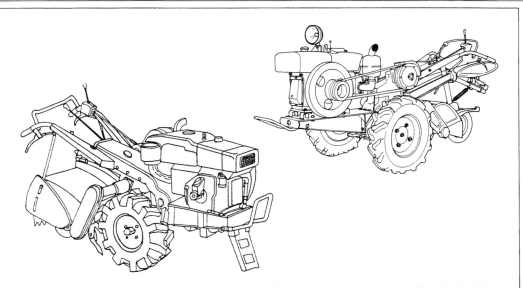

WETLAND TILLERS

HAND TRACTOR/TILLERS
These tillers are suitable for use in paddy fields and for dryland cultivation. They are of a simple and lightweight construction, driven by a diesel engine and V-belt clutch system; they can be supplied with or without the engine, which is easily removed to be used for other purposes. For deep mud conditions, special 'floating' wheels are available and the operator can stand on a towed skid. Each model is supplied with a plough and harrow which can be used together or independently. There are also optional water pump and mower attachments.

Model ER600 has a 4.5kW air-cooled engine and clutch steering. It has a workrate of 14 hours/ha when ploughing or 10 hours/ha when levelling.

The 800 range uses a 5kW engine, either water- or air-cooled, and is supplied without clutch steering. The workrate is somewhat higher at 8 hours/ha for ploughing or 6 hours/ha for levelling.

C.V. KARYA HIDUP SENTOSA
Jl. Magelang 144
Yogyakarta
55241
INDONESIA

A very similar tiller is supplied by:

P.T. RUTAN MACHINERY TRADING CO. .
Jalan Pemuda 1B-1C
P.O. Box 319
Surabaya
INDONESIA

'GOLD LION' WALKING TRACTOR
This is suitable for a wide range of uses including paddy-field and dryland operations and can be coupled to a trailer for general transport. The tractor can also be used as a power source for electricity generating, water pumping, threshing and fodder processing, etc. The tractor is fitted with a single cylinder 4-stroke diesel engine rated at 8.82kW. It has a gross weight of 470kg, including rotary tiller, and a minimum ground clearance of 410mm.

BEIJING TRACTOR COMPANY
1 Xinfeng Street
Outside of Desheng Gate
Beijing
100088
CHINA

POWER TILLER WHEEL ATTACHMENTS

A range of wheels for attachment to power tillers and walking tractors is available from the following company, including:

- Drum type puddling wheel: width 450mm, diameter 51mm, eight cross blades.
- Wet field wheel: width 203mm, diameter 660mm, eight cross blades.
- Four-wheeled cage wheel: width 305mm, diameter 1m, twelve cross blades.

SATHYAWADI MOTORS & TRANSPORTERS
21 Dambulla Road
Kurunegala
SRI LANKA

Cage wheels for attachment to Yanmar power tillers are available from:

NAWINNE AGRICULTURAL IMPLEMENTS MANUFACTURING CO.
128/2 Colombo Road
Kurunegala
SRI LANKA

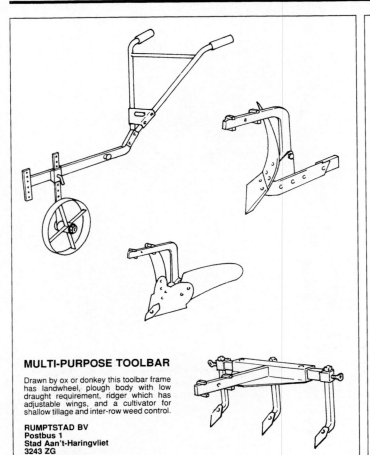

MULTI-PURPOSE TOOLBAR

Drawn by ox or donkey this toolbar frame has landwheel, plough body with low draught requirement, ridger which has adjustable wings, and a cultivator for shallow tillage and inter-row weed control.

RUMPTSTAD BV
Postbus 1
Stad Aan't-Haringvliet
3243 ZG
NETHERLANDS

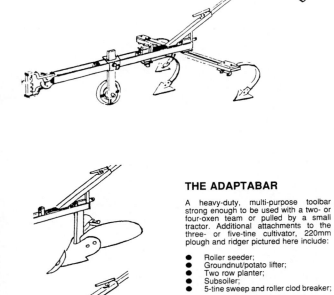

THE ADAPTABAR

A heavy-duty, multi-purpose toolbar strong enough to be used with a two- or four-oxen team or pulled by a small tractor. Additional attachments to the three- or five-tine cultivator, 220mm plough and ridger pictured here include:

● Roller seeder;
● Groundnut/potato lifter;
● Two row planter;
● Subsoiler;
● 5-tine sweep and roller clod breaker;

Attachments are retained by ring blts passing through the stalk, but the thrust is taken by the central frame inserts which are welded in place.

PROJECT EQUIPMENT LTD
Industrial Estate
Oswestry
Shropshire SY11 4HS
UK

NON-WHEELED TOOLBARS

COMBINATION PLOUGH
A simple frame with wooden drawbar and four attachments which convert it into a plough, ridger, cultivator or potato lifter.

CENTRO DE INVESTIGACIÓN,
FORMACIÓN Y EXTENSIÓN
EN MEC. AGRICOLA
Casilla 831
Cochabamba
BOLIVIA

MULTI-PURPOSE TOOLBAR
A simple metal frame with an adjustable handle and wooden drawbar. Four optional tool attachments are available:

● Single tine cultivator (32 hours/ha on fallow land);
● Ridger for furrowing and ridging (8 hours/ha);
● Cultivator with a tine on each side for cultivating and weed control (8 hours/ha);
● Tuber harvesting tool (8 hours/ha).

HERRANDINA
Marte 581
Brena
Lima 5
PERU

'WESTERN HOE' MULTI-PURPOSE FRAME
This versatile toolbar (illustrated) has seven optional attachments as follows:

● Three- or five-tine cultivator;
● Three-tooth duck-foot tine;
● Three-weed cutting blades;
● One 250mm ridger body;
● One 150 or 200mm mouldboard plough;
● One seeder for rice or cereals;
● One 350mm tuber-lifting blade.

SISMAR
20 rue Dr. Thèze
3214
Dakar
SENEGAL

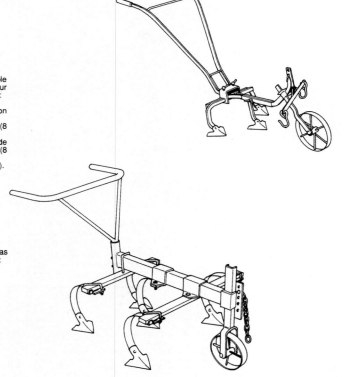

MULTI-PURPOSE TOOLBAR
The basic unit has hitching point, adjustable guide wheel and handles. Attachments include:

● Ridger body;
● Single furrow plough;
● Groundnut (peanut) lifter;
● Spring-tine cultivator;
● Single seeder.

ALVAN BLANCH DEVELOPMENT CO. LTD
Chelworth
Malmesbury
Wilts SN16 9SG
UK

Similar toolbars are available from:

PILTER FRANCE
12 rue Gouverneur
B.P. 3
Dreux 28100
FRANCE

S.M.E.C.M.A.
Zone Industrielle
Route de Sotuba
B.P. 1707
Bamako
MALI

ANIMAL-DRAWN MULTI-PURPOSE TOOLBARS
Two models of this simple toolbar are offered, one for use with smaller draught animals such as donkeys and one for use with oxen.
The attachments available are:

● 150 or 230mm mouldboard plough;
● Three or five spring-tine cultivators;
● High wing ridger bodies.

Both these toolbars have fully adjustable hitch points and depth wheels.

ATELIER PILOTE DE CONSTR. DE MAT. AG
Zone Industrielle de Kossodo
B.P. 2085
Ouagadougou
BURKINA FASO

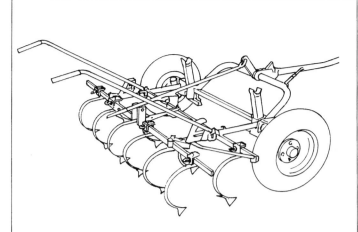

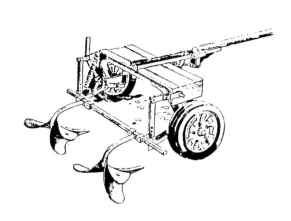

TOOLBAR CULTIVATORS

BAOL POLYCULTIVATOR
A toolbar fabricated from tubular steel, this has pneumatic tyres and an adjustable drawbar, and the track is variable to accommodate different crop row spacings. Attachments include:

- A 250mm plough;
- Two ridging ploughs with adjustable wings;
- Two-row groundnut (peanut) lifter;
- A two-metre toolbar with eight or twelve spring tined hoe;
- Three-row precision seed drill;
- A two-metre long tip-up cart.

SISMAR
20 rue Dr. Thèze
3214
Dakar
SENEGAL

(MULTICULTOR)
This basic two-wheeled cart is similar to the Baol cultivator. It can be adapted for towing by one horse, two horses or two oxen. There is a seat for the driver and either one or two toolbars can be fitted for which a number of different tools are available, including:

- Cultivator tines;
- Double furrow 230mm mouldboard plough;
- Ridger bodies;
- A six-disc harrow, each disc serrated and 406mm in diameter;
- Four-row seed drill for maize;
- Eight-row seed drill for cereals.

ICAT LTDA
Casilla 4636
Santiago
CHILE

MATADOR M.A.D. MACHINE

MULTI-PURPOSE TOOLBAR
This is the basic unit for a whole range of Matador Brand tools and attachments. It is a specially designed tubular chassis on pneumatic wheels, which can be used for transport, tillage, crop planting, crop maintenance and many other tasks. The chassis is adjustable in terms of drawbar position and wheel spacing. The toolbar is adjustable vertically and horizontally and is also spring assisted to ease the raising and lowering of implements. The toolbar operates similarly to a three-point linkage. The basic chassis can be converted into a variety of types of transport. There is a large range of equipment available for use with the toolbar some of which are listed.

- PLOUGH ATTACHMENTS
  Single and double furrow plough attachments are available.

- REVERSIBLE SINGLE FURROW PLOUGH;
- SPRING TINE HARROW ATTACHMENT
  Box frame with rows of spring tines on each side.
- DISC RIDGER ATTACHMENT
  Two disc attachments adjustable across width of bar.
- LAND PLANER ATTACHMENT
  This land planer has been designed to be drawn on a two wheel extension of the basic toolbar. It has a seat for an operator who controls the depth of the blade with an adjusting wheel.
- ROTARY MOWER
  This rotary mower is powered by a 3kW engine sited on top of the 'slasher' casing. It is supported by skids.

FARM IMPLEMENTS (PVT) LTD
Box 55
Glendale
ZIMBABWE

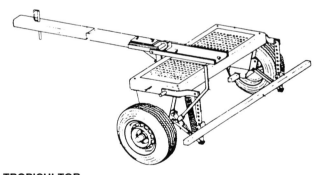

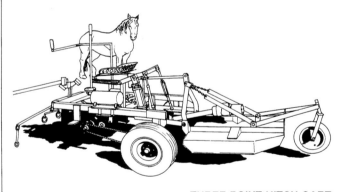

TROPICULTOR

This multi-purpose animal-drawn wheeled tool carrier has been designed by the International Crop Research Institute for the Semi-Arid Tropics and is produced commercially by several companies. Common operations which can be undertaken using the toolbar are ploughing, ridging and seedbed preparation.
The toolbar can also be converted into a cart. Weight 200kg.

ICRISAT
Patancheru P.O.
Andra Pradesh 502 324
INDIA

Produced commercially by:

MEKINS AGRO PRODUCTS (PVT) LTD
6-3-866/A Begumpet
Greenlands
Hyderabad 500 016
INDIA

KALE KRISHI UDYOG
S31/2/2, Hinge Khurd
Vithalwadi, Sinnagad Road
Pune 411 051
INDIA

MULTICULTOR MTA 1200
The basic chassis of this cultivator is made of welded steel tube and supported on pneumatic tyres; the toolbar is mounted on to the chassis using a spring-assisted pantograph system which allows the operator to lift an implement vertically out of work into a transport position. The pneumatic wheels can be exchanged for steel wheels.
In addition to the basic tillage implements available for this toolbar, which include a tandem disc harrow, there is:

- A seven-row seed/fertilizer drill;
- A three-row precision seed drill;
- A trailer body to convert the toolbar into a four-wheeled cart.

SEMEATO DIV. COMERCIO
Av. Presidente Vargas 3800
B.P. 559
99100 Passo Fundo RS
BRAZIL

POLICULTOR 1500
This model has a frame constructed of steel supported on wheels with pneumatic tyres. The toolbar can be lifted, by means of a lever, to bring any implement mounted on it into or out of work; this operation is spring assisted.
Many attachments are available for use with the Policultor 1500 including:

- Double furrow mouldboard plough;
- Reversible mouldboard plough;
- Twin leg subsoiler;
- Land plane;
- Bund former;
- Cultivators;
- Various tanks to carry or distribute liquids;
- Cart body.

CEMAG
Rua João Batista de Oliveira 233
06750 Taboao de Serra
São Paulo
BRAZIL

THREE-POINT HITCH CART

This has a Category I three-point hitch as found on modern tractors. The cart is equipped with a hydraulic system using a hydraulic pump driven from a ground wheel. The cart may also be equipped with a power take-off shaft driven either from a ground wheel or by an engine of 15kW mounted on the cart.
Various implements are available:

- Mouldboard ploughs;
- Single row disc harrow (8 or 10 blades);
- Rake;
- Cultivator;
- Grader blades;
- Hay bale carrier;
- Mowers;
- Spray boom.

The number of horses required to pull the cart depends on the implement being used; up to six can be accommodated.

ELMO REED
Rt. 3
Benton
KY 42025
USA

3. SOWING, PLANTING AND FERTILIZER DISTRIBUTION

In order to achieve good yields when growing vegetables, cereals, legumes and root crops, the depth of seeding and the spacing between the plants should be uniform and optimal for the given growing conditions. However, to facilitate weeding and other operations the plants are often confined to rows, usually with a distance between them that is less than that between the rows. To achieve the best compromise, various designs of hand-operated and animal-drawn seeders and planters have been developed which control, to a greater or lesser extent, the plant density by means of the spacing in each row of seeds and other plant material. Most seeders and planters can also be used to distribute fertilizer. Combined seeder/fertilizer drills are used to drill fertilizer into the soil at optimal distance from the seeds at the same time as sowing.

SEEDERS AND FERTILIZERS

Seeds and planting material are placed in the ground in three ways:

○ Seeds can be broadcast on the soil and are then usually buried by raking, harrowing or scattering earth over them.

○ Seeds and other planting material can be placed in a furrow, which is opened to the appropriate depth, then closed again and lightly compressed.

○ Seed tubers or other vegetable material and seedlings can be placed in holes in the ground when are then refilled with soil.

Wetland rice has special requirements and so is considered in a separate section.

Broadcasting

Broadcasting can be done by hand-scattering or by using a hand-operated broadcaster which is usually slung over the shoulder of the operator (Figure 1). These broadcasters are often called seed fiddles, a name acquired because of the bow-like stick used to drive the spinner. The leather thong of the bow passes around a bobbin which is attached to the ribbed spinner. If the bow is moved from left to right the spinner rotates, scattering the seed which falls on to it from the canvas seed bag. The rate of seeding can be altered by loosening a wing-nut under the fiddle and moving the slide to the setting required, thus altering the size of the aperture through which

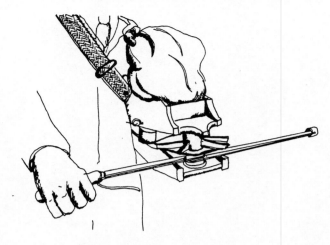

Figure 1   Seed fiddle

the seed trickles. Broadcasting requires considerable skill on the part of the operator to achieve an even distribution.

Alternatively a uniform coverage can be achieved by a spinning disc distributor driven by its wheels through a gear box. These are usually two-wheeled and can be pulled or pushed by one person, with larger versions being animal-drawn. Broadcasters can also be used to distribute granular pesticides (see Chapter 4).

Dibbling

Dibbling seeds and other planting material in holes in the soil is the oldest form of planting. Distances between plants can be precisely determined by the operator. Often more than one seed or plant is placed in each hole. A variety of pointed sticks, some with metal tips, are commonly used for this purpose (Figure 2). Manually operated 'walking stick' and rotary injection 'jab' planters are used for both seeds and fertilizers. Jab planters can be used in quite rough seedbeds or uncultivated land, so long as the ground is soft enough. They are useful for filling gaps in rows and can be used to place fertilizers.

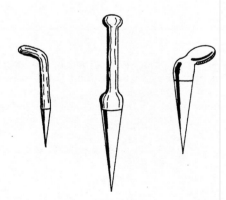

Figure 2   Dibblers: (left to right) steel tipped, steel tipped, all steel

The principle of 'jab-planting' as applied to the rotary injection machine incorporates six jabbing devices around its circumference. Hand-pushed versions of this design have been developed and introduced in Nigeria with some success.

Seed is picked up from the hopper by the feed roller which contains pockets of a suitable size for the crop concerned. The seeds then fall into the jabbing devices which remain closed until just before withdrawal from the soil, at which point they

open and the seeds drop into the hole. The distance between jabs depends on the diameter of the rotary wheel, the length of the jabbing devices, and the depth to which the jabbing devices penetrate the soil; for maize the distance between holes is about 250mm. This is achieved by a wheel of about 350mm diameter with the jabbing devices protruding by about 75mm.

A variation of the dibbler is used to plant large vegetative material (e.g. potatoes), seedlings, or cuttings. The soil-engaging point of the planter can be opened wide enough to allow the material to be placed manually at the correct depth.

Row seeding

Row seeding or planting can, at its simplest, be achieved with a plough or other furrow-making tool and the seeds or other material are dropped in the furrow at the appropriate intervals. The furrow can then be closed. Hand-pushed row seeders (usually single row) normally require a well-prepared seedbed. In unmetered seeders the seed usually trickles into the furrow from a mounted container. Alternatively, in animal-drawn one-and two-row seeders an operator is sometimes required to feed the material manually, either by means of a sowing tube or directly into the furrow.

The design of seed coulter and sowing tube affects the width of line within which the seeds are sown. Figure 3 shows four types of coulter, the narrowest of which, the drag share, is only of use in well-prepared seedbeds. The cultivator and double disc coulters can break up a slightly hardened soil surface to

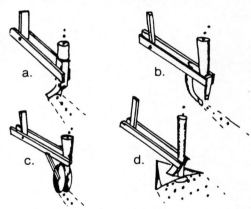

Figure 3   Seed coulters: a. cultivator type share; b. drag share; c. double disc share; d. goose-foot share (for strips)

create a narrow furrow into which the seeds fall. The goose-foot share creates a wide furrow, and a small plate fixed to the bottom of the sowing tube causes the seed to scatter across the width of the furrow, producing a wide band of plants. It is common to trail a metal chain, ring or other small harrow behind the seeder to make the coverage of the seed more complete.

Seed drills

The more sophisticated seed drills usually have seed-metering mechanisms in order to achieve a predetermined spacing of plants in the row. The metering devices are driven by landwheels (ground wheels) which ensure that the rate of seeding is directly related to the distance travelled.

The simplest form of drill is the direct drive seeder in which the metering mechanism takes the seed from the hopper using a seed roller mounted on the same axle as the landwheel. This is usually used for single row vegetable seeders (Figure 4).

More sophisticated precision seeders have metering mechanisms driven from the axle of a landwheel. One type

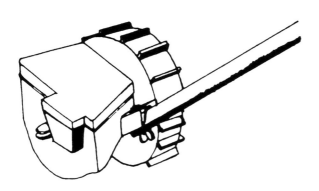

Figure 4   Rolling seed drill — single row vegetable seeder

uses a Pitman drive which connects a drive crank mounted on the axle to a drive crank on the seeder (and also to a second crank on the fertilizer distributor, in the case of seeder/ fertilizers — Figure 5). An improvement on this design is the use of double Pitman drives, both of which connect the seeder and the fertilizer mechanisms to cranks mounted on the landwheel axle.

A second, more common, type of drive uses a chain driven by a sprocket mounted on the landwheel axle. The chain passes around sprockets connected to the seeder mechanism (and fertilizer distributor, if mounted — Figure 6).

Precision seeders, usually chain-driven, are often available for mounting on multi-purpose toolbars (see Chapter 2).

Seed-metering mechanisms

Various mechanical seed-metering systems are used. A rotating brush or agitator controlling the flow of seed through an adjustable opening will handle most types of seed with minimal damage, as will contra-rotating soft rollers, but these mechanisms do not closely control seed spacing in the row.

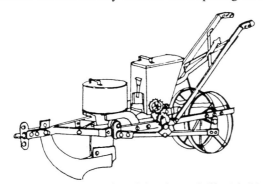

Figure 5   Single row seed and fertilizer drill with Pitman drive

Figure 6   Chain and sprocket driven planter/fertilizer

Fluted roller-feed mechanisms (Figure 7) give more accurate control of overall seed rate per hectare, but again do not control spacing in the row. Cell-wheel and perforated belt-metering systems can give very precise spacing of seeds — particularly those which are approximately spherical in shape. The metal cell wheel (Figure 8) is more likely to cause damage to delicate seeds than the flexible perforated belt. Some seeders can be adjusted to plant groups of seeds at long intervals. Most can be adjusted for various seed sizes and spacing so as to achieve an optimal plant population with a minimal use of seed.

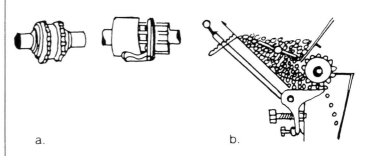

a.   b.

Figure 7   a. Fluted roller and slide roller-feed mechanism; b. Seed roller

Rice planting

Rice is planted in two fundamentally different ways — using dry seed and using pregerminated seed.

Dry seed

Upland rice grown in rainfed systems can be planted in same way as any other grain: by broadcasting, dibbling, or using a mechanical planter, as described above. The same precautions and advice apply for rice grown in this way as for other common grains.

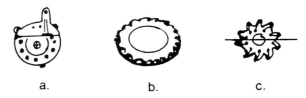

a.   b.   c.

Figure 8   Seed metering wheels and plates: a. vertical cell wheel; b. horizontal feed disc; c. spoon disc

Pregerminated seed

Pregerminating rice seed ensures that an even stand of rice is obtained; that by the time seed comes into contact with the soil it already has a head start on any weeds that may compete with it; and that it can quickly anchor itself to the soil and so minimize dangers of being washed away.

Rice is pregerminated by soaking and then incubating. The rice is soaked in water for a period of 24 hours. Ideally this should be done in buckets of clean water, but good results can also be obtained by soaking the rice in jute sacks in the water channels beside the rice fields as long as the water is moving and not stagnant. After soaking, the rice needs to be incubated for between one and three days depending on the seed vitality. This is done by removing the rice from the water and putting it loosely into sacks (if not already in them): it is important to leave room for the rice to expand as it germinates. The sacks should then be placed covered — by other sacks, leaves or grass — in a shady warm position. Each day the sacks need to be soaked two or three times by having water poured over them, both to cool down the seed and to stop it from drying out. When the seed has just sprouted (the radicles can just be seen emerging) it is ready for planting. Care must be taken that the radicles do not grow too long as they can break during planting.

The pregerminated seed can either be sown directly by broadcasting on to puddled, drained fields or can be planted into beds for later transplanting into the field. If sowing directly into the field, care must be taken to ensure that the field is level and well drained as the seed can be drowned by excess water. The advantage of broadcasting is a greatly reduced labour requirement (mechanical broadcasters can be used if the seed has not been incubated for too long). The disadvantages are the need for very good drainage and good planning so that the field is ready for planting at exactly the right time.

Using a bed to grow seedlings for later transplanting increases the leeway for error, as much greater control can be had over the small area of the bed compared with the whole field. Weed control in the field can be much better as the rice is planted into standing water in puddled fields with a good head start over any weeds that may grow. It aids multiple rice crops as the rice stands in the field for less than its full growing season. The main disadvantage is the large labour requirement required for transplanting the seedlings from the bed to the field. In the equipment section there are a number of pieces of equipment designed to aid transplanting and so reduce and ease this labour requirement.

Fertilizer distributors

The distribution of manure and fertilizer is often done entirely by hand. Organic manures and compost are usually spread over a whole field or between plant rows and incorporated by subsequent cultivation. Similarly, inorganic fertilizers can be broadcast by hand scattering or by using mechanical broadcasters. They can also be placed on the surface between plant rows and then be incorporated, or be dibbled in beside plants or seed placements. Granular or pelleted fertilizer can be drilled into the soil at an appropriate distance from the plants using seeders. This method of distribution is often done at the same time as seeding or planting, frequently using dual-purpose equipment.

ADVANTAGES

The benefits of using precision equipment are higher crop yields. These should be achieved because:
- Correct seeding depths lead to better germination and uniform crop stands.
- Precision seeding results in an optimum plant population and reduces seed consumption.
- Good quality seeders improve the speed and accurate timing of the sowing.
- Use of row seeders/planters allows easier weeding and other operations; it also makes possible contour planting which may help to reduce erosion.

- Fertilizer drilled into the soil provides plants with readily available nutrients; the timing of application can be related to the plants' needs.

Rice planting

Oxfam

ALTERNATIVES

The more labour-intensive methods referred to above have been used since agriculture began. They are still the commonest methods used by poor smallholders. Although precision equipment is not used, the quality of planting need not be any less optimal, given sufficient care and the time of skilled operators. In certain circumstances — for example, when sowing stony uncultivated land, or when using odd corners of fields or in gardens — these labour-intensive methods are the only viable ones.

CHOOSING YOUR EQUIPMENT

Before buying equipment some thought should be given to:
- the possibilities of adapting existing equipment, e.g. by adding a planting tube to a plough;
- the availability and cost of planting material (such as specialist seed) and pelleted fertilizer.

Points to consider when selecting equipment include the size of area to be sown in a single holding and the possibilities of hiring out the equipment to neighbours; the power source available and the typical condition of seedbeds; the possibilities for multi-purpose use with a wide range of seed shapes and sizes; and the level of sophistication required.

Having decided on the particular type of equipment required, the buyer needs to look at each model with regard to:
- robustness, especially that of the seed-metering mechanism;
- ease of maintenance and availability of spares;
- ease with which seed metering and seed size alterations can be made;
- skill level of the operator(s).

The cost spectrum of this type of equipment is very wide and the only point worth emphasizing is that the price increases significantly for precision over and against gravity-flow seeders. Also the repair and maintenance costs of precision seeders and the extra cost of the prepared seed and fertilizer may in the long run exceed the capital cost of the equipment.

Before investing in expensive precision seeders it is necessary to calculate the opportunity costs. To assist in this calculation Table 1 shows average performance data.

Table 1   Performance of equipment

Type of equipment	Draught required (kg)	Average performance per day (8 hours)	Notes
Single row planter/seeder (hand-operated)	15-30	0.3-0.6 ha	Depending on soil conditions as well as row width.
Single row planter (animal-drawn)	25-40	0.5-1.0 ha	Length of field, and thus number of headland turnings, affects performance.
Double row seeder (animal-drawn)	35-65	0.8-1.5 ha	
Seed drill (1.25 m)	55-65	1.0-1.5 ha	
Seed and fertilizer drill (hand-operated)	20-30	0.3-0.6 ha	
Fertilizer distributor (animal-drawn)	35-70	1.0-2.5 ha	Depending on type of equip. & width of swath.

IMPACT

The introduction of mechanical seeders may displace labour. However, in particular circumstances this can be avoided — if, for example:

○ the equipment introduced, such as a plough planter, still requires a similar number of people to operate it, although the workload may be less arduous;

○ the area to be sown increases significantly and the labour is redeployed operating and supplying several seeders;

○ the use of the equipment allows sowing to be carried out where previously it has proven difficult, e.g. the sowing of red peas between the rows in post-harvest sugar cane fields.

SPECIAL CONSIDERATIONS

The health and safety of operators who may be handling material treated with fungicides and insecticides is of paramount importance. Special training should be given in the handling of such poisons and, where appropriate, protective clothing should be provided (see Chapter 4).

Peter Munzinger
GFA-AgriTec

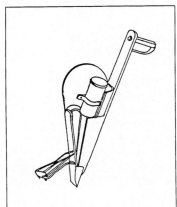

HAND MAIZE PLANTER

This simple spring-action jab planter places single seeds at the required depth. The planter is placed in the ground to the appropriate depth and then pushed forward on to the spring-loaded foot. This action causes the point to open and deposit a seed in the soil. At the same time the seeder is recharged from the hopper. A spring action mechanism returns the planter to a vertical position and the operator then removes the planter from the ground to repeat the process for the next seed. A second person is usually required to apply fertilizer and to cover the seed. Interchangeable discs with different hole sizes can be used for planting single seeds for a range of crops from millet to beans.
Weight 2kg.
25 hours/ha.

COSSUL & CO. PVT LTD
123/367 Industrial Area
Fazalgunj
Kanpur
U.P.
INDIA

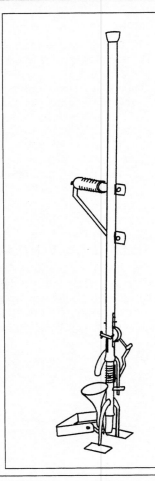

HAND SEEDERS

JAB SEEDER
There are four variations of this jab planter, designed at the Asian Institute of Technology (AIT). The four designs differ only in the shape of the soil-opening mechanisms which are suited to different soil textures and moisture contents. This tool makes a hole in the ground and drops seeds into it in one operation. There is a choice of metering rollers to cater for different seeds. It can be used in both untilled soil in wet conditions and conventionally tilled soil with or without crop residue. The tool is transportable and suitable for use in hilly areas. The seed rate is adjustable as is the tool's ability to sow seeds of different sizes.
Length 1.5m.
Seed tube capacity 0.7 litre.
Work rate 55 to 90 hours/ha.

KUNASIN MACHINERY
107-108 Sri-Satchanalai Road
Sawanankalok
Sukothai
THAILAND

HAND-HELD PLANTER
A form of jab planter. The seed is manually dropped into top seed port and is conducted via the seed tube to the closed planting bit. The seed remains captive in the planting bit until the planter is rocked forward, and the bit is opened.

ALMACO
P.O. Box 296
99 M Avenue
Nevada
IOWA 50201
USA

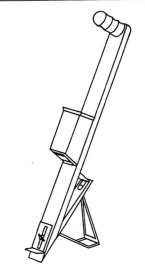

JAB PLANTER

This is a pressed steel hand planter with a seed box fixed to the main upright. When the tool is pushed sideways after it has been jabbed into the ground, a slide plate with a hole of appropriate size extracts a single seed from the bottom of the box. The seed is released into the hole when the planter is returned to vertical position. Planting depth is set by an adjustable guide. Alternative seed slides are available.
Weight 4.1kg

ALVAN BLANCH DEVELOPMENT CO. LTD
Chelworth
Malmesbury
Wilts SN16 9SG
UK

ROTARY INJECTION HAND-PUSHED PLANTER

'TARGET T30'
This is a hand-pushed unit; a seed hopper channels seed towards a selector wheel which is positioned at centre of planting wheel and which meters seed from the hopper to the planting spades. As each spade reaches the ground it penetrates the surface and then opens, releasing seed to the correct depth. Different wheels can be used for different seed types and spacings. The unit can also be tractor-mounted and can be used in rough operating conditions.
Workrate 4 hours/ha.

STANHAY WEBB LTD
Exning
Newmarket
Suffolk CB8 7HD
UK

Similar implements are manufactured by:

GEEST OVERSEAS MECHANISATION LTD
White House Chambers
Spalding
Lincs PE11 2AL
UK

RURAL INDUSTRIES INNOVATION CENTRE
Private Bag 11
Kanye
BOTSWANA

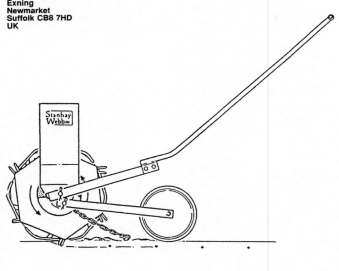

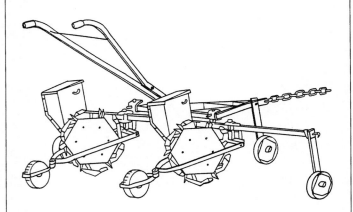

ROTARY PLANTERS

TWO-ROW ROTARY SEEDER
The SR2 is an animal-drawn, two-row rotary injection seeder, fitted with a draught chain, steerage-handles and row marker. Two seed dispensers are fitted on to a toolbar and fed from separate hoppers mounted above them. The dispensers provide seed spacings of 220mm or 440mm and are offered in a range of sizes to suit maize, sorghum, millet, haricot beans and groundnuts (peanuts). Row spacing can be adjusted by moving the dispensers along the toolbar and adjusting the row-marker position accordingly. A furrow press-wheel is fitted behind each dispenser and these wheels can be swung under the seeder to carry it clear of the ground for transport.
Weight 110kg.

UPROMA
B.P. 1086
Lomé
TOGO

MANUAL ROTARY SEEDER
Model SR1 is a single-row version of the same seeder, pushed and steered by the operator using two long handles. An adjustable row-marker and a furrow press-wheel are also included.

MANUAL ROTARY SEEDER
This rotary injection seeder is pushed by the operator using a pair of handles. The seed is gravity fed from a hopper into the injectors and metered out by the wheel rotation.

COBEMAG
B.P. 161
Route de Djougou
Parakou
REPUBLIC OF BENIN

Similar implements are manufactured by:

ISICO
P.O. Box 417
Mbabane
SWAZILAND

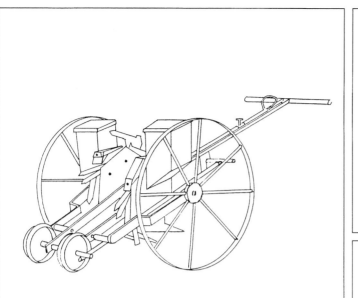

HAND-PUSHED SEED DRILL

This is a very simple hand-pushed seed drill, used for single row sowing of grain and vegetable seeds in dry conditions. Workrate 0.4 ha/day.

THE COMILLA CO-OPERATIVE KARKHANA LTD
Ranir Bazar
P.O. Box 12
Comilla
BANGLADESH

TWO-ROW ROLLING INJECTION PLANTER

This two-row planter is designed to be pulled by one or two people. As the machine is pulled along, seeds are transferred from the hoppers to the planting mechanisms by metering rollers which have slots or circular depressions in them. There is a choice of rollers with different numbers and sizes of seed holes for different crops. The planting mechanisms consist of six inter-connected soil injectors, which spike a hole in the ground into which one or more seeds are dropped as the machine is pulled along. Press wheels mounted behind the injectors cover over the planted seeds. Removable wheels are provided for transport.

Row spacing adjustable from 180-450mm.
Plant spacing 260mm.
Workrate 0.5-0.8 ha/day.

KUNASIN MACHINERY
107-108 Sri-Satchanalai Road
Sawanankalok
Sukothai
THAILAND

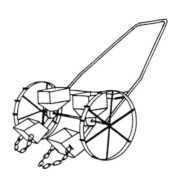

HIGHLAND SEEDER

This manually pulled, two-row seeder is of all-steel construction, with a pair of spiked landwheels driving metering rollers in the hopper outlets. Seeding rate is adjusted by the choice of appropriate metering rollers, and the row spacing can be adjusted from 175-600mm by the positioning of the two seeding units along the landwheel axle.
Workrate 0.5-1.0 ha/day.
Weight 17kg.

FARM MECHANISATION RESEARCH CENTRE
Maha Illuppallama
SRI LANKA

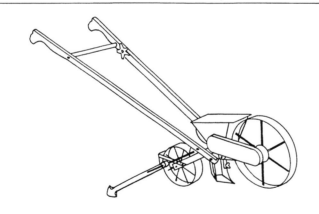

HAND SEEDER

This manual seeder may be used as a drill or as a precision seeder, and can handle a range of seed types. For single-row drilling, the seed is discharged by a rotary brush and regulated by an adjustable drilled disc. For precision seeding, a range of sprocket-type metering wheels are provided, giving alternative seed spacings of 200, 250, 300, 400, 600 or 1200mm. In both modes, the seed flow is constantly visible to the operator. The seeder is mounted between a steel landwheel and a cast iron furrow press-wheel. Adjustments include seeding depth and row-marker position.

THILOT HOLLAND BV
Hoofdstraat 11 - 17
Lottum
5973 ND
NETHERLANDS

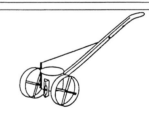

'PUCK' HAND DRILL

This manual row seeder is designed for small quantities of vegetable and grain seeds. A hopper is mounted between a pair of landwheels and its outlet is controlled by a cord on the push handle.

FORTSCHRITT LANDMASCHINEN
Berghausstraße 1
Neustadt
8355
GERMANY

HAND SEED DRILLS

This very simple single row seed drill can be operated by two people and used to sow small plots or for repairing rows which have been incorrectly sown by a larger drill.

A two-row version of the drill is also available which requires two people to pull the implement while a third guides the tool and feeds the seed into the seed tubes.

YANTRA VIDYALAYA
Agricultural Tools Research Centre
Suruchi Campus
P.O. Box 4
Bardoli
Gujarat 394 601
INDIA

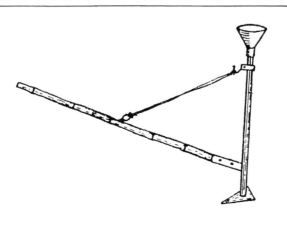

'CASAMANCE' RICE SEED DRILL

This hand-pushed, two-row rice seed drill has two 250mm sowing ploughshares. The distributors are mounted on the wheel axles and can be adjusted to deliver up to 130 seeds per metre.

SISMAR
20 rue Dr. Thèze
3214 Dakar
SENEGAL

CECOCO HAND DIRECT SEEDERS

These light and compact two-row seeders can be operated either in wet field conditions (Type CK-AW) or in dry conditions (Type CK-AD) by one person. The difference between the two models is that for dry field working the sleds are replaced with furrow-opening coulters.

A wide variety of seeds and grain may be sown. Seed spacing is determined by adjusting the brush metering system. Seed is supplied from twin two-litre hoppers. A separate fertilizer attachment is available for the dryland model. Seeding width 300mm.

CECOCO
P.O. Box 8
Ibaraki City
Osaka 567
JAPAN

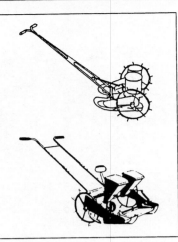

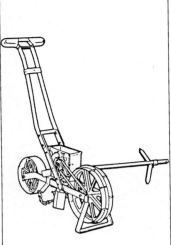

HAND-OPERATED DRILL/PRECISION SEEDER

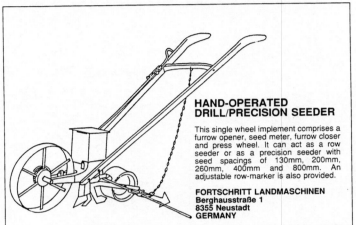

This single wheel implement comprises a furrow opener, seed meter, furrow closer and press wheel. It can act as a row seeder or as a precision seeder with seed spacings of 130mm, 200mm, 260mm, 400mm and 800mm. An adjustable row-marker is also provided.

FORTSCHRITT LANDMASCHINEN
Berghausstraße 1
8355 Neustadt
GERMANY

GARDEN SEEDERS

This is a single row manual precision seeder. Six graduated metering plates are provided and these are stored in a case fitted to the push handles. A furrow press-wheel, row marker and machine stand are also fitted. Weight 5kg.

R. & R. MILL CO. INC.
45 West First North
Smithfield
UT 84335
USA

A similar implement is manufactured by:

OPICO (PANAMA)
P.O. Box 849
Mobile
AL 36601
USA

RUBBER BELT PRECISION SEEDER

This manual, single row seeder features a seed metering belt with seven lines of drilled holes for different seeds and spacings. The seed hopper position is adjusted to align the hopper outlet with the desired line of holes. Seeding depth is adjustable from 10 to 40mm. Weight 12kg.

BIO-INNOKOORD
2040 Budaörs
Pf. 14
HUNGARY

PRECISION SEEDER

Primarily designed for the market gardener, this manual single row seeder employs a cell-plate type seed meter in the hopper outlet. A range of wheels is available to suit different seed types, giving seed spacings of 40-305mm. A machine stand and a row-marker are fitted and an optional fertilizer distributor is available to fit behind the seed hopper.

SOCIÉTÉ NOUVELLE SAELEN SA
Rue Pic au vent CRT
B.P. 359
59813 Lesquin Cedex
FRANCE

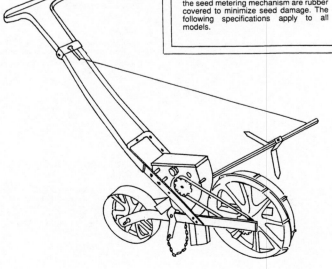

'ROBIN' LIGHTWEIGHT PRECISION DRILL

Four models of this drill are offered: the Robin 820 is a manually pushed single row seeder, the Robin 830 is a two-row model, designed for use in combination with walking tractors, and the Robin 840 and Robin 850 are three- and four-row models, intended for use behind compact and small tractors. The seeding principle is the same for all models and is based on a drilled seed belt driven from a caged rear wheel. Belts are available for different seed sizes and for single, double or triple line seeding, with a very wide range of hole spacings. Belts can be fitted rapidly, without tools, and each belt can itself provide a choice of four seed spacings by a simple adjustment of the drive pulley system. All moving parts of the seed metering mechanism are rubber covered to minimize seed damage. The following specifications apply to all models.

Minimum row spacing 200mm.
Maximum seeding depth 50mm.
Hopper capacity 4 litres per seeding unit.

STANHAY WEBB LTD
Exning
Newmarket
Suffolk CB8 7HD
UK

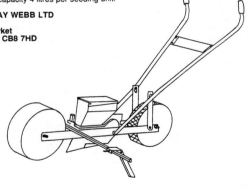

PRECISION PLANTER MS 2TA

This animal-drawn, single row planter can sow any type of grain when supplied with the appropriate seed plate from the manufacturer. The metering mechanism is chain driven from the rear press wheel and the seed spacing can be varied using one of the six interchangeable drive sprockets. The front wheels can be moved along the axle to cater for different row spacings of pre-formed seedbeds and the shoe coulter is adjustable to allow variation in sowing depth.

E.B.R.A.
28 Rue du Maine
B.P. 915
49009 Angers Cedex
FRANCE

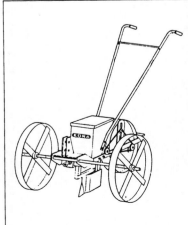

SEBELE STANDARD PLANTER

The Sebele standard planter, manufactured in Botswana, is equipped with a landwheel-driven seed metering mechanism operating by the 'gravity drop' principle. Seed falls through a pre-selected hole in a stationary metering plate, and a chain-driven agitator in the seed hopper keeps the seed flowing steadily. The seed then drops between the two coulter plates in view of the operator who can see if it is planting regularly. The planter has been designed to operate in a well-prepared seedbed. Hopper capacity 3-4kg depending on seed type.
Weight 40kg.

RURAL INDUSTRIES INNOVATION CENTRE
Private Bag 11
Kanye
BOTSWANA

CLIFF ENGINEERING
P.O. Box 282
Gaborone
BOTSWANA

SEROWE BRIGADES DEVELOPMENT TRUST
P.O. Box 121
Serowe
BOTSWANA

SEED ATTACHMENT FOR TWO-FURROW PLOUGH

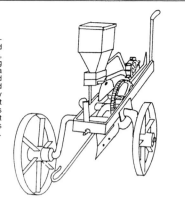

This is attached to the standard two-furrow ox-drawn 'Kifaru' plough and consists of seed hopper, seed plate, operating rod, seed tube and operating wheel. The first plough body cuts a furrow into which the seeds are metered via the seed tube and are then covered by the soil cut by the second plough body as it makes the second furrow. Correct adjustment of the second furrow is essential in order to place a consistent thickness of soil over the seed. Designs are available for potential manufacturers.

CENTRE FOR AGRICULTURAL MECHANISATION & RURAL TECHNOLOGY
P.O. Box 764
Arusha
TANZANIA

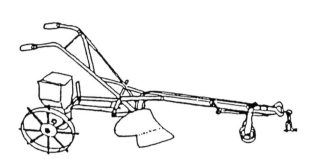

SEBELE PLOUGH PLANTER

The Sebele plough planter, manufactured in Botswana, is a device which may be attached to single or double furrow ox ploughs, or tractor ploughs (when a small electric motor is required to drive the agitator).

The single row seeding mechanism operates by the 'gravity drop' principle and is suitable for planting nearly all seed types including cereals, pulses and groundnuts (peanuts). Seed falls through a pre-selected hole in a stationary metering plate, and a landwheel-driven agitator in the seed hopper keeps the seed flowing steadily. The plough planter has a seed cut off mechanism for use while turning at the end of rows.
Hopper capacity 2-3.5kg depending on seed type.
Weight 11kg including mounting bracket.

RURAL INDUSTRIES INNOVATION CENTRE
Private Bag 11
Kanye
BOTSWANA

CLIFF ENGINEERING
P.O. Box 282
Gaborone
BOTSWANA

SEROWE BRIGADES DEVELOPMENT TRUST
P.O. Box 121
Serowe
BOTSWANA

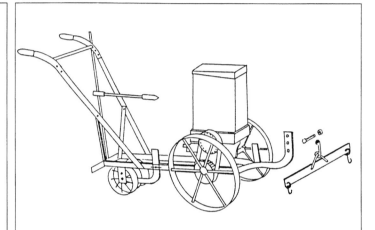

SUPER ECO/TAMBA SEED DRILL

This single row seeder is mounted between two metal landwheels and drawn by a donkey, ox or horse. Two adjustable-height handles are provided for steerage and an adjustable row-marker is also fitted. Two models of the seeder are offered, using the same chassis, landwheels, plough share, coulter, furrow press-wheel and handles, but varying in hopper and seed dispensing mechanism to suit different seed types.

'SUPER-ECO' for:
● Groundnuts (peanuts);
● Sorghum;
● Maize;
● Black-eyed beans and rice.
This seeder is gravity fed from a simple hopper and has a variable discharge rate.

'TAMBA' for:
● Un-delinted cotton seed

This hopper is fitted with a six-blade agitator and force-feed system, the seeder is fitted with a notched disc distributor mounted on the wheel axle. Coulter depth is adjustable from 0 to 50mm.

The following specifications apply to both models offered:
Seed spacing 210mm.
Row marking 440 to 790mm, right- or left-handed.
Ploughshare depth adjustment 0 to 100mm.

SISMAR
20 rue Dr. Thèze
3214
Dakar
SENEGAL

ABI-MÉCANIQUE
B.P. 343
45 rue Pierre et Marie Curie
(Zone 4c)
Abidjan
IVORY COAST

PITMAN DRIVE SINGLE ROW PLANTER

Available with or without a fertilizer attachment, this planter can be used singly or in pairs with the aid of a standard two-section drawbar and stabilizing bar. The fertilizer is deposited below and to the side of the seed and can be regulated to obtain optimum seed germination and growth. A lever is fitted for instant engagement and dis-engagement of planting and fertilizing mechanisms. Seed plates available for all types of commonly used seeds, including cotton. Fertilizer and seed cans are removable, allowing the fertilizer attachment to be used on its own.
Weight 61kg.

ZIMPLOW LTD
P.O. Box 1059
Bulawayo
ZIMBABWE

Similar implements are manufactured by:

G. NORTH (PVT) LTD
P.O. Box 111
Southerton
Harare
ZIMBABWE

ISICO
P.O. Box 417
Mbabane
SWAZILAND

BULAWAYO STEEL PRODUCTS
P.O. Box 1603
Donnington
Bulawayo
ZIMBABWE

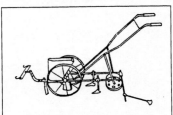

SINGLE ROW SEEDER

This is an animal-drawn seeder, carried between a pair of iron landwheels and with a rear furrow press-wheel, a row-marker and two steering handles. A model suitable for cotton is also available.

COBEMAG
B.P. 161
Route de Djougou
Parakou
REPUBLIC OF BENIN

PITMAN DRIVE PRECISION DRILLS

This animal-drawn seeder is designed for larger seeds and is adjustable to handle corn, sunflower, soya, beans, sorghum and cotton. Other adjustments include seeding depth and the positions of the hitching ring and steering handles. The seeder has a single iron landwheel, shoe coulter and a furrow press-wheel with scraper blade.
Hopper capacity 12 litres.

GHERARDI E HIJOS S.A.
Florida 520 Piso 3° Oficina 318
1005 Buenos Aires
ARGENTINA

JOSÉ J. SANS S.A.
INDÚSTRIA COMÉRCIO
Rua Juscelino Kubitschek de Oliveira 1,450
Santa Barbara d'Oeste SP
BRAZIL

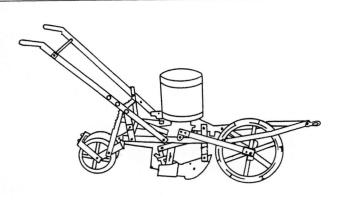

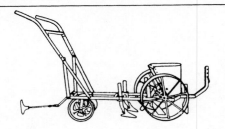

PRECISION SEEDER

This is a single row animal-drawn precision seeder, designed to handle a wide variety of seeds including groundnuts (peanuts), grains and cotton. It is carried on iron landwheels with a 400mm wide axle. Seeding rate is monitored by an adjustable spring-tensioned metering disc driven from the iron landwheels. Coulter depth is adjustable to a maximum of 100mm. The steering handles have a three-position adjustment.

S.M.E.C.M.A.
Zone Industrielle
Route de Sotuba
B.P. 1707
Bamako
MALI

ANIMAL-DRAWN PRECISION DRILL

The T56 precision seeder is supplied with interchangeable seed metering wheels and can be adapted to handle a large range of seeds including cotton and maize. The metering system is driven by a shaft from a gearbox mounted on the front axle of the machine which is turned by the landwheel.

METALURGICA SANTA ANTONIO
Rua Floriano Peixoto, 35
Santa Barbara d'Oeste SP
BRAZIL

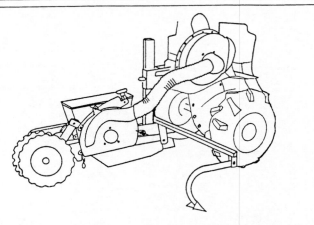

'UPS' PNEUMATIC SEED DRILL

The 'UPS' seed drill is constructed for use with single axle motor cultivators. It operates by means of a vacuum provided by a suction fan which is fitted on to the power take-off shaft of the cultivator. The seed is drawn into a hole in the seed plate by the vacuum created on one side of the plate; the seed plate rotates carrying the seed to an area at atmospheric pressure; and the seed drops down a chute into the furrow prepared by the coulter. A variety of seed plates are available for different types of seeds. There are eight different combinations of seed distances from 25 to 250mm. Seed depth varies from 10 to 60mm and is regulated by a tread wheel. The UPS is available in one-, two- or three-row combinations.
Hopper capacity 1.5 litres.

OLT
54000 Osijek
P. Svačića 4
YUGOSLAVIA

SPARE PARTS FOR SEED DRILLS

SEEDERS, CELL PLATES AND METERING WHEELS
The company below supplies a wide range of manual and animal-drawn seeders (see earlier entries) and also a variety of interchangeable plates, wheels and discs for seed metering. The range of seed types and spacings covered is extremely large and the company welcomes enquiries (with a sample) concerning any seeds not specified in their literature.

E.B.R.A.
28 Rue du Maine
B.P. 915
49000 Angers Cedex
FRANCE

MECHANICAL PLANTERS

Developed primarily for groundnuts (peanuts), this is a four-row seeder mounted on a T-bar and pulled by a pair of draught animals. It consists of a single seed hopper with four outlets, each with metering plates chain-driven from an iron landwheel. This landwheel can be lifted for transport. Coulters and furrow press wheels are fitted and a chain-type seed coverer can be attached for use in dry soil. An optional fertilizer applicator with a hand-metering device is available.

INTERNATIONAL CROP RESEARCH INSTITUTE FOR THE SEMI-ARID TROPICS (ICRISAT)
Patancheru
Andra Pradesh 502 324
INDIA

The machine is also obtainable from the following manufacturers:

K.V. AGRO INDUSTRIES
A-15 Apie
Balanagar
Hyderabad 500 037
INDIA

A.P. STATE AGRO INDUSTRIES DEVELOPMENT CORPORATION LTD
Agro Bhawan 10-2-3, A.C. Guards
Hyderabad 500 004
INDIA

BALAJI INDUSTRIAL AND AGRICULTURAL CASTINGS
4-3-140 Hill Street
P.O. Box 1634
Secunderabad 500 003
INDIA

KALE KRISHI UDYOG
31/2/2 Hinge Khurd
Vithalwadi, Sinnagad Road
Pune 411 051
INDIA

MEKINS AGRO PRODUCTS PRIVATE LTD
6-3-866/A
Begumpet
Greenlands
Hyderabad 500 016
INDIA

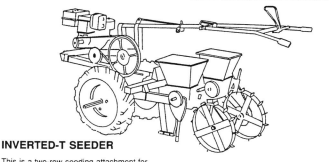

INVERTED-T SEEDER

This is a two-row seeding attachment for a power tiller, working in tilled or untilled soils. It is fitted with a foam pad seed metering device suitable for a wide range of seeds or for the application of granular fertilizers. Design details are available to potential manufacturers.

INTERNATIONAL RICE RESEARCH INSTITUTE
Agricultural Engineering Dept
P.O. Box 933
Manila
PHILIPPINES

CEREAL SEEDER

This is an animal-drawn, six-row seeder, with disc coulters and a single seed hopper. Seeding rate is adjustable between 90-140kg/ha for wheat, or up to 30kg/ha for grass seed, with a fixed row spacing of 180mm.
Hopper capacity 0.54 cubic metres.
Weight 180kg.

I.C.A. PROGRAMA DE MAQUINARIA AGRICOLA
Instituto Colombiano Agropecuario
Apartado Aereo 151123
Bogotá
COLOMBIA

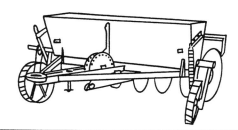

AUTOMATIC SEED DRILL

Both three- and five-row versions of this animal-drawn seed drill are available; each has a single hopper, disc coulters and a fluted-roller seed metering system. Row spacing is adjustable between 150 and 250mm. The drill is also available with a fertilizer distribution attachment.
Weight 94kg (3-row), 110kg (5-row).

COSSUL & CO. PVT LTD
123/367 Industrial Area
Fazalgunj
Kanpur, U.P.
INDIA

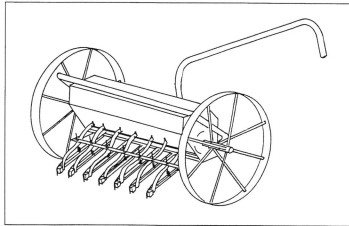

SEED DRILL FOR ANIMAL TRACTION

This seven row seed drill can be pulled by a pair of oxen. A high drawbar enables the oxen to turn very tightly, thus reducing the turning circle and easing problems of manoeuvrability. The seed box and pipes are mounted on two large diameter wheels (which provide the drive for the metering mechanism) and can be turned through 45 degrees in order to avoid damage during transport.

RUMPTSTAD BV
Postbus 1
Stad Aan't-Haringvliet
3243 ZG
NETHERLANDS

1.5m SEED DRILL

This versatile drill comes with a standard three-point linkage, though it may be changed to be either trailer- or animal-drawn by mounting special fittings. It can also be converted to distribute fertilizer while sowing by mounting hopper model GK66 or FG. The drill uses an advanced peg-type sowing system to ensure precision drilling of a wide variety of crops. It can be fitted with double disc coulters for nine rows at 16.6mm spacing, single disc coulters for nine, ten or eleven rows, or shoe coulters for 13 rows.
Overall width 1.75m.
Hopper capacity 150 litres.

SCHEBY MASKINFABRIK A/S
Bogense
DK 5400
DENMARK

INCLINED PLATE PLANTER

Designed for use with a power tiller, this tool has twin seed hoppers and planting mechanisms. Inclined wheels, spiked for positive grip, are connected to a seed metering plate in each hopper. These plates have either slots or circular depressions which transfer a certain number of seeds into the planting tubes as the machine is towed along. The planting tubes are connected to the rear of the soil openers, which make a channel for the seeds to drop into. The seed channel is closed by the inclined wheel. There is a choice of seed metering plates for different seeds.
Row spacing is adjustable from 250 to 980mm.
Workrate 0.96-1.28 ha/day.

KUNASIN MACHINERY
107-108 Sri-Satchanalai Road
Sawanankalok
Sukothai
THAILAND

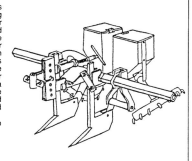

MECHANICAL SEED DRILL

Each unit of this tractor-drawn two-row drill comprises a seed box, horizontal seed plate, sowing mechanism and ploughshare-shaped seed dispenser. A pair of treadwheels operate a chain and sprocket system to run the seed metering mechanism. The chain transmission can be adjusted for twelve different combinations of seed spacing and there are eight types of seed plates available. A dispenser deposits mineral fertilizer to one side of the seed row.
Row spacing 650-800mm.
Sowing depth 40-100mm.
Workrate 0.5ha/hour.
Seed hopper capacity 0.15 cubic metres.
Fertilizer hopper capacity 0.6 cubic metres.
Weight 250kg.

OLT
54000 Osijek
P. Svačića 4
YUGOSLAVIA

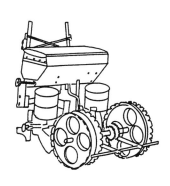

KIMSEED CAMEL PITTER

This machine is designed to regenerate over-grazed and degraded land, in low rainfall areas. It consists of two seed hoppers and two spiked, 600mm diameter discs trailed behind a two- or four-wheel drive vehicle. The discs break the soil crust and make a series of pits, at 1m intervals and in rows 1m apart. These pits then act as small rainfall catchment areas, to reduce runoff and erosion and to provide seedbeds. The machine can be used in a wide variety of soil types and, at a working speed of 8km/hour, can cover 1.6ha/hour.

AUSTRALIAN REVEGETATION CORPORATION LTD
51 King Edward Road
Osborne Park, WA 6017
AUSTRALIA

SEED CUM FERTILIZER DRILL

This tractor-drawn combined drill has separate metering devices for both seed and fertilizer. The metering system is driven from a landwheel and the inter-row spacing can be adjusted from 180mm to 800mm. Depth control wheels are provided but the drill is fully mounted on a standard three-point hitch and has to be lifted out of work for transportation using the tractor's hydraulic system. Weight 270kg.

HINDSONS PVT LTD
The Lower Mall
Patiala
Punjab
147 001
INDIA

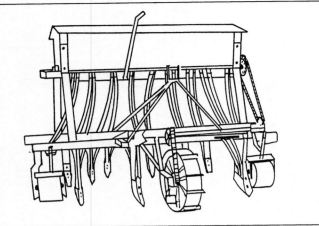

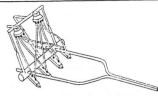

SEED/FERTILIZER DRILL

This is a four-row animal-drawn implement. Similar in principle to the simple hand seed drills, it requires two operators. The frame is steel and plastic feeder tubes are used between the bowls and the coulters.

DANDEKAR BROTHERS & CO.
Shivajinagar
Sangli
Maharashtra 416 416
INDIA

PLANT REPLACER

This hand tool has been designed to lift plants in an undisturbed soil column, thus minimizing root damage.

YANTRA VIDYALAYA
Agricultural Tools Research Centre
Suruchi Campus P.O. Box 4
Bardoli, Gujarat 394 601
INDIA

IRRI MULTI-CROP UPLAND SEEDER

This drill can be used with either a walking tractor or animal draught. It has separate hoppers for seed and fertilizer and can drill a maximum of five rows or a minimum of two. Seeding rate is determined by the interchangeable seed plates fitted, giving possible seed spacings of 200, 250 and 500mm. Sowing depth may also be adjusted to suit the crop.
  The machines hopper capacity is 2.5kg of seed and 3.3kg of fertilizer per row. Row spacing is adjustable from 200mm to 900mm.
Workrate 1.2 ha/day.

JCCE INDUSTRIES
242 Mayondon
Los Baños
Laguna
PHILIPPINES

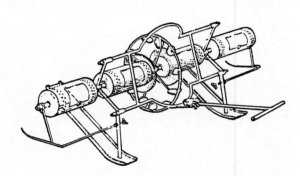

DRUM SEEDERS FOR WETLAND PADDIES

IRRI developed this machine for the seeding of pre-germinated rice in puddled soils, to reduce the high seed requirement of traditional broadcasting. It is a manually pulled eight-row seeder, comprising a central paddle-type drive wheel rotating on a shaft between two skids. Four drum hoppers are fitted on the same shaft, each with a double row of perforations at both ends for seed release. Seeding rate can be set at 60, 90 or 150kg/ha. The machine is constructed of tube and sheet steel and the desired row spacing is fixed, during construction, at any value between 180mm and 250mm. A mud shield and row marker are included in the design, which is available for potential manufacturers. A twelve-row model is also available. The design is available for potential manufacturers.
Workrate 1 ha/day.
Hopper capacity 2kg per drum.

IRRI
Agricultural Engineering Dept
P.O. Box 933
Manila
PHILIPPINES

MULTI-HOPPER SEEDER
This IRRI-designed manual seeder for pre-germinated rice is a six-row machine, giving a seeding rate of 35-50kg/ha, with a row spacing of 250mm. The design includes a drive wheel and shaft, six hoppers with metering rollers, and a handle.
Workrate 1ha/day.
Seed capacity 500g (pre-germinated) per hopper.
Weight 17kg.

Supplied by:

JCCE INDUSTRIES
242 Mayondon
Los Baños
Laguna
PHILIPPINES

ALPHA MACHINERY AND ENGINEERING CORPORATION
1167 Pasong Tamo Street
Makati
Metro Manila
PHILIPPINES

MANUAL SIX-ROW RICE TRANSPLANTERS

This comprises a manually pulled sledge, on which is mounted a seedling tray, holding six mats of 15- to 30-day-old rice seedlings, and a handle which is repeatedly pulled up and pushed down to operate the six-row planting mechanism. With each downward stroke, the picking mechanism removes a number of seedlings from the mat and plants them in six rows. With each upward stroke, the seedling tray is moved horizontally to present new seedlings to the picking mechanism. The transplanter is constructed of steel and wood and weighs 20kg. For fields flooded to a depth of 10-50mm, a workrate of 0.3-0.4ha/day is estimated, with a planting depth of 30-50mm a row spacing of 200mm and with 3-5 seedlings per hill. The designs are available to potential manufacturers.

IRRI
Agricultural Engineering Dept
P.O. Box 933
Manila
PHILIPPINES

Transplanters based on this IRRI design are available from:

JCCE INDUSTRIES
242 Mayondon
Los Baños
Laguna
PHILIPPINES

MEKINS AGRO PRODUCTS (PVT) LTD
6-3-866/A Begumpet
Greenlands
Hyderabad 500 016
INDIA

MAHAWELI AGROMECH
Industrial Complex
Tambuttegama
SRI LANKA

ALPHA MACHINERY AND ENGINEERING CORPORATION
1167 Pasong Tamo Street
Makati
Metro Manila
PHILIPPINES

POTATO PLANTERS

POTATO PLANTER AND FERTILIZER APPLICATOR

This is a tractor-drawn implement, providing simultaneous planting, fertilizer application and insecticide dressing if required. The tubers are planted in two rows, with an adjustable spacing of 150-370mm between tubers. Each furrow is opened by an adjustable-depth shovel tine with a quick-release mechanism to prevent tine damage on contact with fixed obstacles. Tubers, fertilizer and insecticide from separate hoppers are placed in the furrow, which is then closed by a pair of concave discs. Tines at either side of the planter scarify the soil behind the tractor wheels.
Tuber hopper capacity 180kg.
Fertilizer hopper capacity 250kg.
Insecticide hopper capacity 18kg.
Workrate 0.7ha/day.

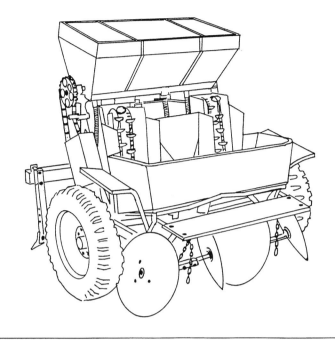

ALFREDO VILLANOVA S.A.
Rue Candelária 1550
B.P. 152
13330 Indaiatuba
São Paulo
BRAZIL

POTATO PLANTER

The basic unit available is a two-wheeled, single-row planter, for mounting on the three-point linkage of a tractor, but two or four of these units can be assembled on a common frame, with a wheel at either end. The specifications for a two-row machine are:
Planting depth 625-750mm.
Required tractor power 15kW.
Workrate 0.5-0.75 ha/hour.

AGRINNOV KFT
4401 Nyíregyháza
Rákóczi út 102
HUNGARY

POTATO PLANTING MACHINE

This two-row machine is towed behind a tractor and comprises a frame for two operators, who load the planting mechanism from boxes of sprouted potatoes. The machine makes the furrow, lays the potatoes and covers them in one operation.

RUDARSKO METALURSKI
KOMBINAT
Ulica 29
Novembra br. 15
Kostajnica
79224 Bos
YUGOSLAVIA

YANTRA FERTILIZER INJECTOR

This is a pointed tube fitted with handles and a foot bar, enabling spot application of fertilizer below the soil surface. After withdrawing the applicator, the operator covers the remaining hole with soil, using his foot.

YANTRA VIDYALAYA
Agricultural Tools Research Centre
Suruchi Campus, P.O. Box 4
Bardoli, 394 601
INDIA

ROTARY DRUM APPLICATOR

This is a very simple, manually pushed device comprising a landwheel fitted with a handle and attached to a fibreglass drum containing the fertilizer. Perforations around the rim of this drum allow the release of fertilizer in a thin band when the device is pushed along.
Drum capacity 10kg.
Weight 5kg.

GRIMALDI MAQUINAS AGRICOLAS
CEP 13830
San Antonio de Posse
São Paulo
BRAZIL

PROTOTYPE AUTOMATIC CASSAVA PLANTERS

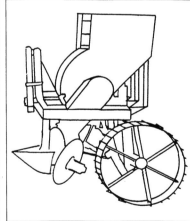

Various single, double and multi-row prototype planters have been developed at the University of Nigeria, to be tractor-mounted or trailed. The planters produce the ridges and then plant the cassava cuttings in them, either vertically or at 45-85 degrees to the horizontal. These machines are not yet in commercial production but the University would welcome enquiries from prospective manufacturers.

UNIVERSITY OF NIGERIA
Department of Agricultural
Engineering
Nsukka
NIGERIA

MANUAL FERTILIZER SPREADER

A metal hopper is fitted between a pair of push-handles, mounted on the axle of a single iron landwheel. A tine coulter is positioned between this landwheel and the hopper outlet, and the fertilizer is gravity-fed through the hopper outlet into the opened furrow. The fertilizer discharge rate is adjusted by a slide in the hopper outlet but application rate is also dependent on the forward speed of the machine, i.e. the walking speed of the operator.
Hopper capacity 14kg.

UPROMA
Kara-Togo B.P. 111
Lome
TOGO

PLOUGH-TRAILED APPLICATOR

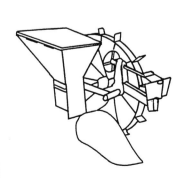

This device was designed by IRRI to be fitted to an existing single mouldboard plough, either animal or tractor powered. Its use increases ploughing time by about 10% but removes the need for a second pass over the land.
Hopper capacity 9kg.
Weight 10kg (without plough).

JCCE INDUSTRIES
242 Mayondon
Los Baños
Laguna
PHILIPPINES

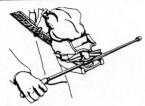

SEED FIDDLE

This shoulder-slung fiddle is suitable for broadcasting seeds, grain and granular fertilizers over small areas or patches of ground affected by flood or drought.

This model features three rate settings.

ALVAN BLANCH DEV CO. LTD
Chelworth
Malmesbury
Wilts SN16 9SG
UK

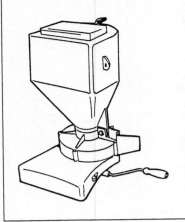

HAND-OPERATED CENTRIFUGAL SPREADERS

LITTLE GIANT X2A
In this spinning disc device, seed or granular fertilizer is broadcast from a polyethylene hopper carried on the operator's shoulder, the distributor disc is spun by manual rotation of a handle at waist height. Distribution width is 1.2-2.4m and the hopper capacity is 9-13kg.

BROADCASTER
A similar but larger centrifugal-type broadcaster is also offered by the company. It can be adjusted to provide granule dispersal either centrally or to the left or right of the operator's path, and with up to 6m throw. Weight 3kg.

SOCIÉTÉ NOUVELLE SAELEN SA
Rue Pic au vent CRT
BP 359
59813 Lesquin Cedex
FRANCE

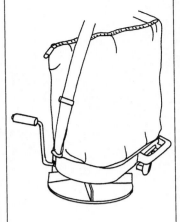

'EV-N-SPRED' BROADCAST SPREADER

This is a shoulder-carried spinning-disc broadcaster for use mainly with grass or other light seeds. The metering device is controlled by one hand and the power to the disc is provided by rotating a handle with the other.

EARTHWAY PRODUCTS INC.
P.O. Box 547
Bristol
IN 46507
USA

OPICO (PANAMA)
P.O. Box 849
Mobile
AL 36601
USA

RICMAR SEED FIDDLE

The Ricmar seed fiddle is a shoulder-slung hand-operated machine for distributing grass seed, grain or granulated fertilizer. It can be used for patching and reseeding areas of poor crop emergence. The shoulder strap can be adjusted and there are three output settings (although distribution also depends on the walking speed of the operator and quality of the seed).

M.E. TUDOR ESQ.
Frogmore Cottage
Sawyers Hill
Minety
Malmesbury SN16 9QL
UK

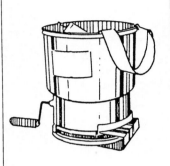

UNIVERSAL SPREADER

This spinning disc device can be used for controlled broadcasting of dry chemicals and seeds. The rate of application can be set on a ten-point scale and an adjustable door controls the width of spread. A spring-loaded release trigger is fitted to stop the flow of material to the disc.

The machine is operated by winding a handle.

SEYMOUR MANUFACTURING CO. INC.
500 North Broadway
P.O. Box 248
Seymour
IN 47274
USA

ROTARY SPREADER

Two models of this spreader are available, supplied either with handles for manual operation by a single operator, or with a towbar and hitch. The conical hopper has an outlet slide in its base and is mounted over a pair of rubber-tyred landwheels. A spinning-disc broadcaster is fitted below the hopper outlet and driven from the landwheels. Application rate is adjusted by the outlet slide position, using a hand-lever. The spreader is also suitable for broadcasting seed.

Spreader model	SP/25-50	SP/25-100
Hopper cap. (litres)	45	80
Range radius (m)	1-3	1-3
Weight (kg)	35.5	37.5

BEZZECCHI S.P.A.
42012 Campagnola Emilia (RE)
ITALY

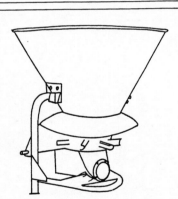

FERTILIZER DISTRIBUTOR SPREADER

The E-600 broadcaster can be mounted on the three-point linkage of a small tractor and driven through its power take-off. It broadcasts fertilizer in either granular or powder form, by the centrifugal action of a spinning disc below the hopper outlet. Application rate is adjustable.
Hopper capacity 0.4 cubic metres.
Tractor power required 4.5kW.

IRMÃOS NOGUEIRA S.A.
Rua 15 de Novembro, 781
Itapira S.P. 13970
BRAZIL

Other suppliers of tractor-mounted granule/powder broadcasters of similar size and performance are:

HOWARD ALATPERTANIAN SDN. BHD.
P.O. Box 8
68107 Batu Caves
Selangor
MALAYSIA

POLJOSTROJ
Industrija mašina i opreme
25250 Odžaci
Karadjordjeva br. 34
YUGOSLAVIA

AIRFLO DIVISION
Kelvin/Cripps Roads
Mashonaland Holdings Ltd
P.O. Box 1914
Harare
ZIMBABWE

LES GRANDS ATELIERS DU NORD
GP1 Km 12 2034
Ez-Zahra Tunis (IE)
TUNISIA

A similar but smaller implement, with a maximum broadcasting radius of 5m and a tractor power requirement of 11kW, is manufactured by:

ZALAGEP BAGODI
MEZÖGAZDASÁGI
GÉPGYÁRTÓ VÁLLALAT
8992 Bagod
Gépállomás út 9
HUNGARY

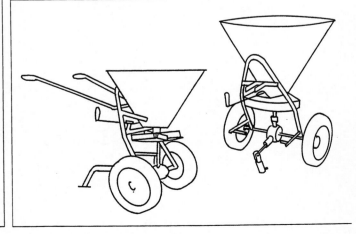

GREEN MANURE TRAMPLER

Four 250mm diameter steel discs with cast iron hubs are mounted along a horizontal shaft. Horizontal blades fitted between these discs chop and trample the green manure crop, pushing it under the soil. Weight 39kg.

COSSUL & CO. PVT LTD
123/367 Industrial Area
Fazalgunj, Kanpur, U.P.
INDIA

'FALCON F10' APPLICATOR

Designed for one-man operation, this applicator comprises a hopper mounted over a single landwheel and fitted with a push-handle and a metering device driven from the landwheel. It is made of mild steel, with pairs of interchangeable, plastic metering wheels to vary and control the fertilizer application rate and to distribute it in a narrow band.
Hopper capacity 12kg.
Weight 9.5kg.

STANHAY WEBB LTD
Exning
Newmarket
Suffolk CB8 7HD
UK

IRRI PLUNGER-AUGER FERTILIZER INJECTOR

This manually pushed injector is used to apply commercial, granular fertilizer in ricefields flooded to a maximum depth of 50mm without dissolving it in the floodwater, thus providing significant savings in the required application rate. The fertilizer is applied 30-50mm below the soil surface and in bands of 40-50mm width. The implement is of metal and wood construction, supported on a pair of skids straddling two rows of plants, each skid carrying a fertilizer hopper. A paddle-type landwheel, mounted between the skids, is pushed along the centre line between these two plant rows and operates the metering device. Each hopper serves two plant rows and thus four rows are treated per pass. The implement is adjustable for 150-225mm row spacings and for five different application rates. Technical details are available for potential manufacturers.
Workrate 0.5 ha/day.
Hopper capacity 2kg per hopper.
Weight 8kg.

IRRI
Agricultural Engineering Department
P.O. Box 933
Manila
PHILIPPINES

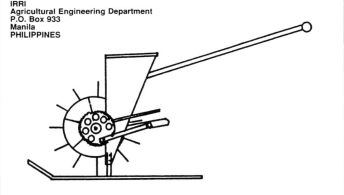

RO-HI GRANULAR CHEMICAL APPLICATOR

This is a two-wheeled unit, designed to be hitched to a tractor but, with a special attachment, can be pulled by two operators. The applicator is chain driven from two 670mm, disc-type wheels with semi-pneumatic tyres; wheel spacing of either 800mm or 1050mm centres is available. Up to four outlet spouts may be used, giving a maximum band width of 720mm and the distance from outlet to ground is adjustable from 25mm to 650mm. There is a rope control shut-off, a spring-loaded chain tensioner, and stainless steel rate control slide and hopper bottom.

GANDY COMPANY
528 Gandrud Road
Owatonna
MN 55060
USA

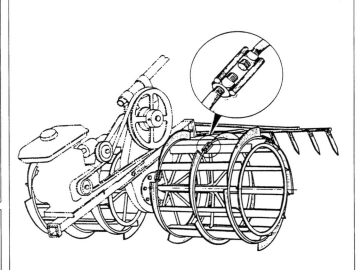

GREEN-MANURE-BURYING TILLER BLADE

This implement is powered by a two-wheeled walking tractor and buries a 510mm swathe of green crop to a depth of 170mm. The tiller pulverizes the top soil, after burying the crop, making the field ready without further tillage for cotton seeding. Manufactured by Dong Thai Farm Equipment, and available through:

CHINA NATIONAL MACHINERY
IMPORT & EXPORT CORPORATION
26 South Yeutan Street
Beijing
CHINA

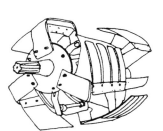

GREEN-MANURE-INCORPORATING KNIVES FOR POWER TILLER

This consists of a hoop with four knives attached, which can be fitted to a power tiller when mouldboard ploughing, to chop a growing green manure crop before incorporation by the plough. Three knife hoop assemblies are slipped over the left-hand cage wheel of the power tiller and tightened with a turnbuckle. The knife hoops must be removed before the power tiller is transported on a hard surface. Technical details are freely available to potential manufacturers.

IRRI
Agricultural Engineering Dept
P.O. Box 933
Manila
PHILIPPINES

Bruce Paton/Panos

4. PEST CONTROL AND OPERATOR SAFETY

Anything that interferes with the growth, development and yield of a crop is called a 'pest'. Pests can be any of a range of species including mammals, insects, viruses, fungi and weeds. These pests may affect the crop plant so severely that, unless they are controlled, the quantity or quality of the crop or the ease of harvest may be seriously reduced.

Over the last half-century the control of pests has increasingly been achieved through the use of specially developed synthetic chemicals, generically called pesticides (a term which embraces herbicides, nematicides, insecticides, fungicides and also poisons used for killing mammalian pests such as rats; some of these are also used to control pests in livestock, for example for the control of ectoparasites). The proven efficacy of chemical control methods in the short term, especially in the protection of 'high yielding varieties', has led to the rapidly increased use of such pesticides in the commercial agriculture sector all over the world, to the point that nearly all large-scale agricultural enterprises and many smallholdings now depend on pesticides, although their use is limited to those farmers who can afford them.

This wide-scale use of pesticides has, particularly over the last decade, raised many concerns including:
○ the safety of farmers and farm workers using pesticides;
○ the build-up of resistance to pesticides, necessitating increased use and/or use of new chemicals;
○ the environmental effects of using large quantities of

pesticides on soil, water and air quality;
○ the build-up of pesticides in the 'food chain' and problems of pesticide residues in food.

The focus of this introduction is on weeding equipment, the safe use of pesticide application equipment, and the safety of smallholder farmers using such equipment. Accordingly, only the first of the above points is addressed; the other three points are equally important but are beyond the scope of this book. First the need for alternative approaches to pest and weed control is highlighted, and the equipment used for weeding described. This is followed by a section describing the hazards that pesticide use can cause to humans, particularly in low-income countries, and the equipment and techniques for operator safety. The final section provides a brief overview of the types of small-scale equipment that are commonly available for pesticide application.

THE NEED FOR ALTERNATIVE APPROACHES

Until the late 1930s the use of synthetic chemical pesticides (including herbicides) in agriculture was not widespread and farmers relied on cultural agronomic methods for the control of pests and weeds. The development of modern pesticides was seen as a great opportunity to reduce the risk to crops from pest attacks while at the same time simplifying crop production by reducing the need for rotations and crop mixtures in order to control pests. However the wide-scale use of chemical pesticides is causing serious environmental problems. These include health risks to humans and animals; unintentional damage through careless or irresponsible use causing spray drift on to neighbouring crops or waterways; runoff from treated fields into watercourses and wells; and careless disposal of material contaminated with pesticides. However, with an increased understanding of environmental and health risks associated with pesticide use, some researchers and practitioners have sought to reduce dependence on these highly toxic substances, by developing new methods of pest control or by reviving earlier crop husbandry techniques. It is now generally gaining acceptance that pesticide use should be considered as the last line of defence, rather than as the first and only means for pest control. With changing pricing policies in richer countries many farmers find that it is more profitable to reduce pesticide use and accept a degree of pest damage than to attempt to achieve 100 per cent control through widespread use of such chemicals.

An example of an approach which is gaining widespread acceptance is integrated pest management (IPM) in which the use of pesticides is considered as a final resort. In some countries (particularly the more wealthy), radical pesticide reduction policies are now being considered or are already being adopted.

A detailed account of these techniques is beyond the scope of this catalogue, so the following section can only provide a very brief outline of what IPM is and where further information can be found.

Integrated pest management

Integrated pest management is a generic term describing an ecological or holistic approach to pest control, which aims to keep crop damage at or below economically acceptable limits. It is achieved mainly through the use of good husbandry techniques and is therefore well suited to traditional smallholdings with access to sufficient labour. Indigenous IPM techniques were, until fairly recently, the only means of pest control and farming communities survived through their ability to invent ways of overcoming pests. These techniques include clearing crop residues; timely tillage, planting and weeding; use of resistant varieties, or indigenous varieties which have not had their endogenous resistance characteristics replaced by yield characteristics; mixed cropping of different species and varieties; crop rotation; and chemical control in emergencies. Such techniques can, when properly used, make conditions less favourable for pests by increasing crop/pest competition and decreasing opportunities for the feeding, breeding and sheltering by pests.

More recently, however, food producers have been joined by scientists in order to accelerate this process of innovation and to introduce some new ideas, including biological controls and the highly reduced and specifically targeted use of chemicals, especially when potential crop losses rise above a predetermined economic threshold. Some biological IPM techniques encourage the establishment of predators, parasites and diseases of the pests themselves. This is achieved both through husbandry practices and, at times, the deliberate introduction of exotic biological controls such as microbial pesticides, inundative release of natural enemies, or the use of pheromones to lure pests into traps. Some of these control measures have only been proven in controlled environments such as greenhouses and are thus of less relevance to low-income smallholders, but others, based on 'organic' farming principles, are very relevant. Organic farming systems

— the common farming system of poorer farmers who cannot afford purchased inputs — use no synthetic chemicals either for pest control or to increase soil fertility. In these systems pest control and soil fertility are maintained through careful husbandry. Developing new IPM techniques should be a priority for all national agricultural research programmes. It requires a detailed understanding of the agro-ecosystem including soils and climate; crop physiology; pests and their predators. However, funding of this research is lower than funding of research for chemical control measures.

Information

Information on IPM techniques is not as widely available as information on pesticide use. The latter also has greater exposure through commercial advertising and many national agricultural extension services. Improved operator safety could be achieved if the producers and operators had access to wider sources of information, including information about the short-and long-term dangers of pesticides, safety precautions and alternative control measures such as IPM, to help them make more informed choices. And if this information is backed up by access to relevant equipment, expertise and training then the impact of improved operator safety will have widespread benefit.

There is a short list of publications on integrated pest management and biological control at the end of this chapter.

WEED CONTROL

Although the use of herbicides has increased dramatically, the majority of smallholder farmers control weeds by cultural methods, usually through manual cultivation (e.g. cutting, uprooting, burying, burning, smothering). Such operations are usually part of highly developed systems that use a number of complementary activities to minimize weed infestation. These systems may include some or all of the following as weed control strategies:

❍ hand-weeding or inter-row cultivation of the standing crop;
❍ mixed cropping;
❍ crop rotations;
❍ minimizing initial weed infestation by:
   — sanitation: use of clean seed, clean tools;
   — prevention of seeds entering the field from field boundaries or in irrigation water (using weed seed traps);
   — late weeding in previous crop to stop the setting of weed seed;
   — post-harvest grazing by livestock, post-harvest cultivations, post-harvest burning of stubble.

Traditional mixed cropping patterns (many with six or more different crops) can involve the use of all of these techniques, spreading the labour requirement through the cropping season. The primary cultivation for a late planted crop becomes the weeding operation of a standing crop; the crop residues from an early harvested crop become the mulch for a later harvested crop; and leaf cover of a spreading crop (e.g. sweet potato) becomes a cover crop for a tall standing plant (e.g. maize). These systems are highly adapted to the weed control demands of each crop (they are also excellent control mechanisms for other pests). Attempts to change such patterns should always stem from an understanding of the relationships in the farming system and the demands made on the farmer by the farming system.

Weeding equipment

Equipment for weeding is often used for primary and/or secondary cultivation, particularly seedbed preparation, as well as weeding. Accordingly much equipment could be included in both this chapter and Chapter 2. To avoid repetition there is cross-referencing where appropriate.

Human-powered

Slashers are used to cut off the part of weeds above ground, leaving them on the surface. This slows down weed growth without disturbing the roots and the soil surface, although it is not as effective as other means of weed control and can require more labour. Where heavy rainfall causes bad erosion problems, slashing can be useful in controlling the severity of erosion as the roots help to hold the soil, and the mulch of weed-tops on the soil surface reduces raindrop impact and slows down the flow of water across the surface. Slashing of weeds is most often used under perennial crops. In much of the world machetes are used for slashing, although some specialist equipment is included in this chapter.

Hoes can be split into three basic types: digging hoes, chopping hoes, and pushing and pulling hoes. Manufacturers of all these types are listed in Chapter 2. Most smallholder farmers possess only one type of hoe, usually a digging type of traditional design, which is used for primary and secondary cultivation, ridging and weeding. Chopping hoes are used to chop the weeds and soil. Pushing and pulling hoes are used to cut the weeds under the soil surface and are less suitable for harder soils as they can have problems penetrating the soil (see Figure 1).

Rotary hoes have been mainly developed for paddy rice grown in rows. The rotors are usually star-shaped or formed from pegs. They are not suited to hard, compacted soils because of soil penetration problems, but can be used for dryland crops grown in friable soil.

Wheeled cultivators can come with a range of attachments: hoes, tines and mouldboards. They can only be used with row-planted crops and are best suited to friable soils.

Cono-weeders have been designed by IRRI especially for weeding row planted paddy rice. They are included in this chapter.

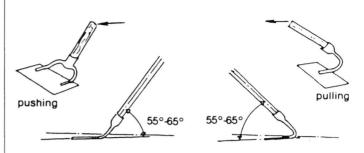

Figure 1   Pushing and pulling hoes, showing working angles

Table 1 provides a guide to the suitability of human-powered equipment for different operating conditions.

Animal-powered

Much information on animal power is provided in the introductions to Chapters 1 and 2. Virtually all cultivation equipment can be used for both soil preparation and for weeding. Accordingly, with the exception of specialist weeding tools, the equipment mentioned here can be found in Chapter 2.

Tined cultivators can be used for both secondary cultivation and for inter-row weeding. These implements come with either rigid or spring tines. Available attachments for the tines are chisel points, duckfoot points, full and half sweeps (see Figure 2). Spring tines are usually used with duckfoot points for weeding; their vibration helps to bring the weeds to the surface and breaks up clods. Rigid tines fixed with full or half sweeps operate a few centimetres under the soil and cut the tops off the weeds, leaving them on the soil surface. Cultivators especially adapted for inter-row weeding can often have their width of operation adjusted.

Rotary tined cultivators have been especially designed for weeding ridges. Two designs are illustrated in this chapter. One straddles the ridge and growing crop (it has a high clearance frame) and cultivates both sides of the ridge. The other is an attachment to a ridger and works between ridges,

Table 1 Suitability of various types of hand-operated equipment for specified intercultivation conditions

	Soil condition			Soil topography			Cropping pattern		
	Hard	Friable	Plastic or muddy	Flat	Ridges	Mounds	Random	Rowcrop	
1. Chopping hoe	✔✔	✔	✗✗	✔✔	✔✔	✔✔	✔✔	✔	decreasing 'drudgery' / increasing cost
2. Pushing/pulling hoe	✗	✔✔	✗	✔✔	✔	✗	✔	✔✔	
3. Rotary hoe/weeder	✗	✔	✔✔	✔✔	✔	✗	✗✗	✔✔	
4. Wheeled hoe/cultivator	✗✗	✔✔	✔	✔✔	✔	✗	✗✗	✔✔	

75°-85°

55°-65°

1

2

3

4

Key:
✔✔ equipment very well suited to the conditions specified.
✔ equipment moderately suited to the conditions specified.

✗ equipment unsuitable for the conditions specified.
✗✗ equipment very unsuitable for the conditions specified.

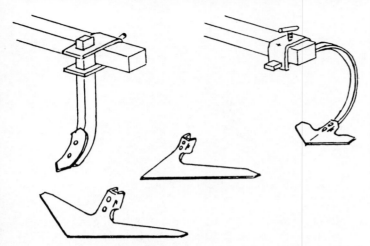

Figure 2   Tines and points: (top left) rigid tine with chisel point; (top right) spring tine with duckfoot print; (bottom) half and full sweeps for use with rigid tine

cleaning the adjacent sides of neighbouring ridges. This latter tool requires ridges to be parallel and equidistant.

Engine-powered cultivators

Narrow single-axle engine-powered cultivators can be used for inter-row weeding. Those suitable for inter-row weeding usually have no wheel or have only one centrally placed wheel or skid. Weeding is carried out by rotovation. These powered cultivators can be found in this chapter; larger ones (with two wheels) are better suited for primary cultivation and can be found in Chapters 1 and 2.

OPERATOR SAFETY

The dangers that the operators of pesticide application equipment experience, particularly in poorer countries, cannot be emphasized too much. This section highlights these dangers and provides information on safety equipment and operational practices needed to lessen these risks.

Pesticide hazards

Pesticides are biologically active substances which have been developed to kill or distort crop pests, including weeds. Unfortunately, chemicals which kill pests can also poison humans and other living organisms and there is mounting world concern that users of pesticides, particularly in low-income countries, face increased risks of pesticide poisoning. The World Health Organization estimates that there are three million global cases of acute and severe pesticide poisonings per year including 20,000 unintentional deaths (WHO/UNEP, 1990). It is estimated that lesser poisonings total more than 25 million cases each year in low-income countries alone, although there are insufficient national data as many poisonings go unrecorded because no medical attention is sought (Jeyaratnam, 1990 43:139-144) and thus the true figures may be much higher. Despite total consumption of pesticides in low-income countries accounting for less than 20 per cent of world production, they suffer half the accidental poisonings and 75 per cent of deaths (Bull, 1984 p.38). With an anticipated doubling of pesticide use in low-income countries in the next ten years, in line with a trend of the doubling of global pesticide production every ten years since 1945 (WHO/UNEP, 1990), such trends are a cause for major concern.

The higher rates of accidents in low-income countries appear to be the result of two main factors:
O lower operator safety;
O the type of pesticides used.

Operator safety is often of a low standard as legislation is, in many countries, either inadequate or ineffective. The problem is compounded by a lack of nearby medical facilities in many rural areas; poor on-farm training, especially of illiterate operators, in the safe use of pesticides and pesticide application equipment and the use of protective clothing; and, even if the other conditions are met, lack of access to equipment and protective clothing of an adequate safety standard for the chemicals being used, especially clothing suited to hot and humid conditions.

Some of the pesticides marketed in low-income countries have been banned or restricted in richer countries, because they are considered too toxic or persistent. Operators may, therefore, be unwitting victims of pesticide poisoning because national legislation has yet to catch up with the recommendations of safety regulations in the richer countries, where the knowledge about the use and dangers of these chemicals often resides.

SAFETY EQUIPMENT AND PROCEDURES

Information on operator safety is supplied by the chemical companies themselves and the following advice is taken with permission from the *Shell Agriculture Safety Guide* (1990) published by the Crop Protection Division of Shell International Chemical Company, Shell Centre, London SE1 7PG, UK.

Measures to be taken to ensure personal protection from exposure for anyone who handles or could otherwise come into contact with chemicals are largely a matter of common sense. Chemicals can enter the body by three routes: through the mouth (ingestion/swallowing), through the skin (dermal exposure), or through inhalation of vapours, small particles of dust or very small droplets (aerosol) of liquid. Of these three routes, dermal exposure represents the most frequent hazard to those who handle crop protection products. Inhalation is important with volatile products, airborne dusts and formulations based on volatile solvents which can themselves present a hazard. Personal protection involves avoiding exposure by taking appropriate precautions, using protective clothing and equipment, and thoroughly washing all exposed parts of the body after work and before eating, drinking, smoking or using the toilet.

The degree of hazard from the many different crop protection products varies widely. Even products containing the same active ingredients can pose different risks. For example, dusts containing low concentrations of active ingredient may be relatively harmless, while liquid formulations may be very hazardous if in contact with the skin or if inhaled. It is therefore important that all personnel handling pesticides should read, or be informed, about the potential hazards of the different products they are handling. When an unfamiliar product is being used, first check information on precautions to be followed as given on the product label and in the Material Safety Data Sheet (MSDS). **Always read the label.**

When leaking containers are found, or in the event of accidents or spillages, the personal protection recommendations given in the relevant Product Advice Sheet must be followed. If a container has leaked and the surfaces of other containers are contaminated this may appear as staining or as a powdery deposit. It may have affected the label, and if this is illegible and the product is unfamiliar, the operator may decide to return the container to the retailer for safe disposal.

When any of these signs are seen, or where the more hazardous products are being handled, care must be aken to prevent skin contamination.

However, the following general recommendations always apply:

○ at least two people wearing appropriate protective clothing should be present when a leaking container is being decanted into a clean empty drum;

○ anyone dealing with an incident should wash hands and exposed skin thoroughly with soap and water as soon as possible and before eating, drinking, smoking and using the toilet.

Protective clothing and equipment

In some parts of the world, clothing to be worn when carrying out certain jobs, and with specified substances, is the subject of legislation. More commonly, it is left to the user to follow advice on the label.

The climate and the economic situation in the more industrialized countries allow for high quality, heavy duty and relatively expensive clothing and equipment to be used. In developing countries, where foreign exchange is often a problem, such clothing and equipment may be either too expensive or unobtainable. In tropical areas, wearing protective clothing and equipment can also be uncomfortable and it is not uncommon to encounter cases of heat stress.

It is known that many of the recommendations which are readily accepted in temperate climates are not practicable in tropical areas and, as a result, are rarely followed. **This is not to say that precautions can be disregarded when working in hot climates; on the contrary, it is in these areas that most poisonings occur and where special attention needs to be paid to safety in use.** [ITDG's emphasis]

A booklet in the GIFAP Guidelines series, *Guidelines for Personal Protection When Using Pesticides in Hot Climates*, provides further advice on the subject of personal protection in hot climates, and this should be read in conjunction with the advice given in this section.

When working with any chemical, it is common sense to avoid exposure. With toxic chemicals, the need is even greater. Normal working clothes afford a degree of protection and the term 'protective clothing' is now taken to refer to clothing additional to or in place of working clothes.

The GIFAP *Guidelines for the Safe and Effective Use of Pesticides* state:

'Even when no specific protective clothing is recommended on the product label, lightweight clothing covering as much of the body as possible should be worn.'

In practice this means a long-sleeved upper garment, long trousers, footwear and hat. This should be taken as the minimum protection required when applying crop protection products.

When dispensing concentrates and mixing formulations, personal protection is required and protective gloves and eye–face protection should be used. Extra protection such as impervious clothing and respirators may (rarely) be needed during application, but this will always be stated on the product label.

Reference to the particular difficulties in hot climates is made in the GIFAP Guidelines and the following extract offers sound advice:

'Protective equipment is uncomfortable to work in, particularly under tropical and sub-tropical weather conditions. Therefore, wherever possible, pesticides which do not require elaborate precautions should be chosen for use. It is sometimes

Jeremy Hartley/Panos

Spraying clove trees: ideally the operator should wear a mask

possible to select a particular pesticide formulation with less stringent precautionary requirements. Application during the cooler hours of the day is more comfortable for operators wearing protective clothing and will encourage [protective clothing] use.'

Protective gloves and gauntlets

These are the most important item of routine protective clothing. Gloves should be worn for all handling operations involving concentrated formulations and, if recommended on the label, during application as well.

The choice between glove and gauntlet should be determined by the job being undertaken. If there is risk of contamination reaching up the arm, then gauntlets should be worn.

The suitability of gloves is important from the point of view of the job being done, comfort and impermeability to the solvents used in formulations. Very thick gloves are appropriate for heavy duty work in formulation plants and storage depots, but they are usually too heavy and inflexible for use during spray application in the field. Conversely, very thin ones are easily damaged.

The best and most economic material for protective gloves is nitrile rubber. PVC gloves may also be suitable and are reasonably resistant to abrasion, but they tend to crack with age. Polyethylene gloves are resistant to many solvents, but are likely to tear. Natural rubber gloves should not be used for handling liquid formulations as they have very poor resistance to many solvents.

Gloves of whatever material have a limited life. Swelling indicates incompatibility with the solvent. If this happens, change to another type of material. If the gloves crack or if leaks develop, discard them and change to a new pair.

Reputable manufacturers publish charts showing the suitability of their gloves for protection against a range of solvents. The label or MSDS for the product being handled will recommend the type of gloves to be used.

Shell has recently introduced the Gardman range of protective clothing specially designed to suit the needs of workers in hot climates. Gardman is supplied as a pack based on a garment made from an air-permeable, synthetic material. Each pack contains a coverall or smock, nitrile rubber gloves, a simple face shield and an impervious apron.

Coveralls

Also known as 'overalls', these are normally made of cotton or synthetic materials and cover most of the body. Some have integral hoods. White coveralls have the advantage of showing up contamination.

Coveralls should not have pockets and ideally should be made with elasticated trouser ends and cuffs. The zip should be secure.

Coveralls provide protection during a wide range of operations, mainly against particulate matter (dust) and light spray. If better protection is required the coverall should be made of a non-permeable material, although this makes the garment 'non-breathable' and hence less comfortable in hot climates.

A number of suppliers now offer special lightweight coveralls designed for use in hot climates. These are made from synthetic fabrics. Some fabrics are coated in order to decrease penetration by liquids. The non-coated fabrics are air-permeable, whereas the coated ones are not. Some are made of long-lasting heavy duty material and can be expensive, but are good value in the long term. More popular are the relatively cheap short-life coveralls.

Cotton coveralls are more robust than many of those made from disposable materials and can withstand repeated washing. Disposable coveralls can usually be laundered a number of times, but if heavily contaminated are best discarded by burning on a bonfire in an open space.

Head coverings

Head covering is generally recommended for comfort in hot climates and as some protection against spray drift. A lightweight cotton brimmed 'beanie' or 'floppy' hat is suitable. Peaked caps, although shielding the eyes from the sun, do not normally protect the neck as well as a brimmed hat, unless they are fitted with a neck-flap.

If overhead spraying is being carried out, then a sou'wester type of waterproof hat and cape may be necessary.

Footwear

Industrial boots (not a type fastened by laces) or long (Wellington) boots need to be worn when dealing with leakage or accidental spillage of hazardous materials, or when handling very toxic products. Boots should be made of an impervious material such as rubber. If toxic products are being poured, the trousers of coveralls should be worn over the boots and not tucked into the boot tops.

Footwear should be regularly inspected for damage and possible leaking. In hot climates, wearing cotton socks may make boots more comfortable to wear.

Boots or shoes should be worn when applying products in the field. Bare feet, 'flip-flops' or sandals are not acceptable.

Protective aprons

Aprons are strongly recommended when handling concentrated products in Class 1a, 1b and II of the WHO Hazard Classification System. Aprons should be made of impermeable material such as neoprene, nitrile rubber or one of the laminated, lightweight, synthetic materials. They should reach from the top of the chest to below the tops of the boots and wrap around sufficiently to cover the sides of the legs.

When a knapsack sprayer is used, protective aprons can be worn on the back to protect the operator against leakage.

Face shields and goggles

Face shields and goggles protect the eyes from splashes. Face shields are cooler than goggles in hot climates and do not 'mist up' as easily.

Respiratory protective equipment

Whenever a product or solvent vapours or dusts disperse in the working area, there is a risk that they might be inhaled. Exposure monitoring studies in the field have shown that inhalation is far less of a hazard than dermal exposure. This is because droplets of spray from medium to high volume application are too large to be inhaled. However, in the case of dusts, ultra-low volume or mistblower application, droplets are very fine and an inhalation hazard exists. Air-purifying respirators are commonly used when handling and applying crop protection products.

Air-purifying respirators These remove the contaminant from the air before it is breathed. Such respirators incorporate dust filters and/or gas adsorbers which are connected to a variety of face pieces. Air-purifying respirators are effective for only a limited time, depending on conditions of use.

A *disposable half mask* (ori-nasal) respirator formed from the filter medium itself, such as paper, synthetic material, gauze (surgical mask) or cellulose protects the nose and mouth against particulate matter (dust). Various types are available, some developed specifically for crop protection products. This is the simplest and most common type of mask.

A *half mask* covers the nose and mouth only and has a single or twin cartridge filter assembly attached. Since it does not protect the eyes, a half face mask should always be worn with goggles or a face shield.

A *full face mask* covers eyes, nose and mouth and the face piece may either have the absorbent cartridge(s) attached directly or be connected by a flexible tube to an adsorbent canister carried on a belt round the waist.

Other types of air-purifying respirators comprise powered devices such as the air-fed blouse, air-fed hood and air-fed visor safety helmet. These are more generally encountered in filling or repacking installations and formulation plants.

Maintaining protective clothing

After use, all items of protective clothing should be washed thoroughly with soap or detergent and water, and well rinsed in accordance with the manufacturers' instructions. Some garments may be single-use only, and should be discarded and destroyed.

Immediately after use, gloves should be well washed with soap or detergent and water before being removed from the hands. After removal, they should be turned inside out and again thoroughly washed, rinsed, rubbed dry and allowed to dry completely in a well-ventilated place before being stored in the safety equipment locker. Dispose of washings as toxic waste. In tropical areas, the preferred approach for dealing with degraded effluent is to evaporate it to dryness in a solar evaporation pond (see Figure 3). The resulting non-toxic residue can then be disposed of in an approved landfill or dumping site.

If organophosphorus or carbamate compounds have been handled, gloves should be soaked in a dilute solution of washing soda (sodium carbonate) for at least eight hours, rinsed and dried before re-use. Long and frequent contact with organophosphorus compounds can result in the glove material becoming impregnated. When there is a risk that this has happened, the gloves should be discarded.

During the rinsing stage, gloves should be filled with air, held under water and firmly squeezed to check that no leaks have developed. If air bubbles are seen, the gloves should be cut up and discarded.

All items of protective clothing and equipment should be checked at regular intervals to ensure that they are in good condition and ready for immediate use. If they become damaged, torn or punctured, they should either be repaired in accordance with manufacturers' instructions or destroyed. *Essential items of protective clothing and equipment should be kept in, or close to, the products store in a specially marked locker.*

Safety in use

Precautions need to be taken when handling and applying crop protection products to safeguard the health of operators, bystanders and the general public, and to protect the environment. Safety recommendations are largely a matter of common sense; for example, following the label directions, avoiding exposure to spray, taking special care when preparing spray solutions, paying attention to personal hygiene and avoiding spray drift.

In some instances however, depending on the nature of the product involved and the job being done, special precautions are required. These may involve the use of certain items of protective clothing or equipment; if so, details will be given on product labels and in the Material Safety Data Sheet.

Handling formulated products

Handling concentrated formulations generally presents more risk to the operator than spraying the diluted product in the field, because of both the high concentration of the undiluted product and the skin-penetrating characteristics of many formulation solvents. Special precautions must therefore be taken to avoid accidentally splashing the skin or eyes.

As a basic precaution when handling undiluted products

Figure 3 Solar evaporation pond for evaporation of degraded effluent

nitrile rubber or neoprene gloves should be worn in addition to a coverall. If there is a likelihood of splashing and spillage, a face shield and apron should also be worn. Suitable items of protective clothing are included in the Gardman kits referred to earlier.

Solid formulations are usually less hazardous to handle and apply than liquids. Granules generally contain low concentrations of active ingredient, and solid formulations are not based on solvents which can assist skin penetration of the active ingredient.

Wettable powders, on the other hand, contain much higher concentrations of active ingredient and also consist of very fine particles. Care is therefore needed to avoid raising a dust cloud that may contaminate the operator and the surroundings during handling operations. Using a simple dust-mask is a sensible precaution while handling and mixing wettable powders.

Application in the field

Conventional water-diluted sprays

These are applied very dilute and, from an acute toxicity standpoint, the spray solution is much less hazardous than the concentrate. From a risk standpoint, however, the potential exposure time will be far greater during spraying because the time spent spraying is greater than the time taken handling the concentrate.

The risk of exposure depends very much on circumstances. For example, a tractor operator in an enclosed cab will be at less risk of exposure than a knapsack sprayer operator spraying a tall crop on a windy day.

Good spraying practice using well-maintained equipment is the key to minimizing the risk of exposure. Details of principles and practices when using knapsack sprayers are given in *A Shell Pocket Guide to Knapsack Sprayers*. The type of equipment used and spraying in the absence of wind are also important factors.

Protective clothing is the next approach for minimizing the risk of exposure. The advice is always related to a particular product and can be found on the product label.

It is a wise, common sense precaution always to wear clothing which covers most of the body (long-sleeved upper garment and long trousers, or Gardman protective clothing) during application and to pay attention to personal hygiene. Operators should not eat, drink or smoke while spraying.

IN CASES OF POISONING

Toxic chemicals can be handled safely, provided the correct precautions are taken. Poisoning nearly always happens as a result of negligence, ignorance or misuse.

Those who store or handle crop protection products must be made aware of the toxic hazards associated with the products with which they work. Equally, they should be made familiar with the first aid procedures appropriate for individual products, and have readily available the information that will assist doctors and hospital in providing the correct treatments.

Prior arrangements should be made with a local physician, who can be contacted at once if a case of poisoning occurs. The doctor should be given a copy of the *Shell Agriculture Safety Guide*, a set of the appropriate Data Sheets, and any other basic medical information on the products handled in order to give appropriate medical treatment. He or she should be asked to hold a stock of antidotes or other essential drugs, e.g. vitamin K1, atropine, diazepam, Toxogonin.

Basic principles

First aid procedures and medical treatment (advice for medically qualified personnel) are given in each Product Advice Sheet. The following general advice is applicable to all cases of over-exposure and to cases of suspected or actual poisoning by crop protection products. Reference may also be made to the GIFAP booklet, *Guidelines for Emergency Measures in Cases of Pesticide Poisoning.*

Poisoning by mixtures

Symptoms of intoxication by mixtures containing two or more active ingredients are usually those presented by the more hazardous ingredient of the mixture. However, symptoms may differ in expression. Potentiation, that is the toxic effect being greater than the sum of the toxic effects of the individual components, may occur. Symptoms may also be deferred. When a solvent is involved, the presentation and onset of symptoms may be influenced considerably.

First aid

In cases of gross contamination or if signs or symptoms of poisoning have developed, first aid measures must be taken.

If not known, try to find out which product was the cause of the poisoning and how it was absorbed, i.e. by mouth, through inhalation, or through the skin.

Carry out the first aid procedures recommended on the Product Advice Sheet for the product involved. The type of first aid measure depends on the route of exposure (skin or eye contact, inhalation or ingestion) and on the chemical and physical properties of the formulation.

There should be no delay in taking first aid measures in all cases of suspected intoxication. The person should be removed from the source of exposure to prevent any further contamination. The rescuer must also take care to avoid self-contamination. Medical attention must be obtained immediately, or the person taken to the nearest hospital or clinic.

If the person is unconscious, ensure that he or she can breathe freely. False teeth should be removed and the mouth cleaned out. The patient should be placed at rest, lying in the recovery position (see Figure 4). If the patient is not breathing, a free airway should be ensured and artificial respiration started immediately, avoiding self-contamination.

These additional actions should be taken by the rescuer:
❍ in case of skin contact, contaminated clothing should be removed and skin washed with water, using soap if available;
❍ in case of eye contact, the eye should be flushed liberally with clean water;
❍ in case of inhalation, the person should be removed to fresh air;
❍ in case of ingestion, vomiting should NOT be induced unless:
— it is specifically advised to do so on the label or in the data for the product;
— the material (if a liquid) swallowed was one of the bipyridylium herbicides (paraquat and diquat). Note: These materials usually have an emetic incorporated in the formulation.

If induction of vomiting is advised, attempt it by stimulating the back of the subject's throat with a finger, but only if the patient is conscious. Induction of vomiting can be very difficult and is best left for a medical practitioner to perform. However, it could be a life-saving measure if medical help is not readily available.

DO NOT USE SALT WATER AS AN EMETIC.
NEVER GIVE ANYTHING BY MOUTH TO AN UNCONSCIOUS PERSON.

If the patient is conscious but induction of vomiting is not called for, give activated charcoal (if available). Keep the patient warm and at rest.

General medical advice

When medical assistance arrives or when delivering the patient to hospital, advise the physician or those concerned of the 'In cases of poisoning' section of the relevant Product Advice Sheet or Material Safety Data Sheet. Tell them how the accident occurred.

The above advice, taken from the *Shell Safety Guide*, should be heeded by all who use chemicals, employ or advise others to use chemicals, sell chemicals, or make grants or loans for the purchase of chemicals. The information given in the next section presupposes that appropriate protection will be taken by the user of the equipment.

SMALL-SCALE APPLICATION EQUIPMENT

The diverse range of available equipment reflects the varying demands of crops, pests and chemicals. It is designed to apply pesticides to various target surfaces that include the soil, crops, weeds and insects. It also needs to be able to handle chemicals some of which are very mobile or systemic — with areas of activity away from the point of deposition — and others which only have an effect on the contact area. The pesticides may also persist for varying lengths of time with some soil-acting residual herbicides effective for months, making it even more important to apply the chemicals at the right time in the development of the pest or crop, at the prescribed dose and in an approved manner, taking the appropriate safety precautions.

A safer method of application of some pesticides is in a powder or granular form and a wide range of equipment for these is described although sometimes equipment is not necessary, e.g. for the treatment of stored grain, but there is still the need to take adequate safety precautions for personal protection.

However, most pesticides are applied when dissolved or suspended in a liquid. The dilution rate depends on the chemical, pest, crop and equipment. Briefly, it is possible to classify the mode of application by the volume applied per hectare:

High volume: around 200 litres/ha.
Low volume: 10-50 litres/ha.
Ultra low volume: less than 10 litres/ha.

Similar equipment can apply the liquid in either high or low volume modes, but equipment for applying chemicals at ultra low volumes is significantly different.

Figure 4   The 'recovery' position

High/low volume sprayers

Knapsack and pressure cylinder sprayers

In these sprayers a diluted spray solution, held in a convenient tank, is forced through a small hole called a nozzle to produce drops that can be directed on to the treatment area. Spray tanks are available in a wide range of sizes but with a maximum limit of about 25 litres (quantities in excess of this amount cannot easily be carried). Tanks are usually slung knapsack fashion on the back but can be hand-carried too. A lever, which comes forward past the side of the body, is pumped up and down by one hand while the other directs the spray-forming nozzle fitted at the distal end of a semi-rigid lance. A small pressure control vessel is incorporated into the pump to smooth out pulsations and reduce the frequency of lever operations. In some models hand-pumping at the time of spraying is eliminated through the use of pressurized metal tanks. Spray liquid is put into the tank and then air-pumped in manually, or from another cylinder, or from a compressed air line. Sometimes the spray liquid is forced into the tank, compressing the remaining air. A convenient on/off tap between the pump and nozzle allows spray to be emitted only when needed.

Figure 5   Different nozzles produce different flow rates, spray widths and droplet shapes

The nozzle performs three main functions which can determine the success of the pesticide.
○ The small hole restricts and thereby partially controls the flow of pressurized spray liquid.
○ The issuing spray forms a sheet which disintegrates into drops that can be directed and distributed over a swath.
○ The size of drops is controlled by the size and design of the nozzle. To meet the varied needs of pesticides, nozzles are available in three main types — namely fan, flood or hollow cone — and a wide range of sizes.

The variety of nozzles available produce different flow rates for a similar pressure, different spray widths, different droplet sizes and ranges of droplet size:
○ Hollow Cone nozzles, which give a fine mist hollow cone spray pattern;
○ Fan Spray nozzles, which give a flat angle fan shaped spray pattern;
○ the Floodjet (e.g. Polijet) range of herbicide application nozzles which can provide a large droplet spray swath from a large orifice. The range of output spray volume rates can vary from 20 to 1000 litres/ha. depending on the nozzle, the pressure and the walking speed of the operator.

Maintenance

Various checks of knapsack sprayers need to be made regularly.
○ The hole in the sprayer nozzle is eroded through use and can corrode when stored. It is imperative that the liquid throughput of the nozzles is regularly and thoroughly checked. Failure to do so may result in more pesticide being applied than is necessary and could damage crops. It is necessary check the throughput of the nozzle and calibrate

the equipment regularly. Visually examine the distribution of the spray too. Spray on to a dry surface and see how uniformly the liquid dries and determine whether the break-up of the liquid sheet from the nozzle is uniform or if there are thick ligaments or partial blockages. Clean and replace the nozzles as necessary.
○ Seals will sometimes leak — often because of trapped dirt. Rinse these in clean water and refit.
○ The spray tank and pipes can split and leak. It is essential that they are repaired or, better, replaced. The on/off trigger must work quickly and completely. Some have devices to lock the trigger open or off. Make sure these work.
○ Before using any sprayer in the field, visually check that the pipes and their clips, the tank, harness or carrying straps are in good order and securely fixed. Use clean water to test the sprayer to make sure it is working properly and the harness is comfortable.

Other hand-operated sprayers

Various types of hand-operated sprayer are commonly used.
○ *Trigger-operated sprayers* Operation of the trigger ejects a small spray or stream of liquid — usually the nozzle is adjustable to allow variation in spray pattern and volume. Capacity 0.25-2 litres.
○ *Piston-operated sprayers* Liquid is sucked into the cylinder when the operator withdraws the piston/plunger, then it is sprayed out when the plunger is pressed home.
○ *Hand compression sprayers* The operator puts the container under pressure by pumping the handle on top. The liquid is then released when a trigger is operated. Capacity 0.5-1 litre (occasionally more).
○ *Hand atomizers* Air, forced out of a small orifice at the end of the piston, sucks up and atomizes liquid from the container which has a capacity of about 150ml upwards.
○ *Slide action sprayers* A back-and-forth pumping action on the hand grip produces a continuous spray.
○ *Hand lever sprayers* The pump is operated by a lever. This type is usually used to spray chemicals from a bucket.
○ *Stirrup pump* The pump is placed in a bucket and the plunger pumped up and down.

Motorized knapsack mistblowers

A third category of high/low volume sprayers are powered by small engines. These are universally available and can be used for atomizing liquids and blowing the particles for considerable distances. Using a different hopper, dusts can also be blown by these machines. If not used carefully the chemicals can easily drift away from the target area.

Ultra low volume sprayers

The are three main categories of hand-held equipment for ultra low volume (ULV) application:
○ rotary atomization controlled droplet application (CDA) sprayers;
○ electrodynamic atomization sprayers;
○ wipers.
High concentrations of chemical are usually used in ULV equipment. These concentrations are more toxic than those used in higher volume applicators; accordingly the dangers from contamination are correspondingly greater.

Rotary atomizers

These produce drops directly or liquid ligaments (which then collapse into drops) from the edge of a high-speed rotating dish, disc or cage. The range of drop sizes is much less than that from conventional nozzles. The size of drop is mainly dependent on the speed of the disc's peripheral edge — higher speeds being used to produce small drops and low speeds large drops. Often small drops are deliberately purposefully produced and emitted into air-streams that are naturally or artificially induced to spread the spray over a very wide swath or penetrate dense leaf canopies. In contrast large drops readily free-fall and a predetermined swath can be applied. The system is always associated with the use of low spray volumes of concentrated pesticide. Less water for spraying is needed and the equipment is often lighter and easier to use than knapsack sprayers.

Electrodynamic atomization

The 'Electrodyn' spraying system comprises a spray stick and 'Bozzle' container, a unique combination of bottle and nozzle, which contains pre-packed pesticide formulations ready for use, thus reducing operator contamination risks. The integral electrically-conductive nozzle supplied with each 'Bozzle' is pre-set for the specific chemical it contains and requires no calibration, always providing the correct droplet size to optimize pest control. The electrodynamic atomization technique uses only 0.5-1.0 litres per hectare. Thus, a single 750ml 'Bozzle' container can treat up to 1.5 crop hectares. The spray stick contains batteries and a solid-state high voltage generator which takes the 6v low voltage input from the four U-2 batteries and converts this to an output at the HV stud of 25kv and a zero potential at the earth field electrode.

Liquid is first formed into a number of evenly spaced ligaments, which in turn break up into uniformly-sized charged droplets. Droplet size and charge can be varied by manipulating the applied voltage. The droplets, which are mutually repellent and of even size, deposit a uniform coat on the crop. The charged droplets 'wrap around' the crop target so that underside coverage of leaves and stems is achieved. Charged droplets are attracted to the nearest earthed target usually the crop, but the operator needs to ensure that at the end of each crop row the apparatus is turned off otherwise the nearest earthed target may be the operator!

Wipers

Wipers allow operators to apply pesticides directly and selectively on to the target plant. Their use is restricted to where the target surface is visually obvious and readily reached. Their main use is for applying non-selective systemic herbicides e.g. glyphosate, to particular weeds above or between crop rows. The cheapness of the equipment compared to other devices, including knapsack sprayers, makes them potentially more viable. They are relatively safe to use if the concentrated chemicals are handled carefully when the apparatus is filled.

CONCLUSION

Smallholder farmers' traditional methods of pest and weed control are often most effective and economical and should be used whenever possible. However, chemical pest control methods are widely used and sometimes abused. For this reason it is imperative that whenever chemical pest control methods are proposed, discussed or used that information on the risks in using them, on personal protection measures, and on safer methods of control is provided (with training, if necessary) to the purchaser, farmer or operator. Adequate protective clothing and necessary safety equipment should not be an optional extra but should be factored into the cost of the chemical, making the effective cost of the products dearer: the cost may be higher but the price of ignoring the safety requirements may be the permanent ill-health of the operator, consumer and the environment at large.

Bill Radley
Principal, Silsoe College
Cranfield Institute of Technology

REFERENCES

Bull A. (1984) *A Growing Problem*, Oxfam

Jeyaratnam, (1990) *Journal of World Health Statistics*, No. 43

WHO/UNEP (1990) *Public Health Impact of Pesticide use in Agriculture*

Information on pesticide hazards supplied by Pesticides Trust, 23 Beehive Place, Brixton SW9, UK

Shell (1990), *Shell Agriculture Guide*, Shell International Chemical Company Ltd, Crop Protection Division, Shell Centre, London SE1 7PG

Further reading on integrated pest management and biological pest control

Allan G. and Rada A. (coordinators) (1984), *The Role of Biological Control in Pest Management*, University of Ottawa Press, Canada

Burn A.J., Coker T.H. and Jetson P.C. (eds.) (1987), *Integrated Pest Management*, Academic Press, London

DeBach P. and Rosen D., *Biological Control by Natural Enemies* (2nd Edition 1991), Cambridge University Press

Samways M.J. (1981) *Biological Control of Pests and Weeds*, Institute of Biology, Studies in Biology Series No. 132, Edward Arnold, London

PROTECTIVE CLOTHING AND EQUIPMENT

The following companies all produce a range of protective equipment for use when handling toxic chemicals. The equipment offered includes visors, goggles, safety spectacles, hard hats, dust masks, respirators (single and double filters), full-face masks (single and twin filter types), backpack respirators, waterproof clothing and gloves.

CHAPMAN & SMITH LTD
Safir Works
East Hoathly
Lewes
East Sussex BN8 6EW
UK

LURMARK LTD
Longstanton
Cambridge CB4 5DS
UK

C.H. DANA COMPANY INC.
Hyde Park
VE 05655
USA

PLUS 50
Lodge Road
Kingswood
Bristol BS15 1JX
UK
H.C. SLINGSBY PLC
Preston Street
Bradford
Yorks BD7 1JF
UK

TOTECTORS LTD
Totector House
Rushden
Northants NN10 9SW
UK

ALFA-LAVAL AGRI LTD
Oakfield
Cwmbran
Gwent NP44 7XE
Wales
UK

COOPER, PEGLER & CO LTD
Burgess Hill
West Sussex RH15 9LA
UK

E.C. GEIGER INC.
P.O. Box 285
Rt 63
Harleysville
PA 19438
USA

GRIPIT OY AB
SF-10330 Billnas
FINLAND

HOCKMAN-LEWIS LTD
200 Executive Drive
West Orange
NJ 07052
USA

3M UNITED KINGDOM
3M House
Bracknell
Berks RG12 1JU
UK

PARMELEE LTD
Middlemore Lane West
Redhouse Industrial Estate
Aldridge
W. Midlands WS9 8DZ
UK

SHELL INTERNATIONAL
Crop Protection Division
Shell Centre
London SE1 7PG
UK

Powered knapsack mistblowers and dusters

Country	Company	Tank material	Function	Tank cap. litres	Fuel tank litres	Power kW	Weight kg
Belgium	Samdow	Plastic	Mist/duster	10	1.5	2.7	*
Brazil	Jacto S.A.	Plastic	Mist/duster	13	1.3	*	12.5
Colombia	Colinagro S.A.	Plastic	Mist/duster	18	1	2.6	9.5
France	Berthoud S.A.	Plastic	Mist blower	12	1	3.7	12
Germany	Holder GmbH	Plastic	Sprayer	10	1.1	*	11.2
	Mesto Spritzenfabrik GmbH	Plastic	Mist/duster	12.5	1.25	3.2	10
Greece	Prapopoulos Bros S.A.	Plastic	Mist blower	12	1.6	2.25	15
India	Aspee	Plastic	Mist/duster	10	1.5	0.9	11.3
	Meakins Agro Products	Plastic	Mist/duster	10	2	1.3	12
	Sigma Steel Ind.	Plastic	Mist/duster	10	1	*	12.8
Italy	Carpi S.R.L.	Plastic	Mist/duster	11	1	3	11.5
	Fox Motori	Plastic	Sprayer	18	1	1	5.9
	Cifarelli S.R.L.	Plastic	Mist/duster	14	2	3.6	10.5
Japan	Hatsuta Industrial Co. Ltd	Plastic	Sprayer	20	1	1.2	9
	Hatsuta Industrial Co. Ltd	Plastic	Mist/duster	16	1.2	2.3	9.8
	Kioritz Corporation	Plastic	Sprayer	22	0.85	*	7.5
	Kioritz Corporation	Plastic	Mist/duster	13-23	0.8-1.2	*	10.8-13
Korea	Korea Farm Mach.	Plastic	Mist/duster	25	-	3.2	10.5
	Korea Farm Mach.	Plastic	Sprayer	25	-	3.2	10.5
Sri Lanka	A. Baur & Co. Ltd	Plastic	Mist/duster	10	1.25	1.3	12
Turkey	MKE	Plastic	Mist blower	13.4	1	1.9	15
UK	Cooper, Pegler & Co. Ltd	Plastic	Mist/duster	12.5	*	2.2	9.1
	Cooper, Pegler & Co. Ltd	Plastic	Sprayer	12.5	*	3	*
USA	E.C. Geiger Inc.	Plastic	Mist/duster	10	*	3.7	11
	Vandermolen Corp.	Plastic	Mist/duster	20	*	2.5	11
Yugoslavia	Morava	Plastic	Sprayer	12	*	*	10.5

*Information not supplied by manufacturer

Manual knapsack sprayers

Country	Company	Tank material		Type of sprayer[1]		Tank cap. litres	Weight kg
Argentina	Efac Pesa S.A.	Plastic	S/steel	PC	KS	3.5-20	*
	Gerhardi	-	S/steel	PC	KS	12,14,16	*
Bangladesh	Mirpur Agric. Workshop	Plastic	-	-	KS	*	5
Belgium	B.V.B.A. Samdow	Plastic	Copper	-	KS	12,16,18	*
	B.V.B.A. Samdow	Plastic	S/steel	PC	-	4,6,8,10	4.15
Brazil	Guarany S.A.	Plastic	Copper	PC	KS	22	4.8
	Jacto S.A.	Plastic	-	-	KS	20	5.7
Cameroon	Tropic	Plastic	-	-	KS	18	4.9
Chile	Parada S.A.	Plastic	Metal	PC	KS	10,20	5.7-9.7
	Wenco S.A.	Plastic	-	-	KS	20	4.6
China	Beijing Changping Sprayer	-	Steel	-	KS	16,17	4-4.6
Colombia	Colinagro S.A.	Plastic	S/steel	PC	KS	10,20,21	7-8.5
	Fumigadoras Triunfo S.A.	Plastic	Brass	-	KS	16,20	5.7-7.5
	Industrias Tequendama S.A.	*	*	-	KS	16,20	7.2
France	Berthoud	Plastic	S/steel	PC	KS	7,18	*
	Pilter	Plastic	-	PC	KS	6,8,16,20	2-4.8
Germany	Holder	Plastic	S/steel	PC	KS	5,18	1.8-5.8
	Mesto Spritzenfabrik GmbH	Plastic	Metal	PC	KS	5,18	2-5.5
Greece	Prapopoulos Bros S.A.	Plastic	Cooper	-	KS	10.5,14,21	*
Hungary	Vegyépszer	Plastic	-	PC	KS	5,14,18	1.9-5.9
India	Aspee	Plastic	Brass	-	KS	12,13,16	*
	Aspee	-	Brass	PC	-	3.5,6,9,12	*
	Asian Agrico Industries	Plastic	Brass	PC	KS	10,16	6-8
	Hindsons Pvt Ltd	Plastic	Metal	-	KS	16	*
	Kumaon Nursery	Plastic	Brass	PC	KS	8,16	*
Italy	Carpi S.P.A.	Plastic	-	-	KS	18	6
	C.M.S. Turbine	Plastic	-	-	KS	10,15,20	*
	Dal Degan	Plastic	Metal	PC	KS	4,6,8,12,18	2.4-4.5
	Di Martino	Plastic	-	PC	-	4,6,8	*
	Di Martino	Plastic	-	-	KS	12,16,22	*
Japan	Hatsuta Industrial	Plastic	-	-	KS	14.5,15,17.5,21	4.8-6.2
	Yanmar	Plastic	-	PC	KS	6,13,16	4-6.1
	Hatsuta Industrial	-	Metal	PC	-	13,17	5.1-6.8
Kenya	Hobra Manufacturing Ltd	Plastic	Brass	-	KS	15,18	5.5
Korea	Korea Farm Mech.	Plastic	-	-	KS	17	4.15
Niger	A.F.M.A.	-	S/steel	-	KS	16	*
Pakistan	Sheikh Nawaz Industries	-	S/steel	PC	KS	14,15	4.5-6
Portugal	Rocha	Plastic	Copper	PC	KS	12,13,14	1.5-7.8
Spain	Mauricio S.A.	Plastic	-	-	KS	18	*
Sri Lanka	A. Baur & Co. Ltd	Plastic	-	-	KS	5,13.75	1.4-5.5
	Agro Technica Ltd	-	S/steel	PC	KS	8-16	*
Thailand	Heng Nguan Seng Factory	-	S/steel	PC	-	8-17	3.7-13.2
UK	Cooper, Pegler & Co. Ltd	Plastic	-	PC	KS	15,20	*
	Lurmark Ltd	Plastic	-	-	KS	16,20	*
	Solo Sprayers Ltd	Plastic	S/steel	PC	KS	10,18	*
USA	Hockman-Lewis Ltd	-	S/steel Galvanized	-	KS	18.9	8
Zimbabwe	Apex Corporation	Plastic	-	-	KS	14	*
	Dunwell Products	Plastic	-	-	KS	14	4.2
	Multi-spray Systems	*	-	-	KS	*	*

*Information not supplied by manufacturer

[1] PC = Pressure cylinder; KS = Knapsac

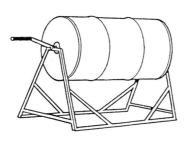

MANUAL SEED DRESSER

A steel mixing drum is supported in a frame also made of steel, with its axis horizontal. The seed and additive are loaded into and removed from the drum through a tightly fitting hatch in the side.

The drum is rotated by a hand-crank, to mix the contained seed and required additive or coating.

COBEMAG
B.P. 161
Parakou
REPUBLIC OF BENIN

RK POWDERED GRAIN PICKLE APPLICATOR

This device is used to coat cereal seeds with a powdered pesticide prior to sowing. It is fitted at the inlet of a grain auger and is driven by the exposed auger flight, thus automatically adjusting to the auger speed. It will fit augers of 100-225mm diameter and has a calibrated flow-rate adjustment. For augers with inaccessible inlets, a variant of the applicator is available to fit over a hole made in the auger casing.

LOXTON ENGINEERING WORKS PTY LTD
P.O. Box 18
Loxton
SA 5333
AUSTRALIA

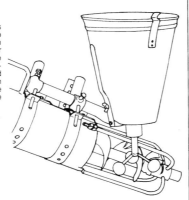

VILLAGE-SCALE SEED TREATER

The Rotostat P500 seed treater consists of a frame with a seat and pedal-operated pulley for driving the mechanism inside the treatment drum. The machine can treat a batch of up to 10kg seed in approximately 15 seconds. The treater is primarily for powder applications but a battery-powered spinning disc may be fitted internally, for the application of a liquid treatment to the seed.

ICI AGROCHEMICALS
Fernhurst
Haslemere
Surrey
GU27 3JE
UK

SLURRY SEED TREATER

This machine is designed to treat seed with a chemical in solution or suspension. An automatic seed-weighing and synchronized dumping mechanism is fitted. The paddles which agitate the slurry of seed and chemical are driven via a V-belt and pulley from a 0.75kW electric motor. The slurry tank has a capacity of 120 litres and the machine can treat 1000-1500kg of seed per hour. A double bagging-off facility is provided to allow continuous operation.

HINDSONS PVT LTD
The Lower Mall
Patiala
Punjab
147 001
INDIA

Similar seed treaters are manufactured by:

COSSUL & CO. PVT LTD
123/367 Industrial Area
Fazalgunj
Kanpur
U.P.
INDIA

ORIENTAL SCIENCE APPARATUS WORKSHOPS
Jawaharlal Nehru Marg
Ambala Cantt
Haryana
133 001
INDIA

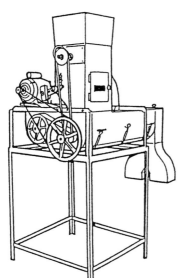

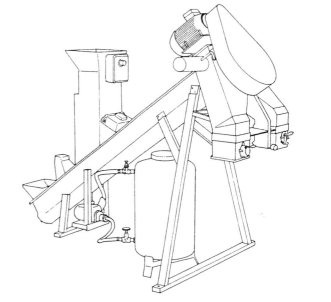

'D-1M' CHEMICAL SEED TREATER

This seed treating machine comprises an auger-type mixer into which seed and chemical can be introduced in measured quantities. The chemical can be applied in either powder or liquid form. Powder chemicals are held in the tall hopper while liquid treatments are stored in a plastic drum and fed to the seed by an electric pump. The machine has a double bagging-off spout to allow continuous operation. It is powered by a 1.3kW motor and can treat six tonnes of seed per hour.

Available from:

JUAN BUSQUETS CRUSAT S.A.
Apartado 74
Reus
SPAIN

A similar dresser is manufactured by:

ALVAN BLANCH DEVELOPMENT CO. LTD
Chelworth
Malmesbury
Wilts SN16 9SG
UK

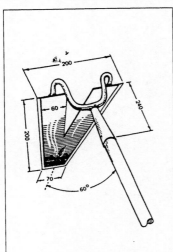

SHARMA HAND HOE

This hoe is designed for very weedy plots. The V-shaped blade cuts the weeds and moves the soil into small ridges on either side. It has a long wooden handle, a choice of three blade-widths and weighs 2.5kg. It is supplied by:

COSSUL & CO. (PVT) LTD
123/367 Industrial Area
Fazalgunj
Kanpur
U.P.
INDIA

AGRICULTURAL IMPLEMENTS
FACTORY
Welisara
Ragama
SRI LANKA

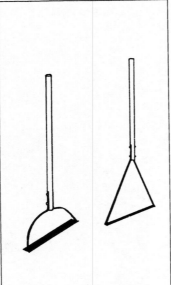

HAND WEEDERS AND BRUSH CUTTERS

This range of long-handled tools includes: plain- and serrated-edge cutters, weeding scythes, brush clearers and a root grubber. All the tools have hardwood handles.

SEYMOUR MANUFACTURING CO.
INC.
P.O. Box 248
500 North Broadway
Seymour
IN 47274
USA

MULTIHOE

The Multihoe hand tool has been designed to perform several tasks which include hoeing, weeding, earthing up plants grown in ridges and producing seed drills in small plots or vegetable gardens. The steel tool-head is attached to a 1.5m hardwood handle.
    Available from:

MULTI-PURPOSE GARDEN TOOLS
LTD
Unit 1X, Dolphin Square
Bovey Tracey
Devon TQ13 9AL
UK

KARJAT HOE

This weeder/cultivator has three arrow-headed, inclined tines and a wedge-fitted handle. The operator walks backwards, pulling the tool along in a single-pass operation, rather than using it as a push-pull tool.
    Available from:

AGRICULTURAL IMPLEMENTS
FACTORY
Welisara
Ragama
SRI LANKA

YANTRA VIDYALAYA
Agricultural Tools Research Centre
Suruchi Campus
P.O. Box 4
Bardoli
Gujarat 394 601
INDIA

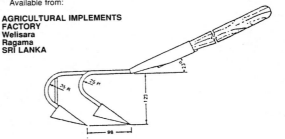

WEEDERS AND HOES

The following companies manufacture a range of hand weeders and hoes, in various sizes and supplied with or without handles. The illustration includes a selection of the range including:

- Culti-hoe;
- Hoe harrow;
- Push/pull hoe with serrated blade;
- Plough hoe;
- Weed grubber.

SAMUEL PARKES & CO. LTD
Pretoria Works
New Road
Willenhall
WV13 2BU
UK

WOLF TOOLS LTD
Ross-on-Wye
Hereford
HR9 5NE
UK

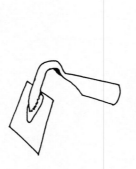

MULTILUTE

This hand tool performs several functions including weeding and seedbed preparation. The central cutter bar breaks up clods, cuts weeds and the front and rear crumbler bars smooth and level the soil. The 300mm wide steel tool-head is attached to a 1.5m hardwood handle.

MULTI-PURPOSE GARDEN TOOLS
LTD
Unit 1X, Dolphin Square
Bovey Tracey
Devon TQ13 9AL
UK

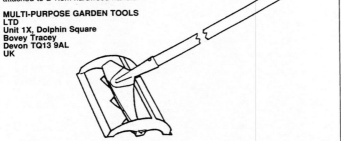

SWISS HOE

This hand weeder has a horizontal cutting blade, riveted to a frame which is mounted on the end of a 1500mm long handle. It is used with a light swinging action while the operator walks along.

AGRICULTURAL IMPLEMENTS
FACTORY
Welisara
Ragama
SRI LANKA

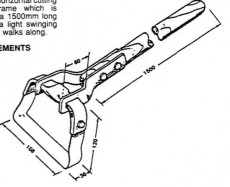

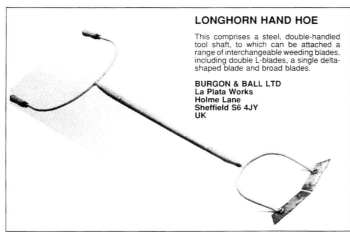

LONGHORN HAND HOE

This comprises a steel, double-handled tool shaft, to which can be attached a range of interchangeable weeding blades, including double L-blades, a single delta-shaped blade and broad blades.

BURGON & BALL LTD
La Plata Works
Holme Lane
Sheffield S6 4JY
UK

GARDEN CULTIVATOR

This is a hand-pushed cultivator with a large range of attachments including: plough, rotary pulverizers, rake, ridger, cultivators, skimmer, hoes, scarifier and aerator. The tubular steel handle is bolted to a 300mm wide cast aluminium toolbar. The toolbar is supported on a single rubber-tyred wheel, and a twin-wheel conversion is available.

JALO ENGINEERING LTD
22-24 Brook Road
Wimborne
Dorset
BH21 2BH
UK

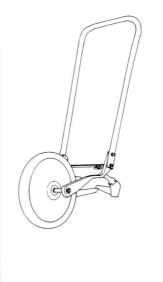

WHEELED HAND HOES

This type of implement is widely used for the weeding and inter-cultivation of row crops, using a push-pull operation. The frame and handle assembly is mounted on a single ground-wheel and a range of interchangeable tools can be fitted. For the implement illustrated, these include a V-blade hoe, a furrower, a narrow tine and a set of three spade tines. Handle height and working depth are both adjustable. It is manufactured by:

MOHINDER & CO. ALLIED
INDUSTRIES
Kurali
Rupnagar District (Ropar)
Punjab
INDIA

Similar implements, with various different blades and tines, are manufactured by:

YANTRA VIDYALAYA
Agricultural Tools Research Centre
Suruchi Campus
P.O. Box 4
Bardoli
Gujarat 394 601
INDIA

COSSUL & CO. (PVT) LTD
123/367 Industrial Area
Fazalgunj
Kanpur
U.P.
INDIA

COMILLA CO-OPERATIVE KARKHANA
LTD
Ranir Bazar
P.O. Box 12
Comilla
BANGLADESH

FORTSCHRITT LANDMASCHINEN
Berghausstraße 1
Neustadt 8355
GERMANY

SOCIÉTÉ NOUVELLE SAELEN SA
Rue Pic au Vent CRT
B.P. 359
59813 Lesquin
FRANCE

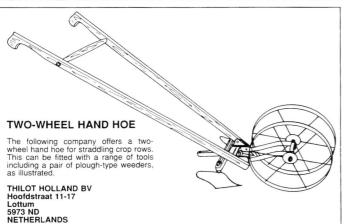

TWO-WHEEL HAND HOE

The following company offers a two-wheel hand hoe for straddling crop rows. This can be fitted with a range of tools including a pair of plough-type weeders, as illustrated.

THILOT HOLLAND BV
Hoofdstraat 11-17
Lottum
5973 ND
NETHERLANDS

'EMCOT' ROTARY WEEDING ATTACHMENT

This was designed by the Institute of Agricultural Research in Samaru, as an attachment for the commercially available 'Emcot' ridging frame. Two gangs of rotary tines are mounted on the frame to clean the sides of the furrow while the ridger share clears the base. The assembly can be pulled by pair of oxen and can achieve an output of 0.1-0.2 hectares per hour.

M/S DALTRADE (NIG) LTD
Plot 45 Chalawa Industrial Estate
P.O. Box 377
Kano
NIGERIA

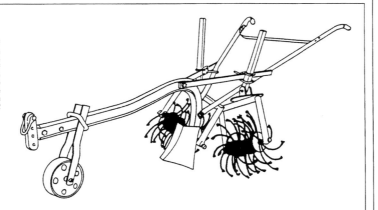

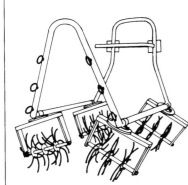

STRADDLE ROW WEEDER

This weeder has four gangs of rotary tines, mounted in a frame and angled to rotate astride a ridge. The mounting frame allows up to one metre clearance for a standing crop. A pair of oxen are required to pull the weeder, which has a seat for the operator fitted on the frame. An output of 0.2 hectares per hour can be achieved and best results are obtained when working on weeds at the 2-3 leaf stage.

M/S DALTRADE (NIG) LTD
Plot 45 Chalawa Industrial Estate
P.O. Box 377
Kano
NIGERIA

INTER-ROW BROAD-BED WEEDER

This is one of many attachments developed for the ICRISAT animal-drawn toolbar. It comprises three duckfoot sweeps positioned along the toolbar for inter-row weeding, plus a ridger fitted at each end of the bar to weed and deepen the furrows between the beds. The spacing of ridgers and sweeps are adjustable.
Available from:

ICRISAT
Patancheru P.O.
Andra Pradesh 502324
INDIA

KALE KRISHI UDYOG
S31/2/2, Hinge Khurd
Vithalwadi
Sinnagad Road
Pune 411 051
INDIA

MEKINS AGRO PRODUCTS (PVT)
LTD
6-3-866/A Begumpet
Greenlands
Hyderabad 500 016
INDIA

RIDGE PROFILE WEEDER

This weeder operates in the furrow between two ridges. A gang of rotary hoes rests on each side of the furrow and these are chain-driven from a pair of landwheels as the implement is pushed manually along the furrow. An engine-driven version is also available.

DEPARTMENT OF AGRICULTURAL ENGINEERING
Faculty of Engineering
University of Nigeria
Nsukka
NIGERIA

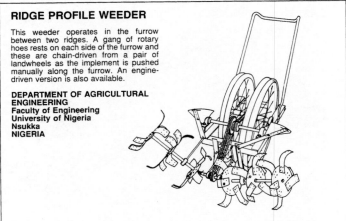

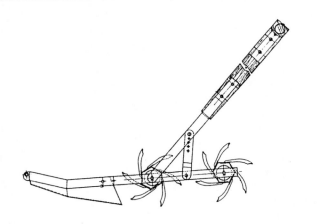

CONO-WEEDERS FOR LOWLAND RICE

This all-steel implement works to a depth of 30mm and weeds in a single-pass operation, without requiring a back-and-forth motion. It has two conical-shaped rotors mounted in tandem, with opposite orientation. Smooth and serrated blades are mounted alternately on the rotors, which provide a scuffing action when pushed along the soil. A small skid on the front of the frame provides flotation and depth control in soft, flooded paddy fields. The rotors can be offset to cope with crop row spacings of 150 to 225mm and the handle height can be adjusted.

A two-row version of the cono-weeder is also available; this has a two-position handle, enabling the tool to be used by either pushing or pulling.

Potential manufacturers can obtain technical details from:

IRRI
Agricultural Engineering Department
P.O. Box 933
Manila
PHILIPPINES

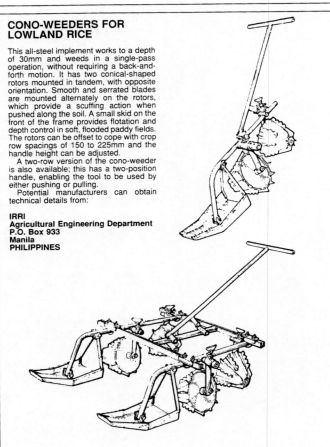

HAND-PUSHED RICE WEEDER

This simple weeder is used for weeding lowland rice planted in rows. Two spiked wheels rotate in a supporting frame, the front of which forms a skid; it also provides depth control for the wheels. When the implement is pushed between rows, the spikes press the weeds under the soil. The two wheels and the skid are made of light sheet metal and the handle is made of wood. The assembly can be dismantled for cleaning and repair. Technical details are available for potential manufacturers.
Available from:

IRRI
Agricultural Engineering Department
P.O. Box 933
Manila
PHILIPPINES

ALPHA MACHINERY & ENGINEERING CORPORATION
1167 Pasong Tamo Street
Makati
P.O. Box 579 MCC
Metro Manila
PHILIPPINES

Rice weeders of similar design are supplied by:

COMILLA CO-OPERATIVE KARKHANA LTD
Ranir Bazar
P.O. Box 12
Comilla
BANGLADESH

COMILLA MODERN MANUFACTURING
Deshawalli Patty
Rajgonj
Comilla
BANGLADESH

RADHARANI MANUFACTURING
Deshawalli Patty
Rajgonj
Comilla
BANGLADESH

COSSUL & CO. PVT LTD
123/367 Industrial Area
Fazalgunj
Kanpur
U.P.
INDIA

KUMAON NURSERY
Ramnagar
Nainital
U.P. 244 715
INDIA

CECOCO
P.O. Box 8
Ibaraki City
Osaka 567
JAPAN

FARM MECHANISATION RESEARCH CENTRE
Maha Illuppallama
SRI LANKA

A.F.M.A.
B.P. 11
619 Niamey
REPUBLIC OF NIGER

CULTIVATOR

This is fitted with a 2.6kW petrol engine mounted at the top of the frame in order to keep it clear of the water in rice fields. The engine provides 120-180 rev/min. shaft drive via a reduction gearbox to a variety of implements which include: four-disc rotary hoe, rotary cultivator and puddling wheels. The weight of the engine is taken on a single wheel or skid at the end of a rear stay.

KOREA FARM MACHINE & TOOL IND. CO-OP.
11-11 Dongja-Dong
Youngsan-Gu
Seoul
KOREA

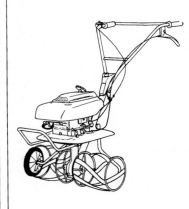

MIO 200 POWER TILLER

This lightweight tiller is powered by an air-cooled, four-stroke petrol engine rated at 1.3kW. It can be fitted with cultivator tines, spiral weeding rotors, pneumatic-tyred or steel paddle wheels.
Weight 30kg.

METALSKA INDUSTRIJA OSIJEK
Vukovarska 219a
Osijek
54000
YUGOSLAVIA

A similar tiller is manufactured by:

AL-KO BRITAIN LTD
Number One Industrial Estate
Medomsley Road
Consett
Co. Durham DH8 6SZ
UK

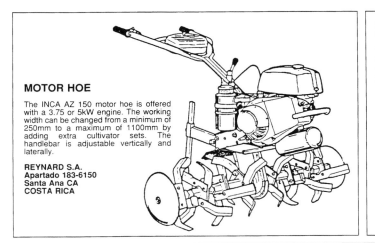

MOTOR HOE

The INCA AZ 150 motor hoe is offered with a 3.75 or 5kW engine. The working width can be changed from a minimum of 250mm to a maximum of 1100mm by adding extra cultivator sets. The handlebar is adjustable vertically and laterally.

REYNARD S.A.
Apartado 183-6150
Santa Ana CA
COSTA RICA

SELF-POWERED CULTIVATOR

This is a 2.6kW petrol engine powered cultivator. The engine and handlebar assembly can be transferred from the cultivator to a grass mower. A set of wheels can be fitted to replace the cultivator tines and the unit used as a lightweight walking tractor.

ROBIX MEZÖGAZDASÁGI
GÉPGYÁRTÓ VÁLLALAT
Pf.210
Viola u. 12
Veszprem 8201
HUNGARY

A similar cultivator is manufactured by:

AGROMACHINA
Russe
BULGARIA

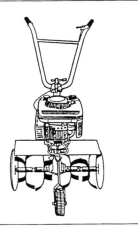

POWER HOES

The motor hoe illustrated is powered by a 2.6kW four-stroke Tecumseh petrol engine. It has a working width adjustable from 350mm to 600mm.

GEBR. HOLDER GmbH & CO.
Stuttgarter Strasse 42-46
Postfach 1555
D-7430 Metzingen
GERMANY

Similar hoes are manufactured by:

BRUMITAL SPA INDUSTRIA
MACCHINE AGR
Zona Industriale
2a Strada
Catania 95030
ITALY

ISHAKAWAJIMA-SHIBAURA
MACHINERY CO.
5-32-7 Sendagaya
Shibuya-ku
Tokyo
JAPAN

YANMAR AGRICULTURAL
EQUIPMENT CO. LTD
1-32, Chayamachi
Kita-ku
Osaka 530
JAPAN

SINGLE-WHEEL MOTOR HOE

The Agria 3100 motor hoe can be fitted with a two- or four-stroke engine. It has a two speed gearbox. A range of tiller attachments is available, giving working widths from 100mm to 500mm. The handlebar is adjustable laterally and vertically which allows an operator to walk behind and to one side of the machine, thus avoiding re-compaction of the ground just worked.
Weight 47kg.

AGRIA-WERKE GmbH
Postfach 1147
D-7108 Moeckmuehl
GERMANY

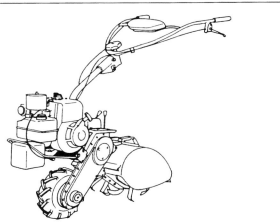

FLAME WEEDERS

BUTANE BURNERS
This range of butane burners includes the following models:

Muguet and Crocus
Knapsack models, each with a hand-held burner lance and with 3kg and 13kg fuel bottles respectively. They are suitable for vineyards, orchards and small-scale horticulture.

Primevere
This weeder is mounted on a three-wheeled steerable frame, suitable for inter-row weeding.

Iris
This is tractor-mounted weeder, with a row of five individually shrouded burners and two 35kg fuel bottles.

Myosotis
This is also tractor-mounted, and has four burners and two 35kg fuel bottles.

Narcisse
Tractor-mounted, the weeder is fitted with two 25kg bottles, and four shrouded blocks of burners which can be adjusted to suit different row spacings.

ETS LEBLANC
Chemin du Gravier
Onzain 41150
FRANCE

PROPANE 'PHYTOFLAME' BURNERS
These flame weeders can be used as pre-emergence weeders, killing the weed seedlings by an intense light-flash rather than by physically burning them. Two models are available:

Manual model
Wheelbarrow-mounted, with double burner, 20-metre hose and two 13kg fuel bottles.

Tractor-mounted model
This has a working width of 1.6-3.0 metres and carries five to eight 13kg bottles or three 30kg bottles. Up to eight double burner units can be used, with adjustable working height, angle and spacing.

U.F.A.B.
B.P. 58
Chateaubriant 44110
FRANCE

PROPANE INFRA-RED WEEDERS
The following company offers a range of flame weeders, including the following examples:

AD-HB25
Four hand-held models with working widths of 150-600mm.

AD-PV60/PV90
Two models, each mounted on a two-wheeled chassis, with up to three 300mm-wide burners and a working width of 300-900mm.
Operating pressure 1.5 bar.
Operating temperature 900°C.

AD-LB
A range of three tractor-mounted models, with working widths of 1.6, 3.2 and 4.5 metres respectively.
Operating pressure 0-3 bar.
Operating temperature 1000°C.
Working speed 4-6 km/hour.

AGRODYNAMIC
Balsemienlaan 238
Den Haag 2555 RH
NETHERLANDS

Also available from:

STÉ CERIMON
B.P. 11
Moncoutant 79320
FRANCE

Propane-fuelled flame weeders are also available from the following two companies, whose product ranges include hand-held and tractor-mounted models.

CATTER/BORST B.V.
Industrie en Handelmij
B.P. 92
Apeldoorn 7300 AB
NETHERLANDS

BIOFARM
Genossenschaft
Kleindietwil be 4936
SWITZERLAND

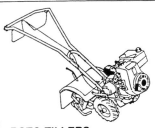

ROTO-TILLERS

A range of six front-wheel-driven rotovators with tilling widths from 360mm to 510mm. The smallest has a 2.25kW engine and the largest 6kW.

TROY-BILT MANUFACTURING CO.
102nd Street & 9th Avenue
Troy
NY 12180
USA

HAND-HELD ROPE-WICK WEED WIPERS

This is used for the direct wiping of weeds with herbicide. It comprises a nylon braided rope, fed by a herbicide reservoir in the tubular handle. Herbicide flow is controlled by tightening the compression-joint nuts retaining the wick.

The weeds should be at least 150mm taller than the crop and, for best results, both sides of the weed leaf should be treated, by using a back-and-forth sweeping motion. A scarlet dye is available as an admix, to identify treated foliage.

Variations on the basic wiper include:
● Single- and double-headed versions;
● Normal or fast flow wicks;
● Head angled at either 90 or 45 degrees to the handle.

HORTICHEM LTD
14 Edison Road
Churchfields Industrial Estate
Salisbury
Wilts SP2 7NU
UK

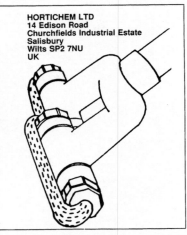

WEED WAND

This hand-held 'weed wand' is shaped like a hockey stick. The herbicide is supplied from a container in the handle to the wettable material fixed to the blade. It is available from:

DONAGHYS INDUSTRIES LTD
Private Bag
123 Crawford Street
Dunedin
NEW ZEALAND

WHEEL-MOUNTED WEED WIPER

This is a wheel-mounted, multi-wick wiper, with the wicks threaded in and out of the wiper bar. It is hand-pushed, using a T-handle fitted with a herbicide flow-control button. The standard 1m long wiper bar can be interchanged with 450mm or 600mm bars for inter-row weeding.

HORTICHEM LTD
14 Edison Road
Churchfields Industrial Estate
Salisbury
Wilts SP2 7NU
UK

ROPE-WICK WIPER FOR FURROWS

A prototype rope-wick weed-wiper has been developed by the following institute, for use with ridge-grown crops. The application head houses a foam wick shaped to follow the contours of a 900mm wide furrow between the ridges. The 600ml herbicide reservoir also serves as a handle.
Application rate 3 litre/ha at 1.5m/sec.

INSTITUTE FOR AGRICULTURAL RESEARCH
Samaru
P.O. Box 1044
Zaria
NIGERIA

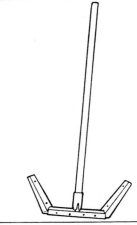

HAND-HELD GRANULE APPLICATOR

This gravity-fed implement is used to apply small, measured doses of granular chemicals to individual plants. Pre-calibrated doses of 0.1 - 1.0g can be applied, through a choice of outlets including pipes, spouts and shields. The metre long handle also serves as a 1 litre granule reservoir and is fitted with a thumb-operated release trigger.
Available from:

HORSTINE FARMERY LTD
North Newbald
Yorks YO4 3SP
UK

'MICROSPREAD' HAND-HELD GRANULE APPLICATOR

This device has been designed to provide a means of spot application for any granular insecticide, nematicide or herbicide where localized treatment is required. Delivery of up to 50g per shot can be set using interchangeable metering units. The 10kg capacity hopper is shoulder mounted and continuously feeds the hand-held metering unit. Also available is the 'Microflow' hand-held unit for applying granular pesticides on a continuous flow basis. This unit can apply granules in a narrow band or in a strip up to half a metre wide.

HORSTINE FARMERY LTD
North Newbald
Yorks
YO4 3SP
UK

GRANULE APPLICATOR

This hand-held applicator comprises a hopper with a manually-cranked, spinning-disc broadcaster. It is made from high-impact polypropylene with nylon gears and the outlet aperture is adjustable to suit different granule sizes and application rates. A separate filling funnel is provided.
Hopper capacity 5 litres (2-8kg granules);
Discharge rate 0-2kg/min;
Granule size range 0.5-5.0mm;
Maximum throw 3-4m (to left of operator).

HORTICHEM LTD
14 Edison Road
Churchfields Industrial Estate
Salisbury
Wilts SP2 7NU
UK

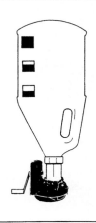

SHOULDER-SLUNG GRANULE APPLICATOR

This spinning-disc type applicator is suitable for any kind of chemical in granular form, and also for seed broadcasting and fertilizer spreading. It has a twelve-blade impeller which disperses the granules in a 1.0 to 1.5 metre band, at a distance of up to 3 metres from the operator. The 8-litre tank has a transparent lid.

HATSUTA INDUSTRIAL CO. LTD
4-39, 1-Chome
Chifune
Nishiyodogawa-ku
Osaka
JAPAN

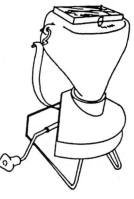

HAND-HELD ROTARY DUSTERS

Various manufacturers produce hand-held rotary dusters. These are all similar and have 4kg hopper capacities, discharge rates of 0-0.6kg/min, and ranges of approximately 2.5m.

CECOCO
P.O. Box 8
Ibaraki City
Osaka 567
JAPAN

B.V.B.A. SAMDOW
9910 Mariakerke
Ghent-Ghant
BELGIUM

KIORITZ CORPORATION
7-2, Suehirocho 1-chome
Ohme
Tokyo 198
JAPAN

HATSUTA INDUSTRIAL CO. LTD
4-39, 1-Chome,
Chifune
Nishiyodogawa-ku
Osaka
JAPAN

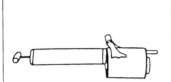

CHAPIN HAND-DUSTERS

A range of hand-held, piston-type dusters with extension tubes, and with capacities from 0.4 to 2.0 litres, is supplied by:

HOCKMAN-LEWIS LTD
200 Executive Drive
West Orange
NJ 07052
USA

ONYX HAND BLOWER

This hand-operated bellows has a capacity of 1100cc and is equally suited to plant and animal insecticide treatments.
    It is manufactured by:

BERTHOUD S.A.
48 Rue Victor Hugo
B.P. 193
Belleville Cedex 69823
FRANCE

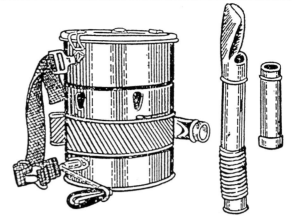

HAND ROTARY DUSTERS

These spinning-disc dust applicators are worn at the operator's waist and supported by a neck strap. They are hand-cranked and the flexible discharge hose is hand-held.

'ASPEE JUBILEE'
This duster is suitable for both powders and granules. It has a 6-litre, aluminium hopper and a polyethylene hose and spout.
    Available from:

AMERICAN SPRING & PRESSING WORKS LTD
P.O. Box 7602
B.J. Patel Road
Malad
Bombay 400 064
INDIA

KRUSHI DUSTER
This is very similar to the 'Aspee Jubilee' above and is supplied by:

ASIAN AGRICO INDUSTRIES
P.O. Box 29
Gandevi Road
Bilimora (W-Rly)
Gujarat 396 321
INDIA

GOLDEN DUSTER
This is another similar duster, available from:

HATSUTA INDUSTRIAL CO. LTD
4-39, 1-Chome,
Chifune
Nishiyodogawa-ku
Osaka
JAPAN

DUSTER
This weighs 5.5kg when empty and holds 6kg of pesticide powder. Available from:

PULVERIZADORES AGRICOLAS PARADA S.A.
Alvarez de Toledo 718
Casilla 2984
Santiago
CHILE

BELLOW-TYPE DUSTERS

This lightweight duster uses a hand-operated bellows to disperse the powder. It is carried on a shoulder strap.

YANTRA VIDYALAYA
Agricultural Tools Research Centre
Suruchi Campus
P.O. Box 4
Bardoli
Gujarat 394 601
INDIA

Similar hand-operated, bellow-type dusters are manufactured by:

COOPER, PEGLER & CO. LTD
Burgess Hill
West Sussex
RH15 9LA
UK

DI MARTINO GIUSEPPE S.R.L.
Via Pavane, 1
Mussolente 36065
ITALY

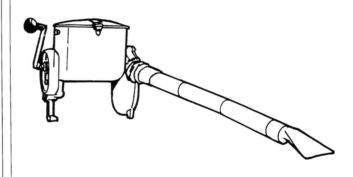

NECK-SLUNG HAND ROTARY DUSTERS

MORAVA 'MRZ-14' DUSTER
The hand-cranked duster illustrated has a manually operated, axial-flow ventilator fan. It can be supplied with a polyethylene or aluminium alloy hopper and the discharge hose is attached by a flexible coupling to enable it to be directed manually. The discharge rate and swath width are variable.
Weight (empty) 6.2kg.
Hopper capacity 14 litres.
Maximum swath width 5m.

DP FABRIKE MAŠINA - 'MORAVA'
Dure Dakovića bb
12000 Požarevac
YUGOSLAVIA

'SAMDOW K5' DUSTER
This duster is very similar to the model illustrated but it has an extendible discharge hose and an optional double outlet spout. It is supplied by:

B.V.B.A. SAMDOW
9910 Mariakerke
Ghent-Ghant
BELGIUM

The following company supplies a similar duster, with a spiral agitator to maintain the flow of dust from the hopper.

HOCKMAN-LEWIS LTD
200 Executive Drive
West Orange
NJ 07052
USA

A similar duster is also supplied by:

HATSUTA INDUSTRIAL CO. LTD
4-39, 1-Chome
Chifune
Nishiyodogawa-ku
Osaka
JAPAN

YELLOW DUSTER

This knapsack duster has a hand-lever mounted on the left-hand side which operates the bellows via a linkage. It has a 10-litre polythene tank which incorporates a mixing device to ensure an even flow of the chemical to the outlet. Air output is 5dm^3 at 6ms^{-1} per stroke. Weight 4.5kg.

BERTHOUD S.A.
48 Rue Victor Hugo
B.P. 193
Belleville Cedex 69823
FRANCE

A similar duster is manufactured by:

CARPI S.R.L.
Via Romana, 90
42028 Poviglio (RE)
ITALY

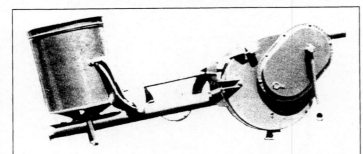

SHOULDER-CARRIED HAND-OPERATED ROTARY DUSTERS

This type of hand-cranked duster can be used for all kinds of powders and dusts. The hopper is separated from the cranking mechanism and carried behind the elbow; this is to improve the balance of the duster when carried on the shoulder strap.

'SIGMA' DUSTER
This has a galvanized steel, 7-litre hopper and lance. The fan casing and impeller are made of mild steel. Weight 7kg.

SIGMA STEEL INDUSTRIES (REGD)
A-2, Industrial Estate
Ludhiana 141003
Punjab
INDIA

'ORIENT' HAND ROTARY DUSTER
This is a similar duster, fitted with a breast-plate for comfortable operation. It is supplied with a flexible hose coupling, metal lance spreader nozzle and adjustable shoulder strap.

AMERICAN SPRING & PRESSING WORKS LTD
P.O. Box 7602
B.J. Patel Road
Malad
Bombay 400 064
INDIA

KRUSHI ROTARY DUSTER
This is very similar to the 'Orient' model, and is supplied by:

ASIAN AGRICO INDUSTRIES
P.O. Box 29
Gandevi Road
Bilimora (W-Rly)
Gujarat 396 321
INDIA

Another duster of similar design, with a 5kg hopper capacity, is available from:

KUMAON NURSERY
Ramnagar
Nainital
U.P. 244 715
INDIA

HAND-OPERATED CENTRIFUGAL SPREADERS

LITTLE GIANT X2A
In this spinning-disc device, dust or granular material is broadcast from a polyethylene hopper carried on the operator's shoulder. The distributor disc is spun by manual rotation of a handle at waist height. Distribution width is 1.2-2.4m and the hopper capacity is 9-13kg.

BROADCASTER
A similar but larger centrifugal-type broadcaster is offered by the company. It can be adjusted to provide granule dispersal either centrally or to the left or right of the operator's path, and with up to 6m throw. Weight 3kg.

SOCIÉTÉ NOUVELLE SAELEN S.A.
Rue Pic au vent CRT
B.P. 359
59813 Lesquin Cedex
FRANCE

TRACTOR-MOUNTED DUSTER

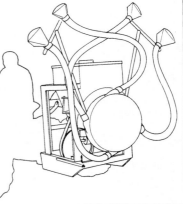

This was designed primarily for vineyards and fruit farms and the four nozzles can be positioned for horizontal discharge of the powder to either side of the tractor.
Hopper capacity of 60kg.
Power requirement: 6kW.
Available from:

PULVERIZADORES AGRICOLAS PARADA S.A.
Alvarez de Toledo 718
Casilla 2984
Santiago
CHILE

POWER DUSTERS

This range of powered knapsack-type dusters is fitted with 35-40cc single cylinder two-stroke air-cooled petrol engines. An optional multi-outlet boom attachment is available: the free end of this is carried by a second operator.
Available from:

KIORITZ CORPORATION
7-2, Suehirocho 1-chome
Ohme
Tokyo 198
JAPAN

Powered knapsack-type dusters are also supplied by:

BUFFALO TURBINE AGRICULTURAL EQUIPMENT CO. INC.
P.O. Box 150
Gowanda
NY 14070
USA

YANMAR AGRICULTURAL EQUIPMENT CO. LTD
1-32, Chayamachi
Kita-ku
Osaka 530
JAPAN

HATSUTA INDUSTRIAL CO. LTD
4-39, 1-Chome
Chifune
Nishiyodogawa-ku
Osaka
JAPAN

A knapsack-type fogger, suitable for both powders and liquid chemicals, and powered by a 4kW motor, is supplied by:

B.V.B.A. SAMDOW
9910 Mariakerke
Ghent-Ghant
BELGIUM

POWER KNAPSACK COMBINED DUSTERS AND MIST BLOWERS

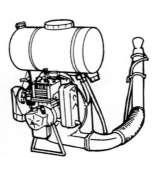

SPRAYMIST
Although primarily designed as a sprayer, this knapsack-type unit is supplied with dusting accessories as standard. An optional attachment is also available for ULV spraying. The unit has a 10-litre (10kg) tank and is powered by a 35cc, two-stroke, air-cooled engine with rope start. The discharge capacity is 0.5-2.0 litre/min for liquid sprays and 0.7-2.0kg/min for dusts.
Available from:

MEKINS AGRO PRODUCTS (PVT) LTD
6-3-866/A Begumpet
Greenlands
Hyderabad 500 016
INDIA

'JUNG ANG' DUST AND MIST BLOWER
This backpack-type blower is fitted with a 4kW, two-stroke, air-cooled engine and a 17-litre chemical tank. It weighs 11.5kg and has a discharge capacity of 5kg/min for dusts and 3.5 litre/min for sprays.

Available from:

KOREA FARM MACHINERY & TOOL INDUSTRY CO-OPERATIVE
11-11 Dongja-Dong
Youngsan-Gu
Seoul
KOREA

Engine-powered, combined powder and mist applicators are also available from the following companies:

INDÚSTRIA E COMÉRCIO GUARANY S.A.
Av. Impératriz Léopoldina 112
B.P. 4951
São Paulo, SP 05305
BRAZIL

COOPER, PEGLER & CO. LTD
Burgess Hill
West Sussex
RH15 9LA
UK

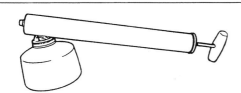

ATOMIZERS

These piston-action hand sprayers are available with either intermittent or continuous action. They are suitable for agricultural use and also commonly for the disinfestation of buildings.

Brass, copper and plastic atomizers of 0.5 to 1.0 litre capacity are available from:

COLINAGRO S.A.
P.O. Box 4671
Bogotá
COLOMBIA

MESTO SPRITZENFABRIK GmbH
Postfach 1154
Ludwigsberger Strasse 71
7149 Freiberg/Neckar
GERMANY

HOCKMAN-LEWIS LTD
200 Executive Drive
West Orange
NJ 07052
USA

TRIGGER-OPERATED AND HAND COMPRESSION SPRAYERS

These small, hand-held sprayers are suitable for the treatment of individual plants or very small plots. They are usually made of plastic or brass, with a calibrated reservoir of 1-1.5 litres capacity. The spray can be gradually adjusted from a fine mist to a continuous jet, by twisting the nozzle. In the simplest type, the liquid is pumped out directly, by trigger action. In other types, the reservoir is first pressurized using a plunger.

Available from:

MESTO SPRITZENFABRIK GmbH
Postfach 1154
Ludwigsberger Strasse 71
7149 Freiberg/Neckar
GERMANY

ASIAN AGRICO INDUSTRIES
P.O. Box 29
Gandevi Road
Bilimora (W-Rly)
Gujarat 396 321
INDIA

KAIVAL AGRO PRODUCTS
119-D, G.I.D.C.
Vitthal Udyognagar
Gujarat 388 121
INDIA

SIGMA STEEL INDUSTRIES (REGD)
A-2, Industrial Estate
Ludhiana
Punjab 141 003
INDIA

AMERICAN SPRING & PRESSING WORKS LTD
P.O. Box 7602
B.J. Patel Road
Malad
Bombay 400 064
INDIA

DI MARTINO GIUSEPPE S.R.L.
Via Pavane, 1
Mussolente 36065
ITALY

SOLO SPRAYERS LTD
Solo Works
4 Brunel Road
Progress Road
Leigh-on-Sea
Essex SS9 5JN
UK

E.C. GEIGER, INC.
P.O. Box 285
Rt 63
Harleysville
PA 19438-0332
USA

EFAC PESA S.A.
Gregorio De Laferrere 3210/12
Buenos Aires 1406
ARGENTINA

BERTHOUD S.A.
48 Rue Victor Hugo
B.P. 193
Belleville Cedex 69823
FRANCE

HOSE END SPRAYER

This trigger-operated sprayer is supplied with a hose-end fitting for attachment to a mains water supply. This enables the reservoir to be filled with a concentrated solution, which is then diluted with water from the hose.

HOCKMAN-LEWIS LTD
200 Executive Drive
West Orange
NJ 07052
USA

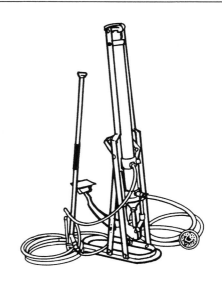

PEDAL-OPERATED SPRAYER

The cylinder of this sprayer is pumped by a double-spring, foot pedal in the manner of a tyre pressure pump. It is easier to use if one person operates the foot pedal while another holds and directs the spray lance. The sprayer is supplied with hoses, lance and nozzle but without the spray container.

ASIAN AGRICO INDUSTRIES
P.O. Box 29
Gandevi Road
Bilimora (W-Rly)
Gujarat 396 321
INDIA

KUMAON NURSERY
Ramnagar
Nainital
U.P. 244 715
INDIA

SIGMA STEEL INDUSTRIES (REGD)
A-2, Industrial Estate
Ludhiana 141003
Punjab
INDIA

KAIVAL AGRO PRODUCTS
119-D, G.I.D.C.
Vitthal Udyognagar 388 121
Gujarat
INDIA

LEVER-OPERATED SPRAYERS

ROCKER SPRAYER
This sprayer is mounted on a small platform on which the operator stands while rocking a long hand lever in a 'push-pull' action. The suction hose is placed in the spray container (not provided) and an eight-metre discharge hose connects to the spraying lance.

ASIAN AGRICO INDUSTRIES
P.O. Box 29
Gandevi Road
Bilimora (W-Rly)
Gujarat 396 321
INDIA

KUMAON NURSERY
Ramnagar
Nainital
U.P. 244 715
INDIA

SIGMA STEEL INDUSTRIES (REGD)
A-2, Industrial Estate
Ludhiana 141001
Punjab
INDIA

KAIVAL AGRO PRODUCTS
119-D, G.I.D.C.
Vitthal Udyognagar 388 121
Gujarat
INDIA

AMERICAN SPRING & PRESSING WORKS LTD
P.O. Box 7602
B.J. Patel Road
Malad
Bombay 400 064
INDIA

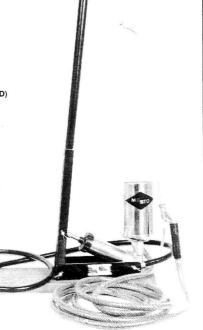

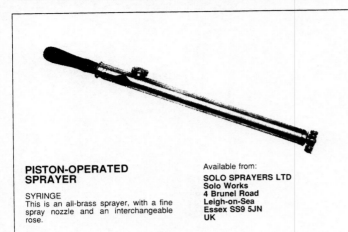

PISTON-OPERATED SPRAYER

SYRINGE
This is an all-brass sprayer, with a fine spray nozzle and an interchangeable rose.

Available from:
SOLO SPRAYERS LTD
Solo Works
4 Brunel Road
Leigh-on-Sea
Essex SS9 5JN
UK

STIRRUP PUMP SPRAYERS

Single- and double-barrel pump units are available for insertion in the spray container (not supplied). Both types are made of brass, and each is supplied with a hose, lance and spray nozzle. An extra-long hose is also available.

ASIAN AGRICO INDUSTRIES
P.O. Box 29
Gandevi Road
Bilimora (W-Rly)
Gujarat 396 321
INDIA

Single-barrel stirrup pump sprayers are also supplied by:

KUMAON NURSERY
Ramnagar
Nainital
U.P. 244 715
INDIA

SIGMA STEEL INDUSTRIES (REGD)
A-2, Industrial Estate
Ludhiana 141003
Punjab
INDIA

AMERICAN SPRING & PRESSING
WORKS LTD
P.O. Box 7602
B.J. Patel Road
Malad
Bombay 400 064
INDIA

A double-barrel pump sprayer, with a 4-metre hose, is also supplied by:

DUNWELL PRODUCTS
P.O. Box 8543
Belmont
Bulawayo
ZIMBABWE

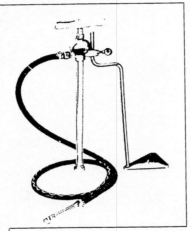

SLIDE-ACTION SPRAYERS

These have a sliding-action pumping and spraying lance and a flexible hose for insertion into a suitable receptacle, which is sometimes supplied with the sprayer.
Suppliers include:

FUMIGADORAS TRIUNFO S.A.
Apartado 4045
Cali
COLOMBIA

AMERICAN SPRING & PRESSING
WORKS LTD
P.O. Box 7602
ASPEE House
B.J. Patel Road
Malad
Bombay 400 064
INDIA

HOBRA MANUFACTURING LTD
P.O. Box 43340
Nairobi
KENYA

SOLO SPRAYERS LTD
Solo Works
4 Brunel Road
Progress Road
Leigh-on-Sea
Essex SS9 5JN
UK

HOCKMAN-LEWIS LTD
200 Executive Drive
West Orange
NJ 07052
USA

DI MARTINO GIUSEPPE S.R.L.
Via Pavane, 1
Mussolente 36065
ITALY

B.V.B.A. SAMDOW
9910 Mariakerke
Ghent-Ghant
BELGIUM

BERTHOUD S.A.
48 Rue Victor Hugo
B.P. 193
Belleville Cedex 69823
FRANCE

WHEELBARROW-MOUNTED, MOTORIZED OR MANUAL SPRAYER

This barrow-mounted sprayer with a stainless-steel tank and a single wheel can be supplied with an engine-powered pump or hand pump operated with a lever arm fitted above the tank. The spray boom is made in two sections with six nozzles on each; these sections can be positioned vertically for treating tree crops (and for transport) or horizontally for spraying ground crops.
Weight 36kg.

CARPI S.R.L.
42028 Poviglio
Reggio Emilia
ITALY

GROUNDSMAN UNIT

This unit comprises a two-wheel trolley fitted with a Falcon 16-litre pressure cylinder sprayer and a four nozzle spray boom. The unit is also fitted with a spray lance and three metres of hose, thus increasing the number of tasks that the unit can perform.

COOPER, PEGLER & CO. LTD
Burgess Hill
West Sussex RH15 9LA
UK

ANIMAL-DRAWN SPRAYERS

HORSE-DRAWN SPRAYER
This sprayer is mounted on a purpose-built, pneumatic-tyred animal cart. It is powered by a 4kW engine and has a 400-litre spray tank. A larger model is also available, with a 10.5kW engine and a 600-litre tank.

FABRIZIO LEVERA
Casilla 42, Isla de Maipo
CHILE

A similar horse-drawn, powered sprayer is supplied by:

PULVERIZADORES AGRICOLAS
PARADA S.A.
Casilla 2984, Santiago
CHILE

PACK HORSE SPRAYER

This is a hand-pumped, compression sprayer, with two 30-litre galvanized steel tanks mounted on a framework and carried by a pack animal.
Weight 89kg.

FUMIGADORAS TRIUNFO S.A.
Apartado 4045
Cali
COLOMBIA

SPRAY SHIELDS

These shields are designed to be mounted on the ends of spray lances and restrict the area sprayed to that covered by the shield. Shields of this type usually have integral spray nozzles and allow the use of broad spectrum herbicides to be used for spot weeding in a standing crop. It must be noted, however, that any contact between the wetted leaves of a weed and the crop plant may cause damage to the crop.

COOPER, PEGLER & CO. LTD
Burgess Hill
West Sussex
RH15 9LA
UK

P.E.S.A. S.A.
Gregorio De Laferrere 3210-12
1406 Buenos Aires
ARGENTINA

HOCKMAN-LEWIS LTD
200 Executive Drive
West Orange
NJ 07052
USA

SOLO SPRAYERS LTD
Solo Works
4 Brunel Road
Progress Road
Leigh-on-Sea
Essex SS9 5JN
UK

TREE GUARDS

These are for spraying herbicide to treat weeds growing in competition with small saplings. They can be attached to a standard lance and comprise a shield fitted with two or more nozzles which spray around the outside of the shield. The model illustrated is made from glass fibre has a spray width of 1.2m and is supplied by:

COOPER, PEGLER & CO. LTD
Burgess Hill
Sussex
RH15 9LA
UK

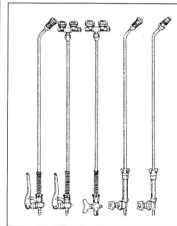

SPRAY LANCES

Most manufacturers provide a wide range of spray lances and triggers or other hand-operated cut-off devices.

Lances range in length from about 600mm up to 3m, these longer implements designed for use in tree crops. Increased health hazards caused by the discharge of toxic chemicals at height may require extra precautions to be taken.

Spray lances can be fitted with a variety of cut-off devices including trigger valves, stopcocks and screw taps. It is usually possible to change nozzles to suit the task being undertaken.

Suppliers include:

MULTI-SPRAY SYSTEMS
P.O. Box HG 570
Highlands
Harare
ZIMBABWE

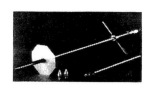

ROOT FEEDER

The following company produces a root feeding attachment for use with a heavy duty spray gun and power sprayer. The pointed injector is fitted with a depth control plate and a T-bar handle.

E.C.GEIGER, INC.
P.O. Box 285
Rt 63
Harleysville
PA 19438
USA

THE SIGMA STEEL INDUSTRIES
(REGD)
A-2 Industrial Estate
Ludhiana
141003
INDIA

COOPER, PEGLER & CO. LTD
Burgess Hill
West Sussex
RH15 9LA
UK

AMERICAN SPRING & PRESSING
WORKS LTD
P.O. Box 7602
B.J. Patel Road
Malad
Bombay 400 064
INDIA

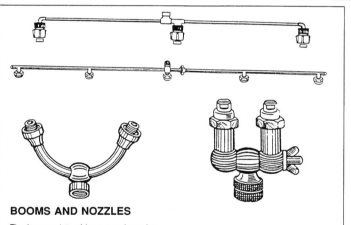

BOOMS AND NOZZLES

The large variety of booms and nozzles supplied by many manufacturers of knapsack sprayers reflects the range of chemicals used and the crops to which they are applied. Illustrated above are a 1.5m five nozzle boom manufactured by American Spring and a 900mm three nozzle boom from Cooper, Pegler.

Two types of double nozzle are also illustrated.

AMERICAN SPRING & PRESSING
WORKS LTD
P.O. Box 7602
B.J. Patel Road
Malad
Bombay 400 064
INDIA

COOPER, PEGLER & CO. LTD
Burgess Hill
Sussex RH15 9LA
UK

P.E.S.A. S.A.
Gregorio De Laferrere 3210-12
1406
Buenos Aires
ARGENTINA

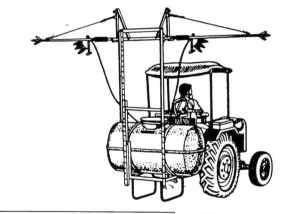

POWER SPRAYER

The Sigma power sprayer comprises a horizontal piston pump and a petrol engine or electric motor mounted on a steel frame. The frame can be provided with wheels or carrying handles (illustrated). The pumps available include single, double or triple cylinder versions and engines of appropriate power are provided to drive them.

The pumps are fitted with a 3m suction hose and a 15m delivery hose which can be coupled to a lance or spray gun.

THE SIGMA STEEL INDUSTRIES
(REGD)
A-2 Industrial Estate
Ludhiana
141003
INDIA

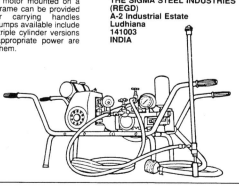

ASPEE 'TRACTORMOUNT' SPRAYER

The sprayer carries 400 litres of chemical in a glass fibre tank or in two steel drums mounted on a steel frame fitted with a standard three-point hitch. The spray pump is driven from the tractor power take-off and can also be used to fill the tank. The version illustrated is fitted with an overhead spray boom for treating tall crops grown in rows. The spray can cover two swaths of 9m to either side. A 2.5m wide path must be provided in the crop every 18m to allow the tractor to pass.

AMERICAN SPRING & PRESSING
WORKS LTD
P.O. Box 7602
Malad
Bombay
400 064
INDIA

CONTROLLED DROPLET APPLICATION

Controlled Droplet Application (CDA) sprayers are all similar in operation and are usually powered by dry-cell or rechargeable batteries. The undiluted chemical is held in a container mounted above a spinning-disc atomizer. This breaks up the spray liquid very evenly, resulting in a controlled, narrow range of spray droplet sizes. Spraying can be halted by either disconnecting the battery or inverting the applicator so that the container is below the spinning disc.

Ultra Low Volume (ULV) CDA sprayers are used for insecticide application. They produce droplets in a narrow size spectrum, generally within a 40-100 micron range, and this fine spray drifts in the air, settling only slowly on the crop. ULV sprayers should therefore always be used downwind of the operator.

Weed control requires larger spray droplets, in order to minimize drift and reduce the evaporation rate. Herbicides are therefore applied with Very Low Volume (VLV) CDA sprayers, which are similar to ULV sprayers in operation but which produce droplets within a 200-250 micron size range; they are generally simpler and of lower cost than ULV sprayers.

Some CDA sprayers are now available with two disc-rotation speeds and a range of nozzles, providing the full range of droplet sizes required for insecticide, fungicide and herbicide application.

GROUND-METERED SHROUDED ULV SPRAYER

This simple sprayer uses a commercially available, ultra-low volume (ULV), spinning-disc applicator, which is shrouded to improve the distribution pattern. This applicator is connected to a peristaltic pump mounted on the axle of a single ground-wheel. The herbicide is pumped out only during forward motion of the sprayer.
Bandwidth 1.5m at 135mm height,
2.0m at 375mm height.

M/S DALTRADE (NIG) LTD
Plot 45 Chalawa Industrial Estate
P.O. Box 377
Kano
NIGERIA

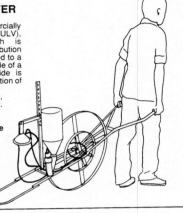

SPINNING-DISC KNAPSACK SPRAYER

This twin CDA sprayer combines the features of conventional knapsack sprayers and CDA sprayers. A spinning-disc applicator is mounted at each end of a spray boom and powered by a 6V rechargeable battery, carried under the chemical tank. The assembly is carried on the back of the operator, who therefore walks ahead of the spray. In ICRISAT trials, the sprayer was found to be suitable for spraying both wettable powders and emulsifiable concentrates, on low-growing crops like groundnut (peanut), chick pea and mung bean. The position of the boom can be adjusted to suit the height of the crop.
Weight (empty) 9kg.
Spray bandwidth 3m.
Spraying rate 15 litre/ha and 1.5 hours/ha
Tank capacity 10 litre.

Developed by:

ICRISAT
Patancheru P.O.
Andra Pradesh 502324
INDIA

Also available from:

KALE KRISHI UDYOG
S31/2/2, Hinge Khurd
Vithalwadi
Sinnagad Road
Pune 411 051
INDIA

MEKINS AGRO PRODUCTS (PVT) LTD
6-3-866/A Begumpet
Greenlands
Hyderabad 500 016
INDIA

HAND-HELD VLV SPRAYERS

'HERBI' RANGE
This range of 6V battery sprayers includes the following models. All are supplied with 2.5-litre spray containers as standard, and with optional 5-litre and 10-litre auxiliary backpack containers. The 'Herbi-Twin' has two applicators fitted on an adjustable frame to enable the spray bandwidth to be varied.

	Bandwidth	Droplet size
HERBAFLEX:	0.1-0.8m	200 micron
HERBI:	1.2m	250 micron
HERBI-TWIN:	1.8-2.4m	250 micron

MICRON SPRAYERS LTD
Three Mills
Bromyard
Hereford HR7 4HU
UK

LANCELOT SPRAYER
This sprayer has a 5-litre backpack spray container and can operate for up to 20 hours on a set of batteries or a rechargeable cell. The application rate is varied by the use of different colour-coded nozzles, stored in the handle. The spray bandwidth can be varied from 0.2 to 1.2m.

HORSTINE FARMERY LTD
North Newbald
Yorks YO4 3SP
UK

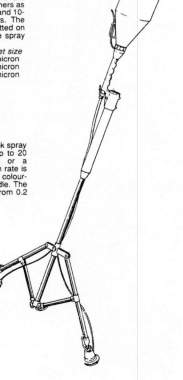

TURBAIR 'WEEDER'

This sprayer has a 6V motor and will operate for 60-90 hours per set of batteries. It has a one-litre spray container and a spraying bandwidth of 0.9-1.3 metres, depending on the chemical used.

TURBAIR LTD
Britannica House
Waltham Cross
Herts EN8 7DR
UK

'H2' SPRAYER

This sprayer has a 6V motor, a 1.4-metre handle, and a set of colour-coded nozzles to adjust the application rate. It is supplied with a 1.5-litre, integral polythene spray container; auxiliary 5-litre or 18-litre shoulder slung containers are optionally available.

BERTHOUD S.A.
B.P. 424
Villefranche - s
S. Cedex 69653
FRANCE

HAND-HELD ULV SPRAYERS

MICRO-ULVA
This sprayer has a telescopic lance and is suitable for both oil-based and water-based sprays. The droplet size can be adjusted by altering the number of batteries fitted, and thus the disc rotation speed. Also, for a given disc speed, droplet size increases with liquid feed rate and this can be adjusted by the use of colour-coded feed nozzles. Combination of these adjustments can provide controlled droplets of any size within a 30-150 micron overall range. A spray container of either 0.5 litre or 1.0 litre is supplied as standard but a 10-litre backpack container is also available.

MICROFIT MINI-ULVA
This is similar to the above model but it does not have a telescopic lance and it produces 50-micron droplets only.

MICRON SPRAYERS LTD
Three Mills
Bromyard
Hereford HR7 4HU
UK

TURBAIR X-J
This sprayer has a 12V motor and will operate for 12-16 hours per set of batteries; these batteries are carried in a separate, shoulder-slung holder. The spray bandwidth is 1-5m, depending on the crop height and windspeed.

TURBAIR LTD
Britannica House
Waltham Cross
Herts EN8 7DR
UK

Other manufacturers of hand-held ULV sprayers include:

TAURUS SPRAYING SYSTEMS (PVT) LTD
P.O. Box AY 18
Msasa
Harare
ZIMBABWE

BERTHOUD S.A.
48, Rue Victor Hugo
B.P. 193
Belleville Cedex 69823
FRANCE

TURBAIR FAN-ASSISTED ULV SPRAYERS

The Turbair range of ULV sprayers includes the following two hand-held, fan-assisted models. Each has a 1-litre spray container and can treat 0.4-1.3 ha/hour. Some form of facial protection is advised with these sprayers.

TURBAIR 'FOX' has a two-stroke petrol engine and is carried in a frame as a 'frontpack'. The droplet size is 70-90 microns, depending on the chemical used.

TURBAIR 'SPRITE' is an electric sprayer, using a 12 volt, 9 amp electric motor with a rechargeable battery. It will operate for up to one hour on a fully charged battery. The droplet size is 60-70 microns, depending on the chemical used.

TURBAIR LTD
Britannica House
Waltham Cross
Herts EN8 7DR
UK

MICRONEX

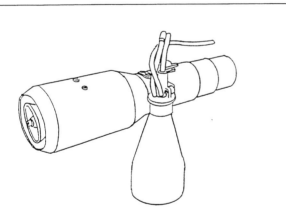

This spinning-disc attachment converts a motorized mist blower to a ULV sprayer, producing droplets of 40-60 micron size. The spray feed to the attachment is from a 0.5-litre plastic bottle, which is re-filled from the main tank of the sprayer. This bottle is pressurized by the airflow of the machine, to provide a constant flow and instant shut-off.

MICRON SPRAYERS LTD
Three Mills
Bromyard
Hereford HR7 4HU
UK

DUAL PURPOSE CDA SPRAYER

BLITZ SPRAYER
This is a two-speed, dual-purpose sprayer. At the lower speed it acts as a CDA sprayer for herbicides and fungicides, producing 240-micron droplets. When set to the higher speed, it becomes a ULV insecticide sprayer, producing droplets in the 90-100 micron size range. The electric motor is powered by dry cell batteries, which provide up to 50 hours of CDA spraying or 15 hours of ULV spraying. A range of models is available, with integral or shoulder-carried spray containers and each with colour-coded interchangeable nozzles.

VOLPI & BOTTOLI
Via F. Altobello, 2
Piadena (CR)
98434
ITALY

ELECTRODYN HAND-HELD SPRAYER

This is a unique system, developed by ICI, in which the sprayer delivers electrically charged droplets of a controlled size. It has been designed to eliminate the drift-prone small droplets and the inefficient large droplets produced by a conventional sprayer. The droplets are propelled at high velocity from the spray nozzle towards the target and, because they are electrically charged, they are mutually repellent. This reduces drift and improves the spray coverage.

The spray chemical is supplied in sealed containers with integral nozzles and the droplet size is pre-set in the range 40-200 microns to suit the product and crop.

ICI AGROCHEMICALS
Fernhurst
Haslemere
Surrey GU27 3JE
UK

earth lead

spray button

'Bozzle' container (incorporating nozzle)

'Bozzle' cap

'Bozzle' holder

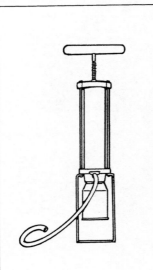

ANT HILL DUSTER

This piston-type duster is designed for the application of powdered insecticides directly into nests and runs. The main body is made of aluminium, supported on a stirrup, with a one-metre long flexible plastic application hose. The aluminium screw-on powder container has a capacity of 500g. The operator places one foot in the support stirrup to steady the duster, while manually operating the plunger.
Weight 4.3kg.

FUMIGADORAS TRIUNFO S.A.
Apartado 4045
Cali
COLOMBIA

TART/TIGA FIELD APPLICATOR

This portable fogger is designed for the application of fungicides and insecticides in large-scale enterprises, including plantations of tree and bush crops. It is also used for emergency defoliation treatment in cases of serious disease outbreak.

Over 200 hectares can be treated in one day by one machine and three operators, with a treatment height of up to 30 metres above ground. The applicator can be pushed or carried by two operators while a third operator carries the knapsack-mounted chemical tank. Alternatively, it can be supplied without wheels and handles, for tractor-mounting or to be carried by jeep.
Weight 114kg.

TIFA (CI) LTD
Cook Lubbock House
Waterside
Maidstone
Kent ME14 1LG
UK

ELECTRIC INSECT TRAP

This ultra-violet insect trap is designed to aid the study of insect pest populations in crops, rather than as a means of routine pest control.

INTRAL S.A.
Rio Grande 130
Zona Kayser
Caixas Do Sul RS
BRAZIL

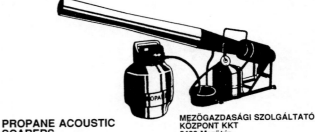

PROPANE ACOUSTIC SCARERS

'PURIVOX - DUPLEX' ACOUSTIC SCARER
This propane-fuelled scarer sits at ground level and 'fires' straight ahead. It is effective over an area of one to two hectares and 5kg of propane is sufficient for approximately 20,000 detonations.

MEZŐGAZDASÁGI SZOLGÁLTATÓ KÖZPONT KKT
5400 Mezőtúr
Szolnoki u.6.sz
HUNGARY

Propane-fuelled scarers of this type are also supplied by:

CECOCO
P.O. Box 8
Ibaraki City, Osaka 567
JAPAN

CARBIDE ACOUSTIC SCARERS

Calcium carbide and water produce acetylene in the main body of the equipment it is then compressed and ignited to produce an explosion. Half a kilogramme of carbide is sufficient for up to twelve hours of operation.

The 'SCARE BANG' model (illustrated) has piezo-electric ignition.

CECOCO
P.O. Box 8
Ibaraki City
Osaka 567
JAPAN

The similar 'TONNFORT 3' is made by:

ETS RELLÉ
2, Rue Diderot
Clamart 92140
FRANCE

ROTATING ACOUSTIC SCARERS

This scarer is a double-detonation model, with weather-proofed, piezo-electronic ignition. The two firing barrels are fitted into a freely rotating head on an adjustable-height tripod; wind vanes are fitted to the firing head assembly. To stabilize the device, the propane cylinder and the detonation timer are suspended by chains from the tripod and additional stays and pegs are also provided. The battery-powered regulator can provide automatic daytime-only or continuous control. The scarer is effective over an area of two to ten hectares, depending on the conditions of use.

ETS RELLÉ
2, Rue Diderot
Clamart 92140
FRANCE

MOTORIZED BARROW SPRAYER

This is a wheel-mounted high pressure pumpset, complete with a 3.7kW petrol engine and a 200-litre tank. The frame, tank and handlebar are made of steel. The steel rim wheels carry pneumatic tyres. Weight 206kg.

PULVERIZADORES AGRICOLAS PARADA S.A.
Casilla 2984
Santiago
CHILE

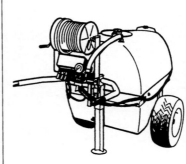

MT 180 SPRAYER

This unit comprises a plastic tank with a capacity of 180 litres mounted on a steel box section chassis. Various options are available for the basic unit to provide the user with the sprayer to suit requirements. The unit can be powered by an electric motor or petrol engine.

COOPER, PEGLER & CO. LTD
Burgess Hill
West Sussex
RH15 9LA
UK

5. HARVESTING AND THRESHING

The crop harvesting equipment available to small farmers in the developing countries has changed very little over the years. Knives, sickles and scythes continue to be the traditional tools used to harvest crops. Some low-horsepower reapers are being developed but, because of their low field capacity, high cost and other problems, they are often not considered a suitable alternative to the manual methods. On the other hand, a large number of efficient, low-cost hand, foot or power-driven threshers have been developed for use on small farms around the world.

The search for more efficient, cost-effective ways of harvesting and threshing crops is important because of the extreme labour-intensity of these tasks. For example, in developing countries, up to 40 per cent of the total labour required to grow a crop is expended in the harvesting and threshing operations. At peak harvest periods, labour shortages often occur — even in regions that normally have surplus labour — and this can lead to higher costs of production or reduced yields because of the delayed harvesting. It should be remembered, however, that the introduction of new equipment can mean the loss of local employment opportunities.

HARVESTING EQUIPMENT

There are three main types of harvesting equipment: manual, animal-powered, and engine-powered.

Manual

A variety of knives, sickles, scythes and reaping hooks are still the principal tools used by small farmers in the developing countries. They are used to harvest the entire plant or, if necessary, can be used selectively to remove mature plants or seed heads in crops that are not uniformly ripe. The cost of such tools is minimal, they are easily maintained or repaired, and they are familiar and dependable. Manual harvesting is, of course, very labour-intensive and in many situations is an important means of providing work to landless labourers who would otherwise be unemployed.

As harvesters, and in particular threshers, are often paid a percentage of the crop, the value of the wage to the recipient is considerably higher than the cost to the farmer, and may be the labourers' main source of food for the coming year.

Knives

Knives are used for cutting plant stalks or grain heads of crops like millet, sorghum and rice. Losses from crop shattering are lower when knife blades are used but labour requirements are very high — about 75 per cent above sickle harvesting. One of the main advantages comes at the threshing stage: selective cutting reduces the moisture content and extra green matter, allowing for safer storage and easier transport.

Sickles

A wide range of sickles is used to harvest the majority of cereals and pulses in developing countries. Basically they consist of a metal blade, usually curved, attached to a wooden handle. The degree of curvature and length of blade, the angle of attachment, and the shape of the handle all vary from area to area. The labour requirements for sickle harvesting vary according to the yield, variety and moisture content of the straw, and the operators' ability, but are likely to be in the range of 100 to 175 person-hours per hectare. The advantages of harvesting with sickles tend to be greatest with heavy crops.

Scythes

A scythe is a curved blade, usually 700–1000mm long, connected to a long shaft which has two handles. The blade is linked to the shaft in various ways, some allowing adjustment of the angle between the two for different crop conditions: the greater the angle, the more material is cut at each stroke (and the more arduous the operation). Scythes are efficient harvesting tools, but require considerable skill to use properly.

For cereal harvesting, a cradle attachment collects the cut crop and allows it to be deposited at the end of the stroke. The most common arrangement is a group of four or five wooden fingers parallel to the blade. Paddy is not normally scythed because rice straw is both softer and tougher than wheat straw and more prone to lodging. However, in a good stand of wheat, scything can reduce the labour to between a third and a quarter of that needed for sickle harvesting.

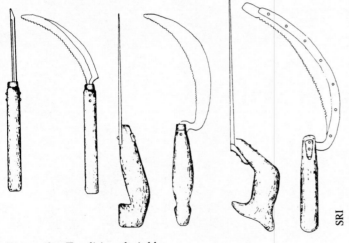

Figure 1   Traditional sickles

Reaping hooks

The reaping hook is a compromise between a sickle and a scythe. It is short handled and has to be used in a crouching position, but the sharp blade will cut the crop without having to hold it. Reaping hooks are frequently used with hooked sticks to gather the crop as it is cut.

Animal-powered harvesters

Animal-powered harvesters are relatively rare in developing countries. Ox-drawn reapers, based upon designs of machines used with horses, have been tried in India but are not used widely. The limited draught available from ox-pairs, the problems of harvesting lodged crops and the cost of the machines compared to tractor-drawn harvesters have limited the commercial development of animal-drawn harvesters.

Engine-powered

A number of prototype reapers and reaper-binders have been designed to meet the harvesting needs in developing countries. In the case of binders, the high cost of twine has made certain machines uneconomic. Other harvesters, because of low field capacity, high cost or other problems have, on the whole, been found unsuitable. However, a Chinese vertical conveyor reaper promoted by IRRI is proving to be an efficient mechanical harvester of crops under conditions existing in developing countries.

THRESHING EQUIPMENT

Threshing equipment involves three quite distinct operations:
- separating the grain from the panicle;
- sorting the grain from the straw;
- winnowing the chaff from the grain.

The first of these requires considerable energy and is the first to be mechanized. Sorting the grain from the straw is relatively easy but is the most difficult stage to mechanize. Winnowing is relatively easy, whether by machine or by hand.

Manual threshing

Most manual threshing methods use some implement to separate the grain from the ears and straw. The simplest method is a stick or hinged flail with which the crop, spread on the floor, is beaten repeatedly. Such tools are simple and cheap, but they are also slow and exhausting to operate. Rice is usually threshed by beating bunches of panicles against the ground, a stone, a bamboo frame, or the edge of a tub or basket. A screen usually surrounds the threshing area to avoid grain loss. Output per person-hour varies considerably, but is generally between 25 and 50 person-hours per tonne.

Slightly more complex mechanical threshers and shellers are available which still rely only on human power. Treadle-operated threshers, consisting of a drum with rows of wire teeth which is rotated by pedalling a treadle, are commonly used for rice. Output is typically 100-150kg per hour for one-person machines. Such threshers are relatively cheap, light and easily manufactured locally. Because of the higher power requirement, they are not suitable for threshing wheat.

Maize shellers consist of a feeder funnel and a shelling disc which is rotated by a hand-crank. The grain is removed as the cob moves down through the machine; output is 100-150kg per hour. Work rates of 750-900kg per hour are claimed for a pedal-operated maize sheller which has a fan to separate light trash from the grain. At an even simpler level are low-cost hand-held maize shellers. These have low work rates but save wear and tear on the hands.

Animal-powered threshing

Animal trampling remains the standard method of threshing grain crops in many parts of the world. While slow, and often resulting in impurities and damage to the grain, it makes threshing less arduous and can be cheap if oxen or buffaloes are readily available. Productivity, at 30-50 person-hours per tonne, is about the same as for manual methods. The animals may pull a heavy object or implement behind them, such as a stone roller, sledge or disc harrows, to increase the rate of work.

Engine-powered threshing

Tractor treading

One method of threshing which has become widespread for rice, wheat, barley and sorghum is driving a tractor round and

Animals threshing rice — still a common method in many parts of the world

round on the crop spread over the threshing floor. If tyre pressure is kept low to minimize grain damage, excellent results are possible, and no added investment in machinery is required. In some areas, near roads, threshing is carried out by spreading the crop on the road and allowing passing traffic to do the threshing. Whilst convenient and cheap, this method relies on the existence of sufficient traffic, and normally leads to dirty and damaged grain. There are also the obvious dangers associated with road traffic.

Hold-on threshers

In areas where whole, undamaged straw is valued, some machines thresh rice by stripping grain from the panicles without damaging the straw. The simplest of these are mechanized versions of the treadle thresher in which the drum is rotated by a 1-3hp engine. Double drum threshers contain two-wire looped cylinders. Most threshing is done in the slower, first cylinder which strips the grain on the panicles from the straw. The second, faster, cylinder is designed to thresh the broken panicles. Double drum threshers are used for wheat and sorghum as well as paddy. Some have a self-feeding mechanism which continuously feeds the bundles into the machine, thus reducing the labour requirement.

Hold-on threshers require that the crop be formed up into even bundles, and this can be laborious if the crop was badly lodged or if even bundles were not harvested in the first place. Their main advantage is that they solve the major problem of all other threshers — how to separate the grain from the straw.

Through-flow threshers

The entire harvested crop is fed into this type of thresher, thus increasing the bulk which has to pass through the machine. Faster feeding is possible but higher power requirements are inevitable. There are two main types:

○ tangential flow machines in which the crop passes directly through the threshing cylinder, around the circumference of the drum;
○ axial flow machines which have spirally positioned fins on the upper concave so that material fed in at one end of the drum passes along the drum as it is rotated, and is ejected at the other end.

In both machines the threshing occurs as the crop passes between a revolving cylinder and a metal grate called the concave, which covers part of the circumference of the drum. Threshed grain falls through the holes in the concave. The mechanism which causes the beating/rubbing which separates grain from straw and chaff can be of several types: wire loop, spike (or peg) tooth, rasp bar, angle bar.

Power for engine-driven threshers may be from a small engine mounted on the machine (2 or 3hp upwards), or from a tractor. Most machines allow adjustments for various crop

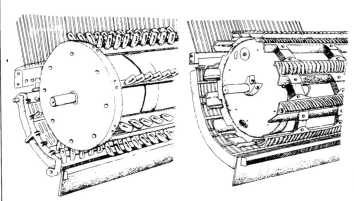

Figure 2   Threshing mechanisms: Peg-tooth drum and slotted metal concave (left); rasp bar and wire concave (right)

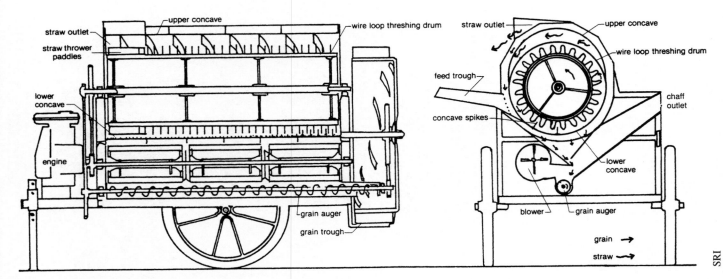

Figure 3   Axial flow thresher

and field conditions, and a large selection is available with varying drum, power supply and winnowing/cleaning arrangements. The simplest consist of little more than the threshing cylinder and concave mounted on a metal framework including feeding chute, outlets and a suitable engine.

More complex threshers which include winnowing fans and sieves to separate grain from straw and chaff include the axial flow thresher developed by IRRI in the Philippines which has been widely adopted by rice producers. The Alvan Blanch Minor thresher from the UK performs successfully with wheat, barley and sorghum; and various Indian-manufactured threshers are used primarily for wheat threshing. They are capable of very high outputs (0.5 to 2 or more tonnes per hour) and remove the need for hand winnowing, but are considerably more expensive and more difficult to repair in rural areas. They are more suitable for contractor operators than individual farmers in developing countries.

Maize shellers

Engine-powered maize shellers operate similarly to the threshers, with rotating cylinders of the peg or bar type and metal concaves. Cobs must be husked before entering the threshing drum.

Some maize shellers have husking rollers which husk the cobs before they are passed to the threshing drum. As with other grain threshers, cleaning fans may be included which remove any trash from the grain. Shellers may have their own engine or be driven from a tractor power take-off (pto), and range in size from 1hp models with 100kg/hr capacity to pto-driven models with a capacity of several tonnes/hr.

Separating grain from straw

The simplest way to separate grain from straw is to pick the straw up and shake it, letting the grain fall out. A better method is to use a pitchfork to do the shaking. The earliest mechanical sorters emulated the pitch fork, and this type consists of three or five troughs mounted on cranks in such a way that the straw is picked up and thrown forward by each trough in turn. This is a very simple and reliable mechanism, but it is also very bulky.

With a well-designed threshing drum, roughly 80 per cent of the grain should be sorted in the drum by passing through holes in the concave. Recent developments with axial flow

threshers have increased this to 100 per cent so that a thresher can do without the very bulky straw walkers. One feature of the axial flow drum is that sorting is more effective at high loadings, whereas the efficiency of straw walkers falls off very rapidly as the throughput rises. For hand-fed machines, where feeding tends to be erratic, the straw walker is probably the most efficient.

Winnowing

Traditional threshing methods leave a lot of trash among the grain and separating this can require almost as much labour as the original threshing. If there is plenty of wind, the threshed material is tossed in the air using forks, shovels, baskets, etc. (see Chapter 8 for information about hand-tools for materials handling) and the lighter chaff and straw is blown to one side while the grain falls vertically. Final cleaning may be done with a winnowing basket, which is shaken until any chaff and dirt separate at the upper edge. This is very simple and effective but, at only about 40-45kg per hour, it is slow. An alternative is to use winnowing sieves, open weave baskets that may be suspended on tripods. They are shaken so that the grain falls through; the chaff and straw remain in the sieve.

Various types of winnowing machines are designed to create artificial wind. The simplest are hand and pedal-operated fans; two, three or four light metal blades are rotated by hand cranks or foot pedals. Slightly more sophisticated is the fanning mill, where the fan is mounted in a wooden housing which contains sieves and screens — the grain is thus graded as well as cleaned. The fan may be manually or engine powered. Fanning mills produce a very clean sample but cannot cope with large amounts of straw, so they are more appropriate for finer winnowing. Details of further cleaners, used primarily for crop-processing operations, are to be found in Chapter 6.

ADVANTAGES

Potential advantages of harvesting and threshing equipment include:
○ eliminating the labour bottlenecks at peak periods;
○ increased yields due to timely cultivation for next crop.

Mechanical harvesting and threshing of crops becomes most advantageous where improved farming practices such as the use of high-yielding varieties, multiple cropping systems and expanded use of irrigation water are introduced. With such systems large quantities of crops mature and need to be harvested at one time, the time for preparation of the land and re-planting of successive crops can be short and, often, labour for manual harvesting is not available during the peak times when it is needed. With higher yields from better production technology, the relative benefits of mechanical over manual harvesting are increased.

ALTERNATIVES

Combined harvester threshers (combines) are the norm for large-scale farms, but they cannot easily be reduced in size and complexity for small farmers. Simple wholecrop harvesters have been developed by Silsoe Research Institute (SRI) to cut the crop and then either to chop it into short (20–50mm) lengths which in effect threshes it or to bruise and break the straw in drums which produces a material that can be used as animal feed. This design is too large for inclusion in this book, but further information can be obtained from SRI if required.

In addition SRI and IRRI have developed a small stripper harvester which separates the grain from the ears without cutting the straw. Information should be sought from SRI or IRRI about the machine's availability.

With hand-powered maize shellers the work gets done faster than by hand-shelling

COSTS AND BENEFITS

Indicative costs

The cost of harvesting and threshing is normally expressed as cost per hectare of crop or as cost per tonne of grain produced; i.e. it can be calculated on the basis of either area or weight. The total operating cost per hectare is the sum of the total fixed cost of the machine, namely interest, depreciation, tax and repairs and total variable cost which comprises the cost of unskilled and skilled labour, fuel, oil, lubricants. In the case of binders, the cost of binding twine is added to the variable cost.

In Table 1, indicative figures are given for the capital costs of a variety of mechanical harvesting devices.

Table 1 Indicative costs

Type		Capital cost ($)
Mometora reaper (5hp)	reaper	693
	Power tiller	1386
TNAU reaper (10hp)	Reaper	590
	Power tiller	2250
Satoh reaper (5.4hp)	Self-propelled machine	1400
Vertical conveyor reaper (8hp)	Reaper	1000
	Power tiller	1750

Source: RNAM (1983).

Economics and scale

Several factors other than capital costs affect decisions about using harvesting and threshing equipment. The size of the farm in physical and economic terms influences the scale of machinery and the size of investment that is appropriate.

If only a small amount of work is undertaken each season, then the capital costs per unit of work done may be so high that a machine is uneconomic compared to alternative methods. This can be avoided where multi-farm use is possible, but this use requires a high degree of organization and co-operation, especially where timeliness is critical.

Small and irregularly shaped fields result in low field efficiency of engine-powered or even animal-drawn machines. Poor access increases the time needed to get to the fields, and lack of access roads sometimes excludes engine-powered machines altogether. Where terraced cultivation is practised, all tools may have to be light enough to be carried on a person's back.

Traditional cropping systems may exclude or make difficult certain types of harvesting technology. Mixed cropping makes mechanized harvesting difficult. Growing a mixture of varieties of single crop can have the same effect; e.g. mixed millet varieties may not all thresh well at a single concave setting and drum speed. Poor land clearing leaving stumps and rocks in the field may prevent the used of animal-drawn and engine-powered implements. Similarly, broadcast or randomly transplanted rice crops cannot always be harvested by machines which rely on crops being grown in rows. These are all factors which must be taken into consideration when deciding to invest in a particular piece of equipment.

Bearing these factors in mind, an example is given of how

Table 2 Fixed and operating costs of harvesting with a 5hp Mometora (RNAM 1983.)

A. Fixed cost ($)

	Reaper	Power tiller
1. Purchase cost (p) ($)	693	1386
2. Fixed cost* per hour ($ per hour)		
a) Depreciation	0.30	0.16
b) Interest (12%)	0.15	0.09
c) Repair (8% of purchase price)	0.18	0.11
d) Tax, insurance, housing (2% of purchase price)	0.05	0.03
Fixed cost per hour	0.68	0.39
3. Total fixed cost (for reaper and power tiller per hour)	1.07	

*Assumes 2100 hours and 7 years of life for harvester and 8000 hours and 8 years life for mounting tractor.

B. Operating cost per ha and per tonne of grain

Prototype		India	Indonesia	Pakistan	Philippines	Thailand	Mometora (Modified) Thailand
Country where tested							
Crop		Rice	Rice	Wheat	Rice	Rice	Rice
Capacity	hr/ha	15.9	15.6	13.2	12.5	10.5	10.0
Yield	t/ha	2.50	4.00	3.86	5.23	3.65	3.16
Grain loss	%	10.7	14.3	10.5	4.87	3.0	4.8
Labour requirement							
unskilled	man-hr/ha	39.9	162.9	57	64.9	33.5	33.5
skilled	man-hr/ha	16.0	27.8	13	12.5	19	19
Fuel consumption							
gasoline	l/ha	11.5	14.7	13	14.9	13.4	10.2
Price of grain	$/kg	0.15	0.15	0.10	0.15	0.15	0.15
Wage rate							
unskilled	$/day	0.76	0.8	1.01	2.27	2.00	2.00
skilled	$/day	1.9	2.0	2.53	5.68	5.00	5.00
Fuel price							
petrol	$/l	0.5	0.5	0.5	0.5	0.5	0.5
diesel	$/l						
Fixed cost	$/hr	1.07	1.07	1.07	1.07	1.07	1.07
Fixed cost	$/ha	17.00	16.69	14.12	13.38	11.23	10.70
Labour							
unskilled	$/ha	3.79	16.29	7.20	18.42	8.38	8.38
skilled	$/ha	3.80	6.95	4.11	8.88	11.88	11.88
Fuel cost	$.ha	5.75	7.35	6.5	7.45	6.70	5.10
Cost of grain loss	$/ha	40.15	85.80	40.53	38.21	16.43	22.75
Total cost per ha	$/ha	70.50 (30.35)	133.08 (47.28)	72.46 (31.93)	86.34 (48.13)	54.62 (38.19)	58.81 (36.06)
Cost per tonne	$/t	28.20	33.27	18.77	16.51	14.96	18.61

Note: Figures in parentheses are values excluding grain loss. Harvesting losses are extremely difficult to assess accurately. One approach is to estimate the yield by sampling and then comparing this with the actual amount harvested, but sampling methods can seldom get closer than 2-3 per cent of the true yield, and this is the range of the expected harvesting loss.

The alternative is to try and collect and count the grains on the ground before harvesting (pre-harvest loss) and after harvesting. The problem here is counting the pre-harvest loss without disturbing the crop and causing more loss. With this method of estimating, the result depends to a large extent on the investigator being able to find the lost grain. A good technician will usually record a much higher percentage loss than a lazy one. It is because most people estimate losses in this way in a very casual manner that in general harvesting losses are hopelessly underestimated.

the cost of harvesting with a 5hp Mometora reaper was worked out in various countries (see Table 2).

These costs can be compared with costs of manual harvesting as shown in Table 3.

HEALTH AND SAFETY

Much harvesting and threshing equipment is potentially dangerous if not manufactured to an adequate standard or not used properly. Costs of locally manufactured equipment are sometimes kept low by omitting safety features. In India, for example, small town artisans are producing threshers without the protective guard needed to take wheat into the machine and keep hands and arms out. This saves sheet metal but raises accident rates — 95 per cent of which occur while crops are being fed into the machines. With the numbers of new machines increasing year by year, the accident rates during threshing are also rising.

SOCIAL IMPACT

The introduction of harvesting and threshing equipment can and does lead to displacement from paid employment of some of the poorest sectors of society unless used in circumstances where they permit higher cropping intensities or yields, thus creating alternative work opportunities in other farm activities. In circumstances where the introduction of such equipment seems desirable from the point of view of the farmer, the

Table 3 Costs of manual harvesting

		India (rice)	Indonesia (rice)	Pakistan (wheat)	Philippines (rice)	Thailand (rice)
Total cost per hectare	$	28	29	31.25	65.76	59
Total cost per tonne	$	7	7.25	7.81	16.44	14.75

employment and equity effects can be taken into consideration by enabling landless workers to purchase machinery through a credit scheme so as to run custom services. This type of scheme is being successfully implemented by various agencies in Bangladesh which have helped groups of landless men and women to benefit from the introduction of pedal threshers rather than be disadvantaged by them.

Ian Johnson
Consultant

Reference

RNAM (1983) *Testing, Evaluation and Modification of cereal Harvesters, Techinical Series No.14* Regional Network of Agricultural Machinery of the Economic and Social Commissiom for Asia and the Pacific. September 1983.

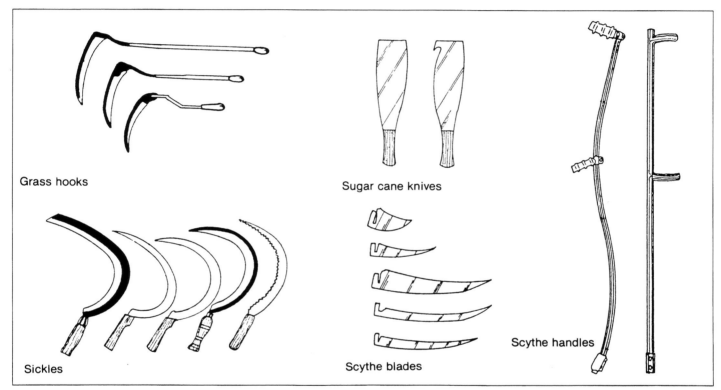

Grass hooks

Sugar cane knives

Sickles

Scythe blades

Scythe handles

Figure 4   Cutting implements

CUTTING IMPLEMENTS

The use of a sharp blade to cut the plant stem is the simplest form of removing a crop. In each culture a different form of blade has been devised for each type of crop. The most renowned manufacturer of scythes and sickles, Falci from Italy, has dozens of designs specifically tailored to particular markets.

Sickles

The degree of curvature, length of blade, angle of attachment and the shape of handle vary from area to area and for different crops. A small selection is shown above. Some sickles have serrated edges but there is little evidence to show this to be an improvement.

The essential dimensions of sickles are shown in Figure 5. A is the length of the implement, including the tang but excluding the handle; D is the total length of the implement. The blade length is measured as the arc B and the development of the blade C is the length around the outer edge, up to but

excluding the tang. The other measurement, not shown here, is blade thickness which is the greatest width of the blade from outer edge to the sharp edge. Similar measurements are used to describe scythes. In both, the curvature and distance between the plane of the tang or the attachment to the snath (scythe handle) and the plane of the blade is also noted sometimes by manufacturers: the 'tang height measurement' and (in scythes) the 'tang opening measurement'.

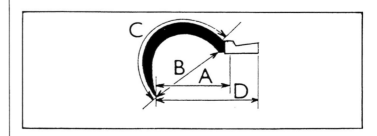

Figure 5   Dimensions of a sickle

Scythes

These are long curved blades, usually 700 to 1000m long measured along the chord of the blade's arc (similar to dimension A in Figure 5) but shorter blades are available for difficult sites (e.g. steep bnaks). The shaft and handle (snath) designs vary in length and curvature to allow the operator to work with outstretched arms and both hands at approximately the same height from the ground. Scythes can be fitted with a cradle attachment which collects the cut crop and allows it to be deposited at the end of the stroke.

Grass or reaping hooks

These are a compromise between sickle and scythe.

Sugar cane knives

This form of implement has been designed to provide considerable momentum at the point of contact with the sugar cane stem. Often there is a hook on the back of the knife with which the cane is picked up for stacking or chopping into short lengths.

Knives

Country	Manufacturer	Implement		
		Cane knives	Corn knives	Misc. knives
Germany	Wolf & Bangert Werkzeugfabrik	●		
India	Kumar Industries	●		
Italy	Eurozappa S.P.A.			●
Malawi	Chillington-Agrimal (Malawi) Ltd	●		
Portugal	Verdugo — Ernesto L. Matias			●
UK	Ralph Martindale & Co. Ltd	●		●
USA	Columbian Cutlery Co. Inc.		●	
	Seymour Manufacturing Co. Inc.	●	●	
Zimbabwe	Toolmaking & Engineering		●	

Sickles and scythes

Country	Manufacturer	Implement		
		Grass hooks	Sickles	Scythes
Austria	Sensenwerke Krenhof A.G.		●	●
Belgium	S. A. Chanic	●		
Cameroon	Tropic	●		
Germany	Schwabische Huttenwerke GmbH		●	●
India	Kumar Industries		●	
Italy	Falci S.P.A.		●	●
Malawi	Chillington-Agrimal (Malawi) Ltd		●	
Nepal	Agricultural Tools Factory Ltd		●	
Niger	A.F.M.A.		●	
Peru	Herramientas S.A.		●	
	Herrandina			●
Portugal	Verdugo — Ernesto L. Matias		●	●
Spain	Eladio Reguillo en C. de B.		●	
	Patricio Echeverria S.A.			●
UK	Alfa-Laval Agri Ltd	●		
	Bulldog Tools Ltd	●		●
	Burgon & Ball Ltd	●	●	●
	Ralph Martindale & Co. Ltd		●	
	Samuel Parkes & Co. Ltd	●		●
	The Stockton Heath Forge Ltd	●	●	●
USA	Columbian Cutlery Co. Inc.	●		●
	Seymour Manufacturing Co. Inc.	●		●
Zimbabwe	Temper Pools (Pvt) Ltd		●	

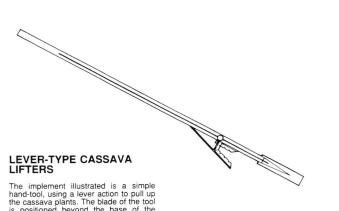

LEVER-TYPE CASSAVA LIFTERS

The implement illustrated is a simple hand-tool, using a lever action to pull up the cassava plants. The blade of the tool is positioned beyond the base of the plant and the handle leant back alongside the plant, which is then wedged into a tapered and notched double jaw near the base of the tool. This jaw holds the stem firmly and levers it out of the ground as the handle is raised. The tool is of all-steel construction and technical details are available to potential manufacturers. Weight 2.5kg.

**AGRICULTURAL MECHANIZATION
DEVELOPMENT PROGRAMME
(AMDP)
CEAT
University of the Philippines
Los Baños College
Laguna 4031
PHILIPPINES**

A similar cassava lifting tool, but with a notched and forked base instead of the blade and jaws of the illustrated tool, is offered by:

**COOPÉRATIVE BÉNINOISE DE
MATÉRIAL AGRICOLE (COBEMAG)
B.P. 161
Parakou
REPUBLIC OF BENIN**

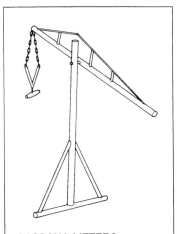

CASSAVA LIFTERS

The following company offers a manual lifter in which the lever arm is raised on to a framework; a chain is used to attach one end of this lever to the plant and the other end is pulled down to lift out the plant.

**COOPÉRATIVE BÉNINOISE DE
MATÉRIAL AGRICOLE (COBEMAG)
B.P. 161
Parakou
REPUBLIC OF BENIN**

This simple, lever-type lifter has a fulcrum which rests on the ground. Two operators are needed; one attaches the tool to the base of the plant, and the handle is then pushed downwards by the other to lift the plant. Design details of the tool are available from:

**BUREAU OF PLANT INDUSTRY
692 San Andres
Malate
Manila
PHILIPPINES**

ROOT CROP HARVESTERS

These animal-drawn implements have a common frame but different blades and tines to suit different crops. Depth control is provided by a skid mounted at the front of the frame, and a wheel is fitted above the frame at the front to provide a means of transport when the tool is inverted. Weight from 36 to 42kg, depending on attachment.

**THILOT HOLLAND BV
Hoofdstraat 11-17
Lottum 5973 ND
NETHERLANDS**

ICRISAT GROUNDNUT DIGGER FOR HARD SOILS

This has been specially designed for hard soil. The digger has two shares which are inclined at 120 degrees to each other and each share has five chisel points on its leading edge to aid penetration. A single digger has a working width of 600mm and can be pulled by a pair of oxen. Alternatively, two or more diggers can be mounted together on a toolbar and the unit tractor-drawn.

**INTERNATIONAL CROPS RESEARCH
INSTITUTE FOR THE SEMI-ARID
TROPICS
Patancheru
Andra Pradesh 502 324
INDIA**

Also available from:

**KALE KRISHI UDYOG
S31/2/2 Hinge Khurd
Vithalwadi
Sinnagad Road
Pune 411 051
INDIA**

**MEKINS AGRO PRODUCTS (PVT)
LTD
6-3-866/A Begumpet
Greenlands
Hyderabad 500 016
INDIA**

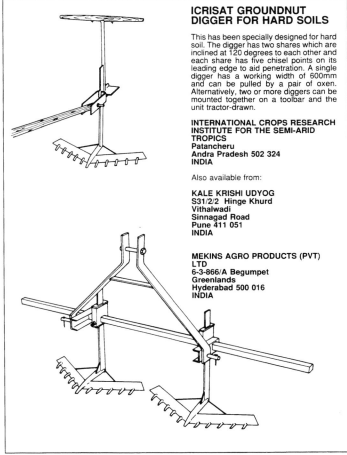

GROUNDNUT LIFTER MODIFICATION

This is a modification of an animal-drawn plough, with a V-shaped cutter blade fitted below the lifter body.

**UPROMA
B.P. 1086
Lomé
TOGO**

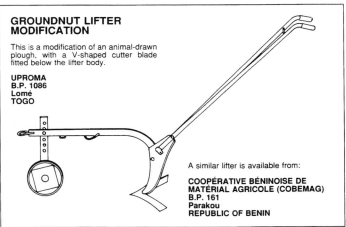

A similar lifter is available from:

**COOPÉRATIVE BÉNINOISE DE
MATÉRIAL AGRICOLE (COBEMAG)
B.P. 161
Parakou
REPUBLIC OF BENIN**

GROUNDNUT AND ROOT LIFTER

The digger body of this animal-drawn implement is mounted on a sprung frame and works to a depth of 100-120mm. The lifted crop passes over a grid which separates it from the soil and deposits it back on to the ground for collection.

**ALVAN BLANCH DEVELOPMENT CO.
LTD
Chelworth
Malmesbury
Wilts SN16 9SG
UK**

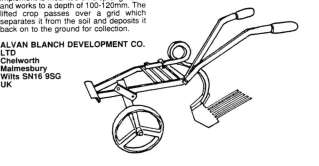

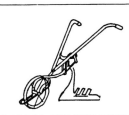

CECOCO PEANUT DIGGER

The Cecoco peanut digger lifts peanut plants from a depth of 100-120mm. Two models are available, one for animal draught the other for power tiller drive (2.25-4.5 kW).

**CECOCO
P.O. Box 8
Ibaraki City
Osaka 567
JAPAN**

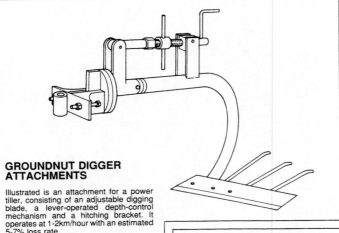

GROUNDNUT DIGGER ATTACHMENTS

Illustrated is an attachment for a power tiller, consisting of an adjustable digging blade, a lever-operated depth-control mechanism and a hitching bracket. It operates at 1-2km/hour with an estimated 5-7% loss rate.

KUNASIN MACHINERY
107-108 Sri-Satchanalai Road
Sawanankalok
Sukothai
THAILAND

TRACTOR-OPERATED GROUNDNUT DIGGER-LIFTER

This is a prototype machine developed at a Malaysian university. It operates from the tractor power take-off, through a chain and sprocket mechanism. There are two digging blades which penetrate under the plant row to loosen the soil and cut the tap root. Lifting rods on the blades raise the plants from the soil up to a conveyor, which separates, shakes and finally discharges the plants for subsequent collection.

UNIVERSITY PERTANIAN MALAYSIA
Fakulti Kejuruteraan
43400 Serdang
Selangor
MALAYSIA

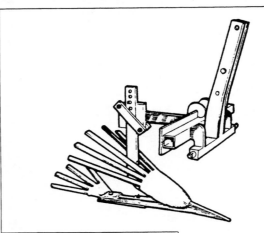

POTATO LIFTERS

The following company offer a range of potato lifting implements with different models suitable for a power tiller or for mounting on the three-point hitch of a tractor. Single-grid and double-grid soil separators are available, and the digger/lifter can be either a shovel type or a horizontal chisel-tine type. The working depth is adjustable.

S.C.A.D. BOURGUIGNON
B.P. 37
Les Tordières
Bourg-de-Peage 26301
FRANCE

CASSAVA HARVESTER

This prototype single-row harvester comprises two separate tractor-mounted units. A powered rotary scythe unit is mounted on the front of the tractor to cut the cassava stems and clear them aside. Mounted at the rear of the tractor is a root lifter and a conveyor belt to transfer the roots to a collection box.
At regular intervals, the harvested roots are dropped in heaps from the machine.

UNIVERSITY OF NIGERIA
Faculty of Engineering
Department of Agricultural Engineering
Nsukka
NIGERIA

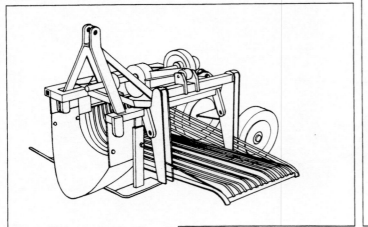

TWO-WHEELED POTATO LIFTER

This two-wheeled implement is attached to the three-point hitch of a tractor. Its main components are a digger/scooper to lift the potatoes, and a shaking grid device to separate them from the soil and deposit them on the surface for collection. Working depth 150-200mm. Weight 110kg.

ZALAGEP BAGODI
MEZŐGAZDASÁGI GÉPGYÁRTÓ VÁLLALAT
8992 Bagod
Gépállomás út 9
HUNGARY

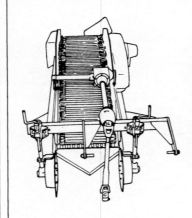

ROOT CROP DIGGER

This is a single-row, semi-mounted unit, requiring a 22kW tractor with a three-point hitch and power take-off. It will handle row widths of 660-760mm, leaving the lifted crop in rows for manual-collection. Two types of digger blade are available for different land conditions and the conveying chains can be fitted with plain or rubber-covered rods. The working depth is controlled by hand-screws acting on depth control wheels.

BLAIR ENGINEERING LTD
Rattray
Blairgowrie
Scotland PH10 7DN
UK

HAND-HELD BRUSH CUTTERS

These can be used to harvest crops from small plots but also for clearing rough grass, bushes and cane fields, cleaning ditches and removing small tree branches.
The range offered by the following company comprises five models which have 1.3kW, two-stroke engines and there is also a 3.6kW model. The cutting heads of each can be fitted with a range of toothed discs, nylon line or replaceable blades and two alternative types are provided as standard with each model. A safety guard and a tool kit are also provided as standard.
One model, C3S, differs from the illustration in that the engine is knapsack-mounted and has a flexible coupling to a hand-held cutter shaft.
Weight 7-9kg.

CIFARELLI S.R.L.
Strada Oriolo, 124
Voghera 27058
ITALY

CUTTER-BAR MOWERS

Two models are offered of this animal-drawn mower with the cutter-bar driven from two pneumatic-tyred landwheels. A seat is provided for the operator. Working width 1.05m or 1.2m.

INDUSTRIAS JOSE TREPAT GALCERAN S.A.
Avenida Jose Trepat Galceran, 9
Apartado 2
Tarrega (Lérida)
SPAIN

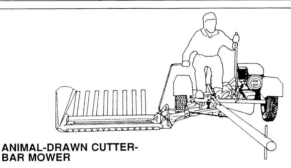

ANIMAL-DRAWN CUTTER-BAR MOWER

This mower can be horse- or ox-drawn and is suitable for both grain and grass crops. It is powered by a 2.2-3.7kW engine with hand and foot controls. The cutting height is adjustable and a choice of cutter-bars provides a working width of 1.07m, 1.22m or 1.37m.

ECOMAT
Le Val Rouge
B.P.132
Morlaix 29210
FRANCE

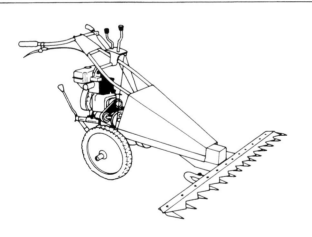

TWO-WHEEL CUTTER-BAR MOWERS

The machine illustrated has the cutter-bar centrally mounted. The mower is carried on two pneumatic-tyred wheels but twin wheels or steel cage wheels can be fitted for use on steep slopes or in difficult soil conditions. Capable of working on slopes of up to 40% incline, it is powered by a 3kW engine.
Cutting width 1m.
Cutting height adjustable in the range 30-150mm.
Workrate 0.2ha/hour.

IMPLEMÁQUINAS LTDA
BR 282, Km 390
Vila Remor
C.P. 381
Joaçaba
Santa Catarina, 89 600
BRAZIL

MF340 MOWER
There are two models of this mower, each with a single cylinder, four-stroke, 6.2kW engine. Both have a dry disc clutch and a seven-speed gearbox (five forward, two reverse). Model MF340 has a rigid axle whereas model 340S has clutch steering through handlebar-mounted control levers. A range of different cutter-bars is offered, fingered or fingerless and with working widths from 1.1 to 1.5m. These cutter-bars are removable to enable the wheeled power unit to be used with other front-mounted implements.
Weight 140kg.

ANTONIO CARRARO TRATTORI S.P.A.
Via Caltana, 18
35011 Campodarsego
C.P. 11
Padua
ITALY

CUTTER-BAR MOWERS

The Agria 5300 (illustrated) is able to harvest grass at the rate of 0.3 ha/hour. It is powered by a four-stroke 3kW petrol engine and can be fitted with pneumatic tyres or cage wheels.
Working width 1000mm.
Weight 75kg.

AGRIA-WERKE GmbH
Postfach 1147
D-7108 Moeckmuehl
GERMANY

A range of similar cutter-bar mowers is supplied by:

CASORZO S.P.A.
Via Asti 31A
Tonco (Asti) 14039
ITALY

GRILLO S.P.A.
Via Cervese 1701
Cesena (Forli) 47027
ITALY

Ten models of a similar design are available, with two-stroke petrol or four-stroke diesel engines, and with a single speed or a three-speed gearbox. The mower is also available with a side-mounted cutter-bar or as a rotary mower unit.

MECCANICA BENASSI S.P.A.
Via Statale 325
Dosso (Ferrara) 44040
ITALY

A range of mowers can be supplied with the cutter-bar mounted centrally (model BRC) or side-mounted (model BRL) and with 5-6kW, four-stroke engines. There are three forward gears plus reverse.
Working width 800, 950, 1100, 1270mm.

BRUMITAL S.P.A. INDUSTRIA MACCHINE AGRICOLE
Zona Industriale
2a Strada Catania
95030
ITALY

The Bertolini mower has a 7kW petrol or 6kW diesel engine, four forward and two reverse gears, and a differential locking device.
Working width 1.15m, 1.27m or 1.37m.

BERTOLINI MACCHINE AGRICOLE S.R.L.
Via Guicciardi n.7
42100 Reggio Emilia
ITALY

A similar machine by Paget is offered with a range of cutter-bar types and widths. An optional fertilizer broadcaster can also be fitted, replacing the cutter-bar. There are three models available, powered by a 3.5, 6.0 or 8.1kW petrol engine.

PAGET
14 & 16 Rue Louis-Jouvet
69632 Venissieux
FRANCE

PASQUALI MACCHINE AGRICOLE S.R.L.
Via Nuova 30
Calenzano (Florence) 50041
ITALY

and also by:

HOLDER, GEBR. GmbH & CO.
Stuttgarter Strasse 42-46
Postfach 1555
D-7430 Metzingen
GERMANY

S.E.P. FABRICA MACCHINE AGRICOLE S.R.L.
Viale della Resistenza, 39
San Martino in Rio (Reggia Emilia)
42018
ITALY

REYNARD SA AGRIC. MACHIN.& EQUIPM.
Apartado 183
Santa Ana Ca
COSTA RICA

VOGEL & NOOT LANDMASCHINENFABR. GmbH
Wartberg
A-8661
AUSTRIA

AL-KO BRITAIN LTD
1 Industrial Estate
Medomsley Road
Consett
Co. Durham DH8 6SZ
UK

COMPANIA AGRIA S.A. DE C.V.
Avenue Ceylan N.897
Col. Industrial Vallejo
C.P. 02300 Mexico, D.F.
MEXICO

MOTORSCYTHE
The Motorscythe has a 5kW, two-stroke petrol engine and two forward gears plus reverse. The mowing mechanism can be replaced by other optional attachments including a rotary mower, a front rake and a semi-trailer with a driving seat.
Working width 1.3m.

MOTOKOV
Na Strži 63
14062 Praha 4
CZECHOSLOVAKIA

The BCS range of four mowers are powered by 4.5-10kW, petrol or diesel engines and have gearboxes with three or five forward, and one or three reverse gears.
Working width 1.1-1.4m.

BCS S.P.A.
Viale Mazzini 161
Abbiategrasso (Milan) 20081
ITALY

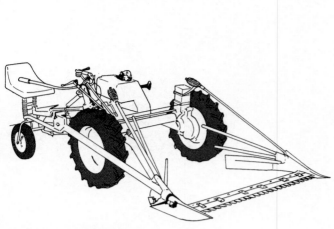

RIDE-ON MOTORIZED MOWERS

This mower has a wide, high-clearance axle, with the cutter-bar positioned between and ahead of the wheels. It is powered by a 7.5-10kW, four-stroke petrol or diesel engine with rope or electric start, and has four forward gears plus reverse. The mower has side controls and a 'Sulky'-type, two-wheeled operator's seat. Reaper-binder and front trailer attachments are available.
Working width 1.1-1.55m.

BCS S.P.A.
Viale Mazzini 161
Abbiategrasso (Milan) 20081
ITALY

The Poljostroj machine is a ride-on, cutter-bar mower, fitted with a 7.5kW diesel engine and steered by a bogie wheel below the driver's seat. The cutting height is adjustable and a hay rake can be fitted at the rear. The machine can also be used to power a number of other agricultural implements.
Working width 1.3m.
Workrate 0.3-0.8ha/hour.

POLJOSTROJ
Industrija masina i opreme
25250 Odžaci
Karađorđeva br. 34
YUGOSLAVIA

HAND-PUSHED ROTARY MOWER

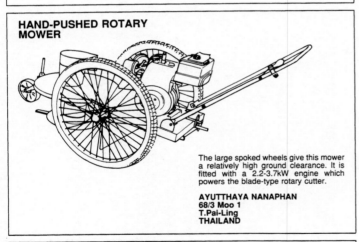

The large spoked wheels give this mower a relatively high ground clearance. It is fitted with a 2.2-3.7kW engine which powers the blade-type rotary cutter.

AYUTTHAYA NANAPHAN
68/3 Moo 1
T.Pai-Ling
THAILAND

ANIMAL-DRAWN ROTARY MOWER

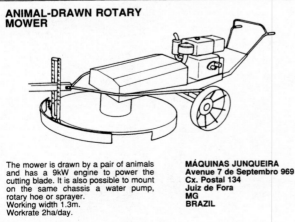

The mower is drawn by a pair of animals and has a 9kW engine to power the cutting blade. It is also possible to mount on the same chassis a water pump, rotary hoe or sprayer.
Working width 1.3m.
Workrate 2ha/day.

MÁQUINAS JUNQUEIRA
Avenue 7 de Septembro 969
Cx. Postal 134
Juiz de Fora
MG
BRAZIL

CUTTER-BAR ATTACHMENTS FOR TRACTORS

REAR-MOUNTED CUTTER-BAR MOWER
This mowing attachment was designed to suit 11-20kW tractors. It has free-floating, adjustable, spring-loaded inner and outer skid shoes to minimize side draught. The hydraulic system for the tractor three-point hitch is used to operate a lifting system for the cutter-bar and enables mowing from 20 degrees below horizontal to 60 degrees above, to cope with banks, slopes and uneven ground. There is also a quick-release system to protect the mower from damage on encountering fixed obstacles.

HABAN MANUFACTURING COMPANY
2100 Northwestern Avenue
Racine
Wisconsin 53404
USA

CUTTER-BAR MOWERS
These mowers are attached to the three-point hitch of a tractor and are driven through the tractor's power take-off. Each has an automatic clutch and a quick-release mechanism to prevent damage on encountering fixed obstacles. Cutting height is adjustable and there are various interchangeable cutter-bar types and widths.
Required tractor power 11 or 18.6kW, dependent on model.
Working width 1.2, 1.5, 1.65, 1.8 or 1.85m.

INDUSTRIAS JOSE TREPAT GALCERAN S.A.
Avenida Jose Trepat Galceran, 9
Apartado 2
Tarrega (Lérida)
SPAIN

Similar implements are manufactured by:

COMPANIA AGRIA S.A. DE C.V.
Avenue Ceylan N.897
Col. Industrial Vallejo
C.P. 02300 Mexico, D.F.
MEXICO

MOWER FOR GRASS CROPS
This is a belt-driven mower attached to the three-point hitch of a small tractor. It can be used on uneven land and its blades are fully protected.
Working width 1.5m.
Tractor power required 3.4kW.
Weight 183kg.

HELWAAN MACHINE TOOLS FACTORY
Ein Helwaan
Cairo
EGYPT

SIDE-MOUNTED MOWER
This is a side-mounted cutter-bar mower for attachment to the back of a small tractor. It is suitable for low-growing fodder crops and for hilly and uneven ground conditions. The cutter-bar section is hinged and can be hooked in an upright position for ease of transport.
Working width 1.6m.

POLJOSTROJ
Industrija masina i opreme
25250 Odžaci
Karađorđeva br. 34
YUGOSLAVIA

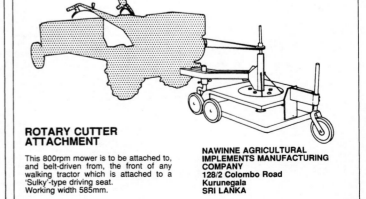

ROTARY CUTTER ATTACHMENT

This 800rpm mower is to be attached to, and belt-driven from, the front of any walking tractor which is attached to a 'Sulky'-type driving seat.
Working width 585mm.

NAWINNE AGRICULTURAL IMPLEMENTS MANUFACTURING COMPANY
128/2 Colombo Road
Kurunegala
SRI LANKA

ROTARY MOWER

The manufacturers of the Agrozet MT8-050 small tractor also offer a three-bladed rotary mower attachment, which fixes on to the front of the tractor via a three-point

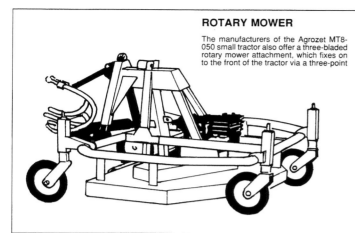

hitch. It is driven from the front output shaft of the tractor.
Cutting height 30-90mm.
Weight 110kg.

AGROZET PROSTĚJOV K.P.
Tř. J. Fučika 41
PSČ 796 21
CZECHOSLOVAKIA

THREE-WHEEL ROTARY MOWER
This mower, powered by an 11kW tractor, is best suited to operation on flat land. The cutting height is adjustable between 200 and 600mm.
Working width 1.5m.
Weight 230kg.

ZALAGEP BAGODI
MEZŐGAZDASÁGI GÉPGYÁRTÓ
VÁLLALAT
8992 Bagod
Gépállomás út 9
HUNGARY

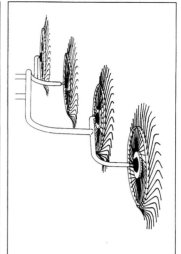

ROTATING DRAG

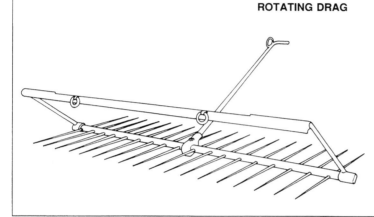

This rake can be drawn by a horse or a tractor. A number of tines are fitted on to either side of a seamless steel tube and these collect the hay as the implement is drawn along. The hay is then discharged on rotation of the tine assembly, effected by a lever-operated trigger mechanism at the centre of the tine-mounting tube. The rake is available in the following sizes:

Working width (m):			
1.8	2.0	2.2	2.4
Number of tines:			
18	20	22	22/24
Weight (kg):			
39	42	47	51

INDUSTRIAS JOSE TREPAT
GALCERAN S.A.
Avenida Jose Trepat Galceran, 9
Apartado 2
Tárrega (Lerida)
SPAIN

TINE-WHEEL WINDROWER

This is a multi-purpose implement carried on the three-point hitch of a 13kW tractor. It comprises four 1.5m diameter 'tine-wheels' mounted on a tubular framework in such a way that they can easily be positioned in one of three alternative arrangements, without the use of tools. This enables the implement to create windrows, or to invert or spread out existing windrows and thus aid and hasten the field-drying process.
Working width 2m.
Working speed 7km/hour.
Weight 180kg.

INDUSTRIAS JOSE TREPAT
GALCERAN S.A.
Avenida Jose Trepat Galceran, 9
Apartado 2
Tárrega (Lerida)
SPAIN

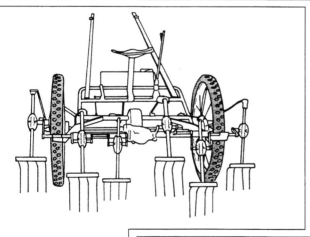

HORSE-DRAWN HAY RAKE

This rake can handle both cereal and hay crops. A row of curved, steel tines is mounted on a frame carried between a pair of metal landwheels. These tines gather the crop and are raised to release it by a pedal-controlled mechanism. The rake is available in the following sizes:

Working width (m):				
1.2	1.5	1.8	2.1	2.2
Number of tines:				
20	24	28	32	34
Weight (kg):				
195	205	210	220	225

INDUSTRIAS JOSE TREPAT
GALCERAN S.A.
Avenida Jose Trepat Galceran, 9
Apartado 2
Tárrega (Lerida)
SPAIN

HORSE-DRAWN TEDDER

Six tedding forks with steel spring-tines are held in bearings on a reinforced tubular chassis. A crank-drive from the landwheels causes the forks to pivot on their bearings, thus providing a tedding action to aerate a cut hay crop. The machine is horse-drawn and the cranking mechanism is chain-driven through a gearbox from the two rubber-tyred, spoked landwheels.
Working width 2.05m.
Weight 262kg.

INDUSTRIAS JOSE TREPAT
GALCERAN S.A.
Avenida Jose Trepat Galceran, 9
Apartado 2
Tárrega (Lerida)
SPAIN

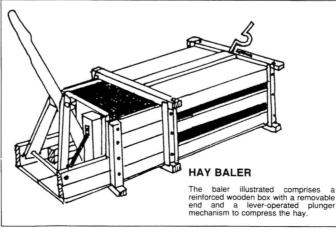

HAY BALER

The baler illustrated comprises a reinforced wooden box with a removable end and a lever-operated plunger mechanism to compress the hay.

Two operators are required: the first places hay in the inlet aperture and the second operates the lever to press the material against the end of the box. Slots in the side of the box allow baler twine to be passed round the compressed material and tied off. Up to 80 bales can be produced a day.

HERRANDINA
Marte 581
Breña
Lima 5
PERU

Manual hay balers are also made by:

CARIB AGRO-INDUSTRIES LTD
Research Centre
Edgehill
St Thomas
BARBADOS

JETMASTER (PVT) LTD
P.O. Box 948
Harare
ZIMBABWE

TWO-WHEEL REAPER

This two-wheel, pedestrian-controlled reaper has a cutter-bar mowing unit and a side stacker. It is powered by a 3.7kW, air-cooled diesel engine and has clutch steering. It is suitable for row crops including rice, wheat and barley. The assembly can be altered for use as an animal-drawn light power tiller.
Cutting height 100mm.
Working width 1.25m.
Weight 300kg.

UNION TRACTOR WORKSHOP
8-B, Phase 11
Mayapuri Industrial Area
New Delhi 110 064
INDIA

FOUR-ROW PADDY REAPER

This manually-steered reaper cuts four rows of rice simultaneously, turning the cut crop to the side of the machine. It is fitted with a Kubota GS2JN, four-stroke 2.8kW petrol engine.
Working width 1.2m.

CENTER FOR DEVELOPMENT OF
APPROPRIATE AGRICULTURAL
TECHNOLOGY
Situgadung, Legok
Tromol Pos 2
Serpong 15310
INDONESIA

IRRI/CAAMS 1M REAPER

This motorized reaper was developed by the International Rice Research Institute in collaboration with the Chinese Academy of Agricultural Mechanization and Sciences. It comprises a reaper built on to a power tiller, with a 2.2kW petrol-engine and cage wheels, but it is adaptable to other walking-type tractor units. It is of all-steel construction, except for the non-metallic star wheels.

Working width 1m;
Cutting height adjustable from 70mm;
Forward speed 2.5-4.5km/hour;
Workrate 2.4 ha/day;
Field losses less than 1%;
Fuel consumption 1 litre/hour;
Weight 48kg (reaper only), 135kg complete.

THE INTERNATIONAL RICE
RESEARCH INSTITUTE
Agricultural Engineering Department
P.O. Box 933
Manila
PHILIPPINES

It is also available from:

JCCE INDUSTRIES
242 Mayondon
Los Baños
Laguna
PHILIPPINES

TRAMATE MERCANTILE INC.
747-749 Gandara St
Santa Cruz
Manila
PHILIPPINES

SIDE-STACKING REAPERS

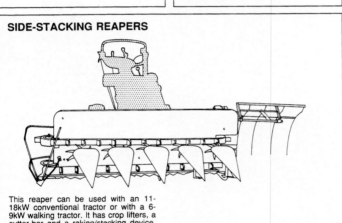

This reaper can be used with an 11-18kW conventional tractor or with a 6-9kW walking tractor. It has crop lifters, a cutter-bar and a raking/stacking device. There is also an operator's seat.
Working width 1.6m.
Stacking distance 2m, 2.5m and 3.2m.
Weight 137kg.

CHINA NATIONAL AGRICULTURAL
MACHINERY IMPORT & EXPORT
CORPORATION
Kwangton Branch
61 Yanjiang
Kwangchow
CHINA

'AGRIMEC' PADDY REAPER
This is similar to the Chinese reaper above, with a windrower to turn the cut crop to the right-hand side. The original design was an attachment for a 3kW (minimum) walking tractor, but a self-propelled version is also available. Power transmission is by V-belt.
Working width 1.2m.
Weight 80kg.

JINASENA LTD
4 Hunupitiya Rd
Colombo 2
SRI LANKA

MADHO WHEAT HARVESTER

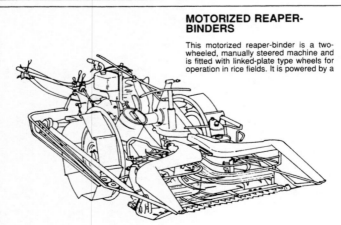

This reaper fits on to the front of a tractor and leaves the cut crop turned and laid to the right-hand side. Cutting height is adjustable, from a minimum of 70mm. The reaper can be tilted back on its mounting frame into a transport position. Working width 2.2m.

MADHO MECHANICAL WORKS
B-49 Industrial Focal Point
G.T. Road
Moga 142-001
Punjab
INDIA

MOTORIZED REAPER-BINDERS

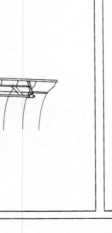

This motorized reaper-binder is a two-wheeled, manually steered machine and is fitted with linked-plate type wheels for operation in rice fields. It is powered by a 7.5-10kW petrol or diesel engine
Working width 1.3m.
Weight 480kg.

BEDOGNI & CO. S.R.L.
(Divisione Giardino)
C.P. 349
Reggio Emilia 42100
ITALY

REAPER-BINDER
This is a ride-on unit with a single or double wheel trailed Sulky-type driving seat. It has a 7.5-10kW, petrol or diesel engine and four forward gears plus reverse. The crop is cut by a reciprocating cutter-bar, collected into sheaves and tied with string. The harvesting mechanism can have a manual or hydraulic lift.
Working width 1.4m.

BCS S.P.A.
Viale Mazzini 161
Abbiategrasso (Milan) 20081
ITALY

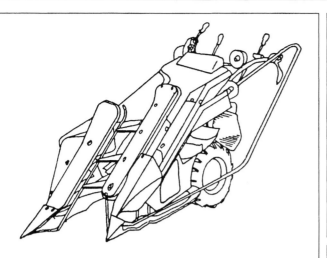

MOTORIZED TWO-ROW REAPER-BINDERS

This two-wheeled machine is designed primarily for row-crops of rice, barley and wheat. It cuts two rows per pass, binding the cut crop into bundles and dropping them to the right-hand side of the machine. Jute or polypropylene string can be used for binding. An optional attachment accumulates the bundles and drops four or five at a time, to ease the subsequent gathering operation. The machine is carried on two wheels with low-pressure pneumatic tyres and is manually steered. It is powered by a 2.6-3.7kW, four-stroke petrol engine and has six forward gears plus two reverse. Working width 550mm. Weight 165kg.

YANMAR AGRICULTURAL EQUIPMENT CO. LTD
1-32, Chayamachi
Kita-ku
Osaka 530
JAPAN

Similar machines are supplied by:

KOREA FARM MACHINERY & TOOL INDUSTRY CO-OPERATIVE
11-11 Dongja-Dong
Youngsan-Gu
Seoul
KOREA

CECOCO
P.O. Box 8
Ibaraki City
Osaka Pref. 567
JAPAN

RICE THRESHER

This treadle rice thresher has an optional hood and collecting box and can be adapted for an independent motor or engine drive if required. The threshing drum is mounted in roller bearings and has spring-steel wire loop beaters. The thresher is a static unit but lifting handles are provided on the chassis for transport. Two models are available: 'Pygmee' weighs 60kg and has an output of 150-200kg/hour whereas 'Sapoo' weighs 100kg and has an output of 200-300kg/hour.

SISMAR
B.P. 3214
20, rue Dr Thèze
Dakar
SENEGAL

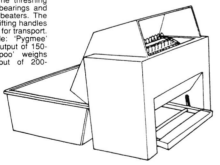

MANUAL PADDY THRESHERS

Two models of this peg-drum thresher are available; both are chain-driven from a manually turned handle. The drive mechanism utilizes the freewheel, sprockets and chain from a bicycle. The smaller of the models has a wooden threshing cylinder and an output of up to 1 tonne/day. The larger model has a sheet metal cylinder, a double chain drive mechanism and an output of up to 1.5 tonne/day.

TANZANIA ENGINEERING AND MANUFACTURING DESIGN ORGANIZATION (TEMDO)
P.O. Box 6111
Arusha
TANZANIA

FRUIT PICKERS

This simple hand-tool consists of a collection bag held open by an oval ring and fixed to the end of a long pole. The ring acts as a shearing device to detach the fruit, which is collected in the bag.

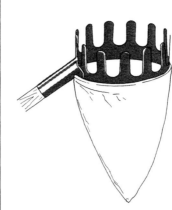

M/S DALTRADE (NIG) LTD
Plot 45 Chalawa Industrial Estate
P.O. Box 377
Kano
NIGERIA

Similar versions of the tool are made by:

SAMUEL PARKES & CO. LTD
Pretoria Works
New Road
Willenhall WV13 2BU
UK

WOLF TOOLS LTD
Ross-on-Wye
Hereford HR9 5NE
UK

TREADLE PEG-DRUM THRESHERS

Treadle-operated drum threshers are widely available and are used primarily for rice but also for other crops. The threshing drum is covered in pegs, spikes or wire loops and is supported, in bearings and on a horizontal axis, by a free-standing framework. Sheaves or bundles of the crop are held against the pegs as the drum is rotated by a foot-operated treadle mechanism. Output is in the region of 70-100kg/hour. Versions of this type of thresher are available from the following companies (the illustration shows the Bangladesh model from Comilla)

THE COMILLA CO-OPERATIVE KARKHANA LTD
Ranir Bazar
P.O. Box 12
Comilla
BANGLADESH

CECOCO
P.O. Box 8
Ibaraki City
Osaka Pref. 567
JAPAN

COSSUL & CO. PVT LTD
123/367 Industrial Area
Fazalgunj
Kanpur
U.P.
INDIA

RAJAN UNIVERSAL EXPORTS (MFRS) PVT LTD
P.O. Box 250
Madras 600 001
INDIA

MIRPUR AGRICULTURAL WORKSHOP & TRAINING SCHOOL
Mirpur Section 12
Pallabi
Dhaka 16
BANGLADESH

AGRICULTURAL ENGINEERS LTD
Ring Road Industrial Area
P.O. Box 12127
Accra North
GHANA

AGRICULTURAL TOOLS FACTORY LTD
P.O. Box 2
Birganj
NEPAL

AGRICULTURAL MECHANIZATION DEVELOPMENT PROGRAMME (AMDP)
CEAT
University of the Philippines
Los Baños College
Laguna 4031
PHILIPPINES

COOPÉRATIVE BÉNINOISE DE MATÉRIAL AGRICOLE (COBEMAG)
B.P. 161
Parakou
REPUBLIC OF BENIN

ATELIER DE FABRICATION DU MATERIEL AGRICOLE (AFMA)
B.P. 11619
Niamey
NIGER

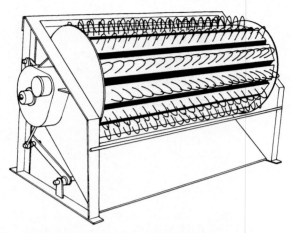

PEDAL THRESHERS FOR RICE

This is a treadle-operated, open-topped rice thresher with the threshing drum mounted in ball bearings. Models are available for one-man and two-man operation (illustrated).
Weight 71kg or 82kg.

COLUMBINI SERGIO & C.S.N.C.
Via Cadorna, 9
P.O. Box 19
Abbiategrasso (Milan) 20081
ITALY

Ecomat produce a small treadle thresher for rice with a 540mm diameter threshing drum, fitted with steel teeth. Options include a transport wheel, a rice collecting box and the replacement of the treadle by an engine drive.
Output 60-200kg/hour.

ECOMAT
Le Val Rouge
B.P.132
Morlaix 29210
FRANCE

The following company offers a similar, two-man treadle thresher and can also supply the machine with a petrol or kerosene engine.

SECA - LE MOTTIER
La Côte St André 38260
FRANCE

A similar implement is manufactured by:

UPROMA
B.P. 111
Kara
TOGO

ANIMAL-DRAWN OLPAD THRESHER

This machine comprises serrated discs of 450mm diameter mounted on a steel shaft and held in position by cast iron spools. The frame is of angle iron and includes a seat with foot- and back-rests. Front and rear safety guards are fitted. The crop is spread on the threshing floor and the machine is drawn round and round over the crop, thus separating the grain from the straw. An extra raking attachment can be fitted for stirring the straw during the threshing operation. Models are available with 8, 11, 14 or 20 discs and the output is 350-850kg/day.

COSSUL & CO. PVT LTD
123/367 Industrial Area
Fazalgunj
Kanpur, U.P.
INDIA

MULTI-CROP THRESHER

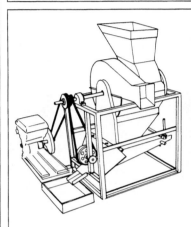

This thresher has a peg drum cylinder which rotates in a housing fitted with a stationary concave.
A blower and set of reciprocating sieves achieve the cleaning process. The machine can be used to thresh sorghum, wheat and millet by selection of the appropriate drum speed, sieve type and cylinder-concave clearance. The machine requires a 3kW power source and has an output of 50-80/hour. Further details can be obtained from:

INSTITUTE FOR AGRICULTURAL RESEARCH
Samaru
P.O. Box 1044
Zaria
NIGERIA

PEDAL-OPERATED MILLET THRESHERS

The AB MINI M is a simple thresher, pedal-operated by two people sitting on bicycle-type seats. The concave bars are of steel and the threshing drum has stout rubber beaters specially designed for millet. A feed hopper, outlet spout and a small winnowing fan are also included and the thresher is fitted with two iron wheels for manoeuvrability. Motorized versions of the thresher are also available.
Output up to 100kg/hour.

AB MINI R PEDAL THRESHER
This is similar to the millet thresher described above but with a peg-tooth drum suitable for rice and many other cereals. The drum is carried in sealed bearings. Optional accessories for sorghum threshing are available. A sloping sieve at the discharge point helps to separate the straw from the grain.
Output up to 200kg/hour.

ALVAN BLANCH DEVELOPMENT CO. LTD
Chelworth
Malmesbury
Wilts SN16 9SG
UK

PORTABLE THRESHERS

The IRRI portable thresher handles rice and some sorghum varieties. It is of all-steel construction, comprising a frame, a pegtooth cylinder with straw-throwing paddles on one end and enclosed by a cover with spiral louvres, and a wire mesh or round rod lower concave. A feeding tray, winnowing fan and a 3.7kW petrol engine complete the unit. It can be carried by two people and removable transport handles are provided.
Material is loaded on to the tray and fed into the opening between the cylinder and the lower concave. The pegs of the threshing cylinder hit the material, separating the grains from the straw and accelerating them around the cylinder. The majority of the grains are threshed during the initial impact but further threshing is performed while the material moves axially towards the opposite, discharge, end. Threshed grain, including impurities such as leaves and short pieces of straw, passes through the openings in the lower concave where it is cleaned by the winnowing fan. Threshing and separation losses are minimized by the cut-off wall installed at the end of the lower concave next to the straw thrower and by the stripper bars opposite the feed opening. The cut-off wall prevents grain going into the straw thrower and the bars cut long straw for ease of axial movement and prevent straw from wrapping around the cylinder during threshing.
Some models of this thresher provide a door in the top cover for 'hold-on threshing' if the straw is to be used for mat and basket weaving. The door is raised and locked in place thereby exposing the entire cylinder length to hold-on threshing.

Power 3.7kW engine;
Output up to 600kg/hour for rice;
Separation recovery 98% by weight;
Grain purity (without cleaning screen) 94%;
Grain breakage less than 2%;
Threshing drum 305mm diameter and 711mm long;
Drum speed 600-630 rev/min;
Fuel consumption 1 litre/hour;
Weight (with engine) 105kg.

THE INTERNATIONAL RICE RESEARCH INSTITUTE
Agricultural Engineering Department
P.O. Box 933
Manila
PHILIPPINES

Similar designs are offered by:

JCCE INDUSTRIES
242 Mayondon
Los Baños
Laguna
PHILIPPINES

MARINAS MACHINERY MANUFACTURING CO. INC.
Rizal Street
Pila
Laguna
PHILIPPINES

PADDY THRESHER
Based on an IRRI design, this thresher consists of a peg-tooth drum in a threshing chamber with spiral internal louvres to move the straw axially. A straw-throwing paddle is fitted at the exit end and a winnowing fan cleans the grain falling through the round-rod concave. The thresher is mounted in a metal frame and can be powered by a 3.7kW, kerosene oil engine. Alternatively, it can be powered from a walking tractor.
Output 400-500kg/hour rice;
Cylinder speed 600-700 rev/min.

AGRO TECHNICA LTD
400 Deans Road
Colombo 10
SRI LANKA

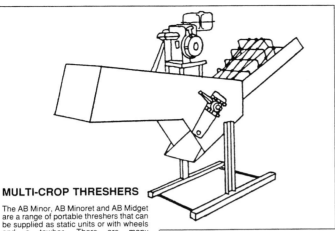

MULTI-CROP THRESHERS

The AB Minor, AB Minoret and AB Midget are a range of portable threshers that can be supplied as static units or with wheels and a towbar. There are many attachments and variations, catering for a wide range of crops, including wheat, barley, oats, beans, peas, sorghum, millet, maize and rice. The threshers are constructed of heavy steel plate and options include:

- A peg-tooth or rasp-bar threshing drum;
- Extra drum-speed reduction pulleys;
- Interchangeable concaves;
- Special attachments for sorghum and millet threshing;
- Power supplied by an electric motor, a diesel or petrol engine or a tractor power take-off;
- Feed via a chute, table or chain-and-slat conveyor;
- Sieves with round or slotted holes, sized to order.

ALVAN BLANCH DEVELOPMENT CO.
LTD
Chelworth
Malmesbury
Wilts SN16 9SG
UK

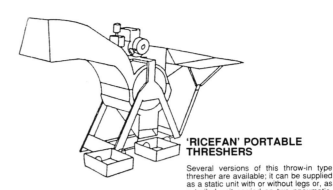

'RICEFAN' PORTABLE THRESHERS

Several versions of this throw-in type thresher are available; it can be supplied as a static unit with or without legs or, as a trailed unit carried on two pneumatic-tyred wheels, it can be powered by an electric motor, a removable petrol or diesel engine or a tractor power take-off, and it can be supplied with or without an additional grain cleaning device. The basic machine comprises a threshing drum with a cross-flow fan and a concave/sieve arrangement covering more than 80% of the drum circumference; this enables the thresher to cope with straw up to one metre long and with up to 75% moisture content, without clogging. By changing the beater bars and concave/sieve arrangement, the machine can also handle a variety of other crops including wheat, sorghum, soya beans and maize.
Output 2 tonne/hour maximum.
Power options:

- 3kW electric motor;
- 3.7kW petrol engine;
- 3.3kW diesel engine;

Weight 151kg petrol model, 194kg diesel model.

VOTEX TROPICAL
Vogelenzang Andelst B.V.
Wageningsestraat 30
Andelst
NL-6673 DD
NETHERLANDS

RICE THRESHER

The three axial-flow threshers offered by the following company are based on IRRI designs. The smallest, TH5, is supplied with a 2.2kW kerosene engine. Models TH2 and TH4 can be powered by a two-wheeled tractor or by a 3-4kW engine. Cylinder speed 600 rev/min. Capacity range 600-900kg/hour.

JINASENA LTD
4 Hunupitiya Road
Colombo 2
SRI LANKA

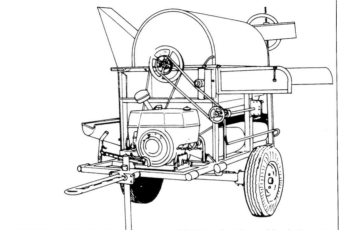

IRRI TH7 & TH8 AXIAL FLOW THRESHERS

These are essentially larger versions of the TH6 axial flow thresher, with screen cleaners. They are heavier and therefore usually mounted on a wheeled chassis and drawn by an animal, power tiller or light truck. The specifications are:

- Power 5-7kW engine;
- Separation recovery 98% by weight;
- Threshing drum 400mm diameter and 1.2m long;
- Drum speed 500-530 rev/min;
- Fan speed 1030 rev/min;
- Weight (with engine) 430kg.

THE INTERNATIONAL RICE
RESEARCH INSTITUTE
Agricultural Engineering Department
P.O. Box 933
Manila
PHILIPPINES

Machines based on this design are offered by several companies, including:

JCCE INDUSTRIES
242 Mayondon
Los Baños
Laguna
PHILIPPINES

FIANSA
Apartado Postal 5017
Avenida Industrial 675
Lima
PERU

C & B CRAFTS
Maginao
San Rafael
Bulacan
PHILIPPINES

STANDARD AXIAL-FLOW THRESHER

The standard axial flow thresher has a power requirement of 7.5kW. It is suitable for a variety of crops and can be converted for use as a maize sheller. Capacity ranges from 800kg/hour for rice to 2500kg/hour for sorghum.

UNION TRACTOR WORKSHOP
8-B Phase 11
Mayapuri Industrial Area
New Delhi 110 064
INDIA

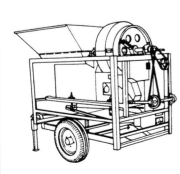

AUTOMATIC-FEED WHEAT THRESHER

This is a hopper-fed, mobile thresher with a bagging-off spout for the threshed grain. It is suitable for a range of grains, including wheat and sorghum. The thresher can be powered by a 15kW electric motor or through the power take-off of a 25-35kW tractor.
Grain cleaning efficiency 99%.
Threshing drum speed 750 rev/min for wheat or 650-700 rev/min for sorghum/pearl millet.
Output 800-1000kg/hour.
Weight 1250kg.

STANDARD AGRICULTURAL
ENGINEERING CO.
824/5 Industrial Area B
Ludhiana 141 003
Punjab
INDIA

MADHO WHEAT THRESHER

This thresher can be powered by either a 3.7kW electric motor or a 4-6kW diesel engine or alternatively from a tractor engine. It is a portable unit, mounted on four cast iron wheels and it has a winnower and a bagging system for the threshed grain.

MADHO MECHANICAL WORKS
B-49, Industrial Focal Point
G.T. Road
Moga
Punjab 142 001
INDIA

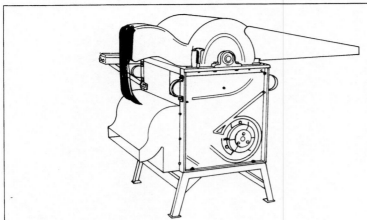

PORTABLE THRESHER

This thresher is suitable for rice and soya beans. It is a portable machine of steel construction and has a 3.7kW power requirement. The whole crop is fed into the machine and the threshed grain, straw, chaff and dust are delivered separately, through four outlets in the machine.
Output: 400-600kg/hour rice, 200kg/hour soya beans.
Weight 115kg.

P.T. RUTAN MACHINERY TRADING CO.
P.O. Box 319
Jalan Pemuda 1B-1C
Surabaya 60271
INDONESIA

CECOCO THRESHERS

Two models of this static thresher are available. The 0.5kW model has a 450mm drum and an output of 300-450kg/hour. The other model is a 0.75kW unit with a 550mm drum and an output of 450-650kg/hour.

CECOCO
P.O. Box 8
Ibaraki City, Osaka 567
JAPAN

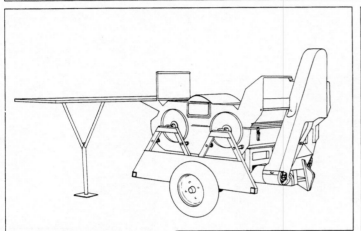

HIGH-SPEED THRESHER

The 'Twinfan 500' portable thresher is suitable for many crops including soya beans, rice, maize and wheat. The crop passes through the threshing chamber and is then auger-fed to an elevator which feeds the bagging-off spout. The threshing drum can be fitted with spike-tooth beaters for rice or rasp-type beater bars for other crops. A cross-flow fan is incorporated in the threshing unit and further aspiration is provided between the grain elevator and the bagging-off spout. The thresher is mounted on a three-wheeled base and can be towed manually or by tractor or animal. It is powered by an integral 7kW diesel engine or can be driven by the power take-off of a tractor.
Weight 710kg.

VOTEX TROPICAL
Vogelenzang Andelst B.V.
Wageningsestraat 30
Andelst
NL-6673 DD
NETHERLANDS

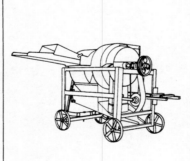

MULTI-PURPOSE ROTARY THRESHER

The following companies supply a range of heavy-duty drum threshers which can be adjusted to handle a variety of crops including grains, pulses, grams and sunflower seeds. There are numerous optional fittings, including fans and cleaners and the threshing drum can be fitted with different types of pegs or teeth as required. The thresher can be powered by a motor, engine, or tractor; a pulley belt or tractor power take-off drive option is offered. All units are mounted on wheeled frames and have safety guards fitted on the intake chutes.

AMAR AGRICULTURAL IMPLEMENTS WORKS
Amar Street
Janta Nagar
Gill Road
Ludhiana 141 003
INDIA

AXIAL-FLOW ALL-CROP THRESHER

This all-steel, throw-in type thresher requires a 3.7kW external power source. It is a mobile unit, mounted on four cast iron wheels, and is suitable for threshing wheat, rice and sorghum. Minor adjustments and some change of parts enable it to handle a range of other crops. Oscillating screens and two winnowing fans are fitted for cleaning the threshed grain.
Weight approximately 700kg.

UNION TRACTOR WORKSHOP
8-B Phase 11
Mayapuri Industrial Area
New Delhi 110 064
INDIA

A similar thresher is manufactured by:

KUNASIN MACHINERY
107-108 Sri-Satchanalai Road
Sawanankalok
Sukothai
THAILAND

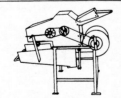

SORGHUM THRESHER

This prototype drum thresher has rasp-bar beaters, reciprocating cleaning sieves and an aspiration fan. The machine requires a 2.5kW power source and has an output of 80-100kg/hour. Further details can be obtained from:

INSTITUTE FOR AGRICULTURAL RESEARCH
Samaru, P.O. Box 1044
Zaria
NIGERIA

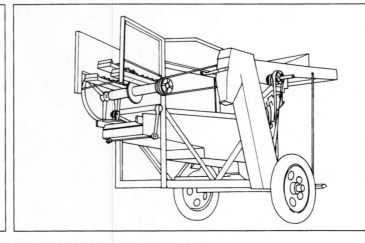

MOBILE MULTI-CROP THRESHER

This thresher has a threshing drum with rasp bars, a choice of concaves and sieves, straw walkers and an adjustable winnowing fan. It is belt-driven and is available with a 3.7kW engine and a 337mm long drum or, alternatively, with a 5.6kW engine and a 560mm long drum. Two concaves are provided, one with linear rods for threshing rice, the other with angle bars for all other grains. The thresher is of steel construction and is mounted on a chassis with two pneumatic-tyred wheels.

RAJAN UNIVERSAL EXPORTS (MFRS) PVT LTD
P.O. Box 250
Madras 600 001
INDIA

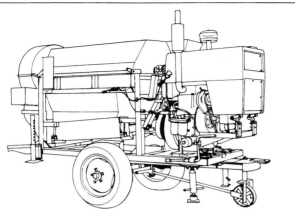

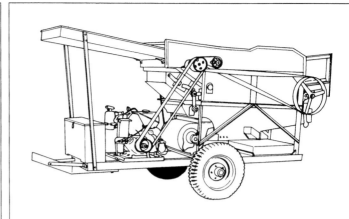

MULTI-CROP THRESHER

This mobile thresher can be used for a wide variety of grains including maize, soya beans, sorghum, millet, wheat and rice; it can accommodate tall traditional rice varieties. It is of all-steel construction and is fitted with a 9kW, single cylinder, water-cooled diesel engine. Alternatively, it can be supplied without the engine. The machine is carried on a single axle with two pneumatic-tyred wheels plus an iron manoeuvring wheel and it can be towed by animal, tractor or suitable vehicle. The threshing assembly comprises an open threshing cylinder with spike and knives, a heavy-duty steel rod concave with replaceable sieves, an oscillating tray and a winnowing fan. Operation of the thresher requires three men, one each to supply, thresh and bag off the grain. Cleaning efficiency 98%.
Weight 1400kg.

PUNJAB TRACTORS LTD
P.O. Box 6, Phase IV
SAS Nagar
Chandigarh 160 055
INDIA

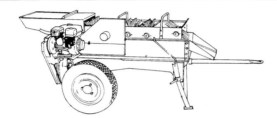

'TONGA' MAIZE HUSKER

The husking mechanism comprises six sets of cast iron and rubber rollers, rotating against each other along the floor of the machine. Cobs are fed on to this floor and carried over the rollers by rubber-fingered press wheels, mounted on cross-shafts. The cob husks are caught between the rotating rollers, stripped from the cobs and then discharged beneath the machine. The husked cobs are carried on to a separate discharge chute. The husker is belt-driven and can be powered by a 4.5-5kW, diesel or petrol engine.

BOURGOIN S.A.
61 Av. Georges-Clemenceau
B.P. 17
Chantonnay 85110
FRANCE

SBI GRAIN THRASHER

This mobile thresher is suitable for most grain types, including rice, wheat, maize, sunflower, sorghum and millet. The threshing unit primarily comprises a threshing drum, winnower and straw walkers. This assembly is mounted on a two-wheeled trailer with pneumatic tyres; a drawbar with a yoke is provided for transportation by a pair of bullocks or the thresher can be drawn by a tractor. An electric motor or small engine is required to power the machine.

SREE BHUVANESHWARI
INDUSTRIES M/S
168/C Avanashi Road
Peelamedu
Coimbatore 641 004
INDIA

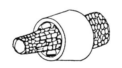

CORN-OFF

This hand-tool has serrated, stainless-steel blades forming a tubular blade around the cob and held against the cob surface by a pair of spring-loaded handles. Each handle is 215mm long and made of plated steel. The cob is stood on end, on a firm surface, and the implement is pushed down over it to strip off the grains. The blade shape adjusts to the size and taper of the cob without damaging the grains.

LEHMAN HARDWARE &
APPLIANCES INC.
P.O. Box 41
4779 Kidron Road
Kidron
OH 44636
USA

MANUAL MAIZE SHELLER

This simple hand-tool has a hollow, conical body with four rows of serrated ribs running axially on the inner side. The sheller is held in one hand while a maize cob is inserted and simultaneously rotated with the other. This rotation causes the internal ribs to strip the grains off the cob. Output is dependent on the size of the cob and on its maturity and moisture content.

INSTITUTE FOR AGRICULTURAL
RESEARCH
Samaru
P.O. Box 1044
Zaria
NIGERIA

Similar shellers are manufactured by:

MULTI-SPRAY SYSTEMS
P.O. Box HG 570
Highlands
Harare
ZIMBABWE

ZIMCAST
P.O. Box 490
Gweru
ZIMBABWE

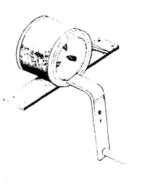

CHITETZE HAND-OPERATED MAIZE SHELLER

This sheller comprises two steel cylinders. The inner cylinder, fitted with two rows of internal teeth, is revolved within the outer by hand-crank. The shellers can be bench mounted using the bracket provided. The shellers are made in three sizes to suit the principal maize varieties grown in Malawi. The sizes relate to the circle formed by the ends of the teeth, and are 40mm, 33mm and 27mm respectively. The sheller has an output of 30kg/hour from dehusked maize.

PETROLEUM SERVICES (MALAWI)
LTD
Barnes Road
Ginnery Corner
P.O. Box 1900
Blantyre
MALAWI

MANUAL MAIZE SHELLER

This single-hole sheller weighs 6kg and can be fitted on to the rim of a box or other container to catch the shelled grain. Cobs are inserted individually through the feed inlet and are held between a serrated disc and a pressure plate; this pressure plate is spring-loaded to accommodate different cob sizes. Rotation of the serrated disc, by a hand-crank, strips the grains from the cob, which is then directed to an outlet outside the container. This type of sheller is very popular and versions are available from many suppliers, including:

COSSUL & CO PVT LTD
123/367 Industrial Area
Fazalgunj
Kanpur
U.P.
INDIA

DANDEKAR BROTHERS & CO
Shivajinagar
Sangli
Maharashtra
416 416
INDIA

G. NORTH & SON (PVT) LTD
P.O. Box 111
Southerton
Harare
ZIMBABWE

CORN SHELLERS

C.S. Bell produce this small maize sheller designed for dry ear maize and walnuts. It includes a cob ejector and tipping attachment. The spring plate adjusts to fit all sizes of ears.

C.S. BELL CO.
170 W. Davis Street
Box 291
Tiffin
OH 44883
USA

Similar implements are manufactured by:

**AGRICULTURAL TOOLS FACTORY
LTD**
P.O. Box 2
Birganj
NEPAL

CECOCO
P.O. Box 8
Ibaraki City
Osaka 567
JAPAN

RAJAN UNIVERSAL EXPORTS
(MFRS) PVT LTD
P.O. Box 250
Madras 600 100
INDIA

CORRADI
Av. Getúlio Vargas 735
Caixa Postal 2
Itaúna
Minas Gerais
BRAZIL

MUELLER IRMÃOS S.A.
Av. Pres. Wenceslau Braz. 1046
Vila Lindóia
C.P. 3336
Curibita (D.P. 57) 80 000
Paraná
BRAZIL

CECCATO OLINDO
Via Giustiniani 1
Arsego (Padua) 35010
ITALY

PRODOMETAL
Carrera 31 No 11-75
Bogotá
COLOMBIA

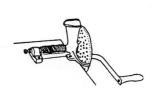

BENCH-MOUNTED MAIZE SHELLER

This is very similar to the manual shellers previously described, but is fitted with a mounting block to enable it to be attached to a bench, container or stand. Models are available from:

ALVAN BLANCH DEVELOPMENT CO. LTD
Chelworth
Malmesbury
Wilts SN16 9SG
UK

ALMACO
P.O. Box 296
99 M Avenue
Nevada
IO 50201
USA

RENSON LANDRECIES S.A.R.L.
37 route d'Happegarbes
B.P. 12
Landrecies 59550
FRANCE

COSSUL & CO. PVT LTD
123/367 Industrial Area
Fazalgunj
Kanpur
U.P.
INDIA

MAIZE SHELLERS

The following two companies supply shellers with optional metal stands:

UPROMA
B.P. 111
Kara
TOGO

COBEMAG
B.P. 161
Parakou
REPUBLIC OF BENIN

A similar free-standing sheller, fitted with a treadle drive, is available from:

CECOCO
P.O. Box 8
Ibaraki City
Osaka 567
JAPAN

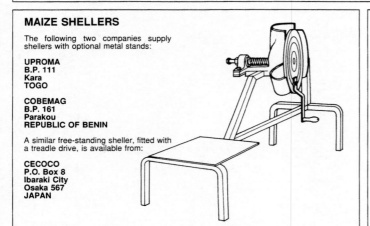

NDUME HAND-OPERATED MAIZE SHELLER

This simple maize sheller is constructed of three basic parts. It can be mounted on a bench, table or post and has an output of up to 30kg/hour.

NDUME PRODUCTS LTD
P.O. Box 62
Gilgil
KENYA

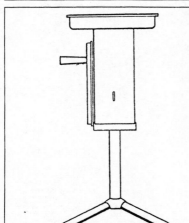

SG2 MAIZE SHELLER

This disc-type sheller is mounted on a tripod and can be operated manually by means of a flywheel with a handle, or it can be powered by an electric motor. Output 300-500kg/hour.
Weight 55kg manual unit, 45kg powered unit.

ABI-MÉCHANIQUE
B.P. 343
45 rue Pierre et Marie Curie
(Zone 4c)
Abidjan
IVORY COAST

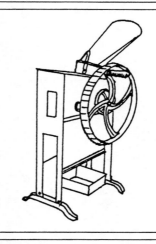

PORTABLE MAIZE SHELLERS

This range of shellers includes single- and double-inlet models. They are portable units, with cleaning fans built into the casings at the grain outlet. Cobs are fed individually through the inlets and are shelled by a rotating cast iron stripper plate. The single-hole model ABMS3 has an output of 300kg/hour and is operated by a hand-turned flywheel fitted with a handle. The double-hole model ABMS8 has an output of 800kg/hour and can be powered by a hand-crank or a foot-pedal. Alternatively, either model can be powered by a 0.4kW electric motor.

ALVAN BLANCH DEVELOPMENT CO. LTD
Chelworth
Malmesbury
Wilts SN16 9SG
UK

Shellers similar to the single-hole model described above are available from:

CORRADI
Av. Getúlio Vargas 735
Caixa Postal 2
Itaúna
Minas Gerais
BRAZIL

MUELLER IRMÃOS S.A.
Av. Pres. Wenceslau Braz. 1046
C.P. 3336
Curibita (D.P.57) 80 000
Paraná
BRAZIL

RENSON LANDRECIES S.A.R.L.
37 route d'Happegarbes
B.P. 12
Landrecies 59550
FRANCE

COBEMAG
B.P. 161
Parakou
REPUBLIC OF BENIN

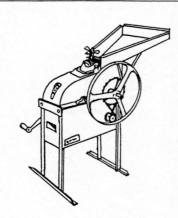

MAIZE SHELLER

This free-standing sheller has a hopper feed system, and a spring-loaded pressure lever which is adjustable to cater for different cob types and sizes. The rotating stripper plate is mounted in split bearings within an outer casing, and a cleaning fan is incorporated into this housing at the grain outlet. The sheller is provided with a hand crank and also a drive-belt pulley for an external 0.2kW power source. Output 300-600kg/hour. Weight 76kg.

PENAGOS HERMANOS & CIA LTD
Apartado Aéreo 689
Búcaramanga
COLOMBIA

Similar machines are available from:

PRODOMETAL
Carrera 31 No 11-75
Bogotá
COLOMBIA

CORRADI
Av. Getúlio Vargas 735
Caixa Postal 2
Itaúna
Minas Gerais
BRAZIL

AGRICULTURAL ENGINEERS LTD
Ring Road Industrial Area
P.O. Box 12127
Accra North
GHANA

AGRO MACHINERY LTD
P.O. Box 3281
Bush Rod Island
Monrovia
LIBERIA

HAND AND POWER MAIZE SHELLER

This free-standing sheller is a single-hole machine, suitable for feed or seed maize. It is of all-steel construction with a built-in cleaning fan and a ratchet-type hand-crank. A belt pulley can be supplied for use with an external power drive; a 0.75kW motor is recommended for optimum performance.
Output:

- 100-120kg/hour if hand-driven.
- 200-300kg/hour if powered.

Weight 94kg.

COSSUL & CO PVT LTD
123/367 Industrial Area
Fazalgunj
Kanpur
U.P.
INDIA

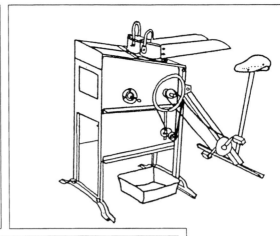

TWO-HOLE MAIZE SHELLER-GRADER

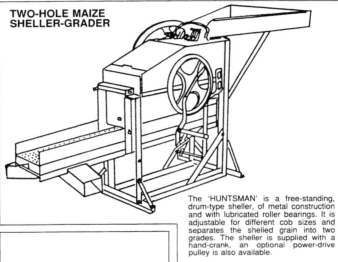

The 'HUNTSMAN' is a free-standing, drum-type sheller, of metal construction and with lubricated roller bearings. It is adjustable for different cob sizes and separates the shelled grain into two grades. The sheller is supplied with a hand-crank, an optional power-drive pulley is also available.

G. NORTH & SON (PVT) LTD
P.O. Box 111
Southerton
Harare
ZIMBABWE

The following company offers a similar machine, again with both manual and power drive options. The manual drive requires two operators, generating a drum speed of 180-250 rev/min and an output of 500kg/hour. If the machine is driven through a tractor power take-off, drum speed can be increased to 380 rev/min to produce a shelling output of 750kg/hour.

TANZANIA ENGINEERING AND MANUFACTURING DESIGN ORGANIZATION (TEMDO)
P.O. Box 6111
Arusha
TANZANIA

PEDAL-OPERATED SHELLER

This is a free-standing, disc-type sheller with a single-hole feed inlet. A bicycle seat and a pedal-and-chain drive mechanism allows the operator to be seated at the sheller. There is also a pulley wheel for a powered belt-drive if desired. Other drive options are available, including a hand-crank, a 0.75kW electric motor or a tractor power take-off connection. If it is to be tractor-powered, the machine must be fixed to the ground. A two-hole powered sheller is also available.

CECCATO OLINDO
Via Giustiniani 1
Arsego (Padua) 35010
ITALY

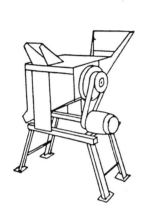

MAIZE HUSKER SHELLER

This is a drum-type sheller, powered by a 1.5kW motor and incorporating a cleaning fan and a bagging-off chute.

MESSRS LAREDO
Industria e Commércio
Rua 1 De Agosto
Bauru (S.P.) 17 100
BRAZIL

A similar sheller is manufactured by:

COMPAHIA PENHA DE MÁQUINAS AGRíCOLAS
Av. Brazil 1724
Ribeirão Preto S.P.
BRAZIL

'MAT 80' MAIZE SHELLER

The standard model of this sheller is a free-standing unit fitted with a belt-drive pulley and powered by a 2-4kW electric motor. The shelled grain is discharged through an outlet chute in the base of the machine. Alternative options include connections for tractor mounting and power take-off, a bulk grain discharge elevator and a bagging-off facility.
Shelling speed 700-750 rev/min.

ECOMAT
Le Val Rouge
B.P. 132
Morlaix 29210
FRANCE

POWER MAIZE SHELLERS

This static sheller is constructed of steel, with a hopper feed, winnowing fan and separate outlets for grain and stripped cobs. It is belt-driven from a 3.7kW electric motor or engine.
Output 1500kg/hour.

DANDEKAR BROTHERS & CO
Shivajinagar
Sangli
Maharashtra 416 416
INDIA

A similar sheller, with the same power requirement, is available from:

MOHINDER & CO. ALLIED INDUSTRIES
Kurali District
Ropar
Punjab
INDIA

BAMBA CORN SHELLER

For shelling millet, sorghum and maize, this machine requires a 5kW engine and has an hourly output of 300kg of millet or 1500kg of maize.

MARPEX
1 rue Thurot
44000 Nantes
FRANCE

PORTABLE SHELLER

This portable sheller is mounted on a metal framework and belt-driven from a 2.6kW diesel or petrol engine, mounted alongside. Output 1.75 tonne/hour.
Weight 68kg.

C.V. KARYA HIDUP SENTOSA
Jl. Magelang 144
Yogyakarta 55241
INDONESIA

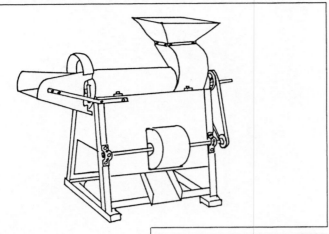

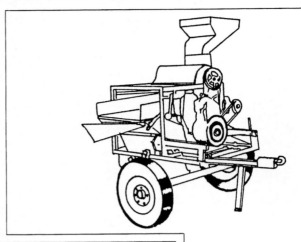

MAIZE SHELLER

This is a powered sheller with a winnowing fan. The cobs are discharged at the top of the machine and the cleaned grain through a bottom chute. Four models are available, ranging from 1.5 to 4kW in power.

RAJAN UNIVERSAL EXPORTS (MFRS) PVT LTD
P.O. Box 250
Madras 600 001
INDIA

A similar sheller is manufactured by:

STANDARD AGRICULTURAL ENGINEERING CO. (SAECO)
824/5 Industrial Area B
Ludhiana
Punjab 141 003
INDIA

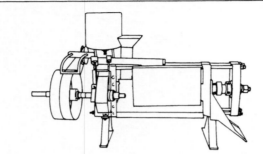

MAIZE SHELLER/THRESHER

This is a static sheller, supported on a pair of two-legged metal stands. It is fitted with a drive-belt pulley, to be powered by any type of motor or engine.

MEKINS AGRO PRODUCTS (PVT) LTD
6-3-866/A Begumpet
Greenlands
Hyderabad 500 016
INDIA

MAIZE SHELLER

The following company offers a sheller that can be towed by a power tiller. It is made of steel, with conical shelling drum, oscillating sieve and adjustable aspirator. It is said to provide 99-100% separation recovery with no broken grains.
   Power required: 6kW petrol engine or 5kW diesel engine.
Weight 280kg.

P.I. FARM PRODUCTS INC.
Km. 16 Malanday
Valenzuela
Metro Manila
PHILIPPINES

Similar machines are manufactured by:

SV AGRO INDUSTRIES ENTERPRISES INC.
65 Commission Civil Street
Jaro
Iloilo City
PHILIPPINES

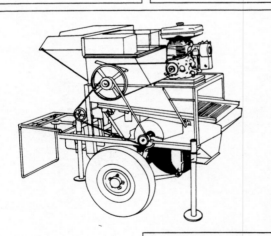

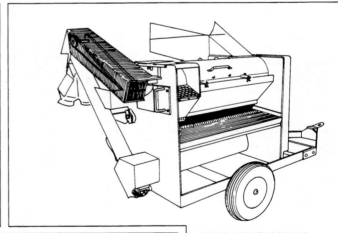

AGAD CORN SHELLER/HUSKER

This mobile sheller is based on an IRRI prototype, mounted on two wheels with pneumatic tyres and shock absorbers. The threshing drum is fitted with spiral beater bars and rotates within an assembly of three concaves, spring-loaded against the drum. Oscillating sieves separate the shelled grain from the trash and a winnowing fan removes light impurities. The sheller is belt-driven from a 5kW petrol engine or from a 2-3kW electric motor.
Weight 303kg.

C & B CRAFTS
Maginao
San Rafael
Bulacan
PHILIPPINES

NAPHIRE MAIZE SHELLER

This all-metal sheller is mounted on a towing chassis with two pneumatic-tyred wheels and a drawbar. It is a drum and concave sheller and can accept any size of cob, with 99.9% shelling recovery. It can be fitted with either a 12kW petrol engine or a 9kW diesel engine and weighs approximately 500kg.

NATIONAL POST-HARVEST INSTITUTE FOR RESEARCH & EXTENSION (NAPHIRE)
Muñoz
Nueva Ecija
PHILIPPINES

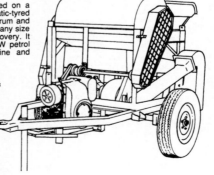

ABMS 1500T MOBILE MAIZE SHELLER

This machine has a single shelling cylinder and a full width shaking screen to separate the grain from pieces of cob. The process is aided by an integral winnowing fan. The screens can be changed to allow other crops such as sorghum and millet to be processed. The cleaned grain is collected in a horizontal screw and elevated by an auger to a bagging-off point. The sheller is driven from a tractor power take-off and can be supplied either with a three-point hitch mounting or wheels.

ALVAN BLANCH DEVELOPMENT CO. LTD
Chelworth
Malmesbury
Wilts SN16 9SG
UK

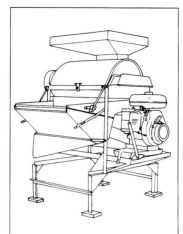

THREE-DRUM MAIZE SHELLER

A trailer-mounted, three-drum sheller has been developed by the University of the Philippines, with a capacity of up to 2.5 tonnes per hour and a shelling efficiency of up to 99%. It can accommodate different sizes of corn cobs and an aspirator/grain cleaner is also fitted. The machine is belt-driven, with a power requirement of 5kW. It is fabricated from round and flat metal bars and galvanized iron sheets, plus bearings. Potential manufacturers can obtain technical drawings and details from:

**AGRICULTURAL MECHANIZATION
DEVELOPMENT PROGRAMME
(AMDP)
CEAT
University of the Philippines
Los Baños College
Laguna 4031
PHILIPPINES**

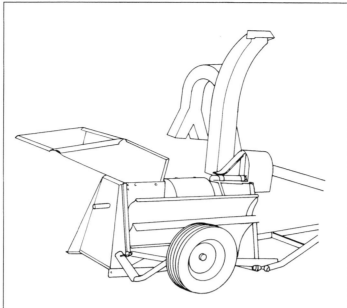

PORTABLE MAIZE HUSKER-SHELLERS

The following company offers a range of portable and static shellers suitable for any size and type of maize. The basic design is similar for each model and includes a feed hopper that can be fitted in three positions. A self-cleaning grain thrower discharges the shelled maize at a height of four metres, while the stripped cobs can be discharged at up to three metres' height and in any direction. Additional options include:

- Connections for tractor three-point linkage and power take-off;
- Two-wheeled chassis with pneumatic-tyres;
- Free-standing chassis;
- 7.5kW electric motor;
- 11-19kW petrol engine;
- Two-spout bagging-off outlet.

**HABAN MANUFACTURING CO.
2100 Northwestern Avenue
Racine
Wisconsin 53404
USA**

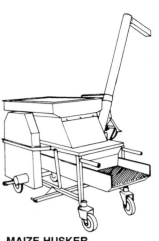

MAIZE HUSKER

This sheller is designed for fodder maize and the discharge spout delivers the shelled maize directly into a trailer or to a bagging-off point. The machine is mounted on four small wheels and powered by a 4kW motor. Alternatively it can be tractor-powered.
Output 4 tonnes/hour.
Weight 400kg.

**POLJOSTROJ
Industrija masina i opreme
25250 Odžaci
Karadjordjeva br. 34
YUGOSLAVIA**

BAMBY MAIZE SHELLER

This sheller can be driven by the power take-off of a tractor or by electric motor rated at 3kW. The model illustrated can shell up to two tonnes of maize per hour and is fitted with a tall discharge auger for loading directly into a trailer. Other attachments include a feed elevator for whole cobs and a discharge blower to deposit chaff and cob pieces away from the working area.

**BOURGOIN S.A.
61 Av. Georges-Clemenceau
85110 Chantonnay
BP 17
FRANCE**

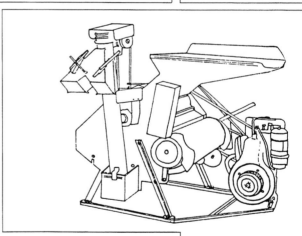

MOBILE MAIZE SHELLER

This mobile sheller will handle both husked and unhusked maize. It has a 275mm diameter shelling cylinder and is belt-driven from a 5.6kW diesel engine. Cylinder speed 700-750 rev/min. Grain recovery 98%.

**NEW RUHAAK INDUSTRIES
Jalan Pintu Besar Utara 11
Jakarta
INDONESIA**

TRAILER-MOUNTED SHELLER

This is a trailer-mounted, disc-type sheller with a single-hole feed inlet. There is a power take-off shaft for powered drive although the machine can be fitted with a separate power source if desired. A two-hole powered sheller is also available.

**CECCATO OLINDO
Via Giustiniani 1
Arsego (Padua) 35010
ITALY**

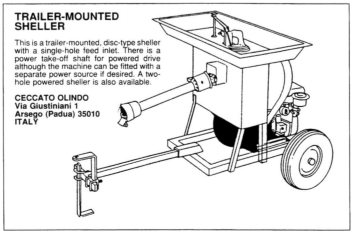

TROPICAL SHELLER

The Bamba tropical sheller is designed for African millet, sorghum and maize and can be operated by one person. It is powered by a 4kW electric motor or 7kW petrol or diesel engine or with the power take-off of any tractor. The output per hour is 1500kg of maize or 300-500kg of millet.

The grain can be collected in bags laid on the ground or a long auger can be attached for discharging directly into a trailer.

**BOURGOIN S.A.
61 Av. Georges-Clemenceau
85110 Chantonnay
BP 17
FRANCE**

Jeremy Hartley/Panos

6. CROP PROCESSING AND STORAGE

Most crops have to be dried, packaged or processed into some slightly different form before storage. This section looks at the processes needed to increase the nutritional or market value of harvested and threshed crops. The emphasis is on small- to medium-scale items of equipment suitable for household or village processing, mainly of seed crops for human food, animal feed and oil extraction, but also of fruit, vegetables and fibre crops.

Inevitably there is the need to ensure the material is dry enough, if it is to be stored for any length of time. Drying and storage is a complex subject in its own right and users concerned with this aspect of post-harvest processing should consult local expert advisers before investing in equipment.

Also included in this section is equipment designed to clean (especially) grain before, and sometimes after, a milling or shelling process. These items precede milling and other processing equipment, which is presented in order of horsepower requirement within each category, starting with manual machinery.

With manual equipment, low efficiency is clearly undesirable even though a technique is effective; this is particularly true for oil processing equipment. There are, however, many occasions where the only feasible solution is a piece of equipment which is hand- or pedal-powered, and the low efficiency, in terms of human effort, is accepted. Improved efficiencies can be achieved with animal-powered equipment,

especially presses and crushers (e.g. sugar cane crushers). Here, the efficient conversion of the animal draught power to rotary motion is the most important consideration.

In the majority of cases, though, crop processing equipment will be powered by motors and these are always a vital factor in the selection of equipment, and may cost far more than the actual process machine. This is particularly so where electricity is not available and small petrol or diesel engines are required.

EQUIPMENT

Grain drying machinery

Although grain can be dried on a continuous or on a batch basis, it is much more convenient at low and medium scale to use the batch system. In the commoner designs, the seed or grain is contained in a large rectangular box or tray. The grain should be spread evenly over the perforated plate in the bottom of the box and heated air will be blown up through a lower chamber.

Typical drying rates would be 1 per cent per hour of moisture removed. The power requirement for this type of operation would be 1.5kW for 1 tonne capacity. The fan may be diesel or electrically operated and the heat may be provided by kerosene, electricity, rice hulls, gas or other fuel. Grain can be loaded in sacks but it is usually loaded in bulk, and discharge spouts are provided with sack mounting hooks.

Storage

Storage equipment must keep the grain dry and free from insect and rodent attack. In some types of store, where the grain may not be quite dry enough for long-term storage, ventilation is considered important. In these stores, and most others, it is common to dust the grain with malathion or similar insecticide to protect it from insect attack. Grain which is sufficiently dry can be stored in airtight containers which may be fumigated with a gas, often derived from aluminium phosphide tablets.

Rodent attack is usually minimized through the use of rodent-proof materials, the use of rat guards on the legs of wooden stores, and other rodent control measures.

Air-screen seed cleaners

These machines will clean seed efficiently, removing leaf, chaff, soil and other rubbish. Small-scale versions are hand-operated and are suitable for sorghum, millet, maize, soya beans and any free-flowing seed crop. Different screen sizes can be provided to suit any size of crop and usually a minimum of two screens is needed for each operation. The upper screen filters out oversize material and the lower screen filters out the undersize. The middle-sized material is blown through a winnowing section to remove the light bits of leaf, chaff, glumes and hollow seed. This machine can be used immediately after a thresher and prior to hulling, milling or resowing.

Simple winnowers are also available with an electric motor-operated fan. These will separate the light material from the heavy, simply by blowing the mass of material up into an air column. In one type, the heavy material continues upwards while the light particles are blown sideways. Another type allows the heavy material to sink to the bottom of the column. This machine is suitable both for pre-cleaning a seed crop or for separating hulled rice, coffee etc. from the husks.

Decorticators

Several crops have an unpalatable husk or shell, which is removed by a decorticator. The most suitable machine for millet or sorghum is the vertical disc mill developed by IDRC and is available in most parts of Africa. Specialized machines are available for sunflower seeds, groundnuts (peanuts), palm kernels, etc. usually by some rasping or impact mechanism.

Grain milling

The milling of grain and grain legumes for human and animal feed is one of the most basic of crop processing requirements.

Plate mill

The plate mill is usually limited to about 7kW and is derived from the stone mill or quern. In the modern plate mill, two chilled iron plates are mounted on a horizontal axis so that one of the plates rotates and the grain is ground between them. The pressure between them governs the fineness of the product and is adjusted by a hand-screw. The grain is usually coarsely cracked in the feed screw to the centre of the plates. Grooves in the plates decrease in depth outwards towards the periphery so that the grain is ground progressively finer until it emerges at the outer edge and falls by gravity into a sack or bowl.

This machine is also very effective in grinding wet products such as wetted maize, tomatoes, peppers and spices. Water may be added by simply pouring it into the feed section as required. Manual versions of the plate mill are available but

the work is hard and throughput is only 1-2kg per hour on cereals. It is more effective than pounding or rubbing stones, however, and will produce fine meal.

Roller mills

For feeding ruminants, grain needs to be crushed rather than ground. A roller mill which simply flattens the grain is adequate for this purpose, a 3kW machine being able to crush up to half a tonne per hour of barley.

Hammer mills

These range in size from 2kW to 20kW in village operation and consist essentially of a circular chamber in which beaters whirl at high speed. Around the tips of the beaters a circular perforated plate allows the shattered grain to filter through either to fall out of the base by gravity or to be sucked through a fan to an elevated delivery point. The size of the holes in the perforated plate determines the particle size, and a 1mm hole size is suitable to most human foods, whereas a 3mm hole is preferred for animal feed.

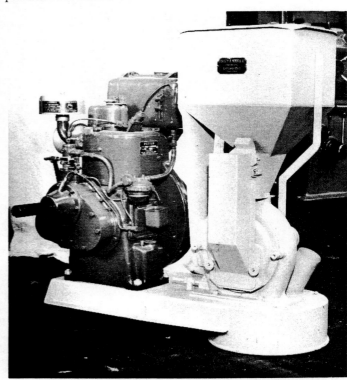

Small grain hammer mill with diesel drive

Most grain crops can be ground in a hammer mill. The input to the mill can be controlled by hand in a feed tray to the centre or side of the mill. Alternatively, bulk hoppers can be mounted over the mill to give a continuous operation. The mill may be driven by a direct-mounted electric motor, by V-belt or flat belt. The simplest type is the direct-mounted, gravity-discharge mill because there are no additional belts or bearings except those of the electric motor. In this case the motor is flange-mounted on the back of the mill and the hammers are keyed directly on to the stub shaft of the motor. The flat belt type is next to be preferred. The V-belt drive type suffers from the problem that all belts have to be replaced when one breaks. The direct drive mill needs no guards and is clearly safer. It is also up to 20 per cent more efficient.

The hammer mill is used just as frequently for animal and poultry meal production as for human food. Oyster shell, an ingredient of poultry meal, can also be ground in the hammer mill, but wear rates are much higher.

The vertical meal mixer is excellent for blending meal with concentrates or other ingredients. A vertical conical-bottomed hopper has a central screw auger which circulates the meal. A 2-tonne hopper would probably have a 3kW mixer drive motor. Several companies supply a complete mill, mix and storage unit containing a feed hopper, and a hammer mill with pneumatic delivery to a vertical mixer set in a round or square hopper. This is usually a good way to buy a matched system for a reasonable price.

Rice hullers

For village use, the Engleberg huller is often quite satisfactory. They are commonly available in small hand-operated sizes or motorized versions of 3-10kW. Throughput, of course, varies with many factors but roughly from 10kg/h for hand operation up to 300kg/h for the bigger models.

The machine comprises essentially a cast steel rotor with rasp bars on it which turns inside a cast housing with a slotted plate in the base. An adjustable knife projects into the side of the housing to increase the stress on the grains of rice. The mill is mounted horizontally on a steel frame so that paddy rice fed in at one end circulates along the rotor to emerge hulled at the other end. Pieces of hull and bran come out through the slotted plate but a separation is still necessary after discharge. A motor-driven aspirator or a hand-winnower can be used for this task. A significant number of grains are broken by this process but the food value is unimpaired. If an unacceptable amount of bran remains on the grain, it can be passed through a second time at the risk of even more grains being broken.

Less rice is broken if it is parboiled first. This is done on about 50 per cent of all rice grown and is simply a soaking and heating process which pre-cooks the grains, loosens the hull, sterilizes and preserves the rice. Village parboiling can be carried out with crude boiling pans but enclosed fires, chimneys and insulation can increase their efficiency significantly.

More sophisticated rice hullers are available, but generally a higher level of maintenance is required. The most popular is the rubber roller-huller which shears the paddy between a pair of rubber rollers of about 150mm diameter, turning in opposite directions at different speeds and with a gap of about 1.5mm. Another alternative is the under-runner disc huller which consists of two flat stones, one of which rotates. The grain is fed through a hole in the centre of the upper stone. It is then sheared in the gap between the horizontal stones as it moves outwards towards the periphery.

Special polishers are available for removing the bran after hulling. One type spins the rice by means of rotor blades to which are attached leather strips. These rotate at high speed abrading the rice grains within a slotted plate drum. Another type uses carborundum stones against the slotted plate. For the village scale of operation, an Engleberg huller with an integral leather-strip polisher is a suitable system.

Groundnut shellers

Simple hand- or motor-operated machines can decorticate groundnuts (peanuts). A rasp bar reciprocates in a semi-circular drum which has a coarse screen in the base. The clearance between the bar and the screen is too small for the nut with the shell. The holes in the screen are large enough to let the broken pieces of shell and whole kernels fall through. The machine can be trickle-fed automatically or simply fed by handfuls.

Coffee pulpers

Both hand- and motor-operated pulpers are manufactured. These strip the flesh off the coffee 'cherries'. The manual type usually comprises a vertical disc covered with rounded projections. It is turned by a handle to rasp the cherries against an adjustable blade. Manual capacities are up to 300kg/h. The motorized versions have a roughened drum, possibly of stainless steel, which rotates to rasp the cherries against a cast iron breast. For both types of pulper, a plentiful supply of water is required to wash away the flesh, leaving the beans to be separated for further processing. A 1kW machine can handle up to 750kg/h of coffee cherries. It is important to use the correct discs and drums for the particular type of coffee.

Coffee hullers

Once the coffee has been dried, it has to be hulled in either a hand- or motor-driven huller. These machines break open the hulls which encase the beans, using a shearing action. Most of them are of the Engleberg type — that is to say, a ribbed, horizontal, cast iron rotor which turns inside a close-fitting housing made of cast iron on top and either solid or woven wire on the underside. The coffee is fed in at one end and the shearing stress may be adjusted by a side-fitting blade. The beans, hulls and dust emerge from the discharge and must be separated by sieves and winnowers. The coffee must be crisp and dry to be satisfactorily treated in this machine.

Oil extractors

The most efficient small-scale press for seeds consists of a machined, tapered screw-auger which rotates in a perforated drum or slotted housing. The slight taper allows adjustment of the flight clearance by screwing it in or out of the housing. The pitch of the screws often decreases towards discharge in order to increase the pressure gradually. The oil emerges from the slots or holes along the housing, and the residue at the discharge annulus at the end of the screw. Careful adjustment of the slot width, temperature generated in the extraction section and insertion of the screw are important factors in efficient operation of this machine. Generally, most small oil seeds can be processed in this machine quite effectively.

Palm oil presses can be very much simpler. A perforated drum or cage is required and the fruitlets are crushed simply by means of a close-fitting ram into the drum. The ram may be hydraulically or screw operated. It can be a manual system developed perhaps from a lorry jack, or motorized.

The oil contained in the inner nut of the palm oil fruitlet is of a different type, and needs separate processing. Centrifugal crackers are usually used to break the shell from around the kernel. In this machine, bars rotate at high speed to throw the nuts against a surrounding chamber wall, thus breaking them open. After this, the two components of shell and kernel are separated by one or more of a variety of means such as screens, winnowers and clay baths. The screw press can then be used to extract oil from the kernel. Alternatively, simply pounding and boiling will extract most of the oil if a manual method is preferred.

Coconut shredders

At domestic and village level the coconut is first of all hand-husked on a firm spike, and is then chopped open with a large knife to expose the meat. The open nut is dried in the sun to release the copra. The shell can also be burnt to provide heat for kilns in which the copra is dried. The white meat is pared by hand and shredded in a machine. Shredding machines are available in various forms. They usually consist of knives mounted on discs which rotate at high speed. A plunger may force the coconut on to a horizontal disc, or sets of rotating vertical discs may inter-leave with a stationary set of discs to tear the meat apart. The blade setting can be adjusted for the production of chips, slices, strips, threads and various other products.

Oil press for coconut

The meat is first passed through a hammer mill with a 6mm screen. It then passes to a plate mill set at the minimum clearance, to produce a finely ground yet soft pulp. This is mixed with hot water and pressed. There are various types of pulp press including the perforated drum mentioned under 'oil extractors', and smaller, cheaper filter presses which pump the slurry through a fine cloth mesh. Separation of the oil from the milk which comes from this process is best carried out in a centrifuge.

Cassava

Medium-scale equipment is available for processing cassava into a pre-cooked meal known as gari in many areas of West Africa. The crop is usually hand-peeled (despite many attempts to develop a machine peeler) and is then washed. A grating drum, which consists of a roughened perforated plate nailed to a wooden cylinder, is driven at about 1000 revolutions per minute beneath a wooden hopper containing the peeled tubers. Tiny chips of cassava are ripped off and collected at the back of the grater ready for bagging and fermenting for about 1-5 days on wooden racks. They are then pressed, about six bags at a time, in a wooden frame with a large capstan-type screw on top. Some of these have a screw at each corner of the square frame; others just have one central screw. Water pours out of the porous sacks.

The blocks of pulp are often disintegrated again in the grater and then fed on to the cooking surface. This may be a series of hemispherical pans, a long flat pan or a semi-circular trough. In this last case, a rotor turns with angled paddles along the length of the trough, keeping the granulated cassava moving down the trough. Heat is provided underneath the trough by firewood, gas, coal or fuel oil. The temperature must be sufficient to gelatinize the raw cassava and stabilize it. Moisture is also driven off and the product emerges hot and dry. After cooling and sifting, it is ready for packaging in sacks or heat-sealed polythene bags. It is often hammer-milled one further time and mixed with other cereals such as ground rice to make other food products.

Sugar cane crushers

The main features of these machines are sets of rollers through which the canes are crushed. They can be powered by hand, animal, or motor and are available with two or three grooved rollers. Most machines have horizontal rollers and are geared down to increase the torque. The cane is fed manually through the rollers and a small 3kW machine can crush from half to one tonne per hour. The grooves have to be re-machined at regular intervals to maintain efficiency. The waste material from sugar cane crushing, called 'bagasse', is sometimes fed to animals, but is often used to fuel the sugar refining process.

Fodder cutters

While livestock can often browse over waste material such as bagasse, a more efficient way of presenting long fodder is in a chopped form. Some cutters are curved knives hinged on a cutting plate. These are dangerous if used without safety

devices. Rotary chaff and hay cutters, if properly guarded, are useful for fodder crops. These are hand- or motor-driven machines for cutting long straw and hay down to a more palatable size for cattle and other ruminants. The crop is also more suitable for storing, mixing and bulk feeding. The usual design incorporates a tray which feeds the bundles to a series of knives which are set as rotors in a wheel. The feed rate determines the chop length and is usually adjustable from about 10mm to 60mm. These machines will cut most types of green or dry fodder.

ADVANTAGES

Advantages of using powered processing machines are:
❍ Considerable time is saved on the performance of onerous and laborious manual tasks.
❍ Production rates are increased, which may lead to an increased cash profit or an increased food supply.
❍ Crops which might otherwise perish can be dried or processed to a state of longer preservation, again leading to greater food availability or cash profit.
❍ A centralized service machine, or a privately owned machine, may open up the way to growing new crops previously considered impossible, or unprofitable.

Improvements to traditional grain stores can be the cheapest way of reducing storage losses

ALTERNATIVES

For a crop which is already being produced in a particular area one alternative to purchasing a (motorized) machine is to use the traditional method. The traditional method invariably involves a machine constructed from wood, stone and twine — local materials — which is powered manually or by animals. Another alternative is to use locally made improved devices, using similar materials and designed and produced in response to locally felt needs and demand in rural workshops.

Traditional methods are available for most crops. Major exceptions are when new crops are introduced, and these are often a cash crop such as oil, gum or beverage.

Solar drying

Many crops are sun-dried for preservation. In most tropical countries this is still the best way to dry many crops even at factory scale. Rice, for example, may be solar-dried after parboiling. Several perishable fruits and vegetables, such as raisins, prunes and yams, are preserved by solar drying. The seeds of any crop need to be dried to below about 15 per cent to ensure good storage.

Simple aids to solar drying have been developed by using black polythene covers and chimney structures. These can be of considerable help in increasing the drying rate and protecting the crop from contamination and rain.

Grain storage

Some of the most common indoor and outdoor structures used for storage on farms are made of mud and split bamboo; in them the grain is usually damaged by insects, fungi and rodents. The structures cannot be effectively fumigated. Some of the indoor bins that are being built are metal bins, structures of burnt bricks plastered with cement, welded wire-mesh bins, and paddy straw and mud structures. The outdoor bins are constructed of metal and brick and appear as flat- and hopper-bottom metal bins, composite bins and reinforced brick bins. They can be hermetically sealed and placed underground or partly above ground. The capacity is about 500kg.

The bins used in villages are either circular or square, with capacities ranging from 500kg to 1000kg, made of standard sizes of galvanized iron sheets. The height may be from 0.5m to 1.0m. The circular bins are easy and economical to fabricate, while the square ones are convenient to keep in the corner of the building. The average life of metal bins is said to be over 20 years.

Bins can also be made of ferrocement, high-density polythene, and wood. Ferrocement bins are made of cement mortar and closely spaced wire mesh in capacities ranging from 0.15m to 1.0m. They are cylindrical and have flat bottoms and domed roofs. Wall thickness is normally 25mm.

Grain milling

The traditional method of grinding is by rubbing between flat stones, or in 'querns', or pounding with a mortar and pestle. The last method, especially, is still widely practised as a means of threshing or hulling and, as a less common application, for grinding. Grinding rates are very limited, usually to less then 0.5kg per hour. Querns and rubbing stones are more effective then pounding, but grinding rates are still less than 1kg per hour.

The rubbing stones rely on a local supply of suitable stones. Volcanic basalt is an excellent material for this purpose, together with granite or sandstone. One rectangular stone, 400-600mm long by 300-500mm wide, is simply scrubbed by a small stone of about 100 × 200mm and 100mm deep in a back-and-forth scrubbing action. Water may be added to prevent blocking and to soften the material.

The quern, as used 2000 years ago by the Romans, consists of two flat stones of about 350mm diameter with a hole in the

The mortar and pestle is still one of the most widely used methods for grinding grain

Jeremy Hartley/Oxfam

centre of the upper stone through which grain is poured. A wooden handle is usually fixed to the upper stone so that it can be rotated. The grain is crushed and sheared between the two stones before emerging at the outer edge. Larger versions of this model can be made for animal power, multiple human power, water-wheels or windmills. Stones over 1m in diameter are common in this case. A certain amount of skill is needed to dress the stones to fit together and to cut channels in each matching face, in order to grind the grain efficiently.

The mortar and pestle is very commonly used in many countries. This usually comprises a hollowed-out section of tree trunk which makes a bowl and large pole, up to 2m long and weighing about 20kg. The end of the pole or pestle is rammed repeatedly into the grain in the bowl until the process is complete. For hulling rice the grains are often placed in a loosely fitted cotton bag during the pounding process; the hulls are then winnowed away later.

Oil extractors

Few traditional techniques exist for oil extraction from seeds and, where they do, they often require considerable skill and force — and even then only meet with limited success. The exception is palm oil for which there are village techniques for sterilizing and squeezing out the oil from the fruitlets. Boiling pans, large pounding sticks and lever presses are all that is required. In some parts of West Africa the squeezing process is achieved partly by tramping fruits with bare feet in specially constructed pits.

Cassava

Domestic processing is common and to be recommended for home consumption, or small-market and roadside sales; large volume production techniques should only be considered when it is sold as an estate or co-operative cash crop. At any size of operation, however, the tubers need to be hand-peeled and washed, and a simple hand-grater or mortar and pestle will then prepare the crop for fermentation in bags or jars. Finally, after two or three days, the water is expelled by heavy stones or lever presses, dried and pre-cooked.

Table 1 Indicative costs

Process equipment	Capital	Running and maintenance p.a. (6h/day excl. fuel costs)	Infrastructure
Hammer mill Elec. 2kW	750	75	Elec. power
Elec. 5kW	1000	100	Elec. power
Diesel 10kW	2500	250	Fuel supply
Plate mill Elec. 1kW	500	20	Elec. power
Elec. 5kW	1000	100	Elec. power
Diesel 10kW	1750	250	Fuel supply
Sugar cane mill 5kW	750	75	Elec. power
Huller			
Rice Diesel 10kW	2000	125	Fuel supply
Electric 10kW	1000	125	Elec. power
Sorghum, Electric 5kW	1250	175	Elec. power
Millet, Electric 5kW	1250	175	Elec. power
Oil extractor, Elec. 5kW	6000	250	Elec. power
Diesel 5kW	7000	250	Fuel supply
Cassava garifier. Electric and gas or heating fuel 50kW	50000	700	Elec. power and fuel supply
Animal feed			
Hammer mill 10kW Electric	1250	50	Fuel supply
Roller mill 5kW Electric	900	50	Power supply
Chaff cutter 3kW Electric	1000	50	Power supply

COSTS AND BENEFITS

The cost of processing most crops is expressed as a cost per tonne of incoming crop. As most crops are seasonal it is convenient to base the costs over a one-year period.

The capital costs of the equipment may involve installation on to a concrete slab in a covered building. The building may or may not have walls and may need to be lockable. The cost of installing the power supply is not shown here but may need consideration. Other costs include depreciation, maintenance and repairs, fuel, loss of interest on capital and labour costs. Rates or ground rent may have to be paid on urban sites.

In Table 1, indicative figures are given for the capital costs and running and maintenance costs of a variety of crop processing machines commonly in use in developing countries. Also indicated are the requirements with respect to power source.

ECONOMICS

In order to establish whether investment in a crop-processing machine will be profitable, factors other than costs need to be taken into consideration. These can include expected capacity utilization over the year (in the case of custom services this is highly dependent on the number of customers and competitors); flexibility of machinery; supporting infrastructure (electricity, transportation, markets); and availability of fuel supplies and spare parts (both now and in the future).

The process of calculating overall costs of a grain hammer mill and a hand-operated plate mill is illustrated below. Once the cost is calculated, it can then be used to estimate whether a satisfactory profit margin can be achieved given local patterns of demand for services.

In the case of a hammer mill the annual throughput must be estimated by gauging the daily throughput and the number of working days per year. A service or contract mill is likely to be running in excess of 300 days per year and the fuel costs,

if it is diesel-driven, will obviously be considerable, outstripping perhaps in one year the capital cost of the mill. The profits from such an operation, however, should cover this. The feasibility of running these machines is clearly linked to the number of people likely to make use of them and the number of hours for which they can be operated.

The performance of machinery cannot always be maintained. Production will be interrupted by the normal turnover of customers, and the efficiency of most machines declines gradually as wear takes place in cutting faces and screens, etc.

Payment for service milling and hulling may also be made as a proportion, say 10 per cent, of the crop being processed. If this is the case, the cash equivalent has to be calculated. One must bear in mind the implications of storing considerable quantities of crop, together with the extra bagging, marketing and labour costs.

Example: Grain hammer mill Annual running costs of a grain hammer mill for the first five years of life:

	$
Cost of capital: mill 2500, 75 per cent financed by loan 15 per cent per year paid over 5 years	37!
Cost of building + concrete plinth: 125 paid in cash.	
Loss of interest @ 8 per cent	10(
Depreciation: mill over 5 years, zero resale value	50(
Maintenance and repairs: mill; new drive belts; bearings; beaters; perforated plates	25(
Engine	20(
Diesel fuel running 300 days @ 5 h per day	350(
Labour	250(
Total running costs	742
Average throughput of maize per year for human feed, flour size below 1mm	7!

Annual cost per tonne of maize = $\dfrac{7425}{75}$ = 9

Example: Hand-operated plate mill Annual running costs of a hand-operated plate mill for the first five years of life:

Cost of capital: mill 125, financed by loan 15 per cent per year over 5 years	19
Depreciation: mill over 5 years, zero resale value (in fact these mills often last much longer than 5 years)	25
Maintenance and repairs, new plates	25
Labour (assumed to be private)	—
Total annual cost	69
Average throughput of maize per year assuming 2h per day use at 1kg/h and 300 days per year	600kg
Annual cost per kg of maize = $\dfrac{69}{600}$	0.115
Annual cost per tonne of maize, 0.115 × 1000 =	115

SCALE OF EQUIPMENT

Perhaps the most important decision to be made when investing in crop processing equipment is that relating to the size and type of machine to be purchased. Purchasers must decide here whether the machine is to be just for their own use, totally for custom work or for a combination of the two. Machinery is more profitable if it is run for a long period each year, and a farmer who buys a larger machine than is needed, in the hope of earning income through custom work, may find it to be a loss-maker if the expected customers fail to materialize.

Before deciding on the appropriate scale of machinery, therefore, an investigation should be made of the local conditions in the crop processing sector. How are crops processed at the moment? Is there a need for custom services and purchasing power to back up this need? Would customers expect to pay on a percentage crop basis and would this cause problems of storage and marketing? Would the machine produce an end-product which suits the taste of local customers compared with that of products prepared in the traditional manner? If not, very few families may be willing to use the custom mill. Will the machine process more than one crop so that demand can be maintained in the event of changing cropping patterns or fluctuations in supply of a single crop?

A final factor affecting the size of equipment will be the size of available prime movers. For example, if a 10kW diesel engine is the best available or already owned prime mover, then it may be wise to buy a 10kW machine to match it.

HEALTH AND SAFETY

Much crop processing equipment contains cutters, knives, rasps and so on. These are potentially dangerous if they are not properly guarded.

Motors and engines incorporate parts which move at high speed, and the machines they drive are often directly coupled to rotate at the same speed. The safety regulations developed in some countries are often disregarded in others.

The two major hazards are, first, unguarded belts and machinery and, second, poorly maintained electrical wire and connections. Careful instruction is needed in the initial stages of operation. Petrol and diesel engines need adequate exhaust pipes to the outside of the building to prevent the build-up of fumes.

The most important features of safety when dealing with high-speed rotational machinery (as most of the foregoing equipment is) are careful retention of guards on belts, pulleys and transmission systems, and the protection of all feed sections against probing fingers. A wise precaution is often to provide a wooden pusher to feed all mills, mixers, hullers, pulpers, etc. or at least to provide a coarse guard screen for the free-flowing crops. Customers or casual visitors should be kept to safe areas. This particularly includes children.

MAINTENANCE

The maintenance schedule for all rotational machinery includes the care of belts, bearings and transmission components. Oiling and greasing of the bearings according to the manufacturers' instructions is essential. V-belts should always be replaced in matched sets, never singly, as otherwise all the load is carried by the shortest belt and this will cause all to break in turn.

Machines with perforated plates should be checked for wear and breakage, the latter occurring most frequently when unscreened samples are fed into the machine. Metal trash and stones can cause intolerable damage. Knives and beaters should be checked frequently for wear and sharpened, reversed or replaced according to the manufacturers' advice. High speed beaters for hammer mills should at least be checked for balance statically, on scales, so as to minimize vibration in operation. Worn beaters are often built up and repaired by welding and grinding them square.

All screens should be checked for wear and blockage; the latter may be corrected by scrubbing with a wooden block or wire brush. Drying in the sun will also loosen many of the stubborn particles or seeds in a screen.

TRAINING

The most difficult aspect of operating much of the motorized process machinery is the maintenance of the diesel engine drive unit. The understanding of the manufacturers' instructions is the only other requirement. Some hullers, for example, require a pregraded sample before they will operate consistently. No formal course of training is required, but the importance of adhering to the recommended maintenance schedules, correct machine settings and cleanliness can all be learnt in half a day of practice and supervision.

Although the operation of the machinery is simple enough, further training may be required if the operator also has to maintain the equipment. The hammer mill, for example, needs regular checking for wear on the hammers, and the plate mill similarly needs to be checked for wear on the plates. Tools may be required, but nevertheless most of these maintenance jobs are fairly simple to learn.

One of the hardest jobs relates to gari production. This is a pre-cooked meal made from grated cassava. The quality of the gari depends on the skill of the garifier operator, who operates in much the same way as a cook. In the continuous systems, which are growing in popularity, the temperature, residence times, additives, etc. all contribute to the quality of the product, and operators should be trained to maintain the quality standards.

SOCIAL IMPACT

Traditionally, crop processing activities are carried out primarily by women. The techniques they use are extremely arduous and they involve a large investment of time for very little result. Two categories of women engage in this type of activity: farm women, who process their own crops for family consumption; and landless women, or the wives of marginal farmers, who process other people's crops as a way of supplementing family income.

The introduction of crop processing equipment has different implications for these different sectors of society. Farm women may find they are released from tiring, unproductive work so that they can devote more time to child-care or, if it is available,

Jeremy Hartley/ITDG

With the introduction of mechanized hulling, millions of the poorest women are losing an important source of income

involve themselves in a more remunerative kind of activity (which would help them pay for the use of machinery). Sometimes, however, the time saved is merely diverted into travelling to the mill and standing in queues for hours on arrival.

Landless women may find themselves relieved of their only means of earning a living. Indeed, the introduction and spread of Engleberg mills in countries like Indonesia and Bangladesh has destroyed millions of part-time jobs for the poorest sections of society. Estimates show that some 7-8 million women lost their jobs following the mechanization of rice milling in Java. Much the same is happening in Bangladesh where each new rice mill puts about 350 women out of part-time employment. Given the greater mechanical efficiency of such equipment compared with traditional techniques, it would be difficult to prevent such changes. It would seem to be very important, however, to plan for the creation of alternative, equally remunerative jobs for the people displaced because of the machines.

The tools and equipment used to process crops in the traditional way are mainly fabricated locally, by farm families themselves or by rural artisans. Commercial machinery is normally manufactured in urban factories or even overseas. The introduction of such machinery means a decline in demand for the products of rural artisans and a flow of cash away from the rural economy. It will also probably involve an increased drain on the country's scarce supplies of foreign exchange for imported machines, spare parts and fuels. In many cases, the largest part of most suitable machines could be made locally by the use of simple machine tools and welding equipment. Measures to encourage this — such as the training of rural artisans, the upgrading of technology in rural workshops, and provision of credit and other support services — should be encouraged.

Brian Clarke
Silsoe College
Cranfield Institute of Technology

COSSUL HAND WINNOWER

This winnowing fan is mounted on a post and driven, via a pulley and belt, by a single operator using a hand crank. Weight 25kg.

COSSUL & CO. PVT LTD
123/367 Industrial Area
Fazalgunj
Kanpur
U.P.
INDIA

Similar implements are manufactured by:

NAWINNE AGRICULTURAL
IMPLEMENTS MANUFACTURING CO.
128/2 Colombo Road
Kurunegala
SRI LANKA

CYCLE WINNOWER

This winnowing fan is fitted with a bicycle seat and pedal drive mechanism. The frame is made of steel and the fan blades have a span of 1200mm.
Weight 80kg.

COSSUL & CO. PVT LTD
123/367 Industrial Area
Fazalgunj
Kanpur
U.P.
INDIA

PEDAL-POWERED WINNOWER

This simple machine is constructed from steel. Power is provided for the fan manually via a set of bicycle pedals. Output is in the range 150-300kg/hour.

C.E.N.E.E.M.A.
B.P. 1040
Yaoundé
CAMEROON

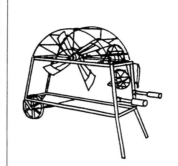

WINNOWING FAN

This winnowing fan is constructed from steel and has four blades with a swept diameter of 610mm. It is driven by hand via a series of chains and sprocket wheels. The company also produce a fan that can be belt driven from a two-wheeled tractor.

SATHYAWADI MOTORS &
TRANSPORTERS
21 Dambulla Road
Kurunegala
SRI LANKA

A similar implement is manufactured by:

MAHAWELI AGRO-MECH IND'L
COMPLEX
Thabuttegama
SRI LANKA

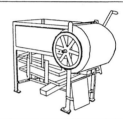

GRADER CUM WINNOWER

This machine is capable of grading all sorts of grains, pulses, and oil seeds whilst winnowing them at the same time. It can be operated by hand or using a 0.3kW motor. Output 200-300kg/hour.

KISAN KRISHI YANTRA UDYOG
64 Moti Bhawan
Collectorganj
Kanpur 208 001
INDIA

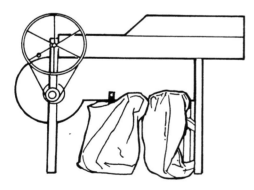

GRAIN WINNOWERS

This free-standing winnower is constructed mainly from wood. The material to be cleaned is fed manually through a slot in the base of the flat bed hopper and falls as a curtain into the airstream produced by the crank-driven fan. The two outlets are provided with hooks from which to suspend sacks. Output is between 200 and 300kg/hour.

HERRANDINA
Marte 581
Brena
Lima 5
PERU

WINNOWER
This winnower is a compact free-standing model, fabricated from mild steel. It is manually operated by cranking a handle, which is connected by pulley and V-belt to the fan.

THE COMILLA CO-OPERATIVE
KARKHANA LTD
Ranir Bazar
P.O. Box 12
Comilla
BANGLADESH

Similar implements are manufactured by:

UNATA
G.V.D. Heuvelstraat 131
3140 Ramsel-Herselt
BELGIUM

CECOCO HAND GRAIN WINNOWER
Cecoco produce two hand-operated winnowers. The A1 model has a capacity of 650kg/hour and an overall weight of 30kg.
The Hand Grain Winnower is a smaller machine and weighs 17kg. It is provided with three outlets:

● for whole grain;
● for broken pieces and immature grain;
● for chaff, hulls and dust.

Both these winnowers are free-standing and can be provided with single phase electric motors on request.

CECOCO
P.O. Box 8
Ibaraki City
Osaka 567
JAPAN

TR50 SEPARATOR

ECOMAT produce this compact winnower/cleaner. It has three oscillating screens and an aspirating fan which are all driven manually via a crank and pulley. The amount of draught produced by the fan can be adjusted by means of sliding shutters over the air intake. The machine is provided with two pneumatic tyred wheels and retractable wheelbarrow-type handles to aid mobility. When in use the winnower is supported on four steel legs.
Output is in the range 1500-2000kg/hour.

ECOMAT
Le Val Rouge
B.P. 132
MORLAIX
29210
FRANCE

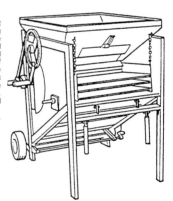

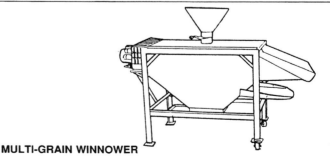

MULTI-GRAIN WINNOWER

This experimental winnower is free-standing and has integral electric motor. It uses a backward curved blade centrifugal fan to produce the airstream required to separate good grain from the chaff. The model works at about 99% winnowing efficiency.

Information is available from:

UNIVERSITY OF NIGERIA
Department Of Agricultural
Engineering
Nsukka
NIGERIA

HAND WINNOWER AND GRAIN CLEANER

The Blair Winnower and grain cleaner is manually operated by turning a handle. The grain to be cleaned is fed into the hopper from which the feed rate to the machine can be controlled by means of an adjustable slide. The grain falls on three different sizes of shaking screens which separate the large and small rubbish from the good grain. During this separation the fan blows air through the grain to aid the removal of the lighter debris. The machine is light enough to be moved by two people. Alternative sizes of screens can be supplied to suit different crops.

BLAIR ENGINEERING LTD
Rattray
Blairgowrie
Scotland PH10 7DN
UK

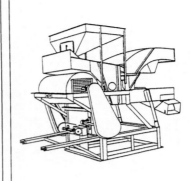

TRACTOR-MOUNTED WINNOWER

This machine has been designed to winnow coffee or other grains immediately after harvesting in order to remove light impurities (leaves, stems and dust), earth, stones and other extraneous material from the crop being cleaned. The machine can be used at the point of harvest, powered by the tractor to which it is mounted, or used at a central location powered by an optional electric motor.

PINHALENSE S/A MAQUINAS AGRICOLAS
rua Honorio Soares, 80
E. Santo de Pinhal
13990
BRAZIL

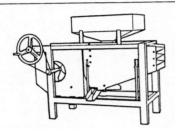

MULTI-CEREAL SEPARATOR

This separator can be powered manually or fitted with an electric motor or diesel engine. It is fitted with three screens which can be changed to suit a variety of different crops. Two outlet chutes are provided: one for cleaned grain; the other for broken grains and small debris.

The separator has four retractable handles to aid transportation.
Output is 250 to 1500kg/hour.
Weight without motor 160kg .

SISMAR
20 rue Dr. Théze
3214
Dakar
SENEGAL

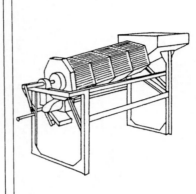

SENEGAL SCREEN

This is a manually operated rotary cleaner. The machine has a double sieve designed to separate groundnuts (peanuts) from husks and other rubbish. It is fitted with a large hopper capacity 80kg (approximately one sack), and two outlet spouts allowing the continuous discharge of cleaned crop into sacks. The sieve axle is mounted in ball bearings and the recommended turning speed is 15 rev/m. Output is in the range 1500 to 2000kg/hour.
Weight 212kg.

SISMAR
20 rue Dr. Théze
3214
Dakar
SENEGAL

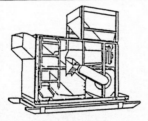

DAROU SEPARATOR

This machine is used for cleaning unshelled groundnuts (peanuts) and all cereals. It is powered by either a 2.3kW electric motor or a 3kW engine. Output is in the range 2500 to 3000kg/hour.

SISMAR
20 rue Dr. Théze
3214, Dakar
SENEGAL

IRRI PORTABLE GRAIN CLEANER

The cleaner illustrated is of wood and steel construction. It has a multi-crop capability as it has two screens, the top one being interchangeable. A 0.3kW electric motor or 0.75kW engine turns a single shaft on which are mounted the fan and the eccentric drive for the oscillating screens. The cleaner can be carried by two people. Grain purity up to 98%. Output 1000kg/hour. Weight with motor 72kg.

ALPHA MACHINERY AND ENGINEERING CORPORATION
1167 Pasong Tamo Street
Makati
Metro Manila
PHILIPPINES

JCCE INDUSTRIES
242 Mayondon
Los Baños, Laguna
PHILIPPINES

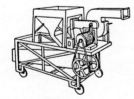

GRAIN PURIFIER

A built-in centrifugal fan blows away light impurities and dust. Clean grain is obtained after being fed into a vibrating sieve which has two different screen sizes. Powered by a 0.75kW electric motor or a 1kW engine.

KISAN KRISHI YANTRA UDYOG
64 Moti Bhawan
Collectorganj
Kanpur 208 001
INDIA

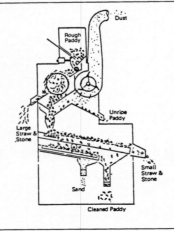

RICE CLEANER

The model SPC 20 is designed to remove impurities such as dust, sand, stones and weeds before the grain is sent through the milling process. It is built entirely of steel and can clean any type of grain at a rate of 1000-2000kg/hour. The machine uses an aspirator fan to remove light impurities and dust. The lower part of the machine contains vibrating sieves which separate the larger impurities. The cleaned grain can be collected in a suitable receptacle.

SOMASIRI HULLER MANUFACTORY
18, S.De S.Jayasinghe Mawatha
Nugegoda
SRI LANKA

A similar implement is manufactured by:

DEVRAJ & COMPANY
Krishan Sudama Marg
Firozpur City
Punjab
INDIA

SEED CLEANER

This is a compact unit mounted on four legs. A bracket is provided to hold a small engine or 2kW electric motor. The design incorporates an aspirating fan and horizontal oscillating screen. There is a large hopper to maintain an even feed rate to the cleaner.
Output 350-400kg/hour seed.
Weight 95kg.

C.V. KARYA HIDUP SENTOSA
Jl. Magelang 144
Yogyakarta
INDONESIA

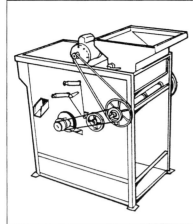

TWO SCREEN GRAIN-SEED CLEANER CUM GRADER

This cleaner is able to clean both large and heavy grains as well as small and light seeds using the adjustable air blast from the integral fan. The oscillating screens are automatically kept clean by brushes mounted beneath them and the design has eliminated any internal ledges where grain may lodge, thus making the cleaner suitable for use with certified seed. Power can be provided by either electric motor or petrol engine.

COSSUL & CO. PVT LTD
123/367 Industrial Area
Fazalgunj
Kanpur
U.P.
INDIA

BLAIR GRAIN CLEANER

This cleaner is a free-standing machine constructed of plywood and steel. An aspirating fan removes dust and light rubbish from the grain as it falls from the hopper on to the riddle case. The first screen removes larger material such as stones and straw; the second screen which has smaller holes allows weed seed and grit to pass through leaving clean grain to be discharged into a chute for collection. The cleaner may be powered by electric motor or by petrol engine. It will winnow, clean and grade all types of grain seeds and pulses, including barley, oats, wheat, rice, maize, coffee, peas, beans, lentils and grasses. Varying sizes of screens are available to suit the crop.

BLAIR ENGINEERING LTD
Rattray
Blairgowrie PH10 7DN
Scotland
UK

GRAIN PRE-CLEANER

Three sizes of this pre-cleaner are offered, with sieve widths of 400, 800 and 1200mm. They have a powerful centrifugal fan to aspirate light impurities and dust. There are two expansion chambers to collect lighter grains and a special mechanism to provide uniform flow of grain throughout the width of the suction box. The unit has a magnetic separator to remove iron contaminants such as nails and screws. Power requirements are 2.3kW for the smallest unit and 3kW for the largest.

Output is in the range 1000-3000kg/hour for rice.

DANDEKAR MACHINE WORKS LTD
Dandekarwadi, Bhiwandi
Dist. Thane
Maharashtra
421 302
INDIA

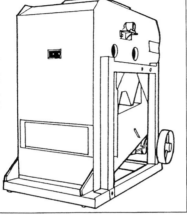

SEED PRE-CLEANER

This is a rotary seed cleaner fabricated from steel. The hopper simultaneously feeds two cylindrical sieves rotating in opposite directions, which remove large debris, straw and other impurities. As the grain falls an aspirating fan draws away light impurities. The cleaner is powered by a 2.5kW three-phase electric motor and the output is in the range 4-5 tonne/hour when the machine is being operated by two people.

HINDSONS PVT LTD
The Lower Mall
Patiala
Punjab
147 001
INDIA

SEED AND GRAIN CLEANER

This cleaner is of all-steel construction. It has a pneumatic grain elevator fed from a low-level hopper. Two-stage adjustable aspiration and twin screens are used to clean the grain. The screens are kept clean continuously by travelling brushes. The machine is powered by an integral three-phase 3.5kW motor. Output is in the range 700-1000kg/hour.

This company produce a wide range of grain cleaning equipment.

ORIENTAL SCIENCE APPARATUS
W'SHOPS
Jawaharlal Nehru Marg
Ambala Cantt
Haryana
133 001
INDIA

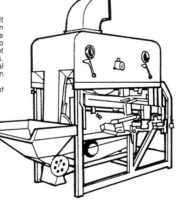

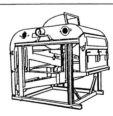

SEED GRADER

This machine uses different sets of sieves for grading and cleaning a variety of grains and beans. It can be powered manually, by animal traction, electric motor or engine.

HINDSONS PVT LTD
The Lower Mall
Patiala
Punjab 147 001
INDIA

THREE-SCREEN GRAIN-SEED CLEANER CUM GRADER

This cleaner has adjustable pitch screens which allows control over the speed at which seed travels on the screen. Aspirating air is also fully adjustable to suit the type and condition of the crop. The cleaner comes equipped with twin metal elevators 4m high; the first of which is used to load the grain into the cleaner from a floor-mounted hopper, the second to unload and lift cleaned grain.
Output 200-400kg\hour.

A larger version of the cleaner is also available with an output of up to 2 tonne/hour.

COSSUL & CO. PVT LTD
123/367 Industrial Area
Fazalgunj
Kanpur
U.P.
INDIA

INDENTED CYLINDER GRADERS

This single cylinder grader is of all-metal construction. It has a variable cylinder speed control, an oscillating trough for rejected seed and the cylinder working surface is hardened to provide wear resistance. Interchangeable cylinders are available for different crop seeds. It is powered by an electric motor of 0.75kW.

The company also produce a twin cylinder version of this grader.

ORIENTAL SCIENCE APPARATUS WORKSHOPS
Jawaharlal Nehru Marg Ambala Cantt
Haryana
133 001
INDIA

A similar indented cylinder grader (illustrated) is manufactured by:

ALVAN BLANCH DEVELOPMENT CO. LTD
Chelworth
Malmesbury
Wilts SN16 9SG
UK

LANE ENGINEERING (PVT) LTD
P.O. Box 43
Southerton
Harare
ZIMBABWE

RICE CLEANER

This is a double aspirating machine for cleaning rice and the removal of rice husk. The aspiration can be regulated to avoid any losses of good grain with the husk.

CONSTRUZIONI MECCANICHE CARDUCCIO COLOMBINI
Via Cadorna, 9
20081, Abbiategrasso (Milan)
ITALY

RICE HUSK FURNACE-DRIER

This is a self-contained rice husk furnace which can be used in conjunction with an electric forced air fan and drying chamber. The burning chamber diameter is 100mm and its husk capacity is 10kg. Husk is consumed at a rate of 4.5kg/hour. The temperature of air coming from the burner can reach 130-200°C which gives a drying air temperature of 40-60°C.
Weight 350kg.

CENTRE FOR DEVELOPMENT OF
APPROPRIATE AGRICULTURAL
ENGINEERING TECHNOLOGY
Situgadung
Legok
Tromol Pos 2, Serpong
15310
INDONESIA

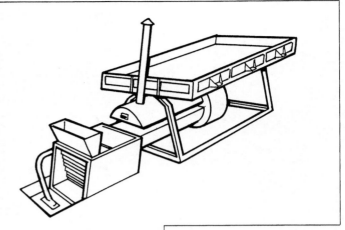

MULTI-CROP DRIER

This is a small flat bed batch drier for use with many grain crops. The drying bed is supported on a frame above the heat exchanger which is fuelled with rice husks or other waste products. A multi-vaned centrifugal fan which can be powered by either diesel engine or electric motor draws air over the heat exchanger and blows it up through the crop. Once the drying process is complete the entire bed can be tilted along its axis to allow the grain to be unloaded through discharge chutes set in the side walls.
Fan speed 1500 rev/min.
Airflow of 1.6 m³s⁻¹.

MARINAS MACHINERY MAN. CO.
INC. Rizal Street
Pila
Laguna
PHILIPPINES

BATCH DRIER

This is a cabinet-type batch drier powered entirely by electricity. The design incorporates an axial flow fan. The heating coils are thermostatically controlled.

TEMDO
P.O. Box 6111
Arusha
TANZANIA

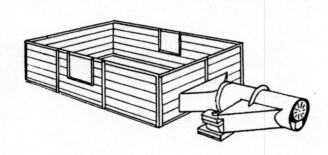

IRRI BATCH DRIER

The illustration shows the drier developed by the International Rice Research Institute. It is constructed from wood or steel. Primary heat is provided by either a rice-husk furnace or kerosine burner. Automatic safety shut-off of burner is provided should the fan shut down during operations. The drier uses a 2.25kW petrol engine or 1.5kW motor to drive 470mm diameter vane-axial type fan and also provide supplementary heat. The grain floor is made from perforated steel sheet, or expanded steel sheet.

- Airflow is 0.85m³s⁻¹ at 2200 rev/min;
- Static pressure 20mm water;
- Drying air temp. 43°C
- Fuel consumption engine: 0.75 l/hour petrol;
- Fuel consumption burner: 2 l/hour kerosene or 3.4kg/hour rice husk;
- Drying rate 23% moisture (w.b.) rice (1 tonne) to 14% in 5-6 hours;
- Weight (without engine) of burner and fan is 40kg.

IRRI
Agricultural Engineering Dept
P.O. Box 933
Manila
PHILIPPINES

These driers are manufactured by:

JCCE INDUSTRIES
242 Mayondon
Los Baños
Laguna
PHILIPPINES

S.V. AGRO INDUSTRIES
ENTERPRISES INC.
65 Commission Civil Street
Jaro
Iloilo City
PHILIPPINES

Similar implements are available from:

ALVAN BLANCH DEVELOPMENT CO.
LTD
Chelworth
Malmesbury
Wilts SN16 9SG
UK

C.V. KARYA HIDUP SENTOSA
Jl. Magelang 144
Yogyakarta
55241
INDONESIA

P.T. RUTAN MACHINERY TRAD. CO.
P.O. Box 319
Surabaya
INDONESIA

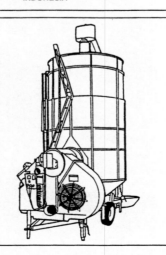

MOBILE DRIER

This is a self-contained recirculating batch drier which is capable of drying many types of grain. It is driven from a tractor power take-off and has an integral generator which is used to provide electric power for the thermostatic control system and the blower on the diesel-fuelled burner. The centrifugal fan, loading and discharge augers are all powered directly by the tractor. The chassis is fitted with pneumatic tyred wheels and a tow hitch to enable the drier to be transported from site to site. Integral mechanical jacks are used to support the machine during use.

EUROPÉENNE DE MATÉRIEL
INDUSTRIEL ET AGRICOLE
Z.i. de Saubion
St Vincent-de-Tyross
40230
FRANCE

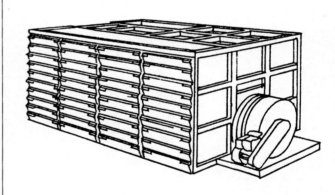

VERTICAL BIN BATCH DRIER

The illustration shows the drier developed by the International Rice Research Institute in co-operation with NGA and MIRDC. The bin is built of wood and steel and is divided into four compartments. It has a capacity of two tonnes. The fan uses either a 2.25kW motor or 3.75kW engine. The air is heated indirectly via a heat exchanger using either a kerosine burner or a rice-husk furnace.
Fuel consumption 1.5 l/hour petrol
Burner consumption 2.7 l/hour kerosine
Drying rate 2% points per hour.
Fan speed 2000 rpm.
Grain bed thickness 460mm.
Drying air temp. 43°C.
Airflow 1.7 m³s⁻¹ at 30mm water static pressure.
Weight with engine 364kg.

THE INTERNATIONAL RICE
RESEARCH INSTITUTE
Agricultural Engineering Dept
P.O. Box 933
Manila
PHILIPPINES

JCCE INDUSTRIES
242 Mayondon
Los Baños
Laguna
PHILIPPINES

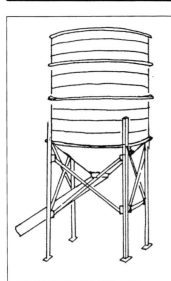

ELEVATED GRAIN AND MEAL STORAGE BINS

Elevated storage bins may be used for keeping either grain or animal feeds dry and safe from vermin. The outlet is situated at the conical base and the bins have the advantage of being self-emptying. The fact that the outlet is above ground level is convenient for loading and distribution operations. The Cossul bins illustrated are available in a wide range of capacities.

COSSUL & CO. PVT LTD
123/367 Industrial Area
Fazalgunj
Kanpur
U.P.
INDIA

SQUARE SILOS

Hopper-bottomed silos made up in 2x2 panel or 3x3 panel units for indoor installations. They are self-emptying, steel silos, which are easily erected and can be supplied with or without sub-frame.

LAW-DENIS ENGINEERING LTD
Lavenham Road
Beeches Industrial Estate
Yate
Bristol BS17 5QX
UK

Similar silos are manufactured by:

PRESIDENT MOLLERMASKINER A/S
Springstrup
Box 20
DK-4300 Holbaek
DENMARK

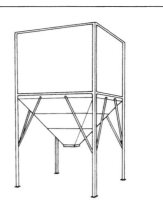

HOUSEHOLD MILL

This is a bench-mounted mill driven by a handle on a flywheel which has a groove for optional motor drive. The case of the mill is cast iron and the main spindle has a worm feed for even feeding and pre-crushing of the raw material. Available with hardened steel grinding plates or artificial stone grinding wheels. Diameter of plates 150mm.
Weight 23kg.

PRESIDENT MØLLERMASKINER A/S
Springstrup
P.O. Box 20
DK-4300 Holbaek
DENMARK

The mill is also available from:

A/S MASKINFABRIKKEN SKIOLD
Saeby, Kjeldgaardswej
P.O. Box 143
Saeby DK 9300
DENMARK

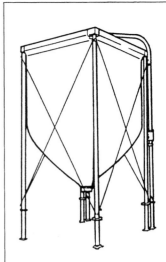

SUSPENDED BAG SILOS

This company can provide a comprehensive range of suspended bag silos from 3.4 tonne capacity upwards. The silo frame is of steel and the body is of reinforced plastic.

ABS SILO UND FORDERANLAGEN
GmbH
Postfach 1226
Osterburken
D-6960
GERMANY

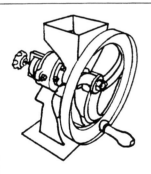

HAND-POWERED MILLS

This mill is equipped with interchangeable 90mm diameter steel grinding wheels. The fineness of the ground product can be adjusted using the screw provided. The output is in the range 10-30kg/hour depending on the fineness of the product. The mill can be powered using a 0.37kW electric motor.
Weight 13kg.

TOY RENÉ S.A.
Impasse des Reclusages
B.P. 10
Montoire
41800
FRANCE

Similar implements are manufactured by:

SAMAP S.A.
1 rue du Moulin
B.P. 1
Andolsheim
68280
FRANCE

RENSON LANDRECIES S.A.R.L.
37 route d'Happegarbes
B.P. 12
Landrecies
59550
FRANCE

GRAIN GRINDING MILL

An all-metal hand-powered maize grinding mill specifically designed for the smallholder. It has a simple adjustment for fine or coarse meal grinding and can also kibble grain for poultry feed. The mill is mounted on a cast iron pedestal and turned by a handle on a large iron flywheel.
Weight 101kg.

G. NORTH (PVT) LTD
P.O. Box 111
Southerton
Harare
ZIMBABWE

FORTIS DUO HAND-POWERED MILL

This is a hand-powered grinding mill with the stones mounted on a horizontal shaft and encased in a 18mm plywood box. Handles are provided to allow two operators to turn the mill. The 20mm diameter main shaft is supported on two dust-protected ball bearings which are maintenance-free. The millstones are held by a thrust bearing ring. A 'worm' cut into the shaft feeds the grain at a constant rate between the millstones. Grinding can be adjusted from very fine to very coarse. Flywheel diameter 500mm, millstone diameter 280mm. Weight 35kg.

HANO
Beukstraat 15
B 3900 Lommel
BELGIUM

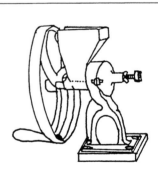

MINI MILLS

HAND-OPERATED MILL
This is a small vertical plate mill designed for hand operation. The mill has a 380mm diameter flywheel which can be replaced by a direct mounted electric motor rated at 0.37kW. The grinding plates are of hardened cast steel. Output for the hand-operated version is in the range 22-30kg/hour.

ALVAN BLANCH DEVELOPMENT CO.
LTD
Chelworth
Malmesbury
Wilts SN16 9SG
UK

HAND FLOUR MILL
This bench-mounted mill has a small hopper, handle and flywheel. Output is between 5 and 50kg/hour. The upper limit can be achieved when using the optional motor drive.

CECOCO
P.O. Box 8
Ibaraki City
Osaka 567
JAPAN

HAND GRIST MILL

This mill can be used to grind all dry material the size of small grains such as maize, beans, peas, coffee. It is fitted with a counter-balanced crank and the grinding surfaces are alloy cone burrs. Weight 13.6kg.

C.S. BELL CO.
170 W Davis Street
Box 291
Tiffin
OH 44883
USA

LEHMAN'S
4779 Kidron Road
P.O. Box 41
Kidron
OH 44636
USA

R & R MILL CO. INC.
45 West First North
Smithfield
UT 84335
USA

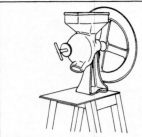

GRAIN GRINDER

This grinding mill can be bench-mounted or supplied with a steel frame stand.

COLOMBO COMMERCIAL CO. (ENG.) LTD
121 Sir James Peiris Mawatha
Colombo 2
SRI LANKA

FORTIS S.H. GRINDING MILL

This is a mill with horizontally mounted millstones encased in a 18mm plywood box. It is powered by a 0.37kW electric motor driving the wooden flywheel with a V-belt. The main shaft is supported on two dust-protected ball bearings which are maintenance-free. The millstones are held by a thrust bearing ring. A 'worm' on the shaft feeds the grain at an even rate between the stones from the integral hopper. Grinding can be adjusted from very fine to very coarse. The flywheel diameter is 460mm, the millstone diameter is 200mm. Weight 40kg.

HANO
Beukstraat 15
B 3900 Lommel
BELGIUM

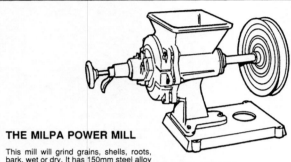

THE MILPA POWER MILL

This mill will grind grains, shells, roots, bark, wet or dry. It has 150mm steel alloy burrs which are adjustable for coarse or fine grinding. The mill is supplied with a 304mm V-belt pulley but a flat, 75mm wide, 304mm diameter pulley is also available. The power required is between 2.25 and 3.75kW. Weight 50kg.

C.S. BELL CO.
170 W Davis Street
Box 291
Tiffin
OH 44883
USA

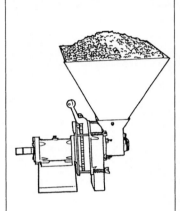

STEEL PLATE MILL

This is a powered grinding mill. It will grind wet, semi-dry and dry materials. It comprises cast iron body, shaft fitted with dust-proof bearings, a hardened steel grinding plate, hopper, and handle to set the distance between grinding plates and hence alter the fineness of the ground product. It can be used to grind maize, wheat, sorghum, millet, cassava, coffee, spices, groundnuts (peanuts) and barley. Power required is a 2.25-4.5kW electric motor or internal combustion engine. Speed range 750-1500 rev/minute. Weight 34kg.

PENAGOS HERMANOS & CIA. LTDA
Apartado Aereo 689
Bucaramanga
COLOMBIA

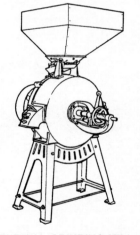

VERTICAL GRINDING MILL

The horizontal mill shaft runs in two heavy dust-proof self-lubricating ball bearings. The mill is equipped with an adjustable shaker device in the hopper to provide an even feed. A safety spring is fitted which allows the stones to separate should any large object enter the mill. A lever can then be operated to part the stones and remove foreign objects without altering the grinding adjustment. The degree of fineness is adjusted by regulating a hand wheel. The millstones are made of emery and flint. Diameter of millstones 400mm. The mill is driven from an external power source of 4.5-6kW via a belt and pulley at 650 rev/min. Weight 167kg.

A/S MASKINFABRIKKEN SKIOLD
Saeby, Kjeldgaardswej
P.O. Box 143
Saeby
DK 9300
DENMARK

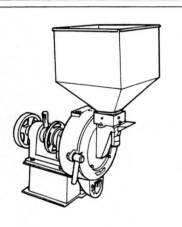

BEAN CURD GRINDER

This machine can be used with dry or wet beans, rice or seeds. Although it is specifically designed for making bean curd (tofu) it is also suitable for chillies, tomatoes and for sambal making. It is driven by belt and pulley from a 3.75kW diesel or petrol engine or electric motor. Capacity is 25kg beans/hour or 100kg rice/hour. Diameter of grinding stones is 250mm. A larger model is also available requiring a 5.25kW power supply but with an output of 40kg beans/hour or 200kg rice/hour.

C.V. KARYA HIDUP SENTOSA
Jl. Magelang 144
Yogyakarta
55241
INDONESIA

VERTICAL GRINDING MILLS

D.S. STYLE VERTICAL GRINDING MILL This mill is suitable for grinding many kinds of grains. Power required is 4.5-6kW for an output of 270kg/hour. Weight 210kg.

DANDEKAR BROTHERS & CO.
Shivajinagar
Sangli
Maharashtra
416 416
INDIA

Similar implements are manufactured by:

RENSON LANDRECIES S.A.R.L.
37 route d'Happegarbes
B.P. 12
Landrecies
59550
FRANCE

TOY RENÉ S.A.
Impasse des Reclusages
B.P. 10
Montoire
41800
FRANCE

KISAN KRISHI YANTRA UDYOG
64 Moti Bhawan
Collectorganj
Kanpur
208 001
INDIA

DIAS & DIAS
690 Negombo Road
Mabola
Wattala
SRI LANKA

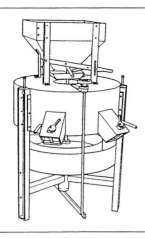

HORIZONTAL GRINDING MILLS

The mill is constructed on a heavy frame with a strong main shaft running in two heavy duty dust-proof self-lubricating ball bearings.

Protection from damage by large objects entering the mill with the feedstock is provided by a safety spring which allows the stones to separate. A lever is used to move the stones apart allowing the removal of the foreign body without altering the grinding setting.

The machine has an adjustable shaker in the hopper to ensure an even feed rate. Grist fineness is adjusted by regulating a hand wheel. Diameter of millstone 500mm. The mill requires a power supply in the range 4-5.5kW at 550-600 rev/min.
Weight 185kg.
Three larger models are also available.

A/S MASKINFABRIKKEN SKIOLD
Saeby, Kjeldgaardswej
P.O. Box 143
Saeby
DK 9300
DENMARK

HORIZONTAL STONE MILL
This machine is similar to the Danish model previously described. The millstones are made of a hard-wearing emery composition containing no flint, known as the 'Garner' brand. They do not absorb oil and so oil-bearing crops can be successfully ground.
Millstone diameter 610mm.

ALVAN BLANCH DEVELOPMENT CO. LTD
Chelworth
Malmesbury
Wilts SN16 9SG
UK

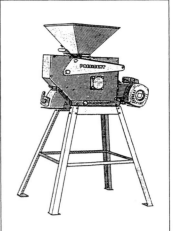

ROLLER MILLS

The R16 mill (illustrated) is suitable for rolling low-fat grains; it is not suitable for rolling beans or maize. Powered by either a 4 or 5.5kW motor, output is in the range 280 to 350kg/hour. The diameter of the cast iron rollers is 225mm.

The R24 and R30 models have power requirements up to 11.2kW and outputs up to 1800kg/hour.

ALVAN BLANCH DEVELOPMENT CO. LTD
Chelworth
Malmesbury
Wilts SN16 9SG
UK

Similar mills are made by:

RENSON LANDRECIES S.A.R.L.
B.P. 12
Landrecies
FRANCE

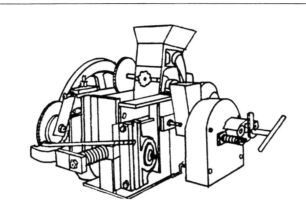

ROLLER MILL TYPE P500

The P500 roller mill is fabricated from heavy duty steel plate. The cast iron rollers are both chain-driven by a 4kW electric motor and each has a spring-loaded scraper to keep it clean. The mill is supplied with inlet hopper, bagging-off chute with bag clamp and either a high-or low-level stand.
Output is up to 600kg/hour for maize.
Weight 235kg including motor.
A range of larger machines of similar design is also produced.

PRESIDENT MOLLERMASKINER A/S
Springstrup
Box 20
DK-4300 Holbaek
DENMARK

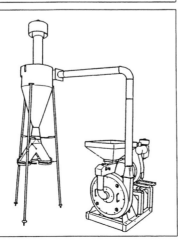

OMAS CEREAL MILLS

These small mills can handle wet or dry products. The mechanics of the M13 and the MS13 are identical with twelve reversible hammers and reinforced screens available in various sizes. The difference is in the power source; the M13 is driven by a 3.75kW three-phase electric motor whilst the MS13 has a 6kW diesel engine. Typical output for both machines is 250-350kg/hour for maize.

ABI-MÉCANIQUE
B.P. 343
45 rue Pierre et Marie Curie
(Zone 4c)
Abidjan
IVORY COAST

A similar mill is manufactured by:

ECMA FRANCE
Z.A. Boussieu Nicolas
Bourgoin-Jallieu 38.300
FRANCE

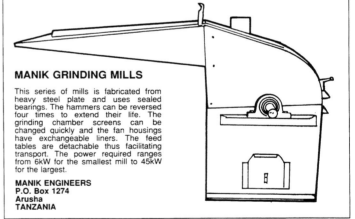

MANIK GRINDING MILLS

This series of mills is fabricated from heavy steel plate and uses sealed bearings. The hammers can be reversed four times to extend their life. The grinding chamber screens can be changed quickly and the fan housings have exchangeable liners. The feed tables are detachable thus facilitating transport. The power required ranges from 6kW for the smallest mill to 45kW for the largest.

MANIK ENGINEERS
P.O. Box 1274
Arusha
TANZANIA

UNIVERSAL HAMMER MILLS

There are three basic models designed for a choice of motors: direct coupled electric motor, V-belt drive for diesel and V-belt drive for electric motor. The DM-2 mill (illustrated) has a built-in fan for pneumatic conveying of the final product to a bagging-off chute mounted under a cyclone. A full 360 degree screen is used, with a replaceable reinforced liner inside the mill housing; the hammers can be reversed four times. The rotor has sixteen hammers and spins at 2800 rev/min. Screen sizes from 0.7-7.0mm.
Weight 103kg.

A/S MASKINFABRIKKEN SKIOLD
Saeby, Kjeldgaardswej
P.O. Box 143
Saeby
DK 9300
DENMARK

HAMMER MILL WITH A CYCLONE SEPARATOR

BELL MINOR MILL
This mill is the smallest in a range of four. It is of all-steel construction and the rotor is fitted with twelve reversible hammers. A cyclone separator is included. The mill has a power requirement of 4.5-6kW and is capable of producing 4kg of ground maize per minute.
Weight 128kg.

H.C. BELL & SON (ENGINEERS) (PVT) LTD
P.O. Box 701
Mutare
ZIMBABWE

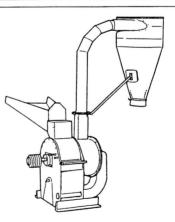

MULTI-PURPOSE HAMMER MILLS

HAMMER MILL
This general purpose mill (illustrated) is mounted on a frame and driven by a belt from a 7.5 or 10kW electric motor. It can be used to grind a very wide range of materials which are either wet or dry.

AGROMAC LTD
449 1/1 Darley Road
Colombo 10
SRI LANKA

HAMMER MILLS
Available in a variety of configurations. Cyclone bagging is also available.

ALVAN BLANCH DEVELOPMENT CO. LTD
Chelworth
Malmesbury
Wilts SN16 9SG
UK

MAIZE MILL
Rotary type mill made from a mild steel plate casing. It has hardened steel hammers and an exhaust system with cyclone collection. It is powered by a direct coupled 22.5kW electric motor, or diesel engine via pulleys and V-belts. Weight 400kg.

STEEL STRUCTURES LTD
Dandora Road
Box 49862
Nairobi
KENYA

HAMMER MILL
This hammer mill grinds bones, coconut, grains, minerals, seeds and shells. 300kg/hour capacity. Powered by a 2.25kW motor.

POLYGON AGRO-INDUSTRIAL CORP.
32 Road B, Project 7
Quezon City
PHILIPPINES

HAMMER MILL FOR COCONUT
The mill can reduce copra to a 2mm mesh size. It will also mill other products such as cassava, corn and coffee. The mill is driven by a 2.25kW electric motor.

APPROPRIATE TECHNOLOGY CENTRE
College of Agriculture
Manresa Heights
Cagayan de Oro 9000
PHILIPPINES

CONVENTIONAL GRAIN MILL
This model requires an 11-15kW diesel engine. The mill is fitted with a cyclone for flour delivery.

NEW MODEL GRAIN MILLING MACHINE
This free-standing mill can be operated without expensive foundations. It can be powered by integral 7.5kW three-phase electric motor or from tractor power take-off. It runs at 4200 rev/min.

DM INVESTMENTS GROUP CT+U (T) LTD
P.O. Box 820
Mwanza
TANZANIA

HAMMER MILL
This mill has 16 reversible hammers and can be used to process millet, maize, sorghum, rice and wheat.
It is powered by a 5.5kW electric motor or an 8kW diesel engine.
Output 300kg/hour.
Weight 317kg.

COMPAGNIE D'APPLICATION MÉCANIQUES
10, avenue Faidherbe
B.P. 397
Dakar
SENEGAL

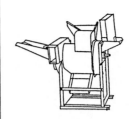

CHOPPER/GRINDERS

The TRIMAQ 200 is a three-in-one hammer mill, with husking, shelling and chopping attachments. The mill can be adjusted to produce fine or coarse meal with or without the maize cob. It is also capable of chopping many fodder crops including sugar cane, grass, green maize (whole plant) and cassava. Power can be supplied by electric motor or diesel engine for which a mounting frame can be supplied which includes a clutch mechanism. This allows the motor or engine to be started with no load. Alternatively the whole unit can be mounted on a three-point hitch and driven by the tractor power take-off shaft.

CIA PENHA MAQ. AGRÍCOLAS
Av, Brazil 1724
C.P. 477
Ribeirão preto
BRAZIL

The DMP-500 is a versatile machine which like the Trimaq can be used both to mill grain or to chop forage crops. This machine is the smallest of a range of four and can be driven by various power sources of 2.25-4.5kW.

IRMÃOS NOGUEIRA S.A.
Rua 15 de Novembro, 781
Itapira S.P. 13970
BRAZIL

BOTTOM DISCHARGE HAMMER MILLS

This mill can be used to process dry grains and wet pulpy products. It can be mounted on a hopper or auger-conveyor or be raised to allow a barrow or tub to be placed beneath. The bottom of the mill is completely open for full and rapid discharge. The basic package includes the mill, feed-regulating table, 6mm screen (or any other size specified), motor mounting bracket, V-belt and pulleys for an 1800 rev/m power source. The mill is available in three sizes.

Model No.	Weight kg	Capacity (shelled maize)	Power kW
10	65	250kg/h	2
20	74	500kg/h	2.5
30	88	2500kg/h	7.5

C.S. BELL CO.
170 W. Davis Street
Box 291
Tiffin
OH 44883
USA

DRY MEAL MIXERS

The MN-150 (illustrated) is the smallest in a range of five ration mixers.
Capacity 150kg mixed in 15 minutes.

IRMÃOS NOGUEIRA S.A.
Rua 15 de Novembro, 781
Itapira S.P. 13970
BRAZIL

The following companies also produce vertical feed mixers:

LAW-DENIS ENGINEERING LTD
Lavenham Road
Beeches Industrial Estate
Yate
Bristol BS17 5QX
UK

FAMIA INDUSTRIAL S.A.
Av. Herooes de la Brena 2790
Ate
Lima 3
PERU

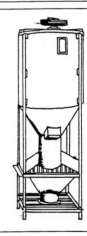

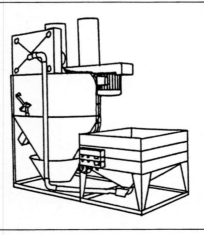

MILL AND MIXER UNITS

MILL AND MIXER INSTALLATION 4K-JU500 (illustrated) contains a mixer of capacity 500kg with a 1.5kW motor, and a hammer mill of capacity 300kg with a 4kW motor.

PRESIDENT MØLLERMASKINER A/S
Springstrup
P.O. Box 20
DK-4300 Holbaek
DENMARK

MILL-N-MIX
This company produce a range of mill and mixers with manual feed and bagging off. These are available in five sizes from 0.5 tonne to 3 tonne.

SCOTMEC (AYR) LTD
Scotmec Works
1a Whitfield Drive, Heathfield
Ayr KA8 9RX
Scotland
UK

JAVA HAND-POWERED RICE HULLER

This is a small machine intended for the grower of small quantities of rice and for domestic use. Rice can be shelled at a maximum rate of about 14kg per hour, but the capacity may vary considerably depending on the type and condition of the crop. The machine has three adjustments which control the feed, the discharge and the hulling knife. Rice is hand fed into the hopper at a constant rate as the handle is turned. As the resistance to turning increases, the discharge regulator is opened. Rice is only shelled when the machine is full. A perforated plate allows dust to escape.

JOHN GORDON & CO. (ENGINEERS) LTD
Gordon House
Bower Hill
Epping
Essex CM16 7AG
UK

A similar huller is manufactured by:

ALVAN BLANCH DEVELOPMENT CO. LTD
Chelworth
Malmesbury
Wilts SN16 9SG
UK

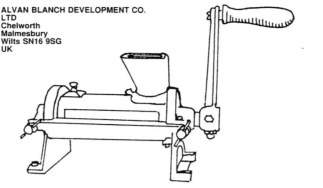

TWO-PERSON HULLER

Twin opposing push-pull handles joined to common crankshaft and gearing allow two people to rotate the huller at about 3000 rev/min. Output 250kg/hour. Weight 63kg.

CECOCO
P.O. Box 8
Ibaraki City, Osaka 567
JAPAN

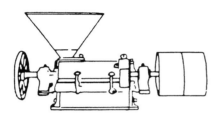

ENGLEBERG RICE HULLERS

These power-driven metal roller rice hullers are used worldwide. A specially chilled, hard, cast iron or steel cylinder shell is rotated inside a double hardened huller screen. The degree of milling is controlled by the outlet flow rate and by adjustment of the huller blade.

The machine may be supplied as a stand alone or in combination with polishers and winnowers. Power requirements are in the range 2.25-12kW.

ENGLEBERG HULLER CO. INC
Export Office 75 West Street
Syracuse
New York
USA

RICE HULLERS

A specially chilled and hardened cast iron cylinder rotates inside a screen to produce shelled and whitened rice in one operation. The degree of milling is controlled by adjustable huller blade, and the outlet slide regulates the time the rice stays in the machine. Milled rice is discharged via a side chute. The huller can be driven by belt from an electric motor or engine of 9-11kW.

LEWIS C. GRANT LTD
East Quality Street
Dysart
Kirkcaldy
Fife KY1 2UA
Scotland
UK

ALVAN BLANCH DEVELOPMENT CO. LTD
Chelworth
Malmesbury
Wilts SN16 9SG
UK

The following manufacturers all produce rice hulling machines that operate on a similar principal to the Lewis C. Grant machine described above.

RAJAN UNIVERSAL EXPORTS (MFRS) LTD
P.O. Box 250
Madras
600 001
INDIA

ABI-MÉCANIQUE
16 rue des Foreurs
B.P. 4019
Abidjan
IVORY COAST

ECOMAT
Le Val Rouge
B.P. 132
Morlaix
29210
FRANCE

RUBBER ROLL RICE HULLERS

This huller has a throughput of 1500kg/hour. It is driven by an external power source of 4kW. Hulling efficiency is 85%.

CHINA NATIONAL MACHINERY IMPORT/EXPORT CORP.
Kwangton Branch
61 Yanjiang
Kwangchow
CHINA

RUBBER ROLL RICE HULLER
Similar in design to the Chinese huller illustrated, this machine has a throughput of 1250kg/hour and a hulling efficiency of 90%. Weight 265kg.

C.V. KARYA HIDUP SENTOSA
Jl. Magelang 144
Yogyakarta
55241
INDONESIA

Similar hullers are manufactured by:

P.T. RUTAN MACHINERY TRADING CO.
P.O. Box 319
Surabaya
INDONESIA

AGROMAC LTD
449 1/1 Darley Road
Colombo 10
SRI LANKA

KISAN KRISHI YANTRA UDYOG
64 Moti Bahwan
Collectorganj
Kanpur 208 001
INDIA

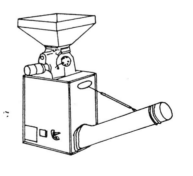

BON ACCORD RICE HULLERS

This company produce a range of rice hullers and hullers with polishers. The output depends on whether the feed material is shelled or unshelled rice but ranges from 30kg/hour for the smallest model to 400kg/hour for the largest. The power required ranges from 2.25kW to 11kW.

WM. MACKINNON & CO. LTD
Spring Garden Ironworks
Aberdeen
Scotland
AB9 1DU
UK

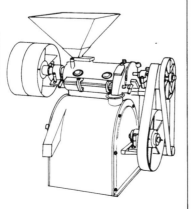

RICE HULLER

This huller uses the Engelberg system. It requires a 3kW engine or electric motor. The huller can be used in conjunction with and driven from the diesel engine on the Votex Ricefan thresher. Weight without motor 93kg.

VOTEX HEREFORD LTD
Friars Street
Hereford HR4 OAT
UK

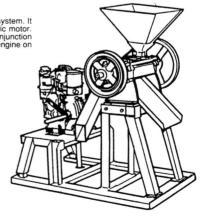

AUTOMATIC TYPE RICE HULLER

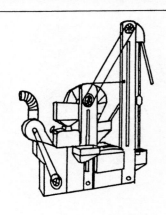

This model comprises a rubber roll huller, husk winnower, an auto-separator and two bucket-type elevators to transfer grain between successive stages. The hulling unit has two rubber rolls which counter-rotate at different speeds. There are two winnowing sections, one high velocity and one low, to remove both unripe rice and husk. The cleaning process is completed with a number of vibrating screens. The dehusked rice is returned by one elevator to the huller, while the second elevator discharges clean brown rice.
Output is in the range 1000-1500kg/hour.

**SOMASIRI HULLER
MANUFACTURING**
18 S.de S. Jayasinghe Mawatha
Nugegoda
SRI LANKA

COMBINATION TYPE RUBBER ROLL RICE HULLERS

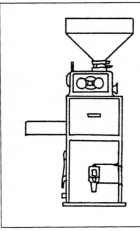

The illustrated machine is a rubber roll hulling unit combined with a husk winnower, driven by 11kW electric motor. Rubber rolls length 150mm, outer diameter 220mm.
Weight 195kg.

**SHANDONG YUTAI MACHINE
MANUFACTORY**
Yutai Shandong
CHINA

**SOMASIRI HULLER
MANUFACTURING**
18 S.de S. Jayasinghe Mawatha
Nugegoda
SRI LANKA

CECOCO
P.O. Box 8
Ibaraki City, Osaka 567
JAPAN

COMPACT RICE MILLS

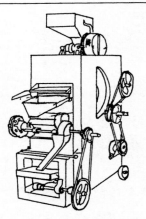

The mill can be used to process both short and long grain rice. Has rubber roller huller, polishing chamber and cleaning device. Powered by 1000 rev/min 18-22kW motor.
Weight 380kg.

EBM INDUSTRIES INC.
115 North Blvd.
Navotas
Metro Manila
PHILIPPINES

SINGLE-PASS RICE MILLING MACHINE
This compact rice mill comprises a rubber roll huller, a winnower and a polishing chamber. Powered by a 15kW electric motor or 18kW diesel engine.
Weight 285kg.

SEA COMMERCIAL CO. INC.
3905 R. Magsaysay Blvd.
Cor. Vivente Cruz Street
Santa Mesa
Manila
PHILIPPINES

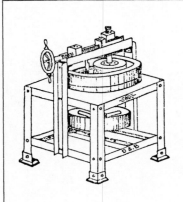

PADDY SEPARATORS

PADDY SEPARATOR (DPS-80)
0.75kW separator with a capacity of between 1000-1300kg/hour. Speed 450 rev/min. Manufactured by Dae Won Machine Work Co.

**KOREA TRADE PROMOTION
CORPORATION**
C.P.O. Box 1621
Seoul
KOREA

RICE FLAKE/POHA MACHINES

RICE FLAKE MACHINE (POHA MILL)
This free-standing power-driven mill has a 280mm roller and 762mm drum. The drum and roller are made of cast iron. The roller only revolves while the paddy is being pressed and can be adjusted to produce the required thickness of poha. By pressing the roller against the rim of the drum, all poha is collected near the centre of the drum and can be removed by hand whilst the machine is running. 60-70kg of rice per hour can be made into poha.

DANDEKAR BROTHERS & CO.
Shivajinagar
Sangli
Maharashtra
416 416
INDIA

A similar mill is manufactured by:

DANDEKAR MACHINE WORKS LTD
Dandekarwadi, Bhiwandi
Dist. Thane
Maharashtra
421 302
INDIA

LOW-COST ROLLER FLAKING MACHINE
This portable machine has a capacity for both cereals and pulses. It comprises a hopper, hollow rollers, gear transmission system and support frame. The rollers are fabricated from mild steel pipe and are surface-plated with nickel. The drive is provided by a 0.75kW single phase electric motor via a belt drive to the central roller.

**CENTRAL INSTITUTE OF
AGRICULTURAL ENGINEERING**
Nabi Bagh
Bersala Road
Bhopal
462 018
INDIA

HAND-OPERATED RICE SEPARATORS

Hulled and winnowed rice is separated into whole brown rice, paddy and broken and immature rice with the use of a woven wire net and an adjustable multi piano wire screen. Four models are available: capacities 600-1000kg/hour. Weight 17-27kg.

CECOCO
P.O. Box 8
Ibaraki City, Osaka 567
JAPAN

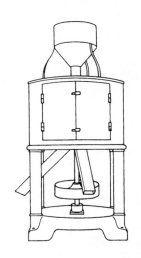

GRAVITY SEPARATOR FOR PADDY

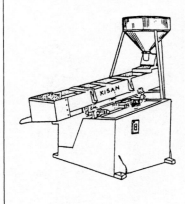

This machine is used to separate paddy from hulled rice prior to the process of polishing. The material to be separated is fed on to the upper end of an oscillating and tilted table from a hopper. The separated fractions are discharged from chutes in the side of the table. The machine is capable of handling 250kg/hour. It is powered by a 0.75kW electric motor.

KISAN KRISHI YANTRA UDYOG
64 moti Bhawan
Collectorganj
Kanpur 208 001
INDIA

WHITE RICE VERTICAL CONE POLISHERS

These machines comprise a balanced conical stone, covered in emery, revolving inside a casing of interchangeable segments, lined with wire screen or perforated sheets. These segments are fitted with rubber brakes. The space between the cone and the segments can be adjusted by raising or lowering the cone and spindle, thus increasing or decreasing the whitening or pearling action. The machines can also be employed to polish wheat and other grains.

BEHERE'S & UNION INDUSTRIAL WORKS
Dahanu Road Dist Thane
Masoli
Jeevan Prakash 401 602
INDIA

EMERY CONE POLISHERS
These models use a conical, cast iron drum which is covered with emery. This revolves inside a casing made with a wooden frame. An adjustable perforated sheet is fitted inside the frame. Power required 4-15kW, depending on size.

DEVRAJ & COMPANY
Krishan Sudama Marg
Firozpur City
Punjab
INDIA

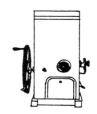

CECOCO HAND RICE POLISHER

This polishes brown rice or paddy. The capacity is 10-15kg/hour. A 0.2kW electric motor can be added which increases the output to 30kg/hour.

CECOCO
P.O. Box 8
Ibaraki City, Osaka 567
JAPAN

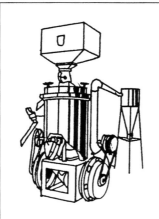

CONE-TYPE RICE POLISHERS

This machine, which is powered by an 6-7.5kW motor, polishes, pearls and delivers the rice and bran separately. Whiteness can be controlled and there is an air blast to ensure that the rice is kept cool during processing.
Output is in the range 750-1000kg/hour.

SOMASIRI HULLER MANUFACTURING
18 S.de S.Jayasinghe Mawatha
Nugegoda
SRI LANKA

A similar polisher is manufactured by:

DEVRAJ & COMPANY
Krishan Sudama Marg
Firozpur City
Punjab
INDIA

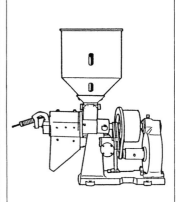

RICE POLISHER

This rice polisher is designed to give a high conversion ratio with low grain breakage. The degree of 'whiteness' is adjustable. The main axle is supported on three bearings. A cooling fan ensures that the temperature is kept low during processing and a rotating screen assists with the extraction of the bran. Two models are available. The H50 has an output of 450-600kg/hour and a power requirement of 9kW. The H70 (illustrated) has an output of 600-700kg/hour and a power requirement of 11.25-13kW.

C.V. KARYA HIDUP SENTOSA
Jl. Magelang 144
Yogyakarta
55241
INDONESIA

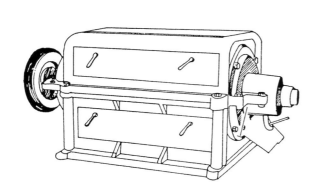

ABRASIVE-TYPE HORIZONTAL EMERY POLISHERS

This is a compact polisher developed for use with raw rice. The machine comprises an abrasive coated roller which is rotated inside a steel screen. The machine can process up to 2000kg per hour and requires an external power source of 15kW.

DANDEKAR MACHINE WORKS LTD
Dandekarwadi, Bhiwandi
Dist. Thane
Maharashtra
421 302
INDIA

A similar polisher is manufactured by:

CECOCO
P.O. Box 8
Ibaraki City, Osaka 567
JAPAN

GROUNDNUT (PEANUT) SHELLERS

This simple decorticator comprises a curved screen in the base of an open tank mounted on a frame. Shelling is achieved by pushing a handle back and forth. This sweeps a scraper across the bottom of the tank. Screen sizes 10mm, 11mm, 13mm and 16mm.

G. NORTH (PVT) LTD
P.O. Box 111
Southerton
Harare
ZIMBABWE

GROUNDNUT DECORTICATOR
Available in screen sizes of 10mm, 11mm, 13mm and 16mm. Operated by pulling a handle back and forth.

ZIMPLOW LTD
P.O. Box 1059
Bulawayo
ZIMBABWE

GROUNDNUT DECORTICATOR
This low-cost model has galvanized steel body sheets, and can produce a high yield of undamaged nuts. It comprises a trough with a wire screen bottom.

ALVAN BLANCH DEVELOPMENT CO. LTD
Chelworth
Malmesbury
Wilts SN16 9SG
UK

GROUNDNUT DECORTICATOR
An alternating hand-operated machine. Seed breakage is only 3-4%. Seed and husk drop down through the sieve and have to be separated from the husk in a further operation. The decorticator can be converted to powered operation.

MEKINS AGRO PRODUCTS (PVT) LTD
6-3-866/A Begumpet
Greenlands
Hyderabad 500 016
INDIA

Similar implements are manufactured by:

SISMAR
20 rue Dr. Thèze
3214
Dakar
SENEGAL

COBEMAG
B.P. 161
Parakou
REPUBLIC OF BENIN

ECOMAT
Le Val Rouge
B.P. 132
Morlaix
29210
FRANCE

UPROMA
B.P. 1086
Lomé
TOGO

PEDAL-OPERATED GROUNDNUT SHELLER

This machine is made from steel. It is pedal-powered and requires two operators to achieve continuous output.

C.E.N.E.E.M.A.
B.P. 1040 Nkolbisson
Yaounde
CAMEROON

SUPER CAYOR ROTARY SHELLER

Output from these machines is 150kg/hour of shelled nuts. Powered or manual versions are available.

SISMAR
20 rue Dr. Thèze
3214
Dakar
SENEGAL

FOOT-OPERATED DECORTICATOR

This treadle-powered machine is free-standing and has a balanced flywheel to help maintain rotation. A winnowing fan is also provided to separate the nuts from the shells. An electric motor may be fitted as an option. Output is 25kg/hour.

HINDSONS PVT LTD
The Lower Mall
Patiala
Punjab 147 001
INDIA

A similar machine is manufactured by:

RAJAN UNIVERSAL EXPORTS (MFRS) LTD
P.O. Box 250
Madras
600 001
INDIA

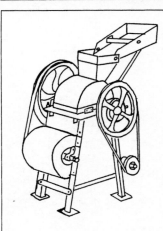

'BABY' GROUNDNUT DECORTICATING MACHINE

The groundnuts are shelled by revolving wooden beaters against a rollbar screen and separated by air from a winnowing fan. Unshelled pods can be fed back into the sheller. The machine can be operated by hand, or by 0.75kW single phase electric motor.

DANDEKAR BROTHERS & CO.
Shivajinagar
Sangli
Maharashtra 416 416
INDIA

PEANUT HUSKER/SHELLER
Free-standing with hand crank and flywheel.
Weight 60kg.

CECOCO
P.O. Box 8
Ibaraki City, Osaka 567
JAPAN

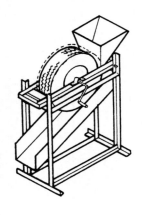

RUBBER-TYRE GROUNDNUT SHELLER

This decorticator comprises a feed hopper, a 'rubber tyre' roller with a fixed cover, concave decorticating plate, and a discharge chute. The roller is turned by a crank handle. Shelling efficiency 95%. Broken kernels 3-5%. Output is in the range 40 to 60kg/hour.

KUNASIN MACHINERY
107-108 Sri-Satchanalai Road
Sawanankalok
Sukothai
THAILAND

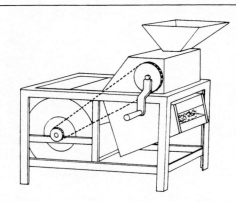

GROUNDNUT DECORTICATORS

ABGD 150
The nuts fall into a shelling chamber from a feed hopper. The winnowing action of a fan blows the shells away from the nuts, which are discharged clean from a chute. Extra strong construction. The model illustrated is hand operated although it can also be powered by a 0.37kW electric motor.

ALVAN BLANCH DEVELOPMENT CO. LTD
Chelworth
Malmesbury
Wilts SN16 9SG
UK

PEANUT HUSKER/SHELLER
This is a free-standing machine, powered by a 1.5kW engine.

CECOCO
P.O. Box 8
Ibaraki City
Osaka 567
JAPAN

GROUNDNUT DECORTICATOR
Comprises a frame, shelling chamber and sieves. The shelling chamber is a sheet metal case which contains a sieve which helps to break the shell. Two different sieves are provided with the machine. Requires a 0.37kW power supply.

RAJAN UNIVERSAL EXPORTS (MFRS) LTD
P.O. Box 250
Madras
600 001
INDIA

AMDP PEANUT SHELLER PS-100
This sheller is suitable for all sizes of peanut pods. It is constructed from steel sheet and is driven by a 1.2kW electric motor. It requires two people to operate it.

AGRICULTURAL MECHANISATION DEVELOPMENT PROGRAM
CEAT
U.P. Los Baños College
Laguna 4031
PHILIPPINES

POWERED RUBBER-TYRE GROUNDNUT SHELLER

This machine is similar to the hand-operated unit but also has an integral winnowing fan for separating and removing the broken shells. Shelling efficiency 95%. Broken kernel 4-6%. Cleaning efficiency 99.5%. It requires a 1.5kW electric motor. Output is 300kg/hour.

KUNASIN MACHINERY
107-108 Sri-Satchanalai Road
Sawanankalok
Sukothai
THAILAND

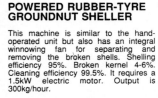
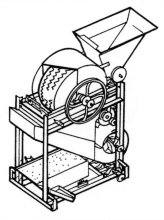

DANDEKAR GROUNDNUT DECORTICATOR

This decorticator is the smallest in a range of four. It is fitted on a steel base with four legs. A hopper for feeding the nuts into the opener is at the top of the machine. From there they pass into the opening cylinder where the shells are broken and then separated from the kernels. Everything drops through a sieve to a chute where the dust and shells are removed by a winnowing fan. Clean kernels fall to the ground.
Beater speed 150-175 revs/min. Fan speed 425 revs/min. Requires 3.75kW motor. Driving pulleys supplied. Weight 750kg.

DANDEKAR BROTHERS & CO.
Shivajinagar
Sangli
Maharashtra
416 416
INDIA

MOBILE GROUNDNUT DECORTICATOR

ABGD 1000
This is a large mobile groundnut decorticator. It is mounted on a chassis with pneumatic-tyred wheels and a drawbar with a screw jack. The nuts fall into a cylindrical shelling chamber from the integral feed hopper and are moved against a screen by a rotating beater. The kernels and shells then pass into an aspiration box through which an adjustable airflow passes to remove the shells. The machine can be powered by electric motor, diesel or petrol engine. Power required is 5.5kW. Capacity is 1000kg/hour.

ALVAN BLANCH DEVELOPMENT CO. LTD
Chelworth
Malmesbury
Wilts SN16 9SG
UK

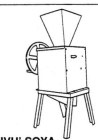

'KIVU' SOYA DECORTICATOR

This is a manually operated soya bean decorticator. The output is 30kg/hour.

DEKLERCK
14 Place Lehon Plein
1030 Brussels
BELGIUM

TROPIC COFFEE PULPER

In this hand-operated drum coffee pulper the ripe coffee cherry is fed into the hopper where it is pulped between a cylinder and screen. This process is fly-wheel assisted.

TROPIC
B.P. 706
Douala
CAMEROON

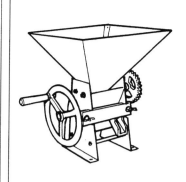

HAND-OPERATED ATOM COFFEE PULPER

This pulper is manufactured for the treatment of Arabica and Robusta coffee. Capacity of ripe coffee is approximately 55kg/hour. This model is unsuitable for use with Liberica coffee for which Mackinnon recommend the special Liberica disc pulpers. Weight 15.5kg.

WM. MACKINNON & CO. LTD
Spring Garden Ironworks
Aberdeen
AB9 1DU
Scotland
UK

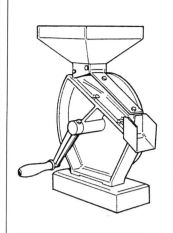

MANUAL MONODISC PULPER

The DMM model has been designed for use by small-scale producers. It is operated by rotating the crank handle mounted on the cast iron flywheel. It can process up to 500kg of coffee cherry per hour.
Weight 150kg.

GAUTHIER S.A.R.L.
Bd. de la Lironde
Parc Agropolis Bât.12
Montferrier-sur-Lez
34980
FRANCE

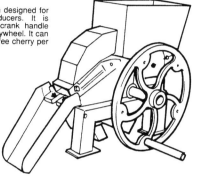

DISC COFFEE PULPERS

IRIMA 67 DISC COFFEE PULPER
Cherries are fed into the hopper with water. The bulbed disc rotates when the handle is turned and, together with the pulping bar, rubs off the outer coatings, leaving a pulp. The pulping bar forms part of the frame of the machine. It is straight and has a renewable steel edge. The skin clearance between the disc and the knife edge can be regulated by altering the position of the disc on the shaft.

JOHN GORDON & CO. (ENGINEERS) LTD
Gordon House
Bower Hill
Epping
Essex CM16 7AG
UK

MACKINNON ONE-DISC COFFEE PULPER
The main shaft of the machine is mounted in ball bearings, a large cast iron flywheel with a handle is used to turn the pulping-disc which has the bulbs cast on to its surface.

WM. MACKINNON & CO. LTD
Spring Garden Ironworks
Aberdeen
Scotland AB9 1DU
UK

Similar implements are manufactured by:

AGRICULTURAL ENGINEERS LTD
Ring Road Industrial Area
P.O. Box 12127
Accra North
GHANA

AGRO MACHINERY LTD
P.O. Box 3281
Bush Rod Island
Monrovia
LIBERIA

MULTI-DISC COFFEE PULPERS

The L.C. series of disc pulpers is available in one-, two-, three- or four-disc versions. All models share the same side and underframe castings. Different discs are available to cater for alternative coffee varieties. The pulping bars on this machine are made of plated steel and can be turned, thus providing four wearing edges. The four-disc model (illustrated) can process 5440kg/hour of ripe cherry coffee with a power input of 3kW.

JOHN GORDON & CO. (ENGINEERS) LTD
Gordon House
Bower Hill
Epping
Essex CM16 7AG
UK

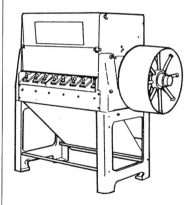

VERTICAL COFFEE PULPERS

DV-256LT
Fitted with six plates, this pulper requires minimum water in use. Totally sealed gearbox is designed to keep out water. All sizes of beans can be pulped simultaneously without adjustment because of helicoidal feed system. The pulper automatically cuts out if any hard material is encountered. Driven by 1.1kW motor or 2.25kW engine. Output is in the rang 2000-2500kg/hour.
Weight 40kg.
A smaller pulper is also offered: the DV-183LT can be operated by hand or with a small electric motor. Output is in the range 300-400kg/hour.
Weight 25kg.

PENAGOS HERMANOS & CIA. LTDA
Apartado Aereo 689
Bucaramanga
COLOMBIA

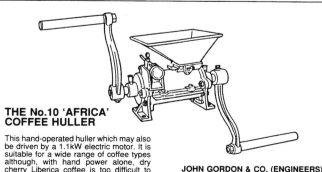

THE No.10 'AFRICA' COFFEE HULLER

This hand-operated huller which may also be driven by a 1.1kW electric motor. It is suitable for a wide range of coffee types although, with hand power alone, dry cherry Liberica coffee is too difficult to shell. Arabica coffee can be shelled at a rate of 22kg/hour of clean coffee or 36kg/hour of parchment coffee. Robusta rates are about 30% more: Liberica about 30% less. Weight 43kg.

JOHN GORDON & CO. (ENGINEERS) LTD
Gordon House, Bower Hill
Epping
Essex CM16 7AG
UK

COFFEE HULLERS

AMUDA 501 COFFEE HULLER
These hullers are capable of treating both dry cherry coffee and dry parchment coffee. It is fitted with a balanced rotating cylinder with steel 'rips' which is mounted on a shaft held in ball bearings. Capacity is in the range 125 to 185kg/hour depending on the coffee variety. Power required is 3.75kW.

RAJAN UNIVERSAL EXPORTS (MFRS) LTD
P.O. Box 250
Madras
600 001
INDIA

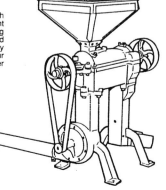

COFFEE HULLERS

COFFEE SHELLER
This huller is powered by either an electric motor or a diesel engine. Capacity is 200kg/hour with a power requirement of 7.5kW. Weight 245kg.

ABI-MÉCHANIQUE
B.P. 343
45 rue Pierre et Marie Curie
(Zone 4c), Abidjan
IVORY COAST

NO.5 'AFRICA' COFFEE HULLER
These hullers are capable of treating both dry cherry and parchment coffee. Two screens are provided, one perforated and the other of woven wire.

JOHN GORDON & CO. (ENGINEERS)
LTD
Gordon House
Bower Hill, Epping
Essex CM16 7AG
UK

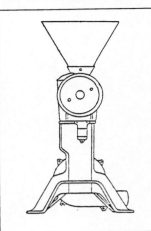

CONGO COFFEE GRADER

The machine is hand operated. Its cylinder is composed of a detachable perforated sheet which has two sizes of perforations, thus giving three products. Spare sheets with different sized perforations can be obtained on request.

JOHN GORDON & CO. (ENGINEERS)
LTD
Gordon House
Bower Hill
Epping
Essex CM16 7AG
UK

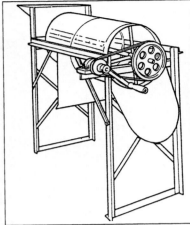

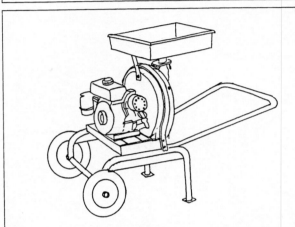

MOBILE PALM NUT CRACKER

The 'Amuda' mobile palm nut cracker is powered by a 1.2kW motor and can process up to 500kg/hour of palm nuts. The legs of the machine can be moved into a horizontal position and the unit may then be carried stretcher-fashion by two people.

RAJAN UNIVERSAL EXPORT (MFRS)
PVT LTD
P.O. Box 250
Madras
600-001
INDIA

A similar cracker is made by:

ALVAN BLANCH DEVELOPMENT CO.
LTD
Chelworth
Malmesbury
Wilts SN16 9SG
UK

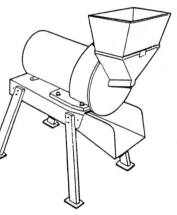

PALM NUT CRACKER

This is a barrow-mounted palm nut cracker. The nuts are fed from a hopper into a cracking chamber which has beaters driven by a 2.25kW engine. The nuts are rendered into small pieces.

ECOMAT
Le Val Rouge
B.P. 132
Morlaix
29210
FRANCE

Similar machines are manufactured by:

SISMAR
20 rue Dr. Thèze
3214
Dakar
SENEGAL

HERCULANO ALFAIAS AGRICOLAS
Loureiro
Oliveira de Azemeis 3720
PORTUGAL

BIELENBERG RAM PRESS

Operated by raising and pulling down a long handle which drives a steel ram into a cage cylinder in which the seed is pressed. The stroke of the handle goes from vertical to about 45 degrees.
   The machine can be operated by one person for several hours. When the handle is in an upright position the steel ram is pushed out and seed is fed from the hopper to the cage. Each time the handle is pressed down, a stream of oil appears from the underside of the cage.

ELCT-DAR
Village sunflower project
P.O. Box 1409
Arusha
TANZANIA

UNATA OIL PRESSES

These are screw presses used for the production of oil. There are two versions available, one for palmfruit and the other for seeds. The difference between them lies in the size and number of holes in the press cages, the seed press having a greater number of smaller holes. The presses can be operated by two people using the long extension handles to turn the press screw.

UNATA C.V.
P.O. Box 50
Nieuwlandlaan B-437
3200 Aarschot
BELGIUM

FABRICACIÓN DE MAQUINARIA
PARA LA INDUSTRIA ALIMETICIA
Jiron Alberto Aberd, 400
San Martin de Porres
Lima
PERU

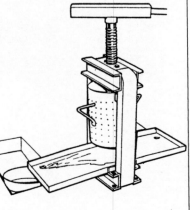

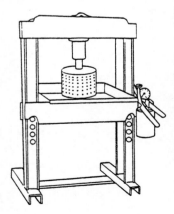

AGRICO HYDRAULIC PRESS

A manually operated two-speed hydraulic pump works a 25-tonne ram. The machine can press 500kg of cassava dough or 100kg of ground sheanuts per hour. The press comprises a frame, a pressing table of adjustable height and top section with vertically-mounted hydraulic press. This pushes a piston down into the circular pressing chamber. The hand-operated pump and reservoir is fitted at the side of the frame.

AGRICULTURAL ENGINEERS LTD
Ring Road Industrial Area
P.O. Box 12127
Accra North
GHANA

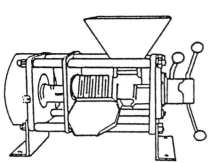

MINI SCREW PRESSES

OIL EXPELLER EXP-10
The expeller is electrically-powered by a 4kW motor. The machine is designed to extract oil from sunflower seed although it can be adjusted to use other types of seed.

TANZANIA ENGINEERING & MANUFACTURING DESIGN ORGANISATION
P.O. Box 6111
Arusha
TANZANIA

AB MINI 40 SCREW PRESS
This is a simple, robust, small capacity screw press, designed to be powered by a 2.25kW 3-phase motor. Seed is gravity fed to the press from an integral feed hopper. When filtered, the extracted oil can be used for cooking purposes and the cake used for animal feed.
Weight 195kg.

ALVAN BLANCH DEVELOPMENT CO. LTD
Chelworth
Malmesbury
Wilts SN16 9SG
UK

POWERED OIL EXPELLERS

The EXP 20 expeller is capable of handling 110kg/hour of sunflower seed. Oil output is dependent on the type of seed used. It is powered by a 7.5kw three-phase electric motor.

TANZANIA ENGINEERING & MANUFACTURING DESIGN ORGANISATION
P.O. Box 6111
Arusha
TANZANIA

POWERED OIL EXPELLER
This machine is suitable for extracting oil from a variety of seeds including mustard, peanut kernel, cotton seed, caster bean, soyabean, rape seed and sesame seed.

CECOCO
P.O. Box 8
Ibaraki City
Osaka 567
JAPAN

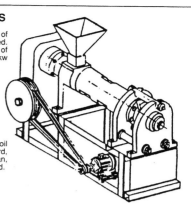

OIL FRUIT CRUSHER AND PRESS

The material to be used is first crushed to a size which the press can then handle. The oil is produced by a cold pressing system and it is unnecessary to heat, boil or steam the raw materials prior to the pressing operation. During the pressing process, there is an increase in temperature and oil is expelled and flows through filtration holes in the cylinder. The residue is expelled in rope form through the centre of the press head thus allowing continuous production. Both machines can be driven from a single power source of 0.37kW.

IBG MONFORTS & REINERS GmbH & CO.
P.O. Box 200853
Munchengladbach 2
D-4050
GERMANY

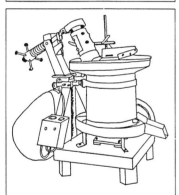

ROTARY OIL MILLS

PORTABLE POWER GHANI
For crushing all types of oil seeds. A 1.5kW motor is required to operate the machine in which a stationary pestle works against a rotating mortar.
A single charge of 12-15kg takes 75 minutes to process.
Weight 530kg.

KISAN KRISHI YANTRA UDYOG
64 Moti Bhawan
Collector Ganj
Kanpur
208 001
INDIA

RAJA ROTARY OIL MILLS
This larger mill requires 3.75-5.25kW. It is equipped with a lever and clutch arrangement which enables the removal of oil cakes and reloading without stopping other mills. Output depends on the type of seed crushed.

RAJAN UNIVERSAL EXPORTS (MFRS) LTD
P.O. Box 250
Madras
600 001
INDIA

ROLLER ROOT CUTTERS

The TYPE B root cutter illustrated left is constructed from cast iron. It has seven helicoidal blades and eight pruning knives. The cutter can be fitted with an electric motor to replace the flywheel and handle. Output is up to 5 tonnes/hour.

RENSON LANDRECIES S.A.R.L.
37 route d'Happegarbes
B.P. 12
Landrecies
59550
FRANCE

A similar cutter manufactured by Cecoco is illustrated right:

CECOCO
P.O. Box 8
Ibaraki City
Osaka 567
JAPAN

CASSAVA PEELER

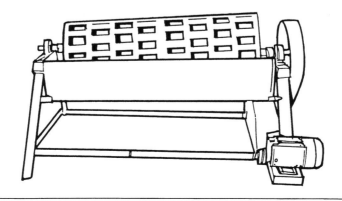

This prototype machine comprises a perforated cylindrical drum eccentrically-mounted on a shaft. The inside of the drum is lined with expanded metal which abrades the cassava skin as the drum rotates.

DEPARTMENT OF AGRICULTURAL ENG.
University of Nigeria
Nsukka
NIGERIA

WADHWA CASSAVA PEELER
This commercially produced machine requires a 5.5kW electric motor or diesel engine. The cassava peel and the top skin of the tuber leave the machine in a granular form, which can then be dried and used for livestock feed.

AGRICULTURAL ENGINEERS LTD
Ring Road Industrial Area
P.O. Box 12127
Accra North
GHANA

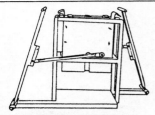

TWO-PERSON CASSAVA GRATER

This manually-powered cassava grater can achieve a reasonable throughput as the lever action provides greater power than hand cranking.

UNATA C.V.
P.O. Box 50
Nieuwlandlaan B-437
3200 Aarschot
BELGIUM

NARDI ROOT CUTTERS

These are manually operated disc cutters with four knives. Three models are available.

NARDI FRANCESCO & FIGLI
06017 Selci Lama
Peruga
ITALY

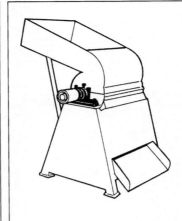

CASSAVA GRATERS

CASSAVA GRATER
The grating blades rotate at high speed. The centre shaft and rollers run in self-aligning ball bearings in dust-proof cast iron housings. 1.5, 2.25 and 3kW versions are available.

RAJAN UNIVERSAL EXPORTS (MFRS) LTD
P.O. Box 250
Madras
600 001
INDIA

WADHWA CASSAVA GRATER
This machine uses a circular grating disc, which is 3-4 times more efficient than cylindrical drum versions. The disc runs at 1550 rev/min and is self cleaning. It is powered by a 3.75kW diesel engine or electric motor.

AGRICULTURAL ENGINEERS LTD
Ring Road Industrial Area
P.O. Box 12127
Accra North
GHANA

MANUAL CASSAVA GRATER
Manually operated by crank handle, the free-standing machine has a rotating abrasive drum. Designed for use by farmers without access to motors or engines. Output is in the range 125-180kg/hour.

DEPARTMENT OF AGRICULTURAL ENGINEERING
Faculty of Engineering
University of Nigeria
Nsukka
NIGERIA

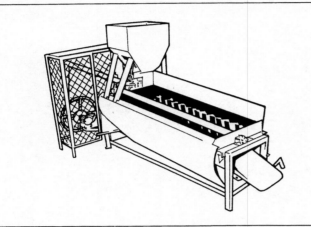

GARI FRYING MACHINE

The machine simulates the traditional manual frying technique. The fryer comprises a 1.7m long metal trough in which spring-loaded paddles are attached to an axially mounted shaft which oscillates through 180 degrees. Gari mash is metered continuously into one end of the heated trough. The oscillating paddles press the mashed gari against the surface of the trough in one direction and then scrape it off and move it along the machine in the other. The machine is powered by an electric motor.
Output 66kg/hour.

DEPARTMENT OF AGRICULTURAL ENGINEERING
Faculty of Engineering
University of Nigeria
Nsukka
NIGERIA

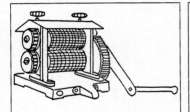

HAND-OPERATED SUGAR CANE CRUSHER

This is a simple two-cylinder machine for household use.

DANDEKAR BROTHERS & CO.
Shivajinagar
Sangli
Maharashtra 416 416
INDIA

HAND-OPERATED SUGAR CANE CRUSHERS

N-15 SUGAR CANE CRUSHER
This is the smallest in a range of three crushers. The cylinders are rotated at 175 rev/min by hand, although it can be powered by an electric motor. Capacity 80 litres/hour.

CIMAG
Rua St Terezinha 1381
13970 Itapira S.P.
BRAZIL

SUGAR CANE CRUSHER
Can be operated by hand or electric motor.

COLOMBO COMMERCIAL CO. (ENG.) LTD
121 Sir James Peiris Mawatha
Colombo 2
SRI LANKA

SUGAR JUICE SQUEEZERS
The hand-powered version is operated by turning the wheel handle at the side of the machine. The machine acts like a mangle. The cane is fed through rollers and the juice is squeezed out.

CECOCO
P.O. Box 8
Ibaraki City
Osaka 567
JAPAN

A similar mill is manufactured by:

DIAS & DIAS
690 Negombo Road
Mabole
Wattala
SRI LANKA

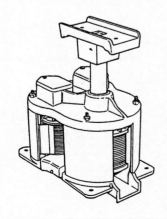

ANIMAL-POWERED SUGAR CANE CRUSHERS

TV-122 VERTICAL SUGAR CANE MILL
This machine has been designed to use the power of one animal. There are three crushing rollers on which the pressure is adjustable externally. The large roller is 250mm in diameter and the smaller pair are 125mm. Output is between 4000-6000kg/day.
Weight 220kg.

PENAGOS HERMANOS & CIA. LTDA
Apartado Aereo 689
Bucaramanga
COLOMBIA

Similar mills are manufactured by:

P.M. MADURAI MUDALIAR & SONS
Madurai Mudaliar Road
P.O. Box 7156
Bangalore
560 053
INDIA

ANIMAL-POWERED HORIZONTAL CANE MILL

This is a horizontal sugar cane crushing mill designed to be powered by a single oxen. The model illustrated is the smallest in a range of three, it has rollers 150mm in diameter and 175mm wide. The frame is made of cast iron and the steel axles run in bronze bearings.

FUNDIÇÁO CORRADI S.A.
Av Getúlio Vargas, 735
Caixa Postal 2
Itaúna M.G.
BRAZIL

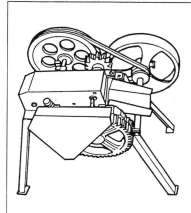

TRITON SUGAR MILL

This crusher is mounted on legs and is driven by flat belt from an independent power source such as a walking tractor. Drive is transferred to the horizontal rollers via V-belt and pulley then through a gear train.

TRITON S.A.
Rue Dois Irmaaos, 262
B.P. 132
Joacaba S.C.
89 604
BRAZIL

A similar mill is made by:

TEMDO
P.O. Box 6111
Arusha
TANZANIA

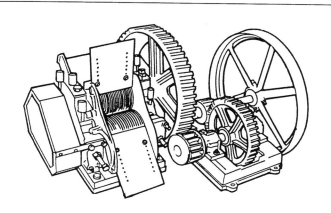

POWERED HORIZONTAL SUGAR CANE CRUSHERS

Penagos build a range of six powered cane mills. The smallest requires a 4.5kW power source; the largest 12kW. The major roller is turned at 15 rev/min through a set of reduction gears by a pulley 970mm in diameter. Construction is of cast iron and steel and the axles run in brass bearings. The largest mill is capable of processing 40 tonnes of cane in 24 hours.
Weight 520kg.

PENAGOS HERMANOS & CIA. LTDA
Apartado Aereo 689
Bucaramanga
COLOMBIA

A similar range of mills are manufactured by:

WM. MACKINNON & CO. LTD
Spring Garden Ironworks
Aberdeen
AB9 1DU
Scotland
UK

AGRICULTURAL ENGINEERS LTD
Ring Road Industrial Area
P.O. Box 12127
Accra North
GHANA

AGRO MACHINERY LTD
P.O. Box 3281
Bush Rod Island
Monrovia
LIBERIA

P.M. MADURAI MUDALIAR & SONS
Madurai Mudaliar Road
P.O. Box 7156
Bangalore
560 053
INDIA

RAJAN UNIVERSAL EXPORTS (MFRS) LTD
P.O. Box 250
Madras
600 001
INDIA

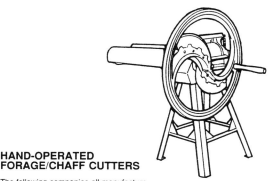

HAND-OPERATED FORAGE/CHAFF CUTTERS

The following companies all manufacture a hand-operated forage cutter of this type. The cutter is mounted on a stand, and is operated by means of a handle on the flywheel so that the turning motion of the two blades within the wheel chops the forage as it is fed manually or mechanically into the cutter. The cutter wheels may or may not be guarded. The Penagos Hermanos machine is illustrated.

PENAGOS HERMANOS & CIA. LTDA
Apartado Aereo 689
Bucaramanga
COLOMBIA

BIO-INNOKOORD
2040 Budaors
Pf. 14
HUNGARY

RURAL INDUSTRIES INNOVATION CENTRE
Private Bag 11
Kanye
BOTSWANA

AGRICULTURAL ENGINEERS LTD
Ring Road Industrial Area
P.O. Box 12127
Accra North
GHANA

DANDEKAR BROTHERS & CO.
Shivajinagar
Sangli
Maharashtra
416 416
INDIA

AGRO MACHINERY LTD
P.O. Box 3281
Bush Rod Island
Monrovia
LIBERIA

DATINI MERCANTILE LTD
Enterprise Road
Box 45483
Nairobi
KENYA

SHEIKH NAWAZ INDUSTRIES (REGD)
Samundry Road
Faisalabad
PAKISTAN

AGRICULTURAL MECHANISATION DEV. PROG
AMDP
CEAT
U.P. Los Baños College
Laguna 4031
PHILIPPINES

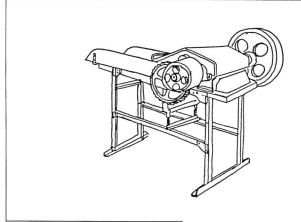

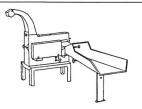

POWERED SILAGE CUTTERS

Nogueira produce two silage cutter models with power requirements of 3.75 to 11.2kW. They have a capacity of between 2000 and 7000kg/hour.

IRMÃOS NOGUEIRA S.A.
Rua 15 de Novembro, 781
Itapira S.P.
13970
BRAZIL

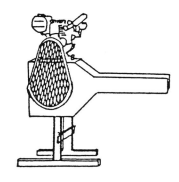

AB FIBRE RIBBONER

This machine is designed for the production of raw fibre from stem fibre crops such as kenaf. It is fitted with a three beater drum and powered by a 3.75kW petrol engine.

ALVAN BLANCH DEVELOPMENT CO. LTD
Chelworth
Malmesbury
Wilts SN16 9SG
UK

POWERED DRUM FORAGE CUTTERS

FORAGE CHOPPERS
The model P-10 chaff cutter has a geared four-blade cylinder cutter and feed mechanism, size of cut 8-12-17mm. It is powered by a 2.25kW electric motor or petrol engine. Output of up to 4000kg/hour.

PENAGOS HERMANOS & CIA. LTDA
Apartado Aereo 689
Bucaramanga
COLOMBIA

CECOCO FORAGE CHOPPERS
Four models are available with a power requirements of 0.37 to 7.5kW.

CECOCO
P.O. Box 8
Ibaraki City
Osaka 567
JAPAN

Jeremy Hartley/Panos

7. WATER LIFTING

Water is essential to all life. Human habitation has always developed where there have been accessible sources of water — streams, rivers, springs, lakes, ponds, rainfall catchment. Subsurface water has also been obtained through the digging of wells. These sources have provided water for humans and their livestock, and also for irrigation when required.

People have developed ways of raising water so that it can be moved to the point where it is required. In the broadest sense all these devices, from simple buckets on the end of some rope to modern centrifugal systems of water raising, can be called pumps. These systems developed as local responses to a wide range of factors:

○ the requirement for water (quality of water; quantity of water by day, through the year, for different uses — human, animal, irrigation);

○ the site of the water source (the depth of the water-table, the height that the water has to be lifted, the capacity of water flow that the site can provide);

○ the type of energy available for powering the pumping system;

○ the type of service that can be provided (local resources, availability of repair and maintenance facilities, cost).

When deciding on the installation of pumping systems these are still the key factors that need to be considered. This chapter provides information to help in assessing these factors and selecting suitable pumping systems. The following will enable non-specialists to begin to identify the basic requirements for pumping systems, thus making them better able to utilize expertise and detailed information.

WATER REQUIREMENTS

Domestic consumption

Basic domestic water requirements include drinking water for humans and some small animals, cooking, bathing, washing clothes and cleaning. The minimum figure for daily human water consumption is usually taken to be 20 litres per person. When water is readily available, with no great effort required to draw or carry it, consumption increases to 30 litres or more per person per day. In Europe, with a ready supply of water piped to individual homes, consumption rises to 150 litres per person per day.

Water for human consumption must be of high quality and so wherever possible chemical, physical and microbiological examination of the source should be carried out. Even when the water is fit to drink at the pump site, care must be taken since it rapidly deteriorates during storage (12-24 hours in pipes, for example). Hygiene rules must therefore be developed and water treatment is highly desirable.

Water consumption by animals

Drinking water for animals can be an important factor in water consumption and should not be ignored. Although water quality is not such an important factor, large animals consume considerably more water than humans. Table 1 gives some guide to the likely requirements, and these amounts can vary considerably according to the season.

Table 1 Typical water requirements of animals

	Wet and/or cold season	Dry season	Dry, hot season
Cattle (zebu)	10-20 l/day	15-40 l/day	50 l/day
sheep, goats	1-2 l/day	4 l/day	5 l/day
Pigs	5-10 l/day		

When animals do not drink every day they will drink more than the above figures at one go. For example: when zebu drink once every two days, they absorb 50-60 litres of water at a time. A camel can drink over 100 litres of water at once.

Where herds of animals need to be watered at the same time, large quantities of water are required quickly. For example, a flow rate of 5m³/hour is required if a herd of 100 cattle is to be watered in one hour. Such flows are often not available, and so for animal water supplies large storage tanks with a capacity of several dozen cubic metres are essential when large numbers of animals are to be supplied in a short period of time.

Agricultural consumption

Water requirements for irrigation are considerably higher than those for both human and animal consumption. Irrigation supplements rainfall during the rainy season, and in the dry season or in arid climates it may supply the entire water requirement. These field requirements are calculated according to complex formulae which involve a number of parameters: type of crop, wind, daily temperature, humidity, shade, and growth stage of the plant (the requirements are usually highest at flowering). The requirement (i.e. the amount of water to be brought to the plot) is evaluated in terms of depth of water, expressed in millimetres per day for a given crop (1mm of irrigation is equivalent to 1 litre per square metre).

In a tropical climate the water requirement (excluding rainfall) will vary between 5mm/day in a humid environment and 15mm/day in an arid area.

In addition to the actual requirement for irrigation, there are also losses of water in pipes or channels carrying water to the fields, perhaps because of poor levelling or excess water flowing out of fields. In order to convert the field requirement to the pumping requirement, the field requirement must be increased by the volume of these water losses. This is known as the *field efficiency*. In general, it is reasonable to expect an efficiency of 60-70 per cent. For example, if the theoretical requirement of the plot is 9mm/day, the amount pumped should be 13mm (9/0.7), or a volume of 130m³ /day for one hectare. Table 2 provides a rough guide to the scale of efficiencies that can be expected with different methods of irrigation.

Table 2 Overall irrigation efficiency

	Average	Range
Flood	60%	80% to 30%
Ridge	55%	70% to 40%
Sprinkler	65%	80% to 50%
Trickle	90%	95% to 70%

When calculating the flow required for a farm, the water raising method must be designed for the maximum requirement of the whole farm during the cropping season. Since such flows are so large the methods for pumping the water can often be expensive, in which case it may well be better to look for alternative means of supplying irrigation water, such as a gravity fed system.

Table 3 Summary of water requirements

Type	Characteristics	Average daily requirement
Small village	300 inhabitants	6m³
Large village	1500 inhabitants	35m³
Small herd	30 zebu, 50 goats	1m³
Large herd	400 zebu, 500 goats	12m³
Small garden	$^1/_{10}$ ha	8m³
Large garden	1ha	80m³
Rice field	20ha	2300m³

SITE CONSIDERATIONS

Most of the rural population have to depend on traditional sources of water for drinking, cooking, washing, livestock and irrigation. Many of the surface sources — lakes, ponds, rivers — are polluted and the community runs the risk of disease when using them. Shallow subsurface water from springs, wells and boreholes is usually of better quality and should be the preferred choice for human consumption. In areas of higher rainfall the collection of water from rooftops can provide good quality water during the wet season; however, its availability is usually limited to times when water is not scarce.

When considering what type of pump would be appropriate for the available water source, there are two main factors to be considered: *the water flow* and the *pumping head*. The water flow is dictated by the requirements outlined in the previous section. The pumping head, or total manometric height (TMH), is determined by two parts (see Figure 1); the height that the water has to be raised and the head loss owing to friction caused by the water flowing through the pipework. The head loss is calculated as a figure in metres. This enables the pumping head to be calculated by adding the height that the water has to be raised to the head loss.

Table 4 Head loss in a pipe of 50mm internal diameter

	Pipe length	
	10m	50m
Flow rate: 10 m³/h	0.4m	2m
Flow rate: 30 m³/h	2.4m	12m

If it is necessary to use a pump that relies on suction, the height of the pump above the water cannot be greater than 8m. Sometimes, when ground level is more than 8m above the water level, it is necessary to lower the pump. This can be done by digging a hole in the ground next to the water source and positioning the pump in the hole, by putting the pump on a raft floating on the water, or by considering some other means of raising the water.

Pumping from a river can also cause installation problems as the water level is often highly variable. The suction height can become too great when the pumping system is installed in a fixed position on the top of the bank, above the high water line. Only easily moved systems, such as engine-driven pumps or some manual pumps, are suitable in such cases. Installation of engine-driven pumps (engines greater than 7.5kW or electric motors) on floating pontoons provides an elegant solution to the problem while reducing the suction height as much as possible, which is always desirable.

Wells and boreholes usually have limited flow rates of a few cubic metres per hour (2-3m³/h). For a well, 5m³/h is a good flow rate. Wells often cannot provide as much water as can be pumped by a motorized system. The flow rate of an engine-driven pump (10m³/hour or more) is often too high for the water catchment system of the well which then starts to deteriorate. Some types of well cannot support water extraction rates of more than 1-2m³/hour. One common source of breakdown is when the level of the water-table drops below the level of the pump, so that the pump is no longer in the water and runs dry! Conversely, not using the well may lead to flooding of the pump.

PUMPING SYSTEMS

Pumping systems can be differentiated into two basic groupings, those which use fossil fuels (petrol, diesel) and all the others which use renewable sources of energy (solar, wind, human, and animal power). At the moment pumps powered by fossil fuels provide a range of powers unrivalled by the other power sources.

The following are the different types of pumps available on the market and the efficiency which should be expected of them. The efficiency of the equipment sometimes varies from one manufacturer to another. A comparison is therefore advisable.

Human-powered pumps

These can be broadly split into 'traditional' and 'factory-made' pumps (Table 5 provides a comparison of some traditional and factory-made pumps).

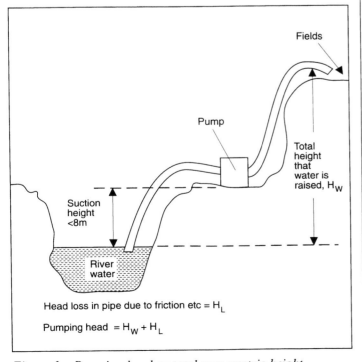

Figure 1   Pumping head or total manometric height

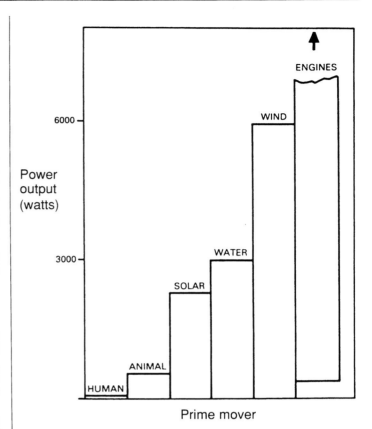

Figure 2   Available power output from various prime movers

Traditional pumps

Although traditional pumps are not represented in this book it is important to have an awareness and understanding of their role and relevance to rural communities.

Traditional pumps are usually made by local artisans and have been developed over a long period of time to satisfy very specific local conditions and requirements. They are primarily for irrigation rather than domestic use. Being human-powered, their capacity is low and they are only suitable for small plots of land up to 0.25ha and for low lifts of a few metres. The simpler types, such as water scoops, are very cheap to make, but are inefficient in their use of energy. The more efficient pumps, such as the archimedean screw, have a greater capital cost, but are able to irrigate larger areas for less effort.

A great advantage of these traditional pumping systems is that they are often portable, thus enabling farmers to move them between their often dispersed smallholdings. In areas where these are already in use, they often provide the most appropriate and secure means of irrigation to crops.

Some successful attempts have been made to develop new pumping devices which are suitable for village manufacture. Their success is a result of matching the design with the resources, skills and specific requirements of the user and maker. The Rower and RDRS pumps described in the equipment pages are examples of this type of technology.

The flow rate of hand (or foot) pumps is very low. A human can produce a continuous 30 watts of hand power, sufficient for pumping 1m³/h at 10m depth. With strenuous effort this may be doubled or trebled for short periods of time. Depths of more than 10m have a very great influence on flow rate — at 40m it falls to 0.3m³/h, so handpumps have little use for irrigation from such depths.

Factory-made handpumps

There is a large number of manufacturers of handpumps. Although each manufacturer will usually only produce two or three models, the range of manufacturers ensures an extremely wide, and often confusing, choice. Since these handpumps are capable of raising water from sealed wells or boreholes they have the potential for providing safer water for domestic consumption. Accordingly many agencies have considered this type of technology to be appropriate for rural water supplies.

In line with this thinking, pump designs for village level operation and maintenance (VLOM) have been developed. The VLOM specifications require that a pump can be easily dismantled, maintained and repaired at village level. In addition VLOM attempts to develop local capacity to manufacture, or part manufacture, pumps and spare parts.

The efficiency of handpumps varies very little from one pump to the next, except when raising water from small depths (less than 4m). However, pumps which incorporate a flywheel are easier and less tiring.

As with traditional pumps, the major drawback of these pumps is the limited power developed by humans. At depths of 15m or more the pumping effort is such that irrigation is no longer an attractive proposition.

When a pump is used for domestic purposes the wear and tear on it is usually very great. It is often used almost continuously through the daylight hours by a wide range of different people, mostly unskilled in its use and without direct responsibility for its upkeep. This puts the pumps under tremendous stress, and durability and robustness become prime selection criteria.

Table 5 Water lifting devices and their application

	Prime mover[1]		Head range				Application	
	Typical	Alter.	V.low[2]	Low[3]	Medium[4]	High[5]	Irrig	Domestic
Traditional			●					
Water jar	H		●				●	
Water scoop	H		●				●	
Swing bucket	H		●				●	
Dhone	H		●				●	
Paddle wheel	H		●				●	
Water ladder	H	AWiEM	●				●	
Arch. screw	H	WiEM	●				●	
Shaduf	H		●				●	●
Picottah	H			●			●	
Rope & bucket	H			●		●		●
Mohte	A			●	●		●	
Circular mohte	A			●			●	
Persian wheel	A	EM		●	●		●	
Sakia/Zawafa	A	EM		●				●
Chain & washer	HA	EM	●	●	●		●	●
Water wheel	Wa			●	●			●
Factory-made pumps							●6	
Shallow well handpump	H	AWiEMS				●		●
Deep well handpump	H	AWiEMS	●	●			●7	●
Diaphragm pump	H	E	●	●	●		●6	●
Semi rotary	H		●	●		●		●
Centrifugal	EM	S		●			●	●
Hydraulic ram	Wa			●	●		●8	●

Notes:
1. Key: H=human; A=animal; Wi=wind; Wa=water; E=engine; M=electric motor; S=solar
2. Surface water up to 2m.
3. Shallow open wells up to 7m.
4. Wells up to 20m.
5. Wells and boreholes over 20m.
6. Applicable to very low lifts and small areas.
7. Applicable when coupled to the more powerful prime movers.
8. Occasionally applicable for small plots in hilly areas.

Animal-powered pumps

Traditional animal-powered systems of pumping have been highly developed in a number of cultures — northern Africa, Middle East and Europe — and can still be found in some countries (Table 5). As with traditional hand powered systems these have developed over time as a response to local needs and opportunities. They are highly adapted to specific local circumstances and provide an essential service. However, as other power sources become available, and as the local situation changes, they are often being replaced by pumps using other sources of power.

In theory animals can provide a very attractive option for pumping since they have a greater power output than humans. However, traditional systems are generally produced by local artisans and are not generally for sale to other countries, although a few commercially available models are listed in this chapter. The introduction of such systems is difficult, not only because of the problems of the design and production of the pumping equipment, but specifically because of the problem of adapting the existing animal-use pattern to the needs of the pumping system. Attempts to introduce animal-powered systems to new areas have not generally proven successful.

The power provided varies greatly from one animal to the next. Some orders of magnitude (for Africa) are:

	Donkey	Ox	Horse or camel	Human
Power (watts)	40-80	150-200	150-300	30

Water-powered pumps

Moving water contains energy corresponding to its speed. This energy can be utilized to pump water by powering water-wheels or turbines, or through the use of hydraulic rams. A major advantage of water power is its continuous availability, and the fact that there is usually no cost attached to its use for the generation of power.

Turbines and water-wheels

Turbines are turned at comparatively high speeds utilizing the energy contained in the speed of a flow of water to turn a pump (usually a centrifugal pump) which then pumps a proportion of the water to a higher level. A water-wheel uses the weight of water falling on the wheel to turn the wheel at low speed. This power is then utilized through a crank to power a simple piston type pump.

The power from both turbines and water-wheels is often used for other purposes than pumping water.

Hydraulic ram

A hydraulic ram utilizes the phenomenon of water hammer to raise a small proportion of the falling water to a higher level. This is described in greater detail in the equipment pages. These types of pumps can, when well made, operate with minimum maintenance for decades without the need for replacement. A top quality model will, however, have a very high initial capital cost. They depend on a continuous supply of water, and so are of no use in arid areas where water is a very scarce resource.

Solar pumps

Although there have been many attempts to develop pumps that utilize the sun's energy directly to raise water (one

Traditional handpump

prototype is shown in this chapter), these have not generally been very successful. The only pumping systems to have gained acceptance are those based on photovoltaic systems or panels of photoelectric cells which produce an electric current to power a conventional electric pump.

Solar cells produce a direct current (dc). It is now usual to convert dc to alternating current (ac) using a converter (efficiency of over 90 per cent); then conventional off-the-shelf ac pumps can be used which are cheaper and more reliable than direct current pumps.

A solar pump involves a very high investment. It only becomes viable over a very long period (ten years or more) and when used all year round (12 months out of 12). For small power requirements, solar energy can be economically viable. Above 5kW it is no longer viable when compared with the costs of a diesel-powered system. Indeed, the cost of diesel power per cubic metre of water pumped falls as the size of motor-driven pumpset increases, whereas the cost of solar power per cubic metre remains stable whatever the size of the system. However, the cost of photoelectric cells has been declining over the past ten years by 5 per cent per year, making them less costly as the years progress so that they are likely to be more competitive in the future.

Solar power does not supply water on demand but, in general, only when there is sufficient light to generate electricity. Therefore, a storage system is essential and this must be considered during planning.

Nowadays, photoelectric cells are very reliable. However, as this technology is not yet very widespread, it is not advisable to become totally dependent on them away from sites where repairs can be undertaken quickly. Installing solar equipment in extremely remote areas should be avoided, unless maintenance facilities are also introduced.

Windpumps

The availability of wind at any particular site can be very variable both from day to day and between seasons. For this reason site selection for wind-pumping is very important. The power output of a windmill is proportional to the cube of the wind speed, i.e. a doubling in wind speed increases the output from the windmill by a factor of eight (2^3=8). Equally a reduction in wind speed by a half reduces the power output by eight. So small changes in wind speed cause large changes in power output. Ideally a site should experience frequent winds of between 4m/s and 8m/s. Below 3m/s pumping is rarely practicable and above 13m/s winds are generally too powerful. As with solar pumping some sort of storage reservoir is necessary to cope with the fluctuations in flow caused by the variability in winds.

Windmills are used to a great extent for pumping water for livestock in remote arid areas in the USA and Australia. Wind power was also used extensively in The Netherlands for drainage, although they have now mainly been superseded by pumps powered by other sources. Wind power has not been used widely for irrigation, although examples in some parts of Peru and in Crete indicate that in favourable circumstances wind power can be a viable option for irrigation from low or medium lifts.

Diesel and petrol pumpsets

Diesel and petrol engine-driven pumps are compact units comprising an engine coupled with a pump, normally a centrifugal pump, on the same chassis. The major advantage of these is their instant start capability and their ready availability at any time. In addition they have a high power to weight ratio. However, they are reliant on a ready supply of clean fuel, and require a high level of regular maintenance to operate efficiently and for their full design life. Where these are not available such pumps become unreliable and an expensive, inefficient, inappropriate means of pumping.

Petrol engines are usually small: 1.5-3kW models are very common because they are comparatively cheap to buy, easy to transport (sometimes even by bicycle) and comparatively simple to repair. However, they have high rotational speeds (3000-4000 rev/min) and a short service life (3000-4000 hours). They are best suited for intermittent use, pumping small amounts of water for short periods of time.

Diesel engines are larger (the smallest diesel engines are 2.25-3kW), heavier and have a greater initial capital cost than petrol engines. They are more fuel efficient, rotate more slowly (e.g. 1500 rev/min) and have a longer service life (6000-8000 hours). They require special precautions in use (clean fuel) and are more difficult to repair (e.g. calibration of injectors), though if well maintained they are very reliable. They are best suited for use in a single fixed installation (particularly the larger engines) and for continuous pumping for long periods.

Pump efficiency

The principle of the centrifugal pump is to expel water from the body of the pump by means of the rotational speed of its turbine, which means that its performance is highly dependent on its rotational speed. The flow rate is proportional to the rotational speed but the power absorbed is proportional to its cube.

The design of each model of engine-driven pump therefore gives it a specific set of characteristics. Each pumping height corresponds to a flow rate for a given rotational speed. These are usually shown as curves on flow rate/height graphs (e.g. Figure 3). When the speed changes there is a different flow rate for each pumping height and the curve is different. Figure 3 shows these curves for a pump operating at three different speeds. Superimposed on the graph are also lines showing the pump efficiency.

The most remarkable feature of this graph is that the optimum operating range is very narrow. At the optimum, the pump efficiency is 75-80 per cent. This efficiency is the ratio of the hydraulic power supplied by the pump to the power absorbed. At speed 1, the optimum efficiency of the pump (80 per cent) corresponds to a flow of 30m³/h, to a height of 45m. If the water is pumped to a height of 15m, then the flow increases to 50m³/h. Although the amount of water flowing has increased, the efficiency of the pump has reduced to under 65 per cent. Therefore fuel is being wasted and the water is costing more to pump. It is also worth noting that if the pump is operated at speed 3, then the maximum efficiency that can be obtained is 70 per cent at a flow of 25m³/h to a height of 20m.

As can be seen operation outside the nominal pumping height and optimum engine speed has dramatic consequences for a centrifugal pump. However, even when the pump is operating at its maximum efficiency, wastage through inefficient distribution (e.g. leaking pipes) and bad irrigation

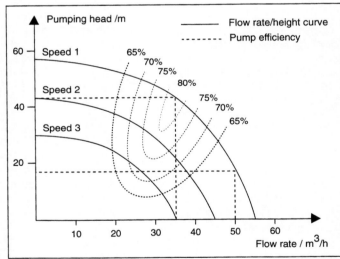

Figure 3   Flow rate/height curves for a pump operating at three different speeds

techniques can significantly lower the efficiency of the system as a whole. Care must therefore be taken over the efficiency of the whole system, not only the pump.

PUMP SELECTION

Manufacturers produce an extensive range of pumps in an attempt to satisfy a wide range of pumping heights and flows. It is important to select a pump that most closely satisfies the requirements of a particular site. To help this selection, manufacturers produce flow rate/height graphs for all their pumps.

Two basic pieces of information are needed when selecting a pump — the pumping head and the volume of water to be pumped (see earlier). With this information and the manufacturers' flow rate/height graphs, pump selection can be easily achieved.

Figure 4 shows flow rate/height graphs for three different pumps. To select a pump the operator identifies the point on the graph that corresponds to the required flow rate and height, and chooses the curve on which it is nearest to the middle.

For example, suppose the pumping head is 18m and the flow rate required is 20m³/h. This corresponds to the point 'a' marked on the graph in Figure 4. Point 'a' is close to the curves for both pump 1 and pump 3. Pump 3 will be chosen because 'a' is closer to the middle of that curve than to the middle of the curve for pump 1.

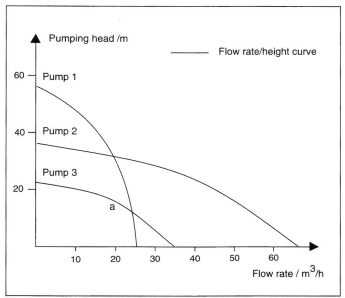

Figure 4   Flow rate/height curves for three different pumps

Costs

When calculating the cost of a pumping system several factors need to be considered — initial capital cost of the pump, installation cost, running cost (fuel or extra food for animal powered systems, lubricants, operator, spare parts), costs of ancillaries (pipes, storage, concrete surround) and eventually the cost of a replacement pump. Table 6 shows some indicative comparative capital costs for different types of pumping system. The extra initial costs can often amount to more than the pump's actual capital cost. The running costs will almost certainly be considerably larger than the initial costs, particularly for diesel- and petrol-engined pumps. It is essential that some means of financing the running costs of any pumping system is set up at the outset, otherwise lack of funds for fuel or repair and maintenance will quickly see the pump inoperable.

A pumping system for irrigation can suffer from cash flow problems because the farmers do not usually receive payment for their crops until after harvest, whereas engine-driven pumps need money constantly from sowing onwards to pay (at the very least) for fuel. Subsistence farmers may not have sufficient funds to pay for the production costs until after harvest. In their case, it may be best to look for a system that does not incur running costs throughout the growing season. However, the advantages of different systems will be highly dependent on a range of local factors, ownership of draught power, fuel prices, government subsidies, etc.

Table 6 Indicative capital costs of various pump types[1]

	0	Cost ($)	10,000
Shallow well handpump			
Deep well handpump[2]			
Deep well handpump[3]			
Animal powered chain & washer pump			
Hydraulic ram pump[4]			
Solar pump[5]			
Lightweight windpump[6]			
Multi-bladed windpump[7]			
Engine-driven pumpset[8]			

Notes

1. These costs are very approximate and are for comparison purposes only.
2. Conventional reciprocating piston type with hand lever.
3. Geared flywheel-assisted type.
4. Imported machine.
5. 250 hydraulic watt system.
6. Locally-manufactured machine.
7. Imported machine.
8. 3kW diesel pumpset.

The problem of financing a pumping system is particularly high in the case of community water supply for domestic use. The increase in productivity resulting from the installation of a pumping system will, at best, only be indirect, and may not be able to generate sufficient increased income to pay for the system.

Finally, it is essential to be able to evaluate the relative importance of the pumping system within the user's activities. In terms of costs, this means evaluating how water costs relate to the user's total expenditure and therefore their influence on profits. Although it is always attractive to reduce expenditure as far as possible, it is also useful to be fully aware of the true limiting factors of the activity which are not necessarily linked to the pumping system. For example, marketing of market garden produce may be the farmer's main concern.

Note also that when the limiting factors are associated with the pumping system, the choice is not always made in terms of costs; ease of use, lack of constraints and amount of water pumped per day can be of at least equal importance.

IMPACT OF PUMPS

The two major potential benefits of pumping water are the provision of greater quantities of water when needed and the provision of higher quality water. The availability of sufficient quantities of irrigation water may make the difference between harvest failure and a surplus. In particular the use of motor-driven pumps can increase the timeliness of application of irrigation water, as well as removing the drudgery of human-powered means of irrigation, releasing time for other work.

Making greater quantities of higher quality water available for domestic consumption will also make possible improvements

Oxfam

Rope and washer pump

in health within the population. However the potential for such improvements can only be realized when combined with other factors such as better nutrition and public health.

Pumps also have the potential of creating problems. Increased use of groundwater resources can lead to the lowering of the water table. This not only increases the cost of pumping, but can detrimentally affect those poorer members of the population who are dependent on shallow wells for their water. These wells are the first to dry out, and their users are those least able to invest in equipment for deeper pumping. A problem frequently encountered in pastoral areas is that the areas surrounding boreholes become subject to overgrazing, leading to the degradation of the environment. There is a clear need for policies on water management to enable the rational use and conservation of water resources.

Another common problem is the misuse and/or underuse of a pumping system because the needs of the users were not fully considered before installation. Where no suitable distribution system is installed, people furthest from the pump may continue to use their traditional water sources, because these are closer and more convenient, and consequently such

individuals do not benefit from improvements in water quality. The pumps may become centres for watering livestock, for doing laundry, etc. leading to the swift degradation of the pump environment with consequent problems of hygiene and excess water wastage. Whenever a pumping system is to be installed it is vital that the planned users are part of the decision-making body so as to be able to take fully into account the possible uses of that water. Only such a process will make it possible for the users to derive the full benefits from the investment.

Bernard Gay
GRET

OUTLINE GUIDE FOR THE SELECTION OF A PUMPING SYSTEM

1 Requirements
❍ For what purpose is the water pumped? Are there any secondary uses?
❍ Estimate the volumes: per day, per day of pumping, max. flow rates according to season or when a number of activities occur at the same time.
❍ Does the water have to have a head (be under pressure)? Does it have to be transported? Does it have to be stored?
❍ Is high quality water required?
❍ If the water is for irrigation, what method is used? What are the losses?

In general, plan for demand to increase once the pumping system is installed.

2 The hydrological site
❍ What is the geometric pumping height?
❍ If the pipework is to be very long, estimate the head losses to give the pumping head or total manometric height.
❍ What is the estimated flow rate of the water outlet? Does it dry up during the year?

3 Maintenance
❍ Are spare parts available? Is the supplier reliable (in the medium term)?
❍ Who is able to carry out repairs? How long will it take? How much will it cost? Do the proposed repairers have experience of this equipment? Will they be able to travel?

4 The service provided
❍ What is the users' economic reasoning? Are they prepared to spend money or do they prefer to invest working time? Does pumping constitute a high proportion of production costs?
❍ Will the service provided be satisfactory? How do the users feel? Have they been able to make a choice in full knowledge of all the constraints?
❍ Prepare a provisional breakdown of costs with the users.

ROWER PUMP

This pump was originally designed and developed for low-lift tubewell irrigation of small plots in Bangladesh but it is now often used for drawing domestic water from shallow sources. A household version is also available. The pump cylinder is inclined at 30 degrees and is made of 65mm diameter PVC, stiffened and protected by split bamboo.

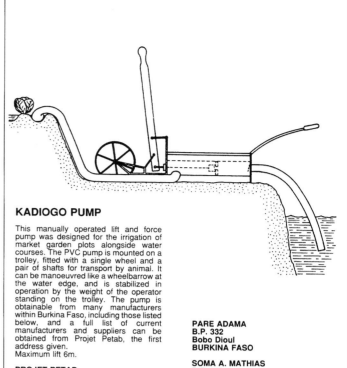

The piston is moved within this cylinder by pulling and pushing directly on a T-handle at the end of the piston rod, thus eliminating the need for a pivot or fulcrum. The foot valve is held in place by a collar at the base of the cylinder. There is a choice of outlets including a 'T' piece diverter spout and a pitcher spout. The pump can be operated from a standing or seated position and an optional surge chamber helps to improve operator comfort.

Low cost and ease of maintenance were prime considerations in the development of this pump and the number of components has been minimized. No special repair tools are required and the piston and valve can be withdrawn through the discharge opening. For protection, the manufacturers recommend that the pump be partly buried in the ground with only the discharge pipe exposed.

The manufacturer hopes to set up workshops in developing countries for local assembly or complete manufacture.
Lift 6m maximum.
Output 2-3m³/hour.

MIRPUR AGRICULTURAL WORKSHOP & TRAINING SCHOOL
Mirpur Section 12
Pallabi
Dhaka 16
BANGLADESH

S.W.S. FILTRATION LTD
Hartburn
Morpeth
Northumberland NE61 4JB
UK

INTERNATIONAL DEVELOPMENT ENTERPRISES
368 St. James Crescent
West Vancouver
B.C. V7S 1J8
CANADA

with offices also at:

10-A Green Road
Dhanmondi
P.O. Box 5055
New Market
Dhaka 5
BANGLADESH

KADIOGO PUMP

This manually operated lift and force pump was designed for the irrigation of market garden plots alongside water courses. The PVC pump is mounted on a trolley, fitted with a single wheel and a pair of shafts for transport by animal. It can be manoeuvred like a wheelbarrow at the water edge, and is stabilized in operation by the weight of the operator standing on the trolley. The pump is obtainable from many manufacturers within Burkina Faso, including those listed below, and a full list of current manufacturers and suppliers can be obtained from Projet Petab, the first address given.
Maximum lift 6m.

PROJET PETAB
B.P. 3573
Ouagadougou
BURKINA FASO

ATELIER NIKIEMA
B.P. 7078
Ouagadougou
BURKINA FASO

PARE ADAMA
B.P. 332
Bobo Dioul
BURKINA FASO

SOMA A. MATHIAS
B.P. 230
Banfora
BURKINA FASO

EMBS
Ouédraogo Noufou
B.P. 59
Ouahigouya
BURKINA FASO

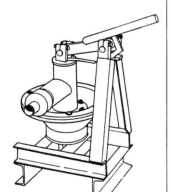

BUMI PUMP

This rugged single-action diaphragm pump was developed to meet the irrigation needs of small-scale and communal farmers in Zimbabwe. It is capable of irrigating over a hectare of land throughout the year
Output 4 litre/stroke.
Maximum lift 6m.

LANE ENGINEERING (PVT) LTD
P.O. Box ST.43
Southerton
Harare
ZIMBABWE

DIAPHRAGM HANDPUMPS

These self-priming handpumps are particularly useful for moving water containing suspended solids. They are generally small and lightweight with few moving parts and with optional flexible suction and delivery hoses for transportation. The diaphragm is usually made of nitrite or butyl rubber and is easily accessed when replacement becomes necessary. Several companies also offer double-acting models with twin diaphragms; an example is shown. These have the advantage that the pumps can continue to be operated if one of the diaphragms becomes damaged.

Diaphragm pumps are suitable for small-scale irrigation, domestic water supply, latrine clearance and for de-watering in shallow well construction. Heavier-duty diaphragm pumps designed for agricultural purposes are also available; these can be trolley-mounted for easier transportation.

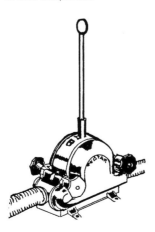

PUMPENFABRIK BEYER
Dorfstraße 25
2361 Wulfsfelde
GERMANY

MUNSTER SIMMS ENGINEERING LTD
Old Belfast Road
Bangor
N. Ireland BT19 1LT
UK

POMPES GRILLOT
2, Rue de l'Observance
B.P. 118
Avignon 84000
FRANCE

MINE-ELECT
P.O. Box 316
Bulawayo
ZIMBABWE

TRACK INDUSTRIES LTD
26 Wickham Street
P.O. Box 19-543
Christchurch 2
NEW ZEALAND

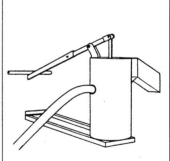

PISTON HANDPUMP

This is a simple, self-priming, piston-type lift pump which operates equally well in clear or dirty water. The piston has three replaceable neoprene sealing rings and is attached to a long pumping handle. There are two non-return valves in the pump base and an anti-surge device which delivers the water in a continuous stream. The pump uses a 50mm diameter suction hose and can operate up to 30 metres away from the water source. It is supplied with either a baseplate or a tubular frame.
Capacity: 175 litre/min. at 2m lift;
            136 litre/min. at 3.6m lift.

ALVAN BLANCH DEVELOPMENT CO. LTD
Chelworth
Malmesbury
Wilts SN16 9SG
UK

STANHAY WEBB LTD
Exning
Newmarket
Suffolk CB8 7HD
UK

IRRIGATION SUCTION PUMP

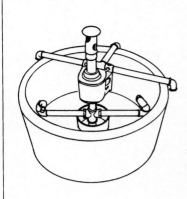

This prototype pump has a novel design, based on centrifugal action. The vertical leg of a T-shaped tube is immersed in water and rotated about its axis; with sufficient speed of rotation, the water is thrown out of the horizontal arms of the tube, creating a lifting effect on the vertical water column. The pump can be manually powered, through a gearbox, by up to eight operators simultaneously.
Maximum lift 8m.
Output 200 litre/min. at 7.5m lift.

UNIVERSITÉ LIBRE DE BRUXELLES
Faculty of Science
Campus Plaine
C.P. 224
Bld. du Triomphe
Brussels 1050
BELGIUM

IRRIPUMP

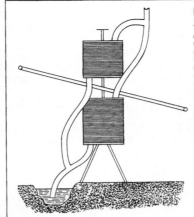

This double-action, lift and force pump comprises a pair of rubber bellows, each with two non-return valves, connected to either side of a pivoted handle. This handle is manually pumped and expands one of the bellows while compressing the other, thus delivering a constant water stream.
Maximum lift 6m.
Output 167 litre/min. at 5m lift.

S.A. BERGOUGNAN BENELUX N.V.
Brugsesteenweg 7
Evergem B-9050
BELGIUM

TWIN CYLINDER TREADLE PUMPS

RDRS TREADLE PUMP
This is a twin cylinder, foot-operated pump for small-scale irrigation. It is designed for local, low-cost manufacture, using hard wood, bamboo and mild steel. The pump is fixed at the bottom of a bamboo framework, which is erected over a small well. The pistons of the two pump cylinders are connected to each end of a rope which passes over a pulley at the top of the frame. Above each piston the rope is attached to a pivoted bamboo treadle. The operator stands with one foot on each treadle, shifting weight from one foot to the other, and thus raises each piston in turn. The treadles can be operated simultaneously by two operators if desired. The basic pump design is available in different sizes and as either a tubewell type for lifts in excess of three metres or as a portable low-lift pump for pumping from waterways, ponds and wells with up to 3m lift.

Several components are interchangeable between these two basic types.
Output 165 litre/min. at 3m lift; 75 litre/min. at 5m lift.

RANGPUR DINAJPUR RURAL SERVICE
G.P.O. Box 618
Dhaka - 1000
BANGLADESH

IRRI TAPAK-TAPAK PUMP
The following institute based the development of their 'Tapak-Tapak' treadle pump on this same design and technical details are available for potential manufacturers.

IRRI
Agricultural Engineering Dept
P.O. Box 933
Manila
PHILIPPINES

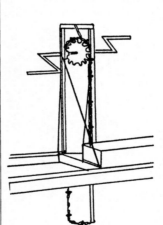

KOUBRI CHAIN PUMP

This pump is suitable for low-lift irrigation of small plots alongside waterways. A chain fitted with a series of rubber washers passes around a hand-cranked pulley and through a partially immersed pipe to draw water from the waterway. The assembly is mounted on a wooden framework and is suitable for one-person operation.
Maximum lift 6m.
Output 17 litre/min. at 3m lift.

CENTRE ARTISANAL DE KOUBRI
B.P. 123
Ouagadougou
BURKINA FASO

LOW-LIFT HANDPUMP

This irrigation pump was designed primarily for low-lift, high delivery applications. It is mounted on three legs and can be fitted with a flexible suction hose if desired. The 200mm diameter piston is moved manually, through a compound lever mechanism with piston guides and removable handles. It can be operated by one or two persons. A foot valve is not required but the manufacturers recommend priming the cylinder before operation. Maximum lift 5.5m (optimum 2-2.5m).

YANTRA VIDYALAYA
Agricultural Tools Research Centre
Suruchi Campus
P.O. Box 4
Bardoli
Gujarat 394 601
INDIA

IRRI DIAPHRAGM PUMP

This is a portable, double-chambered pump for low-lift irrigation. The pump casing consists of a light sheet metal cylinder with a central partition to provide two chambers. Rubber flap valves are used on the intake and outlet ports. The two rubber diaphragms are made from motor car inner tubes and can easily be replaced. The operator stands on two foot-rests and shifts weight from one foot to the other. This compresses the chambers alternately, forcing water from the outlet valves in a continuous flow. The pump is suitable for both clean and dirty water and is simple to construct. Technical details are available for potential manufacturers.

IRRI
Agricultural Engineering Department
P.O. Box 933
Manila
PHILIPPINES

HAND CHAIN PUMPS

The following company offers a chain pump capable of lifting water from a depth of three to four metres, from a tank, canal or pond. The chain wheel is mounted on two heavy duty ball bearings and the pipe is made of galvanized sheet. The rubber washers are easily replaceable. The pump is a portable unit, mounted on a wooden stand, and two people are required to operate it.
Output 300-350 litre/minute.
Weight 125kg.

COSSUL & CO. PVT LTD
123/367 Industrial Area
Fazalgunj
Kanpur
U.P.
INDIA

OHIO CHAIN PUMP
This is similar to the chain pumps described above but the mechanism is enclosed in a galvanized steel housing with a removable top cover. It is designed to be installed at a well head.
Maximum output 68 litre/min.
Maximum lift 12m.

LEHMAN HARDWARE & APPLIANCES INC.
P.O. Box 41
Kidron
OH 44636
USA

SHALLOW WELL DOMESTIC HANDPUMP

This low-cost pump is available in two sizes; model No.4 (80mm) and No.6 (90mm) for very shallow wells. The pump stand which incorporates the cylinder is made from mild steel and connects to a suction pipe and strainer of bamboo or commercial pipe. It is installed by fixing to a sturdy wooden post and fitting a wooden handle. Potential manufacturers can obtain technical details from:

RANGPUR DINAJPUR
REHABILITATION SERVICE
G.P.O. Box 618
Ramna
Dhaka 2
BANGLADESH

OPEN SPOUT PITCHER PUMPS

ORIENT LOW-STAND PUMP
Four sizes of this pump are available, with the following specifications:
Cylinder size 76-114mm.
Output 18-40 litre/min.
Maximum lift 5m.
Stroke 100mm.

SIGMA PUMPING EQUIPMENT
Valves Manufacturing Works
P.O. Box 1111
111 87 Praha 1
CZECHOSLOVAKIA

PITCHER SPOUT PUMP
This pump is available in four sizes, with 85mm to 115mm diameter cylinders. Capacities are in the range 25 to 45 litre/min.

PUMPENFABRIK BEYER
Dorfstraße 25
2361 Wulfsfelde
GERMANY

MYERS PUMP
This pump has a 75mm, cast iron cylinder, and an 85mm stroke.
Maximum lift 6m.

LEHMAN HARDWARE &
APPLIANCES INC.
P.O. Box 41
4779 Kidron Road
Kidron
OH 44636
USA

CLOSED SPOUT PITCHER PUMPS

These handpumps have a closed, pipe-like spout and enclosed base which help reduce splashing and improve sanitation. Apart from these features, they are identical to the classical open spout variety, being suited to cistern and shallow well pumping.

SUCTION PUMP
Three versions of this bolt-down pump are available, with different mounting arrangements and with an optional transport trolley. The pump has a cast-iron body and a rubber valve and it can withstand freezing conditions.
Maximum lift 6m.
Output 20-40 litre/min.

POMPES GRILLOT
2, Rue de l'Observance
Avignon 84 000
FRANCE

'BETTER PITCHER'
This pump has a solid brass cylinder and a 100mm stroke. To prevent damage from freezing, it can be drained after use, by lifting the handle.

LEHMAN HARDWARE &
APPLIANCES INC.
P.O. Box 41
4779 Kidron Road
Kidron
OH 44636
USA

CISTERN PUMP
This closed spout pitcher pump is made of heavy cast iron and is suitable for general shallow well applications.

BAKER (MONITOR DIVISION)
133 Enterprise Street
Evansville
WI 53536
USA

SHALLOW WELL LIFT PUMPS

Like the pitcher pump, shallow well lift (or suction) pumps can draw water from depths of up to 7m. They are suitable for cistern and shallow well applications. The basic design uses a two-pivot hand lever which, via the pump rod, operates the piston inside the cylinder incorporated in the pump stand.

SIGMA 'NP' HANDPUMPS
This pump (illustrated) is intended for domestic water supplies and is available in two sizes. It has a cast iron body and a bronze cylinder.
Cylinder size 75 or 90mm.
Output 28 or 40 litre/min.

SIGMA PUMPING EQUIPMENT
Valves Manufacturing Works
P.O. Box 1111
111 87 Praha 1
CZECHOSLOVAKIA

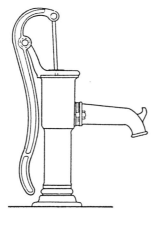

GOLDEN HARVEST SB 38-1
Model SB 38-1 (illustrated below) is a cast iron, shallow well pump. The 100mm cylinder has a porcelain enamelled lining.
Output 50 litre/min. at 45 strokes/min.

CHINA NATIONAL MACHINERY &
EQUIPMENT IMPORT &
EXPORT CORPORATION
59 Zhan Qian Road
Guangzhou
CHINA

KUMAR LIFT HANDPUMP
The following company manufactures a range of shallow well lift pumps of similar design but varying in cylinder sizes, stroke length and minor construction details.
Output 18-37 litre/min.

KUMAR INDUSTRIES
Edathara
Palghat District
Kerala 678 611
INDIA

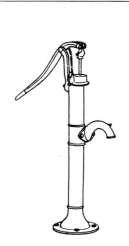

ECONO-GLOBE PUMP

Made from high-impact plastic, this shallow well pump is durable, non-corroding, and weighs less than 1.4kg. It has an output of up to 45 litre/min. for lifts of up to 9 metres. A deep-well version is also available and there are several additional options including:

● Base mounting;
● Open discharge or pressure-pump type;
● Solar or battery operation.

AZTEK INTERNATIONAL
CORPORATION
P.O. Box 11409
Fort Wayne
IN 46858
USA

MONITOR HAND LIFT PUMP

Model 11HA is a shallow well handpump with a multi-position cap and spout.
Cylinder diameter 63.5mm.
Output 19 litre/min. at 40 strokes/min.

BAKER (MONITOR DIVISION)
133 Enterprise Street
Evansville
WI 53536
USA

INDIA SHALLOW WELL HANDPUMP

This is a development of the widely used India Mark II deep well handpump, described later. It has a lighter handle and a cylinder of 63.5mm inside diameter. The riser pipe is supplied in three-metre lengths.
Maximum lift 12m.
Output 0.32 litre/stroke.

RICHARDSON & CRUDDAS (1972) LTD
P.O. Box 1276
Madras 600 001
INDIA

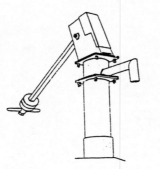

HOUSEHOLD LIFT AND FORCE PUMP

This pump is suitable for domestic use and for raising water to an elevated tank. The cylinder, plunger, rod, guide and spigot are all made of brass and a surge chamber is incorporated for steadier water flow. By lifting the handle, the pump can be drained after use to prevent freezing damage

LEHMAN HARDWARE & APPLIANCES INC.
P.O. Box 41
4779 Kidron Road
Kidron
OH 44636
USA

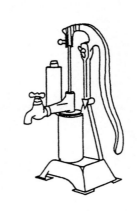

GODWIN HLS LIFT AND FORCE PUMP

This handpump has a valved outlet, three-pivot handle system, rod guide and stuffing box. It is available in the following two sizes:
Cylinder diameter 63.5mm or 90mm.
Output 23 or 44 litre/min. at 40 strokes/min.

H.J. GODWIN LTD
Quenington
Cirencester
Glos GL7 5BY
UK

MANUAL PISTON PUMP

This low-cost pump with foot valve is designed for easy installation and maintenance. It is intended for domestic use and small-plot irrigation by a family rather than for communal use. This pump is widely available in Burkina Faso and a list of manufacturers and suppliers can be obtained from the address below.
Maximum lift 25m.
Output 17 litre/min. at 12m lift.

I.T. DELLO
B.P. 3573
Ouagadougou
BURKINA FASO

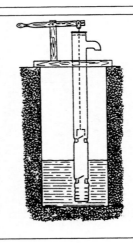

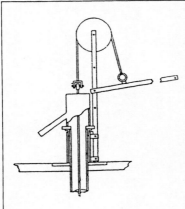

LOTUS VALVE HANDPUMP

The pumping mechanism is operated via a pre-stretched fibre rope over a pulley wheel. This rope is connected to an adjustable-position lever handle, thus avoiding pump rod stress. Composite plastics are mainly used for the construction of the pump and the rising main has solvent-welded screw couplings. Three cylinder diameters provide a range of discharge rates.

LOTUS WATER WELL EQUIPMENT LTD
Thornfield
Banktop
Woodside
Ryton
Tyne & Wear NE40 4QN
UK

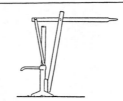

HANDPUMP

The head section is of solid mild steel construction with handle and spout. Pump's suction head is made from a cast iron cylinder and has a non-return valve. For wells with a maximum depth of 30 metres. Output 45-80 litre/min.

STEEL STRUCTURES LTD
Dandora Road
Box 49862
Nairobi
KENYA

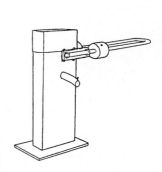

MANUAL PUMPS

This pump has a metal framework and body, a galvanized steel piston, a PVC pipe and a foot valve. The single-pivot handle is connected to the pump rod by a strip of car tyre or similar material. Models of the pump are available for lifts of 6, 14 or 20m.

ATESTA
B.P. 3306
Ouagadougou
BURKINA FASO

NEPTA PUMP
This is a cable-operated pump, similar in operation to the Atesta pump described above. Six cylinder sizes are available to suit different pumping depths, for example:
140mm cylinder for 9m lift, output 83 litre/min.
40mm cylinder for 100m lift, output 9 litre/min.

BRIAU S.A.
B.P. 0903
37009 Tours Cedex
FRANCE

DIRECT ACTION HANDPUMPS

These shallow well domestic pumps are operated directly, by pushing and pulling on the 'T' handle, thus avoiding the complexities of the more conventional two- or three-pivot handle systems.

DOUBLE ACTION HANDPUMP
This pump has a pump rod and rising main made of uPVC and supplied in 2.5m long sections, to be joined by threaded connectors and epoxy cement. The piston is also made of uPVC, with a rubber valve ball. The pump stand and handle are of galvanized steel with a polyethylene bush. Average output 25 litre/min.

WAVIN OVERSEAS BV
Rollepaal 19
P.O. Box 158
7700 AD Dedemsvaart
NETHERLANDS

TARA PUMP
The body of this pump is made of mild steel pipe; other parts are made of plastic, rubber and leather.
Maximum lift 15m.
Stroke length 300mm.

MIRPUR AGRICULTURAL WORKSHOP & TRAINING SCHOOL
Mirpur Section 12
Paliabi, Dhaka 16
BANGLADESH

TRACTA PUMP
This corrosion-protected, self-priming pump can be supplied with a well point and strainer, which enable it to be driven directly into the ground for groundwater extraction without a well.
Maximum lift 15m.
Output 20 litre/min.

BRIAU S.A.
B.P. 0903
37009 Tours Cedex
FRANCE

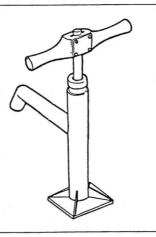

INDIA MARK II DEEP WELL HANDPUMP

This robust pump, fabricated from steel plate, has been developed by UNICEF in India from an original design by the Sholapur Well service. It results from efforts to produce, on a large scale, a strong and reliable pump which can be maintained in operational order at village level.

The pump consists of four major assemblies: pump head, cylinder, connecting rod and riser pipe. Its distinguishing feature is the single-pivot handle system with quadrant and heavy-duty roller chain connecting to the pump rods which facilitates vertical reciprocating motion. The pivot is fitted with sealed ball bearings to minimize friction and wear, and the heavy-duty handle, designed to give a mechanical advantage of 8:1, helps to counterbalance the pump rod weight and improve operator comfort.

The cast-iron cylinder is fitted with a 63.5mm brass liner and the piston with two high quality leather cup washers. The rising main is 32mm. Suitable for fitting to wells or borehole casings from 102 to 127mm and depths up to 70m. Output 13 litre/min. at 40 strokes/min.

Available from many manufacturers and suppliers including the following:

COSSUL & CO. (PVT) LTD
123/367 Industrial Area
Fazalgunj
Kanpur
U.P.
INDIA

MEKINS AGRO PRODUCTS (PVT) LTD
6-3-866/A Begumpet
Greenlands
Hyderabad 500 016
INDIA

RAJAN UNIVERSAL EXPORTS (MFRS) PVT LTD
P.O. Box 250
Madras 600 001
INDIA

RURAL INDUSTRIES INNOVATION CENTRE
Private Bag 11
Kanye
BOTSWANA

PUMPENBOESE KG
P.O. Box 1250
Raiffeisenstraße 2
D-3006 Burgwedel 1
GERMANY

PREUSSAG AG
Postfach 6009
3150 Peine
GERMANY

EXTRA DEEP WELL HANDPUMP
This is suitable for lifts of 60-90m. It has the same basic features as the India Mark II deep well handpump, but with several heavier-duty components, three cup washers instead of two, and an additional foot valve with strainer. The cylinder is positioned at 50-85m depth, depending on water lift. It requires a borehole of 100mm minimum internal diameter.
Output 12 litre/min. at 40 strokes/min.

RICHARDSON & CRUDDAS (1972) LTD
P.O. Box 1276
Madras 600 001
INDIA

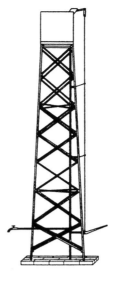

The following company offers another modification of the India Mark II, for filling a raised header tank; a suitable tank with support tower is also available. The riser pipe is extended and the pump handle and outlet connections are modified accordingly, to allow operation of the pump from ground level. Specifications and options include:
Tank capacity 1 or 2m^3.
Tower height 6m.
Pump cylinder diameter 60, 80 or 100mm.
Average working depth 30m.

UPROMA
B.P. 111
Kara-Togo
Lome
TOGO

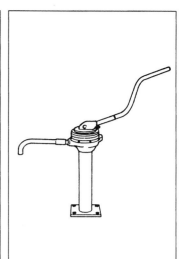

MANUAL PUMP

This is a robust, low-friction, low-maintenance pump, suitable for public use. It can be fitted in wells and boreholes of 100mm minimum internal diameter. The pump is available from several manufacturers in Tunisia and further details can be obtained from the address below.
Maximum lift 60m.
Output 17-33 litre/min, (model-dependent).

SOCIÉTÉ TUNISIENNE D'ENERGÉTIQUE ET DE MÉCANIQUE (SOTEM)
6, Rue 4978
Séjoumi
TUNISIA

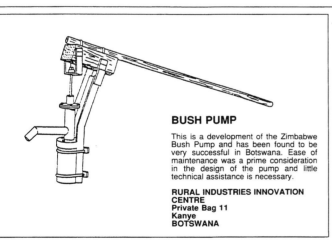

BUSH PUMP

This is a development of the Zimbabwe Bush Pump and has been found to be very successful in Botswana. Ease of maintenance was a prime consideration in the design of the pump and little technical assistance is necessary.

RURAL INDUSTRIES INNOVATION CENTRE
Private Bag 11
Kanye
BOTSWANA

ABI TYPE AM HANDPUMP

This piston pump was designed as a simple, robust pump suitable for wells and boreholes in very rural areas. It is fitted with a foot valve and strainer. The pump stand is of cast iron and fabricated steel and the two-pivot handle is 810mm long and fitted in sealed ball bearings. The connecting rod and cylinder are made of steel and brass respectively.
Cylinder size 60, 70 or 80mm.
Output 15 litre/min. for 30m lift.

ABI-MÉCHANIQUE
B.P. 343
rue Piere et Marie Curie
Abidjan
IVORY COAST

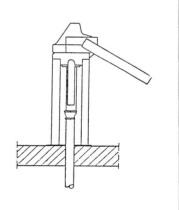

DEEP WELL HANDPUMPS

SWN PUMP
Two models of this pump are available; the standard model SWN 80 for depths up to 40m and model SWN 81 for depths up to 100m. Both models use a two-pivot handle fitted with ball bearings or plain journal bearings. If desired, these can be replaced by locally made oil-soaked hard wood bushes. The pump stand is made of galvanized square section steel tube, with a bituminous coating on the inside. Four cylinder sizes are available, each supplied with a bi-directional neoprene piston washer. The rising main is made of high-impact PVC and the 10mm diameter pump rod is of stainless steel.
Cylinder size 50, 63, 75 or 100mm.
Output 0.3, 0.5, 0.7 or 1.25 litre/stroke.

VAN REEKUM MATERIALS BV
P.O Box 98
Kanaal Noord 115
Apeldoorn 7300 AB
NETHERLANDS

UNATA 3001 PUMP
This is similar to the SWN pump, and is suitable for local construction. It is constructed of galvanized steel plate with a stainless steel cylinder and a galvanized riser pipe. The steel pump arm has two counterweights and is offered in a choice of two lengths.
Cylinder diameter 50, 65 or 80mm.
Output 7-45 litre/min. at 30-60 strokes/min.

UNATA
P.O. BOX 50
3220 Aarschot
BELGIUM

DEEP WELL HANDPUMP
A similar handpump with a maximum lift of 15m is available from:

SARVODAYA KANDY
Palletalawinne
Katugastota
Kandy
SRI LANKA

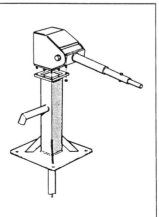

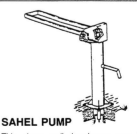

SAHEL PUMP

This deep well handpump can be installed without special equipment on to a concrete pad over a pit or 100mm borehole. Output 22.5 litre/min. at 35m lift. Maximum lift 45m.

APPRO-TECHNO
24 Rue de la Rieze
B-6404 Couvin
Cul-des-Sarts
BELGIUM

AQUADEV HANDPUMP

This piston pump was designed for ease of installation and maintenance and all components are intended for local manufacture, although a maintenance kit can be supplied, with seals and plastic bearings. Installation requires only two people and no special tools or lifting gear. The length of the 'T'-shaped pump handle can be adjusted to suit the pumping depth. The head is made of fabricated steel and all wearing parts are of plastic or rubber. The rising main is of uPVC and the cylinder is of uPVC with a stainless steel liner.
Maximum lift 45m.
Output 22 litre/min. at 50 strokes/min.
Cylinder diameter 50mm.
Rising main diameter 63mm.
Minimum borehole diameter 100mm.

MONO PUMPS LTD
Menca Division
Cromwell Trading Estate
Cromwell Road
Bredbury
Stockport
Cheshire SK6 2RF
UK

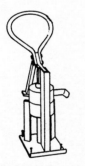

PULSA OSCILLATION HANDPUMPS

This unusual design uses rebound inertia to lift progressively an oscillating column of water. A piston and cylinder assembly at ground level is connected by a flexible pressure hose to a submerged chamber. This chamber is fitted with a foot valve and contains elastic balls which are compressed and expanded by water pressure changes, effected by the pumping action of the lever. The pump has no moving parts below ground level and is equally suitable for water courses and boreholes. The pump is lightweight and can be transported by bicycle. It can be installed by two people in less than half an hour. Up to three pumping units can be installed together in a single borehole of 110mm minimum diameter; four units can be installed in a 130mm borehole. Lifts up to 50m.
Average output 8 litre/min.

FLUXINOS
Via Genoa, 10
58100 Grosseto
ITALY

ELEM POMPE S.A.
B.P. 9
6110 Montigny le Tilleul
BELGIUM

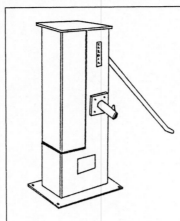

SBF-KARDIA PUMP

This is a deep well piston pump with the cylinder positioned below the water level. The main components of the pump are made from PVC and galvanized or stainless steel. A foot valve with strainer is also included. There is a choice of two models, K65 and K50VA.
Optimum lift 30 or 45m.
Output 0.45 or 0.28 litre/stroke.
Stroke length 150mm.
Minimum borehole diameter 100mm.
Rising main diameter 40mm.

PREUSSAG AG
P.O. Box 6009
3150 Peine
GERMANY

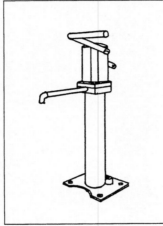

SBF-TURNI ROTARY CRANK PUMP

This piston pump is operated by a two-handled crank, with bevel gearing to transmit reciprocating motion to the piston. There is a choice of gear ratios to suit the required lift.
Lift 3-60m (maximum 90m).

PREUSSAG AG
P.O. Box 6009
3150 Peine
GERMANY

'TROPIC' TYPE II

This heavy duty pump is operated by two people turning the double flywheel. The pump has no reciprocating parts as the water is lifted by a positive displacement device. The pump is equipped with a large oil reservoir to minimize maintenance and all rotating parts are supported in bearings.
Maximum lift 95m.
Output 42.5 litre/min. for 25m lift.

POMPES DEPLECHIN S.A.
Avenue de Maire, 28
Tournai 7500
BELGIUM

HMA COMMUNITY HANDPUMPS

This range of deep well handpumps uses a hand-turned, counterbalanced flywheel made of forged steel fitted in sealed-for-life bearings. The pump stand and head are made from heavy section cast iron. The adjustable pump-rod slide bearing is made from oil-filled bronze. The standard pump is supplied for lift duty only but can be converted to act as a lift and force pump if desired. Both extractable and non-extractable cylinders are available. General specifications include:
Cylinder size 45-102mm.
Stroke length 51 or 102mm.
Maximum head 98 or 124m.
Output   35 litre/min. at 14m lift.
               3.5 litre/min. at 98m lift.

H.J. GODWIN LTD
Quenington
Cirencester
Glos GL7 5BY
UK

UNIMADE HANDPUMPS

This range of lightweight, village-level handpumps has been developed for ease of manufacture and maintenance. It is suitable for mass production in areas with limited facilities and expertise, and this is being encouraged by the development team. The cylinder, piston and foot valve are made of PVC, with joints made by solvent welding and with plastic bearings for all pin joints. The pump stand is constructed from standard mild steel piping. The pump can be installed and removed by two or three people without special skills or tooling and, for servicing, the foot valve can be extracted without removal of the cylinder. Specifications for the range include:
Cylinder diameter 55-76mm.
Maximum lift 8-50m.
Output 22-44 litre/min. at 60 stroke/min.

The pump range was developed by:

JOINT PROJECT IDRC/UM/MOH
Department of Mechanical Engineering
University of Malaya
Lembah Pantai
59100 Kuala Lumpur
MALAYSIA

It is currently being manufactured by the following two companies:

P.I. MANUFACTURING INC.
97, Industrial Ave
Northern Hills
Malaboa
Metro Manila
PHILIPPINES

YAYASAN DIAN DESA
Jl. Kaliurang Km 7
P.O. Box 19
Yogyakarta
INDONESIA

VOLANTA DEEP WELL PUMP

This hand-cranked, flywheel-assisted piston pump can be installed using hand tools and is designed for ease of maintenance. It can also be driven by engine or electric motor.
Maximum lift 80m.
Output 17 litre/min. at 25m lift.

CENTRE DE LA SAINTE FAMILLE
SAABA
B.P. 3905
BURKINA FASO

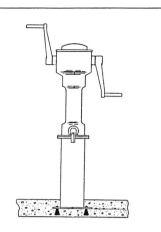

ROTARY HANDPUMPS

These differ fundamentally from the reciprocating piston-type handpump. Instead of a piston and cylinder, the positive displacement pumping element consists of a helical rotor which rotates within a fixed stator, causing a 'progressing cavity' effect which moves water upwards, providing continuous water discharge. The rotary motion for the vertical drive-shaft is achieved through bevel gears turned by crank handles and the discharge rate is directly proportional to the speed of crank rotation.

MONOLIFT HAND-DRIVEN BOREHOLE PUMP
This pump has a cast iron head and stand and a galvanized iron rising main. The pump element comprises a hard chrome-plated, double-spiral, steel rotor and a triple-spiral, moulded nitrile rubber stator. This combination enables the pump to handle water up to 40°C and containing sand or silt, with minimal wear. A conversion kit is available to modify the drive head into a belt-driven motorized unit.
Maximum lift 60m.
Maximum output 57 litre/min.

MONO PUMPS LTD
Menca Division
Cromwell Trading Estate
Cromwell Road
Bredbury
Stockport SK6 2RF
Cheshire
UK

ROBBINS AND MYERS 1V12 and 2V12
These two models are similar to the Monolift pump; they are suitable for 45m or 90m lifts and are designed for one- and two-person operation respectively. Alternatively, they can be power driven from an electric motor or engine.

ROBBINS & MYERS CANADA LTD
Rural Water Systems
P.O. Box 280
Brantford
Ontario N3T 5N6
CANADA

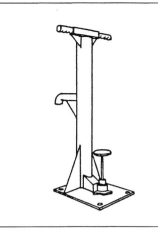

VERGNET ASM HYDRO-PUMP

Designed for use in rural areas, this deep well pump may be operated by a foot pedal as shown or by a lever arm. A water-filled cylinder/piston assembly made of brass is positioned within the pump stand at ground level. A flexible drive hose connects this to an elastic-walled flask inside a submerged stainless steel cylinder. Depression of the piston forces water into the flask and expands it, thereby forcing water out of the surrounding cylinder and up to the surface via a second flexible hose. The piston is then allowed to rise, the flask contracts and water enters the cylinder through a foot valve. Operating depth 10-60m. Output 13 litre/min. for 30m lift and at 40-50 strokes/min.

ABIDJAN INDUSTRIES OI
B.P. 343
Abidjan OI
IVORY COAST

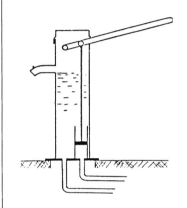

OMEGA HYDROPUMP

Hydraulically operated, the above-ground part of this pump is illustrated. The main piston, cylinder, spring and valve assembly is submerged in the well. Reciprocating motion is achieved by alternate hydraulic compression and extension of the spring. The pump is available in two sizes, as follows:
Maximum lift 30 or 60m.
Output 22 or 11 litre/min.

BRIAU S.A.
B.P. 0903
37009 Tours Cedex
FRANCE

MARUMBY PUMP

This handpump is available with a choice of 25, 31 or 45mm diameter water discharge pipe.

MUELLER IRMAOS S.A.
Av. Pres. Wenceslau Braz, 1046
Vila Lindoia
C.P. 3336
80 000 Curitiba (D.P.57)
Parana
BRAZIL

GODWIN HLD

The deep well pump shown has an all-steel pump stand, a three-pivot handle system with hardened steel bearings and a brass pump-rod guide. There is a choice of extractable or non-extractable, brass cylinders, available in four sizes. A lift and force version of this pump is also available.
Cylinder diameter 51-95mm.
Output 14-50 litre/min. at 40 strokes/min.

H.J. GODWIN LTD
Quenington
Cirencester
Glos GL7 5BY
UK

PUMPS WITH GUIDE RODS

These are similar to the lift and force pumps, but with two main additional features: an adjustable fulcrum position to provide a variable mechanical advantage and stroke length and extra pump-rod guides to maintain vertical reciprocating motion.

JAL JAVAHAR PUMP
Twin, parallel guide rods are fitted to the head of this pump. The normal stroke length is 150mm but this can be altered by changing the position of the fulcrum pin of the handle.
Cylinder diameter 75mm.
Rising main diameter 38mm.
Maximum lift 45m.
Maximum delivery head 21m.

DANDEKAR BROTHERS & CO.
Shivajinagar
Sangli
Maharashtra 416 416
INDIA

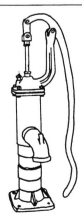

LIFT AND FORCE PUMPS

The following three pumps are capable of both raising water and forcing it up to a level above the pump. They each have a three-pivot handle system with stuffing box and pump rod guide, a surge chamber and a valved outlet spout.

'TROPIC' HANDPUMP
The pump illustrated is available with a choice of six cylinder sizes in the range 50-100mm.
Corresponding output 12-48 litre/min. at 40 stroke/min.

POMPES DEPLECHIN S.A.
Avenue de Maire, 28
Tournai 7500
BELGIUM

DEMPSTER 23F(CS)
This model has an extended rod guide to provide maximum alignment. A lift-only version of the pump, model 23F, is also available.

DEMPSTER INDUSTRIES INC.
P.O. BOX 848
Beatrice
NB 68310
USA

'EASY-PULL' PUMP HEAD
This pump has a cast-iron body, steel handle, stainless steel pivot pins and bronze bushes. There is a choice of cylinder sizes. Other deep well pump heads are also available from the company. Maximum lift 45m.

LEHMAN HARDWARE &
APPLIANCES INC.
P.O. Box 41
Kidron
OH 44636
USA

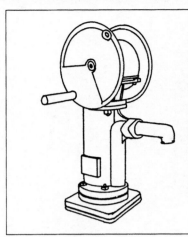

'TROPIC' TYPE III

This piston pump is designed to withstand rough handling and requires no oiling or greasing. It is made mainly of cast iron, with a solid double flywheel connected directly to the totally enclosed crankshaft and drive mechanism. The standard version of the pump is a manual lift-only unit for pits and boreholes, but it can also be adapted to provide a lift and force facility for raising water up to 10m above pump height.
Cylinder diameter 50-100mm (six sizes).
Corresponding lift 50-15m.
Corresponding outputs 13-53 litre/min. at 50 stroke/min.

POMPES DEPLECHIN S.A.
Avenue de Maire, 28
Tournai 7500
BELGIUM

FLYWHEEL-ASSISTED LIFT AND FORCE PUMPS

'BOMBA FUNDO'
The standard version of this deep well pump has a hand-turned flywheel which turns the crankshaft via a reduction drive, but a motorized version is also available.

MUELLER IRMAOS S.A.
Av. Pres. Wenceslau Braz, 1046
Vila Lindoia
C.P. 3336
80 000 Curitiba (D.P.57)
Parana
BRAZIL

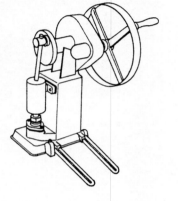

FLYWHEEL-ASSISTED LIFT AND FORCE PUMPS

GODWIN SERIES X
This heavy-duty piston pump can be operated by either one or two persons. It is made mainly of cast iron, with a double flywheel, twin connecting rods and balance weights. The flywheels are sufficiently wide to accommodate an optional belt drive, and a single-flywheel model (illustrated) is also available. The pump can be fitted with a gearbox to increase the maximum lift capability to 20-107m, depending on the cylinder fitted. Extractable or non-extractable cylinders are available, with a choice of eight sizes to suit the required lift.
Cylinder diameter 57-102mm.
Corresponding maximum lift 53-12m.
Corresponding output 13-41 litre/min. at 40 strokes/min.

H.J. GODWIN LTD
Quenington
Cirencester
Glos GL7 5BY
UK

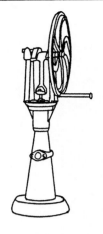

GUILLARD DEEP WELL PUMP
This lift and force, piston pump is made mainly of cast iron with a choice of four cylinder sizes. It is operated by a crank shaft, connected directly to the hand-turned flywheel. The pump stand is fitted with two water outlets so that the water can be delivered directly through a tap or piped to a header tank. The provision of an additional flywheel and handle enables the pump to be operated by two persons simultaneously, increasing the maximum lift obtainable.
Cylinder diameter 63-100mm.
Maximum lift: 30m with single flywheel, 45m with double flywheel.
Water tap height 500mm.

ETS LOUIS GUILLAUD ET CIE S.A.
31, Rue Pierre-Parent
Casablanca
MOROCCO

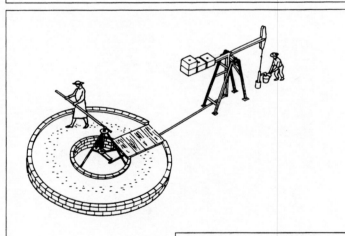

THEBE PUMP

This deep well pump is designed for operation by one person, although it can also be animal-powered for increased output. A capstan assembly is positioned on a tripod and the operator walks in a circle, turning the capstan bar horizontally about the central pivot. The capstan axle has a crank at its lower end, connected to a rod which passes under the circular walkway to a 'see-saw' assembly at the well head. One end of this see-saw is counterweighted; the other is connected to the rod of a borehole pump.

RURAL INDUSTRIES INNOVATION CENTRE
Private Bag 11
Kanye
BOTSWANA

ANIMAL-POWERED CHAIN AND WASHER PUMPS

CHAIN AND WASHER PUMPS
Widely used for irrigation in China, these pumps consist of a rising main through which an endless chain is made to move by rotation of the chain wheel. The chain is fitted with regularly spaced washers which can be provided with rubber discs or 'O'-rings to achieve a closer sliding fit within the rising main. As they move up through the pipe, they lift the water to the surface. They are unsuitable for narrow tubewells owing to the space needed for the circulating chain.

'LIGHT LIBERATION' TUBE AND CHAIN WATERWHEEL
The model illustrated has bevel gear transmission, mounted in a cast-iron frame. The chain has washers with replaceable rubber 'O'-rings and is fitted with a no-return pawl to prevent it from

running backwards. It can be adapted for use with a 3-4kW electric motor or engine.
Maximum lift 12.5m when animal-powered.
Output 110 litre/min. at 4 rev/min. of input shaft.
Minimum well diameter 800mm.

CHINA NATIONAL AGRICULTURAL MACHINERY IMPORT/EXPORT CORPORATION
26 South Yeutan Street
Beijing
CHINA

The following company manufactures a similar pump system, powered by the equivalent of either one or two donkeys.
Maximum lift 12m.
Output 100-120 litre/min. with two donkeys.

ATELIER NIKIEMA
B.P. 7078
Ouagadougou
BURKINA FASO

Cossul produce a similar design. The chain drive mechanism for this pump includes steel gears with a 1:5 gear ratio and gear shafts fitted in ball bearings. The chain has replaceable rubber washers.
Maximum lift 13m.
Output 200-300 litre/min.

COSSUL & CO. (PVT) LTD
123/367 Industrial Area
Fazalgunj
Kanpur
U.P.
INDIA

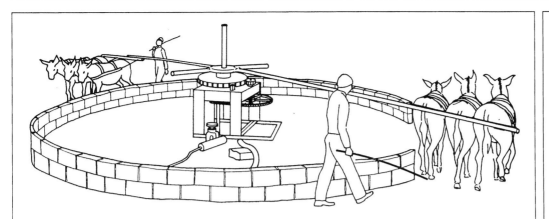

ANIMAL-POWERED IRRIGATION PUMPS

ANIMAL-DRIVEN BOREHOLE PUMP
Originally designed to replace a 2-3kW diesel engine, this animal-draught mechanism is suitable for powering a rotary pump such as the Monolift borehole pump described earlier. Up to eight draught animals can be used, depending on the lift and output required. These animals are harnessed in two teams at the ends of a double capstan bar. The chain transmission is positioned centrally over the well-head and its four sets of sprockets give an 800:1 total speed increase.

As an example of performance, when coupled to a monopump and operated by a capstan speed of 2 rev/min, the system can achieve an output 67 litre/min. for 75m lift.

**RURAL INDUSTRIES INNOVATION
CENTRE
Private Bag 11
Kanye
BOTSWANA**

ANIMAL-POWERED MONOLIFT PUMP
This rotary pump is an adaptation of the Monolift borehole pump described earlier. Its output and lift capabilities are dependent on the number and type of animals used.
Maximum lift 30-110m.
Maximum output 20-80 litre/min.

**MONO PUMPS LTD
Menca Division
Cromwell Trading Estate
Cromwell Road
Bredbury
Stockport SK6 2RF
Cheshire
UK**

MOBILE WATER LIFTER
The capstan of this trolley-mounted shallow-lift pump is provided with a driver's seat mounted over a supporting wheel. For transport, the capstan can be folded and used as a drawbar for the trolley. Two pump sizes are available, one to be powered by a buffalo or two oxen, the other by two buffaloes.
Maximum lift 8m.

**BUNGER ENGINEERING LTD
5260 Højby
Fyn
DENMARK**

ANIMAL-POWERED 'TROPIC' PUMP
This device comprises up to four 'Tropic' Type III handpumps connected to a common gearbox/drive assembly with a capstan. With the smallest cylinder fitted, the pumps can be disengaged from the gearbox and operated manually by fitting a flywheel-mounted handle.

**POMPES DEPLECHIN S.A.
Avenue de Maire, 28
Tournai 7500
BELGIUM**

WATERWHEEL-DRIVEN PUMPS

ROCHFER WATERWHEELS
This range of deep well pumps are powered by waterwheels and are made mainly of cast iron. The waterwheel is connected to an eccentric drive mechanism operating two horizontally opposed, variable stroke piston pumps. Several models and sizes of the pump are available, with 1.1-2.2m wheel diameter and 130-470mm wheel width. Output is dependent on a combination of the required lift and the mass flow and speed of the water arriving at the waterwheel. The minimum flow required to operate the pump varies in the range 60-3000 litre/min, depending on the pressure head and the required lift.
Maximum lift 80-250m, depending on model.

There is also a floating version of the pump, which is mounted on a raft and powered by a paddle-wheel. This has a 6m maximum lift.

**INDUSTRIAS MECANICAS ROCHFER
LTDA
Avenida José da Silva
3765, Jardim Maria Rosa
C.P. 194
Franca SP
BRAZIL**

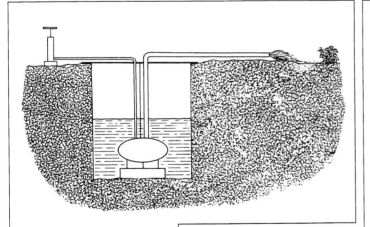

'RCBF' AIR-OPERATED PUMP

This handpump requires no tools for installation but is simply attached to a rope and lowered into a well; water will begin to flow within seconds of starting the pumping operation. A hand-operated air pump is connected by a flexible hose to a submerged, stainless steel tank, ballasted to keep it in position at the well base. The tank fills with water, which is then expelled by pumping air into the tank.
Lift 1-20m.

**FERILAB S.P.R.L.
Av. Albert Elisabeth, 62
Brussels 1200
BELGIUM**

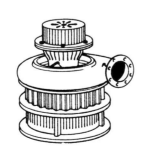

WATER TURBINE PUMP

Pumping systems of this type are very widely used for irrigation purposes, particularly in China. The machine essentially comprises an axial-flow water turbine unit combined with a single-stage centrifugal or axial flow pump mounted on the same shaft. The assembly is totally submerged during operation and is powered by the flow of water through the turbine unit. This power is transmitted through the common shaft to the pump, which draws water from the same flow and discharges it into the delivery pipe. The turbine-pump assembly is usually installed at the end of a supply channel which is fitted with a trash guard and sluice gate.

A wide range of turbine and pump combinations is available to suit different conditions and requirements. Pumping capability varies very widely between models, as indicated by the following general specifications for the range:
Working head 1-20m.
Developed shaft power 0.13-1500kW.
Lift 6-48m.
Output 60-150,000 litre/min.

Two or more units can be installed in series or in parallel, and this will increase the lift and output respectively. The shaft power can alternatively be transmitted by belt and pulley to other equipment or to an electricity generator.

There are several manufacturers of water turbine pumps in China and their equipment is exported by:

**CHINA NATIONAL AGRICULTURAL
MACHINERY IMPORT/EXPORT
CORPORATION
26 South Yeutan Street
Beijing
CHINA**

Similar machines are obtainable from:

**USA ECONOMIC DEVELOPMENT CO.
LTD
56/7 Thung Song Hong Sub Dist.
Bangkhen
Bangkok 10210
THAILAND**

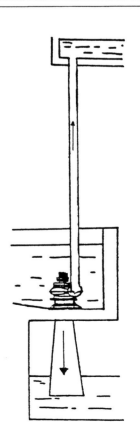

HYDRAULIC RAM PUMPS

The hydraulic ram has been used successfully and reliably for over a hundred years. It requires no external power source and minimal servicing. The energy of a small head of water is used to raise a proportion of this water to a higher level. The water source may be a flowing stream or a spring.

The ram essentially comprises a flow chamber with an open inlet and a valve-controlled outlet. An adjoining air chamber is separated from this flow chamber by a second valve, called the 'grid valve'. Water is gravity-fed from the source, through the flow chamber, passing the closed grid valve, and then out through the open outlet valve into a waste pipe. The pressure of the water flowing through the outlet valve causes this to close suddenly and the momentum of water opens the grid valve and forces a proportion of the water into the air cylinder. The pressure in the flow chamber is thus reduced and the two valves return to their former positions. The water forced into the air cylinder compresses the contained air, which then drives it out of the pump through a delivery pipe. The cycle is repeated up to 90 times per minute and the pump runs continuously as long as the water supply through the flow chamber is not interrupted.

VULCAN RAMS

These rams are constructed from heavy cast iron and gun metal, with moulded rubber valves. A range of sizes is offered, requiring as little as 0.6m of water head to provide a lift of 12-15m. With increased heads, water can be raised up to 100m and delivered over a distance of 2km. Output potential is up to 250,000 litre/24 hours. Reconditioned rams are also available.

GREEN & CARTER
Vulcan Works
Ashbrittle
Wellington
Somerset TA21 0LQ
UK

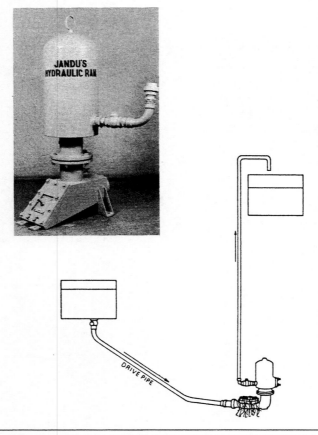

Other companies offering similar ranges of hydraulic ram pumps include:

PREMIER IRRIGATION EQUIPMENT LTD
17/1C Alipore Road
Calcutta 700 027
INDIA

JANDU PLUMBERS
P.O. Box 409
Arusha
TANZANIA

JOHN BLAKE LTD
P.O. Box 43
Royal Works
Accrington
Lancs BB5 5LP
UK

BRIAU S.A.
B.P. 0903
37009 Tours Cedex
FRANCE

CECOCO
P.O. Box 8
Ibaraki
Osaka 567
JAPAN

PILTER FRANCE
12 rue Gouverneur
B.P. 3
Dreux 28100
FRANCE

RIFE HYDRAULIC ENGINE MANUFACTURING COMPANY
Box 367
Millburn
NJ
USA

LEHMAN HARDWARE & APPLIANCES INC.
P.O. Box 41
Kidron
OH 44636
USA

SOLAR-POWERED PUMPS

Using an array of photovoltaic (PV) cells, solar radiation can be converted directly to electricity for powering an electric motor for water pumping. The main components of such a system, as illustrated, are a PV array at ground level connected by electrical cable to a submerged motor driving a pump directly. Alternatively, the motor can be surface-mounted and coupled by a drive-shaft to a submerged pump. Such a system is illustrated. Other components which may be incorporated in the system between the array and the motor are an electronic control system, a battery and an inverter. Provision for water storage may also be included.

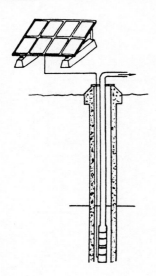

SOLAR PUMPS
The following company offers a range of ten complete pumping systems, using a 12V, DC electric motor charged by a panel of photovoltaic cells. The systems each comprise a solar panel with support structure and hardware, plus a motor and a pump. The range includes both surface and borehole pumps with different capabilities within the range given below. The borehole systems each comprise a submersible motor and multi-stage centrifugal pump controlled by an electronic switchboard.
Lift 6-83m.
Output 7-31 litre/min. averaged over 24-hour day.

HELIODYNÂMICA S.A.
Rodovia Raposo Tavares, Km 41
C.P. 111
06730 Vargem Grande Paulista
São Paulo
BRAZIL

MONO SOLAR PUMP
The Monolift rotary borehole pump, as described earlier, can be driven by an electric motor which is powered by solar panels. These can be fixed panels or 'sun chaser' tracking panels, which provide significantly improved performance.

MONO PUMPS LTD
Menca Division
Cromwell Trading Estate
Cromwell Road
Bredbury
Stockport SK6 2RF
Cheshire
UK

The following companies also supply solar-powered water pumps.

OASIS MANUFACTURING COMPANY INC.
R.R. 4
P.O. Box 571
Mount Vernon
IN 47620
USA

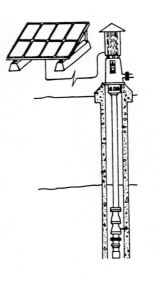

BRIAU S.A.
B.P. 0903
37009 Tours Cedex
FRANCE

BP SOLAR SYSTEMS LTD
Solar House
Bridge Street
Leatherhead
Surrey KT22 8BZ
UK

SOLAR-POWERED SUCTION PUMP

This prototype solar-powered pump comprises a steel drum, painted black and with its ends and base insulated with polyurethane foam. A steel 'pocket' welded to the inside of this cylinder is connected to a small water reservoir. The drum assembly is tilted and the lower end fitted to a water exit valve and to the riser pipe from the intended water source. Adjustable, polished steel mirrors are positioned on each side of the drum to aid solar heating of the contained air and water. The pocket is filled with water, which then evaporates and escapes as vapour through an exit valve. The subsequent entry of cool water to refill the pocket causes negative pressure in the drum and draws water up the riser pipe from the water source. The pump is still under development but tests to date indicate a lift of 5m and an output of 1400 litre/day. Further details can be obtained from:

UNIVERSITÉ LIBRE DE BRUXELLES
Campus Plaine
C.P. 224
Boulevard de Triomphe
Brussels 1050
BELGIUM

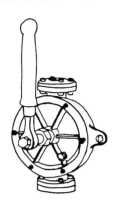

SEMI-ROTARY HANDPUMP

This double-acting handpump is commonly used for lifting small quantities of liquid and delivering it to a higher elevation. Typical applications are the filling of an overhead water tank and the transfer of liquid fuels and oils from a storage tank or barrel. The pump, sometimes known as a 'wing' pump, is operated by moving the handle from side to side in an arc of approximately 90 degrees. The cast-iron body of the pump houses the semi-rotary pump mechanism which is fitted with brass or gun-metal flap valves. The fitting of non-return valves is sometimes suggested for high head installations.
Typical specifications for this type of pump are as follows:
Maximum lift 3-5m.
Maximum delivery head 5-10m.
Output 15-150 litre/min.

PUMPENFABRIK BEYER
Dorfstraße 25
2361 Wulfsfelde
GERMANY

POMPES GRILLOT
2, Rue de l'Observance
Avignon 84 000
FRANCE

RENSON LANDRECIES S.A.R.L.
37 route d'Happegarbes
B.P. 12
Landrecies 59550
FRANCE

WINDLASS

This is used for drawing water from open wells and is suitable for both domestic and public use. Windlass bars can be fitted at both ends of the mild steel axle, which runs in two bearings. The windlass illustrated is available in two sizes, 850mm and 1000mm.

DRAW PULLEY
Also produced is a draw pulley designed for fitting at the head of a domestic bucket-type well. It is made of cast iron with a turned steel axle and has a diameter of 230mm.

Both items are available from:

DANDEKAR BROTHERS & CO.
Shivajinagar
Sangli
Maharashtra 416 416
INDIA

PUMPS FOR WINDMILL CONNECTION

BOREHOLE/DEEP WELL HANDPUMP
The handle pivot position of this pump can be adjusted to provide three different stroke lengths and the pump requires 16mm or 12mm connecting rods. The base and outlet connections have 50mm and 40mm BSP threads respectively. The pump can also be powered by a windmill, and provision for windmill attachment is included.
Maximum lift 40m.
Stroke length 150, 200 or 250mm.
Output with 250mm stroke and at 30 stroke/min:
  62 litre/min. at 7.5m lift (100mm cylinder),
  12 litre/min. at 40m lift (45mm cylinder).

DEEP WELL POWER HEADS
These self-oiling, totally enclosed, borehole power heads can be used for depths of 6m to 215m and can be used for pressure tank or open tank service. They are suitable for windmill connection or they can be driven by flat or V-belt from an engine or electric motor. The crosshead is fitted with sacrificial wearing strips to prevent wear of the casing. The length of stroke can be changed by setting the position of the crank pin in one of two alternative positions.
Driving power required 0.75kW.
Length of stroke 152 or 203mm.
Cylinder size 45-140mm.
Both of the above are available from:

DUNWELL PRODUCTS
P.O. Box 8534
Belmont
Bulawayo
ZIMBABWE

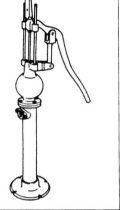

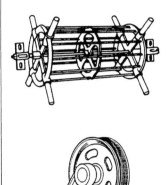

WIND-POWERED PUMPS

In general, water-pumping windmills have multi-bladed rotors. The reason for this is that a high starting torque is needed to get a water pump started, and the provision of many blades eases starting against a heavy load in light winds. Also, multi-bladed rotors run slowly in a given wind which makes this design the natural choice for connecting to reciprocating piston pumps which need to be operated at quite low speeds.
The performance of a windpump is sensitive to the size of pump fitted - fitting a smaller pump will allow the windmill to start in a lower windspeed than a bigger pump. Good judgement is required to fit a pump which will maximize the output from the machine in a given wind regime.
Typical performance figures for a 4.9m diameter windpump are given in the table below.

Windspeed km/hour	Head x Output m x m³/h
8	61
16	122
24	183
32	244
40	305

Most machines are designed to make use of windspeeds in the range 8-50km/hour. They do not function at lower windspeeds and invariably either furl themselves or deliberately shed a lot of the available power at higher windspeeds with the aid of an automatic governing or furling system to prevent any damage.
The three main uses for windpumps are livestock water supplies, village water supplies and irrigation. Water for the latter is characterized by a large variation in requirements from month to month and in order to satisfy peak demand generally it is only economic to lift from shallow depths. Because of the variability of wind, if a supply of water must be guaranteed, it will be necessary to provide either storage or a standby capability.

Most of the following manufacturers and suppliers offer a range of wind-powered pumps, differing in design and size, and suited to different applications including low-lift irrigation and shallow and deep well installation. The following code system is used below to denote the overall specifications for the range offered by a supplier, rather than for any individual model:

R Rotor diameter (m)
P Piston diameter (mm)
V Number of vanes
H Height of tower (m)
L Maximum lift (m)

(R2-5, V6-8)
DEPARTMENT OF RENEWABLE ENERGY
Ministry for Rural Development
C.P. 50
Praia
CAPE VERDE

(R2-3, P50-100, H6-12)
ETS VIAU
23, Avenue du 11 Novembre
Pernes les Fontaines 84210
FRANCE

(R2-5, P64-203, L10-50)
HERCULES INDUSTRIA METALURGICA
J.A. Saglio S.A.
Buenos Aires
1460 Bdo de Irigoyen 1470
ARGENTINA

(R2-8, V4-12, P300, L15-70)
HUMBLOT
8, Rue d'Alger
Coussey 88630
FRANCE

(R2-5, V6-16, H4-13)
ENTERPRISE NATIONALE DE PRODUCTION DES MATERIELS HYDRAULIQUES
B.P. No.1 Baten
Zone Industrielle
Berrouaghia
Wilaya de Medea
ALGERIA

(R2, V4-6, P35-50, L40)
LUBING INTERNATIONAL
66, Rue du Fief
Sailly-sur-la-Lys
Laventie 62840
FRANCE

(R5, V24, P100-150, H10)
AGRO-AIDS
27, Shrunagar Shopping Centre
M.G. Road
Bangalore 560 001
INDIA

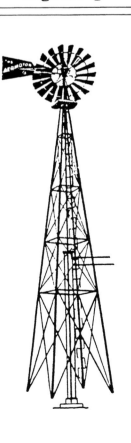

KIJITO WINDPUMP

This windpump (illustrated) is based on an original design by Intermediate Technology.

(R4-7, V3-24, H 10, L180)
BOBS HARRIES ENGINEERING LTD
Kanamaini Estate
P.O. Box 40
Thika
KENYA

(R2-4, V12)
AUTO SPARES INDUSTRIES
Wind Machines Division
C-7 Industrial Estate
Pondichery 605004
INDIA

(R4-5, V12)
INSTITUTE OF ENGINEERING AND RURAL TECHNOLOGY
26 Chatham Lines
Wear Prayag Railway Station
Allahabad 211 002
INDIA

(R6, V6-12, H7-12)
VOLTAS
Agro Industrial Products Division
19 J.N. Heredia Marg.
Ballard Estate
Bombay 400 038
INDIA

(R4-5, V4-8, L4-20)
BOSMAN WATERBEHEERSING EN MILIEUVERBETERING BV
P.O. Box 3701
3265 ZG Piershil
NETHERLANDS

(P51-64, L30)
WIRE MAKERS LTD
P.O. Box 244
Christchurch 4
NEW ZEALAND

(R5, V6)
APPROPRIATE TECHNOLOGY PROJECT
P.O. Box 764
Arusha
TANZANIA

(R2-4, P76-153, L40-92)
THE HELLER-ALLER COMPANY
P.O. Box 29
OH 43545
USA

(R2-5, P44-203, L4-300)
AERMOTOR
The Valley Pump Group
P.O. Box 1364
Conway
AK 72032
USA

(R2-4, P48-102, H6-12)
DEMPSTER INDUSTRIES INC
P.O. Box 848
Nebraska 68310
USA

(L80)
METALÚRGICA ESCOL LTD
Rua Inácio Soares Barbosa, 546
Parelhas (RN)
BRAZIL

(R2-3, V18, H28)
KMP MANUFACTURING INC
P.O. Box 220
Earth
TX 79031
USA

(R2-3, V8-16, P80-150, H4-12, L2 100)
EOTEC
R.N. 117
Lavelanet de Comminges
Cazeres 31220
FRANCE

(R2-3, P46-70, L10-40)
ETS PONCELET ET CIE
Place de la Victoire
B.P. 12
Plancy l'abbaye 10380
FRANCE

(R4, V15)
RURAL INDUSTRIES INNOVATION CENTRE
Private Bag 11
Kanye
BOTSWANA

(R4, V18, P76, H9, L146)
SHEET METAL KRAFT
14 Coventry Street
P.O. Box 1840
Bulawayo
ZIMBABWE

(R4-6, V30-45, P100-400, H6-15)
USA ECONOMIC DEVELOPMENT CO. LTD
56/7 Thung Song Hong Sub Dist.
Bangkhen
Bangkok 10210
THAILAND

(R 2-4m, P 50-200mm, H 4-12m, L 15-150m)
GUILLEMINOT S.A.
Place de l'Eglise
Lusigny sur Barse 10270
FRANCE

(R 3.3-4.3m, P 45-102mm, L 18-90m)
REYMILL STEEL PRODUCTS
Sta Rosa
Nueva Ecija
PHILIPPINES

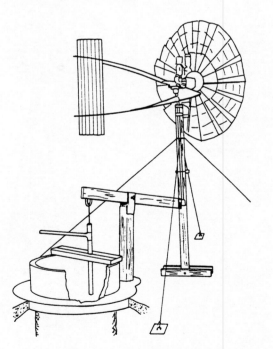

LOW-COST WIND-POWERED PUMP

This low-cost, wind-powered piston pump is made from wood and metal and can be constructed on site in six to ten days. Rotor diameter 3m, with six aluminium vanes. Lift 20m.

BASE DE PERFECTIONNEMENT DES ARTISANS RURAUX
Saint-Louis
SENEGAL

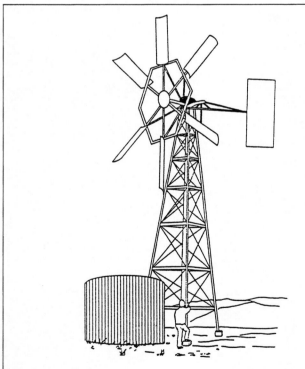

WINDMILL WITH MONOPUMP

MOTSWEDI WINDMILL
This comprises a classic windmill powering a monopump via a horizontal V-belt. Thus the windmill can be offset from the borehole. In 24 hours with an average windspeed of 3.8m/sec it can pump 800 litres of water from 75 metres, depth.

RURAL INDUSTRIES INNOVATION CENTRE
Private Bag 11
Kanye
BOTSWANA

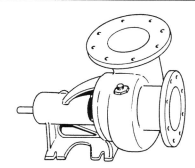
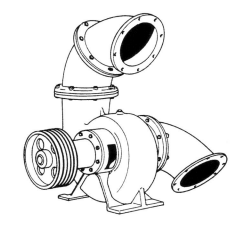

BARE-SHAFTED CENTRIFUGAL PUMPS

The following companies supply ranges of centrifugal pumps with bare drive shafts, for attachment to a power source supplied by the user. Most of the pumps can be either direct-coupled to an engine or electric motor or powered through a belt drive. They are generally made of cast iron and many are self-priming. Power requirements vary from 0.5 to 25kW.

SHAHPORAN ENGINEERING WORKS LTD
6 DIT Avenue (3rd floor)
Motijheel C/A
Dhaka 1000
BANGLADESH

DUNWELL Products
P.O. Box 8543
Belmont
Bulawayo
ZIMBABWE

HIDROSTAL S.A.
Portada del Sol 772
Zarate
Lima 36
PERU

BANGLADESH MACHINE TOOLS FACTORY LTD
Gazipur
Dhaka
BANGLADESH

MIRPUR AGRICULTURAL WORKSHOP & TRAINING SCHOOL
Mirpur Section 12
Pallabi
Dhaka 16
BANGLADESH

CATHOLIC RELIEF SERVICES
P.O. Box 2410
13 Ibrahim Naguib Street
Garden City
Cairo
EGYPT

PUMPENBOESE KG
Postfach 1250
Raiffeisenstraße 2
D-3006 Burgwedel 1
GERMANY

C.V. KARYA HIDUP SENTOSA
Jl. Magelang 144
Yogyakarta 55241
INDONESIA

P.T. RUTAN MACHINERY TRADING COMPANY
P.O. Box 319
Surabaya
INDONESIA

MINE-ELECT
P.O. Box 316
Bulawayo
ZIMBABWE

RAJAN UNIVERSAL EXPORTS (MFRS) PVT LTD
P.O. Box 250
Madras 600 001
INDIA

FUNDIÇAO JACUI S.A.
Avenida Brasil, 1489
CP 190
96500 Cachoeira Do Sul
R.S.
BRAZIL

LANE ENGINEERING (PVT) LTD
P.O. Box 43
Southerton
Harare
ZIMBABWE

ENTERPRISE NATIONALE DE PRODUCTION DES MATERIELS HYDRAULIQUES
B.P. 1 Baten
Berroughia
W. Medea
ALGERIA

AUDOLI & BERTOLA
Z.I. du Nord
9, chemin des Aigais
Brignais 69530
FRANCE

ENGINE-DRIVEN PORTABLE PUMPSETS

The majority of these comprise a self-priming, centrifugal pump supplied with a directly-coupled internal combustion engine. Lightweight models are generally powered by a two- or four-stroke petrol engine, the larger machines by diesel engines. Most of the pumps are made of cast iron but aluminium and stainless steel models are also available from some companies. The pumpsets are portable and are mounted in a frame or on a base with carrying handles.

KOREA FARM MACHINERY & TOOL INDUSTRY CO-OPERATIVE
11-11 Dongja-Dong
Youngsan-Gu
Seoul
KOREA

AGRICULTURAL ENGINEERS LTD
Ring Road Industrial Area
P.O. Box 12127
Accra North
GHANA

AGRO MACHINERY LTD
P.O. Box 3281
Bush Rod Island
Monrovia
LIBERIA

LA BOUR PUMP COMPANY LTD
Denington Estate
Wellingborough
Northants NN8 2QL
UK

HIDROSTAL S.A.
Portada del Sol 772
Zarate
Lima 36
PERU

HARRISONS LISTER ENGINEERING LTD
45, Morgan Road
Colombo 2
SRI LANKA

MEKINS AGRO PRODUCTS (PVT) LTD
6-3-866/A Begumpet
Greenlands
Hyderabad 500 016
INDIA

SIGMA PUMPING EQUIPMENT
Valves Manufacturing Works
P.O. Box 1111
111 87 Praha
CZECHOSLOVAKIA

INDUSTRIAS MECANICAS CONDOR S.A.
Paseo Carlos I, 87-89
Barcelona 18
SPAIN

H.C. SLINGSBY PLC
Preston Street
Bradford
Yorks BD7 1JF
UK

PENAGOS HERMANOS & CIA. LTDA
Apartado Aereo 689
Bucaramanga
COLOMBIA

BANDA METAL INDUSTRIES
Jayanthi Mawatha
Anuradapura
SRI LANKA

AGRO TECHNICA LTD
400 Deans Rd
Colombo 10
SRI LANKA

ENTERPRISE NATIONALE DE PRODUCTION DE MATERIELS HYDRAULIQUES
B.P. 1 Baten
Zone Industrielle
Berrouaghia
ALGERIA

CHINA NATIONAL MACHINERY IMPORT & EXPORT CORPORATION
Wuxi Pump Works
123 Nanmen Tangjingqiao
Wuxi
Jiangsu Province
CHINA

JINASENA LTD
4 Hunupitiya Rd
Colombo 2
SRI LANKA

AUDOLI & BERTOLA
Z.I. du Nord
9, chemin des Aigais
Brignais 69530
FRANCE

YANMAR AGRICULTURAL EQUIPMENT CO.LTD
1-32, Chayamachi
Kita-ku
Osaka 530
JAPAN

ENTERPRISE NATIONALE DE PRODUCTION DES MATERIELS HYDRAULIQUES
B.P. 1 Baten
Berroughia
W. Medea
ALGERIA

FARMLAND ENGINEERING LTD
58/1 Purana Paltan
P.O. Box 629
Dhaka 2
BANGLADESH

FLUXINOS ITALIA SRL
Via Genova, 8
Grosseto 58100
ITALY

SECA
La Côte St André
Le Mottier 38260
FRANCE

COMPAGNIE D'APPLICATION MÉCANIQUES
10, Avenue Faidherbe
B.P. 397
Dakar
SENEGAL

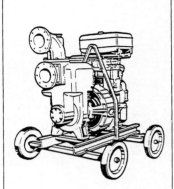

TROLLEY-MOUNTED PUMPSETS

The following companies offer larger pumpsets, similar to the portable sets but mounted on a skid or trolley for ease of transport:

HERCULANO ALFAIAS AGRICOLAS
Loureiro
Oliveira de Azemeis 3720
PORTUGAL

LA BOUR PUMP COMPANY LTD
Denington Estate
Wellingborough
Northants NN8 2QL
UK

SOCIETE POUR L'ENGINEERING INDUSTRIEL ET AGRICOLE
Rue du Textile
Z.I. Sidi Rezig 2033
Mégrine (Tunis)
TUNISIA

ELECTRIC CENTRIFUGAL PUMPSETS

These portable pumpsets comprise a centrifugal pump directly coupled to an electric motor. The majority are low-lift, self-priming pumps, used for irrigation. The pump illustrated is a 'Watt-Miser' powered by a 0.4-1.1kW motor; it was developed by IRRI and potential manufacturers can obtain technical details from:

IRRI
Agricultural Engineering Department
P.O. Box 933
Manila
PHILIPPINES

Similar pumps are manufactured by:

CENTAURO BOMBAS Y EQUIPOS
10 de Agosto
Ascazubi 2646
ECUADOR

TEMDO
P.O. Box 6111
Arusha
TANZANIA

MILNARS PUMPS LTD
Zirat Chamber
31 Bangabandhu Avenue
Dhaka 2
BANGLADESH

MECOL GROUP
6 DIT Avenue, 2nd Floor
Motijheel c/a
Dhaka 1000
BANGLADESH

HIDROSTAL S.A.
Portada del Sol 722
Zarate
San Juan de Lurigancho
Lima 36
PERU

HYDROMECANIQUE S.A.
5, Rue Champlain
Tunis
TUNISIA

MIO STANDARD - OSIJEK
Vukovarska 219a
Osijek 54000
YUGOSLAVIA

CHINA NATIONAL MACHINERY & EQUIPMENT IMPORT & EXPORT CORPORATION
Guangdong Branch
59 Zhan Qian Rd
Guangzhou
CHINA

JINASENA LTD
4 Hunupitiya Rd
Colombo 2
SRI LANKA

Larger electric pumpsets, mounted either on a base frame or a two-wheeled trolleys with towbar, are obtainable from:

GENERAL ELECTRIC COMPANY OF BANGLADESH
Magnet House
72 Dilkusha C/A
Dhaka 2
BANGLADESH

SUBSET 30/11

This hydraulically driven submersible pump is suitable for both irrigation and deep well applications. It can be carried by two people by pushing a pole through two suspension eyes welded to the top of the mounting frame. It can also be mounted on a trolley or raft.

Pump power 2kW at 3000 rev/min.
Output 185 litre/min. for 30m lift.

ARKANA EUROPE B.V.
Joh. van Soesdijkstraat 37
P.O. Box 286
1110 AG
Diemen
NETHERLANDS

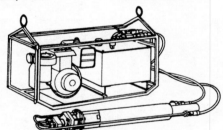

'TORRENTIAL' PUMP

This portable, floating pump has a 3kW petrol engine mounted over a glass fibre-reinforced plastic pump body. It will run for up to four hours between refuellings. The pump is supplied with a 15m plastic water delivery hose.
Maximum lift 3m.

MARINE AVIATION CORPORATION S.A.
8, rue Saint Marc
Paris 75008
FRANCE

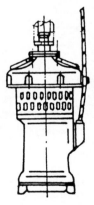

SCREW PUMP

This low-lift pump is a form of Archimedean screw. It consists of a fabricated screw turning about its axis within a casing and powered by either an electric motor or a diesel engine. The pump is sited, typically, on a river bank with its axis inclined at 22-40 degrees to the horizontal. A wide range of sizes is available and the screw can be of one, two or three blades.
Maximum lift 5m.

P.T. RUHAAK PHALA INDUSTRIES LTD
Jl. Pintu Besar Utara 11
Jakarta Barat 11110
INDONESIA

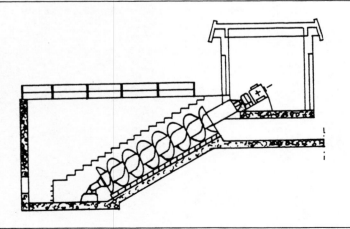

SUBMERSIBLE ELECTRIC PUMPS

This company produce a large range of submersible electric pumps with the following specifications:
Output 125-1600 litre/min.
Lift 3.5-40m.
Power required 0.8-5.5kW.

CHINA NATIONAL AGRICULTURAL MACHINERY IMPORT AND EXPORT CORPORATION
Hangzhou Pump Factory
Hangzhou
Zhejiang
CHINA

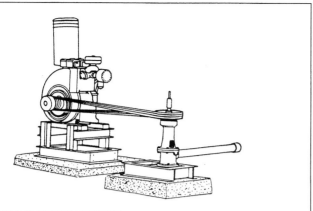

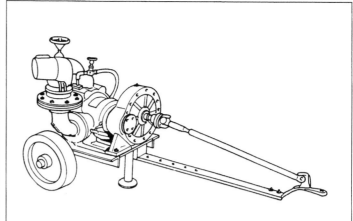

MONOLIFT POWER-DRIVEN BOREHOLE PUMPS

This large range of self-priming borehole pumps can be powered by electric motor or engine, through a belt-drive. The unique 'Mono' design consists of a chrome-plated helical rotor within a nitrile rubber stator. The pump is suspended from a surface-mounted discharge head, which also incorporates the pulley drive. Rubber stabilizers hold the rising main central in the borehole. Various different types of combined discharge and drive heads are available.

MONO PUMPS ZIMBABWE
Box 2049
Graniteside
Harare
ZIMBABWE

MONO PUMPS LTD
Menca Division
Cromwell Road
Bredbury
Stockport
Cheshire SK6 2RF
UK

THREE-POINT HITCH MOUNTED PUMPS

The companies below offer pumps which are to be carried on the three-point linkage of a tractor and driven through its power take-off:

PENAGOS HERMANOS & CIA. LTDA.
Apartado Aereo 689
Bucaramanga
COLOMBIA

BATESCREW SALES
P.O. Box 86
Tocumwal
NSW 2714
AUSTRALIA

TRACTOR-POWERED WATER PUMPS

The following three companies offer low-lift irrigation pumps, to be driven from the engine of a power tiller or walking tractor:

PREMIER IRRIGATION EQUIPMENT LTD
17/1C Alipore Road
Calcutta 700 027
INDIA

V.S.T. TILLERS TRACTORS LTD
P.O. Box 4801
Mahadevapura Post Office
Bangalore 560 048
INDIA

ROBIX M.G.V.
Viola utca 12
Veszprem 8201
HUNGARY

BANDA METAL INDUSTRIES
Jayanthi Mawatha
Anuradapura
SRI LANKA

AXIAL FLOW PUMPS

These low-lift, high output pumps can be powered by engine or electric motor, connected directly or through a belt-drive. They consist of a shaft-driven, axial-flow impeller mounted at the lower end of the discharge pipe. The pump can be installed vertically or at an angle as illustrated.

BATESCREW PUMP
This is offered in a range of sizes with a 2-7kW power requirement. A portable, free-standing model is also available, with an output of 2000 litre/min. at 1m head.

BATESCREW SALES
P.O. Box 86
Tocumwal
NSW 2714
AUSTRALIA

Similar axial-flow pumps are made by:

FARM MECHANISATION RESEARCH CENTRE
Maha Illuppallama
SRI LANKA

JINASENA LTD
4 Hunupitiya Rd
Colombo 2
SRI LANKA

AGRICULTURAL MACHINERY & ENGINEERING CO. LTD
132-134 Samyod
New Road
Bangkok
THAILAND

NEW RUHAAK INDUSTRIES
Jl. Pintu Besar Utara 11
Jakarta
INDONESIA

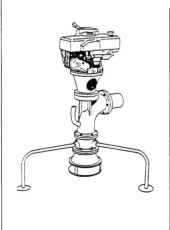

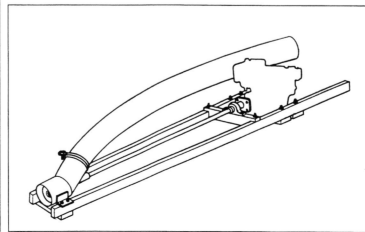

IRRI 'SIPA' PUMP

This is an axial flow pump which has been developed by IRRI. It is of simple construction and is suitable for fabrication from locally obtainable materials in small workshops. Potential manufacturers can obtain technical details from:

IRRI
Agricultural Engineering Department
P.O. Box 933
Manila
PHILIPPINES

Completed IRRI machines are available from:

JCCE INDUSTRIES
242 Mayondon
Los Baños
Laguna
PHILIPPINES

FOOT VALVES AND STRAINERS

These are fitted at the base of rising mains and pump inlets. They are generally made of cast iron with bronze internal parts and are usually designed to be non-clogging or self-cleaning. Various sizes of cast iron and bronze strainers can be obtained from:

DUNWELL PRODUCTS
P.O. Box 8543
Belmont
Bulawayo
ZIMBABWE

and also from:

PUMPENFABRIK BEYER
Dorfstraße 25
2361 Wulfsfelde
GERMANY

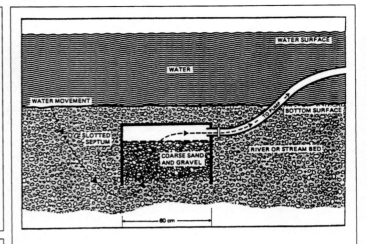

SCREENS

S.W.S. SCREEN, illustrated, is a device to convert an area of sea or river bed into a low-maintenance sand filter. Built of corrosion-free fibre glass, it is a rectangular box with a false ceiling consisting of a compression-moulded, slotted plate. The screen is buried, open end down, in the sea or river bed, after connecting the pump suction pipe to the outlet. The slots are cut in such a way that natural filters are formed soon after the pump is used for the first time. The small village unit has a cross section of 600mm x 300mm and weighs about 8kg.

S.W.S. FILTRATION LTD
Hartburn
Morpeth
Northumberland NE61 4JB
UK

ROBOSCREEN
This water filter unit for hand tubewells has a 12% open area. It is manufactured from ribbed PVC pipe with a spiral slit 0.2mm wide.

MIRPUR AGRICULTURAL
WORKSHOP & TRAINING SCHOOL
Mirpur Section 12
Pallabi
Dhaka 16
BANGLADESH

SELF-JETTING WELLSCREEN

Well-jetting is a technique for inserting a small diameter wellscreen 6-10m deep into a shallow, sandy, water-bearing aquifer. Whereas conventional boreholes require heavy drilling equipment, well-jetting is carried out by hand, using a portable engine pump to produce a powerful jet of water. A specially modified plastic wellscreen is fitted on the end of the bore pipe and 'self-jetted' into the sandy bed. No drilling rig is needed other than a temporary prop for the pipe.

Both of the above items are available from:

S.W.S. FILTRATION LTD
Hartburn
Morpeth
Northumberland NE61 4JB
UK

WELL-DRILLING EQUIPMENT

DEEP WELL EQUIPMENT
The following company offer a very wide range of well-drilling tools, equipment and accessories for surveying, construction and maintenance of hand-drilled wells, including quality testing and control equipment.

VAN REEKUM MATERIALS B V
Postbus 98
Kanaal Noord 115
Apeldoorn
7300 AB
NETHERLANDS

HYDRA-DRILL
This is a complete well-drilling kit, including:

- 2.4m power mast with winch;
- Power swivel for injecting drilling water into system;
- 3kW engine and gearbox;
- Various different drill bits;
- Pump, hoses, fittings, drill fluid additive;
- Forty 1.5m sections of drill stem and plastic well casing.

Maximum drilling depth 60m.
Drilling diameter 90mm.
Weight of complete outfit 119kg.

For drilling to 150m depths, the same company offer a range of rotary air mud drilling rigs with mud pumps and 9-14kW engines.

DEEPROCK CO.
2220 Anderson Road
P.O. Box 1
Opelika
AL 36803
USA

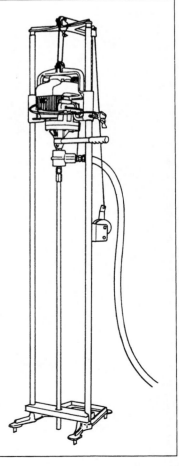

8. TRANSPORT AND MATERIALS HANDLING

TRANSPORT

A significant proportion of agricultural tasks involve moving equipment and materials from one place to another. Tools, fertilizer, seeds and produce must all be moved between field, store and market, which results in a wide variety of types and sizes of load to be moved over different distances and types of terrain. A range of methods of transport and materials handling exists to carry out these tasks in different ways to suit different circumstances. Loads may be carried by hand or on the head, at one extreme, or a self-loading truck may be the most appropriate method at the other.

This chapter covers a very broad range of equipment as it is concerned with both transport and materials handling. In many respects these are different activities, but they are treated as one subject because they are very often complementary, in that materials handling is frequently concerned with loading and unloading vehicles or with transporting goods over very short distances. The guidance given in this introduction is mainly concerned with transport, but much of it can also be applied to materials handling if interpreted with discretion.

In general, transport requirements fall into two categories:
○ On-farm, for the movement of goods between field, store and household. On small farms this will include the collection of firewood and water for domestic purposes — work usually done by women. Loads are generally small

(10-15kg) and distances short (1-10km). Routes are likely to consist of narrow paths and earth tracks, and the goods must also be moved over the fields themselves.
○ Off-farm, for the movement of goods between farm and market. Loads are generally greater, and distances longer. Route conditions may be better, but this is not always the case.

Evidence from a number of surveys in different countries indicates that low-cost (low capital cost) traditional methods of moving goods meet a much greater proportion of these transport requirements then do 'conventional' vehicles, such as tractors, pick-ups, trucks, and buses. There exists a wide range of low-cost vehicles for moving farm goods which can be categorized as follows:
○ carrying aids for head, shoulder and back-loading;
○ wheelbarrows and hand carts;
○ pack animals and animal-drawn carts;
○ pedal-driven vehicles;
○ motor-cycles and converted motor-cycles;
○ trailers for bicycles and motor-cycles;
○ basic motorized vehicles;
○ dual-purpose agriculture/transport equipment.

All of these vehicles have different advantages and disadvantages in terms of load capacity, suitability for route conditions, running costs, speed, range and capital cost, which enable them to meet a broad spectrum of transport

Table 1 The performance characteristics of a range of basic vehicles

Vehicle	Load (kg)	Speed (km/h)	Range (km)	Terrain
Carrying pole	35	3-5	10	Unlimited
Chee-geh	70	3-5	10	Unlimited
Western wheelbarrow	120	3-5	1	Reasonably flat, smooth surface
Chinese wheelbarrow	180	3-5	3-5	Reasonably flat, tolerates rough surfaces
Hand cart	200	3-5	3-5	Reasonably flat; wide paths
Bicycle	80	10-15	40	Reasonably flat paths
Bicycle and trailer	150	10-15	40	Reasonably flat; wide paths
Pack animal	70-150	3-5	20	Unlimited
Animal-drawn sledge (buffalo)	70-150	3-5	20	Reasonably flat; wide track
Animal-drawn cart (oxen)	1000-3000	3-5	50	Reasonably flat; wide track
Motorcycle: 125cc	150-200	30-60	100	Moderate hills
Single axle tractor	1200	10-15	50	Moderate hills; wide track

requirements. Further details and illustrations of the full range of these vehicles is contained in *Low-cost vehicles: options for moving people and goods* by G. Hathway (IT Publications, London 1985).

The performance characteristics of a range of basic vehicles are given in Table 1.

Only a limited range of vehicles is included in Table 1 because many of them are not widely available. Many low-cost forms of transport are used only in certain local areas, and remain unknown in other countries. Sometimes they are unknown even in other areas of the same country. Yet there seems to be no logical reason why many of these methods could not be used elsewhere, if their advantages were known and the equipment available. One obstacle to the widespread availability of some appropriate equipment is that it is usually large relative to its value. Thus freight costs, which are determined by volume as well as weight, will be disproportionately high if the equipment is supplied from a distance. Only when large quantities are ordered at one time can this problem be at least partially overcome. There remains potential in many countries for the local manufacture of a range of types of low-cost transport equipment and of common components such as wheels, bearings and axles. There is also enormous scope for local manufacture of materials handling equipment such as shovels, forks, hoists and elevators. Local manufacture has the advantages of providing the rural community with direct access to the supply and repair of equipment and of generating additional economic activity in rural areas. An example of this approach is the wheel manufacturing technology developed by IT Transport which enables small workshops to set up their own equipment to produce a range of low-cost wheels for various vehicles and agricultural implements.

Transport equipment

Wheelbarrows can carry small loads (up to 100kg) for short distances (up to 1km) over rough ground or on narrow paths. Pneumatic tyres are desirable, to reduce rolling resistance, and a heavy gauge steel load container or barrow will give long service.

Hand carts have two, three or four wheels which support the load directly, so minimizing the load on the operator's arms.

Hand carts operated by one person can carry large loads (up to 200kg) over long distances (up to 10km). Greater loads can be moved by using more than one person. Routes must be sufficiently wide and reasonably flat and smooth. Large diameter wheels, pneumatic tyres and roller bearings are desirable, as is a strong but lightweight structure. Some hand carts may also be used as trailers with a bicycle or motor-cycle.

Special purpose barrows are also available for moving specific loads, such as sacks or water containers.

Animal-drawn carts are constructed in a similar way to hand carts, but the size and capacity is determined by the type and number of animals to be used. Typically, a cart pulled by one donkey can carry up to 500kg, or by one bullock up to 1000kg. Greater loads can be carried by using more than one animal. Route conditions and desirable features are the same as for handcarts. As well as carrying goods, animal carts can also carry people, and special purpose carts are available for specific tasks.

Trailers for single-axle tractors can carry up to 1200kg at up to 10km/h, enabling an agricultural machine to be used for on and off-farm transport as well. A wide track is required, but moderate hills and rough ground can be negotiated. Suspension and brakes are desirable to cope with the relatively high speed. People can be carried, as well as goods.

Engine-powered mono-rail transporters can be useful for carrying loads on steeply sloping land. As the railway is an expensive semi-permanent installation these systems can only be justified for moving substantial quantities over fixed routes in plantations of high-value perennial crops such as citrus fruit and bananas. Lower cost versions use rope or cable operated systems.

MATERIALS HANDLING EQUIPMENT

Shovels and forks are used for handling materials such as grain, fodder and farmyard manure. The rate and distance of movement depends on the skill and strength of the user and also the quality of the tool. Poor quality tools will be unpleasant to use and will fail after a relatively short time, which will reduce output and necessitate frequent replacement.

Hoists enable heavy loads to be moved vertically for loading, unloading or storage. A good quality hoist will reduce the risk of accidents resulting from breakage.

Elevators incorporate a motorized conveyor belt to lift light loads quickly and continuously over short distances.

ADVANTAGES

There are a number of benefits which can result from using better methods of moving goods:

○ Less time or effort may be required to move a given quantity of goods. This benefit will be felt by an individual as an increase in leisure time or a reduction in workload, although the saving may be used, of course, to do more productive work. An employer will benefit by an increase in productivity, enabling more useful work to be done by a given number of people.

○ Labour or other running costs may be reduced.

○ Transport bottlenecks may be relieved, which will reduce the delays and costs caused when transport is not available or is inadequate. Perishable goods can often be sold for a higher price if they reach the market sooner.

○ The efficiency of other operations may be improved by making transport available at the right time and at the right place.

○ Other activities may be permitted to take place, such as the marketing of surplus produce for which transport was not previously available.

ALTERNATIVES

Before purchasing new equipment, however, it should be considered whether the existing methods and equipment could be used more effectively. Could trips be combined or carried out in a different order to minimize empty trips and reduce the total distance covered? Could loading and unloading time be reduced to prevent equipment standing idle? Could equipment and labour be hired temporarily to cover seasonal peaks in demand?

In addition, if new equipment is necessary, there is a wide range of alternatives to the inevitably limited range presented here. First, there are many small-scale suppliers who only advertise and promote themselves locally, and who are thus beyond the scope of this guide. They can be located by reading the local trade or popular press, or by speaking to people who already have the type of equipment sought. Secondly, some of the simpler devices mentioned here can be made by the user or by local craft-workers.

If goods are currently moved by direct head-loading or using

ITDG

Ox-drawn cart with IT Transport-designed split-rim wheels manufactured in Zimbabwe

Jeremy Hartley/Panos

Shoulder pole used for carrying fodder

head or shoulder straps, several simple aids could be used to improve efficiency. These include the shoulder pole and the chee-geh.

The *shoulder pole* is a length of split bamboo 1200-2000m long, and 45m wide in the middle tapering to 30-40m at the ends. Loads are suspended directly or in baskets from the ends and the pole is carried on one shoulder. The most important advantage of this device is that it can be picked up and set down without assistance.

The *chee-geh* is a simple pack frame, carried by one person on the shoulders and back, which can also be picked up and set down without assistance. It is believed to be unique to Korea, where it is invaluable for moving loads on narrow paths and tracks which frequently cross ditches, and on steep and rough terrain.

If domesticated animals are available, *panniers* can be made, as baskets, pack frames or purpose-built containers, to enable the animals to carry loads over any ground which can be traversed on foot. Where there is an earth track or generally flat ground, *sledges* can be used to increase further an animal's load-carrying ability.

COSTS AND RETURNS

Table 2 shows indicative costs for the equipment presented in this section. No currency units are given as the costs are simply relative to others within the table. It is not possible to estimate the cost of providing the necessary infrastructure as this varies so widely both within and between categories. Instead, a qualitative indication of requirements is given.

The cost of transportation is conventionally expressed as the cost per tonne/kilometre, and is derived by dividing the total cost incurred in moving goods during a period of time (such as one year or three months) by the sum of the products of the individual loads moved and distances covered during the same period. In the simple case of moving produce from farm to market, the cost of transporting the load must be less than its increase in value for the trip to be worthwhile.

Costs incurred will include depreciation, maintenance and repairs, fuel, cost of capital (loan repayment or loss of interest), and the cost of the operator's labour (including overheads). Other costs such as tax and insurance may also be applicable. These costs must also be applied to the animal, where relevant, although if the animal is used for transport only part of the time, only an appropriate proportion of its total cost should be

Chee-geh: Korea

included. Similarly, only a proportion of total labour costs should be included where labour is used for other tasks as well.

To obtain the sum of the products of the individual loads moved and distances covered, or 'tonne/km', the product of load moved and distance covered should be calculated for each trip carried out during the period for which costs are calculated. These trip totals are then added together to obtain the required result.

In making calculations of this type to estimate the costs of alternative methods of transport it is important to use the actual loads which will be carried, rather than the maximum loads which could be carried.

Direct costs are not the only factor to be considered when choosing the most suitable type of equipment. Other considerations include intended use(s) of vehicle, technical capability, local availability and social acceptability.

In large or specialized organizations, items of transport and materials handling equipment are often used for only one particular task. For most agricultural work, general purpose equipment is needed, so the first step in choosing an item is to decide the range of tasks which it must be able to perform. The next step is to determine the range of possible options by examining the following aspects.

○ *Capability* Is the equipment capable of performing the required tasks? Is the load capacity high enough? Can the equipment negotiate the route? Can it be operated fast enough?

○ *Costs* Is sufficient cash available to purchase equipment or make loan repayments? Will the equipment result in sufficient cash savings or increased income to pay for itself in a short period of time?

○ *Local availability* Is the equipment itself, and are the necessary animals, fuel or spare parts, available locally, both immediately and in the foreseeable future?

○ *Social acceptability* Are there any social restrictions on people owning or using certain types of equipment or animals, or performing tasks in certain ways?

Once you have determined the range of possible options, a detailed analysis of all the economic factors will then reveal the most suitable choice (from an economic point of view). Where a choice exists between good and poor quality equipment it is important to acknowledge that although the initial cost of the good quality implement will be higher it will usually allow greater productivity and will need replacement less frequently.

Once the most suitable choice has been determined, an economic comparison should always be made with existing methods and with the expected benefits to determine whether the proposed innovation is worthwhile. Some of the benefits described earlier, such as a reduction in effort or increased leisure time, are not directly quantifiable in economic terms, but they must be regarded as having some 'value', in order to make this comparison.

Example: Rubber-tyred bullock cart. Annual transport costs for rubber-tyred bullock cart, for first five years of life:

Cost of capital:

Cart 3000, financed by loan @ 15% per year, paid over 5 years	450
Bullocks 2000, paid in cash. Loss of interest @ 8% 50% of working time used for transport	80

Depreciation

Cart, over 5 years, zero resale value	600
Bullocks, zero depreciation. (Resale value = purchase price)	

Maintenance and repairs:

Cart	150
Bullocks (inc. fodder) 2000 x 50%	1000

Labour

30% of working time used for transport	600
	2880

Average daily load x distance (6 days per week):

January-March	0.6 tonne km/day	= 46.8 tonne km/quarter
April-June	0.8 tonne km/day	= 62.4 tonne km/quarter
July-Sept.	2.0 tonne km/day	= 156.0 tonne km/quarter
October-Dec.	0.5 tonne km/day	= 39.0 tonne km/quarter
		304.2 tonne km/year

Annual cost per tonne kilometre $\frac{2880}{304.2}$ = 9.14

IMPACT

Moving goods not only takes up a considerable proportion of the time available for agriculture work, but it frequently involves debilitating human labour as well. Improvements in transport or material-handling methods will have an important social effect by enabling people to use their time and energy in other ways — either in productive work or by increasing their leisure time. Men tend to have greater access to improvements in transport than women because of their greater ease of access to credit and project inputs. Within households, women are usually unable to use a donkey, a cart or a bicycle owned by men. Thus, women have derived less benefit than men from improved transport devices and must continue in many parts of the world to carry very heavy loads on their heads and backs.

Table 2 Indicative costs

Equipment	Capital	Running (Maintenance and repair)	Required Infrastructure
Transport			
Wheelbarrows	30	5	—
Hand carts	100	10	Wide track or flat ground
Animal carts	500 (exc. animal)	30 (exc. animal)	Wide track or flat ground
Trailers for single-axle tractors	500	30	Wide track
Mono-rail transporters	20000 (1000 m length)	1000 (exc. power)	—
Materials handling			
Shovels and forks	10	1	—
Hoists	80	5	Support structure
Elevators	1600	100 (exc. power)	Power supply

A single axle tractor with trailer can be used for carrying people or goods

Jeremy Hartley/Panos

The use of complex and expensive vehicles and equipment will often create dependence on central or foreign suppliers, for fuel and spare parts as well as the original equipment. Much of the low-cost equipment described here, however, could be made by local manufacturers without continuing dependence on imports and outside assistance. In the long term the use of this type of equipment would assist in developing local industry, thus creating productive employment opportunities in rural towns and saving valuable foreign exchange.

An often unexpected result of improving methods of goods transport is that personal mobility is increased as well. People will always travel further and more often for social purposes when a better form of transport becomes available. This demand for transport is difficult to quantify, but it exists nevertheless. Its value is evidenced by the fact that some means of personal transport, be it an animal, a bicycle or motor car, is so often a highly prized possession.

The use of the most basic methods of moving goods, such as direct head-loading or shifting loads by hand, will often result in harmful effects, especially if used for long periods of time or with excessively heavy loads. These effects may be sudden, such as injuries incurred by falling or dropping loads accidentally, or they may develop over long periods in the form of chronic pain in various parts of the body. In either case, they result in a cost to society in terms of increased demands on health care facilities and reduced availability of productive labour time. All the equipment described here will reduce the effort required to move a given load, though it should always be remembered that if the new equipment is loaded to an excessive level there can still be harmful side effects.

Motorized transport and material-handling equipment will require the same care in use as any other motorized machinery. In the case of vehicles, additional hazards caused by higher speeds and other traffic must also be recognized.

SPECIAL CONSIDERATIONS

When new methods of moving goods are introduced operators must be trained in their use, and time must be allowed for them to become accustomed to the new method before maximum output will be achieved. This is particularly so for some of the very low-cost alternatives, such as carrying aids. Skills and strength in certain parts of the body must be acquired before these devices can be used effectively. The output of engine-and animal-powered devices is also dependent on the operator's care and skill in using and maintaining them.

I T Transport Ltd

EQUIPMENT

Manure forks and drags

Handling loosely packed materials using suitably constructed forks (for lifting) and drags (for pulling) is the manual method most commonly used in European agriculture. The renewed worldwide interest in compost-making gives an increased importance to manure and hay forks: their use for carrying materials for building compost heaps would make feasible the dissemination of composting technologies among smallholder farmers who have a problem handling the required volumes of material. Several tonnes of compost are required to manure one hectare of land effectively.

Oval section fork tines (prongs) penetrate into the mass of heaped material, pushing aside rather than cutting it. When a force is applied perpendicular to the tines, a large mass of inter-knit material can be moved. The number of tines needed for any particular task depends, to some extent, on the particle length of the material to be moved. For example, hay, made from long grass, can be moved effectively using a two-tined pitchfork, while dung and urine-soaked straw cut up by the hooves of stall-fed animals will produce a crumbly material which can be more easily moved by a fork with many tines.

The shape of the handle and its attachment to the head are critical. With a bent handle/shaft or a bent socket attachment the centre of gravity is moved, thus making it easier to handle heavy loads.

Traditional wooden tools made from tree branches are used for moving materials, but it is increasingly hard to find trees of the right shape. These tools, cut from wayside trees when needed, are often discarded after use. Properly designed steel forks will last a lifetime (though the wooden shafts may need replacing) if cleaned and lightly oiled after use, and have proved more efficient and effective.

The forces generated in the shaft are concentrated at its junction with the tines. They can be large if the mass of material to be lifted is heavy. Consequently much attention has been given to strengthening the socket.

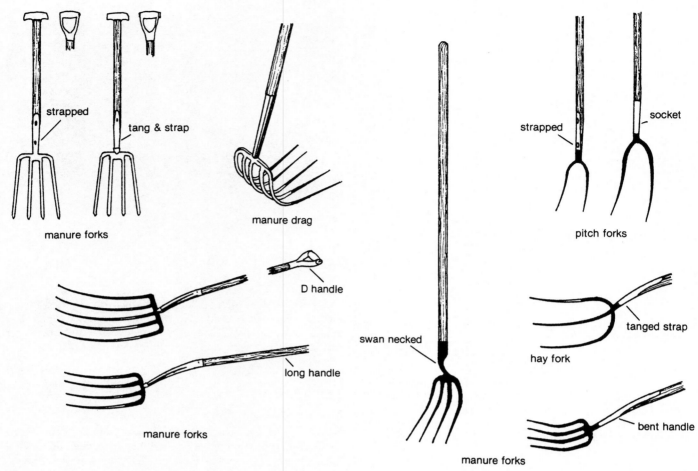

Figure 1 Manure forks and drags

There are three basic forms of attachment that are commonly manufactured, although variations and combinations may occur within and between these divisions. These forms are:

○ *Socket attachments*: usually a split of cylindrical collar into which the shaft is fitted ('open' socket). The shaft may then be secured by one or more screws, nails or rivets.

Variations on this are the solid socket which forms an unbroken collar into which the shaft is placed, and the swan-necked (bent) or sprung-socket.

○ *Strapped attachments* formed from two tapered ferrule straps between which the shaft is fitted. The shaft is then secured into place by screws or rivets. This is the most durable of the attachments included here.

The Scottish and half-straps are variations on this type of attachment.

○ *Tanged attachments*: a simple pin onto which the shaft is fitted. This attachment is often combined with a socket or strapped arrangement to ensure rigidity.

○ *All-metal implements*: A shaft attachment may be strapped, although a welded fitting is more usual.

There are three main tine shapes:

○ *Straight* — the tines are straight, with only slight curvature (forks);

○ *Dished* — the tines are generously curved (forks);

○ *Hooked* — the tines are bent through 90 degrees (drags).

Another variant is the way in which the tines are set relative to one another. Two forms are usual:

○ *Splayed* — where the tines are spread;

○ *Parallel* — where the tines are parallel.

For example, a fork may have four curved tines which are splayed, while a similar model may have a parallel tine formation. Manure drag tines are always parallel.

Types of handle may be classified into three categories:

○ the handle is a short cross-piece forming a T-shape at the top of the shaft;

○ the handle is a D-shaped grip — D-shaped handles may have one or two rivets which strengthen the cross-piece and the join with the shaft;

○ the handle is a (usually) longer, plain shaft, circular in cross-section, sometimes with a small or elongated knob at one end.

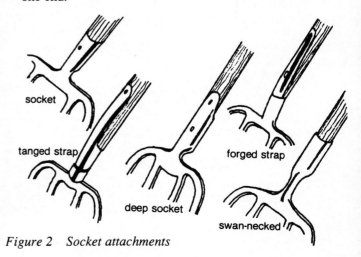

Figure 2 Socket attachments

Material handling forks

Country	Manufacturer	Implement			
		Manure forks and drags	Hay forks and pitchforks	Potato forks and drags	Other forks
Austria	Leonhard Muller & Sohne Kg	●	●		●
	Piesslinger GmbH	●	●		●
	Johann Offner	●	●		
	Sensenwerke Krenhof	●	●		●
	Sonneck GmbH	●	●		
Cameroon	Tropic	●			
Finland	Gripit Oy AB	●			
Germany	Schwabische Huttenwerke GmbH			●	
India	Kumaon Nursery	●	●		
	Kumar Industries	●			●
Italy	Falci S.P.A.	●	●	●	
Peru	Fahena S.A.	●			
	Herramientas S.A.	●			
Portugal	Verdugo — Ernesto I. Matias	●	●	●	
Sri Lanka	Kanthi Industries	●			
Tanzania	Ubungo Farm Implements Manuf. Co. Ltd	●	●		
UK	Bulldog Tools Ltd	●	●		●
	Spear & Jackson Garden Products	●	●	●	●
	The Stockton Heath Forge Ltd	●	●		●
Yugoslavia	Gorenje Muta	●	●	●	●
Zimbabwe	Temper Tools (Pvt) Ltd		●		

Shovels

The shovel, which has been employed since the earliest times in both agricultural and construction activities, is a tool used to move loose or unconsolidated materials short distances. It differs in form and function from the spade (see Chapter 2, Soil Preparation) which is essentially a digging instrument.

The diversity of tasks (and, to a certain extent, conditions) to which the shovel has been applied is reflected in the correspondingly wide range of shovel types developed over the years. As an example, the two very different tasks of grain transport and earth clearance serve to demonstrate how shovel forms have evolved to suit quite specific functions.

In this case the most obvious difference is between the shapes of the shovel heads. On the one hand, the earth-moving shovel is relatively small and rounded or pointed. Such a shape is suited to the penetration and dislodgement of heavy, cohesive materials. On the other hand, the grain shovel, which is used for handling light and incoherent material, is large and broad-mouthed, being better suited to the movement of large quantities at a time, rather than the heavier duty work of earth clearance. Note also that the grain shovel is equipped with a raised edge that increases the capacity of the implement. An earth-moving shovel has no need for this kind of addition, since earth is considerably more cohesive than grain. Further, the nature of its task means that the grain shovel can be lighter and less robust than the shovel used for the movement of earth: lighter, thinner metal is used for making the grain shovel head.

This brief example shows how two very different types of shovel can be described in terms of their function, and accounts in part for the diversity of shovels used throughout the world. The table offers a small range of shovels most useful to agricultural activities. Square-ended shovels are all-purpose implements, though lighter models are useful for tasks such as grain handling. Round-ended shovels are usually heavy-duty implements, whereas scoops are very large-capacity, light-duty shovels. Tapered shovels are usually heavy duty, for specialist work such as trenching.

As a general rule, shovels are not stressed to the same extent as digging tools or manure forks, so the solid socket is the most widely used in shovel manufacture. The handles vary in the same way as forks and drags.

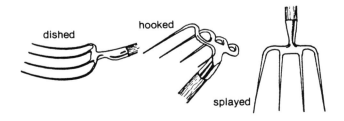

Figure 3   Shape of tines

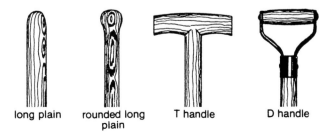

Figure 4   Handle types

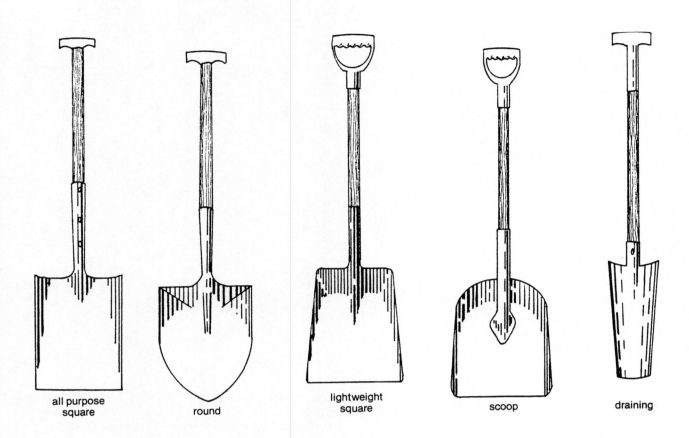

all purpose
square

round

lightweight
square

scoop

draining

Figure 5   Shovels

Shovels

Country	Manufacturer	Implement				
		Square end	Round end	Light-weight	Scoop shovel	Draining shovel
Belgium	S.A. Chanic	●				
Brazil	Acotupy Industrias Metalurgicas Ltd	●	●			●
Chile	Famae	●	●	●	●	●
Germany	Schwabische Huttenwerke GmbH	●	●	●	●	●
Kenya	Datini Mercantile Ltd	●	●			
Nepal	Agricultural Tools Factory Ltd	●	●			
Peru	Herramientas S.A.	●	●	●	●	
	Fahena S.A.		●	●	●	
Portugal	Verdugo — Ernesto L. Matias	●	●		●	
Spain	Patricio Echeverria S.A.	●	●	●	●	
Sri Lanka	Kanthi Industries	●	●			
Tanzania	Ubungo Farm Implements Manuf. Co. Ltd	●	●			
UK	The Stockton Heath Forge Ltd	●	●	●	●	
	Alfa-Laval Agri Ltd	●	●	●	●	
	Bulldog Tools Ltd	●	●	●	●	
USA	Seymour Manufacturing Co. Inc	●	●	●	●	

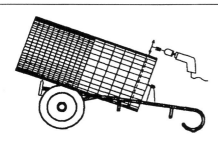

MULTI-PURPOSE HAND CART

This comprises a tubular frame with two pneumatic-tyred wheels. The frame is 500mm wide and various attachments allow it to be put to different uses. These include: *barrel*, capacity 300 litres; *stretcher, barrow*, capacity 80 litres;

platform, 1.6 x 600mm.
Unladen weight 12kg
Maximum load 100-150kg.

MŰSZAKI INTÉZET GÖDÖLLŐ
Tessedik S. u. 4.
2100
HUNGARY

SACK TRUCK

One of a range of sack trucks, this model is made of tubular steel, weighs 6.3kg and has a capacity of 100kg. It has a folding footiron and is mounted on cushion tyred wheels. Hardwood models, aluminium models, all-metal models are also available.

H.C. SLINGSBY PLC
Preston Street
Bradford
Yorks BD7 1JF
UK

A similar truck is manufactured by:

AGRICULTURAL TOOLS FACTORY LTD
P.O. Box No. 2
Birganj
NEPAL

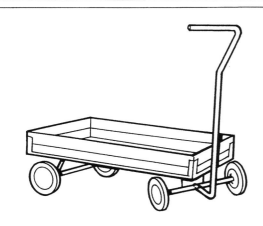

TURNTABLE TRUCK

There is a range of trucks mounted on four wheels with pull handle and wooden platform. This model is made of softwood with tubular steel pull handle and is designed for light loads up to 100kg. A further eight models made of heavy duty hardwood and cast iron are available, which are able to carry loads up to 500kg.

H.C. SLINGSBY PLC
Preston Street
Bradford
Yorks BD7 1JF
UK

PIONEER EQUIPMENT INC.
16392 Western Road
Dalton
OH
44618
USA

PLATFORM TRUCK

The carrying capacity of this type of truck is greater than that of the sack truck. The castor wheels give the truck good manoeuvrability.

H.C. SLINGSBY PLC
Preston Street
Bradford
Yorks BD71JF
UK

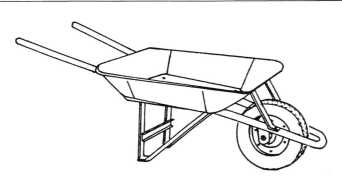
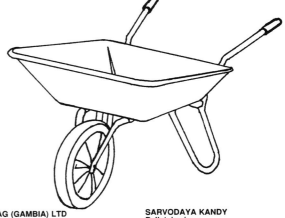

WHEELBARROWS

All the manufacturers listed below offer wheelbarrows which closely follow the traditional design. A frame, usually of tubular steel, which supports the body also provides two handles and the mounting for a single wheel. The materials used for the body can include wood, metal sheet or plastic moulding. The wheels can be of iron, solid rubber tyred or pneumatic tyred.

APICOMA
Zone Industrielle de Kossodo
B.P. 2085
Ouagadougou
BURKINA FASO

FAMAE
Casilla 4100
Santiago
CHILE

THE CHILLINGTON TOOL CO. LTD
71-73 Carter Lane
London EC4V 5EQ
UK

RWANDEX-CHILLINGTON S.A.R.L.
B.P. 356
Kigali
RWANDA

GEORGE H. ELT LTD
Eltex Works
Bromyard Road
Worcester WR2 5DN
UK

H.C. SLINGSBY PLC
Preston Street
Bradford
Yorks BD7 1JF
UK

MEKINS AGRO PRODUCTS (PVT) LTD
6-3-866/A Begumpet
Greenlands
Hyderabad
500 016
INDIA

EAGLE ENGINEERING COMPANY
35 Chittaranjan Avenue
Calcutta
700 012
INDIA

KUMAON NURSERY
Ramnagar
Nainital
U.P.
244 715
INDIA

ESCAPAG (GAMBIA) LTD
B.M.P. 37
Banjul
GAMBIA

DATINI MERCANTILE LTD
Enterprise Road
Box 45483
Nairobi
KENYA

KOREA FARM MACH. & TOOL IND. CO-OP
11-11 Dongja-Dong
Youngsan-Gu
Seoul
KOREA

CHAMIKARA ENGINEERING SERVICES
No.126 Kandy Road
Matale
SRI LANKA

COBEMAG
B.P. 161
Parakou
REPUBLIC OF BENIN

SARVODAYA KANDY
Palletalawinne
Katugastota
Kandy
SRI LANKA

AGRICULTURAL TOOLS FACTORY LTD
P.O. Box No. 2
Birganj
NEPAL

FAHENA S.A.
Calle Las Fraguas 191
Urb. El Naranjal
Lima 31
PERU

HERRAMIENTAS S.A.
Materiales 2215
Lima 1
PERU

THE CHILLINGTON TOOL CO. (UGANDA) LTD
P.O. Box 1391
Jinja
UGANDA

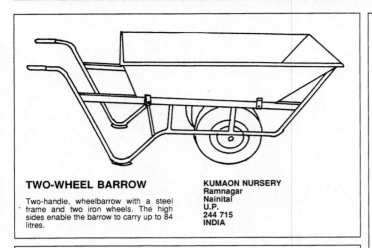

TWO-WHEEL BARROW

Two-handle, wheelbarrow with a steel frame and two iron wheels. The high sides enable the barrow to carry up to 84 litres.

KUMAON NURSERY
Ramnagar
Nainital
U.P.
244 715
INDIA

FOOD BARROW

This food barrow is made of galvanized steel. It can be supplied with any of three types of front wheels: 20mm solid rubber, 355mm solid rubber and 355mm pneumatic tyres. The rear wheel is of jockey type for steering. Capacity 260 litres.

GEORGE H. ELT LTD
Eltex Works
Bromyard Road
Worcester
WR2 5DN
UK

H.C. SLINGSBY PLC
Preston Street
Bradford
Yorks
BD7 1JF
UK

SELF-LOADING MOTORIZED WHEELBARROWS

This self-propelled and self-loading wheelbarrow is fitted with a 3.75kw four-stroke petrol engine. The engine drives the motor-cultivator type wheels via a centrifugal transmission. Forward and reverse gears are provided and the differential can be locked to aid the machine over difficult ground or when loading.

When loading, the whole machine is tilted forwards and the operator drives the front edge of the barrow into a heap of bulk material such as sand, gravel or grain. The machine is then returned to a horizontal position and reversed out of the heap with the barrow filled. Unloading is achieved by releasing a catch holding the pivoted barrow body and tipping it forward. Capacity 180 litres.

COVEM INDUSTRIE
49, rue Jules-Ferry
91390 Morsang/Orge
FRANCE

A-15/6 SELF-POWERED WHEELBARROW
This machine has a tubular steel chassis and a sheet steel barrow. A 3.75kW petrol engine drives the main wheels via a gearbox with three forward speeds and two reverse. A third wheel is mounted at the back of the chassis on a freely rotating castor to allow steering. Maximum load 800kg.

CAVAGION
Stellata PO (FE)
44010
ITALY

WATER BARROW

This barrow has been designed to help with the problem of carrying the water required for domestic use over considerable distance and rough ground. A tubular steel frame which supports four large spherical flasks is fitted with a large diameter single wheel mounted high in the frame, which lowers the centre of gravity thus making the barrow more stable. Six flask models are also manufactured.

APICOMA
Zone Industrielle de Kossodo
B.P. 2085
Ouagadougou
BURKINA FASO

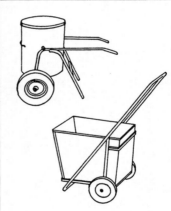

WATER BARROWS

The water container is galvanized and can be lowered to the ground and released from the chassis without lifting. The barrow can have pneumatic or solid rubber tyres. Capacity 133 litres.

GEORGE H. ELT LTD
Eltex Works
Bromyard Road
Worcester WR2 5DN
UK

Similar barrows are manufactured by:

JETMASTER (PVT) LTD
P.O. Box 948
Harare
ZIMBABWE

H.C. SLINGSBY PLC
Preston Street
Bradford
Yorks BD7 1JF
UK

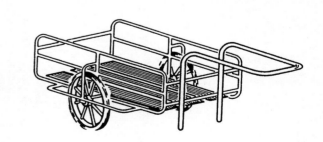

HAND CART

This cart comprises a tubular steel chassis and side rails, wooden load deck and spoked pneumatic-tyred wheels.

APICOMA
Zone Industrielle de Kossodo
B.P. 2085
Ouagadougou
BURKINA FASO

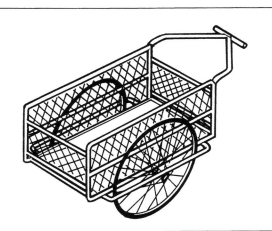

HAND CART

This cart comprises a tubular steel chassis and side rails, wooden load deck and spoked pneumatic-tyred wheels. The sides, front and rear panels are sheeted with wire mesh.

TEMDO
P.O. Box 6111
Arusha
TANZANIA

Similar carts are manufactured by:

UPROMA
B.P. 1086
Lomé
TOGO

COBEMAG
B.P. 161
Parakou
REPUBLIC OF BENIN

SMALL ANIMAL-DRAWN CART

Suitable for single animal draught (e.g. mule or donkey), this cart is equipped with a tubular steel chassis and railings, wooden platform and spoked pneumatic-tyred wheels.

TROPIC
B.P. 706
Douala
CAMEROON

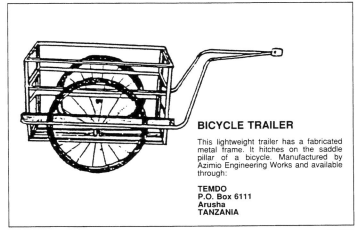

BICYCLE TRAILER

This lightweight trailer has a fabricated metal frame. It hitches on the saddle pillar of a bicycle. Manufactured by Azimio Engineering Works and available through:

TEMDO
P.O. Box 6111
Arusha
TANZANIA

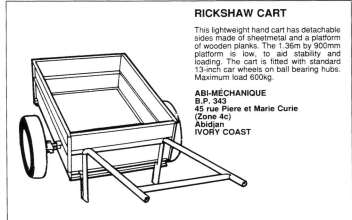

RICKSHAW CART

This lightweight hand cart has detachable sides made of sheetmetal and a platform of wooden planks. The 1.36m by 900mm platform is low, to aid stability and loading. The cart is fitted with standard 13-inch car wheels on ball bearing hubs. Maximum load 600kg.

ABI-MÉCHANIQUE
B.P. 343
45 rue Piere et Marie Curie
(Zone 4c)
Abidjan
IVORY COAST

UTILITY CART

This general purpose cart is fitted with steel wheels on hubs with bearings. The wooden body has removable ends and sides and the drawbar is suitable for tractor or animal draught. Weight 215kg.

ISICO
P.O. Box 417
Mbabane
SWAZILAND

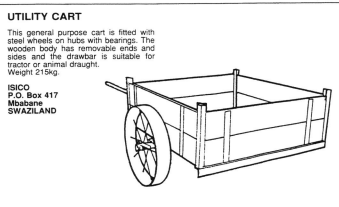

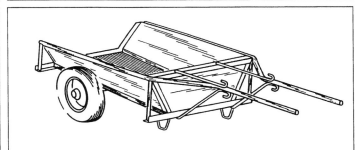

DUMP CART

This is a 500kg capacity cart which can be drawn by a single animal. The cart has sheet-metal floor with similar side and front panels which are bolted to an angle-iron frame. The rear panel can be detached for unloading purposes.

C.....A.
B.P. 7240
Ouagadougou 03
BURKINA FASO

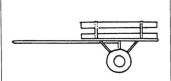

DONKEY CART

The cart frame is constructed from square-section steel tube and the wooden platform and side panels are bolted into place. The pneumatic-tyred wheels run on taper roller bearings.

TROPIC
B.P. 706
Douala
CAMEROON

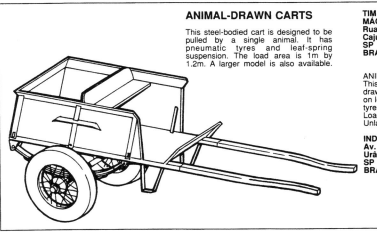

ANIMAL-DRAWN CARTS

This steel-bodied cart is designed to be pulled by a single animal. It has pneumatic tyres and leaf-spring suspension. The load area is 1m by 1.2m. A larger model is also available.

TIM INDÚSTRIA E COMÉRCIO DE MÁQUINAS AGRÍCOLAS LTDA
Rua 7 de Septembro, 600
Cajuru
SP
BRAZIL

ANIMAL-DRAWN CART
This company produce a range of animal-drawn carts. The cart bodies are mounted on leaf-springs, are fitted with pneumatic tyres and have lever-operated brakes. Load capacity is 1000kg. Unladen weight 200kg.

INDÚSTRIA PIGARI
Av. Aliexo Pigari, 665
Urânia
SP
BRAZIL

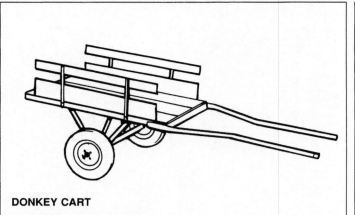

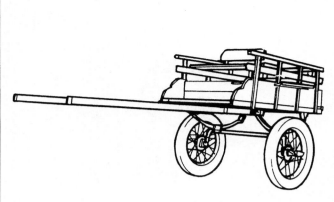

DONKEY CART

This steel framed cart is designed to be pulled by a single donkey or mule. The cart has a wooden deck and provision for fitting side posts. Maximum load 1000kg. Unladen weight 200kg.

APICOMA
Zone Industrielle de Kossodo
B.P. 2085
Ouagadougou
BURKINA FASO

Similar carts are manufactured by:

SISMAR
20 rue Dr. Thèze
3214
Dakar
SENEGAL

A.F.M.A.
B.P. 11 619
Niamy
NIGER

HERCULANO ALFAIAS AGRICOLAS
Loureiro
Oliveira de Azemeis
3720
PORTUGAL

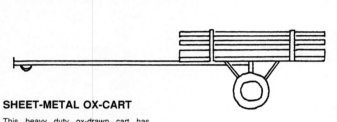

SHEET-METAL OX-CART

This heavy duty ox-drawn cart has pneumatic-tyred wheels and is capable of carrying a load of 1500kg. The sheet metal load deck is 2.4m by 1.5m (wheel track is 1.4m).
Unladen weight 220kg.

SISMAR
20 rue Dr. Thèze
3214
Dakar
SENEGAL

TWO-WHEEL ANIMAL-DRAWN CART

This cart can be used to carry up to four people or a maximum load of 500kg. The pneumatic-tyred wheels are fitted to a high ground clearance axle which is mounted on leaf springs.
Unladen weight 135kg.

DUTRA INDÚSTRIAS REUNIDAS
LTDA
Praca Arthur Bernardes, 33
Araxa
Minas Gerais
BRAZIL

A similar cart is manufactured by:

INDUSTRIAS ZEMA LTDA
Pres. Olegario Maciel, 111
B.P. 150
Araxa
Minas Gerais
BRAZIL

A similar cart is manufactured by:

HERCULANO ALFAIAS AGRICOLAS
Loureiro
Oliveira de Azemeis
3720
PORTUGAL

DONKEY CART

This two-wheeled donkey cart has a mild steel frame and wooden panels. It is fitted with 14 inch car tyres on steel rims with bronze bush hubs. Fitted with a hand operated band brake. Load-space is 1.2m x 950mm. The cart was designed by the Department of Agricultural Engineering, University of Nairobi.
Manufactured by:

GUY ENGINEERING WORKS
P.O. Box 466
Kikuyu
KENYA

SCOTCH CARTS

'HAKA' SCOTCH CART
This steel bodied cart can be supplied in the following configurations: bearing axles and pneumatic tyres; bushed axles and pneumatic tyres; bushed axles and steel wheels. Load area is 1.8m by 1.2m and the carrying capacity is one tonne. The tailgate is bottom hinged. Track width 1430mm.
Unladen weight 230kg.

TINTO INDUSTRIES
P.O. Box 2356
Harare
ZIMBABWE

OX-DRAWN WATER CART/SCOTCH CART
This Scotch cart which can easily be converted into a trailer has a non-corrosive 420-litre water tank for general farm use. It has a fully treated wooden drawbar, reinforced angle iron frame, sealed taper roller axle bearings and stud axles allowing high clearance for cambered roads. It also has a driver platform. Capacity 500kg.

ZFE COMPANY (PVT) LTD
P.O. Box 1180
Harare
ZIMBABWE

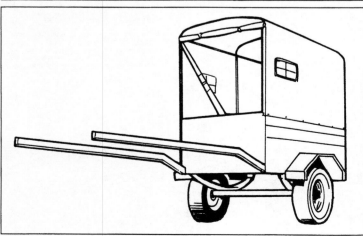

ANIMAL-DRAWN COVERED CART

This cart is made with a wooden floor and steel sheet sides and mudguards. It is equipped with pneumatic-tyred wheels which are mounted on a sprung axle. An adjustable upholstered seat and a waterproof canvas canopy are included. A toolkit is offered as an optional extra and includes: wheel-brace, tyre-pump, pliers, screwdriver, hammer, shovel, axe, cutlass and pickaxe.

E. GHERARDI E HIJOS S.A.
Florida 520 Piso 3° Oficina 318
1005 Buenos Aires
ARGENTINA

A similar cart based on the M.A.D. toolbar is made by:

FARM IMPLEMENTS (PVT) LTD
Box 55
Glendale
ZIMBABWE

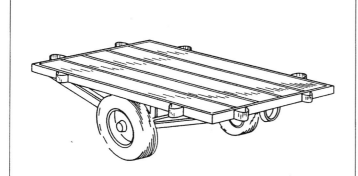

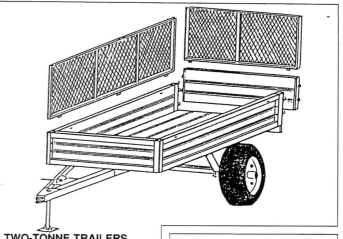

HEAVY DUTY OX-CARTS

This heavy duty cart has a 2m by 1.6m wooden deck on a steel frame. The deck is provided with mountings for wooden side posts and a single wooden drawbar. The cart is carried on steel wheels fitted with pneumatic tyres which are mounted on a rigid axle. The maximum load is 1500kg.

APICOMA
Zone Industrielle de Kossodo
B.P. 2085
Ouagadougou
BURKINA FASO

Similar carts are manufactured by:

ABI-MÉCHANIQUE
B.P. 343
45 rue Piere et Marie Curie
(Zone 4c)
Abidjan
IVORY COAST

OX-CART
This ox-cart can be supplied with iron wheels or pneumatic-tyred wheels. Capacity 1000kg.
Unladen weight 180kg.

MEKINS AGRO PRODUCTS (PVT) LTD
6-3-866/A Begumpet
Greenlands
Hyderabad
500 016
INDIA

AGRICULTURAL ENGINEERS LTD
Ring Road Industrial Area
P.O. Box 12127
Accra North
GHANA

AGRO MACHINERY LTD
P.O. Box 3281
Bush Rod Island
Monrovia
LIBERIA

TWO-TONNE TRAILERS

The trailer is built to be pulled by a small tractor. It has detachable sides and ends which can be extended with mesh panels for use with lightweight but bulky loads such as hay. The trailer uses steel wheels and heavy duty pneumatic tyres. The load deck is 2.36m by 1.5m (wheel track is 1.4m).

ABI-MÉCHANIQUE
B.P. 343
45 rue Piere et Marie Curie
(Zone 4c)
Abidjan
IVORY COAST

A similar trailer is manufactured by:

S.M.E.C.M.A.
Zone Industrielle
Route de Sotuba
B.P. 1707
Bamako
MALI

WATER TANK CARRIERS

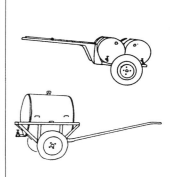

Sismar produce two animal-drawn water tank carriers.

The donkey-drawn 'Marnane' is equipped with two pneumatic-tyred wheels and carries two 200-litre drums held in place on the chassis with steel straps. Its unladen weight is 220kg.

The 'Super Marnane' is designed to be drawn by a single ox. The chassis is made from channel section steel and carries a single 800-litre water tank. Its unladen weight is 290kg.

SISMAR
20 rue Dr. Thèze
3214
Dakar
SENEGAL

A similar carrier to the Marnane is manufactured by:

A.F.M.A.
B.P. 11 619
Niamy
NIGER

'FERLO' HAY WAGON

This large ox-drawn cart has a capacity of 1500kg or 8m³ of hay. The platform is 2.6m long and 1.7m wide (wheel track is 1.4m). Two sizes of pneumatic-tyred wheels are available on request 600 x 19 or 185 x 14.
Unladen weight 340kg.

SISMAR
20 rue Dr. Thèze
3214
Dakar
SENEGAL

WAGON FOR DONKEYS OR OXEN

This four-wheel wagon can be drawn by two donkeys or oxen. The single central drawbar is complete with 'evener' and 'swingle trees'. Car hubs, rims and tyres are used, and the fabricated steel frame has a timber deck and topsides. Connection of the mainframe to the fore-carriage allows both horizontal and vertical flexibility. It has central pivot steering and rear drum brakes which are activated mechanically as in the hand brake of a car. Load space is 2.05m x 1.11m. The cart was designed by the Department of Agricultural Engineering, University of Nairobi. It is manufactured by:

GUY ENGINEERING WORKS
P.O. Box 466
Kikuyu
KENYA

ANIMAL-DRAWN WAGONS

This animal-drawn wagon can be supplied with bearing or bushed axles, both with pneumatic tyres on cast aluminium wheels. The wooden load deck is 3.6m by 1.8m with a carrying capacity of two tonnes. The wagon has friction turntable steering.

TINTO INDUSTRIES
P.O. Box 2356
Harare
ZIMBABWE

INDUSTRIA DE MAQUINARIA
AGRICOLA COLOSA S.A.
Casilla Postal 82 D
San Pablo 9460
Santiago
CHILE

FOUR WHEEL TRAILER
Fabricated from steel sections, this trailer can be drawn by tractor or animal. It has four bearing-mounted pneumatic-tyred wheels on sprung axles and friction turntable steering. The chassis is 4m by 1.05m and can be adapted for many uses and has a load capacity of four tonnes. Unladen weight 560kg.

FARM WAGONS

PIONEER FARM WAGONS
A range of five wagons, with load capacities from 6 to 12 tonnes and steel or pneumatic wheels, is manufactured by:

PIONEER EQUIPMENT INC.
16392 Western Road
Dalton
OH 44618
USA

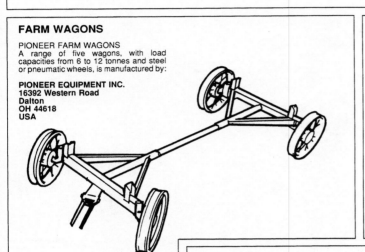

FARM WAGON
This is a wagon frame which has heavy spoked steel wheels running on tapered roller bearings, and 'Ackerman' steering. A telescoping central beam allows the wagon's length to be adjusted according to requirements. The wagon can carry loads of up to 6 tonnes. Accessories available include; wooden eveners and swingle trees; wooden neck yokes; steel clevises.
Height to top of axle 560mm.
Wheels 711mm diameter.
Unladen weight 250kg.

D.A. HOCHSTETLER & SONS
R.R.2 Box 162
Topeka
IN 46571
USA

SINGLE AXLE TRAILER

This two-wheel trailer has a load capacity of 350kg. A seat is provided for the driver and the trailer is fitted with both a footbrake and handbrake.
Unladen weight 162kg.

MOTOKOV FOREIGN TRADE
CORPORATION
Na strži 63
140 62 Praha 4
CZECHOSLOVAKIA

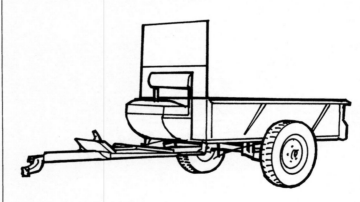

TRAILERS FOR WALKING TRACTORS

This company produce a range of trailers for attaching to 7.5-15kW walking tractors. The trailers are made from steel and are fitted with pneumatic-tyred wheels, and mechanically activated brakes. A tipping bodied trailer is also offered which requires the hydraulics of a conventional tractor to operate.

JIANGMEN AGRICULTURAL
MACHINERY FACTORY
25 Gangkou Road
Jiangmen
Guangdong
CHINA

A similar trailer is manufactured by:

AYUTTHAYA NANAPHAN
68/3 Moo 1, T.Pai-Ling
A.Muang
Ayutthaya
THAILAND

TRACTOR-DRAWN TRAILERS

The company produce a range of trailers for use with conventional tractors. These include two-wheel tipping and non-tipping trailers, a four-wheel water tanker (illustrated) and a four-wheel high-sided wagon with turntable steering.

AGRICULTURAL ENGINEERS LTD
Ring Road Industrial Area
P.O. Box 12127
Accra North
GHANA

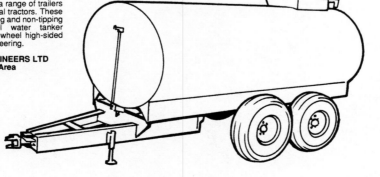

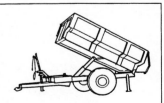

TRACTOR-DRAWN TIPPING TRAILER

Three-tonne single axle trailer with hydraulic tipping.
Unladen weight 550kg.

V.S.T. TILLERS TRACTORS LTD
P.O. Box 4801
Mahadevapura Post Office
Bangalore 560 048
INDIA

PORTABLE AUGER ELEVATOR

This 90mm diameter auger can be supplied in lengths for 3.1m to 10.7m. The shorter lengths can be handled by one person. The augers are driven by electric motor mounted at the head.

Capacities are in the range 2.6 to 3.3 tonnes/hour.

AUSTRALIAN AGRICULTURAL MACHINERY GROUP PTY LTD
P.O. Box 157
Belmont
WA 6104
AUSTRALIA

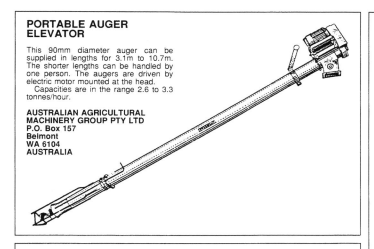

MOBILE AUGER CONVEYORS

These conveyors have bottom-mounted motors and inlet hoppers. They are supplied on a light four-wheel chassis to aid mobility and have hand winches to adjust the discharge height. The augers are available in lengths up to 13m.

PRESIDENT MOLLERMASKINER A/S
Springstrup
Box 20
DK-4300 Holbaek
DENMARK

Similar augers are manufactured by:

LAW-DENIS ENGINEERING LTD
Lavenham Road
Beeches Industrial Estate
Yate
Bristol BS17 5QX
UK

AUSTRALIAN AGRICULTURAL MACHINERY GROUP PTY LTD
P.O. Box 157
Belmont
WA 6104
AUSTRALIA

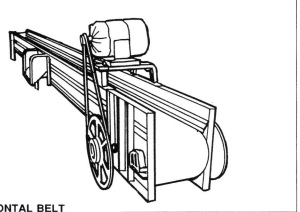

HORIZONTAL BELT CONVEYOR

This conveyor is powered by an integral electric motor unit. The discharge doors can be placed at any position along the length of the conveyor. Appropriate electric motors are supplied depending on the length of conveyor. Available in any length up to 45m.

COSSUL & CO. PVT LTD
123/367 Industrial Area
Fazalgunj
Kanpur
U.P.
INDIA

A similar range of conveyors is manufactured by:

LAW-DENIS ENGINEERING LTD
Lavenham Road
Beeches Industrial Estate
Yate
Bristol BS17 5QX
UK

MOBILE BELT ELEVATORS

COSSUL PORTABLE ELEVATOR
This elevator can handle all types of crops including maize, silage and bales of straw. A 530mm wide trough allows rapid handling of material. An electric motor drives the belt and fitted on a special mounting. A hand-operated winch is used to raise and lower elevator.

COSSUL & CO. PVT LTD
123/367 Industrial Area
Fazalgunj
Kanpur
U.P.
INDIA

MOBILE ELEVATOR
Available in seven sizes from 6-12m. The elevators can be set at 30, 40 and 50 degrees.

HINGHAUS MASCHINENFABRIK GmbH
Postfach 1148
Versmolder Str.
4503 Dissen am Teutoburger Wald
GERMANY

VERTICAL BUCKET ELEVATORS

These elevators are use for lifting granular materials, such as grain, to load hoppers or bins for example. They are constructed from steel and the buckets are fixed to a multiple-ply rubber belt. The elevators can be supplied in various different heights and capacities.

COSSUL & CO. PVT LTD
123/367 Industrial Area
Fazalgunj
Kanpur
U.P.
INDIA

Similar elevators are manufactured by:

ALVAN BLANCH DEVELOPMENT CO. LTD
Chelworth
Malmesbury
Wilts SN16 9SG
UK

AUTOMATIC BAGGER AND WEIGHER

Oriental workshops produce three models of this machine which automatically bags and weighs farm produce such as grain. It is able to handle loads of 1-15kg (Precision model) 5-50kg (Master model) and 10-100kg (Super model) with an accuracy of ±0.1%.

The bagging and weighing process is achieved through a balance assembly which is controlled by a piston set in an oil bath. The piston movements are damped by a rod and rocker mechanism which minimizes oscillations of the balance and speeds up the bag-filling operation.

ORIENTAL SCIENCE APPARATUS WORKSHOPS
Jawaharlal Nehru Marg
Ambala Cannt
Haryana 133 001
INDIA

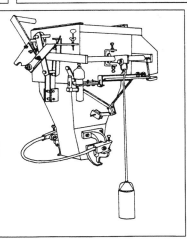

John Young/ITDG

9. LIVESTOCK HUSBANDRY AND HEALTH

It is a paradox that in developing countries, which raise most of the world's livestock (see Table 1) and where livestock forms the backbone of food production systems, most animal husbandry systems use few tools. Animals provide much of the power used in the world's agriculture. They also provide a significant proportion of the protein consumed by people.

An extensive range of equipment has been developed for large-scale intensive livestock production systems, but most of the smaller scale husbandry systems used by poorer livestock farmers in developing countries could not justify the use or support the cost of this equipment. What is attempted in these pages, therefore, is to highlight aspects of livestock health and husbandry which are essential to optimizing productivity, and to make reference to equipment which is available for this purpose and which could enhance lower-cost production systems. This chapter includes reproduction, rearing, feeding, general health care, and notes on milking and sheep shearing, particularly important non-destructive methods of harvesting animal products. Egg production is another non-destructive way of harvesting animal products.

REPRODUCTION

Poor control in maximizing the reproductive abilities of livestock is perhaps the cause of more losses than in any other sphere of livestock husbandry.

Record keeping

A major part of reproduction management is the keeping of accurate records. For instance, dairy cattle calving calendars can be used to remind stock keepers when cows last came into oestrus, when they are due to calve, and so on.

Identification

The ability to identify animals is, of course, important for

Table 1 Livestock populations in the world and developing countries (FAO, 1990)

Type of livestock	World (1000 head)	Developing countries (1000 head)	% in developing countries
Camels	19 072	18 792	98
Cattle	1 281 472	877 777	68
Buffaloes	140 028	139 346	99
Sheep	1 175 524	617 353	52
Goats	526 440	495 098	94
Pigs	846 174	499 467	59
Chickens	10 574 000	6 012 000	57
Mules	14 724	14 292	97
Horses	60 461	44 106	73
Donkeys	43 201	41 612	96

many reasons and is the initial step required in any scheme to improve the productivity of livestock. Table 2 gives a number of identification methods available for animals.

Ear tags are perhaps one of the most widely used methods of identification and are available in both plastic and aluminium. Some companies will provide an individual herd identification of each animal. The one major disadvantage is that they can be pulled or torn out and are therefore likely to have to be replaced from time to time.

Tattooing is also widely used in some countries. The initial cost of the instrument is relatively high but if well looked after one instrument should last for many years. The main advantage of the system is that, if properly used, the tattoo should last for the lifetime of the animal. The disadvantages include the fact they may be difficult to see in dark skinned animals. It is also necessary to catch the animal in order to be able to identify it. It is possible to tattoo in the caudle fold, but it is a method which is less frequently employed than ear tattooing.

Table 2 Identification methods available for animals

	Cattle/ buffalo	Sheep/ goats	Pigs	Poultry	Horses
Ear tags	●	●	●	(wing)	-
Tattoos (ear)	●	●	●	-	-
Leg bands	●	●	-	●	-
Branding	●	-	-	-	●
Ear notching	-	-	●	-	-
Hair/fleece marking	●	●	●	-	-

Leg bands are sometimes used to identify dairy animals when coming through a parlour to be milked, and they are occasionally used on other species as well. Different colours, as well as letters and numbers, can be used to help with identifying particular groups of animals.

Tail bands are also used, particularly in the cattle industry, for the identification of groups of animals.

The traditional *hot branding* of livestock, particularly cattle, is widely used in many countries and results in a permanent scar on the skin. Its main disadvantage lies in the damage to the hide which may be used to make leather.

Freeze-branding using liquid nitrogen is increasing in popularity and is relatively painless, but requires rather more expensive equipment than that for hot branding, including the provision of a liquid nitrogen source.

Hoof branding of horses is carried out in some countries and this is done with a hot iron placed directly on a horse's hoof immediately below the coronet. The brand will obviously grow out with the hoof and will need replacing from time to time.

Ear notching is used in a number of species, but particularly in pigs, to identify animals from different litters. The principal disadvantage of this method is that occasionally the ears get torn and so the ear notches are obliterated.

Marking is widely used for the semi-permanent identification of sheep and other animals — with dye in a paint, wax stick or aerosol spray.

Heat (oestrus) detection

The detection of oestrus in livestock is one of the most important methods of maximizing reproduction. In cattle and goats oestrus is monitored by changes in behaviour. The marking of ewes that have been served by a ram, by means of a raddle attached to the brisket of the ram with a harness, greatly aids the monitoring of mating. The colour of the raddle should be changed every 17 days so as to identify those ewes which are served more than once. It is of principal use in countries away from the equator where there is a distinct reproductive season.

Horses are usually hand-mated and the detection of oestrus in this species is normally done by leading the mare past the stallion and noting the reaction. This method is called teasing.

Sows, when housed next door to a boar, will lie along the fence adjacent to the boar's pen, if they are in oestrus.

Artificial insemination

The use of artificial insemination as a means of reducing the number of entire males and of improving their quality is being increasingly used in most countries. Semen can either be stored chilled at about 4°C, in which case its life is limited to a few days, or stored frozen, usually in liquid nitrogen, which prolongs its life indefinitely. The processing and freezing of cattle semen presents few, if any, problems; that of goats was until recently much more difficult but these problems have largely been overcome. The same is not true of sheep and pig semen which are still usually not frozen. The processing of semen requires relatively complex equipment and is outside the scope of this guide.

Frozen semen is usually stored in either straws or pellets and is kept frozen in flasks of liquid nitrogen until immediately prior to being used. Although modern cylinders do not have to be refilled for up to four months it is important to secure a reliable source before embarking on the keeping of frozen semen.

Provided that suitable training is available, insemination itself requires little or no equipment except for a 'gun' to introduce the semen into the cervix and expel the semen from the straw, and, for smaller species, a speculum to guide the semen into the cervix.

Care of the pregnant animal

Pregnancy diagnosis in cattle and horses is usually done manually by palpation of the uterus through the rectum. In

Farmer being shown how to drench a cow

Table 3 Comparison of reproduction data for goats, sheep, cattle and buffaloes

	Goats	Sheep	Cattle	Buffaloes
Age at puberty: male	4-5	7-8	6-10	18
(months) female	4-5	4-15	6-10	13-19
Age at 1st service: male	6-7	9-12	12	18
(months) female	7-18	9-18	14-22	14-25
Seasonable reproduction	Yes	Yes	No	No
Oestrus cycle (days)	18-21	17	21	21
Duration of oestrus (hours)	36-96	36	18	11-72
Time of ovulation in	36-48	18-40	14	-
relation to oestrus (hours)	after	after	after	
	beginning	beginning	end	
Length of gestation (days)	150	147	280	310
Dependence on corpus	Yes	No	No	-
luteum throughout pregnacy				
Silent ovulation at first cycle of breeding season	No	Yes	-	-
Signs of oestrus in	Yes	No	Yes	Few
absence of male				

sheep, goats and pigs ultrasonic pregnancy diagnosis detectors are available. The probe is either placed externally on the abdomen or introduced into the rectum. These instruments are constantly being improved, but already accurate pregnancy diagnosis is possible from a few weeks after service. Laboratory diagnosis of pregnancy can be achieved by measuring hormone levels in blood or milk. These methods are widely used for pregnancy diagnosis in cattle, horses and goats, but they require a certain amount of sophisticated laboratory equipment and technicians trained in their use.

Table 3 shows the comparative reproduction data for goats, sheep, cattle and buffaloes.

Incubation of eggs

The most useful method of incubating eggs is, of course, a live bird as either the real parent or foster parent. However, poultry incubators with varying degrees of sophistication, including automatic turning of the eggs, and controlled humidity, temperature and airflow, are available for all species.

Table 4 Gestation periods

Buffalo	10 months
Cattle	9 months
Sheep	148 days
Goats	151 days
Horses	11 months
Pigs	113 days
Chickens	21 days
Ducks	28 days
Geese	29-31 days
Turkeys	28 days

Parturition

Many deaths of mothers and newborn animals which occur at or immediately after parturition are avoidable given sufficient attention and equipment to deal with problems. The vast majority of animals will, of course, give birth without any outside interference and it is often a question of fine judgement as to when assistance is required. Table 4 shows the normal gestation period for domestic animals including poultry.

Birthing aids

Calving ropes are useful to aid difficult or delayed parturition

in cattle and horses and they may also be used in sheep and goats. The ropes can be attached to mechanical calf pullers, and these can be used to apply enormous force to the calf. In inexperienced hands they are, however, of considerable danger as, unless the reproductive canal is sufficiently open to allow the calf to come out, great damage can be done to both calf and mother.

On occasions where either the calf is seriously deformed or the reproductive canal is too small, embryotomy may be necessary. The usual method is to cut off parts of the foetus by means of embryotomy wire introduced into the uterus via a double tube, and operated from the outside.

Prolapse retainers

Before parturition, internal pressure from the increased size of the uterus may cause the cervix to prolapse. This must be replaced and held in position until the pressure is released at parturition. Various trusses and retaining aids are available for this purpose. A prolapse of the whole uterus may occur after parturition owing to continued contractions. If this can be replaced it may be held in position until the contractions stop. In this more serious type of prolapse, infection is highly likely.

Farrowing crates

In many intensive systems of pig husbandry, sows are confined in farrowing crates in order to reduce the risk of them lying on or otherwise damaging the piglets. This consists of a set of horizontal tubular rails which restrict the movement of the sow and allow the piglets into an escape area which is usually warmed with an infra-red light in order to attract them when they are not feeding.

Brooding cabinets and lamps

Poultry brooders are also available commercially. The main purpose of these are, of course, to allow temperature and humidity to be closely regulated in the early and most critical days of the chick's life.

REARING

Normally young animals are reared by their mothers. However, if the mother's milk is required for human consumption or the mother dies at parturition the young may have to be artificially reared.

David Hadrill/ITDG

Village animal health-care worker treating goat

Every effort should be made to ensure the young receive colostrum, the first milk produced by the mother, before being transferred to artificial milk replacer. A wide variety of teats, buckets and cafeteria systems are available for artificial rearing. If a newborn animal is very weak a stomach tube may be needed to introduce liquid food directly into the stomach.

If a foster mother is available it may be possible to persuade her to adopt an orphan. Lamb adopting crates can be used to secure a ewe while she becomes accustomed to a lamb and it acquires her smell.

CONCENTRATE FEEDING

A wide variety of equipment is manufactured for providing concentrated feed to animals. The range extends from simple troughs to complex conveyor feeding systems for intensively kept chickens. Only the simplest equipment is covered by this guide — that which might effectively reduce food wastage.

Very rarely will the diet of livestock be complete in all the minerals required for optimum performance. Minerals, especially salt, should be provided, and a number of patent dispensers are available for this purpose. Poultry, while producing eggs, can often benefit from extra calcium provided in the form of crushed sea shells, e.g. oyster shell. To avoid wastage this should be provided in a special container.

GRAZING

Most domestic animals forage for a large portion of their diet. Usually they are carefully herded. In some societies grazing control is exercised communally, but in many the only way of controlling grazing, and hence the productivity of fields and pastures, is through effective fencing, which also limits the range of animals.

Effective fencing is invaluable in both stock and grazing management. The erection of post and wire fences is made easier by the use of post-hole diggers. A post driver is easier for the inexperienced person to use than a sledgehammer and does not split the top of the fencing post. Wire strainers allow barbed and plain wire to be strained tight. Fencing pliers are invaluable for cutting and straining wire and for pulling out or knocking in staples.

Temporary electric fencing is an alternative to permanent fencing. Electric fencing systems are available which are easy to erect and may be run from mains battery supply. Solar-powered electric fences are becoming available.

In many areas living fences are used. These are fences made from closely growing plants with their branches interwoven to form an impenetrable barrier. Although requiring maintenance to ensure that holes do not appear, they have many advantages over other types of fencing including cheapness, use of local materials, and resistance to rotting. When a less permanent fence is required, thorn branches are often used. These have the disadvantage of being susceptible to termite attack, and seldom form a sufficient barrier for more than a season.

WATER

Provision of sufficient clean water will enhance productivity. The watering system chosen for any animal production system will depend on the source available.

If piped water is available then an automatic system will reduce the labour requirement. It must, however, be checked at regular intervals.

A pasture pump can be used to provide water from underground springs or nearby water sources. This simple pump will draw water from a depth of 8 metres and can be operated by the muzzle of an animal.

GENERAL HEALTH CARE: ROUTINE TASKS

Castrating, tailing, disbudding, de-horning, tooth-cutting, de-beaking and foot care are all regular husbandry tasks for which there is a range of equipment available. The most suitable equipment will depend on individual circumstances, and the species and age of the animals concerned.

Animal husbandry tasks are made easier by well thought out handling systems. These range in complexity from a simple bull nose-holder, through head bails to races and crushes in which the animal may be secured for treatment, be it foot trimming or drenching.

For sick or prone cattle there are a number of cow lifting devices available. These range from an inflatable cube to a winch which fits over the animal's pin bones.

Spraying equipment is used to apply insecticides to animals. Insects can be directly deleterious to animals because they are parasitic by nature or they may be vectors of disease.

Emergency treatment

Treatment of serious animal diseases should ideally be carried out by a trained veterinarian. In some countries, however, village animal health workers or 'paravets' are responsible for the notification of the presence of disease and for the implementation of the necessary control and preventative measures. They sometimes diagnose, treat and control diseases. The veterinary equipment covered in this guide is an example of the equipment which might be used by a paravet in the treatment and control of routine animal health problems. Some of the equipment might also be valuable to an informed stock-owner.

MILKING

The simplest method of milk extraction is, of course, hand-milking. If a milking herd or flock increases in size, or if it is desirable to machine-milk for reasons of hygiene, there is a range of small milking machines available.

The simplest machine-milking system consists of a pump to supply vacuum, a pulsator to regulate the alternate collapse and opening of the flexible rubber liners in each teat cup of the cluster, and lastly a bucket or churn into which the milk from the cluster is drawn under vacuum.

This system may be arranged in three ways:
○ The whole system may be mounted on a trolley for ease of mobility.

○ Completely mobile systems are also available in which the vacuum pump is separate from the milk storage vessel. The pump may be trolley-mounted or have a carrying handle.
○ Small vacuum pumps are available for use with an airline. The airline supplies vacuum to a bucket plant which is mobile.

Any milking machine should be designed to maintain the vacuum in the system at the recommended level and minimize vacuum fluctuations. The pulsators must operate at the pulsation rate and ratio of milking to non-milking phase recommended by the manufacturer. Pulsationless machines which work at continuous low vacuum are available. This method is said to ensure maximum milk extraction in minimum time. Milking machines are most commonly powered by electricity but many of the small models may be powered by a diesel or petrol motor. A hand-operated vacuum pump is also available for situations where no mechanical power source is available. This pump produces a continuous low vacuum for use with pulsationless milking equipment. Once milking is completed, milk should be cooled as quickly as possible to prevent the growth of any micro-organisms present. Small bulk tanks and in-churn coolers are available for this purpose.

Additional equipment will be required if the milk is to be processed further. Equipment for processing small quantities of milk is of limited availability. Cream separators and butter churns are supplied by a number of manufacturers but small-scale cheese- and yoghurt-making equipment and small cold stores are scarce and highly priced. Complete dairying installations can be provided by many companies but one company (Alfa-Laval Agri Ltd) specializes in small dairying plants for tropical and sub-tropical conditions.

SHEEP SHEARING

Hand-shearing equipment

This may vary in design and efficiency from simple pivot scissors to precision-made sprung blades of the finest steel. Long or short blades with single or double row bowspring designs are used. These are available wherever sheep are farmed and can be used for full shearing or crutching.

Mechanical shearing equipment

Normally these comprise of a handpiece, a drive-shaft and a source of power. Designs vary with technical progress; mechanical, electrical, electronic and air-powered equipment is available. The handpiece has an oscillating cutter and rigid comb which cuts in both directions. It is slim, lightweight and well balanced. Engineering tolerances are fine. The cutter crosses the comb at speeds of up to 6600 times per minute. The drive-shaft is flexible and made of gut, nylon core or steel shafting, and powered by a separate electric motor. Some earlier designs transmitted power through belt-driven steel shafts to a bank of shearing stands. There are some portable designs of shearing equipment which may be stand-alone, back-pack or fence-hung.

Power can be derived from any convenient source: internal combustion engine, generator or mains electricity. Even hand-cranked gearing has been used. Regular lubrication and maintenance is essential for trouble-free use. General-purpose and handpiece maintenance toolkits are required.

ADVANTAGES

The advantages of using specialist equipment in livestock production systems are to be found in reduced labour requirements or improved ease of operation and operator safety; in the reduction of waste; in the extension of livestock-keeping to people and areas where it has not been traditionally practised; and in the practice of animal health care by livestock farmers.

Equipment for animal handling falls into the first category. Properly constructed races and crushes, hurdles for sheep and bull holders for the safe handling of horned cattle can all improve the productivity and operator safety.

The reduction of wasted feed and water is best achieved by well-made feeders and watering devices. These will also reduce contamination of the feed and water and hence lower exposure to infection.

With suitable housing, animals such as poultry and rabbits can be kept in areas where traditionally this has been difficult, perhaps because of predators. Also the use of reproductive aids, especially artificial insemination, has enabled farmers to own maybe only one female animal and to have it serviced by a premier quality sire, enabling the farmer to raise calves of high potential and hence remain competitive.

Specialist veterinary equipment for dosing animals or for the treatment of minor ailments, if made available to trained livestock farmers, will enhance their animals' productivity. The most useful equipment is that which is adapted to fill a need rather than that which is transferred directly from intensive livestock systems to the less intensive systems of poor livestock owners.

ALTERNATIVES

Livestock husbandry requires few tools. Animals are kept in developing countries without recourse to any of the gadgets used in intensive livestock keeping. These gadgets may not be relevant because of a different scale of enterprise, the local climatic conditions or other circumstances. They may also require operating skills and technical back-up which is not available in developing countries. In addition, village-made equipment, particularly that for handling animals, may be most suitable to the need.

Livestock husbandry may often be improved through education and training with no additional equipment. Improvements in nutrition, hygiene and health care will enhance production, especially of milk, and breed improvements may raise productivity. New equipment is not essential to implement such changes.

Livestock can utilize land unsuitable for other forms of agriculture

David Hadrill/ITDG

ECONOMICS

The costs and benefits of using equipment in the keeping of livestock cannot be summarized in a general way. It is better to consider the desirability of livestock husbandry, which was well summarized by W.J.A. Payne in 1981:

The rationale for increasing livestock production, despite the fact that animals are inevitably relatively inefficient converters of basic materials and energy into human food, is based on the following considerations.

○ Livestock, particularly ruminants, can process forage and waste crop materials inedible by man into nutritionally desirable food products, many of high protein, mineral and vitamin content and including some of high calorific value.

○ Approximately 40 per cent of the total land available in developing countries can be used only for some form of forage production and a further 30 per cent is scheduled as forest with some potential for the production of forage. In addition, some 12 per cent of the world's total population live in areas where food crops cannot be easily grown and where people depend entirely on the products obtained from ruminant livestock.

○ Livestock provides, in addition to food products, additional outputs such as 'work energy', manure that can be used as fertilizer or a source of energy, and many other commodities useful to man, such as wool, hair and hides.

○ Animal, plant and human life are ecologically inter-dependent and the establishment of agricultural systems in which livestock are integrated with field crops, tree crops, forestry and aquaculture are essential for the improvement of overall unit land area productivity.

○ Livestock provides food products that add to the variety and nutritional quality of human diets and although it is possible for humans to exist without them, these foods are relished and sought after by the majority.

Given these overwhelming arguments for livestock production, the benefits of maintaining or intensifying the production through the introduction of equipment will need to be assessed at the macro as well as the micro level. For example, in certain areas it may be deemed desirable to protect livestock production systems which are becoming uneconomic because of, say, the pressure on land, by introducing concentrated animal feeds, possibly subsidized, in order to maintain supplies and to protect incomes. The wastage of these feeds can be minimized by using the appropriate feeder, which will benefit the individual farmer if the feeder is available at the right price.

Another example: if it is the policy of an administration to decentralize animal health care to individual farmers or farmers' groups then the provision of the correct equipment is essential. The pricing of inputs and outputs in this case will probably need adjusting in order to encourage take up of the health-care facilities.

In other words, equipment introduction is likely to be effected more by a system of direct or hidden subsidies than just by extending knowledge about and availability of the equipment.

IMPACT

The use of certain types of livestock equipment can displace labour and can make possible large-scale intensive production systems. It is a matter for policy makers to decide whether extensive or intensive systems should be developed. The problems of intensive livestock raising, which is dependent on imported or centrally produced feeds, is well known. For example, the crises for large-scale farmers in pig production in Jamaica or broiler production around Lima, Peru, stem from this dependence. There is, therefore, some advantage in protecting extensive, low-cost systems, particularly at a time of rising input costs.

However, if in the course of protecting these systems, productivity — particularly in terms of livestock numbers — increases beyond the carrying capacity of the land, or beyond the capacity of the market, a different and very serious crisis can develop for poor livestock owners. It is therefore essential that any new inputs to the livestock husbandry of poor farmers are accompanied by carefully worked-out policies for controlling production.

SPECIAL CONSIDERATIONS

Education and training facilities for improving the livestock husbandry and related skills of poor livestock owners need to be emphasized. Given the large numbers of poor people who depend on livestock for part or all of their income, improvements in their skills and knowledge of the inputs which are available to assist them could have considerable impact. Training and extension facilities for livestock farmers are available and more emphasis on providing these and providing the necessary new inputs at a reasonable cost should be given in the years to come.

Alastair Mews
Consultant

REFERENCES

W.J.A. Payne (1981) 'The desirability and implications of encouraging intensive animal production enterprises in developing countries' *Intensive animal production in developing countries,* occasional publication number 4, British Society of Animal Production, Edited by A.J. Smith and R.G. Gunn.

Information on sheep shearing derived from chapter on Wool Harvesting by Peter Steele in *Tools for Agriculture,* third edition (1985).

FAO (1990) *1989 Production Yearbook,* UN, Rome.

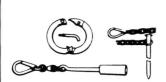

BULL-HANDLING EQUIPMENT

The handling equipment illustrated above includes a nose punch for punching the nasal septum through which the brass nose-ring is placed. To this may be attached the illustrated tethering and leading chains. They may be obtained from:

ANIMATICS LTD
Enterprise Road
Busia Road Corner
P.O. Box 72011
Nairobi
KENYA

ANIVET
1144 Budapest
Remény u.42
HUNGARY

C.H. DANA COMPANY INC.
Hyde Park
Vermont 05655
USA

ALFRED COX (SURGICAL) LTD
Edward Road
Coulsdon
Surrey CR3 2XA
UK

DALTON SUPPLIES LTD
Nettlebed
Henley-on-Thames
Oxfordshire RG9 5AB
UK

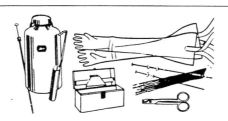

ARTIFICIAL INSEMINATION EQUIPMENT

When suitable equipment support services, liquid nitrogen supply and trained personnel are available, artificial insemination may be used to introduce superior blood lines or to supplement the services provided by local bulls when these are in short supply.
The equipment illustrated includes:
● Liquid nitrogen flask;
● Straws;
● Freezing racks;
● Sheaths;
● Insemination syringes;
● Plastic gloves.
Among many suppliers are:
ANIMATICS LTD
Enterprise Road
Busia Road Corner
P.O. Box 72011
Nairobi
KENYA

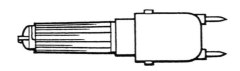

CATTLE PRODS

This battery-operated device is used for loading and moving livestock. A contact switch at the end of the stick causes a mild and harmless electric shock. The prod illustrated has a rubber hand grip, wrist thong and on-off switch. It is supplied by:

C.H. DANA COMPANY INC.
Hyde Park
Vermont 05655
USA

Prods with extension handles and covers are supplied by:

ALFRED COX (SURGICAL) LTD
Edward Road
Coulsdon
Surrey CR3 2XA
UK

BULL HOLDER

A bull holder such as the one illustrated above is useful for grasping a bull or large steer by the nose for treatment or handling. This holder, made of stainless steel with a slide adjuster, is supplied by:

ANIVET
1144 Budapest
Remény u.42
HUNGARY

ALFRED COX (SURGICAL) LTD
Edward Road
Coulsdon
Surrey CR3 2XA
UK

C.H. DANA COMPANY INC.
Hyde Park
Vermont 05655
USA

ALFA-LAVAL AGRI LTD
Oakfield
Cwmbran
Gwent
Wales NP44 7XE
UK

DALTON SUPPLIES LTD
Nettlebed
Henley-on-Thames
Oxfordshire RG9 5AB
UK

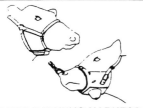

CATTLE-MATING HARNESS

These harnesses are used with coloured crayon or marking fluid and can be fitted on bulls to identify cows which have been served or to indicate those cows which are on heat. They are available from:

ALFRED COX (SURGICAL) LTD
Edward Road
Coulsdon
Surrey CR3 2XA
UK

RAM HARNESS

Ram harnesses enable tupped ewes to be identified with a coloured crayon, so that they can be grouped by expected lambing date. Suppliers include:

ALFRED COX (SURGICAL) LTD
Edward Road
Coulsdon
Surrey CR3 2XA
UK

ALFA-LAVAL AGRI LTD
Oakfield
Cwmbran
Gwent
Wales NP44 7XE
UK

C.H. DANA COMPANY INC.
Hyde Park
Vermont 05655
USA

DALTON SUPPLIES LTD
Nettlebed
Henley-on-Thames
Oxfordshire RG9 5AB
UK

SHEEP TRUSS

Trusses of this type, designed to support the uterus and prevent prolapse, are available from:

DALTON SUPPLIES LTD
Nettlebed
Henley-on-Thames
Oxfordshire RG9 5AB
UK

PLASTIC UTERUS SUPPORT

This simple plastic support is designed to prevent uterine prolapse on ewes close to lambing. It is supplied by:

ALFRED COX (SURGICAL) LTD
Edward Road
Coulsdon
Surrey CR3 2XA
UK

ALFA-LAVAL AGRI LTD
Oakfield
Cwmbran
Gwent
Wales NP44 7XE
UK

C.H. DANA COMPANY INC.
Hyde Park
Vermont 05655
USA

DALTON SUPPLIES LTD
Nettlebed
Henley-on-Thames
Oxfordshire RG9 5AB
UK

ANIVET
1144 Budapest
Remény u.42
HUNGARY

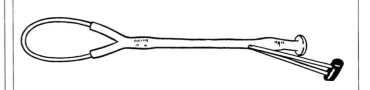

LAMBING INSTRUMENT

A lambing instrument of this type may be used in addition to ropes in a difficult lambing. The loop of the instrument is placed behind the ears of the lamb and tightened so that the 'V' rests under the jaw, thus giving a hold on the head. The lamb may then be manipulated to the correct presentation for delivery. Instruments of this design are supplied by:

ALFRED COX (SURGICAL) LTD
Edward Road
Coulsden
Surrey CR3 2XA
UK

ALFA-LAVAL AGRI LTD
Oakfield
Cwmbran
Gwent
Wales NP44 7XE
UK

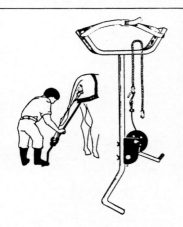

CALVING AIDS

A range of calving aids is available to enable one person to exert a greater pull on the calf during a difficult calving. Each design consists essentially of a frame and winching system. Considerable damage to both cow and calf can be done if such aids are used by unskilled stockmen.

FRANKLIN CALF PULLER
This unit comprises a ratchet-type puller, tubular steel rod, support strap and obstetric chain. It provides a 14:1 power ratio and can also be used as a hoist. It is supplied by:

C.H. DANA COMPANY INC.
Hyde Park
Vermont 05655
USA

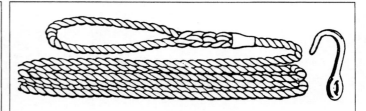

CALVING ROPES, OBSTETRIC PULLEYS AND HOOKS

Strong nylon calving ropes and other obstetrical aids may be required in the event of a difficult calving. Considerable damage can be done to both cow and calf if such aids are used by unskilled stockmen.
   Among many suppliers of this type of equipment are:

ALFRED COX (SURGICAL) LTD
Edward Road
Coulsdon
Surrey CR3 2XA
UK

ALFA-LAVAL AGRI LTD
Oakfield
Cwmbran
Gwent
Wales NP44 7XE
UK

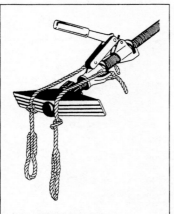

H.K. CALF SAVER

The principle of this calving aid is that it should supplement the natural birth contractions. The rubber head of the instrument is placed close to the cow's vagina and the nylon cords from each side of the ratchet are attached to the calf's pasterns. Each leg can be pulled separately, to optimize the presentation of the calf, and there is a quick-release mechanism, should complications arise.

C.H. DANA COMPANY INC.
Hyde Park
Vermont 05655
USA

ALFRED COX (SURGICAL) LTD
Edward Road
Coulsdon
Surrey CR3 2XA
UK

ALFA-LAVAL AGRI LTD
Oakfield
Cwmbran
Gwent
Wales NP44 7XE
UK

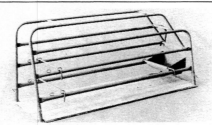

FARROWING CRATES

These are used to restrain the sow during the farrowing and lactation and to prevent her from crushing her young as she lies down. In a crate, the piglets are safe at the sides or end, where a lamp may be provided for warmth. The portable farrowing crate illustrated above is supplied by:

DAVID RITCHIE (IMPLEMENTS) LTD
Whitehills
Forfar DD8 3EE
UK

A similar farrowing crate is made by:

KATTLEWAY BERBAT (PVT) LTD
P.O. Box 489
Marondera
ZIMBABWE

LAMB ADOPTERS

These are used to secure a ewe whilst she is persuaded to adopt a lamb. The adopter illustrated above may be set up in any pen attached to a hurdle. It is manufactured by:

POLDENVALE LTD
Industrial Estate
Williton
Taunton
Somerset TA4 4RF
UK

ARTIFICIAL MILK FEEDING OF CALVES

A variety of teats are manufactured to suit the different methods of feeding milk to calves. From left to right above:
- A valved teat used to wean calves on to bucket feeding;
- Teats which attach to bucket (above) and bar feeders (below);
- Complete cafeteria system for feeding a number of calves simultaneously.

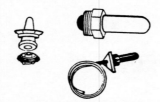

Suppliers of this equipment include:

ALFRED COX (SURGICAL) LTD
Edward Road
Coulsdon
Surrey CR3 2XA
UK

ALFA-LAVAL AGRI LTD
Oakfield
Cwmbran
Gwent
Wales NP44 7XE
UK

C.H. DANA COMPANY INC.
Hyde Park
Vermont 05655
USA

DALTON SUPPLIES LTD
Nettlebed
Henley-on-Thames
Oxfordshire RG9 5AB
UK

LAMB REVIVER

This is a simple bottle and tube which may be used to pass liquid food directly into the stomach of a lamb which is too weak to suckle. One of many suppliers of this reviver is:

DALTON SUPPLIES LTD
Nettlebed
Henley-on-Thames
Oxfordshire RG9 5AB
UK

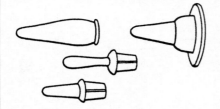

ARTIFICIAL FEEDING OF LAMBS

As for calves, a range of teats and feeders is produced for feeding lambs when ewe's milk is unavailable or insufficient. The equipment used will depend on the number of lambs to be fed and the time available. Supplies can be obtained from:

ALFA-LAVAL AGRI LTD
Oakfield
Cwmbran, Gwent
Wales NP44 7XE
UK

DALTON SUPPLIES LTD
Nettlebed
Henley-on-Thames
Oxfordshire RG9 5AB
UK

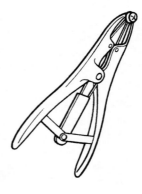

ELASTRATOR

This castrating and tailing tool may be used to castrate very young animals and to remove lambs' tails. The tool is used to apply elastic rings which cut off the circulation. This may be obtained from:

BOVITEC PRODUTOS AGRO-PERCUARIOS
Rua Duarte de Azevento, 449
São Paulo 02036
BRAZIL

A similar tool is available from:

ALFRED COX (SURGICAL) LTD
Edward Road
Coulsdon
Surrey CR3 2XA
UK

BURDIZZO BLOODLESS CASTRATOR

This castrator may be used on animals of all ages up to maturity. It is used to crush the spermatic cords. This equipment should be carefully serviced and adjusted so that the correct separation of the jaws is maintained. Suppliers include:

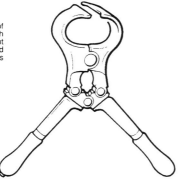

ALFRED COX (SURGICAL) LTD
Edward Road
Coulsdon
Surrey CR3 2XA
UK

C.H. DANA COMPANY INC.
Hyde Park
Vermont 05655
USA

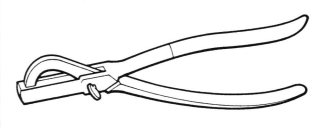

EMASCULATOR

Different designs of these bloodless castrators are supplied by:

ALFRED COX (SURGICAL) LTD
Edward Road
Coulsdon
Surrey CR3 2XA
UK

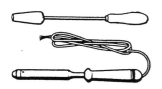

DISBUDDING IRONS

The disbudding of calves with a hot iron prevents the growth of unwanted horns. Two irons are illustrated:
- A simple hot iron, which must be heated in a fire;
- An electrically heated iron.

The calf should have a local anaesthetic before such irons are used. Disbudding irons can be obtained from:

ALFRED COX (SURGICAL) LTD
Edward Road
Coulsdon
Surrey CR3 2XA
UK

ALFA-LAVAL AGRI LTD
Oakfield
Cwmbran
Gwent
Wales NP44 7XE
UK

DALTON SUPPLIES LTD
Nettlebed
Henley-on-Thames
Oxfordshire RG9 5AB
UK

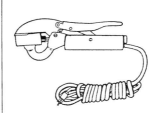

ELECTRIC DOCKER

This instrument for cutting and cauterizing lambs' tails is rustproof and heats in three minutes, using an electrical supply.

C.H. DANA COMPANY INC.
Hyde Park
Vermont 05655
USA

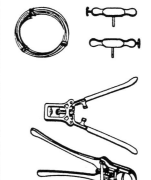

DE-HORNING TOOLS

If de-horning is necessary, the tools illustrated may be used. De-horning wire of two- or four-strand stainless steel may be used to saw through horn with the aid of special handles. Alternatively, powerful shears with a guillotine-like action may be used.
   Tools of this type are supplied by:

ALFA-LAVAL AGRI LTD
Oakfield
Cwmbran
Gwent
Wales NP44 7XE
UK

C.H. DANA COMPANY INC.
Hyde Park
Vermont 05655
USA

DALTON SUPPLIES LTD
Nettlebed
Henley-on-Thames
Oxfordshire RG9 5AB
UK

TOOTH-CUTTING FORCEPS

Tooth-cutting forceps like those illustrated above are used to cut the sharp canine teeth of young piglets. The forceps are available from:

ALFA-LAVAL AGRI LTD
Oakfield
Cwmbran
Gwent
Wales NP44 7XE
UK

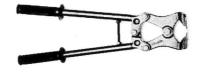

HOOF CUTTERS

The better designs of hoof cutters allow adjustment of the gap between the blades. The hoof cutters illustrated are available with replacement blades, or blades can be sharpened using a small flat stone. Hoof cutters like these can be obtained from:

ANIVET
1144 Budapest
Remény u.42
HUNGARY

C.H. DANA COMPANY INC.
Hyde Park
Vermont 05655
USA

DALTON SUPPLIES LTD
Nettlebed
Henley-on-Thames
Oxfordshire RG9 5AB
UK

FOOT ROT SHEARS

These are used to trim sheep's feet to remove infection and are supplied by:

ALFRED COX (SURGICAL) LTD
Edward Road
Coulsdon
Surrey CR3 2XA
UK

ALFA-LAVAL AGRI LTD
Oakfield
Cwmbran, Gwent
Wales NP44 7XE
UK

HOOF PARING KNIVES

These are supplied with a single or double edge and in right- and left-handed models by, among others:

ANIVET
1144 Budapest
Remény u.42
HUNGARY

ALFA-LAVAL AGRI LTD
Oakfield
Cwmbran, Gwent
Wales NP44 7XE
UK

SHEEP CRADLE

This cradle enables the stress-free examination and treatment of sheep; it is suitable for heavily in-lamb ewes. The device is rested against a wall, gate or hurdle and a cord attachment can be passed across the chest of the animal if necessary. It is available from:

ALFRED COX (SURGICAL) LTD
Edward Road
Coulsdon
Surrey CR3 2XA
UK

CATTLE CRUSHES AND HANDLING CRATE

Handling crates in which cattle may be held secure and immobile are valuable to simplify inspection and treatment. Some crates include a weighing facility whilst others are especially designed for easy foot-trimming, de-horning or castration. Crushes are supplied by, among others:

INDUSTRIAL MICHEL S.A.
Aviacion 1082
La Victoria
Lima 13
PERU

ANIVET
1144 Budapest
Remény u.42
HUNGARY

DAVID RITCHIE (IMPLEMENTS) LTD
Whitehills
Forfar
DD8 3EE
UK

LESLIE P. MORRIS LTD
Dale Street
Craven Arms
Salop
SY7 9NY
UK

MARTING MFG INC.
Washington Court House
OH 43160
USA

KATTLEWAY BERBAT (PVT) LTD
P.O. Box 489
Marondera
ZIMBABWE

CATTLE HEAD BAIL

This all-steel device traps the head of the animal in an adjustable ratchet grip. It has a left- or right-hand action and can be opened fully to allow cattle to walk through. It is supplied by:

WIRE MAKERS LTD
P.O. Box 244
Christchurch 4
NEW ZEALAND

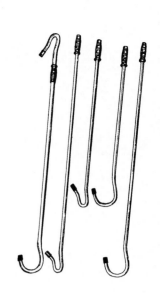

MOBILE SHEEP YARD AND TAILING PEN

The following companies offer a range of sheep pens with galvanized steel gates and hurdles. A typical basic unit, for 120 ewes with lambs, comprises twelve 1.5m gates, one 3m gate and one 0.6m gate.

BORAL CYCLONE EXPORT
P.O. Box 131
Mt Hawthorn
WA 6016
AUSTRALIA

PRATTLEY ENGINEERING LTD
P.O. Box 109
King Street
Temuka
South Canterbury
NEW ZEALAND

A range of sheep-handling equipment including hurdles, gates and crushes is supplied by:

POLDENVALE LTD
Industrial Estate
Williton
Taunton
Somerset
UK

SHEPHERD'S CROOKS

A large range of crooks is available from different suppliers. The range includes leg, neck and dual-purpose crooks, lightweight alloy versions and those especially designed for sheep-dipping. The range illustrated is supplied by:

ALFRED COX (SURGICAL) LTD
Edward Road
Coulsdon
Surrey CR3 2XA
UK

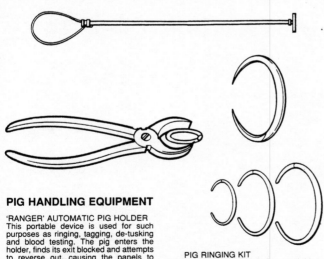

PIG HANDLING EQUIPMENT

'RANGER' AUTOMATIC PIG HOLDER

This portable device is used for such purposes as ringing, tagging, de-tusking and blood testing. The pig enters the holder, finds its exit blocked and attempts to reverse out, causing the panels to close around it.

HOG CATCHER

This is made of steel cable sliding through an outer tube. It is also suitable for cattle.

SORTING PANELS

Single or hinged panels can be useful in manoeuvring groups of small pigs. The steel panels are welded on to braced tubular frames.

ANIVET
1144 Budapest
Remény u.42
HUNGARY

MARTING MFG INC.
Washington Court House
OH 43160
USA

PIG RINGING KIT

A range of ringing pliers and hinged, stainless steel and copper pig rings is available from:

ANIVET
1144 Budapest
Remény u.42
HUNGARY

SEYMOUR MANUFACTURING CO. INC.
P.O. Box 248
500 North Broadway
Seymour
IN 47274
USA

ALFRED COX (SURGICAL) LTD
Edward Road
Coulsdon
Surrey CR3 2XA
UK

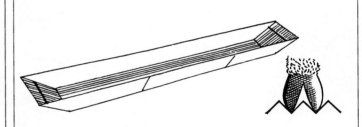

SHEEP FOOT BATH

Foot baths containing a disinfectant and astringent solution may be used in the control of foot rot in sheep. The foot bath should be placed in a race and the sheep made to walk slowly through it.

'BOVI JAK' COW LIFTER

This lifter is a cube-shaped balloon which may be inflated under a recumbent cow to lift her into an upright position for treatment and to assess her ability to stand on her own. It is manufactured by:

ALFRED COX (SURGICAL) LTD
Edward Road
Coulsdon
Surrey CR3 2XA
UK

THE ELTEX SHEEP FOOT BATH (illustrated) has a ridged bottom to force the cloven hoof apart as the animal puts its weight on the bath floor, ensuring that all parts of the foot are treated. (Copper sulphate solutions and acid must not be used in this galvanized bath.) It is made by:

GEORGE H. ELT LTD
Eltex Works
Bromyard Road
Worcester WR2 5DN
UK

Similar foot baths are available from:

POLDENVALE LTD
Industrial Estate
Williton
Taunton
Somerset TA4 4RF
UK

DAVID RITCHIE (IMPLEMENTS) LTD
Whitehills
Forfar DD8 3EE
UK

C.H. DANA COMPANY INC.
Hyde Park
Vermont 05655
USA

CATTLE RUB

This simple insecticide applicator comprises a length of orlon and acrylic padded rope which is loosely suspended between supports so that it will rub along the backs of cattle passing under it. The rope is then periodically soaked in the required insecticide solution. The rub is available in 1, 1.5 or 3m lengths.

FACE FLYPS

These are used in conjunction with the cattle rub to control face flies. When suspended along the length of the cattle rub, they absorb insecticide solution from the rope and wipe it over the face of cattle passing under it.

The cattle rub and face flyps are supplied by:

MARTING MFG INC.
Washington Court House
OH 43160
USA

C.H. DANA COMPANY INC.
Hyde Park
Vermont 05655
USA

ELECTRICALLY POWERED INCUBATOR

'POLYHATCH' EGG INCUBATOR
The following company offers a range of electrically powered, still air incubators, including the 'Polyhatch' with a capacity of 42 hens' eggs. It has electronic temperature control and automatic turning of all types of eggs.

BRINSEA PRODUCTS LTD
Station Road
Sandford
Avon BS19 5RA
UK

Similar electric incubators are available from:

PETERSIME INDUSTRIAL S.A.
Rodovia Municipal Km 3
Bairro São Pedro
Cx. Postal 151
Urussanga (SC) 88840
BRAZIL

LUBING INTERNATIONAL
66, Rue du Fief
Sailly-sur-la-Lys
Laventie 62840
FRANCE

CHINESE MECHANICAL EQUIPMENT
IMP/EXP CORP.
Hang Zhou
Xiao Shan
CHINA

MANUAL CATTLE SPRAYERS

The range of manual sprayers manufactured by the following company includes two models for stock treatment. Model LG-152 is a stirrup pump and LG-180 has a pressure vessel. Both are used in conjunction with a separate container for the spray fluid.

FUMIGADORAS TRIUNFO S.A.
Apartado 4045
Cali
COLUMBIA

KEROSENE-OPERATED INCUBATORS

These incubators are valuable where electricity is not readily available. The 'Amuda' kerosene-operated incubator illustrated has capacity for 150 eggs. A 450-egg model is also available. These incubators are complete with moisture tray, turning mechanism, thermometer and temperature-adjusting screw. They are supplied by:

DE-BEAKERS

Manual and electric de-beakers to prevent feather pecking and cannibalism are available from:

ALFRED COX (SURGICAL) LTD
Edward Road
Coulsdon
Surrey CR3 2XA
UK

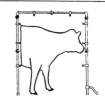

CATTLE-SPRAYING ARCH

This cattle-spraying equipment is designed to improve the ease and accuracy of applying insecticide sprays on to large numbers of stock. The pump can be powered by a 12-volt battery or through a tractor power take-off.

ALFRED COX (SURGICAL) LTD
Edward Road
Coulsdon
Surrey CR3 2XA
UK

RAJAN UNIVERSAL EXPORTS
(MFRS) PVT LTD
Post Bag 250
Madras 600 001
INDIA

The following company offers a low-cost incubator for 200 eggs. It is made of iron sheets, metal, cloth, wood, wire mesh and wire rods, and is heated by a kerosene lamp, with a thermostat to maintain 40°C temperature.

ANIMATICS LTD
Enterprise Road
Busia Road Corner
P.O. Box 72011
Nairobi
KENYA

POULTRY IDENTIFICATION

Padlock-type and numbered wing tabs for poultry are available in a range of colours. Spiral leg bands and poultry and turkey tags for legs are also available. Suppliers include:

ASE EUROPE N.V.
De Keyserlei 58 Bus 1
Century Centre
B-2018 Antwerp
BELGIUM

ALFRED COX (SURGICAL) LTD
Edward Road
Coulsdon
Surrey CR3 2XA
UK

GEORGE H. ELT LTD
Eltex Works
Bromyard Road
Worcester WR2 5DN
UK

FLOORING FOR DUCKS

Perforated, sectional flooring suitable for duck rearing and housing is available from:

LUBING INTERNATIONAL
66, Rue du Fief
Sailly-sur-la-Lys
Laventie 62840
FRANCE

PARAFFIN CHICK BROODERS

The brooding phase is a very vulnerable one for the young bird. Additional heat may be provided at this stage by paraffin brooders. These can be run relatively cheaply where no electricity is available.

THE DELTON PYRAMID BROODER
This brooder, illustrated, comes in a range of sizes with capacity for up to 200 day-old chicks.

GEORGE H. ELT LTD
Eltex Works
Bromyard Road
Worcester WR2 5DN
UK

ALI-BROODER
This low-cost, infra-red brooder uses standard lamp bulbs for heating. It is available from:

BRINSEA PRODUCTS LTD
Station Road
Sandford
Avon BS19 5RA
UK

Other types of electrically-powered brooder are supplied by:

TAYLOR-MADE SHEET METAL
PRODUCTS LTD
Box W99
Waterfalls
Harare
ZIMBABWE

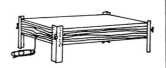

The following company produces two types of thermostatically controlled chick brooders for 100 or 200 chicks.
THE ELECTRIC HEN, illustrated, has a completely enclosed low-watt element, and adjustable legs to suit the size of the chicks.
THE STAR CHICK HEATER is an infra-red heating lamp.

GEORGE H. ELT LTD
Eltex Works
Bromyard Road
Worcester WR2 5DN
UK

POULTRY KILLER

This humane killer for poultry is bloodless and instantaneous. It is available from:

ALFRED COX (SURGICAL) LTD
Edward Road
Coulsdon
Surrey CR3 2XA
UK

CHICK DRINKERS

Simple poultry drinkers of the type illustrated are available from:

TAYLOR-MADE SHEET METAL PRODUCTS LTD
Box W99
Waterfalls
Harare
ZIMBABWE

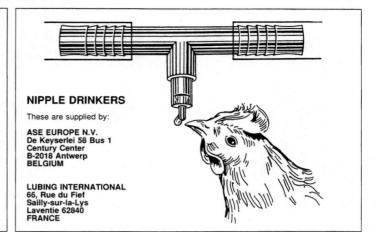

NIPPLE DRINKERS

These are supplied by:

ASE EUROPE N.V.
De Keyserlei 58 Bus 1
Century Center
B-2018 Antwerp
BELGIUM

LUBING INTERNATIONAL
66, Rue du Fief
Sailly-sur-la-Lys
Laventie 62840
FRANCE

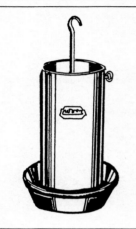

TUBULAR POULTRY FEEDERS

Hanging poultry feeders like the one illustrated are supplied by:

MOHINDER & CO. ALLIED INDUSTRIES
Kurali District
Ropar
Punjab
INDIA

GEORGE H. ELT LTD
Eltex Works
Bromyard Road
Worcester WR2 5DN
UK

TAYLOR-MADE SHEET METAL PRODUCTS LTD
Box W99
Waterfalls
Harare
ZIMBABWE

ALL-WEATHER FEED HOPPERS

All-weather feed hoppers are available for outdoor use. The hopper keeps water and vermin out.

GEORGE H. ELT LTD
Eltex Works
Bromyard Road
Worcester WR2 5DN
UK

CHICK FEEDERS

Small chick-feeding troughs are supplied by, among others:

MOHINDER & CO. ALLIED INDUSTRIES
Kurali District
Ropar
Punjab
INDIA

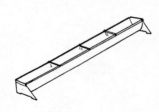

TROUGHS

Simple troughs in sizes to suit all farm species are sold by:

DAVID RITCHIE (IMPLEMENTS) LTD
Whitehills
Forfar
Scotland
DD8 3EE
UK

GEORGE H. ELT LTD
Eltex Works
Bromyard Road
Worcester WR2 5DN
UK

MARTING MFG INC.
Washington Court House
OH 43160
USA

TAYLOR-MADE SHEET METAL PRODUCTS LTD
Box W99
Waterfalls
Harare
ZIMBABWE

Portable water troughs and trough valves for piped water supplies are available from:

TUNNEL TECHNOLOGY LTD
Box 1
Koru
KENYA

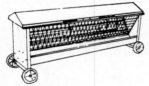

HAY RACKS

Small hay racks prevent fodder being wasted. They are supplied by:

POLDENVALE LTD
Williton
Taunton
Somerset TA4 4RF
UK

DAVID RITCHIE (IMPLEMENTS) LTD
Whitehills
Forfar DD8 3EE
UK

CIRCULAR FEEDERS

Use of circular feeders such as the one illustrated can reduce feed wastage and bullying. These feeders come in semi-circular sections making them portable and ideal for feeding cattle in many

locations. In the circular construction, they are free-standing and highly robust. Alternatively semi-circular sections may be used, backed by a fence.
The many suppliers of this type of feed barrier include:

POLDENVALE LTD
Industrial Estate
Williton
Taunton
Somerset TA4 4RF
UK

Circular feeders for feeding big round bales are available from:

DAVID RITCHIE (IMPLEMENTS) LTD
Whitehills
Forfar DD8 3EE
UK

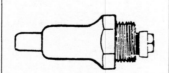

NIPPLE DRINKERS

Bite- and press-operated nipple drinkers for pigs and calves may be obtained from:

ALFA-LAVAL AGRI LTD
Oakfield
Cwmbran
Gwent
Wales NP44 7XE
UK

AUTOMATIC BOWL DRINKERS

These are available in many specifications for all species. They can be obtained from many suppliers, including:

ALFRED COX (SURGICAL) LTD
Edward Road
Coulsdon
Surrey CR3 2XA
UK

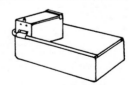

RE-FILLING TROUGHS

This type of trough, which may be used when piped water is available, is supplied by:

GEORGE H. ELT LTD
Eltex Works
Bromyard Road
Worcester WR2 5DN
UK

MARTING MFG INC.
Washington Court House
OH 43160
USA

'NO-TIP' MINERAL DISPENSERS

The reinforced rubber tube of this dispenser is held in a steel frame and protected by a polyethylene hood.

C.H. DANA COMPANY INC.
Hyde Park
Vermont 05655
USA

SALT LICK STAND

The two-in-one salt lick stand and mineral holder illustrated is manufactured in strong polypropylene and supplied by:

ALFRED COX (SURGICAL) LTD
Edward Road
Coulsdon
Surrey CR3 2XA
UK

MARKING STICKS

Marking sticks are available in a range of colours. These pocket-sized markers are wax crayons protected within a metal or plastic tube and are supplied by:

ANIVET
1144 Budapest
Remény u.42
HUNGARY

ALFRED COX (SURGICAL) LTD
Edward Road
Coulsdon
Surrey CR3 2XA
UK

ALFA-LAVAL AGRI LTD
Oakfield
Cwmbran
Gwent
Wales NP44 7XE
UK

C.H. DANA COMPANY INC.
Hyde Park
Vermont 05655
USA

AEROSOL SPRAY MARKERS

Special semi-permanent spray paints are available for livestock identification. They come in a range of colours which do not irreversibly mark the hide or fleece.

ANIVET
1144 Budapest
Remény u.42
HUNGARY

TAIL TAPE

Coloured and numbered adhesive tail tape for temporary identification is supplied by:

DALTON SUPPLIES LTD
Nettlebed
Henley-on-Thames
Oxfordshire RG9 5AB
UK

ALFRED COX (SURGICAL) LTD
Edward Road
Coulsdon
Surrey CR3 2XA
UK

ALFA-LAVAL AGRI LTD
Oakfield
Cwmbran
Gwent
Wales NP44 7XE
UK

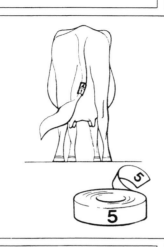

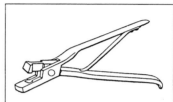

EAR MARKING PLIERS

These pliers are used to make identifying notches in the edge of the ear; several types are available, suitable for cattle or young lambs. They are supplied by:

DALTON SUPPLIES LTD
Nettlebed
Henley-on-Thames
Oxfordshire RG9 5AB
UK

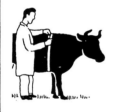

WEIGH BAND

Weigh bands make it possible to assess the approximate live or dead weights of cattle and pigs without the use of scales. The weigh band is placed around the animal's girth and its weight may then be read directly off the band against the linear girth measurement. Weigh bands are supplied by:

DALTON SUPPLIES LTD
Nettlebed
Henley-on-Thames
Oxfordshire RG9 5AB
UK

ALFRED COX (SURGICAL) LTD
Edward Road
Coulsdon
Surrey CR3 2XA
UK

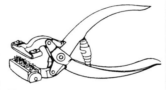

TATTOOING FORCEPS

Tattooing forceps for ear-marking rabbits, piglets, poultry, calves and lambs.

ANIVET
1144 Budapest
Remény u.42
HUNGARY

ALFRED COX (SURGICAL) LTD
Edward Road
Coulsdon
Surrey CR3 2XA
UK

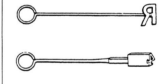

CATTLE BRANDING IRONS

Branding irons in any size or design are available from:

SHEET METAL KRAFT
14 Coventry Street
P.O. Box 1840
Bulawayo
ZIMBABWE

WEIGHING CRATES

Weighing crates are available to suit various farm animals including pigs, sheep and calves. They may rely on mechanical, hydraulic or electronic means of measurement. Suppliers include:

FAMIA INDUSTRIAL S.A.
Av. Heroes de la Brena 2790
Ate
Lima 3
PERU

ANIVET
1144 Budapest
Remény u.42
HUNGARY

KATTLEWAY BERBAT (PVT) LTD
P.O. Box 489
Marondera
ZIMBABWE

DAVID RITCHIE (IMPLEMENTS) LTD
Whitehills
Forfar DD8 3EE
UK

LESLIE P. MORRIS LTD
Dale Street
Craven Arms
Salop SY7 9NY
UK

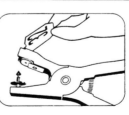

STOCK IDENTIFICATION TAGS

Two-piece plastic ear tags, attached as shown in the illustration, are supplied by:

ANIVET
1144 Budapest
Remény u.42
HUNGARY

ALFRED COX (SURGICAL) LTD
Edward Road
Coulsdon
Surrey CR3 2XA
UK

ALFA-LAVAL AGRI LTD
Oakfield
Cwmbran
Gwent
Wales NP44 7XE
UK

VETERINARY KIT FOR ANIMAL HEALTH AUXILIARIES

The equipment illustrated on this page might be used by an experienced Animal Health Auxiliary (under the supervision of a Veterinarian) in the prevention, diagnosis and treatment of simpler ailments. Preventative treatment might include the use of vaccines or serums given by injection.

In diagnosis, the animal's temperature, heart and respiratory rates are valuable signs in addition to visual symptoms. Even though A.H.As can do little more than recognize the more familiar symptoms of disease, they play an important part in routine collection of smears and specimens and in postmortem examinations.

An A.H.A. is able to administer drugs and medicines prescribed by a Vet. He can repair wounds and assist the Vet with more complex treatments.

The following companies are general suppliers of veterinary equipment:

ANIVET
1144 Budapest
Remény u.42
HUNGARY

ALFRED COX (SURGICAL) LTD
Edward Road, Coulsdon
Surrey CR3 2XA
UK

C.H. DANA COMPANY INC.
Hyde Park
Vermont 05655
USA

LABELVAGE
11, Avenue de Bellevue
Chatenay-Malabry 92290
FRANCE

ALFA-LAVAL AGRI LTD
Oakfield
Cwmbran, Gwent NP44 7XE
Wales
UK

TROCAR AND CANNULA

A trocar and cannula are used in extreme cases of bloat in ruminant animals. In cases where bloat cannot be relieved by less violent methods such as drenching with liquid paraffin or use of a stomach tube, the rumen must be punctured through the left flank of the animal to release the trapped gas.

STETHOSCOPE

A stethoscope may be used by a skilled person to listen to the heart and lungs of an animal, facilitating assessment of its health and condition.

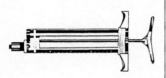

STERILIZABLE SYRINGES

Simple sterilizable syringes are manufactured in a range of sizes and with different needle mountings. They may be made of nylon, glass and metal or all metal.

THE EUROPLEX SYRINGE (illustrated above) will withstand wet heat up to 130-160°C. Syringes of this type are suitable for all types of injection.

MULTI-DOSE SYRINGES

The multi-dose syringe may be useful if a large number of injections are to be given. Two types of multi-dose syringe are available. The first, an example of which is pictured above, does not refill itself but will give a number of repeat doses by pressure on the trigger until the syringe is empty. The second type is refilled after each dose from a suspended canister.

SYRINGE NEEDLES

Needles are available for intravenous, hypodermic and intramuscular injection. Different methods of injection and size of animal demands a range of needles for different tasks. When possible, a freshly sterilized needle should be used for each animal to avoid transferring infection from one animal to another. The Luer lock needles (illustrated) lock on to special syringes. This prevents needles being dropped and lost.

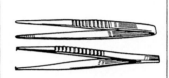

FORCEPS

Forceps are essential tools for precise delicate tasks. A variety of shapes and designs are manufactured to suit each task. For example, pointed splinter forceps, tissue forceps with teeth and angular dressing forceps. Forceps should be made of stainless steel.

SCISSORS

Scissors are required for a variety of tasks and hence a variety of designs are available. Dressing, dissecting and clipping all require sharp scissors. Dressing scissors should be of stainless steel and be kept clean.

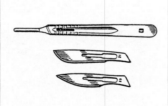

SCALPEL AND BLADES

Scalpels will be necessary if any dissection or surgery is to be undertaken. The blades are renewable and can be obtained in sterile packs in a range of designs and sizes.

SUTURE NEEDLES

These are supplied in a range of sizes in curved and half-curved shapes and with triangular or round points. They are made from stainless steel.

INSTRUMENT DISH

A stainless steel instrument dish such as the one illustrated above provides a clean surface on which to put sterile instruments.

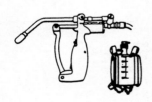

DRENCHING GUNS

Automatic refilling drenching guns like the one illustrated above are invaluable when a large number of animals are drenched routinely. The gun, which may be adjusted to dispense the desired dose, refills automatically from a canister which may be carried on the back or hung over a race.

DRENCHING BOTTLE

A simple drenching bottle is the most straightforward method of administering liquid medicine to animals. It enables the medicine to be poured directly into the animal's mouth.

Drenching must be performed carefully to avoid fluid passing into the animal's lungs. To this end, the animal's head is raised in line with the neck and the dose given slowly with regular pauses to enable the animal to swallow and breathe.

BALLING GUN

Balling guns are made in a range of sizes and types to administer pills or medicinal bullets to animals by placing them at the back of the throat.

The gun illustrated is specially designed to administer cobalt bullets to sheep. It is made of heavy gauge brass, is nickel plated and has a rubber mouthpiece. Balling guns are more difficult to use in pigs because the shape of the pig's throat tends to trap the bolus.

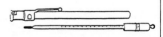

VETERINARY THERMOMETER

An abnormal body temperature is a good indication of a sick animal. Thermometers are available calibrated in Fahrenheit and Centigrade.

THE HOBDAY VETERINARY THERMOMETER (illustrated above) is marked with the normal temperature of the more common farm species (cow, pig, horse) as a reference. It should be noted, however, that normal temperatures will vary between healthy animals because of climate, oestrus, physical activity and food intake.

ANKLE STRAPS

Re-usable ankle straps for easy identification of dairy animals.

ALFRED COX (SURGICAL) LTD
Edward Road
Coulsdon, Surrey CR3 2XA
UK

DALTON SUPPLIES LTD
Nettlebed
Henley-on-Thames
Oxfordshire RG9 5AB
UK

HORN BRANDER

This device has interchangeable sets of letters and numbers, cast in a copper alloy. These castings have 22mm high characters, vented to prevent scorching and concaved to conform to the horn surface. The brander operates from an electricity supply. It is available from:

C.H. DANA COMPANY INC.
Hyde Park
Vermont 05655
USA

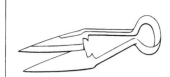

HAND SHEARS

Hand shears can be used for the complete shearing operation in small flocks or when it is desirable not to clip too closely. In larger flocks where mechanical shearing is employed, hand shears are useful for dagging and crutching operations. The illustration shows two popular designs of hand shears, the single-bow (above) and double-bow (above right). These are available from many suppliers including:

KUMAON NURSERY
Ramnagar
Nainital
U.P. 244 715
INDIA

BURGON & BALL LTD
La Plata Works
Holme Lane
Sheffield S6 4JY
UK

COLUMBIAN CUTLERY COMPANY INC.
P.O. Box 123
440 Laurel St.
Reading
PA 19603-0123
USA

DALTON SUPPLIES LTD
Nettlebed
Henley-on-Thames
Oxfordshire RG9 5AB
UK

ALFRED COX (SURGICAL) LTD
Edward Road
Coulsdon
Surrey CR3 2XA
UK

ALFA-LAVAL AGRI LTD
Oakfield
Cwmbran
Gwent
Wales NP44 7XE
UK

C.H. DANA COMPANY INC.
Hyde Park
Vermont 05655
USA

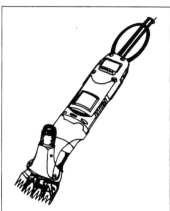

ELECTRIC SHEEP SHEARS

These shears incorporate the motor within the handpiece. Some models are offered with interchangeable heads and blades suitable for clipping goats, horses, and cattle. Machines of this type are available from:

LISTER SHEARING EQUIPMENT LTD
Dursley
Glos GL11 4HR
UK

ANIVET
1144 Budapest
Remény u.42
HUNGARY

ALFRED COX (SURGICAL) LTD
Edward Road
Coulsdon
Surrey CR3 2XA
UK

C.H. DANA COMPANY INC.
Hyde Park
Vermont 05655
USA

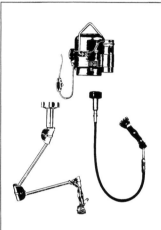

ELECTRIC SHEARING MACHINES WITH SHAFT DRIVE

When large numbers of sheep are to be shorn, the most common type of machine is that in which the handpiece is shaft-driven from an overhead motor. The illustration shows the more conventional rigid shaft-drive (above left) and an alternative flexible drive (above right) which allows greater mobility. Both types are available from:

LISTER SHEARING EQUIPMENT LTD
Dursley
Glos GL11 4HR
UK

ALFRED COX (SURGICAL) LTD
Edward Road
Coulsdon
Surrey CR3 2XA
UK

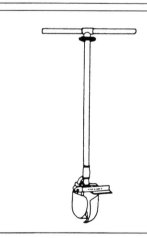

SHEARING HANDPIECES

The handpiece is attached to the drive-shaft of a conventional mechanical shearing machine. It contains a rigid comb and an oscillating cutter which cuts in both directions. Shearing handpieces are available from:

LISTER SHEARING EQUIPMENT LTD
Dursley
Glos GL11 4HR
UK

EARTH AUGERS

Earth augers can be used to prepare holes for fencing posts. The auger illustrated has cutting edges of high carbon steel and is adjustable to bore holes of 150-400mm diameter. It is available from:

KUMAON NURSERY
Ramnagar 244715
Nainital
U.P.
INDIA

Earth augers are also supplied by:

SEYMOUR MANUFACTURING CO. INC.
P.O. Box 248
500 North Broadway
Seymour
IN 47274
USA

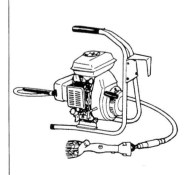

PETROL ENGINE SHEARING/DAGGING SETS

Shearing machines powered by a petrol engine can be used in situations where electricity is not available. The models offered by the two companies listed below are self-contained, portable units with flexible drives, handpieces, combs and cutters. In both cases, the engine is mounted in a free-standing frame which can also be hung from a gate or railings.

LISTER SHEARING EQUIPMENT LTD
Dursley
Glos GL11 4HR
UK

ALFRED COX (SURGICAL) LTD
Edward Road
Coulsdon
Surrey CR3 2XA
UK

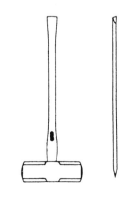

SLEDGEHAMMER AND CROWBAR

These are used for making post holes and driving posts. Suppliers include:

TROPIC
B.P. 706
Douala
CAMEROON

BULAWAYO STEEL PRODUCTS
8, Ironbridge Road
Donnington
P.O. Box 1603
Bulawayo
ZIMBABWE

BULLDOG TOOLS
Clarington Forge
Wigan
Lancs WN1 3DD
UK

POST-HOLE DIGGERS

Manually operated post-hole diggers with a scissor action are supplied by:

SCHWABISCHE HUTTENWERKE GmbH
Postfach 1329
7292 Baiersbronn 1
GERMANY

SEYMOUR MANUFACTURING CO. INC.
P.O. Box 248
500 North Broadway
Seymour
IN 47274
USA

Post-hole diggers mounted on the three-point linkage of a tractor and driven through its power take-off are available from:

HOWARD ALATPERTANIAN SDN BHD
P.O. Box 8
68107 Batu Caves
Selangor
MALAYSIA

ZALAGEP BAGODI MEZOGAZDASAGI
Gepgyarto Vallalat
8992 Bagod
Gépállomás út 9
HUNGARY

KUBOTA LTD
2-47 Shikitsuhigashi 1-chome
Naniwa-Ku
Osaka 556-91
JAPAN

CSN INTERNATIONAL PTY LTD
P.O. Box 396
Dalby
Queensland 4405
AUSTRALIA

GALLAGHER ENGINEERING LTD
Private Bag
Frankton
Hamilton
NEW ZEALAND

FENCING PLIERS

This multi-purpose fencing tool acts as a plier, hammer, wire cutter, and strainer; it also removes staples and nails. It is available from many suppliers, including:

SEYMOUR MANUFACTURING CO. INC.
P.O. Box 248
500 North Broadway
Seymour
IN 47274
USA

BORAL CYCLONE EXPORT
P.O. Box 131
Mt Hawthorn
WA 6016
AUSTRALIA

DALTON SUPPLIES LTD
Nettlebed
Henley-on-Thames
Oxfordshire RG9 5AB
UK

C.H. DANA COMPANY INC.
Hyde Park
Vermont 05655
USA

ALFRED COX (SURGICAL) LTD
Edward Road
Coulsdon
Surrey CR3 2XA
UK

ELECTRIC FENCE INSULATORS

Various designs of insulator, suitable for attachment to standard fencing posts, are offered by:

ALFRED COX (SURGICAL) LTD
Edward Road
Coulsdon
Surrey CR3 2XA
UK

WIRE STRAINERS

This tool can be used for tensioning smooth or barbed wire. An optional 'tensing handle', which ensures correct wire tension, is recommended where high tensile wire is being used. The strainer is supplied by:

BORAL CYCLONE EXPORT
P.O. Box 131
Mt Hawthorn
WA 6016
AUSTRALIA

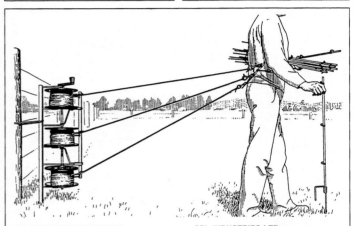

ELECTRIC FENCING

Where mains or battery electricity supply is available, electric fencing can be used as a simple temporary means of stock control. The simplest system consists of a reel of wire, a series of insulated posts and a battery unit to supply an electric pulse. Solar-powered battery packs are also available for use with electric fencing systems. Suppliers of electric fencing equipment include:

HORIZONT AGRARTECHNIK GmbH
Postfach 1329
D-3540
Korbach
GERMANY

GALLAGHER ENGINEERING LTD
Private Bag
Frankton
Hamilton
NEW ZEALAND

KIWITECH INTERNATIONAL LTD
P.O. Box 19
Bulls
NEW ZEALAND

FENCING MATERIALS

The following companies offer different ranges of fencing materials including galvanized wire netting, woven and soldered mesh, chains, springs, barbed wire and fixings.

SIG
Route de Gabes km.2
Sfax
TUNISIA

GEORGE H. ELT LTD
Eltex Works
Bromyard Road
Worcester WR2 5DN
UK

BORAL CYCLONE EXPORT
P.O. BOX 131
Mt Hawthorn
WA 6016
AUSTRALIA

PEL INDUSTRIES LTD
P.O. Box 51-093
Auckland
NEW ZEALAND

DONAGHYS INDUSTRIES LTD
Private Bag
123 Crawford Street
Dunedin
NEW ZEALAND

ALFA-LAVAL AGRI LTD
Oakfield
Cwmbran
Gwent
Wales NP44 7XE
UK

C.H. DANA COMPANY INC.
Hyde Park
Vermont 05655
USA

J. DELGADO S.A.
D. José Ruiz, 26
Socuellamos (Ciudad Real) 13630
SPAIN

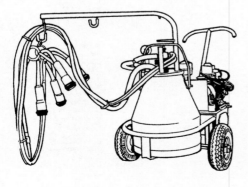

SMALL TROLLEY-MOUNTED MILKING MACHINES

These are supplied by a number of manufacturers. Essentially they all consist of a vacuum pump, a power unit, a milking unit, milk can and pulsation system.

MINIKART
This single-animal milking machine has a stainless steel, trolley-mounted bucket and is driven by an integral 0.75kW electric motor or 2.2kW engine. It is supplied by:

P. STRANGE-HANSEN AS
Stadionvej 16
Horne
Varde 6800
DENMARK

COW TIE

Chain-link cow ties are available from, among others:

ANIVET
1144 Budapest
Remény u.42
HUNGARY

ALFRED COX (SURGICAL) LTD
Edward Road
Coulsdon
Surrey CR3 2XA
UK

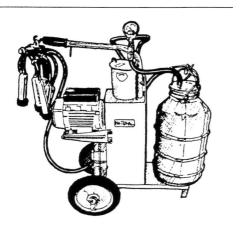

SINGLE AND DOUBLE MILKERS

These are fitted with either one or two clusters (teat-cup assemblies) suitable for cows. They can be powered by electric motor or petrol engine, through a gearbox and piston-type vacuum pump to provide pulsation. Separate pulse regulators are provided for each milking point. The machines are supplied by:

ALFRED COX (SURGICAL) LTD
Edward Road
Coulsdon
Surrey CR3 2XA
UK

Similar machines are available from:

ASE EUROPE N.V.
De Keyserlei 58 Bus 1
Century Center
B-2018 Antwerp
BELGIUM

BUCKET MILKING MACHINES

These machines are used in conjunction with small vacuum pumps. They consist of a bucket or churn of stainless steel, aluminium or polythene, which has a sealed lid. To this lid are attached the pulsator and cluster. Machines of this type are supplied by:

ELECREM
24, Rue Gambetta
92170 Vanves
FRANCE

ALFA-LAVAL AGRI LTD
Oakfield
Cwmbran
Gwent
Wales NP44 7XE
UK

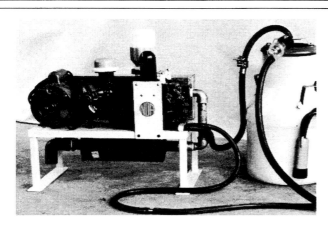

SMALL VACUUM PUMPS

Small vacuum pumps which supply adequate vacuum for two or more clusters may be used directly with a bucket machine or via an airline.

They may be obtained from many manufacturers of dairying equipment, including the following:

NU PULSE (NZ) LTD
P.O. Box 5358
Keddell Street, Hamilton
NEW ZEALAND

R. J. FULLWOOD & BLAND LTD
Fullwood Works
Ellesmere
Salop SY12 9DF
UK

ALFA-LAVAL AGRI LTD
Oakfield
Cwmbran
Gwent
Wales NP44 7XE
UK

MASTITIS DETECTORS

This is a transparent plastic device, fitted into the milk delivery tube of a pipeline milking system. A plastic screen slides into the body of the detector for the in-line detection of mastitis clots. It is supplied by:

ANIVET
1144 Budapest
Remény u.42
HUNGARY

ALFRED COX (SURGICAL) LTD
Edward Road
Coulsdon
Surrey CR3 2XA
UK

An in-line screen of slightly different design is supplied by:

ALFA-LAVAL AGRI LTD
Oakfield, Cwmbran
Gwent NP44 7XE
Wales
UK

KICK BAR

This is used to immobilize a cow's hind leg. The many suppliers include:

ANIVET
1144 Budapest
Remény u.42
HUNGARY

DALTON SUPPLIES LTD
Nettlebed
Henley-on-Thames
Oxfordshire RG9 5AB
UK

ALFRED COX (SURGICAL) LTD
Edward Road
Coulsdon
Surrey CR3 2XA
UK

ALFA-LAVAL AGRI LTD
Oakfield
Cwmbran
Gwent
Wales NP44 7XE
UK

C.H. DANA COMPANY INC.
Hyde Park
Vermont
05655
USA

MILK STRAINERS AND FILTERS

A range of strainers and filters is available to remove foreign material from milk, extending from filter paper to wire gauze. Equipment of this type is supplied by:

UNIPAC INDÚSTRIA E COMÉRCIO LTDA
Rua Pirajá, 45
Pompéia (SP) 17580
BRAZIL

ALFRED COX (SURGICAL) LTD
Edward Road
Coulsdon
Surrey CR3 2XA
UK

ASE EUROPE N.V.
De Keyserlei 58 Bus 1
Century Center
B-2018 Antwerp
BELGIUM

LEHMAN HARDWARE & APPLIANCES INC.
P.O. Box 41
4779 Kidron Road
Kidron
OH 44636
USA

DAIRY BRUSHES AND HYGIENE EQUIPMENT

Ranges of brushes and cleaners for spouts, teat cups and general use can be obtained from:

ALFA-LAVAL AGRI LTD
Oakfield
Cwmbran
Gwent
Wales NP44 7XE
UK

C.H. DANA COMPANY INC.
Hyde Park
Vermont
05655
USA

ALFRED COX (SURGICAL) LTD
Edward Road
Coulsden
Surrey CR3 2XA
UK

MILK HOLDING VESSELS

Stainless steel milking pails can be obtained from:

MDAWI VOCATIONAL TRAINING CENTRE
P.O. Box 304
Moshi
TANZANIA

A range of milk and cream containers including stainless steel and aluminium pails and cans, thermos cans, and cans with mushroom lids is available from:

DAIRY UDYOG
C-229A/230A, Ghatkopar Ind Est
L.B.S. Marg
Ghatkopar (W)
Bombay 400 086
INDIA

J. DELGADO S.A.
D. José Ruiz, 26
Socuellamos (Ciudad Real) 13630
SPAIN

Several types of aluminium milk containers with capacities of 3 to 50 litres are supplied by:

DATINI MERCANTILE LTD
Enterprise Road
Box 45483
Nairobi
KENYA

Plastic milk containers in a similar range of sizes can be obtained from:

UNIPAC INDÚSTRIA E COMÉRCIO LTDA
Rua Pirajá, 45
Pompéia (SP) 17580
BRAZIL

Buckets for mechanical milking are supplied by:

ASE EUROPE N.V.
De Keyserlei 58 Bus 1
Century Center
B-2018 Antwerp
BELGIUM

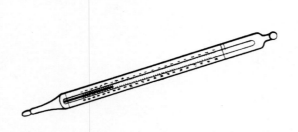

DAIRY THERMOMETER

This mercury-filled, floating thermometer is designed for dairy use and freezing, churning, cheese-making, pasteurizing and sterilizing temperatures are indicated. It can be obtained from:

ALFRED COX (SURGICAL) LTD
Edward Road
Coulsden
Surrey CR3 2XA
UK

CREAM SETTING PAN AND SKIMMER

The pan is made from spun aluminium with a wide, flat rim and with narrow, steeply sloping sides. It has a capacity of 13.5 litres and is used with a hand skimmer, fitted with a flat curved handle. The pan and skimmer are supplied separately, by:

ALFRED COX (SURGICAL) LTD
Edward Road
Coulsden
Surrey CR3 2XA
UK

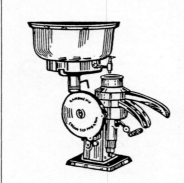

CREAM SEPARATORS

Manual and electric cream separators are available in a range of designs and sizes from:

DAIRY UDYOG
C-229A/230A, Ghatkopar Ind Est
L.B.S. Marg, Ghatkopar (W)
Bombay 400 086
INDIA

INTER-PRODUCT K.F.T.
9700, Szombathely
Schönhertz krt.10
HUNGARY

R. J. FULLWOOD & BLAND LTD
Fullwood Works
Ellesmere
Salop SY12 9DF
UK

GEBR. RADEMAKER
P.O. Box 81
3640 AB Mijdecht
NETHERLANDS

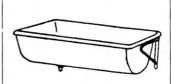

CHURN-WASHING TANK

This range of round-bottom tanks with drain plugs is made of sheet steel and galvanized after manufacture.

GEORGE H. ELT LTD
Eltex Works
Bromyard Road
Worcester WR2 5DN
UK

FARM PASTEURIZER

This machine operates on the same principles as an industrial autoclave, by pressurized heating and vacuum cooling. It is made of anodized aluminium, with a capacity of 21 litres and is supplied by:

ELECREM
24, Rue Gambetta
92170 Vanves
FRANCE

ALFA-LAVAL AGRI LTD
Oakfield
Cwmbran
Gwent
Wales NP44 7XE
UK

TOMEGA S.A.
Rue de la Rochette , 7
Arville B-6904
BELGIUM

LEHMAN HARDWARE & APPLIANCES INC.
P.O. Box 41
4779 Kidron Road
Kidron
OH 44636
USA

ELECREM
24, Rue Gambetta
92170 Vanves
FRANCE

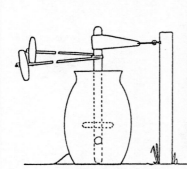

MODIFIED BUTTER CHURN

The traditional churning method in Ethiopia entails shaking the milk container for three to four hours, after several days of acidification. This method results in the loss of much of the fat content in the buttermilk. A simple, wooden agitator has been developed to fit inside the churn, enabling the operation to be completed in only one hour, and the fat content losses are reduced from 1.1% to 0.36%. Details of this modification can be obtained from:

CENTRE INTERNATIONAL POUR L'ELEVAGE EN AFRIQUE (CIPEA)
Addis-Ababa
ETHIOPIA

REDWOOD CYLINDER CHURN

A hand-operated 11 litre churn made of redwood and steel is available from:

LEHMAN HARDWARE & APPLIANCES INC.
P.O. Box 41
4779 Kidron Road
Kidron
OH 44636
USA

Other suppliers of large, manual and electric butter churns include:

DAIRY UDYOG
C-229A/230A, Ghatkopar Ind Est
L.B.S. Marg
Ghatkopar (W)
Bombay 400 086
INDIA

10. BEEKEEPING

Honey has been collected by humans throughout history. For thousands of years it has been known that obtaining a honey crop is made easier and more convenient if bees are encouraged to nest in a hive. This practice, and management of the bees in the hive, is known as beekeeping. However the term beekeeping tends to be used loosely to describe all the techniques involving bees and the subsequent harvesting and processing of the products.

Honey-hunting — plundering wild nests of honey bees to obtain crops of honey and beeswax — is still widely practised where honey bee colonies are abundant in the wild. Although there is no management of the bees, honey-hunting also tends to be considered under the generic term beekeeping, and honey-hunters can benefit from assistance in various ways.

Beekeeping provides a useful side-line income alongside other activities. The presence of honey bees also ensures optimal pollination and thereby quality and yield of nearby crops.

There are various methods for managing honey bees. These methods are determined by the presence (or absence) of traditional skills, whether there have been attempts to introduce new equipment previously, and the type of bee being managed.

BEE SPECIES

The most widely used bees in the World are European *Apis mellifera*. Most of the equipment sold, and thus most of the

entries in this catalogue, is for use with this bee. The modern movable frame hive was developed for this temperate-zone bee. It was not designed for tropical honey bees, and much time and effort has been wasted in the past trying to manage tropical bees in the same type of hive, and by the same methods. In the Americas, Australia, New Zealand and some Pacific islands these are also the main bees used.

Tropical Africa also has native *Apis mellifera*. They are slightly smaller than the European *Apis mellifera*, and their behaviour is notably different. They are more readily alerted to fly off the comb and to sting. Colonies are more likely to abandon their hives if disturbed, and in some areas the colonies migrate seasonally. These are crucial factors governing bee management and hive design.

In Asia there are three native tropical species, *Apis cerana*, *Apis dorsata*, and *Apis floreo*. *Apis cerana* looks like a smaller version of *Apis mellifera* and is the only Asian bee that can be managed in hives. Both *Apis dorsata* and *Apis floreo* build a single comb in the open, and cannot be kept in hives, but honey-hunters do plunder their combs for honey.

In the Americas there are no native honey bees. However European *Apis mellifera* were introduced and used for honey. In 1956 some African *Apis mellifera* queens were introduced into Brazil. Their offspring hybridized with the existing European *Apis mellifera* and proved dominant over them. These 'Africanized' bees have spread through much of South and Central America, and are now spreading into the USA. They have many of the tropical African characteristics, which has necessitated changed management practices, but have also lead to increased yields.

EQUIPMENT SELECTION

Equipment types used for the management of bees can be divided into three main categories: traditional, movable-frame and modern low-technology.

Equipment appropriate for the harvesting and processing of honey and beeswax depends upon the quantities to be processed, and the type of product required. In some areas traditional beekeeping is practised on a large-scale and may well justify the provision of relatively expensive processing equipment capable of dealing effectively with honey in bulk for export.

In selecting equipment the following factors should be considered:

○ If beekeeping is being promoted as a side-line activity then it must be wholly sustainable, using equipment which is available locally. Although equipment can be imported to serve as a prototype, small-scale beekeeping can only be economic in the long-term with equipment which can be serviced and manufactured locally.

The equipment needed for honey-hunting, traditional and low-technology beekeeping can usually be made at village-level.

○ Honey bee species and races vary in size. A honey bee nest consists of a series of parallel beeswax combs. Each comb contains rows of wax, hexagonal compartments containing honey stores, pollen or developing bee larvae (brood). The combs are evenly spaced and are attached to the ceiling of the nest. This spacing, known as the 'bee-space', is critical in maintaining optimal conditions within the nest, with just enough space for bees to walk and work on the surface of the combs while maintaining the optimum nest temperature. Bee-space, dimensions of combs and nest volume all vary with race and species of honey bee. The bee-space is a critical factor in the use of bee equipment and honey bees cannot be managed efficiently using equipment of inappropriate size. When buying equipment it is important to have an understanding of the honey bees to be housed and the specification of the equipment offered. Most equipment is manufactured to the specification for bees of European origin.

○ Honey bee species and races vary in biology and behaviour. Strategies for the management of honey bees have been developed mainly for temperate-zone races of honey bees and most movable-frame equipment is intended for this type of management.

Colonies of tropical honey bees show a tendency to abandon their hive — this is known as absconding, and no reliable management technique has yet been developed to prevent this.

○ During the last two decades there has been a tremendous increase in the spread of bee disease around the world. This has been brought about by the movement of honey bee colonies and used beekeeping equipment by man. There are few remaining regions without introduced honey bee diseases, and most of these are in developing countries. It will be to the future benefit of these countries if they can retain their stocks of disease-free honey bees. It is therefore essential to ensure that used beekeeping equipment is not imported. Honey bee colonies, or even single queen bees must never be moved from one area to another without

expert consideration of the consequences.

○ It can be helpful to import basic equipment (protective clothing, smokers, hive tools) to serve as prototypes leading to local manufacture.

○ For beekeepers practising on a larger scale, for example where a co-operative has established a honey packing plant, there are often items which necessitate importation, because they are specialized and required only in small numbers; for example, honey gates (effective honey 'taps' for use on large containers), specialized gauzes for the filtration of honey, or the equipment for determining honey quality.

As a general rule, attempts to assist or increase beekeeping in any area should start with the existing bees, the existing beekeeping techniques and equipment, and work from there. The local bees will have evolved to survive efficiently under the conditions prevailing. Beekeepers can be assisted in many ways, but will not be helped by the introduction of equipment requiring unfamiliar management techniques and which may well be unsuitable for the local bees.

There are numerous examples of beekeeping being practised by traditional methods which are sustainable and cost-free. These beekeepers often need help, not with their beekeeping, but with transport to get their honey to market and with containers and labels for marketing their honey effectively.

BEEHIVES

A beehive is any container provided for honey bees to nest in. The purpose is to encourage the bees to build their nest in such a way that it is easy for the beekeeper to manage and exploit them.

Traditional hives

These are made from whatever materials are available locally: typically hollowed-out logs, bark formed into a cylinder, clay pots, woven grass or cane. The sole purpose of a traditional hive is to encourage bees to nest in a site that is accessible by the beekeeper.

The bees build their nest inside the container, just as they would build it in a naturally occurring cavity. Eventually the beekeeper plunders the nest to obtain crops of honey and beeswax. Bees may or may not be killed during this process,

Hives can be constructed by village carpenters

depending on the skill of the beekeeper. If the colony is destroyed, the hive will remain empty for a while. If there are plenty of honey bee colonies in the area then eventually a swarm may settle in the empty hive and start building a new nest. Traditional beekeepers often own 200 hives, and expect only a proportion of these to be occupied by bees at any time.

All requirements will be locally available, but traditional beekeepers can be assisted by the provision of protective clothing, smokers, and containers for the honey, and with help in locating markets for their products.

Movable-frame hives

These are the hives used in industrialized countries and in some developing countries such as Mexico and Brazil. Here beekeeping is recognized as an important part of mainstream agriculture and the infrastructure exists to provide specialized expertise and equipment. The objective of movable-frame hive beekeeping is to obtain the maximum honey crop, season after season, with least disruption of the honey bee colony. High populations of honey bees are maintained in the hives. These quickly build up honey stores during flowering seasons and may also be managed specifically for the pollination of particular crops. Rectangular wood or plastic frames are used to support the bees' combs. These frames convey two major advantages:

❍ They allow inspection and manipulation of colonies (e.g. moving frames from a strong colony to strengthen a weaker one).
❍ They allow very efficient honey harvesting because the honeycombs, within their frames, can be emptied of honey and then returned to the hive. This allows increased honey production as the bees' resources are saved in building fresh comb.

Frame hives must be constructed with precision. The spacing between frames must achieve the same spacing as in a natural nest. Frames are contained within boxes and each hive consists of a number of boxes placed on top of one another. Often the bottom-most box is used as the brood chamber. This means that brood is present only in this box: this is achieved by placing a queen excluder between this box and the one above it. The queen excluder is a metal grid with holes of a particular size such that worker bees can pass through but the queen is unable to do so because of her larger size. This ensures that only honey is stored in boxes above the queen excluder and allows for efficient honey harvest.

In addition to the boxes and frames, a floor and roof are required, along with various other specialised items of equipment described in the equipment list.

Frame hive equipment should not be used unless the infrastructure exists for manufacturing it locally. Frame hives require well-seasoned timber, planed and accurately cut as well as other materials like wire, nails and foundation. They are therefore relatively expensive to make. Frames and boxes must fit together precisely and need accurate carpentry. There must be access to supplies of the parts which need frequent renewal, particularly foundation and frames. Centrifugal extractors are needed to achieve full potential in harvesting the honey from frame hives. All these items are described in the equipment listing.

LOW-TECHNOLOGY BEEKEEPING

Low-technology hives have been developed as a means of obtaining the advantages of frame hives (manageability, efficient honey harvest) without the disadvantage of high cost manufacture. To allow manageability, bees are encouraged to

Top-bar from a low-technology hive, showing comb built from its underside

construct their combs from the undersides of a series of top-bars. These top-bars then allow individual combs to be lifted from the hive by the beekeeper.

The container for the hive may, like traditional hives, be constructed from whatever materials are locally available.

Another advantage of this type of equipment is that it opens up beekeeping to new groups of people. (Traditional beekeeping tends to be a male-only activity, practised by forest-dwellers.) Low-technology hives can be kept near home, or can be moved between crops as they flower successively.

All equipment can be made locally. The only items which need construction with precision are the top-bars because they must provide the same spacing of combs within the hive as the bees would use in their natural nest. This spacing will depend upon the species and race of honey bees which are being used. As a very general guide, *Apis mellifera* of European origin need top-bars 35mm wide, *Apis mellifera* in Africa need 32mm, *Apis cerana* in Asia need 30mm. The best way to determine the optimum width is to measure the spacing between combs in a wild nest of the same bees. The volume of the brood box should equate roughly with the volume of the cavity occupied by wild-nesting honey bees. Other necessary items are hive tools, smokers, protective clothing and containers for honey.

Making a start

A good way to start is by transferring a colony from the wild into a hive. The wild colony will already have a number of combs and these can be carefully tied on to the top-bars of the hive. Another way to get started is to set up a hive, perhaps rubbed inside with some beeswax to give it an attractive smell, and wait for a passing swarm of bees to occupy it: this will only be successful in areas where there are still plenty of honey bee colonies.

One of the best ways to get started in beekeeping is with the assistance of a practising, local beekeeper: if you do not know of any locally then write to IBRA at the address below and we will try to help you.

There are many basic texts giving advice on the management of bees, but most relate to frame hive beekeeping using honey bees of European origin. Publications on tropical beekeeping are not widely available, but there are some obtainable from specialist suppliers.

Harvesting honey and beeswax from top-bar hives

Honey is harvested at the end of a flowering season. The beekeeper selects those combs which contain ripe honey, covered with a fine layer of white beeswax. These combs are usually the outside-most ones. Combs containing any pollen or developing bees are left undisturbed.

The honeycomb can be simply cut into pieces and sold as fresh, cut comb honey. Alternatively the honeycomb can be broken up and strained through muslin or another form of filter to separate the honey from the beeswax.

The comb from which bees build their nest is made of beeswax. After honey is separated from the beeswax combs, the beeswax can be melted gently (over water) into a block. Beeswax does not deteriorate with age and therefore beekeepers often save their scraps of beeswax until they have a sufficiently large amount to sell. However, many beekeepers still discard beeswax, unaware of its value. Beeswax is a valuable commodity with many uses in traditional societies: it is used in the lost-wax method of brass casting, as a waterproofing agent for strengthening leather and cotton strings, in batik, in the manufacture of candles, and in various hair and skin ointments.

Beeswax is also in demand on the world market. If groups of beekeepers can combine their beeswax they will have enough to sell. Beeswax for export should be clean and heated as little as possible. Little processing is required: it can be moulded into blocks, which can then be placed in hessian sacks for export: much of the wax on the world market is exported from Africa.

Smoker

A beekeeper needs a source of cool smoke to calm the bees, and this is achieved by use of a smoker. The smoker consists of a fuel box containing smouldering fuel (dried cow dung, hessian or cardboard) with a bellows attached. The beekeeper puffs a little smoke near the entrance of the hive before it is opened, and gently smokes the bees to move them from one part of the hive to another. Imported smokers are useful as prototypes, but smokers can be manufactured by village blacksmiths.

Protective clothing

A broad-brimmed hat with some veiling will serve to protect the head and neck from stings. Adequate protective clothing gives beginner beekeepers confidence, but more experienced beekeepers find that too much protective clothing makes it difficult to work sufficiently gently with the bees, and it is very hot. Some people find that a good way to protect their hands it to put a plastic bag over each hand, secured at the wrist with a rubber band. Rubber bands also prevent bees from crawling up trouser legs or shirt sleeves. Always wear white or light-coloured clothing when working with bees — bees are much more likely to sting dark-coloured clothing. Again imported clothing can provide useful prototypes, but this clothing (basically modified overalls) can be made locally and provides a useful stimulus to local industry.

Hive tools

Bees tend to close up every gap and seal every joint in the hive with a sticky substance known as propolis. The hive tool is a handy piece of metal which is used to prise boxes apart, scrape off odd bits of beeswax, separate frame-ends from their supports, and so on. It is described in the equipment list. It is possible to use an old knife for this job, but knife blades tend to be too flexible and give insufficient leverage. Village blacksmiths should be able to produce a suitable implement and, once again, an imported hive tool could serve as a prototype.

FURTHER INFORMATION

Further information is available from Nicola Bradbear, Advisory Officer for Tropical Apiculture at International Bee Research Association (IBRA), 18 North Road, Cardiff CF1 3DY, UK.

Beekeeping and Development, the quarterly journal for appropriate beekeeping, gives useful information and news, and certain other publications are available free of charge from IBRA to beekeeping projects and educational institutes in developing countries.

Nicola Bradbear
Advisory Officer for Tropical Apiculture, IBRA

Nicola Bradbear

Traditional log hive in Kenya

Low-technology ives in Colombia

Ray Holland/ITDG

GENERAL SUPPLIERS

AUSTRALIA

JOHN L. GUILFOYLE (SALES) PTY
LTD
P.O. Box 18
Darra
Brisbane
Queensland 4076

PENDER BEEKEEPING SUPPLIES
PTY LTD
17 Gardiner Street
Rutherford
N.S.W. 2320

AUSTRIA

STEFAN PUFF GmbH
Neuholdaugasse 36
Graz A-8011

CANADA

F.W. JONES & SON LTD
44 Dutch Street
Bedford
Quebec JOJ 1AO

DENMARK

SWIENTY
Hortoftvej 16
Ragebol
Sonderborg 6400

FRANCE

APICULTURE LEROUGE
91, Rue Mangin
Saint Just-en-Chauss 60130

APICULTURE NEVIERE S.A.R.L.
B.P. 15
Route de Manosque
Valensole 04210

GERMANY

CHR. GRAZE KG.
Strümpfelbacherstraße 21
7056 Weinstadt 2 (Endersbach)

INDIA

LOTLIKAR & COMPANY
A-1/4 Pioneer Co-op Society
Panvel, Dist. Raigad
New Bombay 410 206

JAPAN

GIFU YOHO CO. LTD
Kano-Sakurada-Cho 1
Gifu-Shi
Gifu 500-91

NEW ZEALAND

STUART ECROYD BEE SUPPLIES
P.O. Box 5056
Papanui
Christchurch 5

NORWAY

HONNINGCENTRALEN A/L
Østensjøveien 19
0661 Oslo 6

UK

B.J. ENGINEERING
Swallow Ridge
Hatfield
Norton
Worcs WR5 2PZ

E.H. THORNE (BEEHIVES) LTD
Beehive Works
Wragby
Lincoln LN3 5LA

STEELE & BRODIE (1983) LTD
Stevens Drove
Houghton
Stockbridge
Hants SO20 6LP

USA

A.I. ROOT CO.
P.O. Box 706
623 W. Liberty Street
Medina
OH 44258

DADANT & SONS INC.
Hamilton
IL 62341

MAXANT INDUSTRIES INC.
P.O. Box 454
Ayer
MA   01432

WALTER T. KELLY CO.
3107 Elizabethtown Road
Clarkson
KY 42726

ZIMBABWE

JOHN RAU & COMPANY (PVT) LTD
P.O. Box 2893
Harare

PROTECTIVE CLOTHING

Every beekeeper should have adequate protective clothing, even if he or she sometimes chooses not to wear it all. The most important part to protect is the face, especially the eyes and mouth. Whether arms and hands are covered is a choice to be made by the beekeeper according to the occasion, the work to be done and the character of the bees to be dealt with. Individual items of clothing *must* be impermeable to bee stings, and every joint between them *must* be bee-tight; if not, it could be safer to strip completely than to risk getting bees caught inside the clothing.

Fastening devices such as zip fasteners and Velcro have made it possible for a beekeeper to be completely enveloped in a single garment. Alternatively, separate parts may be used: a veil supported by a hat or hood; gloves; boots and an appropriate overall or boiler suit. Cooler clothing may not provide adequate protection.

Except for the visor of the veil, which must be black to give good vision, all cloth for garments worn when working with bees should be light in colour and of smooth, close-mesh material. For working with tropical African and Africanized bees, it may be best to use a veil with the outside of the wire-mesh visor painted white; otherwise bees are likely to fly against the black mesh and obscure vision. With these bees, stout plastic gloves may also be necessary, although they are hot and clumsy to wear. All general beekeeping suppliers stock protective clothing but it is worth seeing, and *trying on*, different types to find out what is suitable for you and for the conditions under which you work. The outfit illustrated is one used for working with 'aggressive' tropical African bees.

If, in spite of precautions, you find you have a bee inside your protective clothing, go well away from the bees before you investigate. A similar rule applies to removing the clothing.

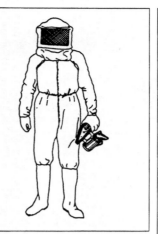

GLOVES AND GAUNTLETS

Gloves (upper illustration) should be light in colour, soft, and sufficiently well fitting to allow the wearer to work delicately when moving frames, in order not to disturb the bees. The material covering the hands should be impervious to stings, and soft leather is ideal. The wider gauntlet part can be of close cotton weave. The upper hem of the gauntlet is elasticated, to be worn over a long sleeve. Never wear black gloves. Rubber gloves are sometimes advertised but they are hot and can be clumsy. On the other hand thin cotton gloves are easily penetrated by a bee's sting.

Some beekeepers prefer to wear gauntlets only (lower illustration), in which case the lower hem is also elasticated and fits snugly over the wrist. Gloves and gauntlets, reaching below or above the elbow as required, can be made locally or can be obtained from:

GENERAL SUPPLIERS

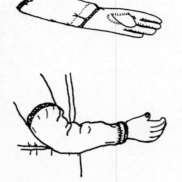

BOOTS

Many beekeepers tuck their trouser bottoms into rubber boots, which can be purchased at a shoe shop. Alternatively, trouser bottoms can be tucked into smooth, light-coloured socks worn with shoes.

You can be stung badly round the ankle through lack of care in ensuring a bee-tight join in the protection there, and bees inside a dark space instinctively run upwards.
Available from:

GENERAL SUPPLIERS

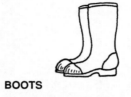

HAT AND VEIL

The choice must depend on the type of work to be done, the temperature and wind, and on personal preference. The drawing shows a folding veil in which the visor is made up of three rigid sections of black wire mesh. The tapes at the front are tied round the waist in such a way that the bottom edge of the cloth is drawn tightly against the clothes beneath. Alternatively, the cloth below the veil can be tucked inside a sleeved jacket at the neck. The brimmed hat shown is soft, but a rigid brimmed hat (with ventilation slits if wanted) is preferred by many. The veil may be integral with a cloth hat, or separate, and held over the brim by an elasticated hem at the top. For light-weight veils, nylon net can be used satisfactorily for the visor, although it may blow against the face or neck in windy weather.

Hats and veils can be made locally or obtained from:

GENERAL SUPPLIERS

OVERALLS

Overalls (and other such clothing for bee work) should be washable, and washed as often as necessary. This is not only to remove any gross dirt, but to remove odours to which bees might respond by stinging, and to minimize the possibility of carrying disease infection from one apiary to another.

A standard overall of a white close-weave material can be made locally or obtained from general suppliers. Custom-made bee suits incorporate elasticated wrists and trouser cuffs. For working with Africanized bees that sting readily, overalls can be made of thin, rip-stop nylon; these are large enough to be worn over clothing and are reported to be 'bee-secure' although hot.

Lightweight overalls convenient for hot climates are available from:

**NORTHWEST PROTECTIVE
GARMENTS LTD
2163B Kingsway
Vancouver V5N 2T4
CANADA**

ALL-IN-ONE SUIT WITH HOOD

The drawing shows a two-piece suit but it can be purchased as a single overall. One-piece smocks with hoods are also available. The wrists are elasticated. The hood is attached by a zip (and sewn on at the back of the neck) and can thus be thrown back when not required, without removing the suit. The visor is of black nylon net and is kept off the face by nylon boning round the edges and by the self-supporting hood. Suitable garments are available from general suppliers and from:

**B.J. SHERRIFF
Five Pines
Mylor Downs
Falmouth
Cornwall TR11 5UN
UK**

In certain countries, hoods have been traditionally preferred to hats, and there has also been a swing towards them in some other countries. If possible try on a veil with a hood and with a hat, to see which you prefer.

air-holes

SMOKER

A good smoker is essential in beekeeping with frame hives or top-bar hives. In traditional beekeeping, smouldering twigs or grass are used to smoke bees, but this does not give the directional flow of cool smoke that is most effective, and best for keeping the bees quiet. (The bees respond to the smoke by gorging themselves with honey, and are then less likely to sting.) Some traditional beekeepers and honey-hunters would probably find a modern smoker very helpful.

The metal firebox illustrated has a directional funnel hinged to the top, which allows the fuel to be inserted. The fuel is kept off the base of the firebox by a perforated metal shelf above an airhole. The bellows on the right, which contain a spring, are used to blow air into the fire box through two holes opposite each other.

The aim is to produce a large and steady supply of cool smoke from the funnel without the need for frequent refuelling. Success depends on the design of the smoker, the use of a large fire box (say 250mm high and 120mm in diameter), and on the type of fuel used. According to what is available, beekeepers may use old sacking, decayed wood, wood shavings or other vegetable matter, and corrugated cardboard.

It is important that only smoke, and no flame, should emerge from the smoker and that the fire should be extinguished immediately after use.

A few suppliers offer a smoker with a clockwork mechanism to maintain a constant flow of smoke, but such a device is not necessary.
Available from:

GENERAL SUPPLIERS

TOP-BAR HIVES

Top-bar hives are 'movable-comb' hives; instead of frames, they have appropriately distanced top-bars. The bees build combs down from the top-bars but they do not attach them to the hive walls, which slope inwards towards the bottom.

OBSERVATION HIVE

Many beekeeping supply firms manufacture a tall narrow observation hive, in which two or three frames are mounted one above the other, so that both sides are visible through the glass. These hives are excellent educational aids, but in hot weather it can be difficult to keep the bees in good condition.

The drawing on the right shows a simpler hive, in which the bees build their own comb from a small piece of foundation (top left of box). Some suppliers provide such a hive in kit form, with detailed drawings and assembly instructions.

The hive can be populated with bees from a special travelling box through the flexible tube (bottom left). The queen is introduced in the queen cage (top left). For health reasons, only order live bees from within your own country.
Available from:

GENERAL SUPPLIERS

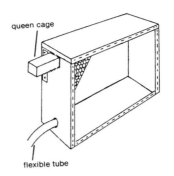

queen cage

flexible tube

MOVABLE-FRAME HIVES FOR *APIS MELLIFERA*

Types of movable-frame hives that are in wide enough use to be considered appropriate are the Langstroth, which is the most widely used throughout the world especially in English speaking countries, and the Dadant or Dadant-Blatt. Both these are designed for the European bee *Apis mellifera*.

In both, the bee-space between hive boxes is at the *top* of each box. This is preferable to a bee-space at the bottom, in which case frames are flush with the hive box at the top. With a top bee-space, a flat wooden cover (e.g. to support a feeder), can be placed directly on the top hive box. (With a bottom bee-space a cover must have a frame below it to lift it above the top of the frames.) Also with a top bee-space, one hive box can be slid into position on top of the one below without crushing the bees.

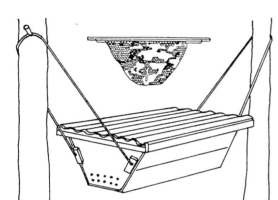

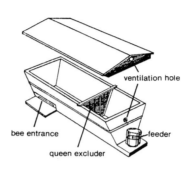

ventilation hole

bee entrance

feeder

queen excluder

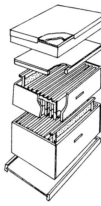
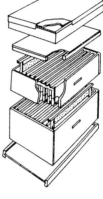

TOP-BAR HIVES

KENYA TOP-BAR HIVES FOR TROPICAL *APIS MELLIFERA*

This design was developed in Kenya before and during the Canadian International Development Agency project (1971-82). Internal measurements of the hive are 889 x 443mm across the top, 889 x 189mm across the bottom, and height 286mm. It has a complement of 28 top bars, each 32mm wide and 483mm long, supported by runners. These top-bars touch each other, and there is no space left between them. This is an important feature when handling tropical African bees, since only one bar-width is open at once, and this opening can be continually smoked, thus minimizing the flight by the bees (and stinging by them).

The illustration shows the entrance holes, roof, and suspension method of support to prevent damage by ants and other enemies.

These hives are manufactured by:

MINISTRY OF AGRICULTURE AND LIVESTOCK DEVELOPMENT
Beekeeping Section
P.O. Box 274
68228 Nairobi
KENYA

They are also sold by:

JOHN RAU & COMPANY (PVT) LTD
2 Moffat Street
P.O. Box 2893
Harare
ZIMBABWE

TOP-BAR HIVE FOR *APIS CERANA*

Several attempts have been made to use top-bar hives for *Apis cerana* in Asia. The hive described and illustrated here is two-thirds (linear) the size of the Kenya top-bar hive. It was designed by the late Father B.R. Saubolle, Kathmandu, and is currently being distributed in Nepal under a UNICEF/Agricultural Development Bank programme. Like the African hives, it is suspended to prevent damage by ants and other enemies. It has full width top-bars, although *Apis cerana* is very little inclined to sting. The slit entrance is taken from an earlier design of the Kenya hive, which was discarded there in favour of a series of holes which the bees can more easily protect.

A strong wire queen excluder is provided with this hive, which is made by:

GANA FURNITURE
Gana Bahal
Kathmandu
NEPAL

LANGSTROTH HIVE

This is the most widely used hive in the world. The frames are separated from the hive wall, and from each other, by a bee-space. The illustration is an exploded view of the Langstroth hive, showing (from the bottom):

● bottom board;
● brood box or chamber;
● super or honey chamber;
● inner cover;
● roof.

Most Langstroth hives have boxes to accommodate ten frames, but eight-frame and twelve-frame hives are also made.

Langstroth hives are available from general suppliers. However, as standard dimensions and certain design details vary slightly from country to country, it is wise to purchase all hives and hive fittings from the same supplier.

MODIFIED DADANT HIVE

This hive is similar to, but larger than the Langstroth, with eleven deeper frames. The filled boxes are heavier, and the extra size is of no advantage unless bees can be managed appropriately.

MODIFIED LONG HIVE

This hive was developed from the Kenya top-bar hive and has been used in Kenya and Tanzania. The sides are vertical and each top-bar has two end-bars, but instead of a bottom bar like a frame, a horizontal strut is fixed between the two end bars to give additional support to the comb. The Kenya top-bars fit this hive and the partial frames can be used in a standard Langstroth hive, so the 'long hive' provides a useful step in advancing from the top-bar hive to a frame hive.

Companies supplying the hive illustrated include:

For tropical African bees:

JOHN RAU & COMPANY (PVT) LTD
2 Moffat Street
P.O. Box 2893
Harare
ZIMBABWE

For European bees:

AMERICAN-KENYA RESEARCH AND DEVELOPMENT CORPORATION
1204-2956 Hathaway Road
Richmond
VA 23225
USA

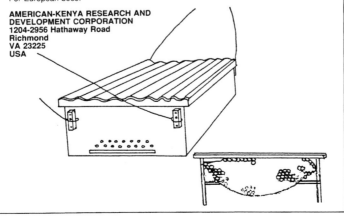

MOVABLE-FRAME HIVE FOR *APIS CERANA*

INDIAN STANDARD HIVE

Hives on the same principle as the Langstroth and the Dadant-Blatt are manufactured for use with the smaller Asiatic hive bee *Apis cerana*; each hive box usually accommodates nine frames. These hives are available from general suppliers in India including:

LOTLIKAR & COMPANY
A-1/4 Pioneer Co-op Society
Panvel
Dist. Raigad
New Bombay 410 206
INDIA

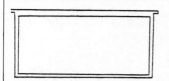

FRAMES

These support the wax foundation and comb that the bees build from it, and maintain the bee-space gap between frames/combs and hive walls (see 'Frame spacers'). Frames are usually made of fine-grained wood, with very strong joints between the bottom and end bars, and where the end bars join the top bar. This is necessary because of the weight of the honey in full combs, subjects the frames to considerable strains during bee management and honey extraction. Available from:

GENERAL SUPPLIERS

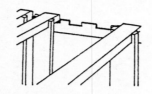

FRAME SPACERS

Some frames have their end-bars widened so that, when they touch, the combs are at the exact spacing required. Alternative methods include the fitting of a plastic or metal spacers on each end of the top-bar, or 'castellated' metal runners into which the top-bars of the frame fit.

Bees tolerate a greater variation in cell depth, and comb spacing, in honey supers (boxes) than in the brood nest. Spacers are viable from:

GENERAL SUPPLIERS

QUEEN EXCLUDER

This is a flat perforated screen, of the same size as the cross-section of the frame hive in which it is to be used. It is inserted above the brood box to separate it from the honey super above, and the slots in it are of such a size that workers can pass through but not the queen. The honey supers are thus kept free from brood.

The dimensions of the slots are critical and vary according to the type of bee used. For tropical *Apis mellifera* they are smaller than for European *Apis mellifera*, and for *Apis cerana* they are smaller still.

Queen excluders can be made from a flat sheet of metal or plastic with slots stamped out by machine. Alternatively (as illustrated), a series of parallel wires can be soldered to cross-strips, and the whole mounted in a wooden frame. The first type is cheaper but the second is more robust and bees pass through the holes more easily.

Queen excluders must be treated with care. If the grid is distorted it may let a queen through, and is thus useless. Before this fault is discovered, however, a honey super may be half full of brood.

For European *Apis mellifera*, the slots should be 4.14mm wide. (For tropical *Apis mellifera* coffee screen can be used.)

Excluders may be purchased from:

GENERAL SUPPLIERS

FEEDERS

In most parts of the world it is necessary to make provision for supplementary feeding of bees, for instance to counteract some unexpected adverse weather, to build up a small nucleus made in order to increase the number of colonies, or to encourage a swarm or other bees newly put into a hive to remain there.

An adequate supply of honey should be left in the hives as a matter of course but other materials are also used for feeding bees. Combs of honey from another source may be used in the hive, but it must be checked that these do not come from a diseased colony. Simple syrup feeders can be made locally, by cutting containers in half and placing these on top of the hive in an empty super (box). Flotation material such as

dried fern or twigs must be provided in these containers, or else large numbers of bees will drown. Other types of feeder can be placed outside the hive with an entrance only from inside. Larger feeders are preferable for food that the bees must store for a shortage period. When it is important that the bees take the syrup immediately, a 'dummy frame' type feeder can be placed inside the hive with the bees.

Dry sugar can be fed instead of syrup in warm weather; it needs no special feeder but can simply be spread over the inner cover of the hive. Dry sugar feeding will not lead to robbing, which syrup or honey feeding can do if other bees have any access to the food (most usual with an outside feeder).

Pollen and/or pollen substitute is fed by beekeepers in some areas where pollen supplies are deficient, but this needs no special feeder.

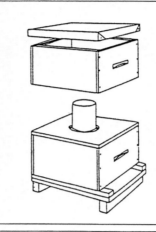

FRICTION-LID TIN

A friction-lid tin or pail with five to ten holes punched in the lid is filled with syrup and put upside down in an empty super on the hive, over the top-bars above the cluster. Friction-lid feeders are easy to make from old coffee tins, and can be refilled with little disturbance to the colony. The main disadvantage is the need to use an extra super and a special inner cover or hive mat with a hole in it.

The holes in the tin lid should be 1.6mm. This size is critical as the syrup must not be able to run out after the tin is inverted. The surface tension of the syrup holds it in the tin and the bees come up and draw syrup, rather like working at a teat. Frame nails are useful for making the right sized holes. Do not put warm syrup in one of these feeders as it will usually run out; wait until it has cooled before feeding. When the tin is first inverted, some syrup will come out anyway so spill this over the colony and not on the ground.

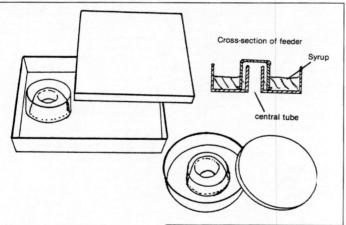

Cross-section of feeder

Syrup

central tube

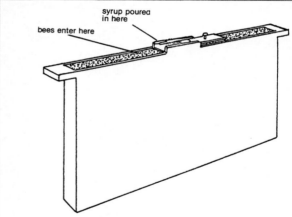

syrup poured in here

bees enter here

FLAT-TOP FEEDER

The illustrations show a large square feeder (the size of the hive cross-section) and also a smaller round feeder. Both have a central tube through which the bees enter from below, plus a provision for them to have access to the syrup by walking down the roughened outer surface of the tube. An outer cylinder closed at the top prevents them from getting access to, or drowning in, the bulk of syrup.

Feeders can be made locally to suit the size and type of hive used, or they are available from:

GENERAL SUPPLIERS

HIVE TOOL

Various designs of hive tool are available commercially. A typical design comprises a strong metal bar, about 200-250mm long and usually of high quality spring steel, with shaped ends. One end, often bent at right angles to the bar itself, is broad and with a sharp edge; this is used for scraping wax or propolis (a sticky resin used by bees as a building material) off a wooden surface. The other end is narrower, or it may be specially shaped, and is used as a lever to separate hive boxes and to loosen frames or top-bars. Any lever with a scraping blade at one end can be used as a simple hive tool and can easily be made locally. The tools illustrated are just two of the many designs available and it is worth trying several in your hand if possible, to see which suits you.
Available from:

GENERAL SUPPLIERS

DUMMY FRAME FEEDER

This is sometimes called a division-board feeder. It conforms to the size of the frame-plus-comb in the brood box, where it replaces a complete frame. The bees enter from the top, and inside there is a float or some other provision to protect the bees from drowning in the bulk of the syrup. This feeder is safe from robbing, and its contents are quickly available to the bees, but the hive must be opened to fill it.

A dummy frame feeder can be made by cutting and folding a piece of aluminium sheet to size. Specially made dummy frame feeders are available in various materials and sizes from:

GENERAL SUPPLIERS

FOUNDATION AND COMB

The following information covers both comb foundation and the equipment for making it. The cell size is critical for both foundation and comb, so different types of bees are dealt with separately.

Foundation is made of beeswax. A mixture of other waxes presents problems when combs are finally melted down and the beeswax recovered. For the use of plastics, see 'Plastic frames' (below right).

The diagram below shows (enlarged) the pattern of hexagons pressed into a flat sheet of beeswax when it is made into comb foundation.

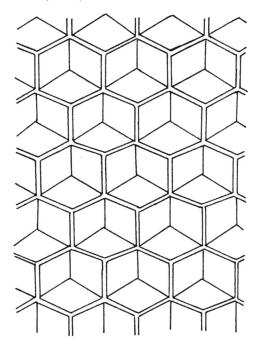

BEESWAX FOUNDATION FOR EUROPEAN *APIS MELLIFERA*

This is obtainable from almost any general beekeeping supplier where *Apis mellifera* is used. In North America, most foundation is sold with strengthening wires embedded in it. Elsewhere, some beekeepers embed the wires themselves, securing them to the frame in the process. Worker and drone foundation is available from many general suppliers and also from:

IMELDA'S BEEKEEPING SUPPLIES
1910 F. Tirona Benitez Street
Malate, Manila
PHILIPPINES

GREWAL WAX SHEETS
Railway Road
Doraha Mandi
141421
INDIA

J. KEMP
10, Rue Boileau
78470 Saint Remy les Chevreuse
FRANCE

FOUNDATION DIES
These provide the least expensive way of making foundation on a small scale. Molten beeswax is poured into a 'forming tray' to form a thin sheet. This sheet is laid between a pair of matched plastic dies, embossed with the hexagon shape of cell bases. The 'sandwich' is then passed through a wringer or under a heavy roller to imprint the pattern of the dies on the wax. Alternatively, an oil drum filled with wet sand, or sand and water, can be rolled over the 'sandwich', which has been laid carefully on a flat board. Hinged plastic dies are generally available in two sizes, 280 x 430mm for Dadant frames and 230 x 430mm for others, with cell sizes for worker or drone.

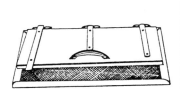

MOULD FOR MAKING EUROPEAN *APIS MELLIFERA* FOUNDATION

Hinged moulds for making European *Apis Mellifera* foundation. Molten beeswax is poured into the base of the tray, which constitutes the lower die, and the hinged lid (upper die) is closed on to it.

LEAF PRODUCTS
24 Acton Road
Long Eaton
Nottingham NG10 1FR
UK

ROLLERS FOR MAKING EUROPEAN *APIS MELLIFERA* FOUNDATION

This produces artificial comb foundation sheets from previously-formed plain beeswax sheets. It comprises a pair of rollers fitted into a cast iron stand and driven by a cranked handle and gears. The rollers are embossed to serve as dies for the foundation.

The first of these companies also supplies a roller mill for the production of plain or laminated beeswax sheets for use with foundation rollers.

LOTLIKAR & COMPANY
A-1/4 Pioneer Co-op Society
Panvel, Dist. Raigad
New Bombay 410 206
INDIA

CHR. GRAZE KG.
Strümpfelbacherstraße 21
7056 Weinstadt 2 (Endersbach)
GERMANY

TOM INDUSTRIES
P.O. Box 800
El Cajon
CA 92022
USA

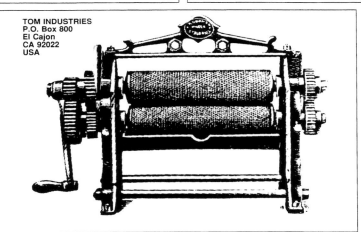

PLASTIC FRAMES WITH INTEGRAL COMB (FOR *APIS MELLIFERA*)

Many plastic frames with integral plastic foundation (or alternatively comb) are produced which are suitable only for large-scale beekeepers. Benefits include greater strength when extracting honey at high speed, ease of sterilization, and saving of time used in assembling wooden frames.

In many conditions bees seem to prefer beeswax to plastic in comb or foundation, when both are used. If plastic is tried, it should be during a good honey flow, and *all* frames in a super should be plastic.

BEESWAX FOUNDATION FOR TROPICAL AFRICAN APIS MELLIFERA

The cell size for these bees is quoted as 1050 cells/dm². The following firms supply suitable foundation and equipment to this specification:

BEESWAX FOUNDATION:
JOHN RAU & COMPANY (PVT) LTD
2 Moffat Street
P.O. Box 2893
Harare
ZIMBABWE

FOUNDATION MOULDS:
LEAF PRODUCTS
24 Acton Road
Long Eaton
Nottingham NG10 1FR
UK

FOUNDATION ROLLERS:
TOM INDUSTRIES
P.O. Box 800
El Cajon, CA 92022
USA

BEESWAX FOUNDATION FOR *APIS CERANA*

The following firms are believed to supply suitable equipment.

BEESWAX FOUNDATION:
IMELDA'S BEEKEEPING SUPPLIES
1910 F. Tirona Benitez Street
Malate
Manila
PHILIPPINES

FOUNDATION DIES
No foundation dies or moulds are known to be on sale. Matched dies like those for *Apis mellifera* (see above) would help many beekeepers in Asia. The initial production of the form from which dies are made is very expensive, and manufacturers would need either to be assured of a large number of orders or to receive some financial support before they could produce these dies.

FOUNDATION ROLLERS
Manufactured by:

TOM INDUSTRIES
P.O. Box 800
El Cajon, CA 92022
USA

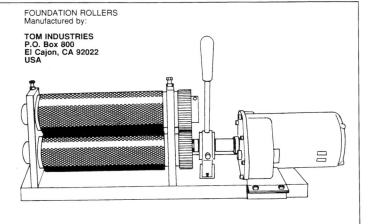

QUEEN REARING

Queen rearing can be a profitable undertaking, both in financial terms and in improvement of colony performance and ease of handling. It must, however, be done to a strict pre-planned timetable. Since queens mate in the air, no control over the male line is possible, except in isolated mating apiaries, or by using artificial insemination. All of the queen rearing equipment described here is designed for European *Apis mellifera,* but most could be used or adapted for other bees.

GRAFTING TOOL

'Grafting' refers to the transfer of a young larva into a cell cup (see right). A small (size 00) paint brush or a pointed piece of yucca or other leaf can be used as a simple grafting tool. Alternatively, retractable grafting tools and instruments like that illustrated are available from:

GENERAL SUPPLIERS

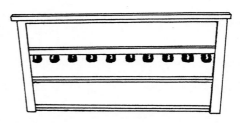

CELL CUPS AND FRAME

The larvae are grafted (see left) into artificial 'cell cups' with a supply of royal jelly. Ten of these filled cups are mounted on each of three horizontal bars fixed between the end-bars of a frame containing no foundation. The frame is then inserted in a strong queenless colony of bees.

Wax cell cups for queen rearing can be made locally, using pure, light-coloured beeswax and a former made from wood 8-9mm in diameter and 8-10mm deep, with a rounded base. Plastic cell cups are available from:

GENERAL SUPPLIERS

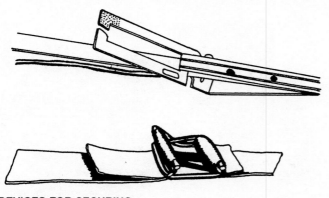

DEVICES FOR SECURING HIVES FOR TRANSPORT

Frame hives are often transported by truck from one honey flow to another. It is essential that all hive boxes, and cover and floorboard, are fastened together so that they do not slip apart and let bees escape. Ventilation for the bees is also essential, and the lid of the hive is usually replaced by a perforated metal screen. The simplest method of securing a hive for transport is to tie a piece of rope around the hive using a knot like those used to secure loads on vehicles. Alternatively, rayon and nylon straps can be used, secured with buckles like those illustrated; styles vary between suppliers.

Apart from tightly secured straps, various metal devices are sold for permanent fitting to the hive boxes, with a closure to be applied before moving which locks the hive together; not all are suitable for large-scale operation. Large metal pointed staples are sometimes knocked into the boxes, but they cause damage and are not to be recommended. Hive securing devices are available from:

GENERAL SUPPLIERS

APPARATUS FOR ARTIFICIAL INSEMINATION

This is a well developed but sophisticated technique used in research and breeding programmes, but in a few countries only. The apparatus required is expensive and it is a waste of time and money to purchase it unless both a properly controlled selection programme can be used for bee breeding and it will be more beneficial to use artificially inseminated queens than naturally mated ones.

The following company is one of the few that sell the apparatus and they also supply an excellent set of full-colour 35mm slides, with a printed manual based on them, taking the operator through every stage of the process.

DADANT AND SONS INC.
Hamilton
IL 62341
USA

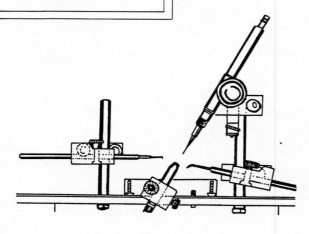

MATING HIVE

After the queen cells have been sealed, each is put into a small mating hive. The queen will shortly emerge and fly out to mate with drones in the air when a few days old. The mating hive can be like part of a brood box, containing two or three frames. Alternatively, it can be a tiny hive (as illustrated) which uses fewer bees. Queens are likely to mate more quickly from a small hive. Such hives are often of polystyrene, which provides better heat insulation than wood. They contain four top-bars from which the bees build sufficient comb to allow the queen to start laying. A feeder is provided. The model shown is fitted with an adjustable entrance at the bottom, and may be suspended for safety. Mating hives can be purchased from:

GENERAL SUPPLIERS

QUEEN MAILING AND INTRODUCTION CAGE

The queen rearer uses this type of cage for sending queens to the purchasers. The cages are made by drilling into a small solid block of wood, and one hole is filled with sugar to provide food for the queen and attendant workers in transit. One side of the cage is of wire mesh to allow ventilation.

The cage can also be used for introduction, provided that the mesh holes are large enough; holes 3mm across are suitable. This is to allow the workers in the new colony to have access to the queen in the cage and to enable pheromones to be transferred between them. It is then more certain that she will be accepted by the new colony. The queen is inserted into this cage without food, and the bees feed her through the mesh.
Available from:

GENERAL SUPPLIERS

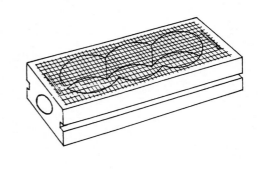

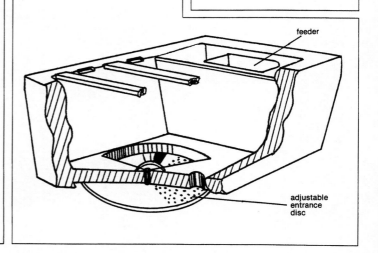

feeder

adjustable
entrance
disc

REMOVING HONEY FROM THE HIVE

The bees must first be made to leave the honey supers. This can be achieved by using an 'escape board' or by brushing and shaking them off the individual combs. Any narrow brush will serve as a bee brush, although specially-made ones are available from general suppliers. Alternatively, the bees can be driven down from the supers and into the brood chamber by using a fume board to apply a bee repellent, or the supers can be taken off the hive and the bees blown out with a bee blower. (These items are described below).

The use of an escape board involves two visits to the hive, one to insert it and another to check that the supers are bee-free, and then to remove them. The other methods need only one visit but they disturb the bees more. It is therefore best to work late in the day, when flight activity is decreasing, to reduce the chance of subsequent robbing of honey by bees from other hives. If robbing seems to be occurring, it can be helpful to apply a fine spray of water to the hive fronts, or wherever bees are congregating. This reduces the temperature and thus makes the bees less active.

FUME BOARD

This is a shallow box or tray made of insulating board such as pressed fibre and of the same cross-section as the hive. The internal depth of the tray is important and depends on the volatility of the repellent to be sprinkled on it. For benzaldehyde (artificial oil of almonds), a depth of 50mm has been recommended. At temperatures above 27°C, a white cloth or an insulated cover is helpful in preventing heat from the sun from vaporizing the repellent too quickly. After sprinkling benzaldehyde on the inside of the fume board, this is inverted over the (uncovered) top super. After a few minutes, the bees should have left the top (shallow) super, which is then removed and, if necessary, the fume board is placed similarly on the one below, and so on. Benzaldehyde is not effective with a full-depth hive box.

If many supers are to be removed from a heavily populated hive (and especially if some of the honey is unsealed) increasing difficulty may be encountered with successive supers, since more and more bees are being crowded into a smaller space. One commonly held objection to the use of any repellent is possible contamination of the honey, but this applies much less to benzaldehyde, which is used as a food flavouring, than to carbolic acid which was used earlier as a bee-repellent.

BEE ESCAPE BOARD

A bee escape board (illustrated near right) is the same size as the cross-section of the hive. It is placed on the hive *below* the honey supers that are to be removed for honey harvesting and it contains a device to ensure that worker bees will pass from boxes above it to those below, but not vice versa, so that the supers can be emptied of bees before removal. Different devices suit different circumstances - according to whether speed of action, certainty that the device will not be blocked by bees, or some other factor is the prime consideration. Any device relying on a spring mechanism can become ineffective if the spring becomes distorted. Nevertheless, the Porter bee escape of this type is the one most commonly sold. The bees 'escape' from above to below by pushing through the gap between two very light springs, but they are unable to return. The Porter escape is illustrated far right, with the upper part slid back to show the spring mechanism. Multiple Porter escapes are also available.

Bees will usually pass through an escape board between one day and the next. They take less time if there are multiple exits. In cool weather they are slow to move. It is *essential* that all honey supers above the escape board are bee-tight, or they will quickly be emptied by bees from other hives.

An escape board with no moving parts is preferred by many. It incorporates holes so shaped and positioned that bees will enter from above (and so 'escape') but do not enter them from below, to return.

Escapes are available from:

GENERAL SUPPLIERS

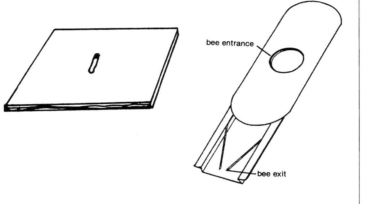

bee entrance

bee exit

BEE BLOWER

Unlike smoke or a bee repellent, the use of an airstream to blow bees out of a hive does not introduce any possibility of honey contamination.

A bee blower is normally powered from an electricity supply, but one could be devised to be operated by some other form of power. It operates rather like a vacuum cleaner in reverse and is used by standing a super (open above and below) either on top of the hive as illustrated, or on a stand constructed like a sawing horse and placed just in front of the hive. The bees blown out of the super find their way back to the hive entrance.
Available from:

GENERAL SUPPLIERS

UNCAPPING TRAY

An uncapping tray (illustrated below) is used to catch the cappings and honey that fall from the comb as uncapping proceeds. It is convenient (but not essential) to use a custom-made tray, which has a sheet of wire mesh near the bottom through which the cappings drain. The frame is held firm by an upward pointing projection on the cross bar. General suppliers sell various types of uncapping tray, some with additional features, which suit individual preferences. Available from:

GENERAL SUPPLIERS

UNCAPPING HONEY COMBS

Framed combs of honey taken from the hive must be uncapped, to remove the wax seals, before they are put in an extractor.

UNCAPPING FORK

These can be obtained in various widths, and many of them are narrower than the depth of a comb. They are operated by sliding the fork under the cappings from one end of the comb to the other. The narrow combs are useful when the shape or surface of the comb is irregular. Forks with offset tines, as illustrated, are also available.

UNCAPPING KNIFE

The knife shown here is of a standard type. The essential features are that the knife is longer than the depth of the frame and that the handle is offset for convenience in use. The knife can be heated by standing it in hot water, but it must then be dried before use. Often two knives are used, one being heated while the other is used.
Available from:

GENERAL SUPPLIERS

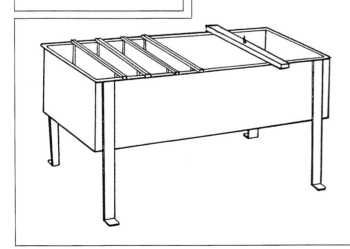

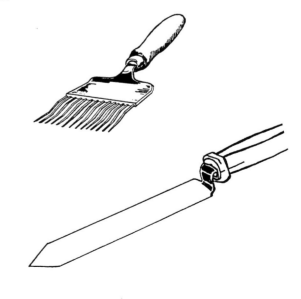

HONEY PROCESSING

All previous operations have been on bees or hives. When starting to work with honey, it is important to remember that honey is a food, and that appropriate standards of hygiene must be maintained. Also, bees quickly get the scent of any honey left unguarded and will collect it to take back to their hives. This can happen in an astonishingly short time. So from the moment the honeycombs free of bees are taken off the hive, *they must be in a bee-tight building or enclosure.*

There is one exception to the above rule: if a good honey flow is still in progress, the bees may continue to work it and ignore the honey being dealt with.

Uncapping and extracting (by whatever method) must be done in a room that allows no access to bees. A few bees may be brought in on clothes or on combs, so vents that allow bees to fly out of the room but not to re-enter are helpful.

Bees in the processing area are objectionable from a hygiene point of view because, when they fly round trying to escape, they release excreta on to walls and floor and this is unacceptable in a food-processing area.

In the simplest operation, pieces of honeycomb are placed in a cloth, which is hung up and left for the honey to drip out (this is 'run honey', the best) and then squeezed to force out as much as possible of the remaining honey.

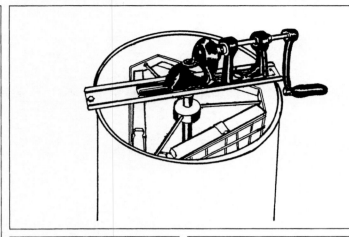

RADIAL EXTRACTOR

A radial honey extractor is like a tangential one, except that the frames are positioned radially in the container, with the top-bar outwards. The cylinder is larger, and is often made to hold all the frames from one honey super (nine or ten) or a multiple of this number. More power is needed to operate these extractors and large ones are electrically operated, but a nine- or ten-frame extractor can be operated by hand, or by foot using an adapted bicycle mechanism. Only one spinning is needed.

A range of manual, pedal and electrically powered radial extractors are available from general suppliers and also from:

PROMETAL M.R.
11 Oriente No.749
Talca
CHILE

HONEY TAP

Taps designed for water flow cannot be used for honey, which is very viscous and flows only slowly. Honey taps or gates for fitting to extractors and tanks should be hygienic and easily cleaned: they should cut off the flow of honey instantly, with no drip, as soon as they are closed, and they must incorporate a safety device (often a screw) to prevent accidental opening from the closed position.

Honey taps are usually made of brass, stainless steel or plastic, and the diameter of the opening can range from 32mm to 76mm. Available from:

GENERAL SUPPLIERS

HONEY EXTRACTORS

These operate by centrifuging the honey out of the combs. The extractor comprises a cylindrical container with a centrally-mounted fitting to support combs or frames of uncapped honey, and a mechanism to rotate the fitting (and the combs) at speed. The honey is thrown out by centrifugal action, to the inner wall of the extractor, whence it falls by gravity to the bottom. Very near the bottom a honey tap is fitted, allowing the honey to be drained out when required. A free space is left below the frames so that a certain amount of honey can accumulate, but honey must be drained off before it reaches the supports of the frames.

The temperature of the room is very important when extracting honey from the combs, because honey flows very much more quickly when warm than when cold, and less is left in the cells. Also, if high speeds have to be used to force the honey out, the combs are more liable to break. With very high-speed (electrically operated) extractors, the speed has to be increased gradually to prevent damage to combs.

TANGENTIAL EXTRACTOR
This was the first type to be developed and is still much used, especially in small-scale beekeeping. The container axis is vertical and the framed combs (often two, three or four) are supported in baskets, or against vertical grids, arranged tangentially within the container (i.e. at right angles to its radius). The frames must normally be spun twice, once with each of the two sides outermost. Some tangential extractors are self-reversing. Extractors can be obtained from most general suppliers or can be made by a local engineering firm.

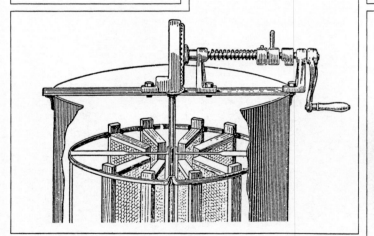

HONEY STRAINERS

Commercially sold honey strainers are designed to receive honey as it leaves the extractor, containing no more than small bits of wax from cappings. Modern quality requirements demand that final straining is through a very fine mesh, and this process is speeded up if all but the smallest particles have been removed first, by one or more strainers of larger mesh. As with other operations on honey, straining is faster if the honey is warm; honey flows roughly twice as fast for every 10°C rise in temperature. Light and dark combs should be strained separately, into different containers, since the flavour of the darker honey may not be as fine.

EXTRACTOR FOR COMBS FROM TOP-BAR HIVES

The combs from top-bar hives have neither the support of a full frame nor the strength of combs built on wired foundation. They cannot withstand the force of a normal extractor, but a small tangential extractor can be adapted by providing wire-mesh baskets in place of the usual grids. Combs (or pieces of comb) are carefully placed in the baskets. The extractor must be spun twice, once with each side of the basket innermost.

A larger extractor (illustrated) for combs from a top-bar hive contains six pairs of baskets mounted horizontally, the whole thus taking twelve combs. The baskets are removed from the top, pair by pair, and combs inserted before they are replaced in the extractor. The extractor is wired for electrical operation but can be adapted for use without electricity. It is produced by:

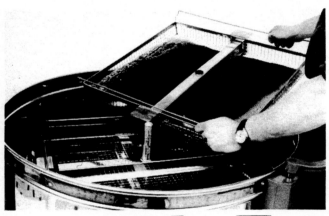

ETS THOMAS FILS SA
65 Rue Abbé G. Thomas
B.P. 2
Fay-aux-Loges 45450
FRANCE

SIMPLE HONEY STRAINERS

Honey can be strained effectively through fine wire mesh or cloth. Alternatively, specially made strainers, available from general suppliers, can be suspended from the honey tap of the extractor. The strainers illustrated include a double strainer with an upper coarse wire mesh to retain the larger particles and speed up the flow through the lower fine wire cloth; the two strainer components are also shown separately in the illustration.

Strainers like those illustrated are practical only for small amounts of honey. For larger quantities, strainers can be purchased with, or to fit at the top of, a honey settling tank (see below right). Available from:

GENERAL SUPPLIERS

DOUBLE BUCKET STRAINER

The Strainaway is a gravity filtration system of two interlocking buckets with a strainer between. The buckets are made from food grade polyethylene and the filters are of stainless steel. The lower bucket is fitted with a honey tap. The rate of filtration can be increased with the use of an optional hand-operated vacuum pump which creates a partial vacuum in the lower bucket.
Capacity 25 litres.

STRAINAWAY
Garn Products
25 & 28 Sages Lane
Peterborough PE4 6AT
Lincs
UK

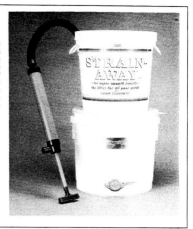

OAC HONEY STRAINER

This strainer was developed at Ontario Agricultural College (now the University of Guelph) in Canada. It is an expensive and relatively sophisticated piece of equipment, suitable only for large-scale operations. It consists of a series of four cylindrical, concentric screens within a cylindrical tank. The sizes of these screens are, from the centre, 0.5, 1.2, 2 and 3 mesh/mm. Honey enters the tank at the top, inside the innermost screen, with the largest mesh. It passes through the screens in turn and is drawn off, also near the top. Each screen, and the tank, has a drainage gate at the bottom.

The OAC strainer has a large straining area for each screen and will handle two tonnes of honey per day at 30°C; it is therefore unsuitable for handling small quantities of honey. In temperate climates, it can be operated successfully without heating the honey. It is available from general suppliers and also from:

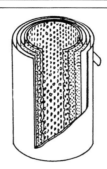

F.W. JONES & SONS LTD
44 Dutch Street
Bedford
Quebec JOJ 1AO
CANADA

HONEY SETTLING TANK

For small-scale operations, many beekeepers use a tank for settling honey. A honey tap is fitted near the bottom for drawing off the honey and the tank can be tilted for final draining. When honey is left standing in the tank at a temperature of 25-30°C, any remaining particles of beeswax rise to the top, hence the term 'settling tank'. Available from:

GENERAL SUPPLIERS

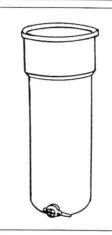

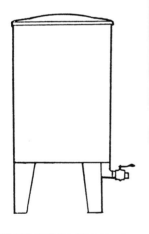

HONEY STORAGE TANKS

Containers for honey storage should be inert (giving no interaction between the vessel and honey) and easy to clean. Honey is a food product and it has a delicate flavour; on both counts it must not be stored in metal drums that are difficult to clean, or that are scratched or damaged. Plastic and stainless steel are ideal materials for smaller and larger honey tanks respectively. The containers must also be tightly closed and moisture-resistant, otherwise the honey in them will absorb moisture and may then ferment.

Suitable storage tanks for honey can be made or obtained locally. Specially made tanks are available, some (as illustrated) holding several tonnes of honey and provided with a stand, a sloping base and an emptying tap. Available from:

GENERAL SUPPLIERS

HONEY CONTAINERS FOR MARKETING

As with honey storage tanks, the material used for the containers must be inert and easily cleaned. Airtightness is essential, especially in humid climates, otherwise the honey will absorb moisture from the air and will then be liable to ferment.

SMALL CONTAINERS (up to 2kg)
For marketing small quantities of honey, use locally-available items such as clean and dry plastic bottles, glass bottles and jars. There is a greater risk of contamination with metal containers (other than stainless steel).

For larger-scale marketing operations, plastic pots are sometimes preferred because glass jars are heavy, liable to break, and cannot be stacked one inside the other, so they are expensive to transport. Specially made plastic containers of 0.5-2.0kg capacity are available, with tightly fitting (re-usable) press-on lids. They may be tall or squat, opaque or transparent. For liquid honey, tall transparent pots are preferable, to minimize the chance of leakage and to show the honey off to advantage. For granulated (crystallized) honey, opaque pots are often used, because surface irregularities in crystal formation are then not visible.

Small honey containers in various styles and materials are available from general suppliers. The supplier of the squat, transparent plastic pots illustrated (above right) is:

SAMAP S.A.
1 Rue du Moulin
B.P. 1
Andolsheim 68280
FRANCE

LARGE CONTAINERS
For quantities of 5-30kg, use food-grade tins or polythene pails. Containers available from general suppliers often have a reinforced rim, a wire handle and a press-on, tightly-fitting lid. A typical design is illustrated.

For quantities of up to 300kg, use 200-litre drums. These should be lined with a food-grade coating like lacquer, or with beeswax. The use of secondhand drums poses a risk of contamination from residues or through corrosion of the drum.

HONEY REFRACTOMETER

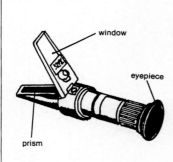

window

eyepiece

prism

A refractometer measures the refractive index of a substance, and one calibrated specifically for honey is very useful because the refractive index shows the total percentage of sugars in the honey. The refractometer is usually calibrated directly in percentage of water (moisture). The upper limit is usually considered to be 21 per cent, but most honey producers and traders prefer a maximum of 18 per cent. Instructions are provided with each refractometer supplied, and these include a table of temperature corrections, since the refractive index is substantially affected by temperature. Some refractometers are calibrated in degrees Brix (a form of measurement of the sugar content in a substance).

In operation, a few drops of honey are placed on the prism (left of drawing), and the hinged window is closed down on to the honey, spreading it into a very thin 'sandwich'. On viewing through the eyepiece (right of drawing) against a good light, the scale will be seen, with an indicating line showing the reading. Since so little honey is used, it is most important that it is representative of the sample, and that the glass surfaces are completely dry. Some refractometers incorporate a thermometer. The following firms supply honey refractometers:

A. ECROYD AND SON LTD
P.O. Box 5056
25 Sawyers Arms Road
Papanni
Christchurch S5
NEW ZEALAND

GIFU YOHO CO LTD
Kano-Sakurado-cho 1
Gifu-Shi
Gifu 500-91
JAPAN

STEFAN PUFF GmbH
Neuholdaugasse, 8011 Graz
AUSTRIA

PFUND COLOUR GRADER

This instrument is used in the world honey market for measuring the 'colour' (darkness) of honey. It compares the opacity of a honey sample with that of a standard 'amber' liquid. The honey sample is placed in a wedge-shaped trough which is moved past a narrow slit in the housing until a colour match is obtained, i.e. the colour density of the honey matches that of the amber wedge. The reading on a millimetre scale is then the 'Pfund scale' reading for the honey. The scale is divided into standardized colour names, which may vary slightly between countries.
Available from:

XPORT
Port Authority Trading Company
1 World Trade Center 55NE
New York
NY 10048
USA

POLLEN TRAP

Honey and beeswax are the most commonly harvested hive products. Pollen, compared with honey, has a high protein, vitamin and mineral content and, in some countries, is harvested and processed for sale. Harvesting is done using a pollen trap, a modified hive entrance in which the incoming bees must pass through two parallel mesh grids, with the result that pollen (loads on the bees' hind legs) are knocked off and fall into a collecting tray below. It would be dangerous to prevent any pollen entering the hive for more than a day or two, because brood rearing would cease, and the use of traps must therefore be organized accordingly.

Most pollen traps on sale are fitted at the bottom of a hive (and must have the same cross-section), either immediately above the normal floorboard or instead of it. Other designs are used at the front of the hive or at the top, with an upper hive entrance. Commercially available pollen traps do not necessarily fulfil all the conditions for successful use in all circumstances without harm to the colony. International Bee Research Association Publication M86, *Pollen and its harvesting*, explains the problems and gives recommended designs not on sale.

Pollen is a highly nutritious food and is thus a good medium for the growth of micro-organisms. Pollen must therefore be either deep-frozen or dried before storage. It must not be subjected to temperatures in excess of 45°C. For safety reasons, pollen traders in technologically advanced countries may be unwilling to import pollen from untried sources.

Pollen traps are available from:

GENERAL SUPPLIERS

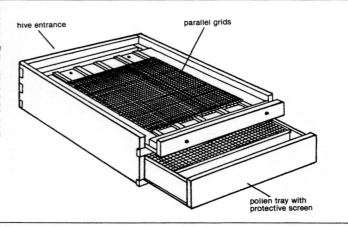

hive entrance

parallel grids

pollen tray with protective screen

BEESWAX PROCESSING EQUIPMENT

Beeswax is a valuable hive product and should bring the beekeeper additional income. Unlike honey, it needs no container and no special care, even in long storage. In spite of this, it is all too often thrown away as there may be little or no local use for it. Beeswax has traditionally been exported from tropical countries but a beekeepers' co-operative or similar body may be needed to organize its sale to traders.

When beeswax cappings, combs, etc. have been washed free of honey, or have been cleaned by bees, the beeswax is melted to let everything that is not pure beeswax separate out by sinking to the bottom. It is essential that light combs are treated separately from dark ones, because light wax will fetch the highest price.

Beeswax *must* be heated in a safe way, or there is danger of a fire. The first apparatus described is ideal in this way, costs nothing to operate, and can produce very high quality wax.

SOLAR WAX EXTRACTOR
The wax pieces are put on a metal base, closed in by four sides and covered with a lid consisting of two sheets of glass 5mm apart. The whole assembly is tilted at a suitable angle to catch the sun's rays. Below the base is a layer of thermal insulation material to trap heat inside the box. The melted wax runs down the sloping base (leaving most of the dross behind), and into a container within the box. A second external container can be incorporated, as in the illustration.

Solar wax extractors can be made from scrap material using the basic design principles shown or they can be purchased from:

GENERAL SUPPLIERS

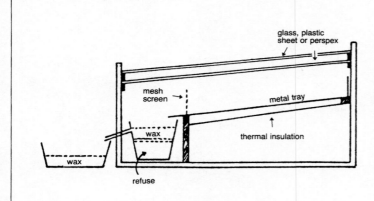

glass, plastic sheet or perspex

mesh screen

metal tray

wax

thermal insulation

wax

refuse

HOT-WATER BEESWAX PROCESSOR

In principle this is a vessel in which water and unprocessed beeswax are heated together. The beeswax floats to the top and can be drained off, leaving behind the dross and the dirty water. More water can then be added at the bottom, to restore the beeswax layer to the correct level for draining. A simple type is illustrated left.

The 'Mountain Grey Beeswax Extractor' works on this principle. It has a two-gallon steel container with a long filling funnel and is fitted with a coarse straining cloth and a wax-collecting channel around the rim. It is made by:

E.H. THORNE (BEEHIVES) LTD
Beehive Works
Wragby
Lincoln LN3 5LA
UK

STEAM BEESWAX PRESS

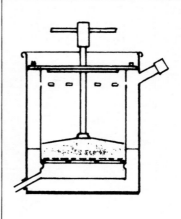

The type illustrated consists of a steamer fitted with a screw plunger. Combs, wrapped in canvas bags, are placed in a perforated basket and separated by wooden boards. The plunger is then screwed down and locked, to maintain pressure on the comb while it is melted by steam generated from water at the bottom of the container. The melted wax runs through the basket and out of the tube. When the wax flow ceases, further pressure is applied. It is necessary to turn the screw back and shake up the bags before renewing the pressure, to extract all the wax, which should be completed in two or three operations, leaving only 1-3 percent dross behind.

Several slightly different models are available. One can be obtained from:

STEFAN PUFF GmbH
Neuholdaugasse
Graz 8011
AUSTRIA

SOURCES OF FURTHER INFORMATION

This book provides the most comprehensive list of manufacturers of small-scale agricultural equipment available today. In addition the introduction to each chapter provides guidelines to help readers in the selection and use of equipment. However, a publication like this cannot possibly provide a totally comprehensive list of manufacturers, nor can it provide sufficient detail in the introductions to cover all equipment and all farming situations. To supplement the information in this book you are advised to consult local information resources wherever possible.

To assist this process we have listed addresses of institutions in as many countries as possible, in alphabetical order by country. Again, it is by no means comprehensive. Please inform Intermediate Technology of any inappropriate inclusions and any appropriate institutions not included in the following list. This will help to make future editions more useful.

We have attempted to show where the institution has indicated that it has information on specific subjects of interest in this book. Even where there is no institution mentioned here on the specific subject of interest, the listed institutions may be able to guide you to other local sources of information not listed in this book.

Subject areas: ag eng = agricultural engineering, bee = beekeeping, bio = biological pest management, har = harvesting, int pest man = integrated pest management, pl pro = plant protection

---

ARGENTINA

National Institute of Agricultural Technology
CC 6
Concepción del Uruguay 3260
Argentina
Tel: 0442-2561
(ag eng)

National Institute of Agricultural Technology
CC 21
Marcos Juárez Córdoba 2580
Argentina
Tel: 0472-25001
(ag eng)

AUSTRALIA

Curtin University of Technology
Muresk Institute of Agriculture
Northam
Western Australia 6401
Australia
Tel: 61-096-22-4548
(ag eng)

University of Sydney
Badham Building
Science Road
Sydney
New South Wales 2006
Australia
Tel: 02-692-2728
(ag eng)

BAHAMAS

Ministry of Agriculture
PB 3028
Nassau
Bahamas
(pl pro)

BANGLADESH

Intermediate Technology Bangladesh
1/13 Iqbal Road
Block A
Mohammadpur
Dhaka
Bangladesh
Tel: 02 811 934

Bangladesh Agricultural Research Institute
(BARI)
Joydebpur
Gazipur
Bangladesh
Tel: 401013
(ag eng)

Bangladesh Rice Research Institute (BRRI)
PO BRRI
Joydebpur
Gazipur
Bangladesh
Tel: 691200
(ag eng)

BELGIUM

ATOL
Blyde Inkomstlaan 9
3000 Leuven
Belgium
(ag eng)

Ministry of Agriculture
National Institute of Agricultural Engineering
Burg. Van Gansberghelaan, 115
B-9220 Merelbeke
Belgium
Tel: 091-52-18-21
(ag eng)

BELIZE

Belize College of Agriculture
Central Farm
Cayo District
Belize
Tel: 092-2131
(ag eng)

Ministry of Agriculture, Forestry and Mariculture
Agriculture Information Unit
Belmopan
Belize
Tel: 08-2241
(pl pro)

BOTSWANA

Botswana Technology Centre
Private Bag 0082
Gaborone
Botswana
Tel: 314161

Department of Agricultural Research
Private Bag 0033
Gaborone
Botswana
Tel: 3152381
(pl pro)

Southern African Centre for Cooperation in Agricultural Research (SACCAR)
Private Bag 00108
Gaborone
Botswana
Tel: Gaborone 352381
(ag eng)

BRAZIL

Confederaçao Nacional do Comércio
Av. General Justo 307, 60 Andar
Rio de Janeiro
Rio de Janeiro 20022
Brazil
Tel: 297-0011
(har)

Empresa Brasileira de Pesquisa Agropecuária
Unidade de Apoio à Pesquisa e
Desenvolvimento de Instrumentaçao
Agropecuária (EMBRAPA, UAPDIA)
Rua XV de Novembro, 1452, PO Box 741
Sao Carlos, Sao Paulo 13560
Brazil
Tel: 016-272-5741
(ag eng)

Fundaçao Getúlio Vargas
Km 47 Da Antiga Rod. Rio Sao Paulo
Itaguaí
Rio de Janeiro 23851
Brazil
Tel: 782-1042
(bio)

BULGARIA

V. Kolarov Higher Institute of Agriculture
D. Mendeleev Str.12
4000 Plovdiv
Bulgaria
Tel: 26-95-40
(ag eng)

BURKINA FASO

Centre Agricole Polyvalent de Matourkou
(CAPM)
BP 130
Bobo Dioulasso
Burkina Faso
Tel: 98-22-27
(ag eng)

BURUNDI

Ministère de l'Agriculture et de l'Elevage
(MINAGRI)
BP 1850
Bujumbura
Burundi
Tel: 2278

CAMEROON

Institute of Agronomic Research
BP 2123
Yaoundé
Cameroon
Tel: 23-26-44
(ag eng)

Institut Panafrican pour le Développement
BP 4078
Douala
Province de Littoral
Cameroon
Tel: 42-37-70
(ag eng)

CANADA

Agriculture Canada
Research Station Beaverlodge
Box 29
Beaverlodge
Alberta T0H 0C0
Canada
Tel: 403-354-2212
(bee)

Brace Research Institute
MacDonald College of McGill University
PO Box 900
Sainte Anne de Bellevue
Quebec H9X 1C0
Canada
Tel: 514-398-7833
(pumps)

International Development and Research
Centre (IDRC)
PO Box 8500
Ottawa
Ontario K1G 3H9
Canada
Tel: 613-236-6163

University of Guelph
Guelph
Ontario N1G 2W1
Canada
Tel: 519-824-4120
(ag eng)

CAPE VERDE

National Agricultural Research Institute
PB 84
Praia
Cape Verde
Tel: 611570
(pl pro)

CHILE

Faculty of Agricultural Sciences
University of Chile
Casila 1004
Santiago
Chile
Tel: 5887041
(ag eng)

Instituto Agricola Metodista 'El Vergel'
Casilla 2-D
Angol
Chile
Tel: 3003
(ag eng, har)

CHINA, PEOPLE'S REPUBLIC OF

Chinese Acadamy of Sciences
Institute of Zoology
19 Zhongguancun Lu
Haidian
Beijing 100080
People's Republic of China
(int pest man, pl pro)

Heilongziang Institute of Agricultural
Mechanization
Haping Road
Nengang District
Harbin
Heilongziang
People's Republic of China
Tel: 61784
(ag eng, pl pro)

Institute of Scientific and Technical
Information of China (ISTIC)
PO Box 640
Beijing
People's Republic of China
(ag eng)

COLOMBIA

Institute of Technological Research
Av.30 No.52A-77, AA 7031
Bogotá, D.E.
Colombia
Tel: 221-0066
(ag eng)

International Centre for Tropical Agriculture
Apartado Aero 6713
Cali
Colombia
Tel: 57-3-675050

National University of Colombia
AA 14490
Bogotá
Colombia
Tel: 244-2871
(ag eng, pl pro)

CONGO

Ministère de Développement Rural (MDR)
BP 2453
Brazzaville
Congo
Tel: 811813
(pl pro)

COSTA RICA

Inter American Institute of Agricultural
Sciences
Apartado 55-2200
Coronado
Costa Rica
Tel: 29-0222

Interamerican Institute of Cooperation for
Agriculture
Apodo 55
Turrialba
Costa Rica
Tel: 56-05-01
(ag eng)

Tropical Agricultural Centre for Research
and Training
7170 Turrialba
Turrialba
Costa Rica
Tel: 506-56-16-32
(pl pro, int pest man)

CUBA

Ministry of Agriculture
GP 4149
Havana 4
Cuba
Tel: 3-3256, 30-9075
(ag eng)

CZECHOSLOVAKIA

Bee Research Institute
Gasperikova 599
033 01 Liptovsky Hrádok
Czechoslovakia
Tel: 2120
(bee)

Institute of Tropical Agriculture
Agricultural University
6 Suchdol
Prague 160 21
Czechoslovakia
Tel: 344107

Research Institute of Agricultural Engineering
Ksancim 50
163 07 Prague 6 — Repy
Czechoslovakia
Tel: 35-95-31
(ag eng)

DENMARK

Royal Veterinary and Agricultural University
Bulowsvej 13, Frederiksberg
DK-1870 Copenhagen V
Denmark
Tel: 01-35 17 88
(ag eng)

DOMINICAN REPUBLIC

Universidad Nacional Pedro Henríquez Ureña
(UNPHU)
Apdo 1423
Santo Domingo
Dominican Republic
Tel: 562-6601
(ag eng)

ECUADOR

Technical University of Manabi
Agricultural Engineering Faculty
Apdo 82
Portoviejo
Manabi
Ecuador
Tel: 652853
(ag eng)

EGYPT

Ain Shams University
Faculty of Agriculture
Shobra El-Khema
Cairo
Egypt
Tel: 941453
(ag eng)

Water Research Centre (WRC)
22 El-Galaa Street
Bulak
Cairo
Egypt
Tel: 760474
(ag eng)

EL SALVADOR

University of El Salvador
Agriculture Science Faculty
Apdo 747
San Salvador
El Salvador
Tel: 25-25-72
(pl pro)

ETHIOPIA

Alemaya Agricultural University
PO Box 138
Dire Dawa
Ethiopia
Tel: 95

Institute of Agricultural Research
PB 2003
Addis Ababa
Ethiopia
Tel: 161055
(ag eng, pl pro)

FIJI

Fiji College of Agriculture (FCA)
PO Box 77
Nausori
Fiji
Tel: 47044
(ag eng)

University of the South Pacific (USP)
PO Box 1168
Suva
Fiji
Tel: 31-3900
(ag eng, pl pro)

FINLAND

Agricultural Research Centre
Institute of Pest Investigation
SF-31600 Jokioinen
Finland
Tel: 358-1688111
(pl pro)

State Research Institute of Engineering in
Agriculture and Forestry
PPA 1
SF-03400 Vihti
Finland
Tel: 358-13-46211
(ag eng)

FRANCE

Centre d'Etude et Expérimentation sur le
Machinisme Agricole Tropical (CEEMAT)
73 rue Jean François Breton
34000 Montpellier
France
Tel: 67-61-57-00

Group de Recherches et d'Échanges
Technologique (GRET)
213 rue Lafayette
75010 Paris
France
Tel: 40-35-13-14

GAMBIA

Gambia Technical Training Institute
PO Box 989
Banjul, Kanifing Industrial Estate
Gambia
Tel: 92600
(har)

Ministry of Agriculture
10B Cameron Street
Banjul
Gambia
Tel: 28752
(ag eng)

GERMANY

Academy of Agricultural Sciences
Max-Eyth-Allee
DDR-1572 Potsdam-Bornim
Germany
Tel: 44-91
(ag eng)

Federal Agricultural Research Centre
Bundesallee 50
D-3300 Braunschweig
Germany
Tel: 0531-596239
(ag eng)

GATE
Postfach 5180
D-6236 Eschborn 1
Germany
Tel: 061-96-790
(ag eng)

GHANA

Technical Training Centre
University of Science and Technology
Kumasi
Ghana
Tel: 5351
(ag eng)

GRENADA

Ministry of Agriculture, Lands, Forestry,
Fisheries and Tourism
Botanic Gardens
St George's
Grenada
Tel: 3195
(pl pro)

GUATEMALA

University of San Carlos of Guatemala
Apdo 1545
Guatemala Zona 12
Tel: 760790

GUINEA

Institut de Sciences Agrozootechniques
Foulaya (ISAF)
BP 156
Kindia
Guinea
Tel: 61-01-48
(ag eng, pl pro)

GUYANA

National Agricultural Research Institute
Mon Repos. East Cost Demerara
Georgetown
Guyana
Tel: 020-2881
(pl pro)

HAITI

Ministère de l'Agriculture des Ressources
Naturelles et du Port-au-Prince, Damien
Haiti
Tel: 2-4592
(ag eng)

HONDURAS

Panamerican School of Agriculture
Apdo 93
Tegucigalpa
Francisco Morazan
Honduras
Tel: 33-2717
(ag eng)

HUNGARY

Cooperative Research Institute
Pf.398
H-1371 Budapest
Hungary
Tel: 761-534
(ag eng)

ICELAND

Agricultural Research Institute
Keldnaholt
112 Reykjavik
Iceland
Tel: 91-82230
(ag eng)

INDIA

Appropriate Technology Development
Association
PO Box 311
Gandhi Bhawan
Lucknow
Uttar Pradesh 226001
India
Tel: 33506

Asian & Pacific Centre for Transfer of
Technology
PO Box 115
Bangalore 560 052
India
Tel: 76931

Central Institute of Agricultural Engineering
(ICAR, CIAE)
Nabi Bagh
Berasia Road
Bhopal 462018, Madhya Pradesh
India
Tel: 75171
(ag eng)

Centre of Science for Villages
Magan Sanagrahalaya
Wardha
Maharashtra 442001
India
Tel: 2412

Consortium on Rural Technology
PO Box 9236
D-320 Laxmi Nagar
New Delhi 110 092
India
Tel: 2244545

Dr Yashwant Singh Parmar University of
Horticulture and Forestry
PO NAUNI
Solan 173230 Himachal Pradesh
India
Tel: 80
(bee)

Indian Council of Agricultural Research
Cuttack 753006 Orissa
India
Tel: PBX ext.236
(ag eng)

Indian Council of Agricultural Research
Santoshnager
PO Saidabad
India
(ag eng)

International Crops Research Institute for the
Semi Arid Tropics Patancheru PO
Hyderabad 502324 Andhra Pradesh
India
Tel: 224016
(ag eng, pl pro)

INDONESIA

Agency for Agricultural Research and
Development (AARD)
Jalan Ir. H. Huanda 20
Bogor
Indonesia
Tel: 0251-24394
(ag eng, pl pro)

Sukarami Research Institute for Food Crops
PO 34
Padang
West Sumatra
Indonesia
Tel: 26435
(ag eng)

IRAN

Agricultural Engineering Dept
Ministry of Agriculture AERTTC
PO Box 1143
Karaj 31585
Iran
Tel: 02221-24046

Shiraz University
College of Agriculture
Shiraz
Iran
Tel: 22109
(ag eng, pl pro)

IRAQ

Scientific Research Council
Agriculture and Water Resources Research
Centre
PO Box 2416
Baghdad
Iraq
Tel: 7512080
(ag eng)

IRELAND

Agricultural & Food Engineering Department
University College
Earlsfort Terrace
Dublin 2
Ireland
Tel: 253-1-693244

IVORY COAST

Bouaké Agricultural Institute
BP 1490
Bouaké 01
Ivory Coast
Tel: 63-33-30
(ag eng)

Centre Invoirien de Machinisme Agricole
(CIMA)
BP 1193
Bouaké
Ivory Coast
Tel: 633695, 633453
(ag eng)

ITALY

International Fund for Agricultural
Development (IFAD)
107 Via del Serafico
00142 Rome
Italy
Tel: 54592307
(ag eng)

United Nations, Food and Agriculture
Organisation (FAO)
Via delle Terme di Caracalla
00100 Rome
Italy
Tel: 5797-3703
(ag eng)

JAMAICA

Ministry of Education
College of Agriculture
PB 170, Passley Gardens
Port Antonio
Jamaica
Tel: 99332468
(ag eng)

JAPAN

National Agricultural Research Centre
(NARC)
3-1-1 Kannondai
Tsukuba
Ibaraki 305
Japan
Tel: 02975-6-8848
(ag eng)

Tokyo University of Agriculture
1-1 Sakuragaoka, 1-chome
Setagayaku
Tokyo 156
Japan
Tel: 03-420-2131
(ag eng)

JORDAN

Ministry of Agriculture
PO Box 226
Amman
Jordan
Tel: 725411
(ag eng)

University of Jordan
Amman
Jordan
Tel: 843555
(ag eng)

KENYA

Intermediate Technology Kenya
PO Box 39493
Nairobi
Kenya
Tel: 446243

Embu Institute of Agriculture
PB 6
Embu
Kenya
Tel: 20117
(ag eng)

International Centre of Insect Physiology and
Ecology (ICIPE)
PO Box 30772
Nairobi
Kenya
Tel: 43081
(int pest man)

Kenya Agricultural Research Institute
PO Box 30148
Nairobi
Kenya
Tel: 0154-32880
(ag eng)

Kenya Institute of Organic Farming (KIOF)
PO Box 34972
Nairobi
Kenya

National Agricultural Research Station
PO Box 450
Kitale
Rift Valley Province
Kenya
Tel: 0325-20107
(ag eng)

University of Nairobi
Department of Agricultural Engineering
Kabete Campus
PO Box 30197
Nairobi
Kenya
Tel: 592211

KOREA, REPUBLIC OF

Seoul National University
College of Agriculture
No.103, Seo-dun Dong
Su-won
Kyung-ki 170
Republic of Korea
Tel: 0331-44-2120
(ag eng)

LEBANON

American University of Beirut
PO Box 11/236
Beirut
Lebanon
Tel: 865250
(pl pro)

LESOTHO

Lesotho Agricultural Production and
Institutional Support Project
Agricultural Research Division
PO Box 829
Maseur
Lesotho
Tel: 322372

LIBERIA

Central Agricultural Research Institute (CARI)
Mailbag 3929
Monrovia
Suakoko Bong County
Liberia
Tel: 223443
(ag eng, pl pro)

West Africa Rice Development Association
(WARDA)
LBDI Building Complex, Tubman Boulevard
Sinkor
PB 1019
Monrovia
Liberia
Tel: 211638
(pl pro)

MADAGASCAR

Ecole Supérieure des Sciences Agronomiques
(ESSA)
BP 175
Antananarivo 101
Madagascar
Tel: 241-14

Ministère de la Production Agricole et de la
Réforme Agraire
Direction de l'Infrastructure Rural (MPARA,
DIR)
BP 1061
Antananarivo
Madagascar
Tel: 40180
(ag eng)

MALAWI

Department of Agricultural Research (DAR)
PO Box 158
Lilongwe
Malawi
Tel: 767-222
(ag eng)

Natural Resources College (NRC)
PO Box 143
Lilongwe
Malawi
Tel: 722744
(ag eng)

MALAYSIA

Department of Agriculture
Menara Khidmat Building
Kota Kinabula
Sabah 88632
Malaysia
Tel: 088-55155
(ag eng, pl pro)

University of Agriculture
Serdang
Selangor Darul Ehsan 43400
Malaysia
Tel: 03-9486688
(ag eng, pl pro)

MALI

International Livestock Centre for Africa
(ILCA)
BP 60
Bamako
Mali
Tel: 22-21-77

Ministère de l'Agriculture
Direction Nationale du Génie Rural
Avenue Mohamed V
BP 155
Bamako
Mali
Tel: 222605
(ag eng)

MAURITIUS

University of Mauritius
Reduit
Mauritius
Tel: 54-1041
(ag eng, pl pro)

MEXICO

CIMMYT
Bueno Lisboa 27
Apdo Postal 6-641
06600 Mexico City
Mexico

Universidad Autonoma de Nuevo Leon
Facultad de Agronomia
Apdo 358
Marin
Nuevo Leon 66450
México
Tel: 824-8-00-99
(ag eng)

University of Sonora
Carretera a Bahia Kino Km 25
Hermosillo
Sonora
México
Tel: 2-10-46
(ag eng)

MOROCCO

Ministère de l'Agriculture et de la Réforme
Agraire
BP 6214
Rabat-Instituts
Morocco
Tel: 717-58
(ag eng)

MOZAMBIQUE

Eduardo Mondlane Unversity
Agronomy Faculty
CP 257
Maputo
Mozambique
Tel: 74-21-42
(pl pro)

NEPAL

International Centre for Integrated Mountain
Development (ICIMOD)
PO Box 3226
Kathmandu
Nepal
Tel: 521575
(ag eng)

Tribhuvan University
Institute of Agriculture and Animal Science
(TU,IAAS)
Rampur
Chitwan
Nepal
Tel: 21211 Chitwan
(ag eng)

NETHERLANDS

Information Centre for Low External Input and
Sustainable Agriculture (ILEIA)
Kastanjelaan 5
PO Box 64
3830 AB Leusden
The Netherlands
Tel: 033 943086

Institute of Agricultural Engineering
PO Box 43
Wageningen 6700 AA
The Netherlands
Tel: 08370-94350
(ag eng)

International Reference Centre for Cummunity
Water Supply and Sanitation
PO Box 93190
2509 AD The Hague
The Netherlands
Tel: 070-331-4133

Royal Tropical Institute (KIT)
63 Mauriskade
Amsterdam 1092 AD
The Netherlands
Tel: 020-5688340
(ag eng)

Technical Centre for Agriculture and Rural
Cooperation (CTA)
PO Box 380
Wageningen 6700 AJ
The Netherlands
Tel: 2-513-7435

TOOL
Sarpathistraat 650
1018 AV Amsterdam
The Netherlands
(ag eng)

Wageningen Agricultural University
PO Box 9100
Wageningen 6700 HA
The Netherlands
Tel: 08370-84440
(ag eng)

NEW ZEALAND

Agricultural Engineering Institute
PO Box 84
Lincoln College
Canterbury
New Zealand
Tel: 03-252-811

University of Canterbury
Private Bag
Christchurch
Canterbury
New Zealand
Tel: 03-66-7001
(ag eng)

NICARAGUA

National School of Agriculture and Livestock
Apdo 1487
Managua
Nicaragua
Tel: 31473

NIGER

Institut National de Recherches Agronomique
du Niger (INRAN)
BP 429
Niamey
Niger
Tel: 72-36-70
(pl pro)

International Crops Research Institute for the
Semi-Arid Tropics
(ICRISAT)
BP 12404
Niamey
Niger
Tel: 72-25-29

NIGERIA

Ahmadu Bello University
Institute for Agricultural Research
PMB 1044
Zaria
Nigeria
Tel: 50571
(ag eng)

Department of Agricultural Engineering
University of Nigeria
Nsukka
Anambra
Nigeria
Tel: 48 771911

International Institute of Tropical Agriculture
(IITA)
PMB 5320
Ibadan
Nigeria
Tel: 022-400300
(ag eng)

National Centre for Agricultural
Mechanization
PMB 1525
Ilorin
Nigeria
(ag eng)

OMAN

Sultan Qaboos University (SQU)
PO Box 32487
El Khod
Muscat
Oman
Tel: 513333
(ag eng)

PAKISTAN

CAB International Institute of Biological
Control
PARC-CIBC Station
PO Box 8
Rawalpindi, Punjab
Pakistan
Tel: 842347
(bio con, pl pro)

National Agricultural Research Centre
(NARC)
L-13 Al-Markaz F/7
PO Box 1031
Islamabad
Pakistan
Tel: 82005
(ag eng)

Rice Research Institute Dokri
District Larkana
Dokri
Sind
Pakistan
Tel: Larkana 60877
(ag eng)

University of Agriculture (AGRIVARSITY)
Faisalabad
Pakistan
Tel: 25911
(ag eng)

PAPUA NEW GUINEA

University of Technology
Appropriate Technology Development
Institute
Private Mail Bag
Lae
Morobe
Papua New Guinea
Tel: 43-4999
(ag eng, pl pro)

PERU

Intermediate Technology Peru
Casilla 18-0620
Lima 18
Peru
Tel: 014 466621

International Potatoe Centre
Apdo 5969
Lima
Peru
Tel: 366920

National Agricultural University la Molina
Apdo 456
Lima
Peru
Tel: 35-2035
(ag eng)

PHILIPPINES

Agricultural Mechanization Devlopment
Program
College of Engineering & Agro-Industrial
Technology
UP College
Laguna 4031
Philippines
Tel: 2307

Institute for Small-Scale Industries
UP Jacinto Street
Diliman
Quezon City 3004
Philippines
Tel: 99-70-76

International Rice Research Institute (IRRI)
PO Box 933
Manila
Philippines
Tel: 9-231

Southeast Asian Regional Centre for Graduate
Study and Research in Agriculture
Laguna 4031
Philippines
Tel: 2317
(ag eng)

Regional Network for Agricultural Machinery
c/o UNDP
PO Box 7285
Domestic Airport PO Lock Box
1300 Domestic Rd
Pasay City
Philippines
Tel: 3522

University of the Philippines at Los Baños
(UPLB)
Los Baños
Laguna 3720
Philippines
Tel: 63-833-2326
(ag eng)

POLAND

Academy of Agriculture and Technology
Kortowo Bl.41
10-957 Olsztyn
Poland
Tel: 27-31-71
(ag eng)

PORTUGAL

Institute of Agriculture
Tapada da Ajuda
1300 Lisbon
Portugal
Tel: 637824
(ag eng)

Institute of Tropical Scientific Research
Rua Jau 47
1300 Lisbon
Portugal
Tel: 63705

SENEGAL

African Regional Centre of Technology
(ARCT)
Information Service (IS)
BP 2435
Dakar
Senegal
Tel: 22-77-12
(har)

Institut Sénégalais de Recherches Agricoles
Centre National de Recherches Agronomiques
(CNRA,ISRA)
BP 53
Bambey
Senegal
Tel: 736050
(pl pro)

Institut Sénégalais de Recherches Agricoles
BP 3120
Dakar
Senegal
Tel: 22-66-99
(ag eng)

SEYCHELLES

Ministry of National Development,
Agriculture Division
Grand Anse Research Station
PB 199
Mahe
Seychelles
Tel: 78252
(pl pro)

SIERRA LEONE

Njala University College
Private Mail Bag
Freetown
Sierra Leone
(ag eng)

Rice Research Station, Rokupr
PMB 736
Freetown
Sierra Leone
(ag eng)

SOLOMON ISLANDS

Agricultural Information Unit
Ministry of Agriculture and Lands
PO Box G13
Honiara
Solomon Islands

SPAIN

Escuela Universitaria de Ingeniería Técnica
Agrícola (EUITA)
Plaza del Triunfo
41004 Seville
Spain
Tel: 954-690750
(ag eng)

National Institute of Agricultural Research
Jose Abascal 56
28003 Madrid
Spain
Tel: 91-4413193
(ag eng)

SRI LANKA

Intermediate Technology Sri Lanka
33 1/1 Queen's Road
Colombo 3
Sri Lanka
Tel: 01 503786

International Irrigation Management Institute
(IIMI)
PO Box 1922
Colombo 1
Sri Lanka
Tel: 546561

University of Ruhuna
Faculty of Agriculture (UR)
Mapalana
Kamburupitiya
Sri Lanka
Tel: 041-2681
(ag eng, pl pro)

SUDAN

Intermediate Technology Sudan
PO Box 2979
Mogran
Khartoum

Arab Organization for Agricultural
Development
(AOAD)
PO Box 474
Khartoum
Sudan
Tel: 40353
(ag eng)

Atbara Technical College
The Nile University
Atbara
Sudan

Small Industries Development Company
PO Box 2718
Khartoum
Sudan
Tel: 611274

University of Khartoum
PO Box 32
Khartoum, North
Sudan
Tel: 612055
(ag eng)

SWAZILAND

Ministry of Agriculture and Cooperatives
Lowveld Experiment Station
PB 11
Matata
Swaziland
Tel: 36311
(pl pro)

Swedish University of Agricultural Sciences
Box 624
S-220 06 Lund
Sweden
Tel: 46-46-117510
(ag eng)

SWITZERLAND

Swiss Federal Station for Farm Management
and Agricultural Engineering
CH-8356 Taenikon
Switzerland
Tel: 052-47-20-25
(ag eng)

SYRIA

Damascus University
Damascus
Syria
Tel: 222003
(ag eng)

International Centre for Agricultural Research
in the Dry Areas (ICARDA)
PO Box 5466
Aleppo
Syria
Tel: 235-221
(ag eng)

TAIWAN

Agricultural Engineering Research Centre
196-1 Chung-Yuan Road
Chungli 32043
Taiwan
Tel: 03-45201314
(ag eng)

Taiwan Agricultural Research Institute (TARI)
189 Chung-Cheng Road
Wu-feng
Taichung
Taiwan 41301
Taiwan
Tel: 04-3302301-5
(ag eng)

TANZANIA

Beekeeping Training Institute
PO Box 62
Tabora
Tanzania
Tel: 2124
(bee)

Mbeya Oxenization Project
PO Box 89
Mbeya
Tanzania

Ministry of Agriculture Training Institutes
(MATI)
PO Box 1400
Dar-Es-Salaam
Tanzania
Tel: 40191
(ag eng)

Sokoine University of Agriculture
PO Box 3022
Morogoro
Tanzania
Tel: 4639

Tanzania Engineering & Manufacturing
Design Organisation
PO Box 6111
Arusha
Tanzania
Tel: 7078

THAILAND

Appropriate Technology Association
61/1 Sawankalok Road
Dusit
Bangkok 110300
Thailand
Tel: 281-3750

Asian Institute of Technology (AIT)
PO Box 2754
Bangkok 10501
Thailand
Tel: 5290100
(ag eng)

Food and Agricultural Organization of the
United Nations, FAO
Regional Office for Asia and the Pacific
Maliwan Mansion
Phra Atit Road
Bangkok 10200
Thailand
(ag eng)

King Mongkut's Institute of Technology
(KMIT)
Faculty of Agriculture Technology
Ladkrabang
Bangkok 10520
Thailand
Tel: 326-7341
(ag eng)

TOGO

Institut National de Formation Agricole de
TOVE (INFA-TOVE)
BP 401
Kpalimé
Togo
Tel: 41-01-29
(ag eng)

TONGA

University of the South Pacific Institute of
Rural Development (IRD)
Nuku'alofa
Tonga
Tel: 21955
(ag eng)

TRINIDAD AND TOBAGO

Ministry of Food Production, Marine
Exploitation, Forestry and the Central
Experiment Station
Centeno
Via Arima PO
Trinidad and Tobago
Tel: 809-6464334
(ag eng, pl pro)

University of the West Indies
St Augustine
Trinidad and Tobago
Tel: 663-1439
(pl pro)

TUNISIA

National Agricultural Institute of Tunis
43 Avenue Charles Nicolle
1002 Tunis
Tunisia
Tel: 01-280-950
(ag eng)

TURKEY

Aegean Agricultural Research Institute
(AARI)
PO Box 9
Menemen
Izmir 35661
Turkey
Tel: 51-149131
(bee)

Black Sea Agricultural Research Institute
PO Box 39
Gelemen
Samsun
Turkey
Tel: 60514
(ag eng)

UGANDA

Ministry of Agriculture and Forestry
Makerere University, Bukalasa Agricultural
College
PB 174
Wobulenzi
Uganda
(ag eng)

Ministry of Agriculture and Forestry
Namulonge Research Station
PO Box 7084
Kampala
Uganda
Tel: Namulonge 3 and 4

UK

Intermediate Technology Transport Ltd
The Old Power Station
Ardington
Oxfordshire OX12 8HP
UK
Tel: 0235 833753

Intermediate Technology Power Ltd
The Warren
Eversley
Hampshire RG27 0PR
UK
Tel: 0734 730073

Institute of Arable Crops Research (IACR)
Agricultural and Food Research Council
(AFRC)
Harpenden
Hertfordshire AL5 2JO
UK
Tel: 05827-63133
(pl pro, pl pro)

International Bee Research Association
(IBRA)
18 North Road
Cardiff
S Glamorgan
Wales CF1 3DY
UK
Tel: 0222 37240
(bee)

International Institute for Biological Pest
Control
Silwood Park
Buckhurst Road
Ascot
Berks SL5 7TA
UK
Tel: 344-872747
(bio)

Overseas Development Natural Resources
Institute (ODNRI)
Central Avenue
Chatham Maritime
Chatham ME4 4TB
UK
Tel: 0634-880088

Silsoe College
Cranfield Institute of Technology
Silsoe
Bedford MK45 4DT
UK
Tel: 0525-60428
(ag eng)

Silsoe Research Institute (SRI)
Agriculture and Food Research Council
(AFRC)
West Park
Silsoe
Bedford MK45 4HS
UK
Tel: 0525-60000
(ag eng)

University of Edinburgh
Centre for Tropical Veterinary Medicine
(CTVM)
Easter Bush
Roslin
Midlothian
Scotland EH25 9RG
UK
Tel: 031-445-2001
(ag eng)

University of Reading
Whiteknights
PO Box 223
Reading
Berks RG6 2AE
UK
Tel: 0734-318770
(ag eng)

Water and Waste Engineering for Developing
Countries
University of Technology
Loughborough
Leicester LE11 3TU
UK
Tel: 0509 263171

Wye College
University of London
Wye
Ashford
Kent TN25 5AH
UK
Tel: 0233-812401

USA

Bio-Integral Resource Centre (BIRC)
PO Box 7414
Berkeley
California 94707
USA
Tel: 415-524-2567
(pl pro)

Inter American Committee on Agricultural
Development
1725 Eye Street NW
Room 805
Washington DC
USA

International Plant Protection Centre (OSU,
IPPC)
Corvallis
Oregon 97331-3094
USA
Tel: 503-754-3541
(pl pro)

Kansas State University
Food and Feed Grain Institute (KSU,FFGI)
Manhattan
Kansas 66506
USA
Tel: 913-532-7452
(ag eng)

National Center for Appropriate Technology
3040 Continental Drive
PO Box 3838
Butte
Montana 59702
USA
Tel: 406-494-4572

United States Department of Agriculture
Agricultural Research Service (USDA,ARS)
Beneficial Insects Lab., Plant Sciences
Institute
Building 476
BARC-East
Beltsville
Maryland 20705
USA
Tel: 301-344-1748
(bio con)

United States Department of Agriculture
Agricultural Research Service
Carl Hayden Bee Research Centre
(USDA,ARS)
2000 East Allen Road
Tucson
Arizona 85719
USA
Tel: 602-629-6380
(bee)

World Bank
International Bank for Reconstruction and
Development (IBRD)
1818 H Street NW
Washington
District of Columbia 20433
USA
Tel: 202-473-8687
(ag eng)

URUGUAY

University of the Republic
Agronomy Faculty
Av.Garzon, 780
Montevideo
Uruguay
Tel: 38-88-68
(ag eng)

VANUATU

University of the South Pacific Institute of
Research, Education and Training
Tagabe Agriculture School (IRETA SOA)
PB 129
Port Vila
Vanuatu
Tel: 2432

VENEZUELA

Central University of Venezuela
Apdo 4579
Maracay
Aragua 2101
Venezuela
Tel: 043-22242
(ag eng)

WESTERN SAMOA

University of the South Pacific
Private Bag
Apia
Western Samoa
Tel: 21671
(ag eng, pl pro)

YUGOSLAVIA

University of Belgrade
Faculty of Agriculture
Nemanjina 6
Zemun, PO Box 127
11080 Belgrade
Yugoslavia
Tel: 215-315
(ag eng)

ZAMBIA

Department of Agriculture
Mount Makulu Central Agricultural Research
Station (DOA)
Private Bag 7
Chilanga
Zambia
Tel: 278655
(ag eng)

Ministry of Agriculture and Water
Development
Zambia College of Agriculture (MAWD)
PO Box 660053
Monze
Zambia
Tel: 505440
(ag eng)

University of Zambia
PO Box 32379
Lusaka
Zambia
Tel: 213221
(ag eng)

ZIMBABWE

Intermediate Technology Zimbabwe
PO Box 1744
156A Samora Machel Avenue
Harare
Zimbabwe
Tel: 04 796420

Institute of Agricultural Engineering
PO Box BW330
Borrowdale
Harare
Zimbabwe
Tel: 725936
(ag eng)

Chiredzi Research Station
PO Box 97
Masvingo
Zimbabwe
Tel: 2397
(ag eng, pl pro)

Ministry of Information (MINIFORM)
Linquenda House
Box 8150
Causeway
Harare
Zimbabwe
Tel: 703891
(bee)

MANUFACTURERS' INDEX

ALGERIA

ENTERPRISE NATIONALE DE PRODUCTION DES MATERIELS HYDRAULIQUES, *159, 161*
B.P. No.1 Baten
Zone Industrielle
Berrouaghia
Wilaya de Medea
ALGERIA

ARGENTINA

GHERARDI E HIJOS S.A., *58, 75, 176*
Florida 520 Piso 3° Oficina 318
1005 Buenos Aires
ARGENTINA
Tel: 01 3939146
Telex: 23614 GHEBA

HERCULES INDUSTRIA MÉTALURGICA, *159*
J.A. Saglio S.A.
Buenos Aires
1460 Bdo de Irigoyen 1470
ARGENTINA

P.E.S.A. S.A., *75, 85, 87*
Gregorio De Laferrere 3210-12
1406 Buenos Aries
ARGENTINA

AUSTRALIA

AUSTRALIAN AGRICULTURAL MACHINERY GROUP PTY LTD, *179*
P.O. Box 157
Belmont
WA 6104
AUSTRALIA
Tel: 227 1555
Telex: 93854 JETAL

AUSTRALIAN REVEGETATION CORPORATION LTD, *59*
51 King Edward Road
Osborne Park
WA 6017
AUSTRALIA
Tel: 09 446 4377
Fax: 09 446 3444
Telex: AA94371 KIMSEED

BATESCREW SALES, *163*
P.O. Box 86
Tocumwal
NSW 2714
AUSTRALIA
Tel: 058 74 2101
Fax: 058 74 2084

BORAL CYCLONE EXPORT, *190, 196*
P.O. Box 131
Mt Hawthorn
Western Australia
6016
AUSTRALIA
Tel: 9 446-4277
Fax: 9 446-6607
Telex: AA 92680

CSN INTERNATIONAL PTY LTD, *196*
P.O. Box 396
Dalby
Queensland 4405
AUSTRALIA
Tel: 76 62 3155
Fax: 76-62 3863
Telex: AA 148720

JOHN L. GUILFOYLE (SALES) PTY LTD, *203*
P.O. Box 18
Darra
Brisbane
Queensland 4076
AUSTRALIA
Tel: 07 375-3677

KANGA FARM EQUIPMENT, *34, 43*
P.O. Box 1177
Dandenong
Victoria 3175
AUSTRALIA
Tel: 03 706 5166
Fax: 03 794 7445

LOXTON ENGINEERING WORKS PTY LTD, *77*
P.O. Box 18
Loxton
SA 5333
AUSTRALIA
Tel: 085 84 7609
Fax: 085 84 6380

PENDER BEEKEEPING SUPPLIES PTY LTD, *203*
17 Gardiner Street
Rutherford
N.S.W. 2320
AUSTRALIA
Tel: 049 327 244
Fax: 049 327 621

AUSTRIA

JOHANN OFFNER, *171*
Werkzeugindustrie GmbH
Postfach 37
A-9400 Wolfsberg
AUSTRIA

LEONHARD MULLER & SOHNE KG, *171*
Zeughammerwerk
A-9413 Frantschach-St. Gertraud
AUSTRIA

PIESSLINGER, GmbH, *171*
Sichel und Gabelwerk
A-3342 Opponitz
AUSTRIA

SENSENWERKE KRENHOF A.G., *30, 98, 171*
Postfach 77
Wien
A-1015
AUSTRIA
Tel: 512 53 91
Fax: 512 5793-75
Telex: 113996

SONNECK GmbH, *171*
Werkzeugschmiederei
Postfach 40
A-3341 Ybbsitz
AUSTRIA

STEFAN PUFF GmbH, *203, 212*
Neuholdaugasse 36
Graz A-8011
AUSTRIA
Tel: 0316 81 1281
Telex: 311988

VOGEL & NOOT, *101*
LANDMASCHINENFABR. GmbH
Wartberg
A-8661
AUSTRIA
Tel: 03858 2441
Fax: 03858 2441 324
Telex: 036778

BANGLADESH

BANGLADESH MACHINE TOOLS FACTORY LTD, *161*
Gazipur
Dhaka
BANGLADESH

COMILLA CO-OPERATIVE KARKHANA LTD, *55, 79, 80, 105, 123*
Ranir Bazar
P.O. Box 12
Comilla
BANGLADESH
Tel: 5428

COMILLA MODERN MANUFACTURING, *80*
Deshawalli Patty
Rajgonj
Comilla
BANGLADESH

FARMLAND ENGINEERING LTD, *161*
58/1 Purana Paltan
P.O. Box 629
Dhaka 2
BANGLADESH
Tel: 283023

GENERAL ELECTRIC COMPANY OF BANGLADESH, *162*
Magnet House
72 Dilkusha C/A
Dhaka 2
BANGLADESH

INTERNATONAL DEVELOPMENT ENTERPRISES, *149*
10-A Green Road
Dhanmondi
P.O. Box 5055
New Market
Dhaka 5
BANGLADESH

MECOL GROUP, *162*
6 Dit Avenue, 2nd Floor
Motijheel c/a
Dhaka 1000
BANGLADESH
Tel: 244846

MILNARS PUMPS LTD, *162*
Zirat Chamber
31 Bangabandhu Avenue
Dhaka 2
BANGLADESH
Tel: 257798

MIRPUR AGRICULTURAL WORKSHOP & TRAINING SCHOOL, *75, 105, 149, 152, 161*
Mirpur Section 12
Pallabi
Dhaka 16
BANGLADESH

RADHARANI MANUFACTURING, *80*
Deshawalli Patty
Rajgonj
Comilla
BANGLADESH

RANGPUR DINAJPUR RURAL SERVICE, *150, 151*
GPO Box 618
Dhaka — 1000
BANGLADESH
Tel: 317872
Telex: 642426 SNHT BJ

SHAHPORAN ENGINEERING WORKS LTD, *161*
6 DIT Avenue (3rd floor)
Motijheel C/A
Dhaka 1000
BANGLADESH

ZAHED METAL INDUSTRIES, *30*
PO & District
Bogra
BANGLADESH

BARBADOS

CARIB AGRO-INDUSTRIES LTD, *103*
Research Centre
Edgehill
St Thomas
BARBADOS
Tel: 425 0075
Telex: 2418 SUGAR BAR WB

BELGIUM

APPRO-TECHNO, *153*
24 Rue de la Rieze
B-6404 Couvin
Cul-des-Sarts
BELGIUM

ASE EUROPE N.V., *191, 192, 197, 198*
De Keyserlei 58 Bus 1
Century Centre
B-2018 Antwerp
BELGIUM

ATELIERS JULES MARCELLE S.A, *29*
Rue de Dinant, 22
Gerpines
B-6280
BELGIUM
Tel: 71 50 10 23

B.V.B.A. SAMDOW, *75, 83, 84, 86*
9910 Mariakerke
Ghent-Gante
BELGIUM
Fax: 091 26 50 22
Tel: 091 26 26 12

DEKLERCK, *134*
14 Place Lehon Plein
1030 Brussels
BELGIUM

ELEM POMPE S.A., *154*
B.P. 9
6110 Montigny le Tilleul
BELGIUM
Tel: 71 51 88 30
Fax: 71 51 98 13
Telex: 51 186

FERILAB S.P.R.L., *157*
Av. Albert Elisabeth, 62
Brussels 1200
BELGIUM
Tel: 02/736 60 90

HANO, *127, 128*
Beukstraat 15
B 3900 Lommel
BELGIUM
Tel: 011/54 44 75

**MADEAR B.V.B.A.
GEREEDSCHAPPEN OUTI,** *29, 30*
Kaaistraat 34 A
ARDOOIE
8850
BELGIUM
Tel: 051 74 40 54

POMPES DEPLECHIN S.A., *154, 155, 156, 157*
Avenue de Maire, 28
Tournai 7500
BELGIUM
Tel: 69/22 81 52
Fax: 69/21 27 64
Telex: 57 399

S.A. BERGOUGNAN BENELUX N.V., *150*
Brugsesteenweg 7
Evergem B-9050
BELGIUM
Tel: 91 53 05 80
Telex: 11551 BBGENT B

S.A. CHANIC, *29, 30, 98, 172*
Chaussee de La Hulpe 177
boite 3
1170 Brussels
BELGIUM

SAMDOW, *76*
Gent-Mariakerke, 9910
BELGIUM
Tel: 091 26 26 12

TOMEGA S.A., *198*
Rue de la Rochette, 7
Arville B-6904
BELGIUM
Tel: 61 61 13 27
Telex: 41 656

UNATA, *123*
G.V.D. Heuvelstraat
3140 Ramsel-Herselt
BELGIUM

UNATA C.V., *136, 138, 153*
P.O. BOX 50
Nieuwlandlaan B-437
3200 Aarschot
BELGIUM
Tel: 16 561 022
Fax: 16 562 025
Telex: 32 21874 PPRB

UNIVERSITÉ LIBRE DE BRUXELLES, *150, 158*
(f.a.o. Professor Lambert)
Campus Plaine
C.P. 224
Boulevard de Triomphe
Brussels 1050
BELGIUM

BENIN

COBEMAG, *31, 35, 36, 41, 54, 58, 77, 99, 105, 110, 133, 173, 175*
B.P. 161
Route de Djougou
Parakou
BENIN
Tel: 61-08-48

BOLIVIA

CENTRO DE INVESTIGACIÓN, FORMACIÓN Y EXTENSIÓN EN MEC.AGRICOLA, *31, 34, 35, 46*
Casilla 831
Cochabamba
BOLIVIA
Tel: 25515

BOTSWANA

CLIFF ENGINEERING, *57*
P.O. Box 282
Gaborone
BOTSWANA

RURAL INDUSTRIES INNOVATION CENTRE, *54, 57, 139, 153, 156, 157, 160*
Private Bag 11
Kanye
BOTSWANA
Tel: 448/449
Telex: 2435 BD

SEROWE BRIGADES DEVELOPMENT TRUST, *57*
P.O. Box 121
Serowe
BOTSWANA

BRAZIL

ACOTUPY INDUSTRIAS METALURGICAS LTD, *29, 30, 172*
Caixa Postal 1664
São Paulo
BRAZIL
Tel: 11 869 6022
Telex: 1123332 FAAT BR

ALFREDO VILLANOVA S.A., *61*
Rue Candelária 1550
B.P. 152
13.330 Indaiatuba
São Paulo
BRAZIL
Tel: 75 21 42

BALDAN IMPLEMENTOS AGRÍCOLAS S.A., *32, 39, 42*
Av. Baldan 1500
C.P.11 15990 Matão SP
BRAZIL
Tel: 0162 82-25 77
Telex: 161 005 VOPE BR

BOVITEC PRODUTOS AGRO-PERCUARIOS, *188*
Rua Duarte de Azevento, 449
São Paulo 02036
BRAZIL

CEMAG, *36, 47*
Rua João Batista de Oliviera 233
06750 Taboao de Serra
São Paulo
BRAZIL

CIMAG, *138*
Rua St Terezinha 1381
13970 Itapira S.P.
BRAZIL
Tel: 0192 63 25 25
Telex: 019 2380 INOG BR

COMPAHIA PENHA DE MÁQUINAS AGRíCOLAS, *111, 130*
Av. Brazil 1724
Ribeirão Preto S.P.
BRAZIL

CORRADI, *110, 138*
Av. Getúlio Vargas 735
Caixa Postal 2
Itaúna
Minas Gerais
BRAZIL

DUTRA INDÚSTRIAS REUNIDAS LTDA, *176*
Praca Arthur Bernardes, 33
Araxa
Minas Gerais
BRAZIL

FUNDIÇAO JACUI S.A., *161*
Avenida Brasil, 1489
CP 190
96500 CACHOEIRA DO SUL
RS
BRAZIL
Tel: 722 2176

GRIMALDI MAQUINAS AGRICOLAS, *61*
CEP 13830
San Antonio de Posse
São Paulo
BRAZIL

HELIODYNÂMICA S.A., *158*
Rodovia Raposo Tavares, Km 41
C.P. 111
06730 Vargem Grande Paulista
São Paulo
BRAZIL

IMPLEMÁQUINAS LTDA, *101*
BR 282, Km 390
Vila Remor
C.P. 381
Joaçaba
Santa Catarina, 89 600
BRAZIL
Tel: 0495 22 0815

INDUSTRIA E COMERCIO GUARANY S.A., *75, 84*
Av.Impératriz Léopoldina 112
B.P. 4951
Sao Paulo
05305
BRAZIL
Tel: 0110 261 1922
Telex: 011 81752 ICGU BR

INDUSTRIAS MECANICAS ROCHFER LTDA, *157*
Avenida José da Silva
3765, Jardim Maria Rosa
C.P. 194
Franca S.P.
BRAZIL

INDÚSTRIA PIGARI, *175*
Av. Aliexo Pigari, 665
Urânia
SP
BRAZIL

INDUSTRIAS ZEMA LTDA, *176*
Pres. Olegario Maciel, 111
B.P. 150
Araxa
Minas Gerais
BRAZIL
Tel: 034 661 1722
Telex: 034 33 06

IRMÃOS NOGUEIRA S.A., *62, 130, 139*
Rua 15 de Novembro, 781
Itapira S.P. 13970
BRAZIL
Tel: 0192 63-1500

JACTO S.A., *75, 76*
Rna Dr. Luis Miranda 6 1650,
Caixa Postal 35,
Pompeia (S.P.)
BRAZIL
Tel: 0144 52 1811
Telex: 142 184 MAJA BR

JOSÉ J. SANS S.A., *58*
Indústria Comércio
Rua Juscelino Kubitschek de Oliveira
1, 450
Santa Barbara d'Oeste SP
BRAZIL

MÁQUINAS JUNQUEIRA, *102*
Avenue 7 de Septembro 969
Cx. Postal 134
Juiz de Fora
MG
BRAZIL

MARCHESAN IMPLEMENTOS E MAQUINAS AGRICOLAS TATU S.A., *33, 35, 39, 42*
Av. Marchesan 1, 979
Matão SP
BRAZIL

MESSRS LAREDO, *111*
Industria E Commércio
Rua 1 De Agosto
Bauru (S.P.) 17 100
BRAZIL

METALÚRGICA ESCOL LTD, *160*
Rua Inácio Soares Barbosa, 546
Parelhas (RN)
BRAZIL

METALÚRGICA SANTA ANTONIO, *58*
Rua Floriano Peixoto, 35
Santa Barbara d'Oeste
SP
BRAZIL

MUELLER IRMAOS S.A., *110, 155, 156*
Av. Pres. Wenceslau Braz, 1046
Vila Lindoia
C.P. 3336
80 000 Curitiba (D.P.57)
Parana
BRAZIL

PETERSIME INDUSTRIAL S.A., *191*
Rodovia Municipal Km 3
Bairro São Pedro
Cx. Postal 151
Urussanga (SC) 88840
BRAZIL
Tel: 0484 65 1533
Telex: 484055 PEIN BR
Fax: 0484 65 1484

PINHALENSE S/A MAQUINAS AGRICOLAS, *124*
rua Honorio Soares, 80
E.SANTO de PINHAL
13990
BRAZIL
Tel: 0196 51 1079
Telex: 192482 MQPI BR

SEMEATO DIV. COMERCIO, *47*
av.Presidente Vargas 3800
B.P. 559
Passo Fundo RS
99 100
BRAZIL
Tel: 054 313 11144
Telex: 05443 855 CSME-BR

TIM INDÚSTRIA E COMÉRCIO DE MÁQUINAS AGRÍCOLAS LTDA, *175*
Rua 7 de Septembro, 600
Cajuru
SP
BRAZIL
Tel: 318-1411

TRITON S.A., *139*
Rue Dois Irmaaos, 262
B.P. 132
Joacaba S.C.
89 604
BRAZIL
Tel: 22 11 44
Telex: 049 2356

UNIPAC INDÚSTRIA E COMÉRCIO LTDA, *197, 198*
Rua Pirajá, 45
Pompéia (SP) 17580
BRAZIL
Tel: 0144 52-1644
Telex: 11 19105 MAJA BR

BULGARIA

AGROMACHINA, *81*
Russe
BULGARIA
Telex: 62235

AGROTECHNICA, *20*
Karlova
4300
BULGARIA
Telex: 44424

SO MTOSS, *37*
55 Hristo Botev bul.
Sofia
BULGARIA
Telex: 22325

BURKINA FASO

APICOMA, *46, 173, 174, 176, 177*
Zone Industrielle de Kossodo
B.P. 2085
Ouagadougou
BURKINA FASO
Tel: 33 67 03

ATELIER NIKIEMA, *149, 156*
B.P. 7078
Ouagadougou
BURKINA FASO

ATESTA, *152*
B.P. 3306
Ouagadougou
BURKINA FASO

BKF-TECH-TERRE, *32*
B.P. 3814
Ouagadougou
BURKINA FASO

CENTRE ARTISANAL DE KOUBRI, *150*
B.P. 123
Ouagadougou
BURKINA-FASO

CENTRE DE LA SAINTE FAMILLE, *154*
SAABA
B.P. 3905
BURKINA FASO

C.N.E.A., *38, 175*
B.P. 7240
Ouagadougou 03
BURKINA FASO
Tel: 30 70 16
Telex: 5439 BF

EMBS, *149*
Ouédraogo Noufou
B.P. 59
Ouahigouya
BURKINA FASO

I.T. DELLO, *152*
B.P. 3573
Ouagadougou
BURKINA FASO

PARE ADAMA, *149*
B.P. 332
Bobo Dioul
BURKINA FASO

PROJET PETAB, *149*
B.P. 3573
Ouagadougou
BURKINA FASO

SOMA A. MATHIAS, *149*
B.P. 230
Banfora
BURKINA FASO

CAMEROON

CENEEMA, *123, 133*
B.P. 1040 Nkolbisson
Yaounde
CAMEROON
Tel: 23 32 50

TROPIC, *29, 30, 75, 98, 135, 171, 175, 195*
BP 706
Douala
CAMEROON

CANADA

F.W. JONES & SON LTD, *203, 211*
44 Dutch Street
Bedford
Quebec J0J 1A0
CANADA
Tel: 514 248 3323

INTERNATIONAL DEVELOPMENT ENTERPRISES, *149*
368 St. James Crescent
West Vancouver
B.C. V7S 1J8
CANADA

NORTHWEST PROTECTIVE GARMENTS LTD, *204*
2163B Kingsway
Vancouver V5N 2T4
CANADA

ROBBINS & MYERS CANADA LTD, *155*
Rural Water Systems
P.O. Box 280
Brantford
Ontario N3T 5N6
CANADA
Tel: 519 752 5447
Telex: 0-618-1131 R AND M

CAPE VERDE

DEPARTMENT OF RENEWABLE ENERGY, *159*
Ministry for Rural Development
C.P. 50
Praia
CAPE VERDE

CHILE

CARS LTDA, *34*
Casilla 2279
Correo Central Santiago
San Bernado
CHILE
Tel: 593636 591254
Telex: 3440278 AVATEX CL

FABRIZIO LEVERA, *86*
Casilla 42
Isla De Maipo
CHILE
Tel: 146

FAMAE, *29, 30, 31, 36, 39, 41, 172, 173*
Casilla 4100
Santiago
CHILE
Tel: 5561011 EXT 222-5
Telex: 0398 FAMAE CZ

ICAT LTDA, *47*
Casilla 4636
Santiago
CHILE
Tel: 6967983 715720
Telex: 241330 TX CENTRO CL

INDUSTRIA DE MAQUINARIA AGRICOLA COLOSA S.A., *178*
Casilla Postal 82 D
San Pablo 9460
Santiago
CHILE
Tel: 739982/735791
Telex: 645110 COLOSA CT

METALURGICA SUDAMERICANA S.A., *34*
Las Violetas 5926
Santiago
CHILE
Telex: 440015 HCHMT CZ
Tel: 572254

PARADA S.A, *75*
Casilla 2984
Santiago
CHILE

PROMETAL M.R., *210*
11 Oriente No.749
Talca
CHILE

PULVERIZADORES AGRICOLAS PARADA S.A., *83, 84, 86*
Alvarez de Toledo 718
Casilla 2984
Santiago
CHILE
Tel: 511819
Telex: 346218 PARADA CK

WENCO S.A., *75*
Casilla 3282
Santiago
CHILE
Tel: 5555302

CHINA, PEOPLE'S REPUBLIC OF

BEIJING CHANGPING SPRAYER FACTORY, *75*
Shahe Zhen
Changping County
Beijing
CHINA
Tel: 48784

BEIJING TRACTOR COMPANY, *20, 21, 45*
1 Xinfeng Street
Outside of Desheng Gate
Beijing
100088
CHINA
Tel: 01 2021188
Fax: 01 3063060
Telex: 20075 SHTU CN

CHINA NATIONAL MACHINERY IMPORT AND EXPORT CORPORATION, *104, 131*
Kwangton Branch
61 Yanjiang
Kwangchow
CHINA

CHINA NATIONAL MACHINERY IMPORT AND EXPORT CORPORATION, *161*
Wuxi Pump Works
123 Nanmen Tangjingqiao
Wuxi
Jiangsu Province
CHINA

CHINA NATIONAL MACHINERY IMPORT AND EXPORT CORPORATION, *151, 162*
Guangdong Branch
59 Zhan Qian Rd
Guangzhou
CHINA

CHINA NATIONAL MACHINERY IMPORT AND EXPORT CORPORATION, *30*
Nantong Branch
Jiangsu
CHINA

CHINA NATIONAL MACHINERY IMPORT AND EXPORT CORPORATION, *162*
Hangzhou Pump Factory
Hangzhou
Zhejiang
CHINA

CHINA NATIONAL MACHINERY IMPORT AND EXPORT CORPORATION, *63, 156, 157*
26 South Yeutan Street
Beijing
CHINA

CHINESE MECHANICAL EQUIPMENT IMPORT AND EXPORT CORPORATION, *191*
Hang Zhou
Xiao Shan
CHINA

JIANGMEN DITY FARM MACH'Y FACTORY, *37, 178*
25 Gangkou Rd
Jiangmen
Guangdong
CHINA
Tel: 56945

RED STAR MACHINE WORKS OF JIANGXI, *20*
Bong Xiang Si
Jiangxi
CHINA
Telex: CABLE 7193

SHANDONG YUTAI MACHINE MAUFACTORY, *132*
Yutai Shandong
CHINA

COLOMBIA

COLINAGRO S.A., *75, 76, 85*
P.O. Box 4671
Bogotá
COLOMBIA
Tel: 775-6200/7351
Telex: 43166 CIGRO CO

FUMIGADORAS TRIUNFO S.A.,
75, 86, 191
Apartado 4045
Cali
COLOMBIA
Tel: 464401 WORKS
Tel: 466789 SALES
Fax: 422068
Telex: 51199

**I.C.A. PROGRAMA DE
MAQUINARIA AGRICOLA,** *34,
37, 41, 59*
Instituto Colombiano Agropecuario
Apartado Aéreo 151123
Bogotá
COLOMBIA

INDUSTRIAS TEQUENDAMA S.A.,
75
Carrera 14 No. 75-77
Oficina 703
Bogotá
COLOMBIA
Tel: 249 3231
Telex: 45346 PASAR CO

**PENAGOS HERMANOS & CIA.
LTDA,** *110, 128, 135, 138, 139,
161, 163*
Apartado Aéreo 689
Bucaramanga
COLOMBIA
Telex: 77735

PRODOMETAL, *110*
Carrera 31 No 11-75
Bogotá
COLOMBIA

COSTA RICA

**REYNARD SA AGRIC. MACHIN.&
EQUIPM.,** *81, 101*
Apartado 183
SANTA ANA CA
COSTA RICA
Tel: 82 79 13
Fax: 23 16 09

CZECHOSLOVAKIA

**AGROZET PROSTEJOV K.P.
MOTOKOV FOREIGN TRADE
CORPORATION,** *40, 43, 101, 103,
178*
Na strzi 63
140 62 Praha 4
CZECHOSLOVAKIA
Tel: 4141111
Telex: PRAHA 121882/121821

SIGMA PUMPING EQUIPMENT,
151, 161
Valves Manufacturing Works
P.O. Box 1111
111 87 Praha
CZECHOSLOVAKIA
Tel: PRAGUE 242951-9
Telex: 121205 IRSIC

DENMARK

A/S MASKINFABRIKKEN SKIOLD,
127, 128, 129
Saeby, Kjeldgaardswej
P.O. Box 143
Saeby
DK 9300
DENMARK
Tel: 98 461311
Fax: 98 467930
Telex: 60737 JESTO DK

BUNGER ENGINEERING LTD, *157*
5260 Højby
Fyn
DENMARK
Tel: 09 958100
Telex: 59823

P. STRANGE-HANSEN AS, *196*
Stadionvej 16
Horne
Varde 6800
DENMARK
Tel: 75 26 0211
Fax: 75 26 0396
Telex: 62451

**PRESIDENT MØLLERMASKINER
A/S,** *127, 129, 130, 179*
Springstrup
P.O. Box 20
DK-4300 Holbaek
DENMARK
Tel: 53 430111
Fax: 53 441821
Telex: 44153 DINESS DK

SCHEBY MASKINFABRIK A/S, *59*
Bogense
DK 5400
DENMARK
Tel: 64 811166
Fax: 64 811930
Telex: 50514

SWIENTY, *203*
Hortoftvej 16
Ragebol
Sonderborg 6400
DENMARK
Tel: 74 486969
Fax: 74 488001

EGYPT

CATHOLIC RELIEF SERVICES, *161*
P.O. Box 2410
13 Ibrahim Naguib Street
Garden City
Cairo
EGYPT

**HELWAAN MACHINE TOOLS
FACTORY,** *40, 102*
Ein Helwaan
Cairo
EGYPT
Tel: 002/02/78 45 93
Telex: 92737 HMTCO-UN

ECUADOR

CENTAURO BOMBAS Y EQUIPOS,
162
10 de Agosto
Ascazubi 2646
ECUADOR
Tel: 550 169

ETHIOPIA

**CENTRE INTERNATIONAL POUR
L'ELEVAGE EN AFRIQUE,
(CIPEA),** *198*
Addis-Ababa
ETHIOPIA

FINLAND

GRIPIT OY AB, *29, 30, 76, 171*
SF-10330 Billnas
FINLAND
Tel: 911 377771
Fax: 911 377351

FRANCE

APICULTURE LEROUGE, *203*
91, Rue Mangin
Saint Just-en-Chauss 60130
FRANCE
Tel: 44 78 54 88

APICULTURE NEVIERE S.A.R.L.,
203
B.P. 15
Route de Manosque
Valensole 04210
FRANCE
Tel: 92 74 85 28
Fax: 92 74 94 16

AUDOLI & BERTOLA, *161*
Z.I. du Nord
9, chemin des Aigais
Brignais 69530
FRANCE
Tel: 7 805 37 77
Telex: 375 564 F AUBERFR

BERTHOUD S.A., *76, 83, 85, 86, 89*
48 Rue Victor Hugo
B.P. 193
Belleville Cedex 69823
FRANCE
Tel: 74 06 50 50
Fax: 74 06 50 77
Telex: 330473

BERTHOUD S.A., *75, 88*
B.P. 424
Villefranche — s
S. Cedex 69653
FRANCE

BOURGOIN S.A., *109, 113*
61 Av. Georges-Clemenceau
B.P. 17
Chantonnay 85110
FRANCE
Tel: 51 94 31 61
Fax: 51 46 93 00
Telex: 710 680 F

BRIAU S.A., *152, 155, 158*
B.P. 0903
37009 Tours Cedex
FRANCE

**COMPAGNIE FRANCAISE POUR
LE DEVELOPPMENT DES
FIBRES TEXTILES (C.F.D.T),**
20
13 rue de Monceau
Paris
75008
FRANCE
Tel: 54 97 13 53
Telex: 750 205 F COFORMI

COVEM INDUSTRIE, *174*
49, rue Jules-Ferry
91390 Morsang/Orge
FRANCE

E.B.R.A., *38, 56, 58*
28 rue de Maine
B.P. 915
49009 Angers Cedex
FRANEC
Tel: 41 43 23 00
Telex: EBRA 720 348F

ECMA FRANCE, *129*
Z.A. Boussieu Nicolas
Bourgoin-Jallieu
38.300
FRANCE
Tel: 74 43 21 44
Telex: 308 186 F

ECOMAT, *101, 106, 111, 123, 131,
133, 136*
Le Val Rouge
B.P. 132
MORLAIX
29210
FRANCE
Tel: 98 88 78 60
Telex: 940 696 F

ELECREM, *197, 198*
24, Rue Gambetta
92170 Vanves
FRANCE

EOTEC, *160*
R.N. 117
Lavelanet de Comminges
Cazeres 31220
FRANCE
Tel: 61 87 69 69
Fax: 61 98 39 52
Telex: ITAMP 530955 F

ETS THOMAS FILS S.A., *210*
65 Rue Abbé G. Thomas
B.P. 2
Fay-aux-Loges 45450
FRANCE
Tel: 59 56 20
Telex: 780 209F

ETS VIAU, *159*
23, Avenue du 11 Novembre
Pernes les Fontaines 84210
FRANCE
Tel: 90 61 32 87

ETS PONCELET ET CIE, *160*
Place de la Victoire
B.P. 12
Plancy l'abbaye 10380
FRANCE
Tel: 25 37 40 15

**EUROPEENNE DE MATERIEL
INDUSTRIEL ET AGRICOLE,**
126
Z.I. de SAUBION
St-Vincent-de-Tyross
40230
FRANCE
Tel: 58 77 44 52
Telex: 560744 F EUMAT

FOX MOTORI, *76*
31 rue Claude Benard
Eragny, 95610
FRANCE
Tel: 1 30 37 09 23

GAUTHIER S.A.R.L., *135*
Bd. de la Lironde
Parc Agropolis Bât.12
Montferrier-sur-Lez
34980
FRANCE
Tel: 67 61 11 56
Fax: 67 54 73 90
Telex: 485 762 F

GUILLEMINOT S.A., *160*
Place de l'Eglise
Lusigny sur Barse 10270
FRANCE
Tel: 25 41 22 26

HUMBLOT, *159*
8, Rue d'Alger
Coussey 88630
FRANCE
Tel: 29 06 93 62

J. KEMP, *207*
10, Rue Boileau
78470 Saint Remy les Chevreuse
FRANCE

LABELVAGE, *194*
11, Avenue de Bellevue
Chatenay-Malabry 92290
FRANCE
Tel: 1 630 43 61
Telex: 201211

LUBING INTERNATIONAL, *159,
191, 192*
66, Rue du Fief
Sailly-sur-la-Lys
Laventie 62840
FRANCE
Tel: 21 27 60 68
Fax: 21 26 26 70
Telex: 130 682 F

**MARINE AVIATION
CORPORATION S.A.**, *162*
8, rue Saint Marc
Paris 75008
FRANCE
Tel: 1 670 52 16
Telex: MAC 250798 F

MARPEX, *38, 111*
1 rue Thurot
44000 Nantes
FRANCE

PAGET, *101*
14 & 16 Rue Louis-Jouvet
69632 Venissieux
FRANCE

PILTER FRANCE, *32, 46, 75, 158*
12 rue Gouverneur
B.P. 3
Dreux 28100
FRANCE
Tel: 37 42 03 13
Telex: 781 155 F

POMPES GRILLOT, *149, 151, 159*
2, Rue de l'Observance
B.P. 118
Avignon 84000
FRANCE
Tel: 90 81 02 12

RENSON LANDRECIES S.A.R.L.,
110, 127, 128, 129, 137, 159
37 route d'Happegarbes
B.P. 12
Landrecies 59550
FRANCE
Tel: 27 77 71 77
Fax: 27 77 13 52
Telex: 820 705 F

SAMAP S.A., *127, 211*
1 Rue du Moulin
B.P. 1
Andolsheim 68280
FRANCE
Tel: 89 71 46 36
Fax: 89 71 48 17
Telex: 870 596

S.C.A.D. BOURGUIGNON, *40, 41,
42, 100*
B.P. 37
Les Tordières
Bourg-de-Peage 26301
FRANCE
Tel: 75 70 23 85
Fax: 75 05 03 71
Telex: 345 951

SECA, *106, 161*
La Côte St André
Le Mottier 38260
FRANCE
Tel: 74 20 48 19
Telex: 340396 CHAMCO PR SECA

**SOCIÉTÉ NOUVELLE SAELEN
SA**, *56, 62, 79, 84*
Rue Pic au vent CRT
B.P. 359
59813 Lesquin Cedex
FRANCE
Tel: 71 09 45 82
Telex: 990 722 F

STÉ CERIMON, *81*
B.P. 11
Moncoutant 79320
FRANCE
Tel: 49 72 61 25
Fax: 49 72 81 58
Telex: CLISSON 790 478 F

TOY RENÉ S.A., *127, 128*
Impasse des Reclusages
B.P. 10
MONTOIRE
41800
FRANCE
Tel: 54 85 01 10
Fax: 54 72 60 67
Telex: 751 484 F

U.F.A.B., *81*
B.P. 58
Chateaubriant 44110
FRANCE
Tel: 40 81 03 30

GAMBIA

ESCAPAG (GAMBIA) LTD, *173*
B.M.P. 37
Banjul
GAMBIA
Tel: 91474
Telex: 2354 ESCA-GV

GERMANY

**ABS SILO UND FORDERANLAGEN
GmbH**, *127*
Postfach 1226
Osterburken
D-6960
GERMANY
Tel: 06291 1034
Fax: 06291 2995

AGRIA-WERKE GmbH, *20, 81, 101*
Postfach 1147
D-7108 Moeckmuehl
GERMANY
Tel: 062 98 39 0

CHR. GRAZE KG., *203, 207*
Strümpfelbacherstraße 21
7056 Weinstadt 2 (Endersbach)
GERMANY
Tel: 07151 61147
Fax: 07151 609239
Telex: 7262213

**FORTSCHRITT
LANDMASCHINEN**, *39, 55, 56,
79*
Berghausstraße 1
Neustadt 8355
GERMANY
Tel: NEUSTADT 70
Telex: 27441 KOFO

GEBR. HOLDER GmbH & CO., *20,
75, 76, 81, 101*
Stuttgarter Strasse 42-46
Postfach 1555
D-7430 Metzingen
GERMANY
Tel: 07123/166-0
Fax: 07123/166-213
Telex: 7245319

**HINGHAUS MASCHINENFABRIK
GmbH**, *179*
Postfach 1148
Versmolder Str.
4503 Dissen am Teutoburger Wald
GERMANY
Tel: 05421/2015
Telex: 944412

**HORIZONT AGRARTECHNIK
GmbH**, *196*
Postfach 1329
D-3540
Korbach
GERMANY
Tel: 05631 565-0

**IBG MONFORTS + REINERS
GmbH + CO.**, *137*
P.O. Box 200853
Munchengladbach 2
D-4050
GERMANY
Tel: 021 66 86 82-0
Fax: 868244
Telex: 8 52 592 IBGRY

**MESTO SPRITZENFABRIK
GmbH**, *75, 76, 85*
Postfach 1154
Ludwigsberger Strasse 71
7149 Freiberg/Neckar
GERMANY
Tel: 07141 71075
Fax: 07141 77444
Telex: 7264839 MEST

MOTORENFABRIK HATZ GmbH,
22
D-8399 Rhustorf a.d. Rott
GERMANY

PREUSSAG AG, *153, 154*
P.O. Box 6009
3150 Peine
GERMANY
Tel: 05171 403-0
Fax: 05171 403-123
Telex: 92670

PUMPENBOESE KG, *153, 161*
P.O. Box 1250
Raiffeisenstraße 2
D-3006 Burgwedel 1
GERMANY
Tel: 05139 8088-0
Fax: 05139 808838
Telex: 921286 NELKE D

PUMPENFABRIK BEYER, *149, 151,
159*
Dorfstraße 25
2361 Wulfsfelde
GERMANY
Tel: 04506 282
Telex: 261487 BEYER D

**SCHWABISCHE HUTTENWERKE
GmbH**, *29, 30, 98, 171, 172, 196*
Postfach 1329
7292 Baiersbronn 1
GERMANY
Tel: 07442 2056/2057
Fax: 07442 7006
Telex: 764225 SHWFR D

**WOLF & BANGERT
WERKZEUGFABRIK**, *98*
Postfach 101047
Sieper Strasse 41
5630 Remscheid 1
GERMANY
Tel: 02191-292048
Telex: 8513 628 WOBA

GHANA

AGRICULTURAL ENGINEERS LTD,
*22, 34, 41, 105, 110, 135, 136, 137,
138, 139, 161, 177, 178*
Ring Road Industrial Area
P.O. Box 12127
Accra North
GHANA
Tel: 228260
Telex: 2232 AGRICO GH

GREECE

**METALLURGY PRAPOPOULOS
BROS S.A.**, *75, 76*
Perivola
260 00 Patras
GREECE
Tel: 061 224 302
Telex: 312285 PRAPGR

HUNGARY

AGRINNOV KFT, *61*
4401 Nyíregyháza
Rákóczi út 102
HUNGARY
Tel: 15-111
Fax: 11-346
Telex: 73242

ANIVET, *187, 189, 190, 193, 194,
195, 196, 197*
1144 Budapest
Remény u.42
HUNGARY
Tel: 183-190, 252-3777
Fax: 183-1190
Telex: 22-3681

BIO-INNOKOORD, *56, 139*
2040 Budaörs
Pf. 14
HUNGARY
Tel: 851-144
Telex: 224281 AND 225110

INTER-PRODUCT K.F.T., *198*
9700, Szombathely
Schönhertz krt.10
HUNGARY

MUSZAKI INTÉZET GÖDÖLL,
173
Tessedik S. u. 4.
2100
HUNGARY
Tel: 28 10200
Fax: 28 20997
Telex: 224892 GATE H

ROBIX MEZOGAZDASÁGI GÉPGYÁRTÓ VÁLLALAT, *81, 163*
Pf. 210
Viola u. 12
Veszprem 8201
HUNGARY
Tel: 80 13 470
Telex: 032203

VEGYÉPSZER CO., *75*
P.O. Box 540
H 1397 Budapest
HUNGARY
Tel: 152-600
Telex: 226930

ZALAGEP BAGODI MEZÖGAZDASÁGI GÉPGYÁRTÓ VÁLLALAT, *40, 41, 62, 100, 103, 196*
8992 Bagod
Gépállomás út 9
HUNGARY
Tel: 92 11 480
Telex: 33207

INDIA

AGRO-AIDS, *159*
27, Shrunagar Shopping Centre
M.G. Road
Bangalore 560 001
INDIA

AMAR AGRICULTURAL IMPLEMENTS WORKS, *108*
Amar Street
Janta Nagar
Gill Road
Ludhiana 141 003
INDIA
Tel: 28985

AMERICAN SPRING & PRESSING WORKS LTD, *83, 84, 85, 86, 87*
P.O. Box 7602
B.J. Patel Road
Malad
Bombay 400 064
INDIA
Tel: 682 2331
Telex: 011-71094 ASPW IN

A.P. STATE AGRO INDUSTRIES DEVELOPMENT CORPORATION LTD, *58*
Agro Bhavan 10-2-3, A.C. Guards
Hyderabad 500 004
INDIA

ASIAN AGRICO INDUSTRIES, *75, 83, 84, 85, 86*
P.O. Box 29
Gandevi Road
Bilimora (W-Rly)
Gujarat 396 321
INDIA
Tel: (02634) 2290/3398

ASPEE, *75, 76*
Aspee House, B.J. Patel Road
P O Box 7602
Malad (W)
Bombay 400 064
INDIA
Tel: 682 2331
Telex: 011 71094 ASPW IN

AUTO SPARES INDUSTRIES, *160*
Wind Machines Division
C-7 Industrial Estate
PONDICHERY 605004
INDIA

BALAJI INDUSTRIAL AND AGRICULTURAL CASTINGS, *42, 58*
4-3-140 Hill Street
P.O. Box 1634
Secunderabad 500 003
INDIA

BEHERE'S & UNION INDUSTRIAL WORKS, *132*
Dahanu Road
Dist Thane
Masoli
Jeevan Prakash 401 602
INDIA
Tel: 2311

BHARAT INDUSTRIAL CORPORATION, *30, 32, 39, 41*
Petit Compound
Nana Chowk, Grant Road
Bombay
400 007
INDIA
Tel: 358061

CENTRAL INSTITUTE OF AGRICULTURAL ENGINEERING, *132*
Nabi Bagh
Bersala Road
Bhopal
462 018
INDIA

COSSUL & CO. PVT LTD, *30, 31, 32, 34, 35, 36, 37, 38, 39, 42, 43, 44, 59, 63, 77, 78, 79, 80, 105, 106, 109, 110, 111, 123, 125, 127, 150, 153, 156, 179*
123/367 Industrial Area
Fazalgunj
Kanpur
U.P.
INDIA
Tel: 221020/070/120
Telex: 0325-309 COSL

DAIRY UDYOG, *198*
C-229A/230A, Ghatkopar Ind Est
L.B.S. Marg
Ghatkopar (W)
Bombay 400 086
INDIA
Tel: 586878

DANDEKAR BROTHERS & CO., *32, 35, 43, 60, 109, 111, 128, 132, 134, 138, 139, 155, 159*
Shivajinagar
Sangli
Maharashtra 416 416
INDIA
Tel: 2758

DANDEKAR MACHINE WORKS LTD, *125, 132, 133*
Dandekarwadi, Bhiwandi
Dist. Thane
Maharashtra
421 302
INDIA
Tel: 02522 21870
Telex: 0135 205

DEVRAJ & COMPANY, *124, 132, 133*
Krishan Sudama Marg
Firozpur City
PUNJAB
INDIA
Tel: 2468

EAGLE ENGINEERING COMPANY, *173*
35 Chittaranjan Avenue
Calcutta
700 012
INDIA
Tel: 26-2077, 26-2180

ENFIELD INDIA LTD, *22*
Thoraipakkam Division (Engines)
Post Bag 892
Madras
600 096
INDIA
Tel: 411229
Fax: (91-44) 416133
Telex: 041 21099 NFLD IN

GREWAL WAX SHEETS, *207*
Railway Road
Doraha Mandi
141421 Pb
INDIA

HINDSONS PVT LTD, *60, 75, 77, 125, 133*
The Lower Mall
Patiala
Punjab 147 001
INDIA
Tel: 77522

INSTITUTE OF ENGINEERING AND RURAL TECHNOLOGY, *160*
26 Chatham Lines
Wear Prayag Railway Station
Allahabad 211 002
INDIA

INTERNATIONAL CROP RESEARCH INSTITUTE FOR THE SEMI-ARID TROPICS (ICRISAT), *42, 47, 58, 79, 88, 99*
Patancheru
Andra Pradesh 502 324
INDIA

K.V. AGRO INDUSTRIES, *58*
A-15 APIE, Balanagar
Hyderabad 500 037
INDIA

KAIVAL AGRO PRODUCTS, *85*
119-D, G.I.D.C.
Vitthal Udyognagar
Gujarat 388 121
INDIA

KALE KRISHI UDYOG, *42, 47, 58, 79, 88, 99*
S31/2/2, Hinge Khurd
Vithalwadi, Sinnagad Road
Pune 411 051
INDIA

KISAN KRISHI YANTRA UDYOG, *123, 124, 128, 131, 132, 137*
64 Moti Bhawan
Collectorganj
Kanpur 208 001
INDIA
Tel: 68945

KUMAON NURSERY, *29, 75, 80, 84, 85, 86, 171, 173, 174, 195*
Ramnagar
Nainital
U.P. 244 715
INDIA
Tel: 85339

KUMAR INDUSTRIES, *29, 30, 98, 151, 171*
Edathara
Palghat Dist.
Kerala 678 611
INDIA
Tel: Parli 1

LOTLIKAR & COMPANY, *203, 205, 207*
A-1/4 Pioneer Co-op Society
Panvel, Dist. Raigad
New Bombay 410 206
INDIA

MADHO MECHANICAL WORKS, *104, 107*
B-49, Industrial Focal Point
G.T. Road
Moga
Punjab 142 001
INDIA
Tel: 3605

MEKINS AGRO PRODUCTS (PVT) LTD, *31, 41, 42, 47, 58, 60, 76, 79, 84, 88, 99, 112, 133, 153, 161, 173, 177*
6-3-866/A Begumpet
Greenlands
Hyderabad 500 016
INDIA
Tel: 91-842 36350
Fax: (91-842) 842477
Telex: 0452-6372

MOHINDER & CO. ALLIED INDUSTRIES, *31, 37, 38, 41, 43, 79, 111, 192*
Kurali district
Rupnagar dist. (Ropar)
Punjab
INDIA
Tel: 62

ORIENTAL SCIENCE APPARATUS WORKSHOPS, *77, 125, 179*
Jawaharlal Nehru Marg
Ambala Cantt
Haryana 133 001
INDIA
Tel: 20796
Telex: 392-204 OSAWIN

P.M. MADURAI MUDALIAR & SONS, *138, 139*
Madurai Mudaliar Road
P.O. Box 7156
Bangalore
560 053
INDIA
Tel: 72524

PREMIER IRRIGATION EQUIPMENT LTD, *158, 163*
17/1C Alipore Road
Calcutta 700 027
INDIA
Tel: 45-7455/7626/5302
Telex: 021-8033

PUNJAB TRACTORS LIMITED, *21, 34, 37, 41, 109*
P.O. Box 6, Phase IV
SAS Nagar
Chandigarh 160 055
INDIA
Tel: 87212-15
Telex: 0395-222

RAJAN UNIVERSAL EXPORTS (MFRS) PVT LTD, *22, 31, 33, 39, 41, 105, 108, 110, 112, 131, 133, 134, 135, 136, 137, 138, 139, 153, 161, 191*
P.O. Box 250
Madras 600 001
INDIA
Tel: 589-711/731/751
Telex: 41-7587/6575 RAJA IN

RAMAKUMAR INDUSTRIES, *40, 42*
P.O. Box No. 5309
G.N.Mills P.O., Coimbatore
641 029
Tamil Nadu
INDIA
Tel: 40056

RICHARDSON & CRUDDAS (1972) LTD, *152, 153*
P.O. Box 1276
Madras 600 001
INDIA
Tel: 456805
Telex: 041-7128

SIGMA STEEL INDUSTRIES (REGD), *76, 84, 85, 86, 87*
A-2, Industrial Estate
Ludhiana
Punjab 141 003
INDIA
Tel: 23839

SREE BHUVANESHWARI INDUSTRIES M/S, *109*
168/C Avanashi Road
Peelamedu
Coimbatore 641 004
INDIA

STANDARD AGRICULTURAL ENGINEERING CO. (SAECO), *37, 107, 112*
824/5 Industrial Area B
Ludhiana
Punjab 141 003
INDIA
Tel: 51888

UNION TRACTOR WORKSHOP, *104, 107, 108*
8-B Phase 11
Mayapuri Industrial Area
New Delhi 110 064
INDIA
Tel: 504615

V.S.T. TILLERS TRACTORS LTD, *20, 21, 40, 41, 42, 43, 163, 178*
P.O. Box 4801
Mahadevapura Post Office
Bangalore 560 048
INDIA
Tel: 58805-6-7
Telex: 0845-8502 VTTL IN

VOLTAS, *160*
Agro Industrial Products Division
19 J.N. Heredia Marg.
Ballard Estate
Bombay 400 038
INDIA
Tel: 268131
Telex: 2239

YANTRA VIDYALAYA, *29, 30, 55, 60, 61, 78, 79, 83, 150*
Agricultural Tools Research Centre
Suruchi Campus
P.O. Box 4
Bardoli
Gujarat 394 601
INDIA
Tel: 258

INDONESIA

C.V. KARYA HIDUP SENTOSA, *20, 44, 45, 111, 124, 126, 128, 131, 133, 161*
Jl. Magelang 144
Yogyakarta
55241
INDONESIA
Tel: 2095/4017
Telex: 25141 KHSYGY IA

CENTER FOR DEVELOPMENT OF APPROPRIATE AGRICULTURAL TECHNOLOGY, *20, 104, 126*
Situgadung, Legok
Tromol Pos 2
Serpong 15310
INDONESIA

NEW RUHAAK INDUSTRIES, *20, 113, 162, 163*
Jalan Pintu Besar Utara 11
Jakarta
INDONESIA
Tel: 676526
Telex: 42048 NRI JKI

P.T. RUTAN MACHINERY TRADING CO., *20, 45, 108, 126, 131, 161*
P.O. Box 319
Surabaya 60271
INDONESIA
Tel: (031) 471643
Fax: 62-31-514668
Telex: 34342 RUTAN IA

YAYASAN DIAN DESA, *154*
Jl. Kaliurang Km 7
P.O. Box 19
Yogyakarta
INDONESIA

ITALY

ALDO BIAGIOLI & FIGLI, *40, 41, 42*
52037 Sansepolcro (Arezzo)
ITALY

ANTONIO CARRARO TRATTORI S.P.A., *101*
Via Caltana, 18
35011 Campodarsego
C.P. 11
Padua
ITALY
Tel: 049/55 64 500
Fax: 049/55 64 517
Telex: 430011

BCS S.P.A., *101, 102, 104*
Viale Mazzini 161
Abbiategrasso (Milan) 20081
ITALY
Tel: 02 94821
Fax: 02 9460800
Telex: 330236 CAST I

BEDOGNI & CO. S.R.L., *104*
(Divisione Giardino)
C.P. 349
Reggio Emilia 42100
ITALY

BERTOLINI MACCHINE AGRICOLE S.c.r.l., *101*
Via Guicciardi n.7
42100 Reggio Emilia
ITALY
Tel: 0522 91000
Telex: 530662 BERMA I

BEZZECCHI S.P.A., *62*
42012 Campagnola Emilia (RE)
ITALY

BRUMITAL S.P.A. INDUSTRIA MACCHINE AGRICOLE, *81, 101*
Zona Industriale
2a Strada
Catania 95030
ITALY
Tel: (095) 592555
Fax: (095) 592526
Telex: 970290 BRUMIT-I

C.M.S TURBINE S.R.L., *75*
Via Roma 37
Lungavilla (Pavia)
27053
ITALY
Tel: 0383 76225 R.A
Fax: 0383 76396
Telex: 311032 TURBIN I

CARPI S.R.L., *75, 76, 83, 86*
Via Romana, 90
42028 Poviglio (RE)
ITALY
Tel: 0522 68 97 41
Telex: 530279 CARPI I

CASORZO S.P.A., *101*
Via Asti 31A
Tonco (Asti) 14039
ITALY
Tel: 0141 991041 R.A
Telex: 214419 CASMAG 1

CAVAGION, *174*
Stellata PO (FE)
44010
ITALY
Tel: (0532) 89504
Telex: 52261 UNIND CAVAGION

CECCATO OLINDO, *110, 111, 113*
Via Giustiniani 1
Arsego (Padua) 35010
ITALY
Tel: 049/5742051
Fax: 049/5742673
Telex: 430886 CECCATATT.ILARIO

CIFARELLI S.R.L., *76, 100*
Strada Oriolo, 124
Voghera 27058
ITALY
Tel: 0383 48938

COLUMBINI SERGIO & C. s.n.c., *106*
Via Cadorna, 9
P.O. Box 19
Abbiategrasso 20081
Milan
ITALY

CONSTRUZIONI MECCANICHE CARDUCCIO COLOMBINI, *125*
Via Cadorna, 9
20081, Abbiategrasso
Milan
ITALY

DAL DEGAN F.lli S.N.C., *75*
Via Turra, 21
36046 Mason Vicentino
ITALY

DEL MORINO s.p.a., *42*
52033 Caprese Michelangelo
ITALY

DI MARTINO GIUSEPPE S.R.L., *75, 83, 85, 86*
Via Pavane, 1
Mussolente
36065
ITALY
Tel: 0424/87 42 23 22
Fax: 0424/87 49 7
Telex: 431210 DMG I

EUROZAPPA S.P.A., *29, 98*
via Stelloni, 12/B
Sala Bolognese Bo
40010
ITALY
Tel: 051 95 41 61
Fax: 051 95 43 00
Telex: 216025 EURZAP I

FALCI s.p.a., *29, 98, 171*
Via Cuneo, 7
12025 Dronero(cn)
ITALY
Tel: 0171 918106
Telex: 21 24 51 FLACI I

FLUXINOS ITALIA SRL, *154, 161*
Via Genova, 8
Grosseto 58100
ITALY
Tel: 0564 451272
Telex: 624043 AINGROL

GRILLO S.P.A., *101*
Via Cervese 1701
Cesena (Forli) 47027
ITALY
Tel: 0547 381333
Fax: 0547 384222
Telex: 550647 GRILLO I

MECCANICA BENASSI S.P.A., *101*
Via Statale 325
Dosso (Ferrara) 44040
ITALY
Tel: 0532 848091/2/3
Fax: 0532 848272
Telex: 213423 EMMEBI I

NARDI FRANCESCO & FIGLI, *33, 36, 42, 138*
06017 Selci Lama
Peruga
ITALY
Tel: 075 8582180
Telex: 660074 NARDI I

PASQUALI MACCHINE AGRICOLE S.R.L., *101*
Via Nuova 30
Calenzano (Florence) 50041
ITALY
Tel: 055 8879541
Telex: PAMA CELENZANO

S.E.P. FABRICA MACCHINE AGRICOLE S.R.L., *20, 101*
Viale della Resistenza, 39
San Martino in Rio (Reggia Emilia)
42018
ITALY
Tel: 0522 698000
Telex: 531 055 SEP I

VOLPI & BOTTOLI, *89*
Via F. Altobello, 2
Piadena (CR)
98434
ITALY
Tel: 0375 98128
Telex: 310023 VEBJET I

IVORY COAST

ABI-MÉCANIQUE, *57, 110, 129, 131, 136, 153, 175, 177*
B.P. 343
45 rue Pierre et Marie Curie
(Zone 4c)
Abidjan
IVORY COAST
Tel: 354560
Telex: 2377/3944(SHELL CI)

ABIDJAN INDUSTRIES 01, *155*
B.P. 343
Abidjan 01
IVORY COAST

JAPAN

CECOCO, *38, 56, 80, 83, 99, 105, 108, 110, 123, 127, 131, 132, 133, 134, 137, 138, 139, 158*
P.O. Box 8
Ibaraki City
Osaka 567
JAPAN
Tel: (0726) 22-2441
Telex: J 65910 CECOCO

GIFU YOHO CO. LTD, *203, 212*
Kano-Sakurada-Cho 1
Gifu-Shi
Gifu 500-91
JAPAN
Tel: (0582)71-3838
Fax: (0582) 75-0855

HATSUTA INDUSTRIAL CO. LTD, *75, 76, 82, 83, 84*
4-39, 1-Chome
Chifune
Nishiyodogawa-ku
Osaka
JAPAN
Tel: 06(471)3356
Telex: J64557 HATSUTA

ISHAKAWAJIMA-SHIBAURA MACHINERY CO., *81*
5-32-7 Sendagaya
Shibuya-ku
Tokyo
JAPAN
Tel: 358-4211
Telex: 232-2128

KIORITZ CORPORATION, *76, 83, 84*
7-2, Suehirocho 1-chome
Ohme
Tokyo 198
JAPAN
Tel: (81) 428-32-6118
Fax: (81) 428-32-6145
Telex: 2852070 KIORIT J

KUBOTA LTD, *21, 40, 196*
2-47 Shikitsuhigashi 1-chome
Naniwa-Ku
Osaka 556-91
JAPAN
Tel: (06) 648 2159
Telex: 526 7785 KUBOTA J

MITSUBISHI CORPORATION, *21*
Central P.O. Box 22
Tokoyo 100-91
JAPAN

YANMAR AGRICULTURAL EQUIPMENT CO. LTD, *21, 81, 84, 105, 161*
1-32, Chayamachi
Kita-ku
Osaka 530
JAPAN
Tel: 06-372-1111
Telex: J63436

KENYA

ANIMAL POWER DEVELOPMENT PROJECT, *43*
Department of Agricultural Engineering
University of Nairobi
Box 30197
Kabete Campus
Nairobi
KENYA
Tel: 592211 EXT 232

ANIMATICS LTD, *187, 191*
Enterprise Road
Busia Road Corner
P.O. Box 72011
Nairobi
KENYA
Tel: 555469

BOBS HARRIES ENGINEERING LTD, *160*
Kanamaini Estate
P.O. Box 40
Thika
KENYA
Tel: THIKA 47234
Telex: 23161 KIJITO

DATINI MERCANTILE LTD, *29, 32, 139, 172, 173, 198*
Enterprise Road
Box 45483
Nairobi
KENYA
Tel: 541713

GUY ENGINEERING WORKS, *176, 177*
P.O. Box 466
Kikuyu
KENYA

HOBRA MANUFACTURING LTD, *75, 86*
P.O. Box 43340
Nairobi
KENYA
Tel: 562590
Fax: 567431
Telex: 25572 ODC KE

MINISTRY OF AGRICULTURE AND LIVESTOCK DEVELOPMENT, *205*
Beekeeping Section
P.O. Box 274
68228 Nairobi
KENYA
Tel: 564301

MUTOMO TECHNICAL CENTRE, *19*
P.O. Box 147
Mutomo
Kitui
KENYA

NDUME PRODUCTS LTD, *110*
P O Box 62
Gilgil
KENYA

OYANI CHRISTIAN RURAL SERV. CENTRE, *30, 41*
Box 771
Suna
KENYA

STEEL STRUCTURES LTD, *34, 130, 152*
Dandora Road
Box 49862
Nairobi
KENYA

TUNNEL TECHNOLOGY LTD, *192*
Box 1
Koru
KENYA
Tel: KORU 14 OR 15

KOREA, REPUBLIC OF

KOREA FARM MACHINERY & TOOL INDUSTRY CO-OP., *22, 75, 76, 80, 84, 105, 161, 173*
11-11 Dongja-Dong
Youngsan-Gu
Seoul
KOREA
Tel: (02)757-1451/6

KOREA TRADE PROMOTION CORPORATION, *132*
C.P.O. Box 1621
Seoul
KOREA

LIBERIA

AGRO MACHINERY LTD, *37, 41, 110, 135, 139, 161, 177*
P.O. Box 3281
Bush Rod Island
Monrovia
LIBERIA

MALAWI

CHILLINGTON-AGRIMAL (MALAWI) LTD, *30, 32, 35, 39, 42, 98*
P.O.Box 143
Blantyre
MALAWI
Tel: 671923
Telex: 4750 AGRIMAL MI

PETROLEUM SERVICES (MALAWI) LTD, *109*
Barnes Road
Ginnery Corner
P.O. Box 1900
Blantyre
MALAWI
Tel: 632597
Telex: 4684 PETSERVE

MALAYSIA

HOWARD ALATPERTANIAN SDN BHD, *62, 196*
P.O. Box 8
68107 Batu Caves
Selangor
MALAYSIA
Tel: (03) 6186637
Fax: 60-3-6188844
Telex: 30535 HRFE MA

JOINT PROJECT IDRC/UM/MOH, *154*
UNIVERSITY OF MALAYA
Department of Mechanical Engineering
Lembah Pantai
59100 Kuala Lumpur
MALAYSIA

UNIVERSITY PERTANIAN MALAYSIA, *100*
Fakulti Kejuruteraan
43400 Serdang
Selangor
MALAYSIA
Tel: 586101-10 EXT 2024
Telex: 37454 UNIPER MA

MALI

S.M.E.C.M.A., *32, 36, 46, 58, 177*
Zone Industrielle
Route de Sotuba
B.P. 1707
Bamako
MALI
Tel: 22 40 71

MEXICO

COMPANIA AGRIA S.A. DE C.V., *101, 102*
Avenue Ceylan N.897
Col. Industrial Vallejo
C.P. 02300 Mexico, D.F.
MEXICO

MOROCCO

ETS LOUIS GUILLAUD et Cie S.A., *156*
31, Rue Pierre-Parent
Casablanca
MOROCCO
Tel: 305971
Telex: 24793 CASABLANCA

NEPAL

AGRICULTURAL TOOLS FACTORY LTD, *29, 30, 32, 37, 38, 41, 98, 105, 110, 172, 173*
P.O. Box No. 2
Birganj
NEPAL

GANA FURNITURE, *204*
Gana Bahal
Kathmandu
NEPAL

NETHERLANDS

AGRODYNAMIC, *81*
Balsemienlaan 238
Den Haag 2555 RH
NETHERLANDS
Tel: 070-68 95 11
Telex: 32207 RODAG NL

ARKANA EUROPE B.V., *162*
Joh. van Soesdijkstraat 37
P.O. Box 286
1110 AG
Diemen
NETHERLANDS
Tel: (020)906296
Telex: 13399 ARBRA NL

BOSMAN WATERBEHEERSING EN MILIEUVERBETERING BV, *160*
P.O. Box 3701
3265 ZG Piershil
NETHERLANDS
Tel: 0031 18691022

CATTER/BORST B.V., *81*
Industrie en Handelmij
B.P. 92
APELDOORN 7300 AB
NETHERLANDS
Tel: 055-335108

GEBR. RADEMAKER, *198*
P.O. Box 81
3640 AB Mijdecht
NETHERLANDS
Tel: 02976 213/261

RUMPTSTAD BV, *31, 32, 35, 43, 59*
Postbus 1
Stad Aan't-Haringvliet
3243 ZG
NETHERLANDS
Tel: 01871-1202
Telex: 22585

THILOT HOLLAND BV, *55, 79, 99*
Hoofdstraat 11-17
Lottum 5973 ND
NETHERLANDS
Tel: (31) (0) 4763-1774
Fax: (31) (0) 4763-2648
Telex: 36493 TCZ NL

VAN REEKUM MATERIALS BV, *153*
Postbus 98
Kanaal Noord 115
Apeldoorn
7300 AB
NETHERLANDS
Tel: 055-213283
Telex: 36316 VRMAP NL

VOTEX TROPICAL, *107, 108*
Vogelenzang Andelst BV
Wageningsestraat 30
Andelst
NL-6673 DD
NETHERLANDS
Tel: 08880 2141
Fax: 31 8880 4041
Telex: 48229 VOTEX NL

WAVIN OVERSEAS BV, *152*
Rollepaal 19
P.O. Box 158
7700 AD Dedemsvaart
NETHERLANDS
Tel: 05230 24911
Fax: 05230-24600
Telex: 30732 WAVOV NL

NEW ZEALAND

A. ECROYD AND SON LTD, *212*
P.O. Box 5056
25 Sawyers Arms Road
Papanni
Christchurch S5
NEW ZEALAND

DONAGHYS INDUSTRIES LTD,
82, 196
Private Bag
123 Crawford Street
Dunedin
NEW ZEALAND
Tel: (024) 792-436
Fax: (024) 792-027

**GALLAGHER ENGINEERING
LTD,** *196*
Private Bag
Frankton
Hamilton
NEW ZEALAND
Tel: (071) 389-800

**KIWITECH INTERNATIONAL
LTD,** *196*
P.O. Box 19
Bulls
NEW ZEALAND
Tel: (64 652) 49036
Fax: (64 652) 49116

NU PULSE (NZ) LTD, *197*
P.O. BOX 5358
Keddell Street, Hamilton
NEW ZEALAND
Tel: (71) 78-713
Telex: NZ 2918 NUPULSE

PEL INDUSTRIES LTD, *196*
P.O. Box 51-093
Auckland
NEW ZEALAND
Tel: 09-274-5762
Fax: 09-274-6199
Telex: 21878 NZ

PRATTLEY ENGINEERING LTD,
190
P.O. Box 109
King Street
Temuka
South Canterbury
NEW ZEALAND
Tel: (056)59-545
Fax: (056)59546

**STUART ECROYD BEE
SUPPLIES,** *203*
P.O. Box 5056
Papanui
Christchurch 5
NEW ZEALAND
Tel: 587-498
Fax: 64 3 588789

TRACK INDUSTRIES LTD, *149*
26 Wickham Street
P.O. Box 19-543
Christchurch 2
NEW ZEALAND
Tel: (03)844-161
Fax: (03)849-767

WIRE MAKERS LTD, *160, 190*
P.O. Box 244
Christchurch 4
NEW ZEALAND
Tel: (03) 842-069
Fax: (03) 842-569

NIGER

A.F.M.A., *75, 80, 98, 105, 176, 177*
B.P. 11
619 Niamey
NIGER

NIGERIA

**INSTITUTE FOR AGRICULTURAL
RESEARCH,** *43, 82, 106, 108, 109*
Samaru
P.O. Box 1044
Zaria
NIGERIA
Tel: 50571-74

M/S DALTRADE (NIG) LTD, *79, 88,*
105
Plot 45 Chalawa Industrial Estate
P.O. Box 377
Kano
NIGERIA

UNIVERSITY OF NIGERIA, *61, 80,*
99, 123, 137, 138
Department of Agricultural Engineering
Faculty of Engineering
Nsukka
NIGERIA
Tel: 48 771911
Telex: 51496 ULIONS NIG

NORWAY

HONNINGCENTRALEN A/L, *203*
Østensjøveien 19
0661 Oslo 6
NORWAY
Tel: (02) 658500

PAKISTAN

HAMDARD AGRO ENGINEERS, *37*
Circular Road
Daska
Dist. Sialkot
PAKISTAN
Tel: (432) 2585

JECO (PRIVATE) LTD, *40, 43*
P.O. Box 46
G.T. Road
Gujranwala
PAKISTAN
Tel: 0431-81343 & 82777
Fax: 0431-84440 (JECO)
Telex: 45328 JECO PK

**SHEIKH NAWAZ INDUSTRIES
(REGD.),** *75, 139*
Samundry Road
Faisalabad
PAKISTAN
Tel: 41139 & 44839

PERU

AGROMONFER S.A., *40*
El Santuario 1035
Zarate
Lima 36
PERU
Tel: 81-2635 81-9331
Fax: 810064

ALGHESA, *34*
Monte Umbroso 140
Santiago de Surco
Lima 33
PERU
Tel: 37-7939

**FABRICACION DE MAQUINARIA
PARA LA INDUSTRIA
ALIMETICA,** *136*
Jiron Alberto Aberd, 400
San Martin De Porres
Lima
PERU

FAHENA S.A., *29, 171, 172, 173*
Calle Las Fraguas 191
Urb. El Naranjal
Lima 31
PERU
Tel: 81-5913
Fax: 720888
Telex: 20250 STEELIND

FAMIA INDUSTRIAL S.A., *130, 193*
Av. Heroes de la Brena 2790
Ate
Lima 3
PERU
Tel: 32-9923 & 31-1395
Telex: 25074 PE

FIANSA, *34, 107*
Apartado Postal 5017
Avenida Industrial 675
Lima
PERU

HERRAMIENTAS S.A., *29, 30, 98,*
171, 172, 173
Materiales 2215
Lima 1
PERU
Tel: 52-2707

HERRANDINA, *29, 30, 35, 46, 98,*
103, 123
Marte 581
Brena
Lima 5
PERU
Tel: 62-9564

HIDROSTAL S.A., *161, 162*
Portada del Sol 722
Zarate
San Juan de Lurigancho
Lima 36
PERU
Tel: 81-2990

INDUSTRIAL MICHEL S.A., *190*
Aviacion 1082
La Victoria
Lima 13
PERU
Tel: 72-4273

JARC DEL PERU S.A., *34, 37*
Santa Natalia 119
Urb. Villa Marina — Chorrillos
Lima 9
PERU
Tel: 67-9201
Telex: 20200 ALBENSA

PHILIPPINES

**AGRICULTURAL
MECHANISATION
DEVELOPMENT PROGRAM,** *30,*
99, 105, 113, 134, 139
CEAT, U.P. Los Banos College
Laguna
4031
PHILIPPINES
Tel: 2307, *3309, 3291*

**ALPHA MACHINERY &
ENGINEERING CORP.,** *60, 80,*
124
1167 Pasong Tamo Street
Makati
Metro Manila
PHILIPPINES
Tel: 865550
Telex: 22579 ALP PH

**APPROPRIATE TECHNOLOGY
CENTRE,** *130*
College Of Agriculture
Manresa Heights
Cagayan de Oro
9000
PHILIPPINES

BUREAU OF PLANT INDUSTRY,
99
692 San Andres
Malate
Manila
PHILIPPINES

C & B CRAFTS, *107, 112*
Maginao
San Rafael
Bulacan
PHILIPPINES

DARMO METAL INDUSTRIES, *44*
Tepaurel Compound
Barrio Putatan
Mantinlupa, Metro Manila
PHILIPPINES

EBM INDUSTRIES INC., *132*
115 North Blvd.
Navotas
Metro Manila
PHILIPPINES
Tel: 236111 & 239371

**IMELDA'S BEEKEEPING
SUPPLIES,** *207*
1910 F. Tirona Benitez Street
Malate
Manila
PHILIPPINES
Tel: 396528

**INTERNATIONAL RICE
RESEARCH INSTITUTE,** *44,*
45, 59, 60, 63, 80, 104, 106, 107,
126, 150, 162, 163
Agricultural Engineering Department
P.O. Box 933
Manila
PHILIPPINES
Tel: 88-48-69
Fax: 63-2-8178470
Telex: 40890 RICE PM

JCCE INDUSTRIES, *44, 45, 60, 61, 104, 106, 107, 124, 126, 163*
242 Mayondon
Los Baños
Laguna
PHILIPPINES
Tel: 50640

MARINAS MACHINERY MANUFACTURING CO. INC., *106, 126*
Rizal Street
Pila
Laguna
PHILIPPINES

NATIONAL POST-HARVEST INSTITUTE FOR RESEARCH & EXTENSION (NAPHIRE), *112*
Muñoz
Nueva Ecija
PHILIPPINES
Tel: 213-107 LOC 524

P.I. FARM PRODUCTS INC., *44, 45, 112*
Km. 16 Malanday
Valenzuela
Metro Manila
PHILIPPINES
Tel: (292) 2181 & 2456

P.I. MANUFACTURING INC., *154*
97, Industrial Ave
Northern Hills
Malaboa
Metro Manila
PHILIPPINES

POLYGON AGRO-INDUSTRIAL CORP., *130*
32 Road B
Project 7
Quezon City
PHILIPPINES
Tel: 967321

POYING'S WELDING SHOP, *44*
262 National Highway
Brgy. Anos
Los Baños
Laguna
PHILIPPINES
Tel: 831 9086
Telex: 63199 ETPI MO PN

REYMILL STEEL PRODUCTS, *160*
Sta Rosa
Nueva Ecija
PHILIPPINES

S V AGRO INDUSTRIES ENTERPRISES INC., *44, 45, 112, 126*
65 Commission Civil Street
Jaro
Iloilo City
PHILIPPINES
Tel: 7-79-17

SEA COMMERCIAL CO. INC., *132*
3905 R. Magsaysay Blvd.
Cor.Vivente Cruz Street
Santa Mesa
Manila
PHILIPPINES
Tel: 611 521-26
Telex: 40178 SEACOM PM

TRAMATE MERCANTILE INC., *104*
747-749 Gandara St
Santa Cruz
Manila
PHILIPPINES
Tel: 472336-39
Telex: 7540404

PORTUGAL

HERCULANO ALFAIAS AGRICOLAS, *32, 42, 136, 162, 176*
Loureiro
Oliveira de Azemeis
3720
PORTUGAL
Tel: (56)64001
Telex: 24501 FMAIHL P

PULVERIZADORES ROCHA, LDA., *75*
Rua da Agra, 945 — Milheiros
Apartado 74
Maia Codex 4471
PORTUGAL
Tel: 901793/4
Telex: 27791 P ROCHA P

VERDUGO — ERNESTO L. MATIAS, *29, 30, 98, 171, 172*
Mangualde-Gare
Mangualde
3530
PORTUGAL
Tel: 032-62325
Telex: 53194 VERDUG P

RWANDA

RWANDEX-CHILLINGTON S.A.R.L., *173*
B.P. 356
Kigali
RWANDA
Tel: Rwanda 2655

SENEGAL

BASE DE PERFECTIONNEMENT DES ARTISANS RURAUX, *160*
Saint-Louis
SENEGAL

COMPAGNIE D'APPLICATION MÉCANIQUES, *130, 161*
10, Avenue Faidherbe
B.P. 397
Dakar
SENEGAL
Tel: (221)23 30 40
Fax: (221)23 30 76
Telex: 21 677 & 21 610 SG

SISMAR, *32, 35, 36, 38, 46, 47, 55, 57, 105, 124, 133, 136, 176, 177*
20 rue Docteur Thèze
B.P. 3214
Dakar
SENEGAL

SPAIN

ELADIO REGUILLO EN C. DE B., *98*
General Aguilera, 6
P.O. Box 6
LA SOLANA(Cdad.real)
SPAIN
Tel: 26 63 15 08

INDUSTRIAS JOSE TREPAT GALCERAN S.A., *101, 102, 103*
Avenida Jose Trepat Galceran, 9
Apartado 2
Tárrega (Lerida)
SPAIN
Tel: 31 05 19

INDUSTRIAS MECANICAS CONDOR S.A., *161*
Paseo Carlos I, 87-89
Barcelona 18
SPAIN
Tel: 309 52 58

J. DELGADO S.A., *196, 198*
D. José Ruiz, 26
Socuellamos (Ciudad Real) 13630
SPAIN
Tel: 9 26 53 10 81
Fax: 9 26 53 17 00
Telex: 48841

JUAN BUSQUETS CRUSAT S.A., *77*
Apartado 74
Reus
SPAIN
Tel: 977 31 00 16

MAURICIO S.A., *75*
46630 Fuente La Higuera
Valencia
SPAIN

PATRICIO ECHEVERRIA S.A., *29, 30, 98, 172*
C/Urola, 10
Legazpia (Guipzcoa)
SPAIN
Tel: 34 43 730 000
Fax: 34 43 733 524
Telex: 38854 PEL-E

SRI LANKA

A. BAUR & CO. LTD, *75, 76*
P.O. Box 11
Colombo
SRI LANKA
Tel: 25035-8
Fax: 21204

AGRICULTURAL IMPLEMENTS FACTORY, *30, 78*
Welisara
Ragama
SRI LANKA

AGRO TECHNICA LTD, *75, 106, 161*
400 Deans Rd
Colombo 10
SRI LANKA
AGROMAC LTD, *130, 131*
449 1/1 Darley Road
Colombo 10
SRI LANKA
Tel: 598855
Telex: 21848 AGROMAC CE

BANDA METAL INDUSTRIES, *161, 163*
Jayanthi Mawatha
Anuradapura
SRI LANKA

CHAMIKARA ENGINEERING SERVICES, *173*
No.126 Kandy Road
Matale
SRI LANKA

COLOMBO COMMERCIAL CO. (ENG.) LTD, *128, 138*
121 Sir James Peiris Mawatha
Colombo 2
SRI LANKA
Tel: 29451-7

DIAS & DIAS, *128, 138*
690 Negombo Road
Mabola
Wattala
SRI LANKA
Tel: WATTALA 070-402

FARM MECHANISATION RESEARCH CENTRE, *55, 80, 163*
Maha Illuppallama
SRI LANKA

HARRISONS LISTER ENGINEERING LTD, *161*
45, Morgan Road
Colombo 2
SRI LANKA

JINASENA LTD, *104, 107, 161, 162, 163*
4 Hunupitiya Rd
Colombo 2
SRI LANKA
Tel: 26558, 26559

KANTHI INDUSTRIES, *29, 171, 172*
Kirinda
Puhulwella
Matara
SRI LANKA

MAHAWELI AGRO-MECH IND'L COMPLEX, *60, 123*
Thabuttegama
SRI LANKA

NAWINNE AGRICULTURAL IMPLEMENTS MANUFACTURING CO., *45, 102, 123*
128/2 Colombo Road
Kurunegala
SRI LANKA

SARVODAYA KANDY, *30, 153, 173*
Palletalawinne
Katugastota
Kandy
SRI LANKA

SATHYAWADI MOTORS & TRANSPORTERS, *45, 123*
21 Dambulla Road
Kurunegala
SRI LANKA

SOMASIRI HULLER MANUFACTURING, *124, 132, 133*
18 S.de S.Jayasinghe Mawatha
Nugegoda
SRI LANKA
Tel: 552258

SWAZILAND

ISICO, *32, 35, 36, 39, 54, 57, 175*
P.O. Box 417
Mbabane
SWAZILAND
Tel: (0194) 22036
Telex: 2213 WD

SWITZERLAND

BIOFARM, *81*
Genossenschaft
Kleindietwil 4936
SWITZERLAND
Tel: 063 56 20 10

TANZANIA

APPROPRIATE TECHNOLOGY PROJECT, *160*
P.O. Box 764
Arusha
TANZANIA

CENTRE FOR AGRICULTURAL MECHANISATION & RURAL TECHNOLOGY, *57*
P.O. Box 764
Arusha
TANZANIA
Tel: 3594/3666
Telex: 42126 AIRSHIP TZ

DM INVESTMENTS GROUP CT+U (T) LTD, *20, 130*
P.O. Box 820
Mwanza
TANZANIA
Tel: (068) 40748
Telex: 46124

ELCT-DAR, *136*
Village sunflower project
P.O. Box 1409
ARUSHA
TANZANIA

JANDU PLUMBERS, *158*
P.O. Box 409
Arusha
TANZANIA

MANIK ENGINEERS, *129*
P.O. Box 1274
Arusha
TANZANIA
Tel: 3520/7187

MDAWI VOCATIONAL TRAINING CENTRE, *198*
P.O. Box 304
Moshi
TANZANIA
Tel: (255)-55-4103

TANZANIA ENGINEERING AND MANUFACTURING DESIGN ORGANIZATION (TEMDO), *105, 111, 126, 137, 139, 162, 175*
P.O. Box 6111
Arusha
TANZANIA
Tel: 7078
Telex: 42121

UBUNGO FARM IMPLEMENTS MANUF. CO. LTD, *29, 30, 32, 41, 171, 172*
Ubungo Industrial Area
Morogoro Road.
P.O.Box 20126
Dar es Salaam
TANZANIA
Tel: 48316-8
Telex: 41206 DSM

ZANA ZA KILIMO LTD, *30*
P.O.Box 1186
Mbeya
TANZANIA
Tel: 2226

THAILAND

AGRICULTURAL MACHINERY & ENGINEERING CO. LTD, *163*
132-134 Samyod
New Road
Bangkok
THAILAND
Tel: 2226648/2226649

AYUTTHAYA TRACTOR FACTORY, *20, 21*
63/4 Moo 1, Rojana Road
T.Pai-Ling, A.Muang
Ayutthaya
13000
THAILAND
Tel: (035)241194/241794

AYUTTHAYA NANAPHAN, *21, 34, 102, 178*
68/3 Moo 1, T.Pai-Ling
A.Muang
Ayutthaya
THAILAND
Tel: 251120, *241288*

CHILLINGTON TOOL (THAILAND) CO. LTD, *30*
60 Old Railway Rd, Samrong Tai
Prapradaeng Samutprakarn 10130
P.O.Box 11-32
BKK 10110
THAILAND
Tel: 2394 1646
Telex: 84183 CROCHOE TH

CHOR CHAROENCHAI FACTORY, *20*
59/7 Rojana Road
T.Pai-Ling, A.Muang
Ayutthaya
THAILAND
Tel: (035)241942/241852

HENG NGUAN SENG FACTORY, *75*
81-83 Soonthorngosa Rd
Klongtoey
Bangkok
10110
THAILAND
Tel: 2492051

JAKPETCH TRACTOR CO. LTD, *20, 34*
14 Moo 3, Soi Orn-Nuch,
Ladkrabang
Bangkok
10520
THAILAND
Tel: (02)326-9214/9395
Telex: 87693 MKV THAI TH

KUNASIN MACHINERY, *54, 55, 59, 100, 108, 134*
107-108 Sri-Satchanalai Road
Sawanankalok
Sukothai
THAILAND
Tel: (055)642119/641653

USA ECONOMIC DEVELOPMENT CO. LTD, *157, 160*
56/7 Thung Song Hong Sub Dist.
Bangkhen
Bangkok 10210
Tel: 5892221 & 5890935
AND

TOGO

UPROMA, *31, 36, 38, 54, 61, 99, 106, 110, 133, 153, 175*
B.P. 1086
Lomé
TOGO
Tel: 21 66 36
Telex: 5328 CNPPNE TO

TUNISIA

HYDROMECANIQUE S.A., *162*
5, Rue Champlain
Tunis
TUNISIA

LES GRANDS ATELIERS DU NORD, *62*
GP1 Km 12 2034
Ez-Zahra Tunis (IE)
TUNISIA
Tel: 292.210
Fax: 216-1-482.534
Telex: 13254 & 13347

SIG, *196*
Route de Gabes km.2
Sfax
TUNISIA

SOCIETE POUR L'ENGINEERING INDUSTRIEL ET AGRICOLE, *162*
Rue du Textile
Z.I. Sidi Rezig 2033
Mégrine (Tunis)
TUNISIA

SOCIÉTÉ TUNISIENNE D'ENERGÉTIQUE ET DE MÉCANIQUE (SOTEM), *153*
6, Rue 4978
Séjoumi
TUNISIA
Tel: 908 274

TURKEY

MKE, *76*
Tandogan Meydani
Ankara
TURKEY
Tel: 13 39 35
Telex: 42 223 MKEA TR

UGANDA

THE CHILLINGTON TOOL CO. (UGANDA) LTD, *30, 173*
P.O. Box 1391
Jinja
UGANDA
Tel: 43-20196
Telex: 64092 CHILTON UG

UK

3M UNITED KINGDOM PLC., *76*
3M House
Bracknell
Berks RG12 1JU
UK
Tel: 0344 426726

AL-KO BRITAIN LTD, *80, 101*
1 Industrial Estate
Medomsley Road
Consett
Co. Durham DH8 6SZ
UK
Tel: (0207) 590295
Fax: (0207) 592144
Telex: 537409 AL-KO UK G

ALFA-LAVAL AGRI LTD, *30, 76, 98, 172, 185, 187, 188, 189, 192, 193, 194, 195, 196, 197, 198*
Oakfield
Cwmbran
Gwent
Wales NP44 7XE
UK
Tel: 0633-838071
Fax: 0633-838054
Telex: 498233

ALFRED COX (SURGICAL) LTD, *187, 188, 189, 190, 191, 192, 193, 194, 195, 196, 197, 198*
Edward Road
Coulsdon
Surrey CR3 2XA
UK
Tel: 081-668-4196
Fax: 081-668-4196
Telex: 947946

ALVAN BLANCH DEVELOPMENT CO. LTD, *19, 32, 38, 41, 43, 46, 54, 62, 77, 99, 106, 107, 110, 112, 125, 126, 127, 129, 130, 131, 133, 134, 136, 137, 139, 149, 179*
Chelworth
Malmesbury
Wilts SN16 9SG
UK
Tel: 06667 333
Fax: 06667 339
Telex: 44304 ALVAN BG

B.J. SHERRIFF, *204*
Five Pines
Mylor Downs
Falmouth
Cornwall TR11 5UN
UK
Tel: 0827-863304

B.J. ENGINEERING, *203*
Swallow Ridge
Hatfield
Norton
Worcs WR5 2PZ
UK
Tel: WORCESTER 820308

BLAIR ENGINEERING LTD, *100, 124, 125*
Rattray
Blairgowrie
Scotland PH10 7DN
UK
Tel: 0250 2244/5
Fax: 0250 2098
Telex: 76596 BLAIR G

BP SOLAR SYSTEMS LTD, *158*
Solar House
Bridge Street
Leatherhead
Surrey KT22 8BZ
UK
Tel: 0372 377899

BRINSEA PRODUCTS LTD, *191*
Station Road
Sandford
Avon BS19 5RA
UK
Tel: 0934 823039
Fax: 0934 820250
Telex: 449752 CHACOM G

BULLDOG TOOLS LTD, *29, 30, 98, 171, 172, 195*
Clarington Forge
Wigan
Lancs.
WN1 3DD
UK
Tel: 0942 44281
Fax: 0942 824316
Telex: 67325 BULLDOG G

BURGON & BALL LTD, *30, 79, 98, 195*
La Plata Works
Holme Lane
Sheffield S6 4JY
UK
Tel: 0742 338262
Fax: 0742 852518
Telex: 547938 EXPERT G

CHAPMAN & SMITH LTD, *76*
Safir Works
East Hoathly
Lewes
East Sussex BN8 6EW
UK
Tel: 082584 323
Fax: 082584 827
Telex: 95263

CHILLINGTON TOOL CO. LTD, *173*
71-73 Carter Lane
London EC4V 5EQ
UK
Tel: 071 236 6135
Fax: 071 628 7411
Telex: 884062 OFGL G

COOPER, PEGLER & CO. LTD, *75, 76, 83, 84, 86, 87*
Burgess Hill
West Sussex
RH15 9LA
UK
Tel: 0444 242526
Fax: 0444 235578
Telex: 87354 COOPEG G

DALTON SUPPLIES LTD, *187, 188, 189, 193, 195, 196, 197*
Nettlebed
Henley-on-Thames
Oxfordshire RG9 5AB
UK
Tel: 0491 641457
Telex: 847547

DAVID RITCHIE (IMPLEMENTS) LTD, *188, 190, 192, 193*
Whitehills
Forfar
Scotland
DD8 3EE
UK
Tel: 0307 62271
Fax: 0307 64081
Telex: 76537 RITCHIE G

E.H. THORNE (BEEHIVES) LTD, *203, 212*
Beehive Works
Wragby
Lincoln LN3 5LA
UK
Tel: 0673 858555
Fax: 0673 857004
Telex: 56353

FISKARS LTD, *29, 30*
Brocastle Avenue
Waterton Industrial Estate
Bridgend, Mid Glam.
CF31 3YN
UK
Tel: 0656 655595
Fax: 0656 659582
Telex: 497584

GEEST OVERSEAS MECHANISATION LTD, *54*
White House Chambers
Spalding
Lincs PE11 2AL
UK
Tel: 0775 76111
Fax: 0775 710427
Telex: 32494 GSTGOM G

GEORGE H. ELT LTD, *173, 174, 190, 191, 192, 196, 198*
Eltex Works
Bromyard Road
Worcester WR2 5DN
UK
Tel: 0905 422377
Fax: 0905 421892

GREEN & CARTER, *158*
Vulcan Works
Ashbrittle
Near Wellington
Somerset TA21 0LQ
UK
Tel: 0823 672365

H.C. SLINGSBY PLC, *76, 161, 173, 174*
Preston Street
Bradford
Yorks BD7 1JF
UK
Tel: 0274 721591
Fax: 0274 723044
Telex: 517450 SLINBY G

H.J. GODWIN LTD, *152, 154, 155, 156*
Quenington
Cirencester
Glos GL7 5BY
UK
Tel: 028 575 271
Telex: 43240

HORSTINE FARMERY LTD, *82, 88*
North Newbald
Yorks YO4 3SP
UK
Tel: 0430 827331
Fax: 0430 827132
Telex: 52470

HORTICHEM LTD, *82*
14 Edison Road
Churchfields Industrial Estate
Salisbury
Wilts SP2 7NU
UK
Tel: 0722 320133

ICI AGROCHEMICALS, *77, 89*
Fernhurst
Haslemere
Surrey
GU27 3JE
UK
Tel: 0428 4061
Telex: 858270/858512 ICIPP G

JALO ENGINEERING LTD, *79*
22-24 Brook Road
Wimborne
Dorset
BH21 2BH
UK
Tel: 0202 885079
Fax: 0202 889329

JOHN BLAKE LTD, *158*
P.O. Box 43
Royal Works
Accrington
Lancs BB5 5LP
UK
Tel: 0254 35441
Telex: 63242 ALLSPD G

JOHN GORDON & CO. (ENGINEERS) LTD, *131, 135, 136*
Gordon House
Bower Hill
Epping
Essex CM16 7AG
UK
Tel: 0378 560731
Fax: 0378 560451
Telex: 817341 PULPER G

LA BOUR PUMP COMPANY LTD, *161, 162*
Denington Estate
Wellingborough
Northants NN8 2QL
UK
Tel: 0933 225080
Fax: 0933 440032
Telex: 31428

LAW-DENIS ENGINEERING LTD, *127, 130, 179*
Lavenham Road
Beeches Industrial Estate
Yate
Bristol BS17 5QX
UK
Tel: 0454 312392
Fax: 0454 325372
Telex: 44396 LAWDEN G

LEAF PRODUCTS, *207*
24 Acton Road
Long Eaton
Nottingham NG10 1FR
UK
Tel: 060 76 727620

LESLIE P. MORRIS LTD, *190, 193*
Dale Street
Craven Arms
Salop SY7 9NY
UK
Tel: 0588 673325

LEWIS C GRANT LTD, *131*
East Quality Street
Dysart
Kirkcaldy, Fife
KY1 2UA
UK
Tel: 0592 55420
Telex: 728241 GRANTX G

LISTER PETTER LTD, *22*
Long Street
Dursley
Glos GL11 4HS
UK
Tel: 0453 544141

LISTER SHEARING EQUIPMENT LTD, *195*
Dursley
Glos GL11 4HR
UK
Tel: 0453 544141
Fax: 0453 545110
Telex: 437152

LOTUS WATER WELL EQUIPMENT LTD, *152*
Thornfield
Banktop
Woodside
Ryton
Tyne & Wear NE40 4QN
UK
Tel: 091 413 6265
Fax: 091 413 4687

LURMARK LTD, *75, 76*
Longstanton
Cambridge CB4 5DS
UK
Tel: 0954 60097
Fax: 0954 60245
Telex: 817714 LURMAK G

M.E. TUDOR ESQ., *62*
Frogmore Cottage
Sawyers Hill
Minety
Malmesbury SN16 9QL
UK
Tel: 0666 860437

MICRON SPRAYERS LTD, *88, 89*
Three Mills
Bromyard
Hereford HR7 4HU
UK
Tel: 0885 482397
Fax: 0885 483043
Telex: 35296 MICRON G

MONO PUMPS LTD, *154, 155, 157, 163*
Menca Division
Cromwell Trading Estate
Cromwell Road
Bredbury
Stockport SK6 2RF
Cheshire
UK
Tel: 061 494 6999
Fax: 061 494 5802
Telex: 668762 MONO G

MULTI-PURPOSE GARDEN TOOLS LTD, *78*
Unit 1X, Dolphin Square
Bovey Tracey
Devon TQ13 9AL
UK

MUNSTER SIMMS ENGINEERING LTD, *149*
Old Belfast Road
Bangor
N. Ireland BT19 1LT
UK
Tel: 0247 270531
Fax: 0247 466421
Telex: 747395

PARMELEE LTD, *76*
Middlemore Lane West
Redhouse Industrial Estate
Aldridge
W. Midlands WS9 8DZ
UK
Tel: 0922 57421
Fax: 0922 743275
Telex: 94017595 PARM G

PLUS 50, *76*
Lodge Road
Kingswood
Bristol BS15 1JX
UK
Tel: 0272 353637
Fax: 0272 352107
Telex: 44273 TUBRI

POLDENVALE LTD, *188, 190, 192*
Industrial Estate
Williton
Taunton
Somerset TA4 4RF
UK
Tel: 0984 32642

PROJECT EQUIPMENT LTD, *31, 33, 41, 46*
Industrial Estate
Oswestry
Shropshire SY11 4HS
UK
Tel: 069 188 263

R. J. FULLWOOD & BLAND LTD, *197, 198*
Fullwood Works
Ellesmere
Salop SY12 9DF
UK
Tel: 0691 622391
Fax: 0691 622355
Telex: 35268 FULWUD G

RALPH MARTINDALE & CO. LTD, *98*
Crocodile Works
Alma Street
Birmingham
B19 2RR
UK
Tel: 021 359 5611
Fax: 021 333 3273
Telex: 336872 RAMACO G

S.W.S. FILTRATION LTD, *149*
Hartburn
Morpeth
Northumberland NE61 4JB
UK
Tel: 067072 214
Fax: 067072 363
Telex: c/o 261540 ATLAIR G

SAMUEL PARKES & CO. LTD, *29,*
30, 78, 98, 105
Pretoria Works
New Road
Willenhall
WV13 2BU
UK
Tel: 0902 366481
Fax: 0902 633789

SCOTMEC (AYR) LTD, *130*
Scotmec Works
1a Whitfield Drive, Heathfield
Ayr, Scotland
KA8 9RX
UK
Tel: 0292 289999
Fax: 0292 610940
Telex: 778770

SHELL INTERNATIONAL, *76*
Crop Protection Division
Shell Centre
LONDON SE1 7PG

SOLO SPRAYERS LTD, *75, 85, 86,*
87
Solo Works
4 Brunel Road
Progress Road
Leigh-on-Sea
Essex SS9 5JN
UK
Tel: 0702 525740
Telex: 99450 CAMCOM SOLO

SPEAR & JACKSON GARDEN
PRODUCTS, *29, 30, 171*
James Neill Tools Limited
Handsworth Road
Sheffield
S13 9BR
UK
Tel: 0742 449911
Fax: 0742 431360
Telex: 54278 J NEILL G

STANHAY WEBB LTD, *54, 56, 63,*
149
Exning
Newmarket
Suffolk CB8 7HD
UK
Tel: 063877 206
Fax: 063877 8359
Telex: 817494

STEELE & BRODIE (1983) LTD,
203
Stevens Drove
Houghton
Stockbridge
Hants SO20 6LP
UK
Tel: 0794 388698
Fax: 0794 388168
Telex: 47388 CHACOM G

STOCKTON HEATH FORGE LTD,
29, 30, 98, 171, 172
Dallam Lane
Warrington
Cheshire
WA2 7PZ
UK
Tel: 0925 36387
Fax: 0925 417762
Telex: 627988

STRAINAWAY, *211*
Garn Products
25 & 28 Sages Lane
Peterborough PE4 6AT
Lincs
UK
Tel: 0733 571172

TOTECTORS LTD, *76*
Totector House
Rushden
Northants NN10 9SW
UK
Tel: 0933 410888
Fax: 0933 410101
Telex: 31638

TURBAIR LTD, *88, 89*
Britannica House
Waltham Cross
Herts EN8 7DR
UK
Tel: 0992 23691
Fax: 0992 26452
Telex: 23957

VICTORWARD LTD, *20*
Bury Farm
Sandridgebury Lane
Sandridge
St. Albans AL3 6JB
UK
Tel: 0727 836005

VOTEX HEREFORD LTD, *131*
Friars Street
Hereford HR4 OAT
UK
Tel: 0432 274361
Fax: 0432 352743
Telex: 35302 (For VOTEX)

WM. MACKINNON & CO. LTD,
131, 135, 139
Spring Garden Ironworks
Aberdeen
Scotland
AB9 1DU
UK
Tel: 0224 634457

WOLF TOOLS LTD, *29, 30, 78, 105*
Ross-on-Wye
Hereford HR9 5NE
UK
Tel: 0989 767600
Fax: 0989 765589

USA

A.I. ROOT CO., *203*
P.O. Box 706
623 W. Liberty Street
Medina
OH 44258
USA
Tel: 216 725 6677
Telex: 753856 (ROOT UD)

AERMOTOR, *160*
The Valley Pump Group
P.O. Box 1364
Conway
Arkansas 72032
USA

ALMACO, *54, 110*
P.O. Box 296
99 M Avenue
Nevada
IOWA 50201
USA
Tel: 515 382 3506
Fax: 515 382 2973
Telex: 759807 ALMACO NEV UD

AMERICAN-KENYA
RESEARCH AND
DEVELOPMENT
CORPORATION, *205*
1204-2956 Hathaway Road
Richmond
VA 23225
USA

AZTEK INTERNATIONAL
CORPORATION, *151*
P.O. Box 11409
Fort Wayne
Indiana 46858
USA
Tel: 219 747 4201
Fax: 219 747 7306
Telex: 3715591 AZTEK

BAKER (MONITOR DIVISION),
151
133 Enterprise Street
Evansville
Wisconsin 53536
USA
Tel: 608 882 5100
Fax: 608 882 6776

BUFFALO TURBINE
AGRICULTURAL
EQUIPMENT CO. INC., *84*
P.O. Box 150
Gowanda
NY 14070
USA
Tel: 716 532 2272

C.H. DANA COMPANY INC., *19,*
76, 187, 188, 189, 190, 191, 193,
194, 195, 196, 197
Hyde Park
Vermont
05655
USA
Tel: 1 800 451 5197

C.S. BELL CO., *110, 128, 130*
170 W. Davis Street
Box 291
Tiffin, OH 44883
USA
Tel: 419 448 0791

COLUMBIAN CUTLERY
COMPANY INC., *98, 195*
P.O. Box 123
440 Laurel St.
Reading
PA 19603-0123
USA
Tel: 215 374 5762

D.A. HOCHSTETLER & SONS, *33,*
178
R.R.2 Box 162
Topeka
IN 46571
USA

DADANT & SONS INC., *203, 208*
Hamilton
IL 62341
USA
Tel: 217 847 3324
Fax: 217 847 3660

DEMPSTER INDUSTRIES INC.,
155, 160
P.O. Box 848
Beatrice
Nebraska 68310
USA
Tel: 312 864 9100
Telex: 724353

E.C. GEIGER INC., *76, 85, 87*
P.O. Box 285
Rt 63
Harleysville
PA 19438
USA
Tel: 215 256 6511
Fax: 215 256 6110

EARTHWAY PRODUCTS INC., *62*
P.O. Box 547
Bristol
IN 46507
USA
Tel: 219 848 7491

ELMO REED, *47*
Rt. 3
Benton
KY 42025
USA
Tel: 527 1087

ENGLEBERG HULLER CO INC.,
131
Export Office 75 West Street
Syracuse
New York
USA

GANDY COMPANY, *63*
528 Gandrud Road
Owatonna
MN 55060
USA
Tel: 507 451 5430
Fax: 507 451 2857
Telex: 263227 GNDYUR

HABAN MANUFACTURING CO.,
102, 113
2100 Northwestern Avenue
Racine
Wisconsin 53404
USA
Tel: 414 637 8388
Fax: 414 637 8389

HOCKMAN-LEWIS LTD, *75, 76,*
83, 85, 86, 87
200 Executive Drive
West Orange
NJ 07052
USA
Tel: 201 325 3838
Fax: 201 325 7974
Telex: 13 8693

KMP MANUFACTURING INC., *160*
P.O. Box 220
Earth
TX 79031
USA
Tel: 257 3411

LEHMAN HARDWARE &
APPLIANCES INC., *30, 109, 128,*
150, 151, 152, 155, 158, 197, 198
P.O. Box 41
4779 Kidron Road
Kidron
OHIO 44636
USA
Tel: 216 857 5441
Fax: 216 857 5785

MARTING MFG INC., *190, 191, 192*
Washington Court House
OH 43160
USA
Tel: 614 335 2090

MAXANT INDUSTRIES INC., *203*
P.O. Box 454
Ayer
Mass. 01432
USA
Tel: 617 772 0576

OASIS MANUFACTURING COMPANY INC., *158*
R.R. 4
P.O. Box 571
Mount Vernon
Indiana 47620
USA

OPICO (PANAMA), *56, 62*
P.O. Box 849
Mobile
AL 36601
USA
Tel: 205 438 9881
Fax: 205 433 2316
Telex: (ITT) 460166

PIONEER EQUIPMENT INC., *33, 36, 173, 178*
16392 Western Road
Dalton
OH 44618
USA

R. & R. MILL CO. INC., *56, 128*
45 West First North
Smithfield
UTAH 84335
USA
Tel: 801 563 3333
Fax: 801 563 3333

RIFE HYDRAULIC ENGINE MANUFACTURING COMPANY, *158*
Box 367
Millburn
New Jersey
USA

SEYMOUR MANUFACTURING CO. INC., *30, 62, 78, 98, 172, 190, 195, 196*
P.O. Box 248
500 North Broadway
Seymour
IN 47274
USA
Tel: 812 522 2900
Telex: 276253

THE HELLER-ALLER COMPANY, *160*
P.O. Box 29
Ohio 43545
USA

TOM INDUSTRIES, *207*
P.O. Box 800
El Cajon, CA 92022
USA
Tel: 619/440 7779

TROY-BILT MANUFACTURING CO., *81*
102nd Street & 9th Avenue
Troy
NY 12180
USA

VANDERMOLEN CORP., *76*
119 Dorsa Avenue
Livingston
NJ 07039-1-92
USA
Tel: (201) 992 8506

WALTER T. KELLY CO., *203*
3107 Elizabethtown Road
Clarkson
KY 42726
USA
Tel: 502 242 2012
Fax: 502 242 4801

XPORT, *212*
Port Authority Trading Company
1 World Trade Center 55NE
New York NY 10048
USA

YUGOSLAVIA

DP FABRIKE MASINA — 'MORAVA', *76, 83*
Dure Dakovica bb
12000 PoÆarevac
YUGOSLAVIA
Tel: (012) 233 580
Fax: 012/222 027
Telex: 10094

GORENJE MUTA, *29, 30, 42, 171*
62366 Muta
YUGOSLAVIA
Tel: +38 62 873140
Fax: (062) 873 414
Telex: 33 257 YU LIMUTA

IMT BEOGRAD, *20, 41*
Fabrika Opreme I Pribora
Industrijska zona bb.
23272 Novi Becej
YUGOSLAVIA
Tel: 023/771 500
Fax: 772 798
Telex: 15620

METALSKA INDUSTRIJA OSIJEK, *80*
Vukovarska 219a
Osijek
54000
YUGOSLAVIA

OLT, *37, 58*
54000 Osijek
P. Svacica 4
YUGOSLAVIA
Tel: (054) 124 277
Fax: 123 600
Telex: 28054 YU OLT

POLJOSTROJ, *62, 102, 113*
Industrija masina i opreme
25250 Odzaci
Karadordeva br. 34
YUGOSLAVIA
Tel: 025/742 331
Telex: 15326

RUDARSKO METALURSKI KOMBINAT, *61*
Ulica 29
Novembra br. 15
Kostajnica
79224 Bos
YUGOSLAVIA
Tel: (079) 63 137/195
Telex: 45 195 YU RMK TBK

ZIMBABWE

AIRFLO DIVISION, *62*
Kelvin/Cripps Roads
Mashonaland Holdings Ltd
P.O. Box 1914
Harare
ZIMBABWE
Tel: 722263
Telex: 24265 ZW

APEX CORPORATION, *75*
P.O. Box 647
Harare
ZIMBABWE

BULAWAYO STEEL PRODUCTS, *30, 32, 35, 36, 38, 39, 42, 57, 195*
P.O. Box 1603
Donnington
Bulawayo
ZIMBABWE
Tel: 62671
Telex: 3257 ZW

DUNWELL PRODUCTS, *75, 86, 159, 161*
P.O. Box 8543
Belmont
Bulawayo
ZIMBABWE
Tel: 76831
Telex: 2316 ZW

FARM IMPLEMENTS (PRIVATE) LTD, *47, 176*
Box 55
Glendale
ZIMBABWE
Tel: (175 8) 345
Fax: 702006
Telex: 26636 MATDOR ZW

G. NORTH (PVT) LTD, *33, 36, 39, 42, 57, 109, 111, 127, 133*
P.O. Box 111
Southerton
Harare
ZIMBABWE
Tel: 63717/9

GARBA INDUSTRIES (PVT) LTD, *30, 36*
P.O.Box 90
Norton
ZIMBABWE
Tel: 162 2063/4

H.C. BELL & SON (ENGINEERS) (PVT) LTD, *129*
P.O. Box 701
Mutare
ZIMBABWE
Tel: 62535 & 64538

JETMASTER (PVT) LTD, *103, 174*
P.O. Box 948
Harare
ZIMBABWE
Tel: 65591 6
Telex: 2362 JETSET

JOHN RAU & COMPANY (PVT) LTD, *203, 204, 207*
2 Moffat Street
P.O. Box 2893
Harare
ZIMBABWE
Tel: 707682

KATTLEWAY BERBAT (PVT) LTD, *188, 190, 193*
P.O. Box 489
Marondera
ZIMBABWE
Tel: 10 128 3610
Telex: 4186 ZW ATTN. HILL

LANE ENGINEERING (PVT) LTD, *125, 149, 161*
P.O. Box 43
Southerton
Harare
ZIMBABWE
Tel: 65354 5 6
Telex: 24659 ZW

MINE-ELECT, *149, 161*
P.O. Box 316
Bulawayo
ZIMBABWE
Tel: 67041, 77506
Telex: 33281 MINLEC ZW

MONO PUMPS ZIMBABWE, *163*
Box 2049
Graniteside
Harare
ZIMBABWE
Tel: 729981/5
Telex: 24148 ZW

MULTI-SPRAY SYSTEMS, *75, 87, 109*
P.O. Box HG 570
Highlands
Harare
ZIMBABWE

SHEET METAL KRAFT, *160, 193*
14 Coventry Street
P.O. Box 1840
Bulawayo
ZIMBABWE
Tel: 74100, *74106*

TAURUS SPRAYING SYSTEMS (PVT) LTD, *89*
P.O. Box AY 18
Msasa
Harare
ZIMBABWE
Tel: 48001

TAYLOR-MADE SHEET METAL PRODUCTS LTD, *191, 192*
Box W99
Waterfalls
Harare
ZIMBABWE
Tel: 65461

TEMPER TOOLS (PVT) LTD, *29, 98, 171*
54 Mafeking Road
P.O.Box 8280
Donnington, Southerton
Harare
ZIMBABWE
Tel: 74541
Telex: 2316 ZW

TINTO INDUSTRIES, *176, 178*
P.O. Box 2356
Harare
ZIMBABWE
Tel: 66781, 64721, 65525
Telex: 22434 ZW

TOOLMAKING & ENGINEERING, *98*
P.O.Box 801
Bulawayo
ZIMBABWE
Tel: 70703
Telex: 3549 TOOMAK ZW

ZFE COMPANY (PVT) LTD, *43, 176*
P.O. Box 1180
Harare
ZIMBABWE
Tel: 10 64764
Telex: 4696 BAIN ZW

ZIMCAST, *109*
P.O. Box 490
Gweru
ZIMBABWE
Tel: 154 2901
Telex: 3474 ZW

ZIMPLOW LTD, *19, 30, 32, 33, 34, 35, 36, 39, 41, 57, 133*
P.O. Box 1059
Bulawayo
ZIMBABWE
Tel: 61357
Telex: 3372 ZW PLOW

EQUIPMENT INDEX

air-screen seed cleaners 116
animal draught equipment 5, 11-14, 25, 28
  beam-pulled implements 12
  chain-pulled implements 12-13
  wheeled tool-carriers 12, 13
  see also carts; pesticide sprayers; ploughs; ridgers
artificial feeding products 188
artificial insemination equipment
  for animals 184, 187
  for bees 208
augers,
  earth 195
  elevators 179

baggers and weighers 179
balers 103
balling guns 194
barrows,
  barrow-mounted pesticide sprayers 86
  food 174
  water 174
  see also wheelbarrows
beam-pulled implements 12
bean curd grinders 128
bed formers 26-7, 42
beehives
  fittings 201, 206, 209
  low-technology 201, 203
  mating hives 208
  modified long hives 205
  movable-frame 200, 201, 205
  observation 205
  top-bar 201-2, 205
  traditional 200-1
beekeeping equipment 200-12
  artificial insemination apparatus 208
  bee blowers 209
  beeswax processing equipment 212
  cell cups and frames 209
  centrifugal extractors 201
  escape boards 209
  feeders 206
  foundation 207
  fume boards 209
  grafting tools 208
  hive tools 200, 202, 206
  honey processing 210-12
  plastic frames with integral combs 207
  protective clothing 200, 202, 204
  queen mailing and introduction cage 208
  smokers 200, 202, 204
  uncapping tools 209
blades,
  levelling 27
  for scalpels 194
branding irons 193, 195
breastband harnesses 13, 15
broad-bed weeders 79
brush cutters 100
bull-handling equipment 187
bullock-driven disc harrows 37
bund formers see ridgers

carts,
  animal-drawn 47, 166, 168, 169, 175, 176, 177, 178
  hand 166, 169, 173, 174, 175
  Scotch 176
  tractor-drawn 177, 178
cassava,
  automatic planters 61
  garifiers 118, 119, 120, 121, 138
  graters 138
  harvesters 99, 100
  peelers 137, 138
castrating tools 188, 189
cattle,
  artificial feeding products 188
  calving aids 183, 188
  crushes 190
  drinkers 192
  face flyps 191
  feeders 192
  identification tags 193
  lifters 190
  prods 187
  rubs 191
  sprayers 191
  weigh bands 193

CDA (Controlled Droplet Application) sprayers 88-9
cereal scythes 92
cereal mills see mills
cereal seeders see seeders and planters
chain harrows 36
chain-pulled implements 12-13
chee-gehs (simple pack frames) 166, 167, 168
chemical fertilizer applicators 63
chisel ploughs see ploughs
chopper/grinders 130
chopping hoes 67
churns see dairying equipment
cleaners,
  grain 123, 124, 125
  pre-cleaners 125
  rice 124
  rotary 124
  seed 125
coconut oil presses 118
coconut shredders 117-18
coffee graders 136
coffee pulpers and hullers 117, 135-6
  disc 135
  hand-operated 135
  vertical 135
collar harnesses 13
collars, oxen 19
combine harvesters 95
cono-puddlers 44
cono-weeders 67, 80
conveyors,
  auger 179
  horizontal belt 179
corn knives 98
corn shellers see maize shellers
cows see cattle; dairying equipment
crackers, palm nut 136
crowbars 195
crushers, sugar cane 138, 139
cultivators 80
  adjustable 39, 40
  engine-powered 68
  garden 79
  horse-drawn 39, 47
  inter-row 40
  light 38
  rotary 15, 24, 26, 27, 67-8
  self-powered 81
  spare parts 39
  spring-loaded 41, 47
  tined 26, 38, 39, 40, 41, 47, 67-8
  toolbar 47
  tractor-mounted 40
  triangular 38
  wheeled 67
cutter-bar attachments for tractors 102
cutter-bar mowers 101
cutters, forage choppers 139

dairying equipment 185, 196-8
  brushes and hygiene equipment 197
  butter churns 198
  churn-washing tanks 198
  cream separators 198
  cream setting pans and skimmers 198
  farm pasteurizers 198
  kick bars 197
  mastitis detectors 197
  milk containers 198
  milk strainers and filters 197
  milking machines 184-5, 196-7
  thermometers 198
de-horning tools 189
decorticators see groundnut shellers; maize shellers
diamond harrows 35
dibblers 50
diggers, post-hole 196
digging hoes 67
disbudding irons 189
disc harrows 26, 37
  see also harrows
disc ploughs see ploughs
donkey carts 175, 176
donkey harnesses 19
double furrow ploughs 33
drenching equipment 194
driers 126
drum seeders 60
dusters 83, 84

elevators 167, 169
  mobile belt 179
  vertical bucket 179
engines,
  diesel 10, 21-2
  driving irrigation pumps 5
  petrol 10, 22
Engleberg hullers 117, 131

farrowing crates 183, 188
feeders 192, 206
feeding products 188
fencing 196
fertilizer applicators 49, 52, 58
  broadcast spreaders 62
  centrifugal spreaders 62
  distributor spreaders 62
  green manure tramplers 63
  manual spreaders 61
  root feeder 87
  rotary drum 61
  tractor-driven 14
fertilizer/seed drills 60
fibre ribboners 139
flame weeders 81
flooring, for duck rearing 191
fodder cutters see forage choppers
foot-rot shears 189
forage choppers 118, 120
  hand-operated 139
  motorized 139
forceps 194
forks see shovels and forks
fruit pickers 105

garden cultivators 79; see also cultivators
garden seeders 56
graders, coffee 136
graders and cleaners 125
graders cum winnowing machines 123
grain drying machinery 115-16
grain mills see mills
grain storage equipment 116
grass hooks 97, 98
grinders see mills
groundnut diggers 99, 100
groundnut lifters 99
groundnut shellers 117, 124, 133
  mobile 134
  pedal-operated 133
  rotary 133
groundnuts, mechanical planters 58

hammer mills see mills
hand carts see carts
harnesses 13, 15, 18, 19, 187
harrow frames 35
harrows,
  adjustable tooth 36
  chain 36
  diamond 35
  disc 26, 37
  ox-drawn 35, 36
  ploughing 26
  rotary 38
  spring-tine 36, 46, 47
  square 35
  tined 26, 35, 36
  triangular 35
  zig-zag 36
harvesting equipment,
  animal-powered 92
  engine-powered 92-7
  manual 91-2, 97-8
  wheat 104
hay balers 103
hay racks 192
hay rakes 103
hay wagons 177
hitch carts 47
hives see beehives
hoes 25, 28, 30, 78, 79
  chopping 67
  digging 67
  motorized 81
  pushing and pulling 67
  rotary 14-15, 67, 79
  tined 25
  wheeled 79
hoists 167, 169

honey processing equipment 210-12
hoof paring knives 189
hoof-cutters 189
horn branders 195
hose-end pesticide sprayers 85
hullers see coffee pulpers and hullers; rice hullers
huskers, maize see maize shellers
hydraulic ram pumps 145, 147, 158

inclined plate planters 59
incubators 191
inverted-T seeders 59
irrigation pumps see pumping systems

jab planters 50, 54

knapsack and pressure cylinder pesticide sprayers 71, 72-3, 75, 76, 84
  spinning disc 88

lambs,
  adopters 188
  artificial feeding products 188
  obstetric instruments 187
  revivers 188
land planers see levellers
levellers 43, 47
levelling blades 27
levelling planks 26
lifters,
  cassava 99
  groundnut 99
  potato 100

machetes 67
maize chopper/grinders 130
maize planters 54
maize shellers 92, 94, 95, 109, 109-13, 122
  bench-mounted 110
  motorized 110, 111, 112, 113
  pedal-operated 111
  portable 111, 113
  three-drum 113
  trailer-mounted 113
manioc see cassava
manure forks and drags 169-70, 171
manure tramplers 63
manure-burying tiller blades 63
marking equipment,
  ankle straps 195
  branding irons 193
  ear-marking pliers 193
  horn branders 195
  identification tags 193
  marking sticks 193
  spray markers 193
  tattooing forceps 193
mattocks 25, 30
  see also hoes
milk strainers and filters 197
milking machines 184-5, 196, 197
  see also dairying equipment
millet threshers 106
mills 5
  bean curd grinders 128
  bottom discharge 130
  chopper/grinders 130
  grain grinding 127, 128, 129
  grist 128
  hammer 116-17, 120, 121, 129, 130
  hand-powered 127, 128
  horizontal 129
  household 127
  mini 127
  and mixer units 130
  motorized 128
  multi-purpose 130
  plate 116, 120, 121, 128
  rice 132
  roller 116, 120, 129
  vertical 128
  see also crushers
mineral dispensers 193
mixers 130
mortar and pestles 119
mouldboard ploughs 25-6, 31, 33, 47
  general purpose 32
  reversible 33, 34, 47
mowers 47, 101-3
multi-crop upland seeders 60

multi-purpose toolbars 27, 46-7
    animal-drawn 46, 47

needles 194

oil presses 117, 118, 119, 120
    hydraulic 136
    mini 137
    motorized 137
    rotary 137
ox ploughs 32
ox-carts *see* carts

paddy *see* rice
palm nut crackers 136
panniers, animal-loaded 167
peanuts *see* groundnuts
pens, mobile 190
pesticide applicators 71
    animal-drawn sprayers 86
    atomizers 85
    barrow-mounted sprayers 86
    CDA (Controlled Droplet Application)
      sprayers 88-9
    dusters 83-4
    hand atomizers 73
    hand compression sprayers 73, 85
    hand lever 73
    hand-held granule applicators 82
    hose-end sprayers 85
    knapsack and pressure cylinders 71, 72-3,
      75, 76, 84
    lever-operated sprayers 85
    micronex 89
    motorized atomizers 73-4
    pedal-operated sprayers 85
    piston-operated 73, 86
    seed treaters 77
    shoulder-slung 82
    slide action 73, 86
    spinning disc distributors 49
    spray lances 87
    spray shields 87
    stirrup pump sprayers 73, 86
    tractor-mounted 14, 87
    tree guards 87
    trigger operated 73, 85
picks 30
pig handling equipment 190
    farrowing crates 183, 188
pitman drive planters 57, 58
plant replacers 50
pliers, fencing 196
ploughs,
    attachments for 46, 47
    chisel 26, 34
    disc 26, 34
    double furrow 33
    light 31
    mouldboard 25-6, 31
    reversible 33, 34, 47
    seed attachments 57
    single furrow 32
    soil-inverting 31
    spare parts 34
    sulky 33
    traditional 25, 31
    turnwrest 34
plows *see* ploughs
plunger-auger fertilizer injectors 63
polishers, rice 132
potatoes,
    lifters 100
    planters 61
poultry
    brooders 183, 191
    de-beakers 191
    drinkers 192
    feeders 192
    humane killers 192
    identification tags 191
    incubators 191
power sprayers 87
prolapse retainers 183, 187
protective clothing 53, 68, 69-71, 76
    for beekeeping 200, 202, 204
    for pesticide applications 69, 70, 71
puddlers 44
pumping systems 142-63, 184
    air-operated 157
    animal-powered 144-5, 147, 156
      chain and washer 156
    engine-driven 5, 143, 146
      axial flow 163
      borehole 163
      centrifugal 161, 162
      diesel 146, 147
      electric 162
      petrol 146, 147

portable 161, 162
    screw pumps 162
    submersible 162
    tractor-powered 14, 163
    trolley-mounted 162
    human-powered 147
      chain and washer pumps 150
      closed spout pitcher 151
      deep well handpumps 153-5
      diaphragm 149, 150
      irrigation suction 150
      lift and force 155, 156
      low-lift 150
      open spout pitcher 151
      piston-type 149, 152-5, 156
      rotary 154, 155, 159
      rower 149
      shallow well 151, 152
      stirrup 73, 86
      traditional 143, 144, 145, 148
      twin cylinder treadle 150
      two-person 154
    irrigation 5, 150, 157
    solar-powered 145-6, 147, 158
    water-powered
      hydraulic rams 145, 147, 158
      turbines and water-wheels 145, 157
    wind-powered 146, 147, 159, 160
      windlasses 159
pushing and pulling hoes 67

rakes 29
    horse-drawn 103
raking blades 43
reapers 104, 105
reaping hooks 92, 97, 98
respirators and masks 69, 70
rice,
    cleaners 124
    cono-weeders 80
    cultivation equipment 44
    drum seeders 60
    flake/poha machines 132
    four-row reapers 104
    hand-pushed weeders 80
    manual transplanters 60
    mechanical broadcasters 52
    mini-tractors 18
    rotary cultivators 27
    seed drills 55
    separators 132
    threshing equipment 93, 94
    weeding equipment 67
rice hullers 117, 120, 131-2
    automatic type 132
    combination type 132
    Engleberg 117, 131
    hand-powered 131
    rubber roll 131, 132
rice mills 132
rice polishers 117, 132, 133
    abrasive-type 133
    cone-type 132, 133
rice threshers 6, 105, 106, 107
    pedal 106
    treadle peg-drum 105
rice-husk furnace-driers 126
ridge profile weeders 80
ridgers (bund formers) 26-7, 40, 41, 43, 47
    adjustable lightweight 41
    animal-drawn 41
    attachments for 46, 47
    tractor-drawn 42
root crop harvesters 99, 100
root cutters,
    disc 138
    roller 137
root feeders 87
rotary cultivators 15, 24, 26, 27, 67-8
rotary dusters 83
rotary fertilizer spreaders 62
rotary harrows 38
rotary hoes 14-15, 67
rotary injection ('jab') planters 50, 54
rotary mowers 47, 103
rotary tillers 44, 81
rotating drag rakes 103

sack trucks 173
salt lick stands 193
scalpels 194
scissors 194
scoops 27
scotch carts *see* carts
scrapers 27
    animal-drawn 43
scythes 92, 97, 98
seed attachments for ploughs 57
seed cleaners 125

seed coulters 50
seed dressers 77
seed drills 50-1, 55
    animal-drawn 58, 59
    hand-pushed 55
    precision 56, 58
    seeder/fertilizer drills 49, 50-1, 60
    spare parts 58
    see also seeders and planters
seed fiddles 49-50, 62
seed treaters,
    slurry 77
    village-scale 77
seed-metering systems 51
seeders and planters 49
    animal-drawn 60
    cassava 61
    cereal 59
    drum seeders 60
    garden 56
    hand-held 54, 55, 56, 62
    hand-operated broadcasters (seed fiddles)
      49-50, 62
    inclined plate 59
    inverted-T 59
    Kimseed camel pitters 59
    maize 54
    mechanical 58
    multi-crop upland 60
    pitman drive 57
    potato 61
    precision 51, 56, 58
    rotary injection ('jab') 50, 54
    row seeders 50
    single-row 58
    spinning disc distributors 49, 50
    two-row rolling injection 55
    walking-stick 50
    see also seed drills
separators,
    cream 198
    multi-cereal 124
    rice 132
shears,
    foot-rot 189
    see also sheep shearing equipment
sheep
    cradles 189
    foot baths 190
    mobile pens 190
    shepherds' crooks 190
    trusses 187
sheep shearing equipment 185
    electric 195
    hand shears 195
    petrol engine-powered 195
shellers 116, 117
    soya 134
    tropical 113
    see also groundnut shellers; maize shellers
shoulder poles 166, 167
shovels and forks 29, 166-7, 169, 170-2
    hay forks and pitchforks 171
    manure forks and drags 169-70, 171
    potato forks and drags 171
sickles 92, 97, 98
silage cutters 139
silos,
    square 127
    suspended bag 127
slashers 67
sledgehammers 195
sledges 167
slurry seed treaters 77
solar-powered pumps 145-6, 147, 158
sorghum, threshing equipment 93, 109
spades 29, 170
spinning disc distributors 49, 50
spray lances 87
spray shields 87
sprayers, pesticide *see* pesticide applicators
spreaders,
    centrifugal 84
    fertilizer 62
stethoscopes 194
stirrup pump pesticide applicators 73, 86
storage bins, elevated grain and meal 127
straddle row weeders 79
sugar cane crushers 115, 118
    hand-operated 138, 139
    motorized 139
sugar cane knives 97, 98
sulky ploughs 33
syringes 194

tailing tools 188, 189
tattooing forceps 193
tedders 103
thermometers,

dairy 198
    veterinary 194
thrashers *see* threshing equipment
threshing equipment
    animal-powered 92, 93, 106
    combine harvesters 95
    engine-powered 92-7
    high-speed 108
    hold-on 93
    manual 92
    multi-crop 106, 107, 108, 109
    portable 106, 107, 108, 109
    rice 6, 105
    simple wholecrop harvesters 95
    sorghum 93, 109
    stripper harvesters 95
    threshing drums 94
    through-flow 93-4, 107
    tractor-driven 14, 92-3
    see also winnowing machines
tillers 40, 41, 44
    manure-burying 63
    power 80
    rotary 44, 81
    wetland 45
    wheel attachments 45
    see also walking tractors
toolbars,
    multi-purpose 27, 46-7
tooth-cutting forceps 189
tractors 5, 9, 10, 14, 17-18
    cutter-bar attachments 102
    four-wheel 14, 18, 21, 25
    mini 18
    walking 18, 20, 25, 45
    see also trailers; walking tractors
trailers,
    bicycle 175
    for single-axle tractors 166, 169
    tractor-drawn 177, 178
transplanters, rice 60
tree guards 87
trek chains 19
triangular harrows 35
    multi-section 35
trocars and cannulas 194
troughs 192
trucks,
    platform 173
    sack 173
    turntable 173
turbines and water-wheels 145, 157
turnwrest ploughs 34

veterinary kit for animal health auxiliaries 194

wagons *see* carts
walking ploughs 32
walking tractors 18, 20, 25, 45
    and cultivators 39, 40
    drawing seeders and planters 60
    rotary cutter attachments 102
    wheel attachments 45
    see also tillers
water carriers 177
weed wipers 82
weeding equipment,
    animal-powered 67-8
    engine-powered 68
    flame weeders 81
    hand-held 78-80
    human-powered 67
    rotary 79
    straddle row 79
weighing crates 193
wetland cultivation equipment 44, 45
wetland tillers 45
wheat,
    scythes 92
    threshing equipment 93, 107
wheelbarrows 166, 169, 173, 174
    motorized 174
wheeled tool-carriers 12, 13, 27
wind-powered pumps 146, 147, 159, 160
winged rakes 35
winnowing machines 116
    fans 94
    hand-operated 123
    motorized 123
    pedal-powered 123
    tractor-mounted 124
    see also threshing equipment

yoke harnesses 13

zig-zag harrows 36

Questionnaire

Please help us to improve future editions of *Tools for Agriculture* by completing this questionnaire and sending to: Tools for Agriculture, ITDG, Myson House, Railway Terrace, Rugby CV21 3HT, UK.

Please tick box(es) where appropriate (tick more than one box if applicable).

Name . . . .

Position/profession . . . .

Address . . . .

. . . .

. . . .

. . . .

User/organization:

Commercial company ☐	Academic institution ☐
Individual ☐	Government organization ☐
International non-gov. organization ☐	National non-gov. organization ☐
Other (please specify) ☐	. . . .

How did you find out about this book?

Word of mouth ☐	Advertisement ☐
Saw it in a bookshop/library ☐	*Books by Post* ☐	IT Publications trade list ☐
Referred to in another book ☐	Other (please specify) ☐	. . . .

Have you used a previous edition of *Tools for Agriculture?*   Yes ☐   No ☐

For what purpose did you buy this book?   To find manufacturers'/suppliers' addresses ☐

To discover the range of tools available ☐   To find information on small-scale agriculture ☐

Other (please specify) ☐   . . . .

Which chapter(s) are of most interest to you? . . . .

Which chapter(s) are of least interest to you? . . . .

If you have any other comments please write them on the back of this questionnaire.